HYUNDAI

COUPES/SEDANS
1986-93 REPAIR MANUAL

President	Dean F. Morgantini, S.A.E.
Vice President–Finance	Barry L. Beck
Vice President–Sales	Glenn D. Potere
Executive Editor	Kevin M. G. Maher, A.S.E.
Manager–Consumer Automotive	Richard Schwartz, A.S.E.
Manager–Marine/Recreation	James R. Marotta, A.S.E.
Production Specialists	Brian Hollingsworth, Melinda Possinger
Project Managers	Will Kessler, A.S.E., S.A.E., Thomas A. Mellon, A.S.E., S.A.E., Richard Rivele, Todd W. Stidham, A.S.E., Ron Webb

CHILTON™ Automotive Books

PUBLISHED BY **W. G. NICHOLS, INC.**

Manufactured in USA
© 1993 Chilton Book Company
1020 Andrew Drive
West Chester, PA 19380
ISBN 0-8019-8412-2
Library of Congress Catalog Card No. 92-054903
0123456789 8765432109

A
8/2011

Contents

Contents

DRIVE TRAIN   **7**

SUSPENSION AND STEERING   **8**

BRAKES   **9**

BODY AND TRIM   **10**

GLOSSARY

MASTER INDEX

See last page for information on additional titles

SAFETY NOTICE

Proper service and repair procedures are vital to the safe, reliable operation of all motor vehicles, as well as the personal safety of those performing repairs. This manual outlines procedures for servicing and repairing vehicles using safe, effective methods. The procedures contain many NOTES, CAUTIONS and WARNINGS which should be followed, along with standard procedures to eliminate the possibility of personal injury or improper service which could damage the vehicle or compromise its safety.

It is important to note that repair procedures and techniques, tools and parts for servicing motor vehicles, as well as the skill and experience of the individual performing the work vary widely. It is not possible to anticipate all of the conceivable ways or conditions under which vehicles may be serviced, or to provide cautions as to all possible hazards that may result. Standard and accepted safety precautions and equipment should be used when handling toxic or flammable fluids, and safety goggles or other protection should be used during cutting, grinding, chiseling, prying, or any other process that can cause material removal or projectiles.

Some procedures require the use of tools specially designed for a specific purpose. Before substituting another tool or procedure, you must be completely satisfied that neither your personal safety, nor the performance of the vehicle will be endangered.

Although information in this manual is based on industry sources and is complete as possible at the time of publication, the possibility exists that some car manufacturers made later changes which could not be included here. While striving for total accuracy, NP/Chilton cannot assume responsibility for any errors, changes or omissions that may occur in the compilation of this data.

PART NUMBERS

Part numbers listed in this reference are not recommendations by Chilton for any product brand name. They are references that can be used with interchange manuals and aftermarket supplier catalogs to locate each brand supplier's discrete part number.

SPECIAL TOOLS

Special tools are recommended by the vehicle manufacturer to perform their specific job. Use has been kept to a minimum, but where absolutely necessary, they are referred to in the text by the part number of the tool manufacturer. These tools can be purchased, under the appropriate part number, from your local dealer or regional distributor, or an equivalent tool can be purchased locally from a tool supplier or parts outlet. Before substituting any tool for the one recommended, read the SAFETY NOTICE at the top of this page.

ACKNOWLEDGMENTS

Chilton expresses appreciation to Hyundai Motor Company for their generous assistance.

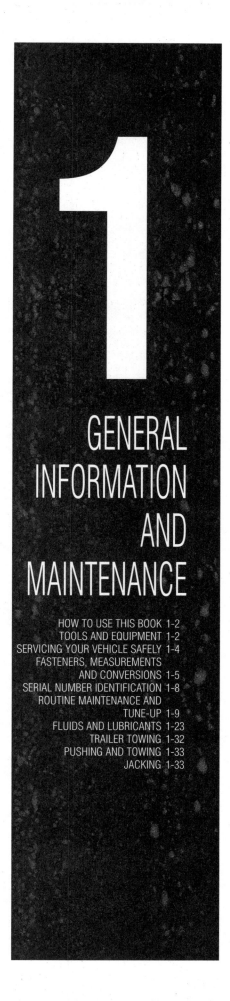

1

GENERAL INFORMATION AND MAINTENANCE

HOW TO USE THIS BOOK

This Chilton's Total Car Care manual for 1986–93 Hyundai Coupes and Sedans is intended to help you learn more about the inner workings of your vehicle while saving you money on its upkeep and operation.

The beginning of the book will likely be referred to the most, since that is where you will find information for maintenance and tune-up. The other sections deal with the more complex systems of your vehicle. Systems (from engine through brakes) are covered to the extent that the average do-it-yourselfer can attempt. This book will not explain such things as rebuilding a differential because the expertise required and the special tools necessary make this uneconomical. It will, however, give you detailed instructions to help you change your own brake pads and shoes, replace spark plugs, and perform many more jobs that can save you money and help you avoid expensive problems.

A secondary purpose of this book is a reference for owners who want to understand their vehicle and/or their mechanics better.

Where to Begin

Before removing any bolts, read through the entire procedure. This will give you the overall view of what tools and supplies will be required. So read ahead and plan ahead. Each operation should be approached logically and all procedures thoroughly understood before attempting any work.

If repair of a component is not considered practical, we tell you how to remove the part and then how to install the new or rebuilt replacement. In this way, you at least save labor costs.

Avoiding Trouble

Many procedures in this book require you to "label and disconnect . . ." a group of lines, hoses or wires. Don't be think you can remember where everything goes—you won't. If you hook up vacuum or fuel lines incorrectly, the vehicle may run poorly, if at all. If you hook up electrical wiring incorrectly, you may instantly learn a very expensive lesson.

You don't need to know the proper name for each hose or line. A piece of masking tape on the hose and a piece on its fitting will allow you to assign your own label. As long as you remember your own code, the lines can be reconnected by matching your tags. Remember that tape will dissolve in gasoline or solvents; if a part is to be washed or cleaned, use another method of identification. A permanent felt-tipped marker or a metal scribe can be very handy for marking metal parts. Remove any tape or paper labels after assembly.

Maintenance or Repair?

Maintenance includes routine inspections, adjustments, and replacement of parts which show signs of normal wear. Maintenance compensates for wear or deterioration. Repair implies that something has broken or is not working. A need for a repair is often caused by lack of maintenance. for example: draining and refilling automatic transmission fluid is maintenance recommended at specific intervals. Failure to do this can shorten the life of the transmission/transaxle, requiring very expensive repairs. While no maintenance program can prevent items from eventually breaking or wearing out, a general rule is true: MAINTENANCE IS CHEAPER THAN REPAIR.

Two basic mechanic's rules should be mentioned here. First, whenever the left side of the vehicle or engine is referred to, it means the driver's side. Conversely, the right side of the vehicle means the passenger's side. Second, screws and bolts are removed by turning counterclockwise, and tightened by turning clockwise unless specifically noted.

Safety is always the most important rule. Constantly be aware of the dangers involved in working on an automobile and take the proper precautions. Please refer to the information in this section regarding SERVICING YOUR VEHICLE SAFELY and the SAFETY NOTICE on the acknowledgment page.

Avoiding the Most Common Mistakes

Pay attention to the instructions provided. There are 3 common mistakes in mechanical work:

1. Incorrect order of assembly, disassembly or adjustment. When taking something apart or putting it together, performing steps in the wrong order usually just costs you extra time; however, it CAN break something. Read the entire procedure before beginning. Perform everything in the order in which the instructions say you should, even if you can't see a reason for it. When you're taking apart something that is very intricate, you might want to draw a picture of how it looks when assembled in order to make sure you get everything back in its proper position. When making adjustments, perform them in the proper order. One adjustment possibly will affect another.

2. Overtorquing (or undertorquing). While it is more common for overtorquing to cause damage, undertorquing may allow a fastener to vibrate loose causing serious damage. Especially when dealing with aluminum parts, pay attention to torque specifications and utilize a torque wrench in assembly. If a torque figure is not available, remember that if you are using the right tool to perform the job, you will probably not have to strain yourself to get a fastener tight enough. The pitch of most threads is so slight that the tension you put on the wrench will be multiplied many times in actual force on what you are tightening.

There are many commercial products available for ensuring that fasteners won't come loose, even if they are not torqued just right (a very common brand is Loctite®). If you're worried about getting something together tight enough to hold, but loose enough to avoid mechanical damage during assembly, one of these products might offer substantial insurance. Before choosing a threadlocking compound, read the label on the package and make sure the product is compatible with the materials, fluids, etc. involved.

3. Crossthreading. This occurs when a part such as a bolt is screwed into a nut or casting at the wrong angle and forced. Crossthreading is more likely to occur if access is difficult. It helps to clean and lubricate fasteners, then to start threading the bolt, spark plug, etc. with your fingers. If you encounter resistance, unscrew the part and start over again at a different angle until it can be inserted and turned several times without much effort. Keep in mind that many parts have tapered threads, so that gentle turning will automatically bring the part you're threading to the proper angle. Don't put a wrench on the part until it's been tightened a couple of turns by hand. If you suddenly encounter resistance, and the part has not seated fully, don't force it. Pull it back out to make sure it's clean and threading properly.

Be sure to take your time and be patient, and always plan ahead. Allow yourself ample time to perform repairs and maintenance.

TOOLS AND EQUIPMENT

▶ **See Figures 1 thru 15**

Without the proper tools and equipment it is impossible to properly service your vehicle. It would be virtually impossible to catalog every tool that you would need to perform all of the operations in this book. It would be unwise for the amateur to rush out and buy an expensive set of tools on the theory that he/she may need one or more of them at some time.

The best approach is to proceed slowly, gathering a good quality set of those tools that are used most frequently. Don't be misled by the low cost of bargain tools. It is far better to spend a little more for better quality. Forged wrenches, 6 or 12-point sockets and fine tooth ratchets are by far preferable to their less expensive counterparts. As any good mechanic can tell you, there are few worse experiences than trying to work on a vehicle with bad tools. Your monetary savings will be far outweighed by frustration and mangled knuckles.

Begin accumulating those tools that are used most frequently: those associated with routine maintenance and tune-up. In addition to the normal assortment of screwdrivers and pliers, you should have the following tools:

• Wrenches/sockets and combination open end/box end wrenches in sizes from ⅛ –¾ in. or 3–19mm, as well as a ¹³⁄₁₆ in. or ⅝ in. spark plug socket (depending on plug type).

➡**If possible, buy various length socket drive extensions. Universal-joint and wobble extensions can be extremely useful, but be careful when using them, as they can change the amount of torque applied to the socket.**

• Jackstands for support.
• Oil filter wrench.

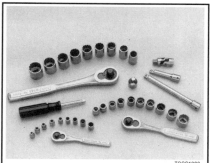

Fig. 1 All but the most basic procedures will require an assortment of ratchets and sockets

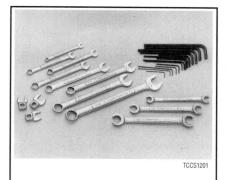

Fig. 2 In addition to ratchets, a good set of wrenches and hex keys will be necessary

Fig. 3 A hydraulic floor jack and a set of jackstands are essential for lifting and supporting the vehicle

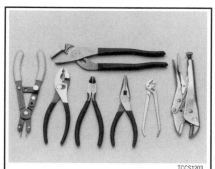

Fig. 4 An assortment of pliers, grippers and cutters will be handy for old rusted parts and stripped bolt heads

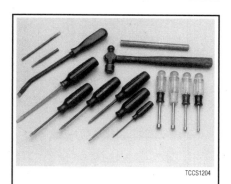

Fig. 5 Various drivers, chisels and prybars are great tools to have in your toolbox

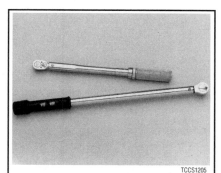

Fig. 6 Many repairs will require the use of a torque wrench to assure the components are properly fastened

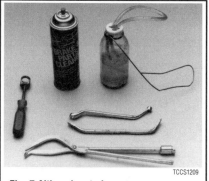

Fig. 7 Although not always necessary, using specialized brake tools will save time

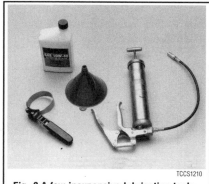

Fig. 8 A few inexpensive lubrication tools will make maintenance easier

Fig. 9 Various pullers, clamps and separator tools are needed for many larger, more complicated repairs

- Spout or funnel for pouring fluids.
- Grease gun for chassis lubrication (unless your vehicle is not equipped with any grease fittings)
- Hydrometer for checking the battery (unless equipped with a sealed, maintenance-free battery).
- A container for draining oil and other fluids.
- Rags for wiping up the inevitable mess.

In addition to the above items there are several others that are not absolutely necessary, but handy to have around. These include an equivalent oil absorbent gravel, like cat litter, and the usual supply of lubricants, antifreeze and fluids. This is a basic list for routine maintenance, but only your personal needs and desire can accurately determine your list of tools.

After performing a few projects on the vehicle, you'll be amazed at the other tools and non-tools on your workbench. Some useful household items are: a large turkey baster or siphon, empty coffee cans and ice trays (to store parts), a ball of twine, electrical tape for wiring, small rolls of colored tape for tagging

lines or hoses, markers and pens, a note pad, golf tees (for plugging vacuum lines), metal coat hangers or a roll of mechanic's wire (to hold things out of the way), dental pick or similar long, pointed probe, a strong magnet, and a small mirror (to see into recesses and under manifolds).

A more advanced set of tools, suitable for tune-up work, can be drawn up easily. While the tools are slightly more sophisticated, they need not be outrageously expensive. There are several inexpensive tach/dwell meters on the market that are every bit as good for the average mechanic as a professional model. Just be sure that it goes to a least 1200–1500 rpm on the tach scale and that it works on 4, 6 and 8-cylinder engines. The key to these purchases is to make them with an eye towards adaptability and wide range. A basic list of tune-up tools could include:

- Tach/dwell meter.
- Spark plug wrench and gapping tool.
- Feeler gauges for valve adjustment.
- Timing light.

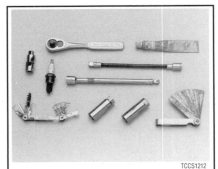

Fig. 10 A variety of tools and gauges should be used for spark plug gapping and installation

TCCS1212

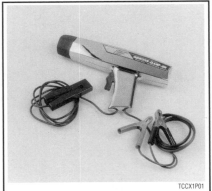

TCCX1P01

Fig. 11 Inductive type timing light

TCCX1P02

Fig. 12 A screw-in type compression gauge is recommended for compression testing

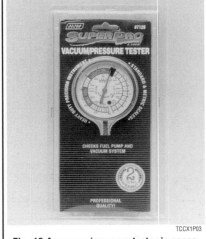

TCCX1P03

Fig. 13 A vacuum/pressure tester is necessary for many testing procedures

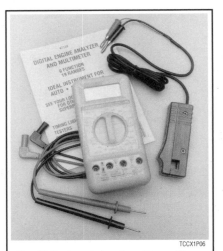

TCCX1P06

Fig. 14 Most modern automotive multimeters incorporate many helpful features

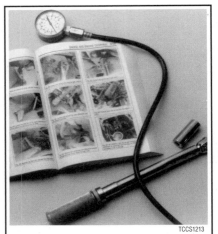

TCCS1213

Fig. 15 Proper information is vital, so always have a Chilton Total Car Care manual handy

The choice of a timing light should be made carefully. A light which works on the DC current supplied by the vehicle's battery is the best choice; it should have a xenon tube for brightness. On any vehicle with an electronic ignition system, a timing light with an inductive pickup that clamps around the No. 1 spark plug cable is preferred.

In addition to these basic tools, there are several other tools and gauges you may find useful. These include:
• Compression gauge. The screw-in type is slower to use, but eliminates the possibility of a faulty reading due to escaping pressure.
• Manifold vacuum gauge.
• 12V test light.
• A combination volt/ohmmeter
• Induction Ammeter. This is used for determining whether or not there is current in a wire. These are handy for use if a wire is broken somewhere in a wiring harness.

As a final note, you will probably find a torque wrench necessary for all but the most basic work. The beam type models are perfectly adequate, although the newer click types (breakaway) are easier to use. The click type torque wrenches tend to be more expensive. Also keep in mind that all types of torque wrenches should be periodically checked and/or recalibrated. You will have to decide for yourself which better fits your pocketbook, and purpose.

Special Tools

Normally, the use of special factory tools is avoided for repair procedures, since these are not readily available for the do-it-yourself mechanic. When it is possible to perform the job with more commonly available tools, it will be pointed out, but occasionally, a special tool was designed to perform a specific function and should be used. Before substituting another tool, you should be convinced that neither your safety nor the performance of the vehicle will be compromised.

Special tools can usually be purchased from an automotive parts store or from your dealer. In some cases special tools may be available directly from the tool manufacturer.

SERVICING YOUR VEHICLE SAFELY

▶ **See Figures 16, 17 and 18**

It is virtually impossible to anticipate all of the hazards involved with automotive maintenance and service, but care and common sense will prevent most accidents.

The rules of safety for mechanics range from "don't smoke around gasoline," to "use the proper tool(s) for the job." The trick to avoiding injuries is to develop safe work habits and to take every possible precaution.

Do's

• Do keep a fire extinguisher and first aid kit handy.
• Do wear safety glasses or goggles when cutting, drilling, grinding or prying, even if you have 20–20 vision. If you wear glasses for the sake of vision, wear safety goggles over your regular glasses.
• Do shield your eyes whenever you work around the battery. Batteries contain sulfuric acid. In case of contact with, flush the area with water or a mixture of water and baking soda, then seek immediate medical attention.

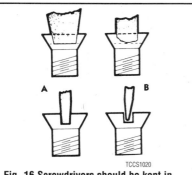

Fig. 16 Screwdrivers should be kept in good condition to prevent injury or damage which could result if the blade slips from the screw

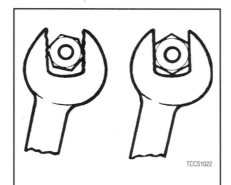

Fig. 17 Using the correct size wrench will help prevent the possibility of rounding off a nut

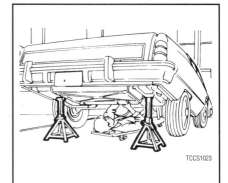

Fig. 18 NEVER work under a vehicle unless it is supported using safety stands (jackstands)

- Do use safety stands (jackstands) for any undervehicle service. Jacks are for raising vehicles; jackstands are for making sure the vehicle stays raised until you want it to come down.
- Do use adequate ventilation when working with any chemicals or hazardous materials. Like carbon monoxide, the asbestos dust resulting from some brake lining wear can be hazardous in sufficient quantities.
- Do disconnect the negative battery cable when working on the electrical system. The secondary ignition system contains EXTREMELY HIGH VOLTAGE. In some cases it can even exceed 50,000 volts.
- Do follow manufacturer's directions whenever working with potentially hazardous materials. Most chemicals and fluids are poisonous.
- Do properly maintain your tools. Loose hammerheads, mushroomed punches and chisels, frayed or poorly grounded electrical cords, excessively worn screwdrivers, spread wrenches (open end), cracked sockets, slipping ratchets, or faulty droplight sockets can cause accidents.
- Likewise, keep your tools clean; a greasy wrench can slip off a bolt head, ruining the bolt and often harming your knuckles in the process.
- Do use the proper size and type of tool for the job at hand. Do select a wrench or socket that fits the nut or bolt. The wrench or socket should sit straight, not cocked.
- Do, when possible, pull on a wrench handle rather than push on it, and adjust your stance to prevent a fall.
- Do be sure that adjustable wrenches are tightly closed on the nut or bolt and pulled so that the force is on the side of the fixed jaw.
- Do strike squarely with a hammer; avoid glancing blows.
- Do set the parking brake and block the drive wheels if the work requires a running engine.

Don'ts

- Don't run the engine in a garage or anywhere else without proper ventilation—EVER! Carbon monoxide is poisonous; it takes a long time to leave the

human body and you can build up a deadly supply of it in your system by simply breathing in a little at a time. You may not realize you are slowly poisoning yourself. Always use power vents, windows, fans and/or open the garage door.
- Don't work around moving parts while wearing loose clothing. Short sleeves are much safer than long, loose sleeves. Hard-toed shoes with neoprene soles protect your toes and give you a better grip on slippery surfaces. Watches and jewelry is not safe working around a vehicle. Long hair should be tied back under a hat or cap.
- Don't use pockets for toolboxes. A fall or bump can drive a screwdriver deep into your body. Even a rag hanging from your back pocket can wrap around a spinning shaft or fan.
- Don't smoke when working around gasoline, cleaning solvent or other flammable material.
- Don't smoke when working around the battery. When the battery is being charged, it gives off explosive hydrogen gas.
- Don't use gasoline to wash your hands; there are excellent soaps available. Gasoline contains dangerous additives which can enter the body through a cut or through your pores. Gasoline also removes all the natural oils from the skin so that bone dry hands will suck up oil and grease.
- Don't service the air conditioning system unless you are equipped with the necessary tools and training. When liquid or compressed gas refrigerant is released to atmospheric pressure it will absorb heat from whatever it contacts. This will chill or freeze anything it touches.
- Don't use screwdrivers for anything other than driving screws! A screwdriver used as an prying tool can snap when you least expect it, causing injuries. At the very least, you'll ruin a good screwdriver.
- Don't use an emergency jack (that little ratchet, scissors, or pantograph jack supplied with the vehicle) for anything other than changing a flat! These jacks are only intended for emergency use out on the road; they are NOT designed as a maintenance tool. If you are serious about maintaining your vehicle yourself, invest in a hydraulic floor jack of at least a 1½ ton capacity, and at least two sturdy jackstands.

FASTENERS, MEASUREMENTS AND CONVERSIONS

Bolts, Nuts and Other Threaded Retainers

▶ **See Figures 19 and 20**

Although there are a great variety of fasteners found in the modern car or truck, the most commonly used retainer is the threaded fastener (nuts, bolts, screws, studs, etc.). Most threaded retainers may be reused, provided that they are not damaged in use or during the repair. Some retainers (such as stretch bolts or torque prevailing nuts) are designed to deform when tightened or in use and should not be reinstalled.

Whenever possible, we will note any special retainers which should be replaced during a procedure. But you should always inspect the condition of a retainer when it is removed and replace any that show signs of damage. Check all threads for rust or corrosion which can increase the torque necessary to achieve the desired clamp load for which that fastener was originally selected. Additionally, be sure that the driver surface of the fastener has not been compromised by rounding or other damage. In some cases a driver surface may

become only partially rounded, allowing the driver to catch in only one direction. In many of these occurrences, a fastener may be installed and tightened, but the driver would not be able to grip and loosen the fastener again.

If you must replace a fastener, whether due to design or damage, you must ALWAYS be sure to use the proper replacement. In all cases, a retainer of the same design, material and strength should be used. Markings on the heads of most bolts will help determine the proper strength of the fastener. The same material, thread and pitch must be selected to assure proper installation and safe operation of the vehicle afterwards.

Thread gauges are available to help measure a bolt or stud's thread. Most automotive and hardware stores keep gauges available to help you select the proper size. In a pinch, you can use another nut or bolt for a thread gauge. If the bolt you are replacing is not too badly damaged, you can select a match by finding another bolt which will thread in its place. If you find a nut which threads properly onto the damaged bolt, then use that nut to help select the replacement bolt.

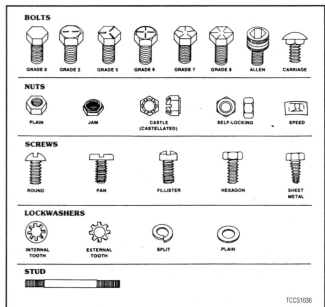

Fig. 19 There are many different types of threaded retainers found on vehicles

☀ WARNING

Be aware that when you find a bolt with damaged threads, you may also find the nut or drilled hole it was threaded into has also been damaged. If this is the case, you may have to drill and tap the hole, replace the nut or otherwise repair the threads. NEVER try to force a replacement bolt to fit into the damaged threads.

Torque

Torque is defined as the measurement of resistance to turning or rotating. It tends to twist a body about an axis of rotation. A common example of this would be tightening a threaded retainer such as a nut, bolt or screw. Measuring torque is one of the most common ways to help assure that a threaded retainer has been properly fastened.

When tightening a threaded fastener, torque is applied in three distinct areas, the head, the bearing surface and the clamp load. About 50 percent of the measured torque is used in overcoming bearing friction. This is the friction between the bearing surface of the bolt head, screw head or nut face and the base material or washer (the surface on which the fastener is rotating). Approximately 40 percent of the applied torque is used in overcoming thread friction. This leaves only about 10 percent of the applied torque to develop a useful clamp load (the force which holds a joint together). This means that friction can account for as much as 90 percent of the applied torque on a fastener.

TORQUE WRENCHES

♦ See Figure 21

In most applications, a torque wrench can be used to assure proper installation of a fastener. Torque wrenches come in various designs and most automotive supply stores will carry a variety to suit your needs. A torque wrench should be used any time we supply a specific torque value for a fastener. Again, the general rule of "if you are using the right tool for the job, you should not have to strain to tighten a fastener" applies here.

Beam Type

The beam type torque wrench is one of the most popular types. It consists of a pointer attached to the head that runs the length of the flexible beam (shaft) to a scale located near the handle. As the wrench is pulled, the beam bends and the pointer indicates the torque using the scale.

Click (Breakaway) Type

Another popular design of torque wrench is the click type. To use the click type wrench you pre-adjust it to a torque setting. Once the torque is reached, the wrench has a reflex signaling feature that causes a momentary breakaway of the torque wrench body, sending an impulse to the operator's hand.

Pivot Head Type

♦ See Figure 22

Some torque wrenches (usually of the click type) may be equipped with a pivot head which can allow it to be used in areas of limited access. BUT, it must be used properly. To hold a pivot head wrench, grasp the handle lightly, and as you pull on the handle, it should be floated on the pivot point. If the handle comes in contact with the yoke extension during the process of pulling, there is a very good chance the torque readings will be inaccurate because this could alter the wrench loading point. The design of the handle is usually such as to make it inconvenient to deliberately misuse the wrench.

➡**It should be mentioned that the use of any U-joint, wobble or extension will have an effect on the torque readings, no matter what type of wrench you are using. For the most accurate readings, install the socket directly on the wrench driver. If necessary, straight extensions (which hold a socket directly under the wrench driver) will have the least effect on the torque reading. Avoid any extension that alters the length of the wrench from the handle to the head/driving point (such as a crow's foot). U-joint or wobble extensions can greatly affect the readings; avoid their use at all times.**

Rigid Case (Direct Reading)

A rigid case or direct reading torque wrench is equipped with a dial indicator to show torque values. One advantage of these wrenches is that they can be held at any position on the wrench without affecting accuracy. These wrenches are often preferred because they tend to be compact, easy to read and have a great degree of accuracy.

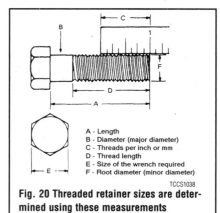

Fig. 20 Threaded retainer sizes are determined using these measurements

A - Length
B - Diameter (major diameter)
C - Threads per inch or mm
D - Thread length
E - Size of the wrench required
F - Root diameter (minor diameter)

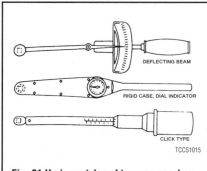

Fig. 21 Various styles of torque wrenches are usually available at your local automotive supply store

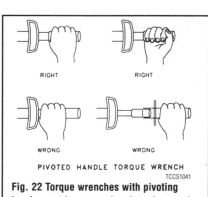

Fig. 22 Torque wrenches with pivoting heads must be grasped and used properly to prevent an incorrect reading

TORQUE ANGLE METERS

Because the frictional characteristics of each fastener or threaded hole will vary, clamp loads which are based strictly on torque will vary as well. In most applications, this variance is not significant enough to cause worry. But, in certain applications, a manufacturer's engineers may determine that more precise clamp loads are necessary (such is the case with many aluminum cylinder heads). In these cases, a torque angle method of installation would be specified. When installing fasteners which are torque angle tightened, a predetermined seating torque and standard torque wrench are usually used first to remove any compliance from the joint. The fastener is then tightened the specified additional portion of a turn measured in degrees. A torque angle gauge (mechanical protractor) is used for these applications.

Standard and Metric Measurements

▶ See Figure 23

Throughout this manual, specifications are given to help you determine the condition of various components on your vehicle, or to assist you in their installation. Some of the most common measurements include length (in. or cm/mm), torque (ft. lbs., inch lbs. or Nm) and pressure (psi, in. Hg, kPa or mm Hg). In most cases, we strive to provide the proper measurement as determined by the manufacturer's engineers.

Though, in some cases, that value may not be conveniently measured with what is available in your toolbox. Luckily, many of the measuring devices which are available today will have two scales so the Standard or Metric measurements may easily be taken. If any of the various measuring tools which are available to you do not contain the same scale as listed in the specifications, use the accompanying conversion factors to determine the proper value.

The conversion factor chart is used by taking the given specification and multiplying it by the necessary conversion factor. For instance, looking at the first line, if you have a measurement in inches such as "free-play should be 2 in." but your ruler reads only in millimeters, multiply 2 in. by the conversion factor of 25.4 to get the metric equivalent of 50.8mm. Likewise, if the specification was given only in a Metric measurement, for example in Newton Meters (Nm), then look at the center column first. If the measurement is 100 Nm, multiply it by the conversion factor of 0.738 to get 73.8 ft. lbs.

CONVERSION FACTORS

LENGTH–DISTANCE

Inches (in.)	x 25.4	= Millimeters (mm)	x .0394	= Inches
Feet (ft.)	x .305	= Meters (m)	x 3.281	= Feet
Miles	x 1.609	= Kilometers (km)	x .0621	= Miles

VOLUME

Cubic Inches (in3)	x 16.387	= Cubic Centimeters	x .061	= in3
IMP Pints (IMP pt.)	x .568	= Liters (L)	x 1.76	= IMP pt.
IMP Quarts (IMP qt.)	x 1.137	= Liters (L)	x .88	= IMP qt.
IMP Gallons (IMP gal.)	x 4.546	= Liters (L)	x .22	= IMP gal.
IMP Quarts (IMP qt.)	x 1.201	= US Quarts (US qt.)	x .833	= IMP qt.
IMP Gallons (IMP gal.)	x 1.201	= US Gallons (US gal.)	x .833	= IMP gal.
Fl. Ounces	x 29.573	= Milliliters	x .034	= Ounces
US Pints (US pt.)	x .473	= Liters (L)	x 2.113	= Pints
US Quarts (US qt.)	x .946	= Liters (L)	x 1.057	= Quarts
US Gallons (US gal.)	x 3.785	= Liters (L)	x .264	= Gallons

MASS–WEIGHT

Ounces (oz.)	x 28.35	= Grams (g)	x .035	= Ounces
Pounds (lb.)	x .454	= Kilograms (kg)	x 2.205	= Pounds

PRESSURE

Pounds Per Sq. In. (psi)	x 6.895	= Kilopascals (kPa)	x .145	= psi
Inches of Mercury (Hg)	x .4912	= psi	x 2.036	= Hg
Inches of Mercury (Hg)	x 3.377	= Kilopascals (kPa)	x .2961	= Hg
Inches of Water (H₂O)	x .07355	= Inches of Mercury	x 13.783	= H₂O
Inches of Water (H₂O)	x .03613	= psi	x 27.684	= H₂O
Inches of Water (H₂O)	x .248	= Kilopascals (kPa)	x 4.026	= H₂O

TORQUE

Pounds–Force Inches (in–lb)	x .113	= Newton Meters (N·m)	x 8.85	= in–lb
Pounds–Force Feet (ft–lb)	x 1.356	= Newton Meters (N·m)	x .738	= ft–lb

VELOCITY

Miles Per Hour (MPH)	x 1.609	= Kilometers Per Hour (KPH)	x .621	= MPH

POWER

Horsepower (Hp)	x .745	= Kilowatts	x 1.34	= Horsepower

FUEL CONSUMPTION*

Miles Per Gallon IMP (MPG)	x .354	= Kilometers Per Liter (Km/L)	
Kilometers Per Liter (Km/L)	x 2.352	= IMP MPG	
Miles Per Gallon US (MPG)	x .425	= Kilometers Per Liter (Km/L)	
Kilometers Per Liter (Km/L)	x 2.352	= US MPG	

*It is common to covert from miles per gallon (mpg) to liters/100 kilometers (1/100 km), where mpg (IMP) x 1/100 km = 282 and mpg (US) x 1/100 km = 235.

TEMPERATURE

Degree Fahrenheit (°F)	= (°C x 1.8) + 32
Degree Celsius (°C)	= (°F – 32) x .56

TCCS1044

Fig. 23 Standard and metric conversion factors chart

SERIAL NUMBER IDENTIFICATION

Vehicle Identification Number

▶ See Figure 24

The vehicle identification number plate is mounted on the instrument panel, adjacent to the lower corner of the windshield on the driver's side, and is visible through the windshield. The seventeen digit vehicle number is composed of an identification number and a five or six digit serial number.

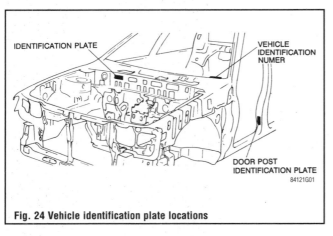

Fig. 24 Vehicle identification plate locations

Engine Model Number

The engine model number is cast on the lower left side of the engine block or stamped near the engine serial number on the upper front side of the engine block.

Engine Serial Number

▶ See Figure 25

The engine serial number is stamped on a boss usually located on the right front top edge of the cylinder block.

Fig. 25 Engine serial number location, the number is stamped into the block

ENGINE IDENTIFICATION

Year	Model	Engine Displacement Liters (cc)	Engine Series (ID/VIN)	Fuel System	No. of Cylinders	Engine Type
1986	Excel	1.5 (1468)	M	2bbl	4	OHC
1987	Excel	1.5 (1468)	M	2bbl	4	OHC
1988	Excel	1.5 (1468)	M	2bbl	4	OHC
1989	Excel	1.5 (1468)	M	2bbl	4	OHC
	Sonata	2.4 (2351)	S	MPI	4	OHC
1990	Excel	1.5 (1468)	M	2bbl	4	OHC
	Excel	1.5 (1468)	J	MPI	4	OHC
	Sonata	2.4 (2351)	S	MPI	4	OHC
	Sonata	3.0 (2972)	T	MPI	6	OHC
1991	Excel	1.5 (1468)	M	2bbl	4	OHC
	Excel	1.5 (1468)	J	MPI	4	OHC
	Sonata	2.4 (2351)	S	MPI	4	OHC
	Sonata	3.0 (2972)	T	MPI	6	OHC
	Scoupe	1.5 (1468)	J	MPI	4	OHC
1992	Excel	1.5 (1468)	M	2bbl	4	OHC
	Excel	1.5 (1468)	J	MPI	4	OHC
	Sonata	2.0 (1997)	F	MPI	4	DOHC
	Sonata	3.0 (2972)	T	MPI	6	OHC
	Scoupe	1.5 (1468)	J	MPI	4	OHC
	Elantra	1.6 (1596)	R	MPI	4	DOHC
1993	Excel	1.5 (1468)	M	2bbl	4	OHC
	Excel	1.5 (1468)	J	MPI	4	OHC
	Sonata	2.0 (1997)	F	MPI	4	DOHC
	Sonata	3.0 (2972)	T	MPI	6	OHC
	Scoupe	1.5 (1495)	N	MPI	4	OHC
	Scoupe ①	1.5 (1495)	N	MPI	4	OHC
	Elantra	1.6 (1596)	R	MPI	4	DOHC
	Elantra	1.8 (1796)	M	MPI	4	DOHC

MPI—Multipoint fuel injection
OHC—Overhead camshaft
① Scoupe Turbo

84121C01

Vehicle Body Number/Identification Plate Location

The body number and identification plate are located on the firewall in the engine compartment.

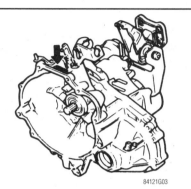

Fig. 26 Manual transaxle number location, the number is stamped into the transaxle body

Transaxle Identification Number

♦ See Figures 26 and 27

The manual transaxle serial number is stamped on the clutch housing portion of the transaxle case. On automatic transaxle models, the number is on a plate attached to the side of the transaxle, or stamped on a boss at the oil pan flange.

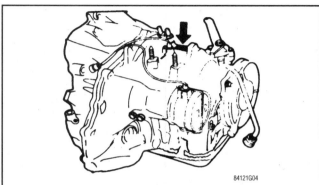

Fig. 27 Automatic transaxle number location, the number is stamped into the transaxle body

ROUTINE MAINTENANCE AND TUNE-UP

♦ See Figures 28 and 29

Proper maintenance and tune-up is the key to long and trouble-free vehicle life. Studies have shown that a properly tuned and maintained vehicle can achieve better gas mileage than an out-of-tune vehicle. As a conscientious owner and driver, set aside a Saturday morning, say once a month, to check or replace items which could cause major problems later. Keep your own personal log to jot down which services you performed, how much the parts cost you, the date, and the exact odometer reading at the time. Keep all receipts for such items as engine oil and filters, so that they may be referred to in case of related problems or to determine operating expenses. As a do-it-yourselfer, these receipts are the only proof you have that the required maintenance was performed. In the event of a warranty problem, these receipts will be invaluable.

The literature provided with your vehicle when it was originally delivered includes the factory recommended maintenance schedule. If you no longer have this literature, replacement copies are usually available from the dealer.

Air Cleaner

The air cleaner contains a dry filter element that keeps most dirt and dust from entering the engine via the carburetor or throttle body air intake system. Never run the engine (other than for adjusting) without a filter element. The dirt and dust entering the engine can cause expensive damage to the pistons, bearings, etc.

Proper maintenance of the cleaner element is vital. A clogged filter element will fail to supply sufficient fresh air to the carburetor, causing an overly rich

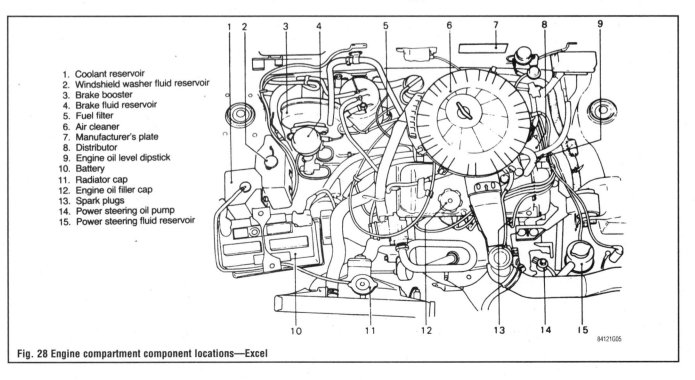

1. Coolant reservoir
2. Windshield washer fluid reservoir
3. Brake booster
4. Brake fluid reservoir
5. Fuel filter
6. Air cleaner
7. Manufacturer's plate
8. Distributor
9. Engine oil level dipstick
10. Battery
11. Radiator cap
12. Engine oil filler cap
13. Spark plugs
14. Power steering oil pump
15. Power steering fluid reservoir

Fig. 28 Engine compartment component locations—Excel

TYPICAL UNDERHOOD MAINTENANCE COMPONENT LOCATIONS—SONATA SHOWN

1. Battery
2. Brake master cylinder
3. Air cleaner assembly
4. Oil dipstick
5. Oil fill cap
6. PCV valve
7. Power steering reservoir
8. Power steering belt
9. Upper radiator hose
10. Radiator cap/neck
11. Washer solvent bottle

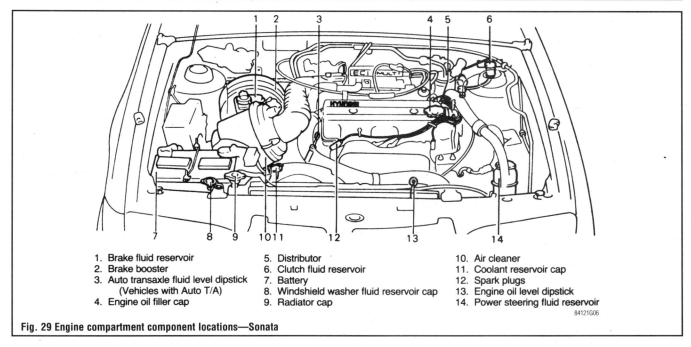

1. Brake fluid reservoir
2. Brake booster
3. Auto transaxle fluid level dipstick
   (Vehicles with Auto T/A)
4. Engine oil filler cap
5. Distributor
6. Clutch fluid reservoir
7. Battery
8. Windshield washer fluid reservoir cap
9. Radiator cap
10. Air cleaner
11. Coolant reservoir cap
12. Spark plugs
13. Engine oil level dipstick
14. Power steering fluid reservoir

84121G06

Fig. 29 Engine compartment component locations—Sonata

fuel/air mixture. Such a condition will result in poor engine performance and economy.

Periodic cleaning or replacing of the filter element will help your car last longer and run better.

REMOVAL & INSTALLATION

1986–89 Excel

♦ See Figure 30

To clean or replace the air cleaner filter element, remove the top wing nut/nuts and loosen the side mounted spring clips (if equipped). Lift off the top of the air cleaner and remove the filter element. Replace the filter element if mileage or extreme dirt clogging is indicated.

1990–93 Excel, Elantra, Scoupe And Sonata

♦ See Figures 31 thru 37

1. Loosen the hose clamp that connects the intake flexible hose to the air cleaner cover.
2. Separate the hose from the cover.
3. Disconnect the air flow sensor connector.
4. Release the air cleaner cover clips. Move the flexible air intake out of the way to allow you to remove the air cleaner cover.

➡**Remove the air cleaner cover carefully because it contains the air flow sensor. The air flow sensor is very delicate.**

5. Remove the air cleaner element from the housing and wipe the housing clean with a dry rag.

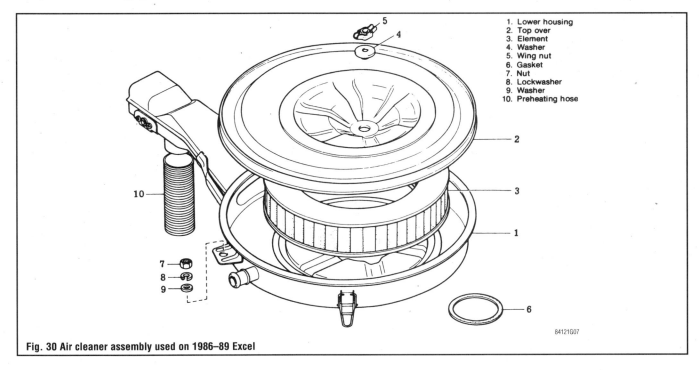

1. Lower housing
2. Top over
3. Element
4. Washer
5. Wing nut
6. Gasket
7. Nut
8. Lockwasher
9. Washer
10. Preheating hose

84121G07

Fig. 30 Air cleaner assembly used on 1986–89 Excel

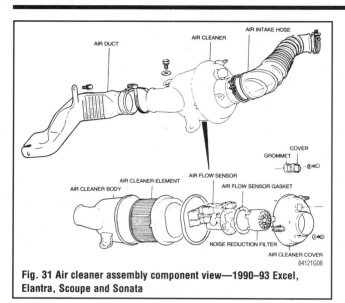

Fig. 31 Air cleaner assembly component view—1990–93 Excel, Elantra, Scoupe and Sonata

6. Place the new filter element into the housing making sure that it seats properly in the body of the air cleaner.

7. Replace the air cleaner cover and connect the air flow sensor and pressure relief valve multi-connectors.

8. Connect the air intake hose to the air cleaner cover and tighten the hose clamp.

Fuel Filter

The fuel filter should be replaced, or at least checked for clogging every 12,000 miles. The fuel filter is of the inline type and is located on the firewall.

REMOVAL & INSTALLATION

1986–89 Excel

♦ See Figure 38

To remove the filter, loosen the hose clamps at both ends of the filter and remove the fuel lines from the filter ends. Unclip the filter from the mounting bracket. Install a new filter in the reverse order of removal. Start the engine and check for leaks. If a clogged filter is suspected, remove the filter and blow compressed air through the inlet and outlet fittings, reinstall the filter. Replace the old filter as soon as possible.

Fig. 32 The air flow sensor uses a weatherproof connector. Inspect the seal for damage and replace as necessary

Fig. 33 Unscrew the clamp that attaches the air hose duct to the air filter assembly

Fig. 34 Take care when removing the air hose duct. The air flow sensor inside the air filter is easily damaged

Fig. 35 Unfasten the air filter cover clips by unlatching them as shown—Excel, Scoupe and 1994–95 Elantra

Fig. 36 Carefully remove the air filter cover. The air flow sensor (arrow) is at the center of the cover

Fig. 37 The round air filter element is made of paper and cannot be cleaned. When dirty, it must be replaced

Fig. 38 Fuel filter location on the 1986–89 Excel

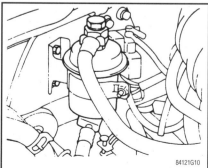

Fig. 39 Fuel filter location on the 1990–93 Excel

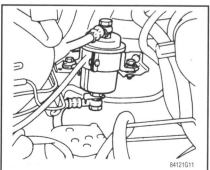

Fig. 40 Fuel filter location on the Elantra, Scoupe and Sonata

1990–93 Excel, Elantra, Scoupe and Sonata

♦ See Figures 39, 40, 41 and 42

On these models the fuel injection system is always under constant pressure even when the engine is not running. This residual pressure must be relieved from the fuel system before changing the fuel filter element. Release the fuel pressure as follows:

Fuel pressure relief

• From under the vehicle, disconnect the fuel pump harness connector located at the rear of the fuel tank.
• Start the engine and allow it to run until it stops by itself.
• Turn the ignition switch to the OFF position.
• Disconnect the negative battery cable.
• Reconnect the fuel pump harness connector.
1. Remove the inlet and outlet union bolts while holding the fuel lines stationary. Inspect the union bolt gaskets for damage and replace them as necessary.
2. Remove the fuel filter mounting bolts.
3. Pull the old filter from the mounting bracket.
4. Place the new fuel filter into the mounting bracket.
5. Install and tighten the fuel filter mounting bolts.
6. Connect the fuel inlet and outlet lines to the filter and tighten the union bolts.
7. Connect the negative battery cable.
8. Start the engine and check the filter connections for leaks by running the tip of your finger around each union bolt connection.

PCV Valve

♦ See Figure 43

A closed crankcase ventilation system is used on your car. The purpose of the closed system is to prevent blow-by gases, created by the engine, from escaping into the air.

The PCV system supplies fresh air to the crankcase through the air cleaner. Inside the crankcase, the fresh air mixes with the blow-by gases. The mixture of fresh air and blow-by gases is then passed through the PCV valve and into the intake manifold. The PCV valve (mounted on the top end of the valve cover) is a metered orifice that reacts to intake manifold vacuum, and has an adequate capacity for all normal driving conditions. However, under heavy engine loads or high speed driving there is less intake manifold vacuum and the blow-by gases exceed the PCV valve's capacity. When this happens, the blow-by gases back up into the air cleaner through the front hose, mix with fresh air and are reburned in the engine.

TESTING

To test the operation of the PCV valve with the engine running, apply the parking brake, start the engine and allow it to operate at a normal idle speed. Remove the PCV valve from the valve cover mounting. A hissing noise should be heard as air passes through the valve and a strong vacuum should be felt if you place a finger over the opened end of the valve. To check the PCV valve with the engine not running, remove the PCV valve from the valve cover mounting, and insert a thin rod into the opening on the threaded end of the PCV valve and check that the plunger moves freely back and forth. Blow air through the threaded end of the valve. If air is not felt passing through the valve, it is clogged. Clean the valve in solvent, recheck for air flow. Replace valve and/or hose if necessary.

REMOVAL & INSTALLATION

♦ See Figures 44, 45 and 46

To remove the PCV valve, disconnect the vacuum hose from the valve and unscrew the valve from the rocker arm cover by engaging the flats of the valve with an open end wrench. Thread the new valve into the rocker arm cover and tighten to 1.4 ft. lbs. (2.0 Nm). Connect the vacuum hose to the valve.

Evaporative Emission Canister

Fuel vapors from the gas tank and carburetor (created by changes in temperature) are absorbed by a charcoal filled canister. When the engine is operating, the stored vapors are sucked out of the canister and fed back to, and burned in the combustion chambers. The canisters are sealed, making cleaning unnecessary. The canister should be checked every 50,000 miles. Make sure all hoses are clamped and not dry rotted or broken. A number of types of valves are used

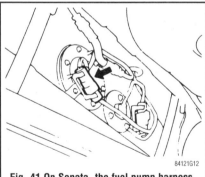

Fig. 41 On Sonata, the fuel pump harness is located at the rear of the fuel tank

Fig. 42 Firewall mounted fuel filter location. Use a wrench and socket to remove the banjo bolt securing the fuel line

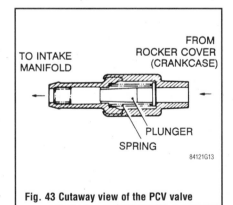

Fig. 43 Cutaway view of the PCV valve

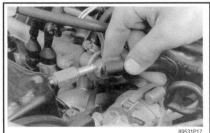

Fig. 44 When removing the PCV hose, check it for obstructions by blowing through the hose

Fig. 45 Carefully loosen the PCV valve with a wrench and remove it from the rocker cover

Fig. 46 When removed, shake the PCV valve. If a rattle is heard, the valve is operational

in the canister; refer to the Section 4 for a detailed description of their function and necessary servicing.

REMOVAL & INSTALLATION

▶ See Figure 47

The charcoal canister on early Excel models and all Elantra, Sonata and Scoupe models is located at the firewall on the passengers side of the vehicle. On all 1990–93 Excel models the charcoal canister is located below the battery tray.

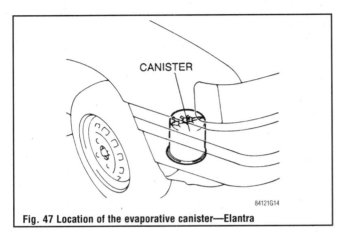

CANISTER

84121G14

Fig. 47 Location of the evaporative canister—Elantra

Except 1990–93 Excel

1. Label the hoses according to their position on the canister.
2. Remove the connecting hoses from the canister.
3. Loosen and remove the canister retaining band bolt or clip.
4. Remove the canister.
5. Check the hoses, replace any that are cracked, soft or collapsed. Install the new canister.

1990–93 Excel

1. Disconnect the battery cables and remove the battery.
2. Remove the battery tray mounting bolts and remove the tray.
3. Label the hoses according to their position on the canister.
4. Remove the connecting hoses from the canister.
5. Loosen and remove the canister retaining band bolt or clip.
6. Remove the canister.
7. Check the hoses, replace any that are cracked, soft or collapsed. Install the new canister.
8. Install the battery tray and the battery.

Battery

PRECAUTIONS

Always use caution when working on or near the battery. Never allow a tool to bridge the gap between the negative and positive battery terminals. Also, be careful not to allow a tool to provide a ground between the positive cable/terminal and any metal component on the vehicle. Either of these conditions will cause a short circuit, leading to sparks and possible personal injury.

Do not smoke or all open flames/sparks near a battery; the gases contained in the battery are very explosive and, if ignited, could cause severe injury or death.

All batteries, regardless of type, should be carefully secured by a battery hold-down device. If not, the terminals or casing may crack from stress during vehicle operation. A battery which is not secured may allow acid to leak, making it discharge faster. The acid can also eat away at components under the hood.

Always inspect the battery case for cracks, leakage and corrosion. A white corrosive substance on the battery case or on nearby components would indicate a leaking or cracked battery. If the battery is cracked, it should be replaced immediately.

GENERAL MAINTENANCE

Always keep the battery cables and terminals free of corrosion. Check and clean these components about once a year.

Keep the top of the battery clean, as a film of dirt can help discharge a battery that is not used for long periods. A solution of baking soda and water may be used for cleaning, but be careful to flush this off with clear water. DO NOT let any of the solution into the filler holes. Baking soda neutralizes battery acid and will de-activate a battery cell.

Batteries in vehicles which are not operated on a regular basis can fall victim to parasitic loads (small current drains which are constantly drawing current from the battery). Normal parasitic loads may drain a battery on a vehicle that is in storage and not used for 6–8 weeks. Vehicles that have additional accessories such as a phone or an alarm system may discharge a battery sooner. If the vehicle is to be stored for longer periods in a secure area and the alarm system is not necessary, the negative battery cable should be disconnected to protect the battery.

Remember that constantly deep cycling a battery (completely discharging and recharging it) will shorten battery life.

BATTERY FLUID

▶ See Figure 48

Check the battery electrolyte level at least once a month, or more often in hot weather or during periods of extended vehicle operation. On non-sealed batteries, the level can be checked either through the case (if translucent) or by removing the cell caps. The electrolyte level in each cell should be kept filled to the split ring inside each cell, or the line marked on the outside of the case.

If the level is low, add only distilled water through the opening until the level is correct. Each cell must be checked and filled individually. Distilled water should be used, because the chemicals and minerals found in most drinking water are harmful to the battery and could significantly shorten its life.

If water is added in freezing weather, the vehicle should be driven several miles to allow the water to mix with the electrolyte. Otherwise, the battery could freeze.

Although some maintenance-free batteries have removable cell caps, the electrolyte condition and level on all sealed maintenance-free batteries must be checked using the built-in hydrometer "eye." The exact type of eye will vary. But, most battery manufacturers, apply a sticker to the battery itself explaining the readings.

➡**Although the readings from built-in hydrometers will vary, a green eye usually indicates a properly charged battery with sufficient fluid level. A dark eye is normally an indicator of a battery with sufficient fluid, but which is low in charge. A light or yellow eye usually indicates that electrolyte has dropped below the necessary level. In this last case, sealed batteries with an insufficient electrolyte must usually be discarded.**

Checking the Specific Gravity

▶ See Figures 49, 50 and 51

A hydrometer is required to check the specific gravity on all batteries that are not maintenance-free. On batteries that are maintenance-free, the specific gravity

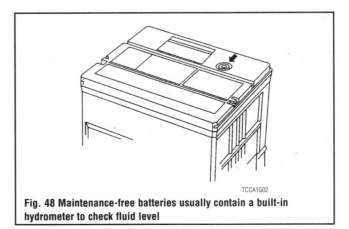

TCCA1G02

Fig. 48 Maintenance-free batteries usually contain a built-in hydrometer to check fluid level

Fig. 49 On non-sealed batteries, the fluid level can be checked by removing the cell caps

Fig. 50 If the fluid level is low, add only distilled water until the level is correct

Fig. 51 Check the specific gravity of the battery's electrolyte with a hydrometer

is checked by observing the built-in hydrometer "eye" on the top of the battery case.

✳✳ CAUTION

Battery electrolyte contains sulfuric acid. If you should splash any on your skin or in your eyes, flush the affected area with plenty of clear water. If it lands in your eyes, get medical help immediately.

The fluid (sulfuric acid solution) contained in the battery cells will tell you many things about the condition of the battery. Because the cell plates must be kept submerged below the fluid level in order to operate, the fluid level is extremely important. And, because the specific gravity of the acid is an indication of electrical charge, testing the fluid can be an aid in determining if the battery must be replaced. A battery in a vehicle with a properly operating charging system should require little maintenance, but careful, periodic inspection should reveal problems before they leave you stranded.

At least once a year, check the specific gravity of the battery. It should be between 1.20 and 1.26 on the gravity scale. Most auto stores carry a variety of inexpensive battery hydrometers. These can be used on any non-sealed battery to test the specific gravity in each cell.

The battery testing hydrometer has a squeeze bulb at one end and a nozzle at the other. Battery electrolyte is sucked into the hydrometer until the float is lifted from its seat. The specific gravity is then read by noting the position of the float. If gravity is low in one or more cells, the battery should be slowly charged and checked again to see if the gravity has come up. Generally, if after charging, the specific gravity between any two cells varies more than 50 points (0.50), the battery should be replaced, as it can no longer produce sufficient voltage to guarantee proper operation.

CABLES

◆ See Figures 52, 53, 54 and 55

Once a year (or as necessary), the battery terminals and the cable clamps should be cleaned. Loosen the clamps and remove the cables, negative cable first. On top post batteries, the use of a puller specially made for this purpose is recommended. These are inexpensive and available in most parts stores. Side terminal battery cables are secured with a small bolt.

Clean the cable clamps and the battery terminal with a wire brush, until all corrosion, grease, etc., is removed and the metal is shiny. It is especially important to clean the inside of the clamp thoroughly (an old knife is useful here), since a small deposit of oxidation there will prevent a sound connection and inhibit starting or charging. Special tools are available for cleaning these parts, one type for conventional top post batteries and another type for side terminal batteries. It is also a good idea to apply some dielectric grease to the terminal, as this will aid in the prevention of corrosion.

After the clamps and terminals are clean, reinstall the cables, negative cable last; DO NOT hammer the clamps onto battery posts. Tighten the clamps securely, but do not distort them. Give the clamps and terminals a thin external coating of grease after installation, to retard corrosion.

Check the cables at the same time that the terminals are cleaned. If the cable insulation is cracked or broken, or if the ends are frayed, the cable should be replaced with a new cable of the same length and gauge.

CHARGING

✳✳ CAUTION

The chemical reaction which takes place in all batteries generates explosive hydrogen gas. A spark can cause the battery to explode and splash acid. To avoid personal injury, be sure there is proper ventilation and take appropriate fire safety precautions when working with or near a battery.

A battery should be charged at a slow rate to keep the plates inside from getting too hot. However, if some maintenance-free batteries are allowed to discharge until they are almost "dead," they may have to be charged at a high rate to bring them back to "life." Always follow the charger manufacturer's instructions on charging the battery.

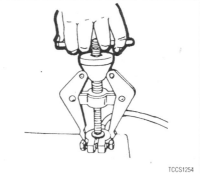

Fig. 52 A special tool is available to pull the clamp from the post

Fig. 53 The underside of this special battery tool has a wire brush to clean post terminals

Fig. 54 Place the tool over the battery posts and twist to clean until the metal is shiny

Fig. 55 The cable ends should be cleaned as well

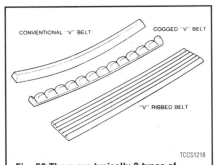

Fig. 56 There are typically 3 types of accessory drive belts found on vehicles today

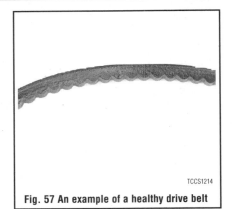

Fig. 57 An example of a healthy drive belt

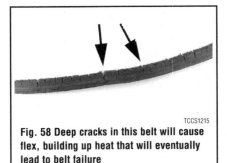

Fig. 58 Deep cracks in this belt will cause flex, building up heat that will eventually lead to belt failure

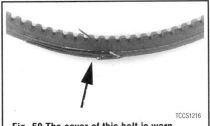

Fig. 59 The cover of this belt is worn, exposing the critical reinforcing cords to excessive wear

Fig. 60 Installing too wide a belt can result in serious belt wear and/or breakage

REPLACEMENT

When it becomes necessary to replace the battery, select one with an amperage rating equal to or greater than the battery originally installed. Deterioration and just plain aging of the battery cables, starter motor, and associated wires makes the battery's job harder in successive years. This makes it prudent to install a new battery with a greater capacity than the old.

Accessory Drive Belts

INSPECTION

▶ See Figures 56, 57, 58, 59 and 60

Inspect the belts for signs of glazing or cracking. A glazed belt will be perfectly smooth from slippage, while a good belt will have a slight texture of fabric visible. Cracks will usually start at the inner edge of the belt and run outward. All worn or damaged drive belts should be replaced immediately. It is best to replace all drive belts at one time, as a preventive maintenance measure, during this service operation.

It is a good idea, therefore, to visually inspect the belts regularly and replace them, routinely, every two to three years.

ADJUSTING

▶ See Figures 61, 62, 63, and 64

Except Sonata V6

▶ See Figures 65 and 66

Belts are normally adjusted by loosening the bolts of the accessory being driven and moving that accessory on its pivot points until the proper tension is applied to the belt. Some models also have belt tension adjusting bolts that are used to take up any slack in the belt. The accessory is held in this position while the bolts are tightened. To determine proper belt tension, you can purchase a belt tension gauge or simply use the deflection method. To determine deflection, press inward on the belt at the midpoint of its longest straight run. The belt should deflect (move inward) 0.35–0.43 in. (9–11mm). Some long V-belts and

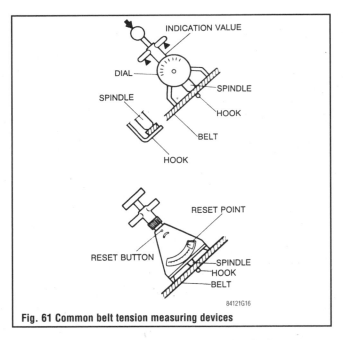

Fig. 61 Common belt tension measuring devices

most serpentine belts have idler pulleys which are used for adjusting purposes. Just loosen the idler pulley and move it to take up tension on the belt.

Sonata V6

▶ See Figures 67, 68, 69 and 70

ALTERNATOR AND POWER STEERING PUMP BELT

To increase the tension on the belt, first loosen the power steering nut pulley locknut. Then, with the proper size wrench, turn the adjusting bolt CLOCKWISE to loosen the pulley (this a left-hand threaded bolt). Move the tensioner pulley to tension the belt. Once the belt is tensioned, position the adjusting bolt back to the far side of the recess in the tensioner pulley mounting bracket and tighten the locknut to 11 ft. lbs. (15 Nm).

AIR CONDITIONER BELT

First loosen the tensioner pulley bolt that is labeled A in the accompanying illustration. Next, turn adjuster bolt B to adjust the belt deflection to 0.177–0.216 in. (4.5–5.5mm). Once the belt is tensioned, tighten bolt A and check the tension again after the bolt is tight. Crank the engine a few times and recheck the belt tension.

REMOVAL & INSTALLATION

▶ **See Figures 71 and 72**

To remove a drive belt, simply loosen the accessory being driven and move it on its pivot point to free the belt. Then, remove the belt. If an idler

pulley is used, it is often only necessary to loosen the idler pulley to provide enough slack the remove the belt. It is important to note, however, that on engines with many driven accessories, several or all of the belts may have to be replaced.

Hoses

INSPECTION

▶ **See Figures 73, 74, 75 and 76**

Upper and lower radiator hoses, along with the heater hoses, should be checked for deterioration, leaks and loose hose clamps at least every 15,000 miles (24,000 km). It is also wise to check the hoses periodically in early spring and at the beginning of the fall or winter when you are performing other mainte-

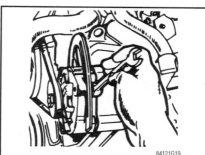

Fig. 62 To adjust the belt tension or to replace the belts, first loosen the component's mounting and adjusting bolts slightly

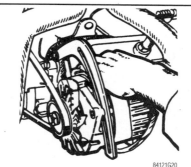

Fig. 63 Pull outward on the component and tighten the mounting and adjusting bolts

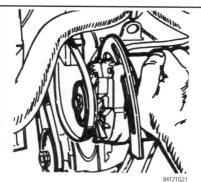

Fig. 64 To remove the belt, push the component inward and remove the belt

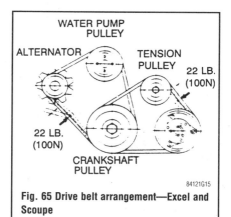

Fig. 65 Drive belt arrangement—Excel and Scoupe

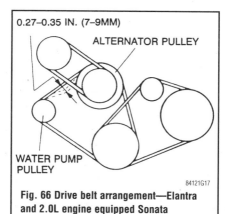

Fig. 66 Drive belt arrangement—Elantra and 2.0L engine equipped Sonata

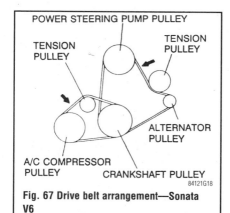

Fig. 67 Drive belt arrangement—Sonata V6

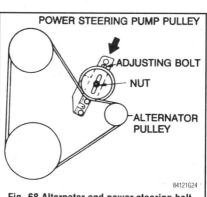

Fig. 68 Alternator and power steering belt adjustment on the Sonata V6

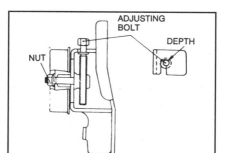

Fig. 69 Alternator and power steering belt adjusting bolt on the Sonata V6. This bolt has left hand threads, so turn it CLOCKWISE to loosen it

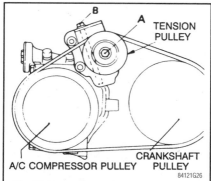

Fig. 70 Air conditioning compressor belt adjustment on the Sonata V6

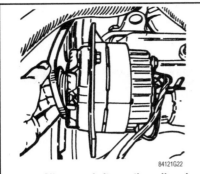

Fig. 71 Slip a new belt over the pulley, do not use prying tools to get the belt on

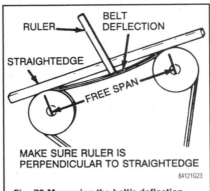

Fig. 72 Measuring the belt's deflection

Fig. 73 The cracks developing along this hose are a result of age-related hardening

Fig. 74 A hose clamp that is too tight can cause older hoses to separate and tear on either side of the clamp

Fig. 75 A soft spongy hose (identifiable by the swollen section) will eventually burst and should be replaced

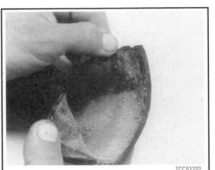

Fig. 76 Hoses are likely to deteriorate from the inside if the cooling system is not periodically flushed

nance. A quick visual inspection could discover a weakened hose which might have left you stranded if it had remained unrepaired.

Whenever you are checking the hoses, make sure the engine and cooling system are cold. Visually inspect for cracking, rotting or collapsed hoses, and replace as necessary. Run your hand along the length of the hose. If a weak or swollen spot is noted when squeezing the hose wall, the hose should be replaced.

REMOVAL & INSTALLATION

1. Remove the radiator pressure cap.

> ☀☀ **CAUTION**
>
> **Never remove the pressure cap while the engine is running, or personal injury from scalding hot coolant or steam may result. If possible, wait until the engine has cooled to remove the pressure cap. If this is not possible, wrap a thick cloth around the pressure cap and turn it slowly to the stop. Step back while the pressure is released from the cooling system. When you are sure all the pressure has been released, use the cloth to turn and remove the cap.**

2. Position a clean container under the radiator and/or engine draincock or plug, then open the drain and allow the cooling system to drain to an appropriate level. For some upper hoses, only a little coolant must be drained. To remove hoses positioned lower on the engine, such as a lower radiator hose, the entire cooling system must be emptied.

> ☀☀ **CAUTION**
>
> **When draining coolant, keep in mind that cats and dogs are attracted by ethylene glycol antifreeze, and are quite likely to drink any that is left in an uncovered container or in puddles on the ground. This will prove fatal in sufficient quantity. Always drain coolant into a sealable container.**

3. Loosen the hose clamps at each end of the hose requiring replacement.

Clamps are usually either of the spring tension type (which require pliers to squeeze the tabs and loosen) or of the screw tension type (which require screw or hex drivers to loosen). Pull the clamps back on the hose away from the connection.

4. Twist, pull and slide the hose off the fitting, taking care not to damage the neck of the component from which the hose is being removed.

➡️**If the hose is stuck at the connection, do not try to insert a screwdriver or other sharp tool under the hose end in an effort to free it, as the connection and/or hose may become damaged. Heater connections especially may be easily damaged by such a procedure. If the hose is to be replaced, use a single-edged razor blade to make a slice along the portion of the hose which is stuck on the connection, perpendicular to the end of the hose. Do not cut too deep so as to prevent damaging the connection. The hose can then be peeled from the connection and discarded.**

5. Clean both hose mounting connections. Inspect the condition of the hose clamps and replace them, if necessary.

To install:

6. Dip the ends of the new hose into clean engine coolant to ease installation.

7. Slide the clamps over the replacement hose, then slide the hose ends over the connections into position.

8. Position and secure the clamps at least ¼ in. (6.35mm) from the ends of the hose. Make sure they are located beyond the raised bead of the connector.

9. Close the radiator or engine drains and properly refill the cooling system with the clean drained engine coolant or a suitable mixture of coolant and water.

10. If available, install a pressure tester and check for leaks. If a pressure tester is not available, run the engine until normal operating temperature is reached (allowing the system to naturally pressurize), then check for leaks.

> ☀☀ **CAUTION**
>
> **If you are checking for leaks with the system at normal operating temperature, BE EXTREMELY CAREFUL not to touch any moving or hot engine parts. Once temperature has been reached, shut the**

engine OFF, and check for leaks around the hose fittings and connections which were removed earlier.

Air Conditioning System

SYSTEM SERVICE & REPAIR

➡**It is recommended that the A/C system be serviced by an EPA Section 609 certified automotive technician utilizing a refrigerant recovery/recycling machine.**

The do-it-yourselfer should not service his/her own vehicle's A/C system for many reasons, including legal concerns, personal injury, environmental damage and cost.

According to the U.S. Clean Air Act, it is a federal crime to service or repair (involving the refrigerant) a Motor Vehicle Air Conditioning (MVAC) system for money without being EPA certified. It is also illegal to vent R-12 refrigerant into the atmosphere. State and/or local laws may be more strict than the federal regulations, so be sure to check with your state and/or local authorities for further information.

➡**Federal law dictates that a fine of up to $25,000 may be levied on people convicted of venting refrigerant into the atmosphere.**

When servicing an A/C system you run the risk of handling or coming in contact with refrigerant, which may result in skin or eye irritation or frostbite. Although low in toxicity (due to chemical stability), inhalation of concentrated refrigerant fumes is dangerous and can result in death; cases of fatal cardiac arrhythmia have been reported in people accidentally subjected to high levels of refrigerant. Some early symptoms include loss of concentration and drowsiness.

Also, some refrigerants can decompose at high temperatures (near gas heaters or open flame), which may result in hydrofluoric acid, hydrochloric acid and phosgene (a fatal nerve gas).

It is usually more economically feasible to have a certified MVAC automotive technician perform A/C system service on your vehicle.

PREVENTIVE MAINTENANCE

Although the A/C system should not be serviced by the do-it-yourselfer, preventive maintenance should be practiced to help maintain the efficiency of the vehicle's A/C system. Be sure to perform the following:

• The easiest and most important preventive maintenance for your A/C system is to be sure that it is used on a regular basis. Running the system for five minutes each month (no matter what the season) will help ensure that the seals and all internal components remain lubricated.

➡**Some vehicles automatically operate the A/C system compressor whenever the windshield defroster is activated. Therefore, the A/C system would not need to be operated each month if the defroster was used.**

• In order to prevent heater core freeze-up during A/C operation, it is necessary to maintain proper antifreeze protection. Be sure to properly maintain the engine cooling system.

• Any obstruction of or damage to the condenser configuration will restrict air flow which is essential to its efficient operation. Keep this unit clean and in proper physical shape.

➡**Bug screens which are mounted in front of the condenser (unless they are original equipment) are regarded as obstructions.**

• The condensation drain tube expels any water which accumulates on the bottom of the evaporator housing into the engine compartment. If this tube is obstructed, the air conditioning performance can be restricted and condensation buildup can spill over onto the vehicle's floor.

SYSTEM INSPECTION

Although the A/C system should not be serviced by the do-it-yourselfer, system inspections should be performed to help maintain the efficiency of the vehicle's A/C system. Be sure to perform the following:

The easiest and often most important check for the air conditioning system consists of a visual inspection of the system components. Visually inspect the system for refrigerant leaks, damaged compressor clutch, abnormal compressor drive belt tension and/or condition, plugged evaporator drain tube, blocked condenser fins, disconnected or broken wires, blown fuses, corroded connections and poor insulation.

A refrigerant leak will usually appear as an oily residue at the leakage point in the system. The oily residue soon picks up dust or dirt particles from the surrounding air and appears greasy. Through time, this will build up and appear to be a heavy dirt impregnated grease.

For a thorough visual and operational inspection, check the following:

• Check the surface of the radiator and condenser for dirt, leaves or other material which might block air flow.

• Check for kinks in hoses and lines. Check the system for leaks.

• Make sure the drive belt is properly tensioned. During operation, make sure the belt is free of noise or slippage.

• Make sure the blower motor operates at all appropriate positions, then check for distribution of the air from all outlets.

➡**Remember that in high humidity, air discharged from the vents may not feel as cold as expected, even if the system is working properly. This is because moisture in humid air retains heat more effectively than dry air, thereby making humid air more difficult to cool.**

Windshield Wipers

ELEMENT (REFILL) CARE & REPLACEMENT

◗ **See Figures 77 thru 86**

For maximum effectiveness and longest element life, the windshield and wiper blades should be kept clean. Dirt, tree sap, road tar and so on will cause streaking, smearing and blade deterioration if left on the glass. It is advisable to wash the windshield carefully with a commercial glass cleaner at least once a month. Wipe off the rubber blades with the wet rag afterwards. Do not attempt to move wipers across the windshield by hand; damage to the motor and drive mechanism will result.

To inspect and/or replace the wiper blade elements, place the wiper switch in the **LOW** speed position and the ignition switch in the **ACC** position. When the wiper blades are approximately vertical on the windshield, turn the ignition switch to **OFF**.

Examine the wiper blade elements. If they are found to be cracked, broken or torn, they should be replaced immediately. Replacement intervals will vary with usage, although ozone deterioration usually limits element life to about one year. If the wiper pattern is smeared or streaked, or if the blade chatters across the glass, the elements should be replaced. It is easiest and most sensible to replace the elements in pairs.

If your vehicle is equipped with aftermarket blades, there are several different types of refills and your vehicle might have any kind. Aftermarket blades and arms

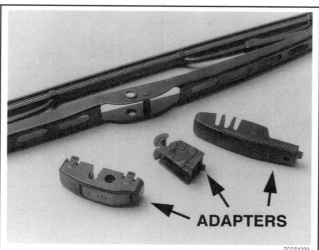

TCCS1223

Fig. 77 Bosch® wiper blade and fit kit

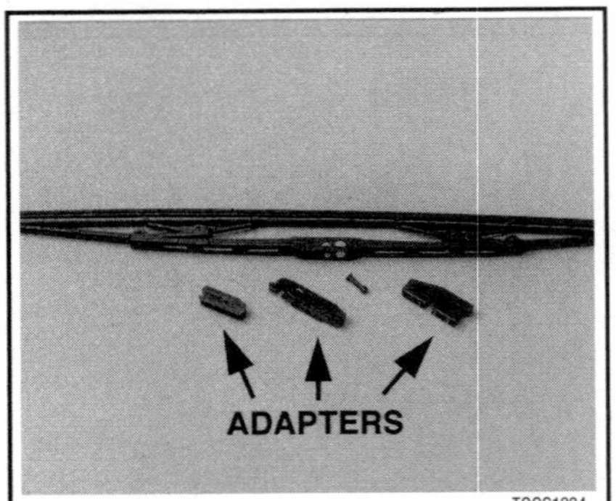

TCCS1224

Fig. 78 Lexor® wiper blade and fit kit

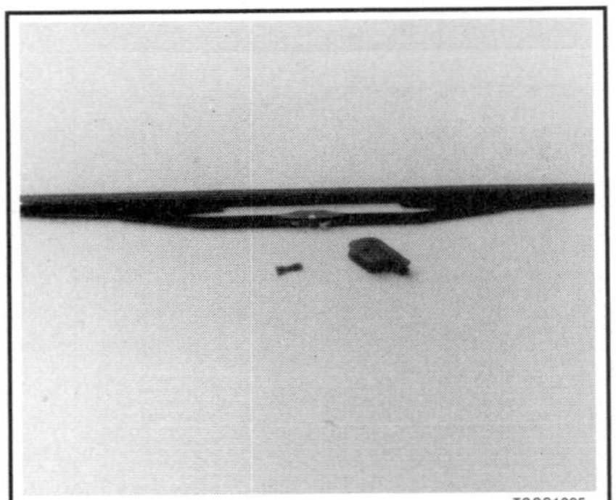

TCCS1225

Fig. 79 Pylon® wiper blade and adapter

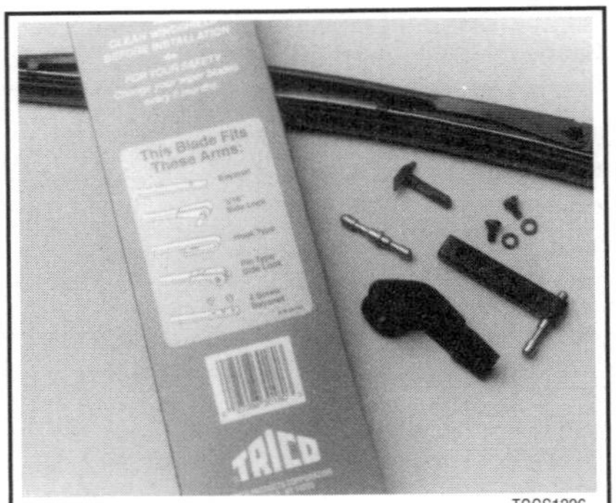

TCCS1226

Fig. 80 Trico® wiper blade and fit kit

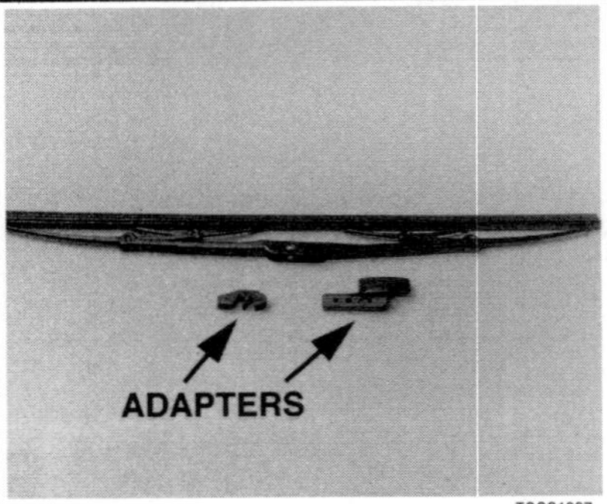

TCCS1227

Fig. 81 Tripledge® wiper blade and fit kit

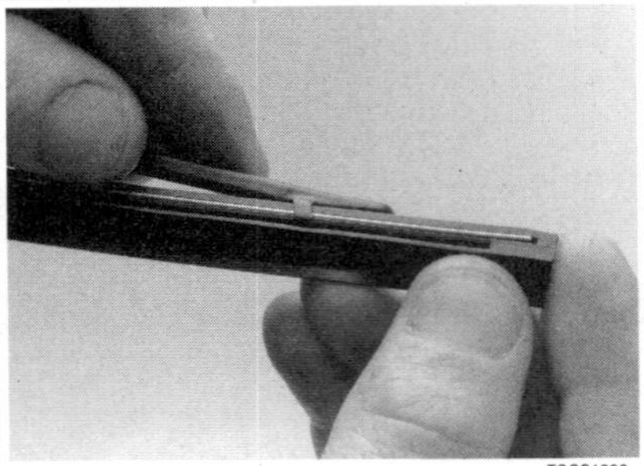

TCCS1228

Fig. 82 To remove and install a Lexor® wiper blade refill, slip out the old insert and slide in a new one

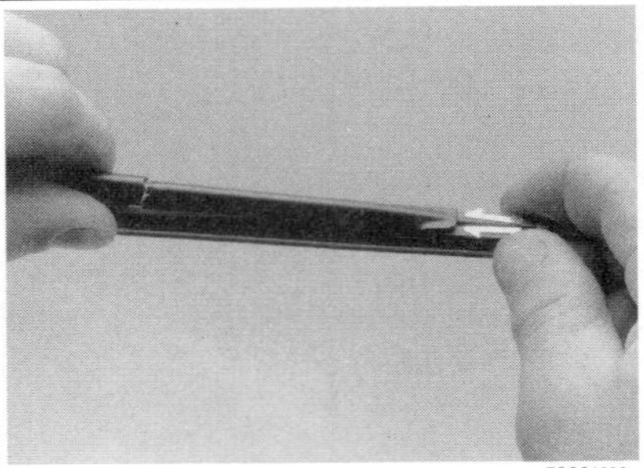

TCCS1229

Fig. 83 On Pylon® inserts, the clip at the end has to be removed prior to sliding the insert off

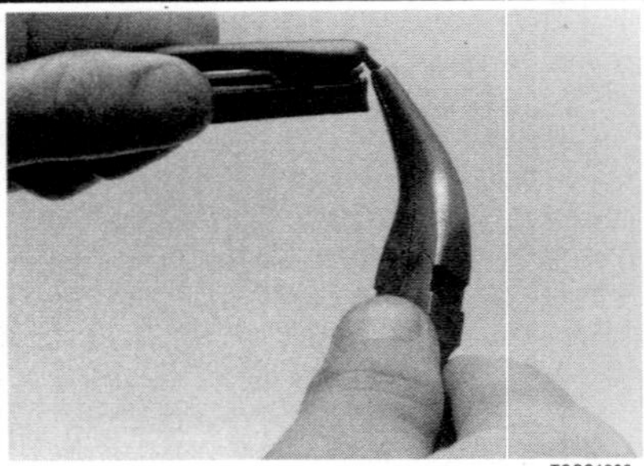

TCCS1230

Fig. 84 On Trico® wiper blades, the tab at the end of the blade must be turned up . . .

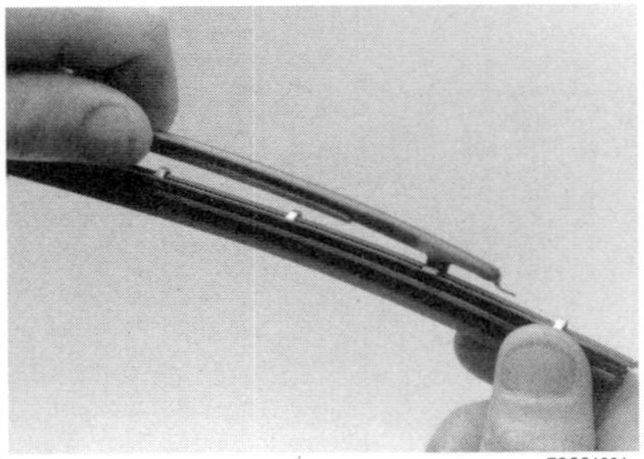

TCCS1231

Fig. 85 . . . then the insert can be removed. After installing the replacement insert, bend the tab back

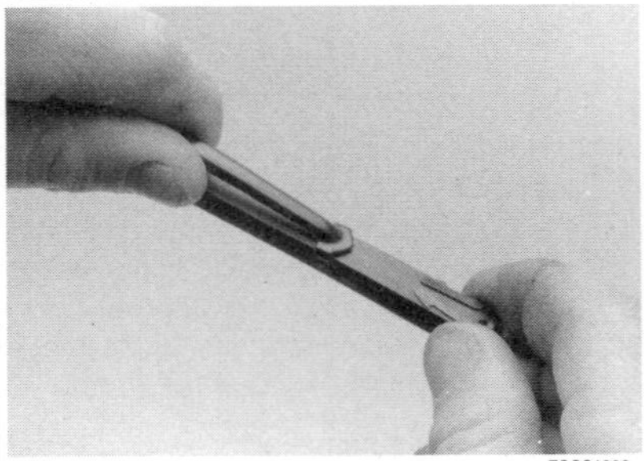

TCCS1232

Fig. 86 The Tripledge® wiper blade insert is removed and installed using a securing clip

rarely use the exact same type blade or refill as the original equipment. Here are some typical aftermarket blades; not all may be available for your vehicle:

The Anco® type uses a release button that is pushed down to allow the refill to slide out of the yoke jaws. The new refill slides back into the frame and locks in place.

Some Trico® refills are removed by locating where the metal backing strip or the refill is wider. Insert a small screwdriver blade between the frame and metal backing strip. Press down to release the refill from the retaining tab.

Other types of Trico® refills have two metal tabs which are unlocked by squeezing them together. The rubber filler can then be withdrawn from the frame jaws. A new refill is installed by inserting the refill into the front frame jaws and sliding it rearward to engage the remaining frame jaws. There are usually four jaws; be certain when installing that the refill is engaged in all of them. At the end of its travel, the tabs will lock into place on the front jaws of the wiper blade frame.

Another type of refill is made from polycarbonate. The refill has a simple locking device at one end which flexes downward out of the groove into which the jaws of the holder fit, allowing easy release. By sliding the new refill through all the jaws and pushing through the slight resistance when it reaches the end of its travel, the refill will lock into position.

To replace the Tridon® refill, it is necessary to remove the wiper blade. This refill has a plastic backing strip with a notch about 1 in. (25mm) from the end. Hold the blade (frame) on a hard surface so that the frame is tightly bowed. Grip the tip of the backing strip and pull up while twisting counterclockwise. The backing strip will snap out of the retaining tab. Do this for the remaining tabs until the refill is free of the blade. The length of these refills is molded into the end and they should be replaced with identical types.

Regardless of the type of refill used, be sure to follow the part manufacturer's instructions closely. Make sure that all of the frame jaws are engaged as the refill is pushed into place and locked. If the metal blade holder and frame are allowed to touch the glass during wiper operation, the glass will be scratched.

Tires and Wheels

Common sense and good driving habits will afford maximum tire life. Make sure that you don't overload the vehicle or run with incorrect pressure in the tires. Either of these will increase tread wear. Fast starts, sudden stops and sharp cornering are hard on tires and will shorten their useful life span.

➡For optimum tire life, keep the tires properly inflated, rotate them often and have the wheel alignment checked periodically.

Inspect your tires frequently. Be especially careful to watch for bubbles in the tread or sidewall, deep cuts or underinflation. Replace any tires with bubbles in the sidewall. If cuts are so deep that they penetrate to the cords, discard the tire. Any cut in the sidewall of a radial tire renders it unsafe. Also look for uneven tread wear patterns that may indicate the front end is out of alignment or that the tires are out of balance.

TIRE ROTATION

◆ See Figure 87

Tires must be rotated periodically to equalize wear patterns that vary with a tire's position on the vehicle. Tires will also wear in an uneven way as the front steering/suspension system wears to the point where the alignment should be reset.

Rotating the tires will ensure maximum life for the tires as a set, so you will not have to discard a tire early due to wear on only part of the tread. Regular rotation is required to equalize wear.

When rotating "unidirectional tires," make sure that they always roll in the same direction. This means that a tire used on the left side of the vehicle must not be switched to the right side and vice-versa. Such tires should only be rotated front-to-rear or rear-to-front, while always remaining on the same side of the vehicle. These tires are marked on the sidewall as to the direction of rotation; observe the marks when reinstalling the tire(s).

Some styled or "mag" wheels may have different offsets front to rear. In these cases, the rear wheels must not be used up front and vice-versa. Furthermore, if these wheels are equipped with unidirectional tires, they cannot be rotated unless the tire is remounted for the proper direction of rotation.

➡The compact or space-saver spare is strictly for emergency use. It must never be included in the tire rotation or placed on the vehicle for everyday use.

TIRE DESIGN

◆ See Figure 88

For maximum satisfaction, tires should be used in sets of four. Mixing of different brands or types (radial, bias-belted, fiberglass belted) should be avoided. In most cases, the vehicle manufacturer has designated a type of tire on which the vehicle will perform best. Your first choice when replacing tires should be to use the same type of tire that the manufacturer recommends.

When radial tires are used, tire sizes and wheel diameters should be selected to maintain ground clearance and tire load capacity equivalent to the original specified tire. Radial tires should always be used in sets of four.

✳✳ CAUTION

Radial tires should never be used on only the front axle.

When selecting tires, pay attention to the original size as marked on the tire. Most tires are described using an industry size code sometimes referred to as

P-Metric. This allows the exact identification of the tire specifications, regardless of the manufacturer. If selecting a different tire size or brand, remember to check the installed tire for any sign of interference with the body or suspension while the vehicle is stopping, turning sharply or heavily loaded.

Snow Tires

Good radial tires can produce a big advantage in slippery weather, but in snow, a street radial tire does not have sufficient tread to provide traction and control. The small grooves of a street tire quickly pack with snow and the tire behaves like a billiard ball on a marble floor. The more open, chunky tread of a snow tire will self-clean as the tire turns, providing much better grip on snowy surfaces.

To satisfy municipalities requiring snow tires during weather emergencies, most snow tires carry either an M + S designation after the tire size stamped on the sidewall, or the designation "all-season." In general, no change in tire size is necessary when buying snow tires.

Most manufacturers strongly recommend the use of 4 snow tires on their vehicles for reasons of stability. If snow tires are fitted only to the drive wheels, the opposite end of the vehicle may become very unstable when braking or turning on slippery surfaces. This instability can lead to unpleasant endings if the driver can't counteract the slide in time.

Note that snow tires, whether 2 or 4, will affect vehicle handling in all non-snow situations. The stiffer, heavier snow tires will noticeably change the turning and braking characteristics of the vehicle. Once the snow tires are installed, you must re-learn the behavior of the vehicle and drive accordingly.

➡Consider buying extra wheels on which to mount the snow tires. Once done, the "snow wheels" can be installed and removed as needed. This eliminates the potential damage to tires or wheels from seasonal removal and installation. Even if your vehicle has styled wheels, see if inexpensive steel wheels are available. Although the look of the vehicle will change, the expensive wheels will be protected from salt, curb hits and pothole damage.

TIRE STORAGE

If they are mounted on wheels, store the tires at proper inflation pressure. All tires should be kept in a cool, dry place. If they are stored in the garage or basement, do not let them stand on a concrete floor; set them on strips of wood, a mat or a large stack of newspaper. Keeping them away from direct moisture is of paramount importance. Tires should not be stored upright, but in a flat position.

INFLATION & INSPECTION

◆ See Figures 89 thru 94

The importance of proper tire inflation cannot be overemphasized. A tire employs air as part of its structure. It is designed around the supporting strength of the air at a specified pressure. For this reason, improper inflation drastically reduces the tire's ability to perform as intended. A tire will lose some air in day-to-day use; having to add a few pounds of air periodically is not necessarily a sign of a leaking tire.

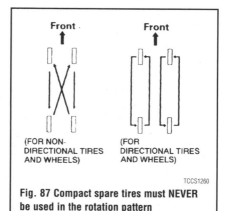

TCCS1260

Fig. 87 Compact spare tires must NEVER be used in the rotation pattern

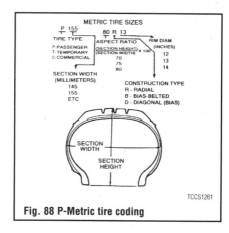

TCCS1261

Fig. 88 P-Metric tire coding

TCCS1095

Fig. 89 Tires with deep cuts, or cuts which bulge, should be replaced immediately

Two items should be a permanent fixture in every glove compartment: an accurate tire pressure gauge and a tread depth gauge. Check the tire pressure (including the spare) regularly with a pocket type gauge. Too often, the gauge on the end of the air hose at your corner garage is not accurate because it suffers too much abuse. Always check tire pressure when the tires are cold, as pressure increases with temperature. If you must move the vehicle to check the tire inflation, do not drive more than a mile before checking. A cold tire is generally one that has not been driven for more than three hours.

A plate or sticker is normally provided somewhere in the vehicle (door post, hood, tailgate or trunk lid) which shows the proper pressure for the tires. Never counteract excessive pressure build-up by bleeding off air pressure (letting some air out). This will cause the tire to run hotter and wear quicker.

❊❊ CAUTION

Never exceed the maximum tire pressure embossed on the tire! This is the pressure to be used when the tire is at maximum loading, but it is rarely the correct pressure for everyday driving. Consult the owner's manual or the tire pressure sticker for the correct tire pressure.

Once you've maintained the correct tire pressures for several weeks, you'll be familiar with the vehicle's braking and handling personality. Slight adjustments in tire pressures can fine-tune these characteristics, but never change the cold pressure specification by more than 2 psi. A slightly softer tire pressure will give a softer ride but also yield lower fuel mileage. A slightly harder tire will give crisper dry road handling but can cause skidding on wet surfaces.

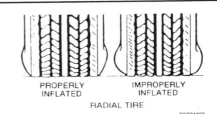

Fig. 90 Radial tires have a characteristic sidewall bulge; don't try to measure pressure by looking at the tire. Use a quality air pressure gauge

Unless you're fully attuned to the vehicle, stick to the recommended inflation pressures.

All automotive tires have built-in tread wear indicator bars that show up as ½ in. (13mm) wide smooth bands across the tire when ¹⁄₁₆ in. (1.5mm) of tread remains. The appearance of tread wear indicators means that the tires should be replaced. In fact, many states have laws prohibiting the use of tires with less than this amount of tread.

You can check your own tread depth with an inexpensive gauge or by using a Lincoln head penny. Slip the Lincoln penny (with Lincoln's head upside-down) into several tread grooves. If you can see the top of Lincoln's head in 2 adjacent grooves, the tire has less than ¹⁄₁₆ in. (1.5mm) tread left and should be replaced. You can measure snow tires in the same manner by using the "tails" side of the Lincoln penny. If you can see the top of the Lincoln memorial, it's time to replace the snow tire(s).

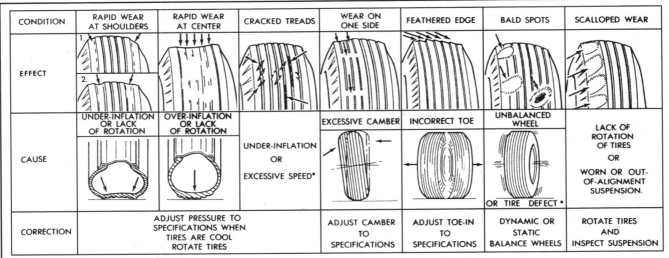

Fig. 91 Common tire wear patterns and causes

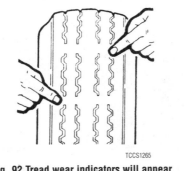

Fig. 92 Tread wear indicators will appear when the tire is worn

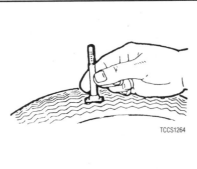

Fig. 93 Accurate tread depth indicators are inexpensive and handy

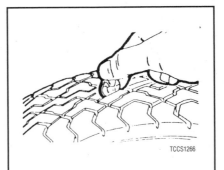

Fig. 94 A penny works well for a quick check of tread depth

FLUIDS AND LUBRICANTS

Waste Fluid Disposal

Used fluids such as engine oil, transmission fluid, anti-freeze and brake fluid are hazardous wastes and must be disposed of properly. Before draining any fluids, consult your local authorities; in many areas, waste oil, etc. is being accepted as a part of recycling programs. An increasing number of service stations and auto parts stores are also accepting waste fluids for recycling.

Be sure of the recycling center's policies before draining fluids, as many will not accept fluids which have been mixed together.

Fuel and Oil Recommendations

FUEL

All Hyundai vehicles covered in this manual are designed to run on unleaded fuel only.

You should be careful to use quality fuels having an octane rating of 86 or greater when measured by the R/M method, which averages "Research" and "Motor" octane ratings. Too low an octane rating will produce combustion knock, which will prove to be damaging to the engine over a long period. Always buy fuel from a reputable dealer, preferably where a regular volume is pumped so that the fuel is always fresh.

OIL

♦ See Figure 95

When using engine oil, there are two types of ratings with which you should be familiar: viscosity and service (quality). There are several service ratings, resulting from tests established by the American Petroleum Institute. Use only SE rated oil or SF (for better fuel economy). SF oil passes SE requirements and also reduces fuel consumption. No other service ratings are acceptable.

Oil can be purchased with two types of viscosity ratings, single and multi-viscosity. Oil viscosity ratings are important because oil tends to thin out at high temperatures while getting too thick and stiff at low temperatures. Single viscosity oil, designated by only one number (SAE 30), varies in viscosity or thickness, a great deal over a wide range of temperatures. The single rating number comes from the fact that the oil is basically a single, straight grade of petroleum. A multi-viscosity oil rating is given as two numbers (for example: SAE 10W-40, the **W** standing for **winter**). Multi-viscosity oils slow changes in viscosity with temperature. These changes occur with changes in engine temperature conditions, such as cold starts versus eventual engine warm-up and operation. The double designation refers to the fact that the oil behaves like straight 10W oil at 0°F and like straight 40W oil at 200°F. The desirable advantage of multi-viscosity oil is that it can maintain adequate thickness at high engine operating temperatures (when oil tends to get too thin) while it resists the tendency to thicken at very low temperatures. A straight 30W oil gets so thick near 0°F that the engine will usually not crank fast enough to start. Because of its versatility, a multi-viscosity oil would be the more desirable choice.

When adding oil, try to use the same brand that's in the crankcase since not all oils are completely compatible with each other.

Engine

OIL LEVEL CHECK

♦ See Figures 96, 97 and 98

At every stop for fuel, check the engine oil as follows:
1. Park the car on a level surface.
2. The engine may be either hot or cold when checking oil level. However, if it is hot, wait a few minutes after the engine has been shut off to allow the oil to drain back into the crankcase. If the engine is cold, do not start it before checking the oil level.
3. Open the hood and locate the dipstick, which is on the front of the engine. Pull the dipstick from its tube, wipe it clean, and reinsert it.
4. Pull the dipstick again and, holding it horizontally, read the oil level. The oil should be between the MIN and MAX mark. If the oil is below the MIN mark, add oil of the proper viscosity through the capped opening of the valve cover.
5. Replace the dipstick, and check the level again after adding any oil. Be careful not to overfill the crankcase. Approximately one quart of oil will raise the level from the low mark to the high mark. Excess oil will generally be consumed at an accelerated rate even if no damage to the engine seals occurs.

OIL AND FILTER CHANGE

♦ See Figures 99 thru 107

Oil changes should be performed at intervals as described in your owners manual. However, it is a good idea to change the oil and oil filter at least three to four times a year depending on how many miles the car is driven. If your car is being used under dusty conditions, change the oil and filter sooner. The same thing goes for cars being driven in stop and go city traffic, where acid and

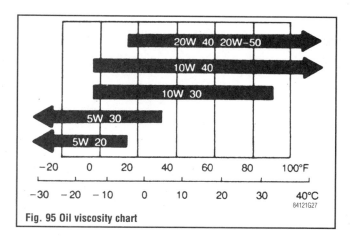

Fig. 95 Oil viscosity chart

Fig. 96 The engine oil dipstick is located at the front of the engine compartment, either on the passenger's side . . .

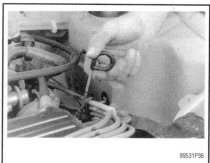

Fig. 97 . . . or on the driver's side

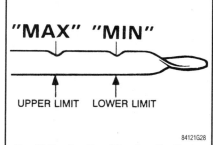

Fig. 98 Reading the oil level on the dipstick

sludge buildup is a problem. The oil should also be changed more frequently in cars which are constantly driven at high speeds on expressways. The relatively high engine speeds associated with turnpike driving mean higher operating temperatures and a greater instance of oil foaming.

Always drain the oil after the engine has been run long enough to bring it to the normal operating temperature. Hot oil will flow easier and more contaminants will be removed with the oil than if it were drained cold. The cost of a large capacity drain pan, which can be purchased at any automotive supply store, will be more than paid back by savings from do-it-yourself oil changes. Another necessity is containers for the used oil. You will find that plastic bleach containers make excellent storage bottles.

To change the oil:

1. Run the engine until it reaches the normal operating temperature. Raise and safely support the front of the car.
2. Remove the filler cap, wipe it off and set it aside.
3. Slide a drain pan under the oil pan drain plug.
4. Loosen the drain plug with a socket or box wrench, and then remove it by hand. Push in on the plug as you turn it out, so that no oil escapes until the plug is completely removed.
5. Allow the oil to drain into the pan.
6. Clean and install the drain plug, making sure that the gasket is still on the plug. Tighten the drain plug to 25–33 ft. lbs. (34–44 Nm).
7. Refill the engine with oil and replace the filler cap. Start the engine and check for leaks.

The car manufacturer recommends changing the oil filter at every other oil change, but it is more beneficial to replace the filter every time the oil is changed. Aside from the obvious improved filtration that a new filter affords, what most people don't realize is that a quantity of the old oil remains in the filter at all times. If the oil filter is not changed with the oil, the old, contaminated oil has a chance to mix with and dilute the new oil. Not renewing the oil filter at every oil change, in reality, only constitutes a partial oil change.

✳✳ CAUTION

Prolonged and repeated skin contact with used engine oil, with no effort to remove the oil, may be harmful.

Manual Transaxle

FLUID RECOMMENDATIONS

These units use SAE 75-85W or 85W-90 GL-4/GL-5 gear oil.

Fig. 99 The engine oil drain plug is located at the bottom of the oil pan, directly below the engine

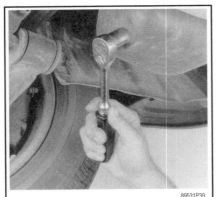

Fig. 100 Using the proper size wrench, loosen, but do not remove the oil drain plug

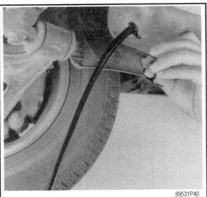

Fig. 101 Carefully unscrew the drain plug with your fingers, keeping pressure on the plug to prevent spills

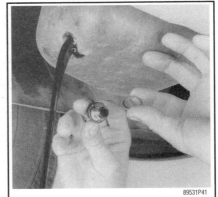

Fig. 102 Always check the drain plug gasket for damage and replace it as necessary

Fig. 103 The oil filter is located beneath the engine, near the oil pan rail, and can be easily unscrewed with a wrench

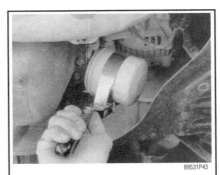

Fig. 104 Be sure to slide the oil filter wrench as far up on the filter as possible, to avoid crushing it during removal

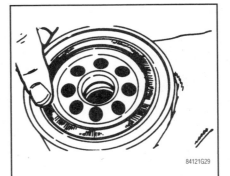

Fig. 105 Apply a thin film of clean engine oil to the filter gasket, before installing it

LEVEL CHECK

◆ See Figure 108

Check the lubricant level at the interval specified in the maintenance chart.

1. With the car parked on a level surface, remove the filler plug from the side of the transmission case.

2. If lubricant begins to trickle out the hole, there is enough. Otherwise, carefully insert a finger (watch out for sharp threads) and check to see if the oil is up to the edge of the hole.

3. If not, add lubricant through the hole to raise the level to the edge of the filler hole. Most gear lubricants come in a plastic squeeze bottle with a nozzle, making additions easy, you can also use a squeeze bulb. Add gear oil GL-4/GL-5.

4. Replace the plug and check for leaks.

DRAIN AND REFILL

It is relatively easy to change your own gear oil. The oil level should be checked twice a year and changed every 36,000 miles or three years, whichever comes first. The only equipment required is a drain pan, a socket to fit the filler and drain plugs, and an oil suction gun or gear oil in a squeeze bottle. Gear oil can be purchased in quarts or gallon cans at automotive supply stores.

To change the oil:

1. Raise and safely support the front end on jackstands.

2. Slide a drain pan under the drain plug.

3. Remove the filler plug and then the drain plug.

4. When the oil has been completely drained, install the drain plug.

5. Using the squeeze bottle or suction gun, refill the gearbox to the level of the filler plug.

6. Install and tighten the filler plug.

Automatic Transaxle

FLUID RECOMMENDATIONS

These units use DEXRON®II automatic transmission fluid.

LEVEL CHECK

◆ See Figure 109

Check the level of the automatic transaxle fluid every 2,000 miles. There is a dipstick at the right side of the engine or transaxle.

❋❋ CAUTION

The electric cooling fan may switch on any time the engine is running. Keep hands away. The dipstick has a high and low mark which are accurate for level indications only when the transmission is hot (normal operating temperature). The transmission is considered hot after 15 miles of highway driving.

1. Park the car on a level surface with the engine idling. Apply the parking brake.

2. Shift the transmission to Park.

3. Remove the dipstick, wipe it clean, then reinsert it firmly. Be certain that it has been pushed fully home. Remove the dipstick and check the fluid level while holding the dipstick horizontally. The level should be at or near the high mark.

4. If the fluid level is below the low mark in the HOT range, add Dexron®II type automatic transmission fluid through the dipstick tube. This is more easily accomplished with the aid of a funnel and hose. Check the level often between additions, being careful not to overfill the transmission. Overfilling will cause slippage, seal damage, and overheating. Approximately one pint of fluid will raise the level from low to high.

➡**The fluid on the dipstick should be bright red color. If it is discolored (brown or black), or smells burnt, serious transmission troubles, probably due to overheating, should be suspected. The transmission should be inspected to locate the cause of the burnt fluid.**

DRAIN AND REFILL

◆ See Figures 110 and 111

1. Jack up the front of the car and support it on jackstands. Remove the lower cover.

Fig. 106 Twist and remove the oil filler cap . . .

Fig. 107 . . . then pour new oil into the engine. Always use the proper grade of oil for your driving conditions

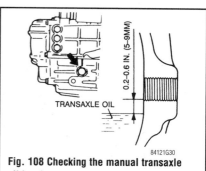

Fig. 108 Checking the manual transaxle oil level

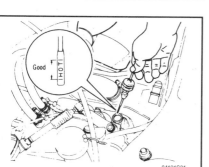

Fig. 109 Check the automatic transaxle fluid level by using the dipstick in the transaxle

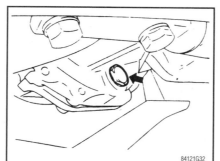

Fig. 110 The automatic transaxle drain plug is located in the transaxle oil pan—location on Excel

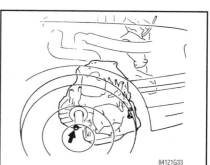

Fig. 111 The automatic transaxle drain plug is located in the transaxle oil pan—location on Sonata

2. Slide a drain pan under the differential and remove the drain plug. When the differential is completely drained, move the pan under the transmission, remove the plug and drain. If the plug gasket is worn, replace it with a new one.

3. Reinstall the two drain plugs. Fill the transmission with 4.2 qts. of Dexron®II fluid. Start the engine and allow to idle for at least two minutes. With the parking brake applied, move the selector to each position ending in Neutral.

4. Add sufficient fluid to bring the level to the lower dipstick mark. Recheck the fluid level after the transmission is up to normal operating temperature.

PAN AND FILTER SERVICE

▶ **See Figures 112, 113, and 114**

1. Raise the front of the vehicle and support it safely.
2. Remove the drain plug from the bottom of the differential and allow the fluid to drain.
3. Position a large drain pan under the oil pan and have plenty of rags on hand.
4. Slightly loosen all the pan bolts. Tap one corner of the pan with a soft hammer to break the seal.
5. Once the pan is broken loose, support it, remove all the bolts, and then tilt it to one side to drain the fluid.
6. Check the oil filter for clogging and damage and replace as necessary.
7. Clean all the gasket surfaces and the inside of the pan thoroughly. Then, raise the pan and gasket in position with bolt holes lined up. Support the pan and replace the bolts, tightening them only very gently with your fingers.
8. Tighten the pan bolts diagonally in several stages to 7.5–8.5 ft. lbs. (10–12 Nm).
9. Install the drain plug and torque to 22–25 ft. lbs. (30–35 Nm).
10. Pour fluid in carefully through the dipstick hole until it reaches the lower mark on the dipstick.
11. Start the engine and allow to idle for about two minutes so that the fluid has a chance to warm to normal operating temperature.
12. Check the fluid level as described above and add fluid as necessary.

Engine Coolant

FLUID RECOMMENDATIONS

A good quality ethylene glycol based or other aluminum compatible antifreeze is recommended for use in the vehicles covered by this Manual. It is best to add a 50/50 mix of antifreeze and distilled water to avoid diluting the coolant in the system.

LEVEL CHECK

▶ **See Figure 115**

Allow the engine to cool down. Using a rag, turn the radiator cap 1/4 turn to the stop and allow all pressure to escape. Then, remove the cap. Check the level visually in the expansion tank. It should be above the low mark. Never fill the tank over the upper mark. Fill the radiator until the level is within 25mm (1 in.)

of the radiator cap. It is best to add a 50/50 mix of ethylene glycol antifreeze and water to avoid diluting the coolant in the system. Use permanent type antifreeze only. Avoid using water that is known to have a high alkaline content or is very hard, except in emergency situations. Drain and flush the cooling system as soon as possible after using such water.

✳✳ CAUTION

Cover the radiator cap with a thick cloth before removing it from a radiator in a vehicle that is hot. Turn the cap counterclockwise slowly until pressure can be heard escaping. Allow all pressure to escape from the radiator before completely removing the radiator cap. It is best to allow the engine to cool if possible, before removing the radiator cap. After filling the radiator, run the engine until it reaches normal operating temperature, to make sure that the thermostat has opened and all the air is bled from the system.

TESTING FOR LEAKS

▶ **See Figures 116, 117, 118, 119 and 120**

If the fluid level of your cooling system is constantly low, the chances of a leak are probable. There are several ways to go about finding the source of your leak.

The first way should be a visual inspection. During the visual inspection, look around the entire engine area including the radiator and the heater hoses. The interior of the car should be inspected behind the glove box and passenger side floorboard area, and check the carpet for any signs of moisture. The smartest way to go about finding a leak visually is to first inspect any and all joints in the system such as where the radiator hoses connect to the radiator and the engine. Another thing to look for is white crusty stains that are signs of a leak where the coolant has already dried.

If a visual inspection cannot find the cause of your leak, a pressure test is a logical and extremely helpful way to find a leak. A pressure tester will be needed to perform this and if one is not available they can be purchased or even rented at many auto parts stores. The pressure tester usually has a standard size radiator cap adapter on the pressure port, however, other adapters are available based on the size of the vehicle's radiator neck or recovery tank depending on where the pressure tester connects. when pressurizing the cooling system, make sure you do not exceed the pressure rating of the system, which can be found on the top of the radiator cap, however, if you have and aftermarket or replacement cap that does not have the rating on it, 16psi is a standard to use but some cars are higher. Overpressurizing the system can cause a rupture in a hose or worse in the radiator or heater core and possibly cause an injury or a burn if the coolant is hot. Overpressurizing is normally controlled by the radiator cap which has a vent valve in it which is opened when the system reaches it's maximum pressure rating. To pressure test the system:

➡**The pressure test should be performed with the engine OFF.**

1. Remove the radiator or recovery tank cap.
2. Using the proper adapter, insert it onto the opening and connect the pressure tester,
3. Begin pressurizing the system by pumping the pressure tester and watching the gauge, when the maximum pressure is reached, stop.

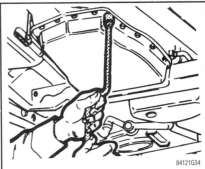

Fig. 112 To remove the transaxle oil pan, remove the pan retaining bolts

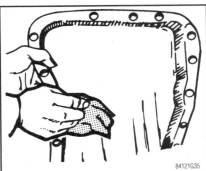

Fig. 113 Clean the pan thoroughly before installing it

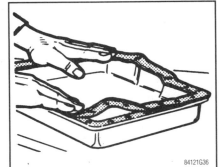

Fig. 114 Install a new transaxle oil pan gasket whenever the pan is removed

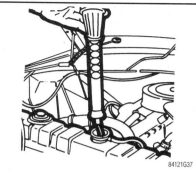

Fig. 115 Use a float type tester to check the coolant

Fig. 116 Remove the recovery tank cap to allow the pressure tester to be connected to the system

Fig. 117 This cooling system requires a threaded adapter for the recovery tank to allow the pressure tester to be connected

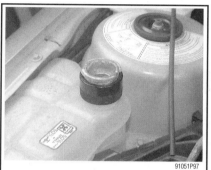

Fig. 118 Thread the adapter onto the recovery tank

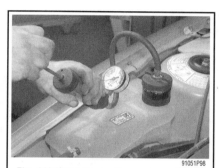

Fig. 119 Pump the cooling system with pressure, making sure not to overpressurize the system or damage can occur

Fig. 120 Watch the gauge on the system and observe the pressure reading

4. Watch the gauge slowly and see if the pressure on the gauge drops, if it does, a leak is definitely present.

5. If the pressure stayed somewhat stable, visually inspect the system for leaks. If the pressure dropped, repressurize the system and then visually inspect the system.

6. If no signs of a leak are noticed visually, pressurize the system to the maximum pressure rating of the system and leave the pressure tester connected for about 30 minutes. Return after 30 minutes and verify the pressure on the gauge, if the pressure dropped more than 20%, a leak definitely exists, if the pressure drop is less than 20%, the system is most likely okay.

Another way coolant is lost is by a internal engine leak, causing the oil to be contaminated or the coolant to be burned in the process of combustion and sent out the exhaust. To check for oil contamination, remove the dipstick and check the condition of the oil in the oil pan. If the oil is murky and has a white or beige "milkshake" look to it, the coolant is contaminating the oil through an internal leak and the engine must be torn down to find the leak. If the oil appears okay, the coolant can be burned and going out the tailpipe. A quick test for this is a cloud of white smoke appearing from the tailpipe, especially on start-up. On cold days, the white smoke will appear, this is due to condensation and the outside temperature, not a coolant leak. If the "smoke test" does not verify the situation, removing the spark plugs one at a time and checking the electrodes for a green or white tint can verify an internal coolant leak and identify which cylinder(s) is the culprit and aiding your search for the cause of the leak. If the spark plugs appear okay, another method is to use a gas analyzer or emissions tester, or one of several hand-held tools that most professional shops possess. This tools are used to check the cooling system for the presence of Hydrocarbons (HC's) in the coolant.

DRAINING, FLUSHING AND REFILLING THE COOLING SYSTEM

To drain the cooling system, allow the engine to cool down BEFORE ATTEMPTING TO REMOVE THE RADIATOR CAP. Then turn the cap until it hisses. Wait until all pressure is off the cap before removing it completely.

1. At the dash, set the heater TEMP control lever to the fully HOT position.

2. With the radiator cap removed, drain the radiator by loosening the petcock at the bottom of the radiator. Locate any drain plugs in the block and remove them. Flush the radiator with water until the fluid runs clear.

3. Remove the expansion tank and drain it.

4. Close the petcock and replace the plug(s), then refill the system with a 50/50 mix of ethylene glycol antifreeze. Fill the system to 25mm from the bottom of the filler neck. Reinstall the radiator cap.

5. Install the expansion tank and fill it to the FULL mark with pure antifreeze.

6. Operate the engine at 1,500 rpm for a few minutes and check the system for signs of leaks.

RADIATOR CAP INSPECTION

♦ See Figures 121 and 122

Allow the engine to cool sufficiently before attempting to remove the radiator cap. Use a rag to cover the cap, then remove by pressing down and turning counterclockwise to the first stop. If any hissing is noted (indicating the release of pressure), wait until the hissing stops completely, then press down again and turn counterclockwise until the cap can be removed.

Check the condition of the radiator cap gasket and seal inside of the cap. The radiator cap is designed to seal the cooling system under normal operating conditions which allows the build up of a certain amount of pressure (this pressure rating is stamped or printed on the cap). The pressure in the system raises the

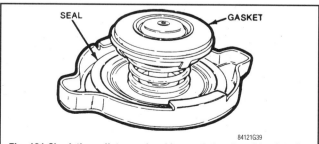

Fig. 121 Check the radiator cap's rubber gasket and seal for deterioration

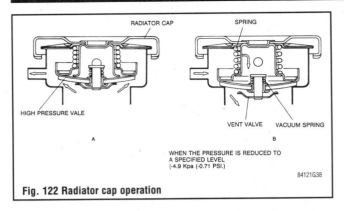

Fig. 122 Radiator cap operation

boiling point of the coolant to help prevent overheating. If the radiator cap does not seal, the boiling point of the coolant is lowered and overheating will occur. If the cap must be replaced, purchase the new cap according to the pressure rating which is specified for your vehicle.

Prior to installing the radiator cap, inspect and clean the filler neck. Make sure that the stop tabs are straight. If not, straighten them with needle nose pliers. If you are reusing the old cap, clean it thoroughly with clear water. After turning the cap on, make sure the arrows align with the overflow hose.

CLEANING RADIATOR OF DEBRIS

▶ **See Figure 123**

Periodically clean any debris leaves, paper, insects, etc. from the radiator fins. Pick the large pieces off by hand. The smaller pieces can be washed away with a water hose.

Carefully straighten any bent radiator fins with a pair of needle nose pliers. Be careful as the fins are very soft. Don't wiggle the fins back and forth too much. Straighten them once and try not to move them again.

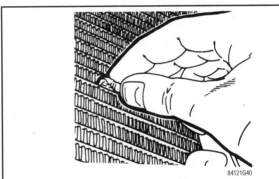

Fig. 123 Keep the radiator fins clear of debris and keep the fins straight

Brake Master Cylinder

FLUID RECOMMENDATION

When making additions of fluid, use only fresh, uncontaminated brake fluid meeting or exceeding DOT 3 standards.

LEVEL CHECK

▶ **See Figures 124 and 125**

Check the level of brake fluid in the brake master cylinder reservoir every two weeks. The fluid should be maintained to a level not below the bottom line on the reservoir and not above the top line. Any sudden decrease in the level in the reservoir indicates a probable leak in the system and should be checked out immediately.

When making additions of fluid, use only fresh, uncontaminated brake fluid meeting or exceeding DOT 3 standards. Be careful not to spill any brake fluid on painted surfaces, because it eats paint. Do not allow the fluid container or master cylinder reservoir to remain open any longer than necessary; brake fluid absorbs moisture from the air, reducing its effectiveness and causing brake line corrosion.

Clutch Master Cylinder

FLUID RECOMMENDATIONS

When making additions of fluid to the clutch master cylinder, use only fresh, uncontaminated brake fluid meeting or exceeding DOT 3 standards.

LEVEL CHECK

▶ **See Figure 126**

Check the fluid level in the clutch master cylinder reservoir every two weeks. The fluid should be maintained to a level between the "MIN" and "MAX" lines on the reservoir and not above the top line. Any sudden decrease in the level in the reservoir indicates a probable leak and should be investigated and repaired immediately.

When making additions of fluid, use only fresh, uncontaminated brake fluid meeting or exceeding DOT 3 standards. Be careful not to spill any brake fluid on painted surfaces, because it eats paint. Do not allow the fluid container or master cylinder reservoir to remain open any longer than necessary; brake fluid absorbs moisture from the air, reducing its effectiveness and causing clutch line corrosion.

Power Steering Pump

FLUID RECOMMENDATIONS

The power steering pump uses Dexron®II automatic transmission fluid.

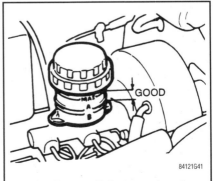

Fig. 124 Master cylinder reservoir on the Excel

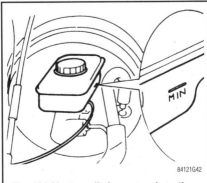

Fig. 125 Master cylinder reservoir on the Sonata

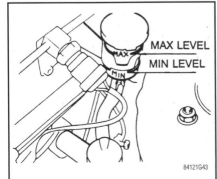

Fig. 126 Clutch master cylinder level on the Sonata

LEVEL CHECK

It is a good idea to perform the power steering fluid level check at the same time as all the other fluid levels.

To check the fluid level, first park the car on a level surface. Start the engine and turn the steering several times to raise the temperature of the fluid. With the engine idling, turn the wheel all the way to the left and right several times. Turn the engine off and remove the dipstick from the reservoir. The level should be between the "MIN" and "MAX" marks on the dipstick. If the level is not as specified, add fluid as necessary. Stop the engine and compare the levels in the power steering pump reservoir with and without the engine running. If the level varies 5mm (0.2 in) or more, there is air in the system. If the fluid level rises suddenly after stopping the engine, this is also an indication that air is trapped in the system.

➡**If checking the level in extremely cold weather, a grinding noise may be heard from the power steering pump as soon as the engine is started and you begin to turn the steering wheel. This is not abnormal and is due to the flow characteristics of the power steering fluid in cold temperatures.**

Chassis Greasing

BALL JOINT AND STEERING LINKAGE SEALS, STEERING AND DRIVESHAFT BOOTS

Ball joint and steering linkage seals and steering and driveshaft boots are permanently lubricated at the factory. They require no periodic lubrication. Inspect the seals and boots for damage and signs of leakage. Replace damaged boots and seals as necessary.

Body Lubrication

LOCK CYLINDERS

Apply graphite lubricant sparingly through the key slot. Insert the key and operate the lock several times to be sure that the lubricant is worked into the lock cylinder.

DOOR HINGES

Spray a silicone lubricant or white lithium grease on the hinge pivot points to eliminate any binding conditions. Open and close the door several times to be sure that the lubricant is evenly and thoroughly distributed.

HATCH

Spray a silicone lubricant or white lithium grease on all of the pivot and friction surfaces to eliminate any squeaks or binds. Work the tailgate to distribute the lubricant

Rear Wheel Bearings

Removal, packing and installation of the rear wheel bearings is covered in this Section. In addition to bearing service we also tell you how to replace the bearing races and grease seals if such service is required, but you need use only the steps that apply to packing the bearings.

For front wheel bearing service, please refer to Section 7.

REMOVAL, PACKING AND INSTALLATION

▶ **See Figures 127, 128 and 129**

➡**Sodium based grease is not compatible with lithium based grease. Read the package labels and be careful not to mix the two types. If there is any doubt as to the type of grease used, completely clean the old grease from the bearing and hub before replacing.**

Before handling the bearings, there are a few things that you should remember to do and not to do.

Remember to DO the following:
- Remove all outside dirt from the housing before exposing the bearing.
- Treat a used bearing as gently as you would a new one.
- Work with clean tools in clean surroundings.
- Use clean, dry canvas gloves, or at least clean, dry hands.
- Clean solvents and flushing fluids are a must.
- Use clean paper when laying out the bearings to dry.
- Protect disassembled bearings from rust and dirt. Cover them up.
- Use clean rags to wipe bearings.
- Keep the bearings in oil-proof paper when they are to be stored or are not in use.
- Clean the inside of the housing before replacing the bearing.

Do NOT do the following:
- Don't work in dirty surroundings.
- Don't use dirty, chipped or damaged tools.
- Try not to work on wooden work benches or use wooden mallets.
- Don't handle bearings with dirty or moist hands.
- Do not use gasoline for cleaning. Use a safe solvent.
- Do not spin dry bearings with compressed air. They will be damaged.
- Avoid using cotton waste or dirty cloths to wipe bearings.
- Try not to scratch or nick bearing surfaces.
- Do not allow the bearing to come in contact with dirt or rust at any time.

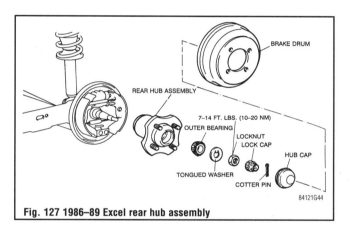

Fig. 127 1986–89 Excel rear hub assembly

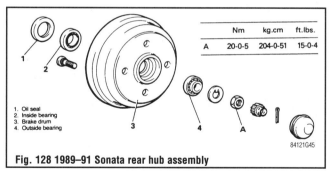

Fig. 128 1989–91 Sonata rear hub assembly

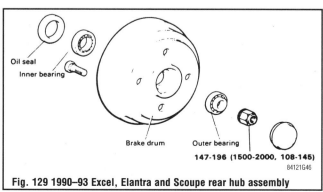

Fig. 129 1990–93 Excel, Elantra and Scoupe rear hub assembly

Elantra

1. Safely raise and support the rear of the vehicle. Remove the tire and wheel assembly.
2. Remove the grease cap, axle shaft nut and washer.
3. Pull outward on the brake drum slightly to remove the outer wheel bearing.
4. Slide the drum down the spindle and remove from the vehicle.
5. Pry the inner grease seal from the rear hub of the drum and discard.
6. Remove the inner wheel bearing. If the bearings are being replaced, drive the bearing races from the hub taking care not to damage the inner surface of the drum.

To install:

7. Coat the new races with EP lithium wheel bearing grease and drive them into the hub, making sure they are fully and squarely seated.
8. Pack the hub cavity with new EP lithium wheel bearing grease.
9. Install the inner bearing and drive a new grease seal into place. Make sure to pack the bearings completely with grease prior to installing into the drum.
10. Before installing the rear drum assembly, inspect the rear bearing nut as follows:
    a. Thread the wheel nut onto the spindle until the gap between the shoulder of the spindle and the nut is 0.07–0.11 in. (2.0–3.0mm).
    b. Measure the torque required to rotate the rear wheel bearing nut while turning counterclockwise. The limit is 48 ft. lbs. (5.5 Nm). If torque is less than the limit, replace the nut.
11. Install the brake drum and bearing assembly onto the spindle and install the outer bearing and shaft nut. Tighten the nut to 108–145 ft. lbs. (150–200 Nm).
12. Check for correct bearing end play by placing a dial indicator on the hub surface and moving the hub outward. Note the movement of the gauge and compare to the desired reading of 0.008 in. or less (0.2mm or less). If end-play exceeds the desired reading, retighten the rear hub bearing nut and recheck end-play. If reading is still excessive, replace the hub unit.
13. If end-play is correct, check the starting torque by attaching a spring balance to the hub lug bolts and pulling at a 90 degree angle while noting the required force to turn the hub. If the torque required is above the desired reading of 4.9 lbs. or less (22 Nm or less), loosen the nut and again tighten to the desired torque. Recheck the starting torque. If torque is still above the desired reading, replace the rear bearings.
14. Install the tire and wheel assembly and lower the vehicle. Prior to moving the vehicle, pump the brakes until a firm pedal is obtained.

Excel

1. Safely raise and support the rear of the vehicle. Remove the tire and wheel assembly.
2. Remove the grease cap, cotter pin, serrated nut cap, axle shaft nut and washer from the spindle as equipped.
3. Pull outward on the brake drum slightly to remove the outer wheel bearing.
4. Slide the drum down the spindle and remove the assembly from the vehicle.
5. Pry the inner grease seal from the rear hub of the drum and discard.
6. Remove the inner wheel bearing. If the bearings are being replaced, drive the bearing races from the hub taking care not to damage the inner surface of the drum.

To install:

7. Coat the new races with EP lithium wheel bearing grease and drive them into the hub, making sure they are fully and squarely seated.
8. Pack the hub cavity with new EP lithium wheel bearing grease.
9. Install the inner bearing and drive a new grease seal into place. Make sure to pack the bearings completely with grease prior to installing into the drum.
10. Install the brake drum onto the spindle. Install the outer bearing, washer and shaft nut onto spindle.
11. On 1986–90 vehicles equipped with castellated nut and cotter pin, torque the bearing nut to 15 ft. lbs. (20 Nm) while turning the drum. Back off the nut until it is loose, then torque it to 48 inch lbs. Install the serrated nut cap and a new cotter pin. If the cotter pin holes have to be re-aligned, back off on the nut no more than 15 degrees; if not, repeat the adjustment procedure.
12. On 1991–93 vehicles equipped with bearing locknut, install and tighten bearing locknut as follows:
    a. Prior to installation, inspect the rear bearing nut by threading the nut onto the spindle until the distance between the shoulder of the spindle and the inner flat on the nut is 0.07–0.11 in. (2.0–3.0mm).
    b. Measure the torque required to rotate the rear wheel bearing locknut

while turning counterclockwise. The limit is 48 ft. lbs. (5.5 Nm). If required torque is less than the limit, replace the nut.
    c. Install the brake drum and outer bearing onto the spindle. Install and torque the nut to 108–145 ft. lbs. (147–196 Nm).
    d. Check for correct bearing end-play by placing a dial indicator on the hub surface and moving the drum outward. Note the movement of the gauge and compare to the desired reading of 0.0043 in. or less (0.11mm or less). If end-play exceeds the desired reading, retighten the rear hub bearing nut and recheck end-play. If reading is still excessive, replace the hub unit.
    e. If end-play is correct, check the starting torque by attaching a spring balance to the hub lug bolts and pulling at a 90 degree angle while noting the required force to turn the hub. If the torque required is above the desired reading of 4.9 lbs. or less (22 N or less), loosen the nut and again tighten to the desired torque. Recheck the starting torque. If torque is still above the desired reading, replace the rear bearings.
    f. After final tightening the wheel bearing nut, align with the spindle's indentation and crimp the edge of the nut to wedge in position.
13. Install the tire and wheel assembly and lower the vehicle. Prior to moving the vehicle, pump the brakes until a firm pedal is obtained.

Scoupe

1. Safely raise and support the rear of the vehicle. Remove the tire and wheel assembly.
2. Remove the grease cap, axle shaft nut and washer.
3. Pull outward on the brake drum slightly to remove the outer wheel bearing.
4. Slide the drum down the spindle and remove from the vehicle.
5. Pry the inner grease seal from the rear hub of the drum and discard.
6. Remove the inner wheel bearing. If the bearings are being replaced, drive the bearing races from the hub taking care not to damage the inner surface of the drum.

To install:

7. Coat the new races with EP lithium wheel bearing grease and drive them into the hub, making sure they are fully and squarely seated.
8. Pack the hub cavity with new EP lithium wheel bearing grease.
9. Install the inner bearing and drive a new grease seal into place. Make sure to pack the bearings completely with grease prior to installing into the drum.
10. Before installing the rear drum assembly, inspect the rear bearing nut as follows:
    a. Thread the wheel nut onto the spindle until the gap between the shoulder of the spindle and the nut is 0.07–0.11 in. (2.0–3.0mm).
    b. Measure the torque required to rotate the rear wheel bearing nut while turning counterclockwise. The limit is 48 ft. lbs. (5.5 Nm). If torque is less than the limit, replace the nut.
11. Install the brake drum and bearing assembly onto the spindle and install the outer bearing and shaft nut. Tighten the nut to 108–145 ft. lbs. (150–200 Nm).
12. Check for correct bearing end play by placing a dial indicator on the hub surface and moving the hub outward. Note the movement of the gauge and compare to the desired reading of 0.0043 in. or less (0.11mm or less). If end-play exceeds the desired reading, retighten the rear bearing nut and recheck end-play. If reading is still excessive, replace the rear bearings.
13. Once end-play is correct, check the hub and drum starting force by attaching a spring balance to the lug bolts and pulling at a 90 degree angle while noting the required force to turn the drum assembly. If the torque required is above the desired reading of 4.8 lbs. or less (22 N or less), loosen the nut and again tighten to the desired torque. Recheck the starting torque. If torque is still above the desired reading, replace the rear bearings.
14. After final tightening the wheel bearing nut, align with the spindle's indentation and crimp the edge of the nut to wedge in position.
15. Install the tire and wheel assembly and lower the vehicle. Prior to moving the vehicle, pump the brakes until a firm pedal is obtained.

Sonata

1989–91

➡**The rear hub bearing unit cannot be disassembled. If the hub shows signs of wear or damage, replacement of the unit is required.**

1. Safely raise and support the rear of the vehicle. Remove the tire and wheel assembly.

2. If equipped with rear disc brakes, remove the brake caliper and support out of the way using wire. Do not disconnect the brake hose from the caliper. Remove the brake rotor. If equipped with drum brakes, remove the brake drum from the hub assembly.

3. Remove the grease cap, cotter pin, serrated nut cap, axle shaft nut and washer from the spindle as equipped.

4. Pull outward on the rear hub assembly slightly to remove the outer wheel bearing.

5. Slide the hub down the spindle and remove the assembly from the vehicle.

6. Pry the inner grease seal from the hub and discard.

7. Remove the inner wheel bearing. If the bearings are being replaced, drive the bearing races from the hub taking care not to damage the inner surface of the hub.

To install:

8. Coat the new races with EP lithium wheel bearing grease and drive them into the hub, making sure they are fully and squarely seated.

9. Pack the hub cavity with new EP lithium wheel bearing grease.

10. Install the inner bearing and drive a new grease seal into place. Make sure to pack both bearings completely with grease prior to installing into the hub.

11. Install the hub assembly onto the spindle. Install the outer bearing, washer and shaft nut onto the spindle.

12. Torque the bearing nut to 14 ft. lbs. (20 Nm) while turning the hub or drum. Back off the nut until it is loose, then torque it to 7 ft. lbs. (10 Nm). Install the serrated nut cap and a new cotter pin. If the cotter pin holes have to be re-aligned, back off on the nut no more than 15 degrees; if not, repeat the adjustment procedure.

13. If equipped with drum brakes, install the brake drum to the hub assembly and adjust the brake shoes as required. If equipped with disc brakes, install the rotor and caliper.

14. Install the tire and wheel assembly and lower the vehicle. Pump the brake pedal to seat the brake pads against the rotors prior to moving the vehicle.

1992–93

➥**The rear hub bearing unit can not be disassembled. If the hub shows signs of wear or damage, replacement of the unit is required.**

1. Safely raise and support the rear of the vehicle. Remove the tire and wheel assembly.

2. If equipped with rear disc brakes, remove the brake caliper and support out of the way using wire. Do not disconnect the brake hose from the caliper. Remove the brake rotor. If equipped with drum brakes, remove the brake drum from the hub assembly.

3. Remove the grease cap, wheel bearing nut and washer from the center of the hub bearing unit. Remove the rear hub unit from the vehicle.

To install:

4. Install the rear bearing unit onto the spindle. Install the outer bearing and the tonged washer into the rear hub unit.

➥**Press the inner race further until the inner race contacts with the spindle end.**

5. Install and tighten the rear wheel bearing nut to 174–217 ft. lbs. (240–300 Nm).

6. Check for correct bearing end-play by placing a dial indicator on the hub surface and moving the hub outward. Note the movement of the gauge and compare to the desired reading of 0.004 in. or less (0.01mm or less). If end-play exceeds the desired reading, retighten the rear hub bearing nut and recheck end-play. If reading is still excessive, replace the hub unit.

7. If end-play is correct, check the starting torque by attaching a spring balance to the hub lug bolts and pulling at a 90 degree angle while noting the required force to turn the hub. If the torque required is above the desired reading of 7 lbs. or less (31 N or less), loosen the nut and again tighten to the desired torque. Recheck the starting torque. If torque is still above the desired reading, replace the rear hub bearing unit.

8. After final tightening the wheel bearing nut, align with the spindle's indentation and crimp the edge of the nut to wedge in position.

9. If equipped with rear disc brakes, install the brake disc and caliper to the vehicle. If equipped with drum brakes, install drum to hub assembly.

10. Install the tire and wheel assembly and lower the vehicle. Pump the brake pedal to assure correct brake operation, prior to moving the vehicle.

ADJUSTMENT

Excel

1. Raise the vehicle and support it safely. Remove the rear wheel assembly.

2. Remove the dust cover from the hub.

3. On 1986–90 vehicles equipped with castellated nut and cotter pin, remove the cotter pin and nut cap. Torque the bearing nut to 15 ft. lbs. (20 Nm) while turning the drum. Back off the nut until it is loose, then torque it to 48 inch lbs. Install the serrated nut cap and a new cotter pin. If the cotter pin holes have to be re-aligned, back off on the nut no more than 15 degrees; if not, repeat the adjustment procedure.

4. On 1991–93 vehicles equipped with bearing locknut, adjust bearing locknut as follows:

a. Loosen the nut and then torque the nut to 108–145 ft. lbs. (147–196 Nm).

b. Check for correct bearing end-play by placing a dial indicator on the hub surface and moving the drum outward. Note the movement of the gauge and compare to the desired reading of 0.0043 in. or less (0.11mm or less). If end-play exceeds the desired reading, retighten the rear hub bearing nut and recheck end-play. If reading is still excessive, replace the hub unit.

c. If end-play is correct, check the starting torque by attaching a spring balance to the hub lug bolts and pulling at a 90 degree angle while noting the required force to turn the hub. If the torque required is above the desired reading of 4.9 lbs. or less (22 N or less), loosen the nut and again tighten to the desired torque. Recheck the starting torque. If torque is still above the desired reading, replace the rear bearings.

d. After final tightening the wheel bearing nut, align with the spindle's indentation and crimp the edge of the nut to wedge in position.

5. Fill the dust cap with grease and install.

6. Install the tire and wheel assembly.

Sonata

1989–91

1. Safely raise and support the rear of the vehicle. Remove the tire and wheel assembly.

2. Remove the grease cap, cotter pin and serrated nut cap.

3. Torque the bearing nut to 14 ft. lbs. (20 Nm) while turning the hub or drum. Back off the nut until it is loose, then torque it to 7 ft. lbs. (10 Nm). Install the serrated nut cap and a new cotter pin. If the cotter pin holes have to be re-aligned, back off on the nut no more than 15 degrees; if not, repeat the adjustment procedure.

4. Install the nut lock and a new cotter pin.

5. Install the tire and wheel assembly and lower the vehicle. Pump the brake pedal to seat the brake pads against the rotors prior to moving the vehicle.

1992–93

1. Safely raise and support the rear of the vehicle. Remove the tire and wheel assembly.

2. If equipped with rear disc brakes, remove the brake caliper and support out of the way using wire. Do not disconnect the brake hose from the caliper. Remove the brake rotor. If equipped with drum brakes, remove the brake drum from the hub assembly.

3. Remove the grease cap and loosen the wheel bearing nut.

4. Tighten the rear wheel bearing nut to 174–217 ft. lbs. (240–300 Nm).

5. Check for correct bearing end-play by placing a dial indicator on the hub surface and moving the hub outward. Note the movement of the gauge and compare to the desired reading of 0.004 in. or less (0.01mm or less). If end-play exceeds the desired reading, retighten the rear hub bearing nut and recheck end-play. If reading is still excessive, replace the hub unit.

6. If end-play is correct, check the starting torque by attaching a spring balance to the hub lug bolts and pulling at a 90 degree angle while noting the required force to turn the hub. If the torque required is above the desired reading of 7 lbs. or less (31 N or less), loosen the nut and again tighten to the desired torque. Recheck the starting torque. If torque is still above the desired reading, replace the rear hub bearing unit.

7. After final tightening the wheel bearing nut, align with the spindle's indentation and crimp the edge of the nut to wedge in position.

8. If equipped with rear disc brakes, install the brake disc and caliper to the vehicle. If equipped with drum brakes, install drum to hub assembly.

9. Install the tire and wheel assembly and lower the vehicle. Pump the brake pedal to assure correct brake operation, prior to moving the vehicle.

Elantra

1. Safely raise and support the rear of the vehicle. Remove the tire and wheel assembly.
2. Remove the grease cap and loosen the axle shaft nut.
3. Tighten the nut to 108–145 ft. lbs. (150–200 Nm).
4. Check for correct bearing end play by placing a dial indicator on the hub surface and moving the hub outward. Note the movement of the gauge and compare to the desired reading of 0.008 in. or less (0.2mm or less). If end-play exceeds the desired reading, retighten the rear hub bearing nut and recheck end-play. If reading is still excessive, replace the hub unit.
5. If end-play is correct, check the starting torque by attaching a spring balance to the hub lug bolts and pulling at a 90 degree angle while noting the required force to turn the hub. If the torque required is above the desired reading of 4.9 lbs. or less (22 Nm or less), loosen the nut and again tighten to the desired torque. Recheck the starting torque. If torque is still above the desired reading, replace the rear bearings.
6. Install the tire and wheel assembly and lower the vehicle. Prior to moving the vehicle, pump the brakes until a firm pedal is obtained.

Scoupe

1. Safely raise and support the rear of the vehicle. Remove the tire and wheel assembly.
2. Remove the grease cap and loosen the axle shaft nut.
3. Tighten the nut to 108–145 ft. lbs. (150–200 Nm).
4. Check for correct bearing end-play by placing a dial indicator on the hub surface and moving the hub outward. Note the movement of the gauge and compare to the desired reading of 0.0043 in. or less (0.11mm or less). If end-play exceeds the desired reading, retighten the rear bearing nut and recheck end-play. If reading is still excessive, replace the rear bearings.
5. Once end-play is correct, check the hub and drum starting force by attaching a spring balance to the lug bolts and pulling at a 90 degree angle while noting the required force to turn the drum assembly. If the torque required is above the desired reading of 4.8 lbs. or less (22 Nm or less), loosen the nut and again tighten to the desired torque. Recheck the starting torque. If torque is still above the desired reading, replace the rear bearings.
6. After final tightening the wheel bearing nut, align with the spindle's indentation and crimp the edge of the nut to wedge in position.
7. Install the tire and wheel assembly and lower the vehicle. Prior to moving the vehicle, pump the brakes until a firm pedal is obtained.

TRAILER TOWING

➡ **Although your Hyundai can be used for light trailer hauling, it is generally considered not to be a good choice in heavy applications.**

General Recommendations

Your car was primarily designed to carry passengers and cargo. It is important to remember that towing a trailer will place additional loads on your vehicle's engine, drive train, steering, braking and other systems. However, if you find it necessary to tow a trailer, using the proper equipment is a must.

Local laws may require specific equipment such as trailer brakes or fender mounted mirrors. Check your local laws.

Trailer Weight

The weight of the trailer is the most important factor. A good weight-to-horsepower ratio is about 35:1, 35 lbs. of GCW (Gross Combined Weight) for every horsepower your engine develops. Multiply the engine's rated horsepower by 35 and subtract the weight of the car passengers and luggage. The result is the approximate ideal maximum weight you should tow, although a numerically higher axle ratio can help compensate for heavier weight.

Hitch Weight

Figure the hitch weight to select a proper hitch. Hitch weight is usually 9–11% of the trailer gross weight and should be measured with the trailer loaded. Hitches fall into three types: those that mount on the frame and rear bumper or the bolt-on or weld-on distribution type used for larger trailers. Axle mounted or clamp-on bumper hitches should never be used.

Check the gross weight rating of your trailer. Tongue weight is usually figured as 10% of gross trailer weight. Therefore, a trailer with a maximum gross weight of 2,000 lb. will have a maximum tongue weight of 200 lb. Class I trailers fall into this category. Class II trailers are those with a gross weight rating of 2,000-3,500 lb., while Class III trailers fall into the 3,500-6,000 lb. category. Class IV trailers are those over 6,000 lb. and are for use with fifth wheel trucks, only.

When you've determined the hitch that you'll need, follow the manufacturer's installation instructions, exactly, especially when it comes to fastener torques. The hitch will subjected to a lot of stress and good hitches come with hardened bolts. Never substitute an inferior bolt for a hardened bolt.

Cooling

ENGINE

One of the most common, if not the most common, problems associated with trailer towing is engine overheating.

Check the cooling system to make sure that it is in good working condition. Make sure that the radiator is no blocked in any way. By doing these simple checks you can avoid any engine damage caused by overheating.

Aftermarket engine oil coolers are helpful for prolonging engine oil life and reducing overall engine temperatures. Both of these factors increase engine life.

While not absolutely necessary in towing Class I and some Class II trailers, they are recommended for heavier Class II and all Class III towing.

Engine oil cooler systems consist of an adapter, screwed on in place of the oil filter, a remote filter mounting and a multi-tube, finned heat exchanger, which is mounted in front of the radiator or air conditioning condenser.

TRANSMISSION

An automatic transmission is usually recommended for trailer towing. Modern automatics have proven reliable and, of course, easy to operate, in trailer towing.

The increased load of a trailer, however, causes an increase in the temperature of the automatic transmission fluid. Heat is the worst enemy of an automatic transmission. As the temperature of the fluid increases, the life of the fluid decreases.

It is essential, therefore, that you install an automatic transmission cooler.

The cooler, which consists of a multi-tube, finned heat exchanger, is usually installed in front of the radiator or air conditioning compressor, and hooked inline with the transmission cooler tank inlet line. Follow the cooler manufacturer's installation instructions.

Select a cooler of at least adequate capacity, based upon the combined gross weights of the car and trailer.

Cooler manufacturers recommend that you use an after market cooler in addition to, and not instead of, the present cooling tank in your radiator. If you do want to use it in place of the radiator cooling tank, get a cooler at least two sizes larger than normally necessary.

➡A transmission cooler can, sometimes, cause slow or harsh shifting in the transmission during cold weather, until the fluid has a chance to come up to normal operating temperature. Some coolers can be purchased with or retrofitted with a temperature bypass valve which will allow fluid flow through the cooler only when the fluid has reached operating temperature, or above.

PUSHING AND TOWING

If your Hyundai's rear axle is operable, you can tow your vehicle with the rear wheels on the ground. Due to its front wheel drive, the Hyundai is a relatively easy vehicle to tow with the front wheels up. Before doing so, you should release the parking brake.

If the rear axle is defective, the vehicle must then be towed with the rear wheels off the ground. Before attempting this, a dolly should be placed under the front wheels. If a dolly is not available, and you still have to tow it with the

Handling A Trailer

Towing a trailer with ease and safety requires a certain amount of experience. It's a good idea to learn the feel of a trailer by practicing turning, stopping and backing in an open area such as an empty parking lot.

rear wheels up, then you should first shift the transaxle into Neutral and then lock the steering wheel so that the front wheels are pointing straight ahead. In such a position, the vehicle must not be towed at speeds above 35 mph or for more than short distances (50 miles). **It's critically important that you observe these limitations to prevent damage to your transaxle due to inadequate lubrication.**

JACKING

♦ **See Figures 130, 131 and 132**

The vehicle is supplied with a scissors jack for emergency road repairs. The scissors jack may be used to raise the car via the notches on either side at the front and rear of the doors. Do not attempt to use the jack in any other places. Always block the diagonally opposite wheel when using a jack. When using a garage jack, support the car at the center of the front suspension member or at the differential carrier. Block both wheels at the opposite end of the car. When using stands, use the side members at the front and the differential or trailing

axle front mounting crossmember at the back for placement points.

Whenever you plan to work under the car, you must support it on jackstands or ramps. Never use cinder blocks or stacks of wood to support the car, even if you're only going to be under it for a few minutes. Never crawl under the car when it is supported only by the tire-changing jack.

Small hydraulic, screw, or scissors jacks are satisfactory for raising the car. Drive-on trestles or ramps are also a handy and safe way to both raise and support the car.

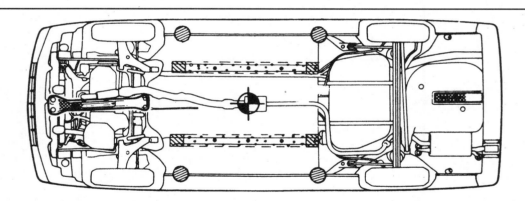

 Jack provided with the vehicle

 Rigid jack, single or double post lift

 Garage jack

H bar lift

84121G49

Fig. 130 Floor jack and jackstand points for the Sonata.

When using a garage jack

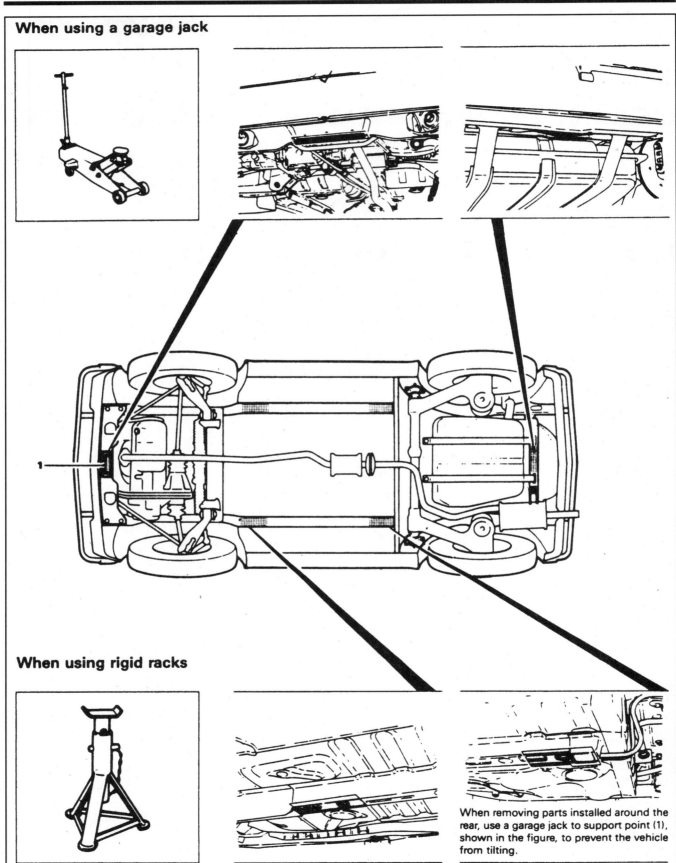

When using rigid racks

When removing parts installed around the rear, use a garage jack to support point (1), shown in the figure, to prevent the vehicle from tilting.

84121G47

Fig. 131 Floor jack and jackstand points for the 1986–89 Excel

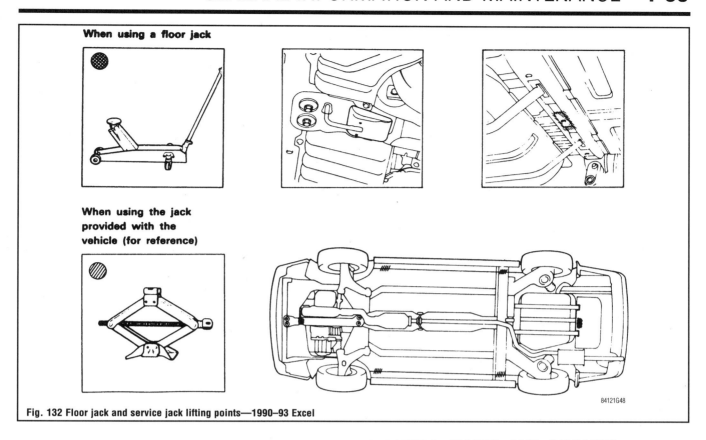

Fig. 132 Floor jack and service jack lifting points—1990–93 Excel

MAINTENANCE INTERVALS CHART—ELANTRA, EXCEL AND SCOUPE

No.	Description	Miles x 1000	7.5	15	22.5	30	37.5	45	50	60
		Kilometers x 1000	12	24	36	48	60	72	80	96
		Months	6	12	18	24	30	36	40	48
	Emission Control System Maintenance									
1	Engine Oil		R	R	R	R	R	R	R	R
2	Engine Oil Filter		R	R	R	R	R	R	R	R
3	Drive Belt			I		R		I		R
4	Valve Clearance			I		I		I		I
5	Ignition Timing								I	
6	Idle Speed			I		I		I		I
7	Carburetor Choke Mechanism					I				I
8	Fuel Filter/Lines					I/I			R/I	
9	Vacuum, Secondary Air, Crankcase Ventilation Hoses								R	
10	Air Cleaner Filter					R				R
11	PCV Valve								I	
12	Evaporative Emission Control System								I	
13	Spark Plugs					R				R
14	Ignition Wirings								R	
15	Oxygen Sensor								R	
16	EGR System								I	
17	Canister								R	
18	Throttle Positioner			I						I

R: Replace   I: Inspect. After inspection, clean, adjust, repair or replace if necessary.

84121C02

MAINTENANCE INTERVALS CHART—ELANTRA, EXCEL AND SCOUPE (CONT'D)

No.	Description	Miles x 1000							
		Kilometers x 1000							
		Months							
		7.5	15	22.5	30	37.5	45	52.5	60
		12	24	36	48	60	72	84	96
		6	12	18	24	30	36	42	48
	General Maintenance								
1	Cooling System (Hoses, Connections, etc.)		I		I		I		I
2	Engine Coolant				R				R
3	Timing Belt								R
4	Manual T/Oil				R				R
5	Auto T/A Oil				R				R
6	Brake Hoses, Lines		I		I		I		I
7	Brake Fluid		I		R		I		R
8	Rear Brake Drums/Linings		I		I		I		I
9	Brake Pads, Calipers, Rotors	I		I		I		I	
10	Parking Brake		I		I		I		I
11	Exhaust Pipe Connections, Muffler and Suspension Bolts		I		I		I		I
12	Steering Gear Box, Linkage and Boots		I		I		I		I
13	Rear Wheel Bearing Grease						I		
14	Driveshafts and Boots		I		I		I		I

84121C03

MAINTENANCE INTERVALS CHART — SONATA

NO	DESCRIPTION	MILES X 1000 — 7.5 / KILOMETER X 1000 — 12 / MONTHS — 5	15 / 24 / 10	22.5 / 36 / 20	30 / 48 / 30	37.5 / 60 / 40	45 / 72 / 50	52.5 / 84 / 60	60 / 96 / 70
	EMISSION CONTROL ITEMS								
1	ENGINE OIL AND FILTER	R	R	R	R	R	R	R	R
2	FUEL FILTER							R	
3	FUEL LINES AND CONNECTIONS							I	
4	VACUUM, CRANKCASE VENTILATION HOSES							I	
5	FUEL HOSE, VAPOR HOSE & FUEL FILLER CAP							I	
6	AIR FILTER				R				R
7	SPARK PLUGS (2.0 DOHC)				R				R
8	SPARK PLUGS (3.0 V6)								R
	GENERAL ITEMS								
1	DRIVE BELT (WATER PUMP)		I		I		I		I
2	ENGINE COOLANT				R				R
3	TIMING BELT		I						R
4	MANUAL TRANSAXLE OIL		I		I				I
5	AUTO TRANSAXLE OIL				R		I		R
6	BRAKE FLUID				R				R
7	BRAKE HOSES, LINES				I				I
8	REAR BRAKE DRUMS/LININGS/PARKING BRAKE		I		I		I		I
9	BRAKE PADS, CALIPERS, ROTORS		I		I		I		I
10	EXHAUST PIPE CONNECTIONS, MUFFLER & SUSPENSION BOLTS				I				I
11	STEERING GEAR RACK, LINKAGE & BOOTS		I						I
12	WHEEL BEARING GREASE								I
13	DRIVESHAFTS & BOOTS		I				I		I

84121C04

CAPACITIES

Year	Model	Engine ID/VIN	Engine Displacement Liters (cc)	Engine Crankcase with Filter	Transmission (pts.)			Transfer Case (pts.)	Drive Axle		Fuel Tank (gal.)	Cooling System (qts.)
					4-Spd	5-Spd	Auto.		Front (pts.)	Rear (pts.)		
1986	Excel	M	1.5 (1468)	3.6	4.4	4.4	12.2	—	—	—	10.6 ①	5.6
1987	Excel	M	1.5 (1468)	3.6	4.4	4.4	12.2	—	—	—	10.6 ①	5.6
1988	Excel	M	1.5 (1468)	3.6	4.4	4.4	12.2	—	—	—	10.6 ①	5.6
1989	Excel	M	1.5 (1468)	3.6	4.4	4.4	12.2	—	—	—	10.6 ①	5.6
	Sonata	S	2.4 (2351)	4.0	—	5.3	12.3	—	—	—	10.6 ①	5.6
1990	Excel	M	1.5 (1468)	3.6	4.4	4.4	12.2	—	—	—	10.6 ①	5.6
	Excel	J	1.5 (1468)	3.6	4.4	4.4	12.2	—	—	—	10.6 ①	5.6
	Sonata	S	2.4 (2351)	4.0	—	5.3	12.3	—	—	—	16	7.4
	Sonata	T	3.0 (2972)	4.0	—	—	12.3	—	—	—	17	7.4
1991	Excel	M	1.5 (1468)	3.6	4.4	4.4	12.2	—	—	—	10.6 ①	5.6
	Excel	J	1.5 (1468)	3.6	4.4	4.4	12.2	—	—	—	10.6 ①	5.6
	Sonata	S	2.4 (2351)	4.0	—	5.3	12.3	—	—	—	16	7.4
	Sonata	T	3.0 (2972)	4.0	—	—	12.3	—	—	—	17	7.4
	Scoupe	J	1.5 (1468)	3.6	3.8	3.8	12.8	—	—	—	11.9 ①	5.6
1992	Excel	M	1.5 (1468)	3.6	4.4	4.4	12.2	—	—	—	10.6 ①	5.6
	Excel	J	1.5 (1468)	3.6	4.4	4.4	12.2	—	—	—	10.6 ①	5.6
	Sonata	F	2.0 (1997)	4.0	—	4.0	12.8	—	—	—	17.2	7.7
	Sonata	T	3.0 (2972)	4.0	—	—	12.3	—	—	—	17	7.4
	Scoupe	J	1.5 (1468)	3.6	3.8	3.8	12.8	—	—	—	11.9 ①	5.6
	Elantra	R	1.6 (1596)	4.6	—	3.8	12.8	—	—	—	13.8	5.4
1993	Excel	M	1.5 (1468)	3.6	4.4	4.4	12.2	—	—	—	10.5 ①	5.6
	Excel	J	1.5 (1468)	3.6	4.4	4.4	12.2	—	—	—	10.5 ①	5.6
	Sonata	F	2.0 (1997)	4.0	—	4.0	12.8	—	—	—	17.2	7.7
	Sonata	T	3.0 (2972)	4.0	—	—	12.3	—	—	—	17	7.4
	Scoupe	N	1.5 (1495)	3.4	—	4.4	12.8	—	—	—	11.9	5.6
	Scoupe ②	N	1.5 (1495)	3.4	—	4.4	12.8	—	—	—	11.9	5.6
	Elantra	R	1.6 (1596)	4.6	—	3.8	12.8	—	—	—	13.8	5.4
	Elantra	M	1.8 (1796)	4.6	—	3.8	12.8	—	—	—	13.8	5.4

① Optional 13.2 gallon tank
② Scoupe Turbo

84121C05

ENGLISH TO METRIC CONVERSION: MASS (WEIGHT)

Current **mass** measurement is expressed in pounds and ounces (lbs. & ozs.). The metric unit of mass (or weight) is the kilogram (kg). Even although this table does not show conversion of masses (weights) larger than 15 lbs, it is easy to calculate larger units by following the data immediately below.

To convert ounces (oz.) to grams (g): multiply th number of ozs. by 28
To convert grams (g) to ounces (oz.): multiply the number of grams by .035

To convert pounds (lbs.) to kilograms (kg): multiply the number of lbs. by .45
To convert kilograms (kg) to pounds (lbs.): multiply the number of kilograms by 2.2

lbs	kg	lbs	kg	oz	kg	oz	kg
0.1	0.04	0.9	0.41	0.1	0.003	0.9	0.024
0.2	0.09	1	0.4	0.2	0.005	1	0.03
0.3	0.14	2	0.9	0.3	0.008	2	0.06
0.4	0.18	3	1.4	0.4	0.011	3	0.08
0.5	0.23	4	1.8	0.5	0.014	4	0.11
0.6	0.27	5	2.3	0.6	0.017	5	0.14
0.7	0.32	10	4.5	0.7	0.020	10	0.28
0.8	0.36	15	6.8	0.8	0.023	15	0.42

ENGLISH TO METRIC CONVERSION: TEMPERATURE

To convert Fahrenheit ($^\circ$F) to Celsius ($^\circ$C): take number of $^\circ$F and subtract 32; multiply result by 5; divide result by 9

To convert Celsius ($^\circ$C) to Fahrenheit ($^\circ$F): take number of $^\circ$C and multiply by 9; divide result by 5; add 32 to total

Fahrenheit (F)	Celsius (C)			Fahrenheit (F)	Celsius (C)			Fahrenheit (F)	Celsius (C)		
°F	°C	°C	°F	°F	°C	°C	°F	°F	°C	°C	°F
−40	−40	−38	−36.4	80	26.7	18	64.4	215	101.7	80	176
−35	−37.2	−36	−32.8	85	29.4	20	68	220	104.4	85	185
−30	−34.4	−34	−29.2	90	32.2	22	71.6	225	107.2	90	194
−25	−31.7	−32	−25.6	95	35.0	24	75.2	230	110.0	95	202
−20	−28.9	−30	−22	100	37.8	26	78.8	235	112.8	100	212
−15	−26.1	−28	−18.4	105	40.6	28	82.4	240	115.6	105	221
−10	−23.3	−26	−14.8	110	43.3	30	86	245	118.3	110	230
−5	−20.6	−24	−11.2	115	46.1	32	89.6	250	121.1	115	239
0	−17.8	−22	−7.6	120	48.9	34	93.2	255	123.9	120	248
1	−17.2	−20	−4	125	51.7	36	96.8	260	126.6	125	257
2	−16.7	−18	−0.4	130	54.4	38	100.4	265	129.4	130	266
3	−16.1	−16	3.2	135	57.2	40	104	270	132.2	135	275
4	−15.6	−14	6.8	140	60.0	42	107.6	275	135.0	140	284
5	−15.0	−12	10.4	145	62.8	44	112.2	280	137.8	145	293
10	−12.2	−10	14	150	65.6	46	114.8	285	140.6	150	302
15	−9.4	−8	17.6	155	68.3	48	118.4	290	143.3	155	311
20	−6.7	−6	21.2	160	71.1	50	122	295	146.1	160	320
25	−3.9	−4	24.8	165	73.9	52	125.6	300	148.9	165	329
30	−1.1	−2	28.4	170	76.7	54	129.2	305	151.7	170	338
35	1.7	0	32	175	79.4	56	132.8	310	154.4	175	347
40	4.4	2	35.6	180	82.2	58	136.4	315	157.2	180	356
45	7.2	4	39.2	185	85.0	60	140	320	160.0	185	365
50	10.0	6	42.8	190	87.8	62	143.6	325	162.8	190	374
55	12.8	8	46.4	195	90.6	64	147.2	330	165.6	195	383
60	15.6	10	50	200	93.3	66	150.8	335	168.3	200	392
65	18.3	12	53.6	205	96.1	68	154.4	340	171.1	205	401
70	21.1	14	57.2	210	98.9	70	158	345	173.9	210	410
75	23.9	16	60.8	212	100.0	75	167	350	176.7	215	414

TCCS1C01

ENGLISH TO METRIC CONVERSION: LENGTH

To convert inches (ins.) to millimeters (mm): multiply number of inches by 25.4

To convert millimeters (mm) to inches (ins.): multiply number of millimeters by .04

Inches		Decimals	Milli-meters	Inches to millimeters		Inches		Decimals	Milli-meters	Inches to millimeters	
				inches	mm					inches	mm
	1/64	0.051625	0.3969	0.0001	0.00254		33/64	0.515625	13.0969	0.6	15.24
	1/32	0.03125	0.7937	0.0002	0.00508		17/32	0.53125	13.4937	0.7	17.78
	3/64	0.046875	1.1906	0.0003	0.00762		35/64	0.546875	13.8906	0.8	20.32
1/16		0.0625	1.5875	0.0004	0.01016	9/16		0.5625	14.2875	0.9	22.86
	5/64	0.078125	1.9844	0.0005	0.01270		37/64	0.578125	14.6844	1	25.4
	3/32	0.09375	2.3812	0.0006	0.01524		19/32	0.59375	15.0812	2	50.8
	7/64	0.109375	2.7781	0.0007	0.01778		39/64	0.609375	15.4781	3	76.2
1/8		0.125	3.1750	0.0008	0.02032	5/8		0.625	15.8750	4	101.6
	9/64	0.140625	3.5719	0.0009	0.02286		41/64	0.640625	16.2719	5	127.0
	5/32	0.15625	3.9687	0.001	0.0254		21/32	0.65625	16.6687	6	152.4
	11/64	0.171875	4.3656	0.002	0.0508		43/64	0.671875	17.0656	7	177.8
3/16		0.1875	4.7625	0.003	0.0762	11/16		0.6875	17.4625	8	203.2
	13/64	0.203125	5.1594	0.004	0.1016		45/64	0.703125	17.8594	9	228.6
	7/32	0.21875	5.5562	0.005	0.1270		23/32	0.71875	18.2562	10	254.0
	15/64	0.234375	5.9531	0.006	0.1524		47/64	0.734375	18.6531	11	279.4
1/4		0.25	6.3500	0.007	0.1778	3/4		0.75	19.0500	12	304.8
	17/64	0.265625	6.7469	0.008	0.2032		49/64	0.765625	19.4469	13	330.2
	9/32	0.28125	7.1437	0.009	0.2286		25/32	0.78125	19.8437	14	355.6
	19/64	0.296875	7.5406	0.01	0.254		51/64	0.796875	20.2406	15	381.0
5/16		0.3125	7.9375	0.02	0.508	13/16		0.8125	20.6375	16	406.4
	21/64	0.328125	8.3344	0.03	0.762		53/64	0.828125	21.0344	17	431.8
	11/32	0.34375	8.7312	0.04	1.016		27/32	0.84375	21.4312	18	457.2
	23/64	0.359375	9.1281	0.05	1.270		55/64	0.859375	21.8281	19	482.6
3/8		0.375	9.5250	0.06	1.524	7/8		0.875	22.2250	20	508.0
	25/64	0.390625	9.9219	0.07	1.778		57/64	0.890625	22.6219	21	533.4
	13/32	0.40625	10.3187	0.08	2.032		29/32	0.90625	23.0187	22	558.8
	27/64	0.421875	10.7156	0.09	2.286		59/64	0.921875	23.4156	23	584.2
7/16		0.4375	11.1125	0.1	2.54	15/16		0.9375	23.8125	24	609.6
	29/64	0.453125	11.5094	0.2	5.08		61/64	0.953125	24.2094	25	635.0
	15/32	0.46875	11.9062	0.3	7.62	31/32		0.96875	24.6062	26	660.4
	31/64	0.484375	12.3031	0.4	10.16		63/64	0.984375	25.0031	27	690.6
1/2		0.5	12.7000	0.5	12.70						

ENGLISH TO METRIC CONVERSION: TORQUE

To convert foot-pounds (ft. lbs.) to Newton-meters: multiply the number of ft. lbs. by 1.3

To convert inch-pounds (in. lbs.) to Newton-meters: multiply the number of in. lbs. by .11

in lbs	N-m	in lbs	N-m	in lbs	N-m	in lbs	N-m	in lbs	N-m
0.1	0.01	1	0.11	10	1.13	19	2.15	28	3.16
0.2	0.02	2	0.23	11	1.24	20	2.26	29	3.28
0.3	0.03	3	0.34	12	1.36	21	2.37	30	3.39
0.4	0.04	4	0.45	13	1.47	22	2.49	31	3.50
0.5	0.06	5	0.56	14	1.58	23	2.60	32	3.62
0.6	0.07	6	0.68	15	1.70	24	2.71	33	3.73
0.7	0.08	7	0.78	16	1.81	25	2.82	34	3.84
0.8	0.09	8	0.90	17	1.92	26	2.94	35	3.95
0.9	0.10	9	1.02	18	2.03	27	3.05	36	4.0

ENGLISH TO METRIC CONVERSION: TORQUE

Torque is now expressed as either foot-pounds (ft./lbs.) or inch-pounds (in./lbs.). The metric measurement unit for torque is the Newton-meter (Nm). This unit—the Nm—will be used for all SI metric torque references, both the present ft./lbs. and in./lbs.

ft lbs	N-m	ft lbs	N-m	ft lbs	N-m	ft lbs	N-m
0.1	0.1	33	44.7	74	100.3	115	155.9
0.2	0.3	34	46.1	75	101.7	116	157.3
0.3	0.4	35	47.4	76	103.0	117	158.6
0.4	0.5	36	48.8	77	104.4	118	160.0
0.5	0.7	37	50.7	78	105.8	119	161.3
0.6	0.8	38	51.5	79	107.1	120	162.7
0.7	1.0	39	52.9	80	108.5	121	164.0
0.8	1.1	40	54.2	81	109.8	122	165.4
0.9	1.2	41	55.6	82	111.2	123	166.8
1	1.3	42	56.9	83	112.5	124	168.1
2	2.7	43	58.3	84	113.9	125	169.5
3	4.1	44	59.7	85	115.2	126	170.8
4	5.4	45	61.0	86	116.6	127	172.2
5	6.8	46	62.4	87	118.0	128	173.5
6	8.1	47	63.7	88	119.3	129	174.9
7	9.5	48	65.1	89	120.7	130	176.2
8	10.8	49	66.4	90	122.0	131	177.6
9	12.2	50	67.8	91	123.4	132	179.0
10	13.6	51	69.2	92	124.7	133	180.3
11	14.9	52	70.5	93	126.1	134	181.7
12	16.3	53	71.9	94	127.4	135	183.0
13	17.6	54	73.2	95	128.8	136	184.4
14	18.9	55	74.6	96	130.2	137	185.7
15	20.3	56	75.9	97	131.5	138	187.1
16	21.7	57	77.3	98	132.9	139	188.5
17	23.0	58	78.6	99	134.2	140	189.8
18	24.4	59	80.0	100	135.6	141	191.2
19	25.8	60	81.4	101	136.9	142	192.5
20	27.1	61	82.7	102	138.3	143	193.9
21	28.5	62	84.1	103	139.6	144	195.2
22	29.8	63	85.4	104	141.0	145	196.6
23	31.2	64	86.8	105	142.4	146	198.0
24	32.5	65	88.1	106	143.7	147	199.3
25	33.9	66	89.5	107	145.1	148	200.7
26	35.2	67	90.8	108	146.4	149	202.0
27	36.6	68	92.2	109	147.8	150	203.4
28	38.0	69	93.6	110	149.1	151	204.7
29	39.3	70	94.9	111	150.5	152	206.1
30	40.7	71	96.3	112	151.8	153	207.4
31	42.0	72	97.6	113	153.2	154	208.8
32	43.4	73	99.0	114	154.6	155	210.2

TCCS1C03

ENGLISH TO METRIC CONVERSION: FORCE

Force is presently measured in pounds (lbs.). This type of measurement is used to measure spring pressure, specifically how many pounds it takes to compress a spring. Our present force unit (the pound) will be replaced in SI metric measurements by the Newton (N). This term will eventually see use in specifications for electric motor brush spring pressures, valve spring pressures, etc.

To convert pounds (lbs.) to Newton (N): multiply the number of lbs. by 4.45

lbs	N	lbs	N	lbs	N	oz	N
0.01	0.04	21	93.4	59	262.4	1	0.3
0.02	0.09	22	97.9	60	266.9	2	0.6
0.03	0.13	23	102.3	61	271.3	3	0.8
0.04	0.18	24	106.8	62	275.8	4	1.1
0.05	0.22	25	111.2	63	280.2	5	1.4
0.06	0.27	26	115.6	64	284.6	6	1.7
0.07	0.31	27	120.1	65	289.1	7	2.0
0.08	0.36	28	124.6	66	293.6	8	2.2
0.09	0.40	29	129.0	67	298.0	9	2.5
0.1	0.4	30	133.4	68	302.5	10	2.8
0.2	0.9	31	137.9	69	306.9	11	3.1
0.3	1.3	32	142.3	70	311.4	12	3.3
0.4	1.8	33	146.8	71	315.8	13	3.6
0.5	2.2	34	151.2	72	320.3	14	3.9
0.6	2.7	35	155.7	73	324.7	15	4.2
0.7	3.1	36	160.1	74	329.2	16	4.4
0.8	3.6	37	164.6	75	333.6	17	4.7
0.9	4.0	38	169.0	76	338.1	18	5.0
1	4.4	39	173.5	77	342.5	19	5.3
2	8.9	40	177.9	78	347.0	20	5.6
3	13.4	41	182.4	79	351.4	21	5.8
4	17.8	42	186.8	80	355.9	22	6.1
5	22.2	43	191.3	81	360.3	23	6.4
6	26.7	44	195.7	82	364.8	24	6.7
7	31.1	45	200.2	83	369.2	25	7.0
8	35.6	46	204.6	84	373.6	26	7.2
9	40.0	47	209.1	85	378.1	27	7.5
10	44.5	48	213.5	86	382.6	28	7.8
11	48.9	49	218.0	87	387.0	29	8.1
12	53.4	50	224.4	88	391.4	30	8.3
13	57.8	51	226.9	89	395.9	31	8.6
14	62.3	52	231.3	90	400.3	32	8.9
15	66.7	53	235.8	91	404.8	33	9.2
16	71.2	54	240.2	92	409.2	34	9.4
17	75.6	55	244.6	93	413.7	35	9.7
18	80.1	56	249.1	94	418.1	36	10.0
19	84.5	57	253.6	95	422.6	37	10.3
20	89.0	58	258.0	96	427.0	38	10.6

TCCS1C04

2

ENGINE
PERFORMANCE
AND TUNE-UP

TUNE-UP PROCEDURES

A tune-up is performed periodically to make a complete check of the operation of the engine and several associated systems, to bring various minor adjustments to the best possible position, and to replace fast-wearing ignition parts. The tune-up is a good time to perform a general preventive maintenance check-out on everything in the engine compartment. Look for things like loose or damaged wiring, fuel leaks, frayed drive belts, etc.

Refer to the car's owners manual for the recommended intervals between tune-ups as a guide, but after one or two tune-ups, according to the vehicle's performance, you can determine your own tune-up interval. Whether it is 8,000, 13,000, 24,000 miles, or once every year; set up a definite schedule for your car and follow it religiously. Regular tuning will head off disappointing performance and help prevent roadside breakdowns.

Spark Plugs

▶ **See Figures 1 and 2**

A typical spark plug consists of a metal shell surrounding a ceramic insulator. A metal electrode extends downward through the center of the insulator and

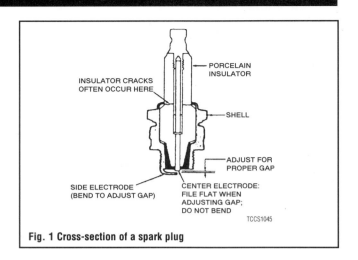

Fig. 1 Cross-section of a spark plug

GASOLINE ENGINE TUNE-UP SPECIFICATIONS

Year	Engine ID/VIN	Engine Displacement Liters (cc)	Spark Plugs Gap (in.)	Ignition Timing (deg.) MT	Ignition Timing (deg.) AT	Fuel Pump (psi)	Idle Speed (rpm) MT	Idle Speed (rpm) AT	Valve Clearance In.	Valve Clearance Ex.
1986	M	1.5 (1468)	0.039–0.043	5B	5B	2.8–3.6	750	750	0.006	0.010
1987	M	1.5 (1468)	0.039–0.043	5B	5B	2.8–3.6	750	750	0.006	0.010
1988	M	1.5 (1468)	0.039–0.043	5B	5B	2.8–3.6	750	750	0.006	0.010
1989	M	1.5 (1468)	0.039–0.043	5B	5B	2.8–3.6	750	750	0.006	0.010
	S	2.4 (2351)	0.039–0.043	5B	5B	48	750	750	Hyd.	Hyd.
1990	M	1.5 (1468)	0.039–0.043	5B	5B	2.8–3.6	700	700	0.006	0.010
	J	1.5 (1468)	0.039–0.043	5B	5B	48	700	700	0.006	0.010
	S	2.4 (2351)	0.039–0.043	5B	5B	48	750	750	Hyd.	Hyd.
	T	3.0 (2972)	0.039–0.043	5B	5B	48	750	750	Hyd.	Hyd.
1991	M	1.5 (1468)	0.039–0.043	5B	5B	2.8–3.6	700	700	0.006	0.010
	J	1.5 (1468)	0.039–0.043	5B	5B	48	700	700	0.006	0.010
	S	2.4 (2351)	0.039–0.043	5B	5B	48	750	750	Hyd.	Hyd.
	T	3.0 (2972)	0.039–0.043	12B	12B	48	750	750	Hyd.	Hyd.
1992	M	1.5 (1468)	0.039–0.043	5B	5B	2.8–3.6	700	700	0.006	0.010
	J	1.5 (1468)	0.039–0.043	5B	5B	48	700	700	0.006	0.010
	F	2.0 (1997)	0.039–0.043	5B	5B	48	750	750	Hyd.	Hyd.
	T	3.0 (2972)	0.039–0.043	12B	12B	48	750	750	Hyd.	Hyd.
	R	1.6 (1596)	0.039–0.043	5B	5B	48	750	750	Hyd.	Hyd.
1993	M	1.5 (1468)	0.039–0.043	5B	5B	2.8–3.6	700	700	0.006	0.010
	J	1.5 (1468)	0.039–0.043	5B	5B	48	700	700	0.006	0.010
	N	1.5 (1495)	0.039–0.043	9B	9B	43	800	800	0.007	0.009
	N①	1.5 (1495)	0.039–0.043	9B	9B	43	800	800	0.007	0.009
	F	2.0 (1997)	0.039–0.043	5B	5B	48	750	750	Hyd.	Hyd.
	T	3.0 (2972)	0.039–0.043	12B	12B	48	750	750	Hyd.	Hyd.
	R	1.6 (1596)	0.039–0.043	5B	5B	48	750	750	Hyd.	Hyd.
	M	1.8 (1796)	0.039–0.043	5B	5B	48	750	750	Hyd.	Hyd.

NOTE: The lowest cylinder pressure should be within 75% of the highest cylinder pressure reading. For example, if the highest cylinder is 134 psi, the lowest should be 101. Engine should be at normal operating temperature with throttle valve in the wide open position.
The underhood specifications sticker often reflects tune-up specification changes in production. Sticker figures must be used if they disagree with those in this chart.
① Scoupe Turbo

84122C01

Fig. 2 A variety of tools and gauges are needed for spark plug service

protrudes a small distance. Located at the end of the plug and attached to the side of the outer metal shell is the side electrode. The side electrode bends in at a 90° angle so that its tip is just past and parallel to the tip of the center electrode. The distance between these two electrodes (measured in thousandths of an inch or hundredths of a millimeter) is called the spark plug gap.

The spark plug does not produce a spark, but instead provides a gap across which the current can arc. The coil produces anywhere from 20,000 to 50,000 volts (depending on the type and application) which travels through the wires to the spark plugs. The current passes along the center electrode and jumps the gap to the side electrode, and in doing so, ignites the air/fuel mixture in the combustion chamber.

SPARK PLUG HEAT RANGE

▶ **See Figure 3**

Spark plug heat range is the ability of the plug to dissipate heat. The longer the insulator (or the farther it extends into the engine), the hotter the plug will operate; the shorter the insulator (the closer the electrode is to the block's cooling passages) the cooler it will operate. A plug that absorbs little heat and remains too cool will quickly accumulate deposits of oil and carbon since it is not hot enough to burn them off. This leads to plug fouling and consequently to misfiring. A plug that absorbs too much heat will have no deposits but, due to the excessive heat, the electrodes will burn away quickly and might possibly lead to preignition or other ignition problems. Preignition takes place when plug tips get so hot that they glow sufficiently to ignite the air/fuel mixture before the actual spark occurs. This early ignition will usually cause a pinging during low speeds and heavy loads.

The general rule of thumb for choosing the correct heat range when picking a spark plug is: if most of your driving is long distance, high speed travel, use a

colder plug; if most of your driving is stop and go, use a hotter plug. Original equipment plugs are generally a good compromise between the 2 styles and most people never have the need to change their plugs from the factory-recommended heat range.

REMOVAL & INSTALLATION

▶ **See Figures 4 and 5**

A set of spark plugs usually requires replacement after about 20,000–30,000 miles (32,000–48,000 km), depending on your style of driving. In normal operation plug gap increases about 0.001 in. (0.025mm) for every 2500 miles (4000 km). As the gap increases, the plug's voltage requirement also increases. It requires a greater voltage to jump the wider gap and about two to three times as much voltage to fire the plug at high speeds than at idle. The improved air/fuel ratio control of modern fuel injection combined with the higher voltage output of modern ignition systems will often allow an engine to run significantly longer on a set of standard spark plugs, but keep in mind that efficiency will drop as the gap widens (along with fuel economy and power).

When you're removing spark plugs, work on one at a time. Don't start by removing the plug wires all at once, because, unless you number them, they may become mixed up. Take a minute before you begin and number the wires with tape.

1. Disconnect the negative battery cable, and if the vehicle has been run recently, allow the engine to thoroughly cool.

2. Carefully twist the spark plug wire boot to loosen it, then pull upward and remove the boot from the plug. Be sure to pull on the boot and not on the wire, otherwise the connector located inside the boot may become separated.

3. Using compressed air, blow any water or debris from the spark plug well to assure that no harmful contaminants are allowed to enter the combustion chamber when the spark plug is removed. If compressed air is not available, use a rag or a brush to clean the area.

➡**Remove the spark plugs when the engine is cold, if possible, to prevent damage to the threads. If removal of the plugs is difficult, apply a few drops of penetrating oil or silicone spray to the area around the base of the plug, and allow it a few minutes to work.**

4. Using a spark plug socket that is equipped with a rubber insert to properly hold the plug, turn the spark plug counterclockwise to loosen and remove the spark plug from the bore.

✳✳ WARNING

Be sure not to use a flexible extension on the socket. Use of a flexible extension may allow a shear force to be applied to the plug. A shear force could break the plug off in the cylinder head, leading to costly and frustrating repairs.

To install:
5. Inspect the spark plug boot for tears or damage. If a damaged boot is found, the spark plug wire must be replaced.

6. Using a wire feeler gauge, check and adjust the spark plug gap. When using a gauge, the proper size should pass between the electrodes with a slight drag. The next larger size should not be able to pass while the next smaller size should pass freely.

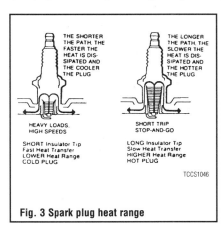

Fig. 3 Spark plug heat range

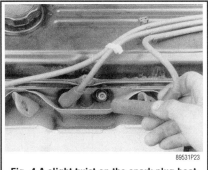

Fig. 4 A slight twist on the spark plug boot will allow the wire to be removed from the spark plug more easily

Fig. 5 Using a spark plug socket equipped with a rubber insert, carefully remove the spark plug from the engine

7. Carefully thread the plug into the bore by hand. If resistance is felt before the plug is almost completely threaded, back the plug out and begin threading again. In small, hard to reach areas, an old spark plug wire and boot could be used as a threading tool. The boot will hold the plug while you twist the end of the wire and the wire is supple enough to twist before it would allow the plug to crossthread.

✳✳ WARNING

Do not use the spark plug socket to thread the plugs. Always carefully thread the plug by hand or using an old plug wire to prevent the possibility of crossthreading and damaging the cylinder head bore.

8. Carefully tighten the spark plug. If the plug you are installing is equipped with a crush washer, seat the plug, then tighten about ¼ turn to crush the washer. If you are installing a tapered seat plug, tighten the plug to specifications provided by the vehicle or plug manufacturer.

9. Apply a small amount of silicone dielectric compound to the end of the spark plug lead or inside the spark plug boot to prevent sticking, then install the boot to the spark plug and push until it clicks into place. The click may be felt or heard, then gently pull back on the boot to assure proper contact.

INSPECTION & GAPPING

▶ **See Figures 6, 7, 8 and 9**

Check the plugs for deposits and wear. If they are not going to be replaced, clean the plugs thoroughly. Remember that any kind of deposit will decrease the efficiency of the plug. Plugs can be cleaned on a spark plug cleaning machine, which can sometimes be found in service stations, or you can do an acceptable job of cleaning with a stiff brush. If the plugs are cleaned, the electrodes must be filed flat. Use an ignition points file, not an emery board or the like, which will leave deposits. The electrodes must be filed perfectly flat with sharp edges; rounded edges reduce the spark plug voltage by as much as 50%.

Check spark plug gap before installation. The ground electrode (the L-shaped one connected to the body of the plug) must be parallel to the center electrode and the specified size wire gauge (please refer to the Tune-Up Specifications chart for details) must pass between the electrodes with a slight drag.

➡ **NEVER adjust the gap on a used platinum type spark plug.**

Always check the gap on new plugs as they are not always set correctly at the factory. Do not use a flat feeler gauge when measuring the gap on a used plug,

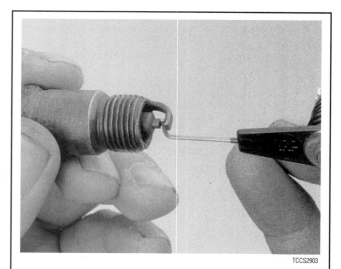

Fig. 6 Checking the spark plug gap with a feeler gauge

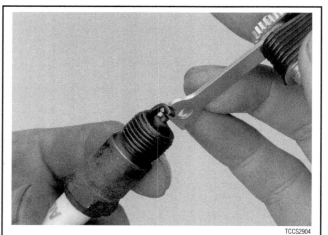

Fig. 7 Adjusting the spark plug gap

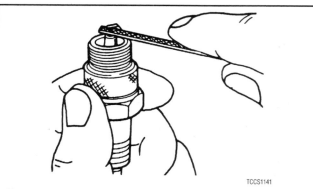

Fig. 8 If the standard plug is in good condition, the electrode may be filed flat—WARNING: do not file platinum plugs

because the reading may be inaccurate. A round-wire type gapping tool is the best way to check the gap. The correct gauge should pass through the electrode gap with a slight drag. If you're in doubt, try one size smaller and one larger. The smaller gauge should go through easily, while the larger one shouldn't go through at all. Wire gapping tools usually have a bending tool attached. Use that to adjust the side electrode until the proper distance is obtained. Absolutely never attempt to bend the center electrode. Also, be careful not to bend the side electrode too far or too often as it may weaken and break off within the engine, requiring removal of the cylinder head to retrieve it.

Spark Plug Wires

CHECKING & REPLACING

▶ **See Figures 10, 11 and 12**

Visually inspect the spark plug cables for burns, cuts, or breaks in the insulation. Check the spark plug boots and the nipples on the distributor cap and coil. Replace any damaged wiring. If no physical damage is obvious, the wires can be checked with an ohmmeter for excessive resistance. Resistance should be about 8,000 ohms per foot of cable length. The resistance reading on the No. 4 wire will be greater than the No. 1 wire because it is slightly longer. When installing a new set of spark plug cables, replace the cables one at a time so there will be no mixup. Start by replacing the longest cable first. Install the boot firmly over the spark plug. Route the wire exactly the same as the original. Insert the nipple into the tower on the distributor cap. Repeat the process for each cable.

A normally worn spark plug should have light tan or gray deposits on the firing tip.

A carbon fouled plug, identified by soft, sooty, black deposits, may indicate an improperly tuned vehicle. Check the air cleaner, ignition components and engine control system.

This spark plug has been **left in the engine too long,** as evidenced by the extreme gap- Plugs with such an extreme gap can cause misfiring and stumbling accompanied by a noticeable lack of power.

An oil fouled spark plug indicates an engine with worn poston rings and/or bad valve seals allowing excessive oil to enter the chamber.

A physically damaged spark plug may be evidence of severe detonation in that cylinder. Watch that cylinder carefully between services, as a continued detonation will not only damage the plug, but could also damage the engine.

A bridged or almost bridged spark plug, identified by a buildup between the electrodes caused by excessive carbon or oil build-up on the plug.

TCCA1P40

Fig. 9 Inspect the spark plug to determine engine running conditions

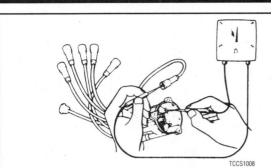

Fig. 10 Checking plug wire resistance through the distributor cap with an ohmmeter

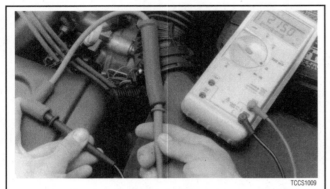

Fig. 11 Checking individual plug wire resistance with a digital ohmmeter

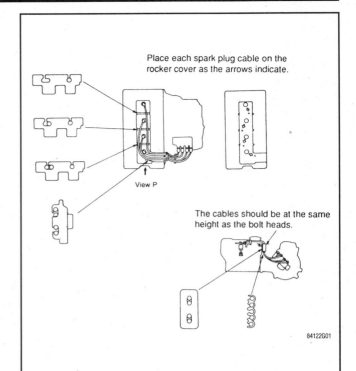

Place each spark plug cable on the rocker cover as the arrows indicate.

View P

The cables should be at the same height as the bolt heads.

Fig. 12 Proper routing of the spark plug wires is extremely important on the Elantra, incorrect wire routing will cause ignition system problems

HYUNDAI ELECTRONIC IGNITION SYSTEM

General Information

EXCEL EQUIPPED WITH FEEDBACK CARBURETOR

♦ **See Figure 13**

The electronic ignition system used on engines with a Feedback Carburetor (FBC), uses a magnetic pulse/igniter distributor and a conventional type ignition coil. The distributor cap, rotor, advance mechanism (vacuum and centrifugal) and secondary ignition wires are also of standard design. The distributor contains the igniter, signal rotor and mechanical advance components.

SCOUPE, SONATA, ELANTRA, EXCEL EQUIPPED WITH MULTI-POINT INJECTION

♦ **See Figures 14 and 15**

The electronic ignition used on the Scoupe and Excel engine with Multi-Point Fuel Injection (MPI), has timing controlled by the Electronic Control Unit (ECU). The standard reference ignition timing data from the engine operating conditions are programmed in the memory of the ECU. The engine conditions, rpm, load and temperature are detected by the ECU sensors and the ignition timing data signals to interrupt the primary current are sent to the power tran-

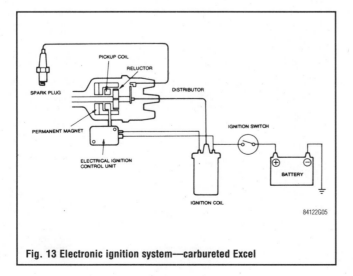

Fig. 13 Electronic ignition system—carbureted Excel

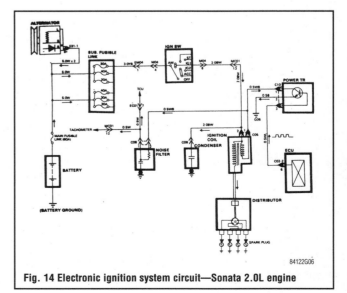

Fig. 14 Electronic ignition system circuit—Sonata 2.0L engine

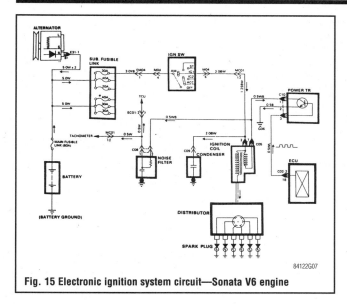

Fig. 15 Electronic ignition system circuit—Sonata V6 engine

sistor. The ignition coil is activated and timing is controlled by this ECU control method.

The electronic ignition used on Sonata and Elantra with Multi-Point Fuel Injection (MPI) is the same system as used on the Excel with MPI. Timing is controlled by the ECU. The standard reference ignition timing data is programmed in the memory of the ECU. The engine conditions, rpm, load and temperature are detected by the ECU sensors and the ignition timing data signals to interrupt the primary current are sent to the power transistor. The ignition coil is activated and timing is controlled by the ECU.

Diagnosis and Testing

♦ **See Figures 16 and 17**

SERVICE PRECAUTIONS

- Make sure all connectors are fastened securely. A poor connection can cause an extremely high surge voltage in the coil and condenser and result in damage to integrated circuits.
- Keep all parts and harnesses dry during service.
- Before attempting to remove any parts, turn **OFF** the ignition switch and disconnect the battery ground cable.
- Always use a 12 volt battery as a power source.

Probable condition	Probable cause	Remedy
Engine will not start or is hard to start. (Cranks OK)	Incorrect ignition timing	Adjust ignition timing
	Ignition coil faulty	Inspect ignition coil
	Power transistor faulty	Inspect power transistor
	Crank angle sensor faulty	Replace crank angle sensor
	High tension cable faulty	Inspect high tension cable
	Spark plugs faulty	Replace plugs
	Ignition wiring disconnected or broken	Inspect wiring
Rough idle or stalls	Spark plugs faulty	Replace plugs
	Ignition wiring faulty	Inspect wiring
	Incorrect ignition timing	Adjust ignition timing
	Ignition coil faulty	Inspect ignition coil
	Power transistor faulty	Inspect power transistor
Engine hesitates/poor acceleration	Spark plugs faulty	Replace plugs
	Ignition wiring faulty	Inspect wiring
	Incorrect ignition timing	Adjust timing
Poor mileage	Spark plugs faulty	Replace plugs
	Incorrect ignition timing	Adjust ignition timing
Engine overheats	Incorrect ignition timing	Adjust ignition timing

Fig. 16 Ignition system troubleshooting—all models

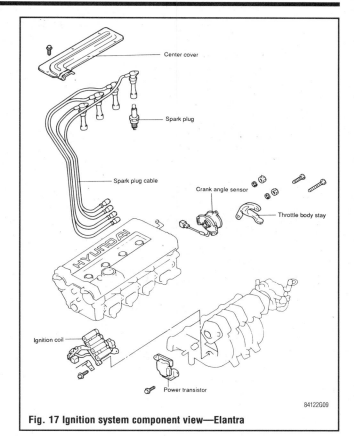

Fig. 17 Ignition system component view—Elantra

- Do not attempt to disconnect the battery cables with the engine running.
- Do not depress the accelerator pedal when starting.
- Do not rev up the engine immediately after starting or just prior to shutdown.
- If a battery cable is disconnected, the memory will return to the ROM (programmed) values. Engine operation may vary slightly, but this is not an indication of a problem. Do not replace parts because of a slight variation.
- If installing a 2-way or CB radio, keep the antenna as far as possible away from the electronic control unit. Keep the antenna feeder line at least 8 in. away from the ECU harness and do not let the 2 run parallel for a long distance. Be sure to ground the radio to the vehicle body.

SECONDARY SPARK TEST

♦ **See Figures 18, 19, 20 and 21**

The best way to perform this procedure is to use a spark tester (available at most automotive parts stores). Three types of spark testers are commonly available. The Neon Bulb type is connected to the spark plug wire and flashes with each ignition

Fig. 18 This spark tester looks just like a spark plug, attach the clip to ground and crank the engine to check for spark

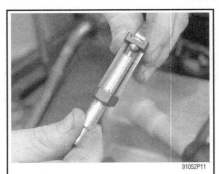

Fig. 19 This spark tester has an adjustable air-gap for measuring spark strength and testing different voltage ignition systems

Fig. 20 Attach the clip to ground and crank the engine to check for spark

Fig. 21 This spark tester is the easiest to use just place it on a plug wire and the spark voltage is detected and the bulb on the top will flash with each pulse

pulse. The Air Gap type must be adjusted to the individual spark plug gap specified for the engine. The last type of spark plug tester looks like a spark plug with a grounding clip on the side, but there is no side electrode for the spark to jump to. The last two types of testers allows the user to not only detect the presence of spark, but also the intensity (orange/yellow is weak, blue is strong).

1. Disconnect a spark plug wire at the spark plug end.
2. Connect the plug wire to the spark tester and ground the tester to an appropriate location on the engine.
3. Crank the engine and check for spark at the tester.
4. If spark exists at the tester, the ignition system is functioning properly.
5. If spark does not exist at the spark plug wire, perform diagnosis of the ignition system using individual component diagnosis procedures.

CYLINDER DROP TEST

▶ See Figures 22, 23 and 24

The cylinder drop test is performed when an engine misfire is evident. This test helps determine which cylinder is not contributing the proper power. The easiest way to perform this test is to remove the plug wires one at a time from the cylinders with the engine running.

1. Place the transaxle in **P**, engage the emergency brake, and start the engine and let it idle.
2. Using a spark plug wire removing tool, preferably, the plier type, carefully remove the boot from one of the cylinders.

✳✳ WARNING

Make sure your body is free from touching any part of the car which is metal. The secondary voltage in the ignition system is high and although it cannot kill you, it will shock you and it does hurt.

3. The engine will sputter, run worse, and possibly nearly stall. If this happens reinstall the plug wire and move to the next cylinder. If the engine runs no differently, or the difference is minimal, shut the engine off and inspect the spark plug wire,

spark plug, and if necessary, perform component diagnostics as covered in this section. Perform the test on all cylinders to verify the which cylinders are suspect.

IGNITION COIL

▶ See Figure 25

Testing

EXCEL WITH FEEDBACK CARBURETOR

1. Using a suitable volt/ohmmeter, measure the resistance. An open or short circuited coil should be replaced. The standard resistance values are as follows:
   a. Primary coil resistance—1.2 ohms
   b. Secondary coil resistance—13.7 kilo-ohms
   c. External resistor resistance—1.35 ohms
2. Check the resin portion for cracks. If there are any cracks present, replace it.
3. Check for any fluid (oil) leaks. If there are any leaks present, replace it.

SCOUPE, SONATA AND EXCEL WITH MPI

1. Using a suitable volt/ohmmeter, measure the resistance. An open or short circuited coil should be replaced. The standard resistance values are as follows:
   a. Primary coil resistance—0.72–0.88 ohms
   b. Secondary coil resistance—10.9–13.3 kilo-ohms
2. Check the resin portion for cracks. If there are any cracks present, replace it.
3. Check for any fluid (oil) leaks. If there are any leaks present, replace it.

ELANTRA

▶ See Figures 26 and 27

1. Using a suitable volt/ohmmeter, measure the primary and secondary resistances. An open or short circuited coil should be replaced. The standard resistance values are as follows:
2. Primary coil resistance—0.77–0.95 ohms. Measure resistance between con-

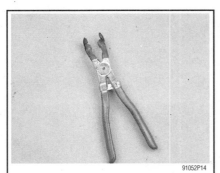

Fig. 22 These pliers are insulated and help protect the user from shock as well as the plug wires from being damaged

Fig. 23 To perform the cylinder drop test, remove one wire at a time and . . .

Fig. 24 . . . note the idle speed and idle characteristics of the engine. the cylinder(s) with the least drop is the non-contributing cylinder(s)

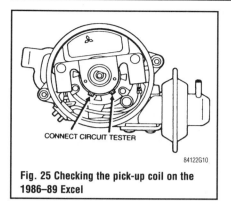

Fig. 25 Checking the pick-up coil on the 1986–89 Excel

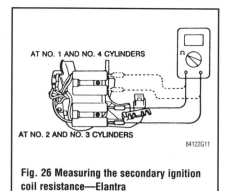

Fig. 26 Measuring the secondary ignition coil resistance—Elantra

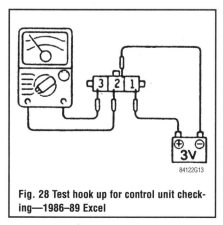

Fig. 27 Measuring the primary ignition coil resistance—Elantra

nector terminals 3 and 1, the coils at the No.1 and No.4 cylinder sides of the ignition coil, and between terminals 3 and 2, the coils at the No.2 and No.3 cylinder sides.

3. Secondary coil resistance—10.3–13.9 kilo-ohms. Measure the resistance between the high voltage terminal for the No.1 and No.4 cylinders and between the high voltage terminals for the No.2 and No.3 cylinders.

➡**When measuring the resistance of the secondary coil, disconnect the ignition coil connector.**

4. Check the resin portion for cracks. If there are any cracks present, replace it.
5. Check for any fluid (oil) leaks. If there are any leaks present, replace it.

CONTROL UNIT

Testing

1986–89 EXCEL ONLY

♦ **See Figure 28**

The control unit is internally mounted (in the distributor). Connect the igniter unit, battery, lamp or ohmmeter as shown in the illustration. Apply signal voltage. If the lamp lights or ohms are read when voltage is applied, and goes out or reads 0 ohms when the voltage signal is removed, the igniter may be considered good.

➡**Only the switching section of the control unit is checked with this test. Even if the unit tests as good, it could still be defective.**

RELUCTOR GAP

Adjustment

♦ **See Figure 29**

1986–89 EXCEL ONLY

The reluctor gap is adjustable on the Hitachi Electric distributor used on the Excel. While service is not required as a part of normal maintenance, if you have worked on the distributor or if you suspect the reluctor gap might be incorrect because of ignition problems, you can check and adjust it.

1. Get a feeler gauge of non-magnetic material (brass, plastic or wood) of 0.8mm thickness. Remove the distributor cap and rotor.
2. Rotate the engine (you can use a large socket wrench on the bolt that attaches the front pulley) until one of the prongs of the rotor is directly across from the igniter pickup.
3. Insert or attempt to insert the feeler gauge between the prong and pickup. If the gap is correct, there will be a very slight drag. If the gauge fits loosely or cannot be inserted, loosen both mounting screws and then (if necessary widen the gap) insert the gauge. Slowly close the gap by pivoting the igniter assembly on the left screw and rotating it at the right side, where it's slotted. When the gauge is just touching, tighten first the right side screw and then the screw on the left. Recheck the gap and re-adjust as necessary. Reinstall the cap and rotor.

POWER TRANSISTOR

Testing

♦ **See Figure 30**

SCOUPE, SONATA AND EXCEL WITH MPI

1. Connect an analog type ohmmeter across terminals 2 and 3 of the power transistor.
2. There should be no continuity.
3. Connect the negative terminal of a 3 volt battery to terminal 2 and the positive terminal to terminal 1 of the power transistor. The ohmmeter should show continuity.
4. Replace the power transistor, if there is a malfunction.

ELANTRA

1. Check the power transistor for coil No.1 and No.4 as follows:
   a. Connect the negative lead of a 1.5 volt battery source to terminal 3 of the power transistor; then check for continuity between terminal 5 and terminal 3 when the terminal 4 and the positive terminal are connected.
   b. Continuity should exist when terminal 4 is connected. Continuity should not exist when terminal 4 is disconnected.
2. Check the power transistor for coil No.2 and No.3 as follows:

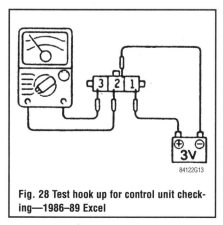

Fig. 28 Test hook up for control unit checking—1986–89 Excel

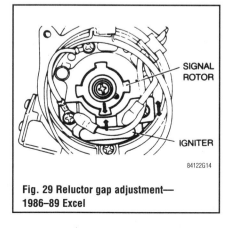

Fig. 29 Reluctor gap adjustment—1986–89 Excel

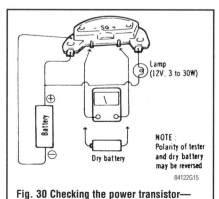

Fig. 30 Checking the power transistor—Sonata and Excel with MPI

a. Connect the negative lead of a 1.5 volt battery source to terminal 3 of the power transistor; then check for continuity between terminal 1 and terminal 3 when the terminal 2 and the positive terminal are connected.

b. Continuity should exist when terminal 2 is connected. Continuity should not exist when terminal 2 is disconnected.

3. If the problem is still evident after tests are completed, replace the power transistor.

Component Replacement

DISTRIBUTOR

Removal & Installation

EXCEL WITH FEEDBACK CARBURETOR

1. Rotate the engine and bring up the No. 1 cylinder to top dead center of its compression stroke.

2. Disconnect the negative battery cable. Disconnect and tag (if necessary) the electrical connectors along with the spark plug wires from the distributor.

3. Disconnect the wiring harness from the distributor lead wire. Disconnect the vacuum hoses from the vacuum controller.

4. Using a scribe tool or a marker, scribe or mark an alignment mark on the base of the distributor and the cylinder head. This can be used for an easier installation procedure.

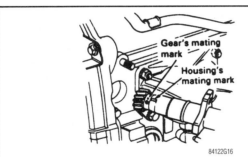

Fig. 31 Distributor gear installation marks—Sonata and Excel with MPI

5. Remove the distributor mounting nut and remove the distributor assembly from the engine cylinder head.

To install:

6. Install the distributor assembly into the cylinder block, being sure to align the scribe marks made previously. Lightly tighten the distributor mounting bolt.

7. Connect the wiring harness to the distributor lead wire. Connect the vacuum hoses to the vacuum controller.

8. Connect all the electrical connectors along with the spark plug wires to the distributor.

9. Connect the negative battery cable. Start the engine and set the timing. Then tighten the distributor mounting bolt.

SCOUPE, SONATA AND EXCEL WITH MPI

▶ See Figures 31, 32, 33 and 34

1. Rotate the engine and bring up the No.1 cylinder to TDC of its compression stroke.

2. Disconnect the negative battery cable. Disconnect and tag the electrical connectors and spark plug wires from the distributor.

3. Unclip the distributor cap and set aside.

4. Disconnect the wiring harness from the distributor.

5. Remove the distributor mounting nut and remove the distributor assembly.

To install:

6. If necessary, turn crankshaft so that No. 1 cylinder is at TDC on compression stroke.

7. Align the distributor housing and gear mating marks.

8. Install the distributor to the engine while aligning the fine cut of the distributor flange with the center of the distributor stud.

CRANK ANGLE SENSOR

Removal & Installation

ELANTRA

1. Disconnect the negative battery cable.

2. Remove the crank angle sensor mounting bolts and carefully pull the sensor from the engine.

To install:

3. Rotate the crankshaft until No.1 cylinder is at TDC.

4. Align the punch mark on the crank angle sensor housing with the notch in the plate.

5. Install the crank angle sensor on the cylinder head.

Fig. 32 Distributor housing installation marks—Sonata and Excel with MPI

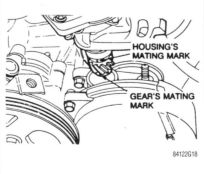

Fig. 33 Installing the distributor—Sonata V6 engine

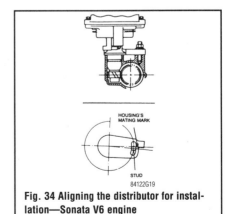

Fig. 34 Aligning the distributor for installation—Sonata V6 engine

FIRING ORDERS

▶ **See Figures 35, 36 and 37**

➡ **To avoid confusion, remove and tag the spark plug wires one at a time, for replacement.**

If a distributor is not keyed for installation with only one orientation, it could have been removed previously and rewired. The resultant wiring would hold the correct firing order, but could change the relative placement of the plug towers in relation to the engine. For this reason it is imperative that you label all wires before disconnecting any of them. Also, before removal, compare the current wiring with the accompanying illustrations. If the current wiring does not match, make notes in your book to reflect how your engine is wired.

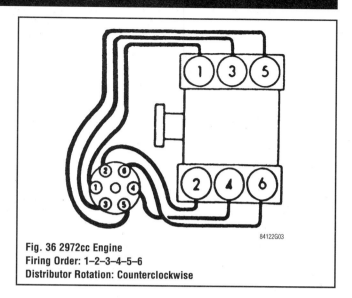

Fig. 36 2972cc Engine
Firing Order: 1–2–3–4–5–6
Distributor Rotation: Counterclockwise

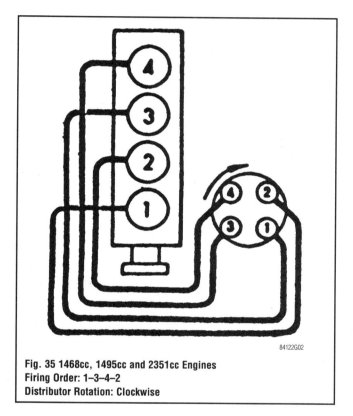

Fig. 35 1468cc, 1495cc and 2351cc Engines
Firing Order: 1–3–4–2
Distributor Rotation: Clockwise

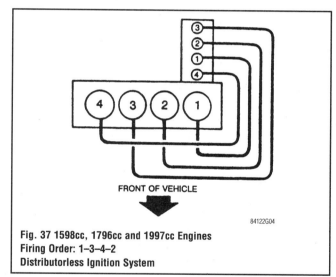

FRONT OF VEHICLE

Fig. 37 1598cc, 1796cc and 1997cc Engines
Firing Order: 1–3–4–2
Distributorless Ignition System

IGNITION TIMING

Ignition timing is the measurement, in degrees of crankshaft rotation, of the point at which the spark plugs fire in each of the cylinders. It is measured in degrees before or after Top Dead Center (TDC) of the compression stroke. Ignition timing is controlled by turning the distributor body in the engine. Ideally, the air/fuel mixture in the cylinder will be ignited by the spark plug just as the piston passes TDC of the compression stroke. If this happens, the piston will be beginning the power stroke just as the compressed and ignited air/fuel mixture then forces the piston down on the power stroke and turns the crankshaft. Because it takes a fraction of a second for the spark plug to ignite the mixture in the cylinder, the spark plug must fire a little before the piston reaches TDC. Otherwise, the mixture will not be completely ignited as the piston passes TDC and the full power of the explosion will not be used by the engine.

The timing measurement is given in degrees of crankshaft rotation before the piston reaches TDC (BTDC). If the setting for the ignition timing is 5 BTDC, each spark plug must fire 5 before each piston reaches TDC. This only holds true, however, when the engine is at idle speed. As the engine speed increases, the pistons go faster. The spark plugs have to ignite the fuel even sooner if it is to be completely ignited when the piston reaches TDC. To do this, the distributor has a means to advance the timing of the spark as the engine speed increases. On the 1986-89 Excel this is accomplished by centrifugal weights

within the distributor and a vacuum diaphragm mounted on the side of the distributor. On Elantra, Scoupe, Sonata and 1990–93 Excel, as engine speed increases ignition timing advance and retard adjustments are made by the ECU based on input from crankshaft angle sensor and engine sensor network.

If the ignition is set too far advanced (BTDC), the ignition and expansion of the fuel in the cylinder will occur too soon and tend to force the piston down while it is still traveling up. This causes engine ping. If the ignition spark is set too far retarded after TDC (ATDC), the piston will have already passed TDC and started on its way down when the fuel is ignited. This will cause the piston to be forced down for only a portion of its travel. This will result in poor engine performance and lack of power.

The timing is best checked with a timing light. This device is connected in series with the No. 1 spark plug or the coil wire, depending on type of timing light. The current that fires the spark plug also causes the timing light to flash.

✳✳ CAUTION

When making any adjustments with the engine running, be careful of the fan blades and/or drive belt.

Timing

ADJUSTMENT

Excel with Feedback Carburetor

♦ **See Figures 38 and 39**

1. Place the vehicle in **P** or **N** , the emergency brake applied and the drive wheels blocked. Start the engine and let it reach normal operating temperature.
2. Connect a suitable tachometer and timing light to the engine. Turn **OFF** all accessories. Check the curb idle and adjust as necessary. The curb idle should be as follows:
   a. Manual Transmissions—600–800 rpm
   b. Automatic Transmission—650–850 rpm
3. If the timing marks are difficult to see, use chalk or a dab of paint to make them more visible.
4. On the Canadian engines, disconnect the vacuum line from the distributor vacuum advance and plug the line.
5. Aim the timing light onto the timing marks and check the engine timing. If the timing is out of specifications, loosen the distributor mounting bolt and advance or retard the timing as necessary.
6. Once the proper timing has been reached, tighten the distributor mounting bolt and then recheck the timing again. The correct timing specifications are as follows:
   a. California—1–5 degrees BTDC
   b. Federal—3–7 degrees BTDC
   c. Canada—2–6 degrees BTDC
7. When the timing has been set properly, recheck the curb idle speed and adjust as necessary.
8. When all final adjustments have been made, shut **OFF** the engine, reconnect all vacuum lines and remove all test equipment.

Scoupe, Sonata and Excel with Multi-Point Fuel Injection (MPI)

♦ **See Figures 40, 41, 42 and 43**

1. Place the vehicle in **P** or **N**, the emergency brake applied and the drive wheels blocked. Start the engine and let it reach normal operating temperature.
2. Connect a suitable tachometer and timing light to the engine. Turn **OFF** all accessories. Check the curb idle and adjust as necessary to 650–850 rpm.
3. Stop engine and connect a jumper wire from the ignition timing adjustment connector (located at the rear of the engine compartment) to ground.
4. Start engine and allow to idle.
5. Loosen the distributor hold-down nut and turn distributor as needed to obtain a basic timing of 3–7 degrees BTDC.
6. Tighten distributor hold-down nut.
7. Stop engine and remove the jumper wire.
8. Start engine and recheck timing at idle. The correct ignition timing without ignition timing connector grounded is 10 degrees BTDC.

Elantra

♦ **See Figure 44**

1. Place the vehicle in **P** or **N**, the emergency brake applied and the drive wheels blocked. Start the engine and let it reach normal operating temperature.
2. Connect a suitable tachometer and timing light to the engine. Turn **OFF** all accessories. Check the curb idle and adjust as necessary to 750–800 rpm.
3. Stop engine and connect a jumper wire from the ignition timing adjustment connector (located at the rear of the engine compartment) to ground.
4. Start engine and allow to idle.
5. Check the basic ignition timing and adjust as required. The basic timing should be 3–7 degrees BTDC.

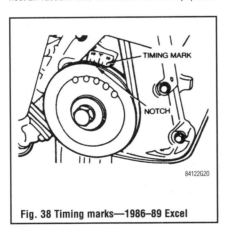

Fig. 38 Timing marks—1986–89 Excel

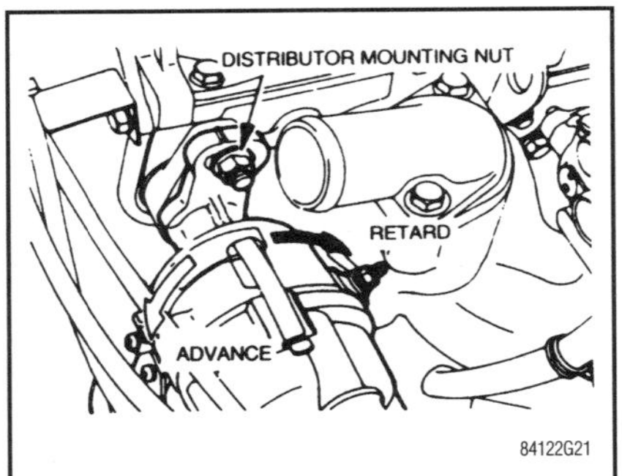

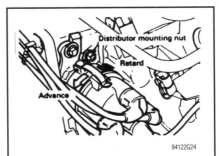

Fig. 39 Adjust the ignition timing by rotating the distributor housing—1986–89 Excel

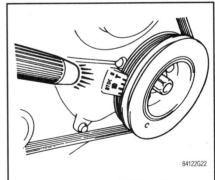

Fig. 40 Timing marks—1990–93 Excel, Elantra, Scoupe and Sonata

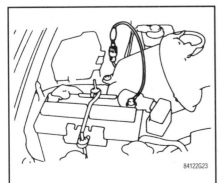

Fig. 41 Grounding the ignition timing connector on the Sonata

Fig. 42 Adjusting the ignition timing on 2.0L engine Sonata and 1990–93 Excel. Turn the distributor clockwise to retard timing and counterclockwise to advance it

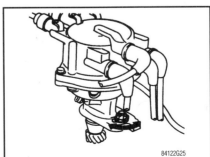

Fig. 43 Adjusting the ignition timing on V6 engine Sonata. Turn the distributor clockwise to advance timing and counterclockwise to retard it

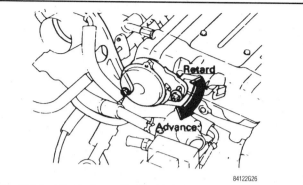

Fig. 44 Adjust the timing on the Elantra by turning the crank angle sensor

6. If the timing is incorrect, loosen the crank angle sensor mounting nut and rotate the sensor until the correct timing is obtained.
7. Tighten the crank angle mounting nut to 7–9 ft. lbs. (10–13 Nm).
8. Stop engine and remove the jumper wire.
9. Start engine and recheck timing at idle. The correct ignition timing without ignition timing connector grounded is 8 degrees BTDC.

VALVE LASH

Valve adjustment determines how far the valves enter the cylinder and how long they stay open and closed.

If the valve clearance is too large, part of the lift of the camshaft will be used in removing the excessive clearance. Consequently, the valve will not be opening as far as it should. This condition has two effects: the valve train components will emit a tapping sound as they take up the excessive clearance and the engine will perform poorly because the valves don't open fully and allow the proper amount of gases to flow into and out of the engine. If the valve clearance is too small, the intake valve and the exhaust valves will open too far and they will not fully seat on the cylinder head when they close. When a valve seats itself on the cylinder head, it does two things: it seals the combustion chamber so that none of the gases in the cylinder escape and it cools itself by transferring some of the heat it absorbs from the combustion in the cylinder to the cylinder head and to the engine's cooling system. If the valve clearance is too small, the engine will run poorly because of the gases escaping from the combustion chamber. The valves will also be come overheated and will warp, since they cannot transfer heat unless they are touching the valve seat in the cylinder head.

Valve Lash

ADJUSTMENT

➡The Sonata and Elantra engines are equipped with hydraulic valve lash adjusters, which require no adjustment or regular maintenance.

1468cc and 1495cc Engines

◆ See Figures 45, 46, 47 and 48

Valve clearance is adjusted with the engine off.
1. Run the engine until it reaches normal operating temperature and then turn it off.

2. Remove the air cleaner. Pull the large crankcase ventilation hose off the front of the air cleaner. Disconnect the 2 smaller hoses, one goes to the rear of the rocker arm cover and the other to the intake manifold.
3. Loosen and remove the nuts and bracket which attach the air cleaner to the rocker arm cover.
4. On carburetor equipped vehicles, lift the bottom housing of the air cleaner off of the carburetor and the hose coming up from the exhaust manifold heat stove.
5. Remove the spark plug wires from their clips on the rocker arm cover.
6. Using a deep socket or box wrench, remove the rocker arm cover bolts.
7. Carefully lift the rocker arm cover off the cylinder head. Using a 5/16 in. (8mm) Allen socket and a torque wrench, make sure the cylinder head bolts are all tightened to specification.
8. Hot valve clearance is 0.006 in. (0.25mm) for the intake valves and 0.010 in. (0.30mm) for the exhaust.
9. Turn the crankshaft pulley to bring the piston to TDC of the compression stroke on the cylinder being adjusted.
10. Loosen the rocker arm adjusting screw locknuts.
11. Using the correct thickness feeler gauge, turn the adjusting screw until the gauge just snaps through the valve stem and the rocker arm.
12. Repeat the procedure to adjust the valves of each cylinder.

➡**Loose valve clearances will result in excessive wear and valve train chatter. Tight valve clearance will result in burnt valves. Make sure to set the valve clearance to the exact specifications.**

13. Apply non-hardening sealer to the rocker arm cover gasket. Always use a new gasket.
14. Install the cover, hoses, spark plug wires and the air cleaner in the reverse order of removal. Tighten the rocker arm cover bolts to 48–60 inch lbs. (5.4–6.7 Nm)
15. Start the engine and check for leaks.

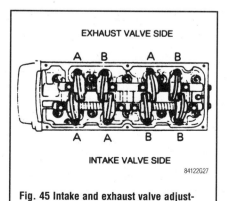

Fig. 45 Intake and exhaust valve adjustment sequence—1986–89 Excel

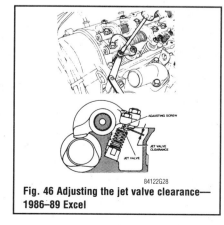

Fig. 46 Adjusting the jet valve clearance—1986–89 Excel

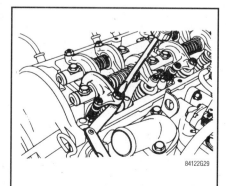

Fig. 47 Adjusting the valve clearance on models with a jet valve

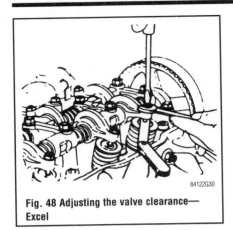

Fig. 48 Adjusting the valve clearance—Excel

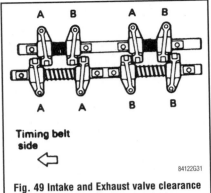

Fig. 49 Intake and Exhaust valve clearance adjusting sequence—1990–93 Excel

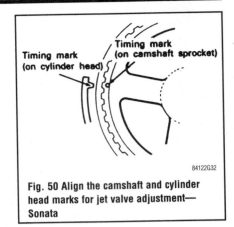

Fig. 50 Align the camshaft and cylinder head marks for jet valve adjustment—Sonata

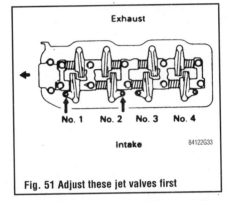

Fig. 51 Adjust these jet valves first

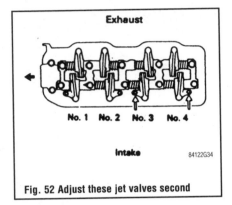

Fig. 52 Adjust these jet valves second

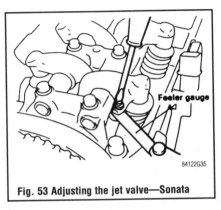

Fig. 53 Adjusting the jet valve—Sonata

Jet Valve

ADJUSTMENT

1468cc And 2351cc Engine

▶ **See Figures 49, 50, 51, 52 and 53**

The jet valve clearance is normally adjusted with the engine stopped and at normal operating temperature. However, after the engine has been rebuilt or a valve job done, the valves should first be set and adjusted with the engine cold. The basic procedure is the same, hot or cold, the only differences being the engine temperature and the jet valve clearance setting. The cold setting is 0.007 in. (0.17mm). The hot setting is 0.010 in. (0.25mm).

1. Start the engine and allow it to reach normal operating temperature.
2. Turn the engine off and disconnect the negative battery cable. Remove the air cleaner. Disconnect the large crankcase ventilation hose from the front of the air cleaner. Disconnect the smaller hoses from the rear of the rocker arm cover and the intake manifold.
3. Loosen and remove the nuts and bracket which secure the air cleaner to the rocker arm cover.
4. Lift the bottom housing of the air cleaner off of the intake, with the hose from the exhaust manifold heat stove attached.
5. Unsnap the spark plug wires from their clips on the rocker arm cover.
6. Remove the rocker arm cover bolts.
7. Carefully lift the rocker arm cover off the cylinder head. Using a 5/16 in. (8mm) Allen socket and a torque wrench, torque the cylinder head bolts. Turn each bolt, in sequence, to specifications. After the first bolt, in sequence, has been torqued, move on to the second one, repeating the procedure. Continue, in order, until all the bolts have been torqued. Make sure the cylinder head bolts are all tightened, in sequence, to specification.
8. Remove the spark plugs.
9. Remove the distributor cap.

➡**A crankshaft pulley access hole is located on the left side frame member. Remove the covering plug and use a ratchet extension to turn the crankshaft when adjusting the valves.**

10. Rotate the crankshaft until the No. 1 cylinder is at TDC of the compression stroke. Turn the engine by using a wrench on the bolt in the front of the crankshaft until the **TDC** or **0** timing mark on the timing cover lines up with the notch in the front pulley. Observe the valve rockers for No. 1 cylinder. If both are in identical positions with the valves up, the engine is in the right position. If not, rotate the engine exactly 360 degrees until the **TDC** or **0** degree timing mark is again aligned. Each jet valve is associated with an intake valve that is on the same rocker lever. In this position, adjust No. 1 and No. 2 jet valves, which are located on the rockers on the intake side only.

11. To adjust the appropriate jet valves, first loosen the regular (larger) intake valve adjusting stud, by loosening the locknut and backing the stud off 2 turns (1468cc only). Now, loosen the jet valve (smaller) adjusting stud locknut, back the stud out slightly and insert a 0.010 in. (0.25mm) feeler gauge between the jet valve and stud. Make sure the gauge lies flat on the top of the jet valve. Being careful not to twist the gauge or otherwise depress the jet valve spring, rotate the jet valve adjusting stud back in until it just touches the gauge. Now, tighten the locknut. Make sure the gauge still slides very easily between the stud and jet valve and they both are still just touching the gauge. Readjust, if necessary. Note that, especially with the jet valve, the clearance must not be too tight. Repeat the entire procedure for the other jet valves associated with rockers labeled No. 1 and 2.

12. Turn the engine exactly 360 degrees, until the timing marks are again aligned at **TDC** or **0**. Perform the adjustment procedure for all the jet valves on rockers labeled No. 3 and 4, intake side only.

➡**Loose valve clearances will result in excessive wear and valve train chatter; tight valve clearance will result in burnt valves.**

13. Apply non-hardening sealer to the rocker arm cover gasket. Always use a new gasket.
14. Install the cover, hoses, spark plug wires and the air cleaner in the reverse order of removal. Tighten the rocker arm cover bolts to 48–60 inch lbs. (5.4–6.7 Nm).
15. Start the engine and check for leaks. It's best to install new gaskets and seals wherever they are used and to observe torque specifications for the cam cover bolts.

FUEL SYSTEM ADJUSTMENTS

➡The adjustments included here are related to tune-up procedures, complete fuel system coverage can be found in Section 5 of this manual.

Idle Speed

IDLE SPEED ADJUSTMENT

Carbureted Engines

▶ See Figures 54 and 55

The idle speed is adjusted periodically to compensate for engine wear or after engine work is performed. Idle mixture adjustments are not required as routine adjustments, but only when major carburetor work has been completed. If idle speed adjustment is required, adjust under the following conditions:

- Lights Off
- All accessories Off
- Electric cooling fan Off
- Transaxle in neutral and parking brake applied

1. Start and run the engine at idle until normal operating temperature is reached.
2. Check the underhood decal or the tune-up specification charts for the correct curb idle speed.
3. Connect a tachometer, according to the manufacturer's instructions and adjust the idle speed screw until the correct rpm is reached.
4. Run the engine for at least 5 seconds at 2000–3000 rpm. Then, reduce the speed to idle rpm for at least 2 minutes.
5. If the idle speed is not at the specified rpm, turn the idle speed adjusting screw until the proper rpm is reached.
6. Check the underhood specifications sticker for the correct idle speed rpm.

Fuel Injected Engines

1468CC ENGINE

▶ See Figures 56, 57, 58, 59 and 60

1. Warm the engine to operating temperature, leave lights, electric cooling fan and accessories **OFF**. The transaxle should be in **N**. The steering wheel in a neutral position for vehicles with power steering.
2. Loosen the accelerator cable.
3. Turn the ignition switch **ON** but do not start the engine. Leave the key in this position for at least 15 seconds. Check to see that the ISC servo is fully retracted to the curb idle position.

➡When the ignition switch is turned to the ON position, the ISC plunger extends to the fast idle position opening. After 15 seconds, it retracts to the fully closed (curb idle) position.

4. Turn the ignition switch **OFF**.
5. Disconnect the ISC motor connector and secure the ISC motor at the fully retracted position.
6. In order to prevent the throttle valve from sticking, open it 2 or 3 times, then allow it to click shut and loosen the fixed SAS sufficiently.
7. Start the engine and allow it to run at idle speed. Ensure that the engine is running at idle speed of 700 rpm plus or minus100. Adjust as necessary by turning the ISC adjust screw.
8. Tighten the fixed SAS until the engine speed starts to increase. Then, loosen the screw until the engine speed ceases to drop (touch point) and loosen an additional ½ turn.
9. Turn the ignition switch to the **OFF** position.
10. Adjust the accelerator cable to 0–0.04 in. (0–1mm) for a manual transaxle and 0.08–0.12 in. (2–3mm) for an automatic transaxle.
11. Connect the ISC motor connector.
12. Start the engine and check to be sure that the idle speed is correct.

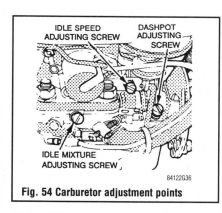

Fig. 54 Carburetor adjustment points

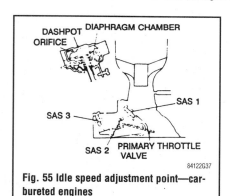

Fig. 55 Idle speed adjustment point—carbureted engines

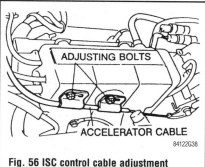

Fig. 56 ISC control cable adjustment points

Fig. 57 Multi-tester connections for ISC adjustment

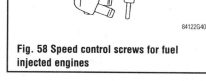

Fig. 58 Speed control screws for fuel injected engines

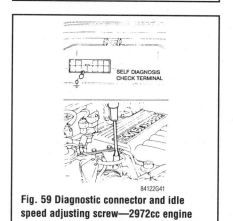

Fig. 59 Diagnostic connector and idle speed adjusting screw—2972cc engine

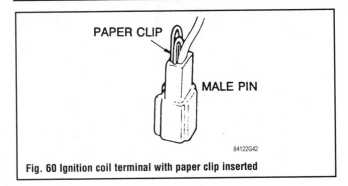

Fig. 60 Ignition coil terminal with paper clip inserted

13. Turn the ignition switch **OFF** and disconnect the negative battery cable for 15 seconds and re-connect. This will erase the data stored in memory during ISC adjustment.

2351CC ENGINE

1. Warm the engine to operating temperature, leave lights, electric cooling fan and accessories **OFF**. The transaxle should be in **N**. The steering wheel in a neutral position for vehicles with power steering.
2. Loosen the accelerator cable.
3. Insert the paper clip into the 1 terminal rpm connector in the engine compartment, and connect the primary voltage detection type tachometer to the paper clip.
4. Ground the self-diagnostic control terminal of the diagnostic connector with a jumper wire.
5. Turn the ignition switch **ON** but do not start the engine. Leave the key in this position for at least 15 seconds. Check to see that the ISC servo is fully retracted to the curb idle position.

➡**When the ignition switch is turned to the ON position, the ISC plunger extends to the fast idle position opening. After 15 seconds, it retracts to the fully closed (curb idle) position.**

6. Turn the ignition switch **OFF**.
7. Disconnect the ISC motor connector to secure the ISC motor at the fully retracted position.
8. In order to prevent the throttle valve from sticking, open it 2 or 3 times, then allow it to click shut and loosen the fixed SAS sufficiently.
9. Start the engine and allow it to run at idle speed. Ensure that the engine is running at idle speed of 700 rpm plus or minus 50. Adjust as necessary by turning the ISC adjust screw.
10. Tighten the fixed SAS until the engine speed starts to increase. Then, loosen the screw until the engine speed ceases to drop (touch point) and loosen an additional ½ turn.
11. Turn the ignition switch to the **OFF** position.
12. Adjust the accelerator cable to 0–0.04 in. (0–1mm) for a manual transaxle and 0.08–0.12 in. (2–3mm) for an automatic transaxle.
13. Connect the ISC motor connector.
14. Start the engine and check to be sure that the idle speed is correct.
15. Turn the ignition switch to the **OFF** and disconnect the negative battery cable for 15 seconds and re-connect. This will erase the data stored in memory during ISC adjustment.

1596CC, 1997CC AND 2972CC ENGINES

1. Warm the engine to operating temperature, leave lights, electric cooling fan and accessories **OFF** . The transaxle should be in **N** . The steering wheel in a neutral position for vehicles with power steering.
2. Loosen the accelerator cable.
3. Connect a multi-use tester to the diagnostic connector in the fuse box. If a multi-use tester is not being used, connect a tachometer to the engine and ground the self-diagnostic terminal.
4. Ground the ignition timing adjustment terminal in the engine compartment.
5. Run the engine for more than 5 seconds at an engine speed of 2000–3000 rpm. Allow the engine to return to idle for a minimum of 2 minutes.
6. Check that the engine is within the desired reading of 700–750 rpm. If the multi-use tester is being used, press code No. 22 and read the engine timing.

➡**The engine speed on a new vehicle driven less than 300 miles may be 100 rpm lower than the desired rpm, in which case it would not require**

adjustment. Break-in should take approximately 300 miles. If the vehicle stalls or has a very low idle speed, suspect a deposit buildup on the throttle valve which must be cleaned.

7. If the basic engine idle speed is out of specification, adjust by turning the Speed Adjusting Screw.(SAS), until the desired reading is obtained.
8. Turn the ignition switch **OFF** and stop the engine. Disconnect the jumper wire from the diagnosis connector, disconnect the jumper wire from the ignition timing connector and reconnect the waterproof connector. Disconnect the tachometer.
9. Restart the engine, allow to run for 10 minutes and check for good idle quality.

IDLE MIXTURE ADJUSTMENT

Carbureted Engines

➡**The idle mixture adjustment is preset at the factory. The mixture adjusting screw is inaccessible without removing and modifying the carburetor. Since this adjustment is preset, it should not be changed as part of a routine tune-up.**

USA VEHICLES

1. Disconnect the negative battery cable. Remove the carburetor. The idle mixture screw is located in the base of the carburetor, just to the left of the PCV hose. Mount the carburetor, carefully, in a soft-jawed vise, protecting the gasket surface and with the mixture adjusting screw facing upward.
2. Drill a 1/8 in. (2mm) hole through the casting from the underside of the carburetor. Make sure the hole intersects the passage leading to the mixture adjustment screw just behind the plug. Now, widen that hole with a 3mm (⅛ in.) drill bit.
3. Insert a blunt punch into the hole and tap out the plug. Install the carburetor on the engine and connect all hoses, lines, etc. Connect the negative battery cable.
4. Start the engine and run it at fast idle until it reaches normal operating temperature. Make sure all accessories are **OFF** and the transaxle is in neutral. Turn the ignition switch **OFF** and disconnect the negative battery cable for about 3 seconds, then, reconnect it. Disconnect the oxygen sensor.
5. Start the engine and run it for at least 5 seconds at 2000–3000 rpm. Then, allow the engine to idle for about 2 minutes.
6. Connect a tachometer and allow the engine to operate at the specified curb idle speed. Adjust it, if necessary, to obtain this speed. Connect a CO meter to the exhaust pipe. A reading of 0.1–0.3 percent is necessary. Adjust the mixture screw to obtain the reading. If, during this adjustment, the idle speed is varied more than 100 rpm in either direction, reset the idle speed and readjust the CO until both specifications are met simultaneously. Shut off the engine, reconnect the oxygen sensor and install a new concealment plug.

CANADIAN VEHICLES

1. Disconnect the negative battery cable. Turn off all of the electrical accessories and place the transaxle in the neutral position. Then remove the carburetor from the engine.
2. Position the carburetor in a vise with idle mixture adjusting screw facing up. Make sure the gasket surface does not become damaged when the carburetor is placed in the vise.
3. Drill a 1/8 in. (2mm) pilot hole in the casting surrounding the idle mixture adjusting screw, then redrill the hole to ⅛ in. (3mm). Insert a blunt punch into the hole and drive out the plug.
4. Reinstall the carburetor. Run the engine until it reaches normal operating temperature.
5. Run the engine for 5 seconds or more at 2000–3000 rpm. Allow the engine to idle for 2 minutes.
6. Set the idle CO and the engine speed to specifications, by adjusting the idle speed adjusting screw No. 1 (SAS-1) and the idle mixture adjusting screw. Idle CO should be 1.8 percent when the curb idle speed is set between 850–900 rpm.
7. Install the concealment plug to seal the idle mixture adjusting screw.

Fuel Injected Engines

The fuel mixture is controlled and governed by the Electronic Control Unit (ECU). No mixture adjustment is necessary on the system.

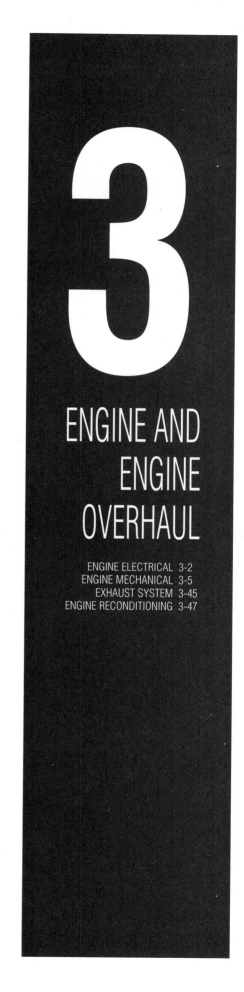

3

ENGINE AND ENGINE OVERHAUL

ENGINE ELECTRICAL

Ignition Coil, Distributor and Ignition System

For full coverage of the engine ignition system and the distributor, refer to Section 2 of this manual.

Charging System

GENERAL INFORMATION

The automobile charging system provides electrical power for operation of the vehicle's ignition and starting systems and all the electrical accessories. The battery serves as an electrical surge or storage tank, storing (in chemical form) the energy originally produced by the engine driven alternator. The system also provides a means of regulating generator output to protect the battery from being overcharged and to avoid excessive voltage to the accessories.

The storage battery is a chemical device incorporating parallel lead plates in a tank containing a sulfuric acid/water solution. Adjacent plates are slightly dissimilar, and the chemical reaction of the 2 dissimilar plates produces electrical energy when the battery is connected to a load such as the starter motor. The chemical reaction is reversible, so that when the generator is producing a voltage (electrical pressure) greater than that produced by the battery, electricity is forced into the battery, and the battery is returned to its fully charged state.

The vehicle's alternator is driven mechanically, by a belt(s) that is driven by the engine crankshaft. In an alternator, the field rotates while all the current produced passes only through the stator winding. The brushes bear against continuous slip rings rather than a commutator. This causes the current produced to periodically reverse the direction of its flow creating alternating current (A/C). Diodes (electrical one-way switches) block the flow of current from traveling in the wrong direction. A series of diodes is wired together to permit the alternating flow of the stator to be converted to a pulsating, but unidirectional flow at the alternator output. The alternator's field is wired in series with the voltage regulator.

The regulator consists of several circuits. Each circuit has a core, or magnetic coil of wire, which operates a switch. Each switch is connected to ground through one or more resistors. The coil of wire responds directly to system voltage. When the voltage reaches the required level, the magnetic field created by the winding of wire closes the switch and inserts a resistance into the generator field circuit, thus reducing the output. The contacts of the switch cycle open and close many times each second to precisely control voltage.

ALTERNATOR PRECAUTIONS

Several precautions must be observed when performing work on alternator equipment.
- If the battery is removed for any reason, make sure that it is reconnected with the correct polarity. Reversing the battery connections may result in damage to the one-way rectifiers.
- Never operate the alternator with the main circuit broken. Make sure that the battery, alternator, and regulator leads are not disconnected while the engine is running.
- Never attempt to polarize an alternator.
- When charging a battery that is installed in the vehicle, disconnect the negative battery cable.
- When utilizing a booster battery as a starting aid, always connect it in parallel; negative to negative, and positive to positive.
- When arc (electric) welding is to be performed on any part of the vehicle, disconnect the negative battery cable and alternator leads.
- Never unplug the PCM while the engine is running or with the ignition in the **ON** position. Severe and expensive damage may result within the solid state equipment.

TESTING

Voltage Test

1. Make sure the engine is **OFF**, and turn the headlights on for 15–20 seconds to remove any surface charge from the battery.

2. Using a DVOM set to volts DC, probe across the battery terminals.
3. Measure the battery voltage.
4. Write down the voltage reading and proceed to the next test.

No-Load Test

1. Connect a tachometer to the engine.

✳✳ CAUTION

Ensure that the transmission is in PARK and the emergency brake is set. Blocking a wheel is optional and an added safety measure.

2. Turn off all electrical loads (radio, blower motor, wipers, etc.)
3. Start the engine and increase engine speed to approximately 1500 rpm.
4. Measure the voltage reading at the battery with the engine holding a steady 1500 rpm. Voltage should have raised at least 0.5 volts, but no more than 2.5 volts.
5. If the voltage does not go up more than 0.5 volts, the alternator is not charging. If the voltage goes up more than 2.5 volts, the alternator is overcharging.

➡Usually under and overcharging is caused by a defective alternator, or its related parts (regulator), and replacement will fix the problem; however, faulty wiring and other problems can cause the charging system to malfunction. Further testing, which is not covered by this book, will reveal the exact component failure. Many automotive parts stores have alternator bench testers available for use by customers. An alternator bench test is the most definitive way to determine the condition of your alternator.

6. If the voltage is within specifications, proceed to the next test.

Load Test

1. With the engine running, turn on the blower motor and the high beams (or other electrical accessories to place a load on the charging system).
2. Increase and hold engine speed to 2000 rpm.
3. Measure the voltage reading at the battery.
4. The voltage should increase at least 0.5 volts from the voltage test. If the voltage does not meet specifications, the charging system is malfunctioning.

➡Usually under and overcharging is caused by a defective alternator, or its related parts (regulator), and replacement will fix the problem; however, faulty wiring and other problems can cause the charging system to malfunction. Further testing, which is not covered by this book, will reveal the exact component failure. Many automotive parts stores have alternator bench testers available for use by customers. An alternator bench test is the most definitive way to determine the condition of your alternator.

REMOVAL & INSTALLATION

1986–89 Excel and Sonata with 2.4L Engine

♦ See Figures 1 and 2

1. Disconnect the battery ground (negative) cable. Tag (location) and remove the wires connected to the alternator.
2. On Sonata, lay a couple of rags on top of the rocker arm cover. Remove the power steering pump mounting bolt, separate the pump from the block and rest the pump on the top of the rags. DO NOT disconnect the oil lines from the power steering pump.
3. Loosen and remove the top mounting nut and bolt. Loosen the bottom mounting nut and bolt. Push the alternator towards the engine and slip the drive belt from the pulley.
4. Remove the bottom mounting nut and bolt; remove the alternator. On Sonata, the alternator must be maneuvered so that the pulley is facing up (towards you) before it can be removed from the engine.

➡When removing the bottom mounting bolt do not lose any of the adjustment shims.

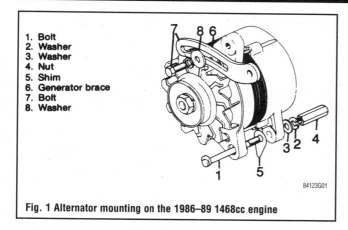

1. Bolt
2. Washer
3. Washer
4. Nut
5. Shim
6. Generator brace
7. Bolt
8. Washer

Fig. 1 Alternator mounting on the 1986–89 1468cc engine

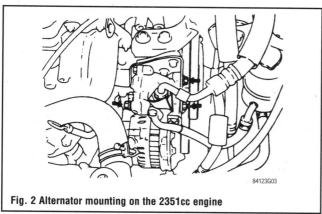

Fig. 2 Alternator mounting on the 2351cc engine

To install:

5. Align the hole in the lower alternator leg with the hole in the mounting and insert the lower bolt. Remember to install any adjustment shims you removed. Install the mounting nut but do not tighten at this time.

6. Install the top mounting bolt and nut but do not tighten. Slip the drive belt onto the pulley and pull the alternator away from the engine to put pressure on the belt.

7. Adjust the drive belt to the proper tension and tighten top mounting bolt. Tighten the lower mounting nut and bolt. (See Section 1 for proper belt adjustment).

8. On Sonata, lift the power steering pump from the rocker arm cover and position it onto the block. Install and tighten the mounting bolt.

9. Connect the alternator wires to their respective terminals and connect the negative battery cable. Make sure the wire nuts are tight and the rubber wire protectors firmly pushed onto the wire nuts.

1990–93 Excel

♦ **See Figure 3**

1. Disconnect the negative battery cable.
2. Loosen the alternator mounting bolts to relieve the belt tension and remove the drive belt from the alternator pulley.
3. Raise the front of the vehicle and support safely.
4. Remove the left side mud guard.
5. Disconnect the B+ terminal wire from the alternator.
6. Support the alternator by hand, finish removing the mounting bolts and lift the unit up and out of the engine compartment.

To install:

7. Position the alternator onto it's mounting and install the mounting bolts.
8. Connect the B+ wire to the alternator terminal. Make sure the wire nut is tight and the protective cap is firmly placed over the wire connection.
9. Install the left side mud guard.
10. Lower the vehicle.

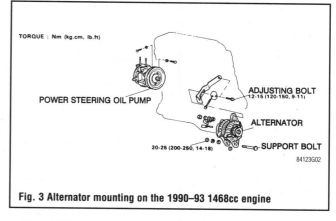

TORQUE : Nm (kg.cm, lb.ft)

POWER STEERING OIL PUMP

ADJUSTING BOLT
12-15 (120-150, 9-11)

ALTERNATOR

20-25 (200-250, 14-18)   SUPPORT BOLT

Fig. 3 Alternator mounting on the 1990–93 1468cc engine

11. Install the drive belt and adjust the tension as described in Chapter 1.
12. Connect the negative battery cable.

Sonata With 2.0L Engine and Elantra

♦ **See Figure 4**

1. Disconnect the negative battery cable.
2. Raise and safely support the vehicle. Remove the left side mud guard and engine cover panel from under the vehicle.
3. Lower the vehicle. Remove the radiator attaching bolts.
4. Disconnect the coolant reserve hose, oil pressure switch and the fan motor connectors.
5. Loosen the belt tensioner and remove the accessory drive belt.
6. Remove the terminal nut and the wire from the B terminal of the alternator.
7. While lifting up on the radiator, remove the alternator from the vehicle.

To install:

8. While lifting the radiator, position the alternator on the engine mounting fixture. Install the lower mounting bolt and nut. Tighten the nut just enough to allow for movement of the alternator.

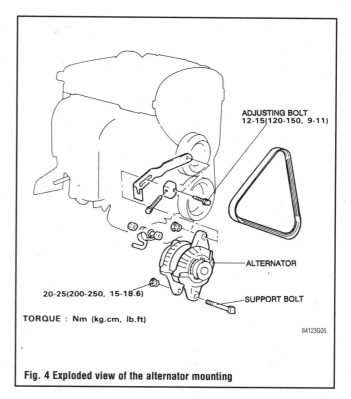

ADJUSTING BOLT
12-15(120-150, 9-11)

ALTERNATOR

20-25(200-250, 15-18.6)   SUPPORT BOLT

TORQUE : Nm (kg.cm, lb.ft)

Fig. 4 Exploded view of the alternator mounting

9. Lower the radiator and install the radiator attaching bolts.

10. Install the wire to the B terminal of the alternator and secure.

11. Install the belt and adjust the tensioner to apply the correct belt tension. Secure the alternator in position, tightening the upper adjuster bolt to 11 ft. lbs. (15 Nm), and the lower support bolt to 18 ft. lbs. (25 Nm).

12. Connect the coolant reserve hose, oil pressure switch and the fan motor connectors.

13. Install the left side cover and panel under the vehicle.

14. Connect the negative battery cable and check the charging system for proper operation.

Scoupe

♦ **See Figure 5**

1. Disconnect the negative battery cable.
2. Loosen the belt tension and remove the belt.
3. Raise and safely support the vehicle.
4. Remove the left hand mud guard.
5. Disconnect the alternator B+ terminal wire.
6. Remove the alternator assembly.
7. Install the alternator by reversing the removal procedure. Adjust the drive belt to the proper tension.

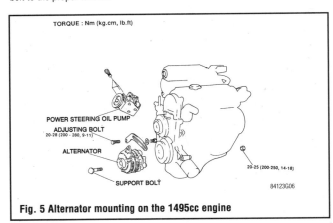

Fig. 5 Alternator mounting on the 1495cc engine

Sonata V6

♦ **See Figure 6**

1. Disconnect the negative battery cable.
2. Remove the distributor cap and power steering pressure hose nut.
3. Loosen the tension and remove the belt.
4. Remove the timing belt cover cap and timing belt upper cover.
5. Disconnect the electrical connectors.
6. Remove the alternator from the engine.

To install:

7. Install the alternator and torque the through bolt to 18 ft. lbs. (25 Nm) and the small bolt to 11 ft. lbs. (15 Nm).

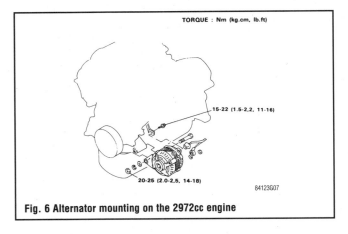

Fig. 6 Alternator mounting on the 2972cc engine

8. Reconnect the electrical connectors.

9. Install the timing belt cover and alternator belt.

10. Install the power steering pressure hose and distributor cap.

11. Connect the battery cable, start the engine and check the power steering fluid.

Starter

GENERAL INFORMATION

The starting system includes the battery, starter motor, solenoid, ignition switch, circuit protection and wiring connecting the components. An inhibitor switch located in the Transmission Range (TR) sensor is included in the starting system to prevent the vehicle from being started with the vehicle in gear.

When the ignition key is turned to the **START** position, current flows and energizes the starter's solenoid coil. The solenoid plunger and clutch shift lever are activated and the clutch pinion engages the ring gear on the flywheel. The switch contacts close and the starter cranks the engine until it starts.

To prevent damage caused by excessive starter armature rotation when the engine starts, the starter incorporates an over-running clutch in the pinion gear.

TESTING

Voltage Drop Test

➡ **The battery must be in good condition and fully charged prior to performing this test.**

1. Disable the ignition system by unplugging the coil pack. Verify that the vehicle will not start.

2. Connect a voltmeter between the positive terminal of the battery and the starter **B+** circuit.

3. Turn the ignition key to the **START** position and note the voltage on the meter.

4. If voltage reads 0.5 volts or more, there is high resistance in the starter cables or the cable ground, repair as necessary. If the voltage reading is ok proceed to the next step.

5. Connect a voltmeter between the positive terminal of the battery and the starter **M** circuit.

6. Turn the ignition key to the **START** position and note the voltage on the meter.

7. If voltage reads 0.5 volts or more, there is high resistance in the starter. Repair or replace the starter as necessary.

➡ **Many automotive parts stores have starter bench testers available for use by customers. A starter bench test is the most definitive way to determine the condition of your starter.**

REMOVAL & INSTALLATION

Except Scoupe

♦ **See Figure 7**

1. Disconnect the negative battery cable. On some models, it may be helpful to remove the battery and the battery tray from the engine compartment during this procedure.

2. Raise and support the vehicle safely.

3. Remove the engine under cover. Disconnect the electrical harness from the starter solenoid, noting position of wires for correct installation.

4. Remove the starter mounting bolts and the starter from the vehicle.

5. Clean the surfaces of the starter motor flange and the flywheel housing where the starter attaches.

To install:

6. Install the starter motor and secure with the retainer bolts. Tighten the bolts to 23 ft. lbs. (30 Nm) for 4 cylinder engines and 20–25 ft. lbs. (27–34 Nm) for the V6.

7. Connect the electrical harness to the starter solenoid. Install the battery and tray, if removed.

8. Reconnect the negative battery cable.

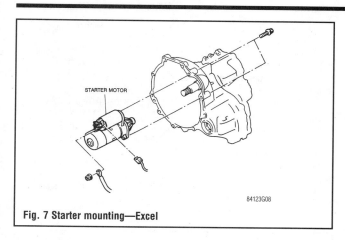

STARTER MOTOR

84123G08

Fig. 7 Starter mounting—Excel

Scoupe

1. Disconnect the negative battery cable.
2. Remove the EGR valve assembly.
3. Remove the speedometer cable and the heater valve.
4. Disconnect the starter motor connector and terminal.
5. Remove the starter motor retainer bolts and the starter assembly from the vehicle.

To install:

6. Install the starter assembly to the engine and secure using the retainer bolts, tightening to 20–25 ft. lbs. (26–33 Nm).
7. Connect the starter motor electrical connector and terminal.
8. Install the speedometer cable and the heater valve.
9. Install the EGR valve assembly and torque the retaining bolts to 7–11 ft. lbs. (10–15 Nm).
10. Connect the negative battery cable and check the starting system for proper operation.

ENGINE MECHANICAL

Engine

REMOVAL & INSTALLATION

The manufacturer recommends that the engine and transaxle be removed as a unit on all models.

Tag all hoses, wires, tubes, cables, etc., so you'll remember where they go when it comes time for installation. If you have a camera handy, a couple of pre-removal photographs of the engine compartment may also be useful.

➡ The 1993 Scoupe has a different engine/transaxle layout then the 1991–92 models, the engine/transaxle assembly has been reversed. The removal and installation procedures, as well as all torque specifications are the same for all years of the Scoupe.

GENERAL ENGINE SPECIFICATIONS

Year	Engine ID/VIN	Engine Displacement Liters (cc)	Fuel System Type	Net Horsepower @ rpm	Net Torque @ rpm (ft. lbs.)	Bore × Stroke (in.)	Compression Ratio	Oil Pressure @ rpm
1986	M	1.5 (1468)	2bbl	77 @ 5300	84 @ 3000	2.97 × 3.23	9.4:1	45 @ 2000
1987	M	1.5 (1468)	2bbl	77 @ 5300	84 @ 3000	2.97 × 3.23	9.4:1	45 @ 2000
1988	M	1.5 (1468)	2bbl	77 @ 5300	84 @ 3000	2.97 × 3.23	9.4:1	45 @ 2000
1989	M	1.5 (1468)	2bbl	77 @ 5300	84 @ 3000	2.97 × 3.23	9.4:1	45 @ 2000
	S	2.4 (2351)	MPI	126 @ 5100	180 @ 2600	3.41 × 3.94	8.5:1	45 @ 2000
1990	M	1.5 (1468)	2bbl	77 @ 5300	84 @ 3000	2.97 × 3.23	9.4:1	45 @ 2000
	J	1.5 (1468)	MPI	81 @ 5500	91 @ 3000	2.97 × 3.23	9.4:1	45 @ 2000
	S	2.4 (2351)	MPI	126 @ 5100	180 @ 2600	3.41 × 3.94	8.5:1	45 @ 2000
	T	3.0 (2972)	MPI	142 @ 5000	168 @ 2500	3.59 × 2.99	8.9:1	30–80 @ 2000
1991	M	1.5 (1468)	2bbl	77 @ 5300	84 @ 3000	2.97 × 3.23	9.4:1	45 @ 2000
	J	1.5 (1468)	MPI	81 @ 5500	91 @ 3000	2.97 × 3.23	9.4:1	12 @ 750
	S	2.4 (2351)	MPI	126 @ 5100	180 @ 2600	3.41 × 3.94	8.5:1	45 @ 2000
	T	3.0 (2972)	MPI	142 @ 5000	168 @ 2500	3.59 × 2.99	8.9:1	30–80 @ 2000
1992	M	1.5 (1468)	2bbl	77 @ 5300	84 @ 3000	2.97 × 3.23	9.4:1	45 @ 2000
	J	1.5 (1468)	MPI	81 @ 5500	91 @ 3000	2.97 × 3.23	9.4:1	12 @ 750
	F	2.0 (1997)	MPI	128 @ 6000	120.7 @ 5000	3.35 × 3.46	9.0:1	12 @ 750
	T	3.0 (2972)	MPI	142 @ 5000	168 @ 2500	3.59 × 2.99	8.9:1	30–80 @ 2000
	R	1.6 (1596)	MPI	113 @ 6000	102 @ 5000	3.24 × 2.95	9.2:1	12 @ 750
1993	M	1.5 (1468)	Carb.	81 @ 5500	91 @ 3000	2.97 × 3.23	9.4:1	12 @ 750
	J	1.5 (1468)	MPI	81 @ 5500	91 @ 3000	2.97 × 3.23	9.4:1	12 @ 750
	N	1.5 (1495)	MPI	92 @ 5500	97 @ 4500	2.97 × 3.29	10.0:1	21 @ 800
	N ①	1.5 (1495)	MPI	115 @ 5500	123 @ 4500	2.97 × 3.29	7.5:1	21 @ 800
	F	2.0 (1997)	MPI	128 @ 6000	120.7 @ 5000	3.35 × 3.46	9.0:1	12 @ 750
	T	3.0 (2972)	MPI	142 @ 5000	168 @ 2500	3.59 × 2.99	8.9:1	30–80 @ 2000
	R	1.6 (1596)	MPI	113 @ 6000	102 @ 5000	3.24 × 2.95	9.2:1	12 @ 750
	M	1.8 (1796)	MPI	124 @ 6000	116 @ 5000	3.17 × 3.46	9.2:1	12 @ 750

NOTE: Horsepower and torque are SAE net figures. They are measured at the rear of the transmission with all accessories installed and operating. Since the figures vary when a given engine is installed in different models, some are representative rather than exact.
MPI—Multipoint fuel injection
① Scoupe Turbo

84123C01

All Models Except Sonata V6

◆ **See Figures 8 thru 13**

➡The factory recommends that the engine and transaxle be removed as a unit. Slight variations in this procedure may occur due to extra connections, etc., but the basic procedure will cover all 4 cylinder engines.

1. If equipped with fuel injection, relieve the fuel system pressure as follows:

    a. Turn the ignition to the **OFF** position.

    b. Loosen the fuel filler cap to release fuel tank pressure.

    c. Disconnect the fuel pump harness connector located under the rear seat cushion on Elantra or in the area of the fuel tank on the remaining models.

    d. Start the vehicle and allow it to run until it stalls from lack of fuel. Turn the key to the **OFF** position.

    e. Disconnect the negative battery cable, then reconnect the fuel pump connector.

2. Matchmark the hood and hinges and remove the hood assembly. Remove the air cleaner assembly and all adjoining air intake duct work.

3. Remove the under cover if equipped.

4. Disconnect the purge control vacuum hose from the purge valve. Remove the purge control valve mounting bracket. Remove the windshield washer reservoir, radiator tank and carbon canister.

5. Drain the coolant from the radiator. Disconnect the upper and lower radiator hoses and then remove the radiator assembly with the electric cooling fan attached. Be sure to disconnect the fan wiring harness prior to removal.

6. Disconnect the electrical connectors for the back-up lights and engine harness, located near the battery tray. If equipped with a 5 speed transaxle, dis-connect the select control valve connector. Disconnect the alternator harness connectors and the oil pressure sending unit.

7. Label and disconnect the automatic transaxle oil cooler hoses. Avoid spilling oil and cap the openings.

8. Label and disconnect all low tension wires and the one high tension wire going to the coil from the distributor. Disconnect the engine ground.

9. Disconnect the brake booster vacuum hose at the intake manifold.

10. Disconnect the fuel supply, return and vapor hoses at the side of the engine. Before disconnecting the fuel supply and return lines, wrap shop towels around the fuel fitting that is being disconnected to absorb any fuel spray caused by residual pressure in the lines.

11. Disconnect the heater hoses from the side of the engine. Disconnect the accelerator cable at the engine side.

12. Disconnect the clutch control cable for manual transaxle or transaxle shifter control cable for automatic transaxle from the transaxle.

13. Unscrew and disconnect the speedometer cable at the transaxle.

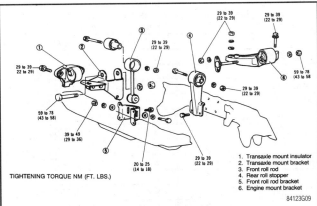

Fig. 8 1986–89 Excel engine mounting components—manual transaxle

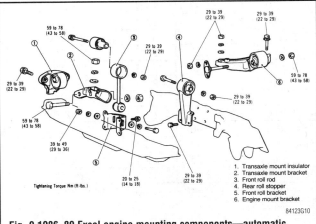

Fig. 9 1986–89 Excel engine mounting components—automatic transaxle

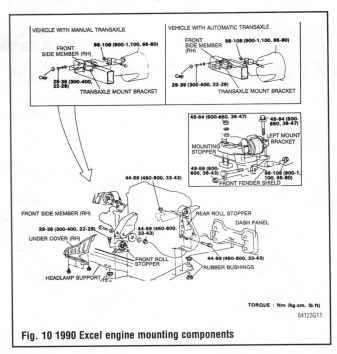

Fig. 10 1990 Excel engine mounting components

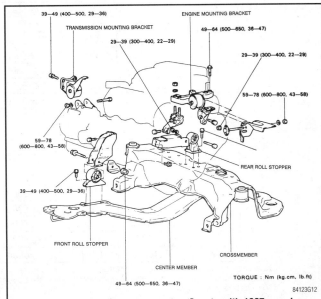

Fig. 11 Engine mounting components—Sonata with 1997cc and 2351cc engines

14. Remove the air conditioner drive belt and the air conditioning compressor. Leave the hoses attached. Do not discharge the system. Wire the compressor aside.

15. Raise and safely support the vehicle. Remove the splash shield. Remove the drain plug and drain the transaxle fluid. Disconnect the exhaust pipe at the manifold and suspend the pipe securely with wire.

16. If equipped with a manual transaxle, remove the shift control rod and extension rod.

17. Disconnect the stabilizer bar at both lower control arms. Remove the bolts that attach the lower control arms to the body on either side. Support the arms from the body.

18. Remove the front halfshafts. Then, seal off the openings in the transaxle to prevent damage caused by the introduction of foreign substances into the transaxle. Be sure to replace the circlips holding the halfshafts in the transaxle during assembly.

19. Attach an engine lift, via chains or cables, to both the engine lifting hooks. Put just a little tension on the cables. Then, remove the nut and bolt from the front roll stopper; unbolt the brace from the top of the engine damper.

20. Separate the rear roll stopper from the No. 2 crossmember. Remove the attaching nut from the left mount insulator bolt, but do not remove the bolt.

21. Raise the engine just enough that the lifting device is supporting its weight. Check that everything is disconnected from the engine.

22. Remove the blind cover from the inside of the right fender inner shield. Remove the transaxle mounting bracket bolts.

23. Remove the left mount insulator bolt. Then, press downward on the transaxle while lifting the engine/transaxle assembly to guide it up and out of the vehicle.

➡**Make sure the transaxle does not hit the battery bracket during engine and transaxle removal.**

To install:

24. Using a lifting device, lower the engine and transaxle carefully into position and loosely install the mounting bolts. Temporarily tighten the front and rear roll control rods mounting bolts. Lower the full weight of the engine and transaxle onto the mounts and tighten the nuts and bolts. Loosen and retighten the roll control rods.

25. Install the transaxle mounting bracket bolts. Install the blind cover to the inside of the right fender inner shield.

26. Assemble the rear roll stopper to the No. 2 crossmember. Install retaining nut and bolt.

27. Install new circlips on the halfshafts and install in position.

28. Attach the lower control arms to the body on either side. Connect the stabilizer bar to both lower control arms.

29. If equipped with a manual transaxle, install the shift control rod and extension rod.

30. Raise the vehicle and support it safely. Connect the exhaust pipe at the manifold. Install the splash shield.

31. Connect the speedometer cable at the transaxle. Connect the air conditioning compressor to the mounting bracket.

32. Install the clutch control cable, for manual transaxle, or shifter control cable, for automatic transaxle, to the transaxle.

33. Lower the vehicle. Connect the heater hoses to the engine. Connect the accelerator cable at the engine side.

34. Connect the fuel supply, return and vapor hoses with new O-rings installed.

35. Connect the brake booster vacuum hose at the intake manifold.

36. Connect all low tension wires and the high tension wire going to the coil from the distributor. Connect the engine ground and the fuel injectors.

37. Connect the automatic transaxle oil cooler hoses.

38. Connect the electrical connectors for the back-up lights and engine harness, located near the battery tray. If equipped with 5 speed, connect the select control valve connector. Connect the alternator harness connectors and the oil pressure sending unit.

39. Install the radiator and electric cooling fan assembly. Connect the upper and lower radiator hoses.

40. Fill all fluids to the proper levels. Adjust the transaxle control cables, accessory drive belts and accelerator linkages as required. Reconnect the negative battery cable.

41. Start the engine and check for leaks as well as proper gauge operation. Allow the vehicle to reach normal operating temperature and recheck all fluid levels.

42. Replace the hood making sure to align the matchmarks made during removal. Allow the engine to cool and recheck the coolant level.

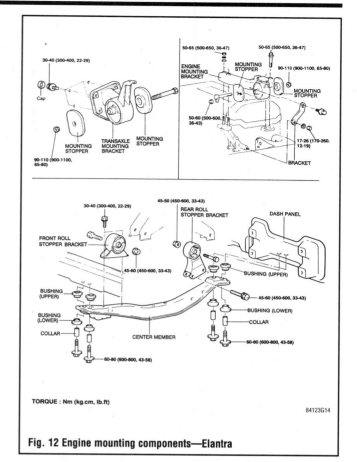

Fig. 12 Engine mounting components—Elantra

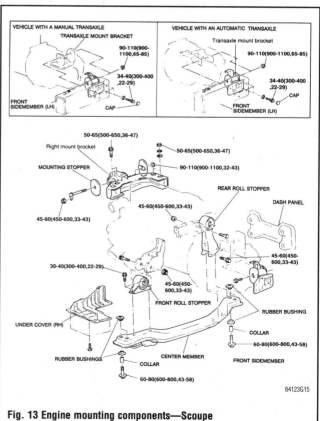

Fig. 13 Engine mounting components—Scoupe

Sonata V6

♦ **See Figure 14**

➡️ **The factory recommends that the engine and transaxle be removed as a unit.**

1. If equipped with fuel injection, relieve the fuel system pressure as follows:
   a. Turn the ignition to the **OFF** position.
   b. Loosen the fuel filler cap to release fuel tank pressure.
   c. Disconnect the fuel pump harness connector normally located under the vehicle towards the rear of the fuel tank.
   d. Start the vehicle and allow it to run until it stalls from lack of fuel. Turn the key to the **OFF** position.
   e. Disconnect the negative battery cable, then reconnect the fuel pump connector.
2. Remove the under cover, if equipped.
3. Matchmark the hood and hinges and remove the hood assembly. Remove the air cleaner assembly and all adjoining air intake duct work.
4. Disconnect the fuel supply line, return line and vent hoses. Prior to disconnecting the fuel supply or return lines, wrap shop towels around the fitting that is being disconnected to absorb any fuel spray caused by residual pressure in the lines.
5. Disconnect the backup light, engine, alternator and oil pressure harnesses.
6. Drain the engine coolant.
7. Label and disconnect the transaxle oil cooler lines, radiator hoses and remove the radiator assembly.
8. Disconnect the brake booster, fuel, evaporative canister and heater hoses.
9. Disconnect the accelerator, transaxle, cruise control and speedometer cables.
10. Detach the air conditioning compressor from the mounting bracket and hang out of the way with a piece of wire. Do not disconnect the refrigerant lines.
11. Remove the power steering pump and wire aside.
12. Raise the vehicle and support safely.
13. Remove the oil pan shield and drain the transaxle.
14. Disconnect the front exhaust pipe.
15. Remove the lower arm ball joint and stabilizer bar at the point where it is mounted to the lower arms.
16. Remove the halfshaft from the housing by prying against the transaxle housing with a prybar.
17. Suspend the lower arm and driveshafts aside using wire attached to the vehicle underbody.
18. Attach an engine lifting device to the engine. Raise the engine just enough to take the tension off the engine mounts.
19. Remove the front roll stopper, engine damper and rear roll stopper.
20. Remove the engine mount bolts.
21. Remove the blind plugs from the inside of the right fender shield and remove the transaxle mounting bracket bolts.

22. Remove the left mount insulator bolt.
23. Raise the engine and transaxle slightly and inspect to make sure all cables, hoses and harness connectors are disconnected.
24. While directing the transaxle side downward, lift the engine and transaxle assembly up and out of the vehicle.

To install:

25. While directing the transaxle side downward, direct the engine and transaxle assembly into the vehicle. Install all mounting hardware and control bracket retainers.
26. Tighten the center crossmember-to-body bolts to 43–58 ft. lbs. (58–77 Nm).
27. Once the engine is securely in place, remove the engine lifting device.
28. Connect the lower arm and the remaining suspension components disassembled during engine removal.
29. Install the halfshafts to the transaxle housing. Make sure the new C-clips are fully engaged into the differential assembly.
30. Connect the front exhaust pipe. Refill the transaxle with fluid.
31. Install the oil pan shield and lower the vehicle.
32. Install the power steering pump.
33. Reconnect the fuel lines using new O-rings where required.
34. Install the air conditioning compressor to the mounting bracket.
35. Connect the accelerator, transaxle, cruise control and speedometer cables.
36. Connect the brake booster, fuel, evaporative canister and heater hoses.
37. Install the radiator. Connect the transaxle oil cooler lines and radiator hoses.
38. Refill the engine coolant.
39. Connect the backup light, engine, alternator and oil pressure harnesses.
40. Connect the negative battery cable. Install the air cleaner assembly.
41. Start the engine and check for leaks. Allow the engine to run until normal operating temperature is reached and recheck all fluid levels.
42. Replace the hood making sure to align the matchmarks made during removal. Allow the engine to cool and recheck the coolant level.

Rocker Arm Cover

REMOVAL & INSTALLATION

All Models

♦ **See Figures 15, 16, 17, 18 and 19**

1. Remove air cleaner, air cleaner snorkel, mounting brackets and remove plug wires from mounting clip if necessary. Label vacuum hoses that are disconnected for reinstallation identification.

➡️ **On the Sonata and Elantra with DOHC engines, the upper timing belt cover must be removed to remove the rocker arm cover.**

2. Disconnect breather hoses and remove cover mounting bolts. Remove valve cover and valve cover gasket.
3. Clean all valve cover mating surfaces. Inspect the breather seal, camshaft end seal and valve cover end seals that are mounted on the cylinder head. Replace as necessary.
4. On V6 engines, apply a small amount of Threebond No. 1324 or equivalent sealant to four places on each cylinder head. Do this before installing the rocker cover. Make certain that the sealant does not leak out into the cam journal surface during application. If it does, make sure that all the excess is wiped away.
5. Install a new valve cover gasket into the mounting slot. Apply RTV sealant to the end seals and install the valve cover. Torque the valve cover bolts on Excel to 1.1–1.4 ft. lbs. (1.5–2.0 Nm), 4.0–5.0 ft. lbs. on 2.4L Sonata, 2–3 ft. lbs. (2.5–3.5 Nm) on 2.0L Sonata and Elantra, and 6.0–7.0 ft. lbs. on V6 Sonata.

➡️ **Do not overtighten the valve cover bolts, because warpage of the valve cover and oil leakage could result.**

6. On V6 engines, once the valve cover is in place, apply Threebond No. 1212D or equivalent sealant to circular packing and top cylinder head surfaces on each side of the rocker cover for both heads.
7. Run the engine until normal operating temperature is reached. Shut the engine off and check for oil leaks.

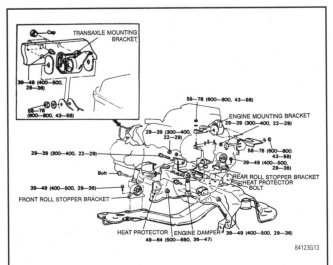

Fig. 14 Engine mounting components—Sonata with 2972cc engine

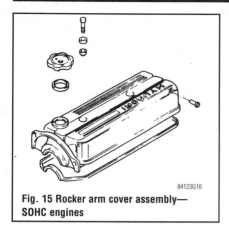

Fig. 15 Rocker arm cover assembly—SOHC engines

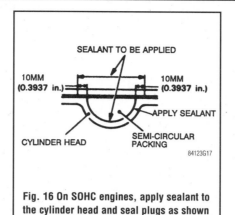

Fig. 16 On SOHC engines, apply sealant to the cylinder head and seal plugs as shown

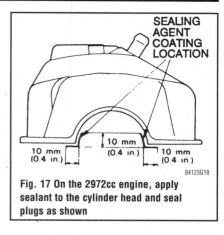

Fig. 17 On the 2972cc engine, apply sealant to the cylinder head and seal plugs as shown

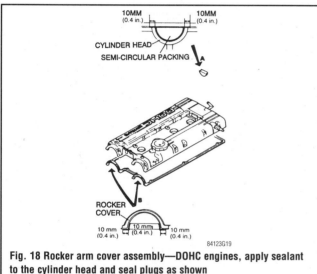

Fig. 18 Rocker arm cover assembly—DOHC engines, apply sealant to the cylinder head and seal plugs as shown

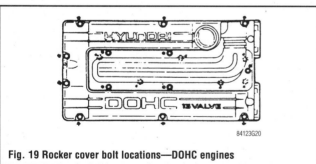

Fig. 19 Rocker cover bolt locations—DOHC engines

Identification mark	Installation position
1–3	No. 1 and 3 cylinders (positions A and C in illustreation shown below)
2–4	No. 2 and 4 cylinders (positions and B and D in illustration shown below)

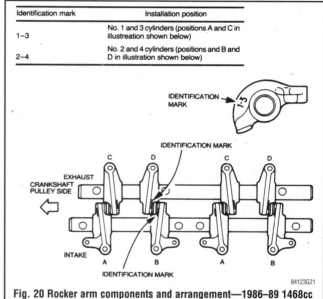

Fig. 20 Rocker arm components and arrangement—1986–89 1468cc engine

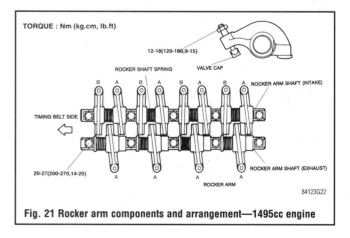

Fig. 21 Rocker arm components and arrangement—1495cc engine

Rocker Arms and Shafts

REMOVAL & INSTALLATION

1468cc and 1495cc Engines

▶ See Figures 20 thru 25

1. Disconnect the negative battery cable. Remove the PCV hose running from the rocker cover and the air cleaner. Remove the air cleaner.

2. Remove the upper timing belt cover. Remove the rocker cover.

3. Loosen the bearing cap bolts or the rocker shaft mounting bolts but do not remove them. Remove each rocker shaft, rocker arms and springs as an assembly. Disassemble the whole assembly by progressively removing each bolt and then the associated springs and rockers, keeping all parts in the exact order of disassembly. The left and right springs have different tension ratings and free length. Observe the location of the rocker arms as they are removed. Exhaust and intake, right and left are different. Do not mix them up.

4. Check the rocker arm face contacting the cam lobe and the adjusting screw that contacts the valve stem for excess wear. Inspect the fit of the rockers on the shaft. Replace adjusting screws, rockers, and/or shafts that show exces-

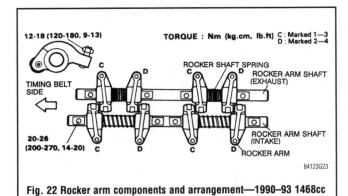

Fig. 22 Rocker arm components and arrangement—1990–93 1468cc engine

sive wear. Pay special attention to the contact pad ends of the rocker arms and the ball surface of the adjusting studs. Check the diameter of the shaft at the rocker mounting points and subtract that number from the measured inside diameter of the corresponding rocker arm. Clearance should be 0.0005–0.0017 in. (0.013–0.043mm). The service limit is 0.004 in. (0.1mm). Check the rocker shaft bend. Total rocker shaft bend should be 0.002 in. (0.05mm). Check the spring free length. Maximum free length should be 2.1 in. (53.3mm) for the exhaust side springs; 2.6 in. (66mm) for intake side springs.

To install:

5. Assemble all the parts, noting the differences between intake and exhaust parts. The intake rocker shaft is much longer; the intake rocker shaft springs are over 3 in. long, while those for the exhaust side are less than 2 in. long; intake rockers have the extra adjusting screw for the jet valve; rockers are labeled 1–3 and 2–4 for the cylinder with which they are associated. Torque the rocker shaft mounting bolts to 15–19 ft. lbs. (20–26 Nm).

6. Adjust the valve clearances. This step may be omitted only if all parts are being reused.

7. Install the rocker cover with a new gasket, torquing the bolts to 12–18 inch lbs. (1.5–2.0 Nm).

8. Install the air cleaner and PCV valve. Connect the battery cable.

9. Run the engine at idle speed until it is hot. Then, unless valves did not require adjustment, remove the valve cover again and adjust the valve clearances with the engine hot.

10. Replace the rocker cover and timing belt cover, air cleaner and PCV valve.

2351cc Engine

♦ See Figures 26, 27, 28 and 29

➡A special tool 09246-32000 (MD998443) or equivalent, is required to retain the automatic lash adjusters in this procedure.

1. Disconnect the negative battery cable. Remove the rocker cover and gasket and the timing belt cover.

2. Turn the crankshaft so the No. 1 piston is at TDC compression. At this point, the timing mark on the camshaft sprocket and the timing mark on the head to the left of the sprocket will be aligned.

3. Remove the camshaft bearing cap bolts.

4. Install the automatic lash adjuster retainer tool 09246-32000 (MD998443) or equivalent, to keep the adjuster from falling out of the rocker arms.

5. Lift off the bearing caps and rocker arm assemblies.

6. The rocker arms may now be removed from the shafts.

➡Keep all parts in the order in which they were removed. None of the parts are interchangeable. The lash adjusters are filled with diesel fuel, which will spill out if they are inverted. If any diesel fuel is spilled, the adjusters must be bled.

To install:

7. Check all parts for wear or damage. Replace any damaged or excessively worn part.

8. Service as required, assemble all parts. Note the following:

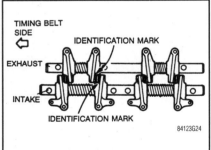

Fig. 23 Measuring the rocker arm shaft diameter. Note that the shaft with 8 oil holes is the exhaust side; the shaft with 4 holes is the intake side—1468cc engines

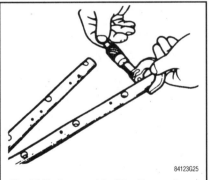

Fig. 24 Rocker arm identification marks on carbureted 1468cc engines

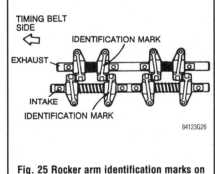

Fig. 25 Rocker arm identification marks on fuel injected 1468cc engines

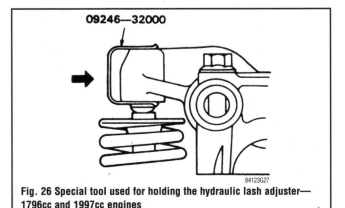

Fig. 26 Special tool used for holding the hydraulic lash adjuster—1796cc and 1997cc engines

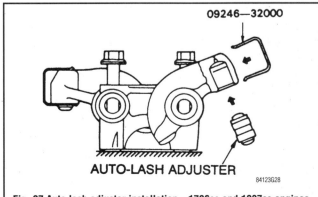

Fig. 27 Auto lash adjuster installation—1796cc and 1997cc engines

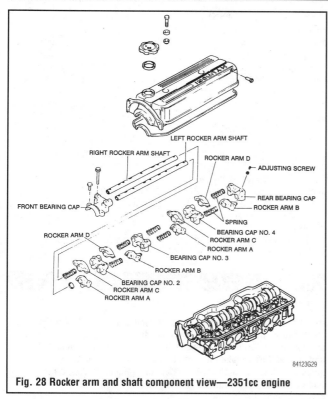

Fig. 28 Rocker arm and shaft component view—2351cc engine

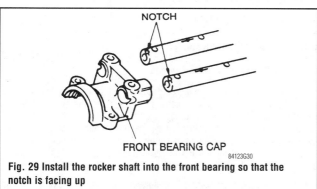

Fig. 29 Install the rocker shaft into the front bearing so that the notch is facing up

a. The rocker shafts are installed with the notches in the ends facing up.

b. The left rocker shaft is longer than the right.

c. The wave washers are installed on the left shaft.

d. Coat all parts with clean engine oil prior to assembly.

e. Insert the lash adjuster from under the rocker arm and install the special holding tool. If any of the diesel fuel is spilled, the adjuster must be bled.

f. Tighten the bearing cap bolts, working from the center towards the ends, to 15 ft. lbs. (20 Nm).

g. Check the operation of each lash adjuster by positioning the camshaft so the rocker arm bears on the low or round portion of the cam. Insert a thin steel wire, tool MD998442 or equivalent, in the hole in the top of the rocker arm, over the lash adjuster and depress the check ball at the top of the adjuster. While holding the check ball depressed, move the arm up and down. Looseness should be felt. Full plunger stroke should be 2.2mm. If not, remove, clean and bleed the lash adjuster.

2972cc Engine

▶ **See Figures 30, 31, 32 and 33**

➡The V6 engine is equipped with hydraulic lash adjusters. To prevent the lash adjusters from falling out during removal of the rocker arms, special holding clips 09426 32000 are needed to hold the adjusters in place.

1. Remove the breather hoses, purge hose and air cleaner. Disconnect the spark plug cables. Remove the distributor.

2. Remove the rocker arm cover and gasket.

3. Before removing the rocker arm and shaft assemblies, install special holding clip 09246 3200 on each rocker arm to prevent the automatic lash adjusters from falling out of the rocker during removal (and installation).

4. Loosen the rocker shaft bolts from the cylinder head but do not remove them from the caps or shafts. Lift the rocker assembly from the cylinder head as a unit.

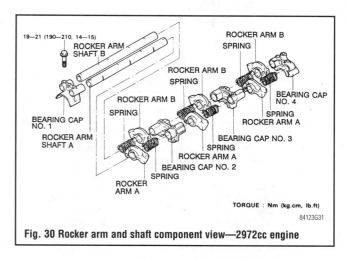

Fig. 30 Rocker arm and shaft component view—2972cc engine

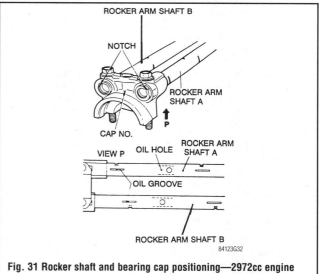

Fig. 31 Rocker shaft and bearing cap positioning—2972cc engine

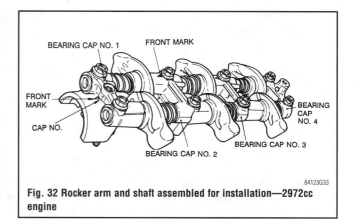

Fig. 32 Rocker arm and shaft assembled for installation—2972cc engine

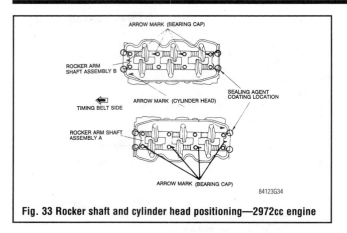

Fig. 33 Rocker shaft and cylinder head positioning—2972cc engine

5. The rocker arm assembly can be disassembled by the removal of the mounting bolts from the bearing caps and shafts. The bearing caps are marked, so make a mental note or drawing of their positions during disassembly.

6. Keep the rocker arms and springs in the same order as disassembly. The left and right springs have different tension ratings and free length.

7. Observe the location of the rocker arm as they are removed. Exhaust and intake, right and left are different. Do not get them mixed up.

8. Remove the lash adjuster holding tools and remove each lash adjuster and label it according to "CYLINDER NUMBER" and "INTAKE" or "EXHAUST". This must be done to ensure that each adjuster is installed in its original location. The lash adjuster is filled with diesel fuel. Store the adjusters in the upright position or cover with masking tape to prevent the diesel fuel from spilling out. If the fuel spills out the adjusters will have to be bled.

9. Inspect all parts for wear or damage as follows:

a. Areas of concern are the contact pad ends of the rocker arms and the ball surface of the adjusting studs.

b. Make sure all the oil holes are clear by cleaning them out with a piece of wire.

c. This engine uses roller type rockers. Pay special attention to the rollers at the end of the rocker. Inspect the roller wear surface for nicks, dents, damage and evidence of seizure. Check the rotation of the roller. It should not bind or have excessive play. If eccentric rotation or backlash is evident, replace the rocker arm. Inspect the inside diameter of the roller for signs of seizure or similar damage. Inspect the tips of the valve adjusting stud for wear. Replace the rocker arm as required.

To install:

10. Lubricate the rocker arm and shafts with clean engine oil.

11. Observe the mating marks and reassemble the rocker arm shafts, springs, bearing caps and rocker arms in the reverse order of removal, after all necessary service has been done. Insert the rocker arm shaft into the front bearing cap so the notch on the end of the shaft is facing up, then insert the bolts.

➡The No. 2, 3 and 4 bearing caps have roughly the same shape and are stamped with identification marks. When assembling the caps on the rocker shafts, make sure that they are installed in their original positions.

12. Insert the auto lash adjusters into their original rockers, being careful not to spill any of the diesel fuel inside. As each adjuster is installed, capture the rocker with the tip of your finger to keep it from falling out, then reinstall the special holding clips.

13. Install the rocker arm shaft assemblies A and B so that the stamped arrow mark on the bearing caps is facing the same direction as the arrow marks on the cylinder heads. Torque the rocker arm shaft bolts to 14–15 ft. lbs. starting from the center and working out. Remove the special holding tools from the auto lash adjusters.

14. Apply a small amount of Threebond No. 1324 or equivalent sealer to four places at the top surface of each cylinder head. Make certain that the sealant does not leak out into the cam journal surface during application. If it does, make sure that all the excess is wiped away.

15. Install the rocker arm cover with a new gasket. After the rocker cover is in place, apply Threebond No. 1212D or equivalent sealant to circular packing and top cylinder head surfaces to both sides of the cover on each head.

16. Connect all the rocker arm cover hoses and spark plug wires. Install the distributor.

17. Run the engine until normal operating temperature is reached. Shut the engine off and check for oil leaks.

Hydraulic Lash Adjusters

Hydraulic lash adjusters are used in the 4 and 6 cylinder engines on Sonata.

➡The hydraulic lash adjuster is a precision component that relies on a clean operating environment. When handling the lash adjuster, make certain that no dirt or foreign particles are allowed to get inside the unit. DO NOT try to take the unit apart as it is not rebuildable. The adjuster is filled with diesel fuel. Hold the adjuster in the upright position so that the diesel fuel does not spill out. When cleaning the unit, only use clean diesel fuel.

REMOVAL & INSTALLATION

◗ **See Figures 34, 35, 36 and 37**

1596cc, 1796cc and 1997cc Engines

1. Release the fuel system pressure. Disconnect the negative battery cable.

2. Disconnect the accelerator cable, PCV hoses, breather hoses, spark plug cables and the remove the valve cover.

3. Rotate the crankshaft clockwise and align the timing marks so No. 1 piston will be at TDC of the compression stroke. At this time the timing marks on the camshaft sprocket and the upper surface of the cylinder head should coincide, and the dowel pin of the camshaft sprocket should be at the upper side.

➡Always rotate the crankshaft in a clockwise direction. Make a mark on the back of the timing belt indicating the direction of rotation so it may be reassembled in the same direction if it is to be reused.

4. Remove the timing belt upper and lower covers.

5. Remove the timing belt.

6. Remove the crank angle sensor.

7. Remove the camshafts.

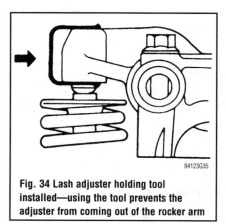

Fig. 34 Lash adjuster holding tool installed—using the tool prevents the adjuster from coming out of the rocker arm

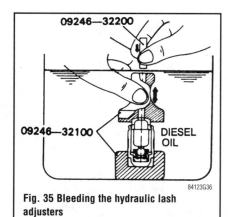

Fig. 35 Bleeding the hydraulic lash adjusters

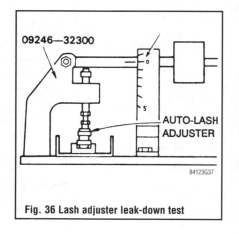

Fig. 36 Lash adjuster leak-down test

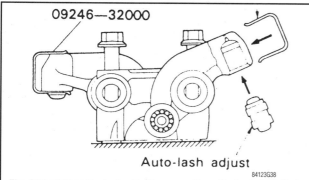

Fig. 37 Installing the lash adjuster—once the adjuster is installed, use the holding tool to keep it in position

8. Visually inspect the rocker arm roller and replace if dent, damage or seizure is evident. Check the roller for smooth rotation. Replace if excess play or binding is present. Also, inspect valve contact surface for possible damage or seizure. It is recommended that all rocker arms and lash adjusters be replaced together.

To install:

9. Install the lash adjusters and rocker arms into the cylinder head. Lubricate lightly with clean oil prior to installation.

10. Apply engine oil to the lobes and journals of each camshaft. Install the camshafts into the cylinder head taking care not to confuse the intake and the exhaust camshaft; the intake camshaft has a slit on its rear end for driving the crank angle sensor. Align shafts so dowel pins on camshaft sprocket end are located on the top.

11. Install and tighten the camshaft bearing caps in the proper sequence tightening to 14–15 ft. lbs. (19–21 Nm), in 3 even progressions.

12. Replace the camshaft oil seals and install the sprockets.

13. Locate the dowel pin on the sprocket end of the intake camshaft at the top position, if not already done.

14. Align the punch mark on the crank angle sensor housing with the notch on the sensor plate. Install the crank angle sensor into the cylinder head.

15. Install the timing belt, covers and related components.

16. Install the valve cover using a new gasket. Reconnect all related components.

17. Reconnect the negative battery cable.

2351cc and 2972cc Engines

1. Disconnect the negative battery cable. Remove the air cleaner assembly.

2. Remove the valve cover.

➡**The lash adjuster is incorporated in the rocker arm on the side of the valve spring. When removing the rocker arm, a special tool must be used the prevent the lash adjuster from falling out.**

3. Using the lash adjuster retainer tools MD998443 or equivalent, install them on the rocker arms.

4. On the right side cylinder head, remove the distributor extension.

5. Hold the rear end of the camshaft down. If the rear of the camshaft cannot be held down, the belt will dislodge and the valve timing will be lost. Loosen the camshaft cap bolts but do not remove them from the caps. Remove the caps, arms, shafts and bolts all as an assembly.

6. Remove the lash adjuster(s) from the rocker arm(s).

7. Lubricate the lash adjuster(s) and their bore(s) with clean engine oil.

8. The installation is the reverse of the removal procedure.

9. Connect the negative battery cable and check the lash adjusters for proper operation.

BLEEDING HYDRAULIC LASH ADJUSTERS

Removed from the Engine

To bleed the hydraulic lash adjusters when disassembling the rocker arms or as part of an engine overhaul, perform the following:

1. Mount the adjuster into special bleeding tool 09246–32100 and immerse the tool and adjuster in a container of clean diesel fuel.

2. With air bleed wire 09246–32200 inserted in the adjuster, lightly press down on the steel ball and compress the plunger four or five times.

3. Remove the air bleed wire from the adjuster and push down firmly on the plunger. If the plunger moves even slightly, repeat Steps 1 and 2 until the plunger stops moving. If the plunger continues to move, replace it.

During Driving

If the lash adjuster is removed and the diesel fuel contained inside is spilled, submerge the adjuster in clean diesel fuel and compress it several times to expel the air using the procedure described above. If air is still trapped after assembly and installation, and a clattering noise is heard when the engine is started, the air can be bled by increasing engine speed from idle to 3000 rpm and back to idle over a one minute period. Do this several times, or until the clattering stops. If this does not stop the clattering, remove and submerge the lifter in clean diesel fuel, compressing it several times as described above. If clattering continues, replace the lash adjuster.

Thermostat

REMOVAL & INSTALLATION

1468cc Engine

▶ **See Figure 38**

1. Disconnect the negative battery cable. Remove the air cleaner.

2. Drain the cooling system to a point below the level of the tubes in the top tank of the radiator.

3. Disconnect the hose at the thermostat water pipe.

4. Remove the water pipe support bracket nut.

5. Unbolt and remove the thermostat housing and pipe.

6. Lift out the thermostat. Discard the gasket.

To install:

7. Clean the mating surfaces of the housing and manifold thoroughly.

8. Install the thermostat with the spring facing downward and position a new gasket. The jiggle valve in the thermostat should be on the manifold side.

9. Install the housing and pipe assembly. Torque the housing bolts to 10 ft. lbs. (14 Nm); the intake manifold nut to 14 ft. lbs. (19 Nm).

10. Refill the cooling system. Connect the negative battery cable.

1495cc, 1596cc, 1796cc and 1997cc Engines

▶ **See Figures 39, 40, 41 and 42**

1. Disconnect the negative battery cable.

2. Drain the cooling system.

3. Disconnect the upper radiator hose from the thermostat housing.

4. Remove the thermostat housing and gasket.

5. Remove the thermostat, taking note of its original positioning in the housing.

To install:

6. Install the thermostat so its flange seats tightly in the machined groove in the thermostat case. Refer to its location prior to removal.

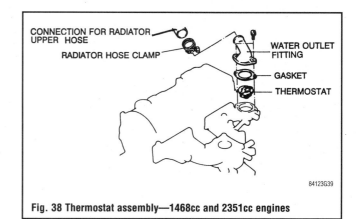

Fig. 38 Thermostat assembly—1468cc and 2351cc engines

7. Use a new gasket and reinstall the thermostat housing. Torque the housing mounting bolts to 12–14 ft. lbs. (17–20 Nm).

8. Fill the system with coolant.

9. Connect the negative battery cable, run the vehicle until the thermostat opens and fill the radiator completely.

10. Once the vehicle has cooled, recheck the coolant level.

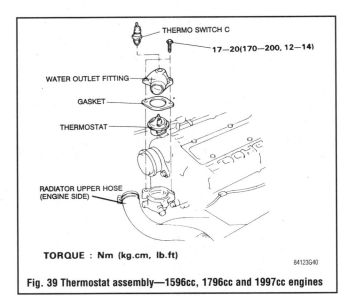

Fig. 39 Thermostat assembly—1596cc, 1796cc and 1997cc engines

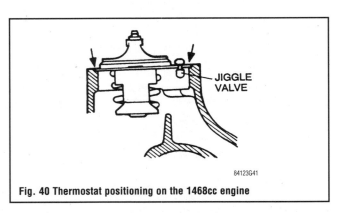

Fig. 40 Thermostat positioning on the 1468cc engine

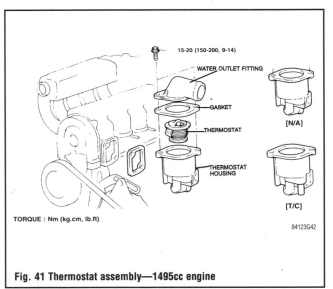

Fig. 41 Thermostat assembly—1495cc engine

2351cc Engine

1. Connect the negative battery cable. Remove the air cleaner.

2. Drain the cooling system down well below the level of the tubes in the top tank of the radiator.

3. Disconnect the hose at the thermostat water pipe.

4. Unbolt and remove the thermostat housing.

5. Lift out the thermostat. Discard the gasket.

6. Clean the mating surfaces of the housing and manifold thoroughly.

To install:

7. Install the thermostat with the spring facing downward and position a new gasket.

8. Install the housing. Torque the housing bolts to 14 ft. lbs. (19 Nm).

9. Refill the cooling system. Connect the negative battery cable.

2972cc Engine

1. Disconnect the negative battery cable. Remove the air cleaner.

2. Drain the cooling system down well below the level of the tubes in the top tank of the radiator.

3. Disconnect the hose at the thermostat water pipe.

4. Unbolt and remove the thermostat housing.

5. Lift out the thermostat. Discard the gasket.

6. Clean the mating surfaces of the housing and manifold thoroughly.

To install:

7. Install the thermostat with the spring facing downward and position a new gasket.

8. Install the housing. Torque the housing bolts to 14 ft. lbs. (19 Nm).

9. Refill the cooling system. Connect the negative battery cable.

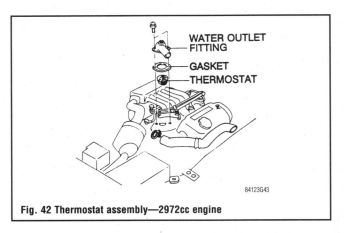

Fig. 42 Thermostat assembly—2972cc engine

Intake Manifold

REMOVAL & INSTALLATION

1986–89 1468cc Engine

♦ See Figure 43

1. Disconnect the negative battery cable. Remove the air cleaner assembly.

2. Disconnect the fuel line and the EGR lines, if equipped with EGR. Tag and disconnect all vacuum hoses.

3. Disconnect the throttle positioner and fuel cut-off solenoid wires.

4. Disconnect the throttle linkage.

5. If equipped with an automatic transaxle, disconnect the shift cable linkage.

6. Disconnect the power brake booster vacuum line.

7. Drain the cooling system.

8. Disconnect the choke water hose at the manifold.

9. Remove the heater and water outlet hoses, disconnect the water temperature sending unit.

10. Remove the mounting nuts that hold the manifold to the cylinder head. Remove the intake manifold.

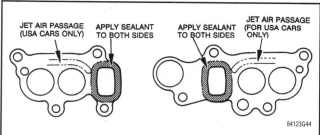

Fig. 43 Intake manifold sealant application points—1986–89 1468cc engine

To install:

11. Clean all mounting surfaces. Before installing the manifold, coat both sides of a new gasket with a gasket sealer.

➡**If equipped with jet air system, take care not to get any sealer into the jet air intake passage.**

12. Install the intake manifold assembly to the engine block.

13. Reconnect the heater and water outlet hoses. Connect the water temperature sending unit.

14. Connect the brake booster vacuum line. Connect the choke hose at the manifold.

15. Connect the throttle and shift cable linkages, the fuel lines and all vacuum hoses. Install the air cleaner.

16. Refill the engine with coolant. Connect the negative battery cable.

1990–93 1468cc and 1495cc Engines

▶ **See Figures 44 and 45**

1. Disconnect the air intake hose from the throttle body. Position the hose off to the side and out of the way.

2. Disconnect the accelerator cable from the throttle lever. To do this loosen the two cable adjusting bracket bolts so that there is enough play in the cable to disengage the cable end from the throttle lever. Move the cable out of the way.

3. Disconnect the water hose from the water outlet fitting.

4. Remove the throttle body and gasket.

5. Disconnect the PCV hose from the rocker cover and disconnect the brake vacuum hoses.

6. Disconnect all vacuum hoses from their respective connections on the intake manifold. Make sure that you label them to avoid confusion during installation. On turbocharged engines, disconnect the air intake pipe from the turbocharger.

7. Relieve the fuel system pressure, then disconnect the high pressure fuel hose connection from the fuel delivery pipe. Cover the connection joint with a rag to absorb the excess fuel.

8. Unbolt and remove the air intake surge tank (and gasket) from the intake manifold.

9. Disconnect the fuel injector harness connectors.

10. Unbolt and remove the fuel delivery pipe (with pressure regulator) from the intake manifold. Take care not to drop the injectors when removing the delivery pipe.

11. Disconnect the wiring harness that runs between the water temperature gauge and the water temperature sensor assembly.

12. Remove the water outlet fitting and gasket from the intake manifold. Remove the thermostat.

13. Disconnect the spark plug wires from the distributor cap. Make sure that you label them first.

14. Remove the distributor and the ignition coil.

15. Remove the intake manifold stay.

16. Remove the intake manifold retaining nuts. Rock the intake manifold back and forth to separate it from the cylinder head. Remove the intake manifold gasket.

17. Clean all the intake manifold and cylinder head gasket surfaces making sure that all existing gasket material is removed. Do the same for the surge tank and all other gasket mating surfaces. Inspect the intake manifold and surge tank for cracks and check the coolant passages for restrictions. Replace all gaskets.

To install:

18. Install the intake manifold gasket. Position the intake manifold to the cylinder head studs and lower it onto the gasket. Install the intake manifold retaining nuts and torque them to 11–14 ft. lbs, starting from the center and working outwards.

19. Install the intake manifold stay and torque the retaining bolts to 13–18 ft. lbs.

20. Install the ignition coil, distributor, and spark plug wires.

21. Install the thermostat into the intake manifold.

22. Install the water outlet fitting with a new gasket. Torque the retaining bolts to 12–14 ft. lbs.

23. Connect the wiring harness that runs between the temperature sensor and temperature gauge.

24. Install the fuel delivery pipe onto the intake manifold. Torque the retaining bolts to 7–9 ft. lbs.

25. Connect the fuel injector harness connectors.

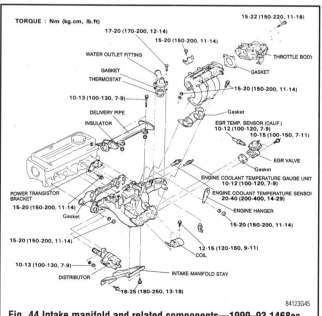

Fig. 44 Intake manifold and related components—1990–93 1468cc fuel injected engine

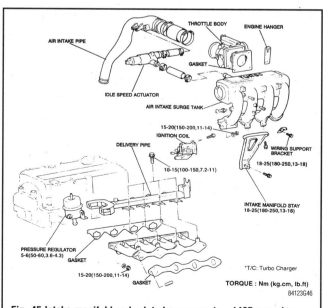

Fig. 45 Intake manifold and related components—1495cc engine

26. Place the surge tank and gasket onto the intake manifold. Install the retaining bolts and torque them to 11–14 ft. lbs.
27. Connect the high pressure hose to the fuel delivery pipe.
28. Connect the intake manifold, brake and PCV vacuum hoses.
29. Install the throttle body with a new gasket. Torque the throttle body bolts to 7–9 ft. lbs.
30. Connect the water hose to the outlet fitting.
31. Connect the accelerator cable to the throttle lever and tighten the cable bracket adjusting bolts.
32. Connect the air intake hose to the throttle body.
33. Start the engine and check/adjust the ignition timing and the idle speed. Check for fuel and coolant leaks.

2351cc Engine

♦ **See Figure 46**

1. Disconnect the negative battery cable. Remove the air cleaner assembly.
2. Release fuel system pressure. Disconnect the fuel line and the EGR lines. Tag and disconnect all vacuum hoses.
3. Disconnect the throttle positioner and fuel cut-off solenoid wires.
4. Disconnect the throttle linkage. If equipped with automatic transaxle, disconnect the shift cable linkage.
5. Remove the heater and water outlet hoses and disconnect the water temperature sending unit. Disconnect the oxygen sensor connector, power transistor connector, ISC connector, ignition coil connector, etc. and the distributor.
6. Remove the mounting nuts that hold the manifold to the cylinder head. Remove the intake manifold lower and upper sections with injector assembly as a unit.
7. Clean all mounting surfaces. Before installing the manifold, coat both sides with a gasket sealer.

To install:

8. Clean all mounting surfaces. Before installing the manifold, coat both sides of a new gasket with a gasket sealer.

➡ **If equipped with jet air system, take care not to get any sealer into the jet air intake passage.**

9. Install the intake manifold lower and upper sections with injector assembly as a unit. Install the mounting nuts that hold the manifold to the cylinder head.
10. Install the heater and water outlet hoses, disconnect the water temperature sending unit. Connect the oxygen sensor connector, power transistor connector, ISC connector, ignition coil connector, etc. and the distributor.
11. Connect the throttle linkage. If equipped with automatic transaxle, connect the shift cable linkage.

12. Connect the throttle positioner and fuel cut-off solenoid wires.
13. Connect the fuel line and the EGR lines. Connect all vacuum hoses.
14. Refill the engine with coolant. Connect the negative battery cable.

1596cc, 1796cc and 1997cc Engines

♦ **See Figure 47**

1. Relieve the fuel system pressure.
2. Disconnect battery negative cable and drain the cooling system.
3. Disconnect the accelerator cable, breather hose and air intake hose.
4. Disconnect the upper radiator hose, heater hose and water bypass hose.
5. Remove all vacuum hoses and pipes as necessary, including the brake booster vacuum line.
6. Disconnect the high pressure fuel line, fuel return hose and remove throttle control cable brackets.
7. Tag and disconnect the electrical connectors from the oxygen sensor, coolant temperature sensor, thermo-switch, idle speed control connection, spark plug wires, etc. that may interfere with the manifold removal procedure.
8. Remove the fuel delivery pipe, fuel injectors, pressure regulator and insulators from the engine. Be careful not to drop the injectors when removing the assembly from the engine.
9. Disconnect the water hose connections at the throttle body, water inlet, and heater assembly.
10. If the thermostat housing is preventing removal of the intake manifold, remove it.
11. Disconnect the vacuum connection at the power brake booster and the PCV valve, if still connected.
12. Remove the intake manifold mounting bolts and remove the intake manifold assembly.

To install:

13. Clean all gasket material from the cylinder head intake mounting surface and intake manifold assembly. Check both surfaces for cracks or other damage. Check the intake manifold water passages for clogging and clean if necessary.
14. Install a new intake manifold gasket to the head and install the manifold. Torque the manifold in a criss-cross pattern, starting from the inside and working outwards to 11–14 ft. lbs. (15–19 Nm).
15. Install the fuel delivery pipe, injectors and pressure regulator from the engine. Torque the retaining bolts to 7–9 ft. lbs. (10–13 Nm).
16. Install the thermostat housing, intake manifold brace bracket, distributor and throttle body stay bracket.
17. Connect or install all hoses, cables and electrical connectors that were removed or disconnected during the removal procedure.

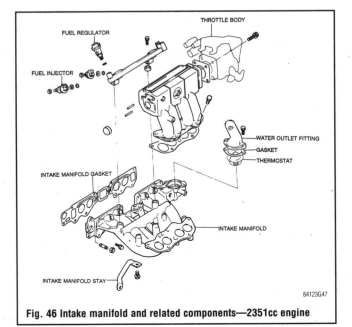

Fig. 46 Intake manifold and related components—2351cc engine

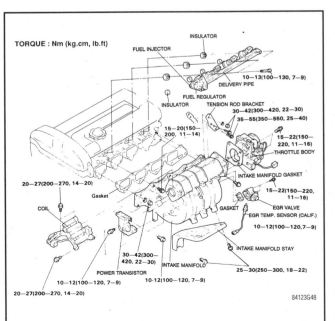

Fig. 47 Intake manifold and related components—1596cc, 1796cc and 1997cc engines

18. Fill the system with coolant.

19. Connect the negative battery cable, run the vehicle until the thermostat opens, then fill the radiator completely.

20. Adjust the accelerator cable. Check and adjust the idle speed as required.

21. Once the vehicle has cooled, recheck the coolant level.

2972cc Engine

▶ See Figures 48 and 49

1. Disconnect the negative battery cable. Relieve the fuel system pressure.

2. Drain the cooling system.

3. Remove the throttle body to air cleaner hose.

4. Remove the throttle body and transaxle kickdown linkage.

5. Remove the AIS motor and TPS wiring connectors from the throttle body.

6. Remove and label the vacuum hose harness from the throttle body.

7. From the air intake plenum, remove the PCV and brake booster hoses and the EGR tube flange.

8. Disconnect and label the charge and temperature sensor wiring at the intake manifold.

9. Remove the vacuum connections from the air intake plenum vacuum connector.

10. Remove the fuel hoses from the fuel rail.

11. Remove the air intake plenum mounting bolts and the plenum.

12. Remove the vacuum hoses from the fuel rail and pressure regulator.

13. Disconnect the fuel injector wiring harness from the engine wiring harness.

14. Remove the fuel pressure regulator mounting bolts and the regulator from the fuel rail.

15. Remove the fuel rail mounting bolts and the fuel rail from the intake manifold.

16. Separate the radiator hose from the thermostat housing and heater hoses from the heater pipe.

17. Remove the intake manifold mounting bolts and the manifold from the engine.

18. Clean the gasket mounting surfaces on the engine and intake manifold.

To install:

19. Using new gaskets, position the intake manifold on the engine and install the mounting nuts and washers.

20. Torque the mounting nuts gradually and evenly, in sequence, to 15 ft. lbs. (20 Nm).

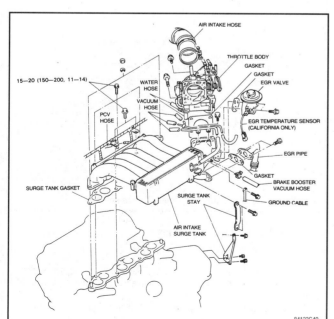

Fig. 48 Upper intake manifold and surge tank components—2972cc engine

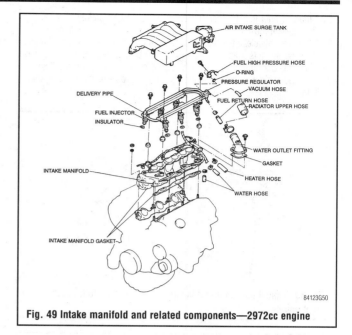

Fig. 49 Intake manifold and related components—2972cc engine

21. Make sure the injector holes are clean. Lubricate the injector O-rings with a drop of clean engine oil and install the injector assembly onto the engine.

22. Install and torque the fuel rail mounting bolts to 10 ft. lbs. (14 Nm).

23. Install the fuel pressure regulator onto the fuel rail.

24. Install the fuel supply and return tube and the vacuum crossover hold-down bolt.

25. Connect the fuel injection wiring harness to the engine wiring harness.

26. Connect the vacuum harness to the fuel pressure regulator and fuel rail assembly.

27. Remove the cover from the lower intake manifold and clean the mating surface.

28. Place the intake plenum gasket with the beaded sealant side up, on the intake manifold. Install the air intake plenum and torque the mounting bolts gradually and evenly, in sequence, to 10 ft. lbs. (14 Nm).

29. Connect or install all remaining items that were disconnected or removed during the removal procedure.

30. Refill the cooling system. Connect the negative battery cable and check for leaks using the DRB I or II to activate the fuel pump.

Exhaust Manifold

Exhaust system fasteners are notorious for rusting which makes removing them without snapping or rounding an almost impossible task. Before working on any exhaust system component, identify which flanges, brackets, U-bolts, manifold, etc. have to be removed and inspect the material condition of the fasteners. If necessary, wire brush any rusted fastener to remove loose rust particles, then spray the area with penetrating oil and allow it to soak overnight.

REMOVAL & INSTALLATION

1468cc and 1495cc Engines

▶ See Figures 50, 51 and 52

1. Disconnect the negative battery cable. Remove the air cleaner. Remove the heat stove and/or heat shield on the exhaust manifold, if equipped. With the manifold cool, soak all manifold nuts and studs with a liquid penetrant.

2. Disconnect the exhaust pipe at the exhaust manifold. Disconnect and remove the oxygen sensor. If there is a secondary air line connected to the exhaust manifold, disconnect it. On turbocharged Scoupe models, disconnect the air intake hose from the turbocharger. First remove the exhaust pipe, then the secondary air supply pipe.

3. Support the manifold and remove all attaching nuts and washers. Slide the manifold from the cylinder head. Remove the converter mounting bolts.

When the converter is disconnected, remove the exhaust manifold. If necessary, rock it to break it loose.

4. Thoroughly clean the sealing surfaces on the cylinder head and manifold. Replace any nuts, washers or studs that are excessively rusted or may have been damaged during removal. Use a straightedge to check the manifold and cylinder head sealing surfaces for flatness. Correct problems by replacing the manifold or machining the cylinder head surface.

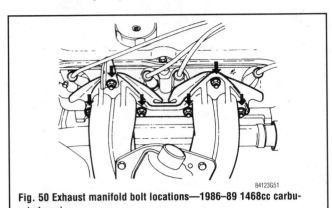

Fig. 50 Exhaust manifold bolt locations—1986–89 1468cc carbureted engine

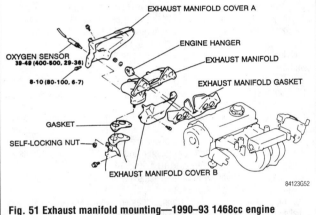

Fig. 51 Exhaust manifold mounting—1990–93 1468cc engine

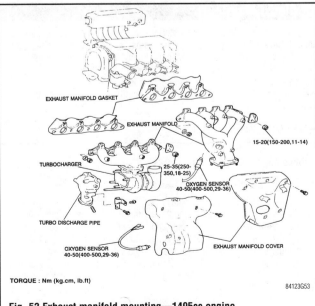

Fig. 52 Exhaust manifold mounting—1495cc engine

To install:

5. Install new gaskets in such a way that all bolt holes and ports are aligned.

6. Make sure all the nuts turn freely, oiling them lightly, if necessary. Also, make sure all the studs are screwed all the way into the block.

7. Place the manifold in position and support it, install all washers and nuts hand tight.

8. Torque the exhaust manifold-to-cylinder head nuts to 14 ft. lbs. (20 Nm), alternately and in several stages on non-turbocharged engines. On turbocharged engines, torque the mounting nuts to 18–25 ft. lbs. (25–35 Nm).

9. Install piping, heat stoves and shields. Connect the exhaust pipe or primary catalytic converter. On turbocharged engines, connect the air intake line to the turbocharger.

10. Connect the negative battery cable. Operate the engine and check for leaks.

2351cc Engine

▶ **See Figure 53**

1. Disconnect the negative battery cable. Remove the air cleaner assembly.
2. Disconnect any EGR or heat lines. Disconnect the reed valve, if equipped.
3. Remove the exhaust pipe support bracket from the engine block, if equipped.
4. Remove the exhaust pipe from exhaust manifold by removing the exhaust pipe flange nuts. It may be necessary to remove 1 nut or bolt from underneath the vehicle.
5. If equipped with a catalytic converter mounted between the exhaust manifold and exhaust pipe, remove the exhaust pipe and the secondary air supply pipe.
6. Remove the nuts mounting the exhaust manifold to the cylinder head. Slide the manifold from the cylinder head, to provide enough room to remove the converter mounting bolts. When the converter is disconnected, remove the exhaust manifold.
To install:
7. Installation is the reverse order of the removal procedure. Install the exhaust manifold with new gaskets. New gaskets should be used and on some engines, port liner gaskets are used.
8. Torque the exhaust manifold-to-cylinder head bolts to 14 ft. lbs. (20 Nm).

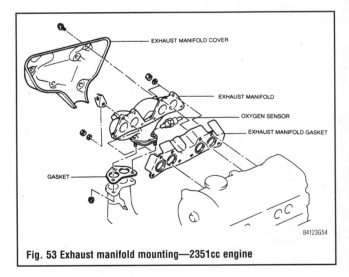

Fig. 53 Exhaust manifold mounting—2351cc engine

1596cc, 1796cc and 1997cc Engines

▶ **See Figure 54**

1. Disconnect the negative battery cable. Remove the air cleaner. Remove the heat shield on the exhaust manifold. With the manifold cool, soak all manifold nuts and studs with a liquid penetrant.
2. Disconnect the exhaust pipe at the exhaust manifold. Disconnect and remove the oxygen sensor.
3. Support the manifold and remove all attaching nuts and washers. Slide the manifold from the cylinder head.

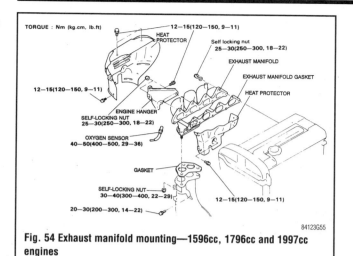

Fig. 54 Exhaust manifold mounting—1596cc, 1796cc and 1997cc engines

4. Thoroughly clean the sealing surfaces on the cylinder head and manifold. Replace any nuts, washers or studs that are excessively rusted or may have been damaged during removal. Use a straightedge to check the manifold and cylinder head sealing surfaces for flatness. Correct problems by replacing the manifold or machining the cylinder head surface.

To install:

5. Install new gaskets in such a way that all bolt holes and ports are aligned.

6. Make sure all the nuts turn freely, oiling them lightly, if necessary. Also, make sure all the studs are screwed all the way into the block.

7. Place the manifold in position and support it, install all washers and nuts hand tight.

8. Torque the exhaust manifold-to-cylinder head nuts to 22 ft. lbs. (30 Nm), alternately and in several stages.

9. Connect the exhaust pipe.

10. Connect the negative battery cable. Operate the engine and check for leaks.

2972cc Engine

♦ See Figure 55

1. Disconnect the negative battery cable. Raise the vehicle and support safely.

2. Disconnect the exhaust pipe from the rear exhaust manifold at the articulated joint.

3. Disconnect the EGR tube from the rear manifold and unplug the oxygen sensor wire.

4. Remove the crossover pipe to manifold bolts.

5. Remove the rear manifold to cylinder head nuts and the manifold.

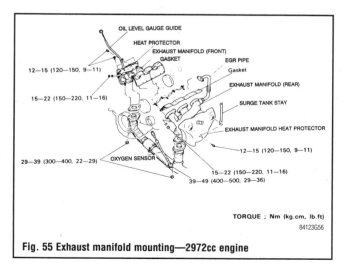

Fig. 55 Exhaust manifold mounting—2972cc engine

6. Lower the vehicle and remove the heat shield from the manifold.

7. Remove the front manifold-to-cylinder head nuts and the manifold.

8. Clean the gasket mounting surfaces. Inspect the manifolds for cracks, flatness and/or damage.

To install:

9. When installing, the numbers 1–3–5 on the gaskets are used with the rear cylinders and 2–4–6 are on the gasket for the front cylinders. Torque the manifold-to-cylinder head nuts to 14 ft. lbs. (20 Nm).

10. Install the crossover pipe to the manifold.

11. Connect the EGR tube and oxygen sensor wire.

12. Connect the exhaust pipe to the rear exhaust manifold, at the articulated joint.

13. Connect the negative battery cable and check the manifolds for leaks.

Turbocharger

REMOVAL & INSTALLATION

1993 Scoupe Turbo

1. Disconnect the negative battery cable.

2. Remove the turbocharger air intake pipe and the air intake hose..

3. Disconnect the oil feed and drain pipe connectors from the turbo housing.

4. Remove the turbocharger discharge pipe and bracket from the outlet (exhaust) side of the turbo.

5. Remove the turbo-to-exhaust manifold mounting bolts and remove the turbo.

To install:

6. Install the turbo in position on the manifold, using a new gasket. Tighten the turbo-to-manifold bolts to 18–25 ft. lbs. (25–35 Nm).

7. Connect the discharge pipe and bracket to the turbo, tighten the bolts to 18–25 ft. lbs. (25–35 Nm).

8. Connect the oil lines to the turbo housing.

9. Connect the air intake pipe and hose. Connect the negative battery cable, run the engine and check for exhaust and oil leaks.

Radiator

REMOVAL & INSTALLATION

♦ See Figures 56 and 57

1. Disconnect the negative battery cable.

2. On Scoupe and Elantra, set the warm water flow control knob of the heater control to the hot position.

3. Drain the radiator. Raise the vehicle and support it safely. Remove the splash shield from under the vehicle.

4. Remove the fan shroud and disconnect the fan motor wiring harness.

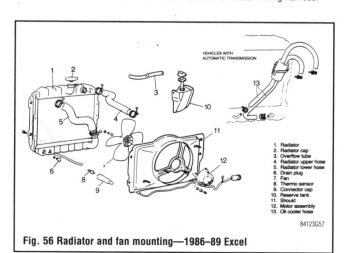

Fig. 56 Radiator and fan mounting—1986–89 Excel

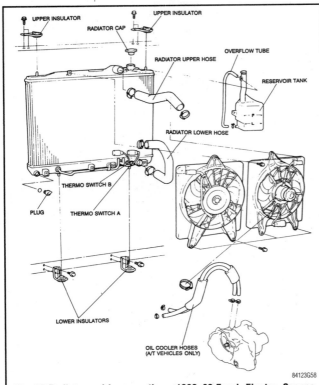

Fig. 57 Radiator and fan mounting—1990–93 Excel, Elantra, Scoupe and Sonata

5. Disconnect the radiator hoses and, if equipped, the automatic transaxle cooler hoses. Plug the end of the oil cooler hoses to prevent the transaxle fluid from spilling out and foreign material from getting in.

6. Disconnect the expansion tank hose.

7. Remove the radiator mounting bolts and lift out the radiator and fan assembly. The fan and motor may be left attached to the radiator and removed with the radiator as one unit.

To install:

8. Install the radiator. Tighten the retaining bolts gradually in a crisscross pattern.

9. Connect the expansion tank hose, the radiator hoses and the automatic transaxle oil cooler lines.

10. Install the fan shroud and connect the fan wiring.

11. Install the splash shield and refill the engine with coolant.

12. Connect the negative battery cable, run the vehicle until the thermostat opens, fill the radiator completely and check the automatic transaxle fluid level, if equipped.

13. Once the vehicle has cooled, recheck the coolant level.

Electric Cooling Fan and Auxiliary Fan

REMOVAL & INSTALLATION

1. Disconnect the negative battery cable.
2. Remove the upper cooling fan shroud-to-radiator support bolts.
3. Disconnect the electrical leads from the fan motor. Remove the fan and shroud as an assembly.

To install:

4. Position the fan and shroud assembly onto the radiator support and install the mounting bolts.
5. Connect the electrical leads to the fan motor.
6. Connect the negative battery cable. Start the engine and check for proper fan operation.

TESTING

▶ **See Figures 58, 59 and 60**

If the cooling fan fails to operate, there are 2 items to be checked; the first is the fan motor itself and the second is the thermo- switch. The fan motor can be checked as follows:

1. Start the engine and allow it to reach normal operating temperature.
2. When the radiator temperature reaches 230°F, the electric cooling fan should turn on.
3. If the fan fails to operate, turn the engine OFF and perform the following procedures:

   a. Disconnect the electrical connector from the electric cooling fan.

   b. Using a fused jumper wire, apply battery voltage to the appropriate terminals.

   c. Make sure the motor runs smoothly, without abnormal noise or vibration.

4. Reconnect the cooling fan connector and the negative battery cable.

The thermo switch or switches (some models have an auxiliary fan) control the operation of the engine fan, by completing an electrical circuit when the coolant temperature in the radiator reaches a certain operating temperature, usually around 185°F.

Check the thermo sensor/sensors by removing them from their mounting position and immersing them in hot water up to the top of the threads. Using a volt-ohmmeter, check for continuity with the sensor in the hot water, there should be continuity at 185°F–5°F and NO continuity at 172°F. If the sensor fails this test and the motor checks out OK, replace the thermo switch.

Water Pump

REMOVAL & INSTALLATION

1468cc and 1495cc Engines

▶ **See Figures 61 and 62**

1. Disconnect the negative battery cable.
2. Loosen the 4 bolts attaching the water pump pulley to the pulley flange.

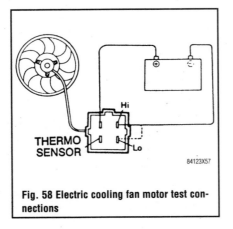

Fig. 58 Electric cooling fan motor test connections

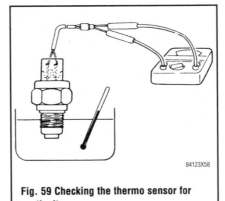

Fig. 59 Checking the thermo sensor for continuity

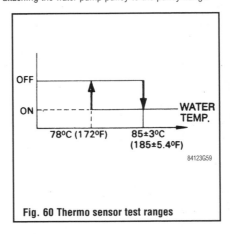

Fig. 60 Thermo sensor test ranges

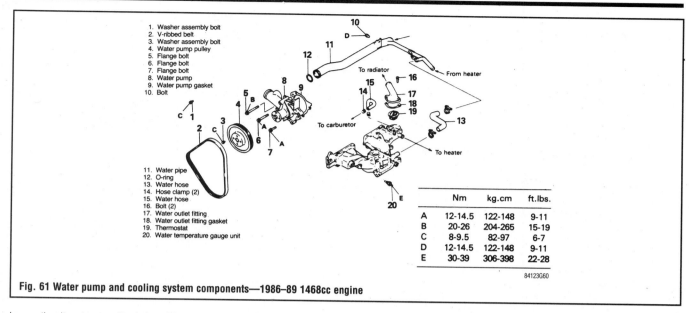

1. Washer assembly bolt
2. V-ribbed belt
3. Washer assembly bolt
4. Water pump pulley
5. Flange bolt
6. Flange bolt
7. Flange bolt
8. Water pump
9. Water pump gasket
10. Bolt
11. Water pipe
12. O-ring
13. Water hose
14. Hose clamp (2)
15. Water hose
16. Bolt (2)
17. Water outlet fitting
18. Water outlet fitting gasket
19. Thermostat
20. Water temperature gauge unit

	Nm	kg.cm	ft.lbs.
A	12-14.5	122-148	9-11
B	20-26	204-265	15-19
C	8-9.5	82-97	6-7
D	12-14.5	122-148	9-11
E	30-39	306-398	22-28

84123G60

Fig. 61 Water pump and cooling system components—1986–89 1468cc engine

Loosen the alternator mounting bolts, slide the alternator toward the engine and remove the belt. Remove the radiator cap, open the draincock at the bottom of the radiator and drain the coolant from the radiator into a clean container.

3. Remove the timing belt covers, timing belt and tensioner.

4. Remove the water pump mounting bolts, noting the 3 different lengths and locations. Remove the pump and gasket, disconnecting the outlet at the water pipe (don't lose the O-ring).

To install:

5. Clean gasket surfaces and coat a new gasket with sealer. Then, position the gasket on the front of the block with all bolt holes aligned. Replace the O-ring for the outlet water pipe.

6. Install the pump connecting the outlet water pipe. Install the bolts with the shortest at the bottom; 2 just slightly longer at the 1 and 4 o'clock positions on the right side of the pump; next-to-longest bolt at the 8 o'clock position, just under the outlet; and the longest bolt at the 11 o'clock position and also attaching the alternator brace. Torque the bolts with a head mark 4, to 9–11 ft. lbs. (12–15 Nm); those with a head mark 7, to 14–20 ft. lbs. (20–26 Nm).

7. Install the remaining parts in reverse order. Final tightening of the water pump pulley bolts is done after the V-belt has been installed and tensioned. Recheck tension after the pulley bolts are tightened. Close the radiator drain and refill the system. Run the engine until the thermostat opens and then add coolant until the level stabilizes before replacing the radiator cap. Check for leaks. Connect the negative battery cable.

1596cc, 1796cc and 1997cc Engines

♦ See Figure 63

1. Disconnect the negative battery cable. Drain the cooling system.

2. Remove all drive belts and water pump pulley.

3. Rotate the crankshaft clockwise and align the timing marks so No. 1 piston will be at TDC of the compression stroke. Remove the timing belt covers and the timing belt tensioner.

4. Remove the water pump mounting bolts and the alternator mounting brace.

5. Remove the water pump assembly from the engine block.

6. Thoroughly clean all gasket mounting surfaces to prevent leaks after reassembly.

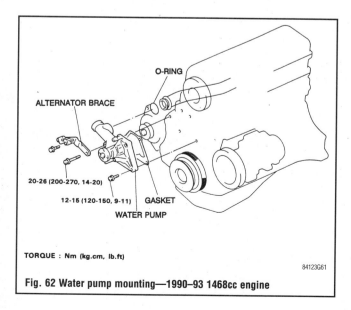

TORQUE : Nm (kg.cm, lb.ft)

84123G61

Fig. 62 Water pump mounting—1990–93 1468cc engine

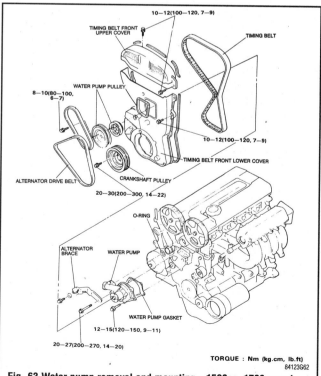

TORQUE : Nm (kg.cm, lb.ft)

84123G62

Fig. 63 Water pump removal and mounting—1596cc, 1796cc and 1997cc engines

To install:

7. Install new O-rings on the front end of the water pipe, then wet the O-ring with water to aid in installation. Do not apply oil or grease to the O-ring.

8. Install the water pump onto the block with a new gasket in place. Position the alternator brace on pump and install the mounting screws. Tighten mounting bolts as follows:

    a. Head mark 4 bolt—9–11 ft. lbs. (12–15 Nm)

    b. Head mark 7 bolt—14–20 ft. lbs. (20–27 Nm)

9. Install the timing belt tensioner and the timing belt. Install the timing belt front covers.

10. Install the water pump pulley and drive belts. Adjust the drive belt tension.

11. Refill the cooling system and reconnect the negative battery cable.

12. Start the vehicle and run until normal operating temperature is reached. Check the operation of the heating system and inspect for leaks.

13. Shut the engine **OFF** and allow to cool. Carefully remove the radiator cap. Add coolant as required to fill the system to the appropriate level.

2351cc Engine

▶ **See Figure 64**

1. Disconnect the negative battery cable. Drain the cooling system.
2. Remove all drive belts and the water pump pulley.
3. Remove the timing belt covers, timing belt tensioner and timing belt.
4. Remove the water pump mounting bolts.
5. Remove the water pump from the engine block.

➡**The pump is not rebuildable. If there are signs of damage or leakage from the seals or vent hole, the unit must be replaced.**

6. Discard the O-ring in the front end of the water pipe. Install a new O-ring coated with water.

7. Using a new gasket, mount the water pump. Torque the bolts with a head marked 4, to 10 ft. lbs. (14 Nm) or the bolts with a head marked 7, to 20 ft. lbs. (27 Nm).

8. Install the timing belt tensioner, timing belt and belt covers.

9. Install the water pump pulley and accessory drive belts.

10. Connect the negative battery cable and fill the cooling system to the proper level.

11. Start the vehicle and run until normal operating temperature is reached. Check the operation of the heating system and inspect for leaks.

12. Shut the engine **OFF** and allow to cool. Carefully remove the radiator cap. Add coolant as required to fill the system to the appropriate level.

2972cc Engine

▶ **See Figures 65, 66 and 67**

1. Disconnect the negative battery cable.
2. Drain the cooling system.

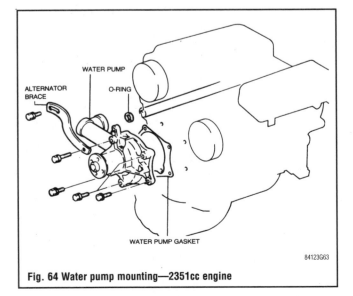

Fig. 64 Water pump mounting—2351cc engine

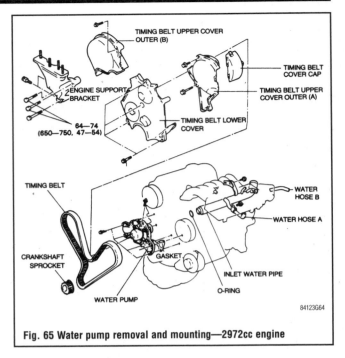

Fig. 65 Water pump removal and mounting—2972cc engine

3. Remove the timing cover. If the same timing belt will be reused, mark the direction of the timing belt's rotation, for installation in the same direction. Make sure the engine is positioned so the No. 1 cylinder is at the TDC of its compression stroke and the sprocket timing marks are aligned with the engine's timing mark indicators.

4. Loosen the timing belt tensioner bolt and remove the belt. Position the tensioner as far away from the center of the engine as possible and tighten the bolt. Remove the water pump mounting bolts, separate the pump from the water inlet pipe and remove the pump from the engine.

To install:

5. Install the pump with a new gasket to the engine. Torque the water pump mounting bolts to 20 ft. lbs. (27 Nm).

6. If not already done, position both camshafts so the marks align with those on the alternator bracket (rear bank) and inner timing cover (front bank). Rotate the crankshaft so the timing mark aligns with the mark on the oil pump.

7. Install the timing belt on the crankshaft sprocket and while keeping the belt tight on the tension side (right side), install the belt on the front camshaft sprocket.

8. Install the belt on the water pump pulley, then the rear camshaft sprocket and the tensioner.

9. Rotate the front camshaft counterclockwise to tension the belt between the front camshaft and the crankshaft. If the timing marks became misaligned, repeat the procedure.

10. Install the crankshaft sprocket flange.

11. Loosen the tensioner bolt and allow the spring to tension the belt.

12. Turn the crankshaft 2 full turns in the clockwise direction only until the timing marks align again. Now that the belt is properly tensioned, torque the tensioner lock bolt to 21 ft. lbs. (29 Nm).

13. Refill the cooling system. Connect the negative battery cable and road test the vehicle.

Cylinder Head

REMOVAL & INSTALLATION

➡**Do not remove the cylinder head unless the engine is cold, a hot cylinder head will warp.**

1468cc and 1495cc Engines

▶ **See Figures 68 thru 74**

1. Release the fuel system pressure and disconnect the negative battery cable.

2. Drain the cooling system and then disconnect the upper radiator hose. Remove the PCV hose that runs between the air cleaner and the rocker cover.

3. Remove the air cleaner. Label and disconnect any vacuum lines running to the cylinder head, manifold or carburetor from other parts of the engine compartment. Disconnect the heater hoses going to the head.

4. Disconnect the fuel supply line, return line and vent hoses. Prior to disconnecting the fuel supply or return lines, wrap shop towels around the fitting that is being disconnected to absorb any fuel spray caused by residual pressure in the lines.

5. Label and disconnect the spark plug wires, injectors and any other elec-

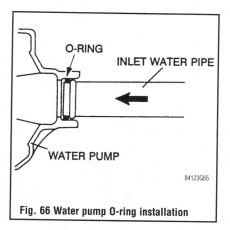

Fig. 66 Water pump O-ring installation

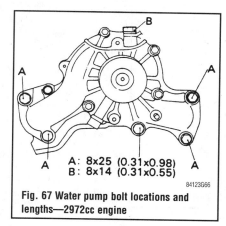

Fig. 67 Water pump bolt locations and lengths—2972cc engine

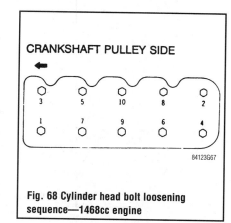

Fig. 68 Cylinder head bolt loosening sequence—1468cc engine

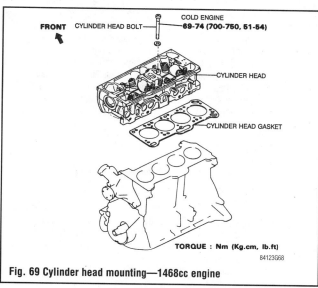

Fig. 69 Cylinder head mounting—1468cc engine

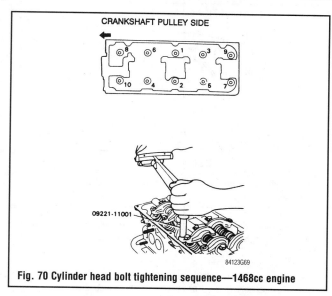

Fig. 70 Cylinder head bolt tightening sequence—1468cc engine

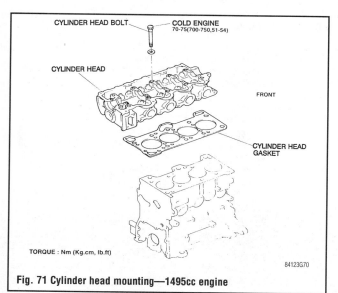

Fig. 71 Cylinder head mounting—1495cc engine

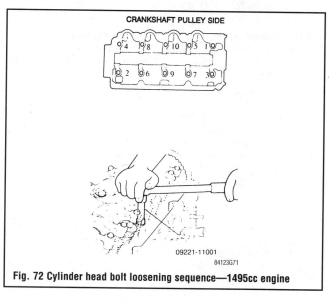

Fig. 72 Cylinder head bolt loosening sequence—1495cc engine

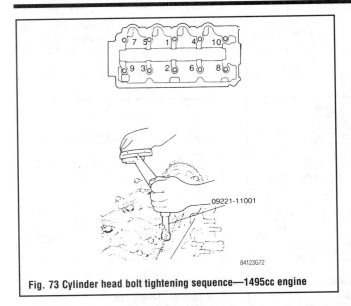

Fig. 73 Cylinder head bolt tightening sequence—1495cc engine

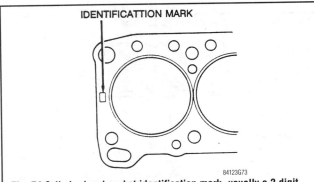

Fig. 74 Cylinder head gasket identification mark, usually a 2 digit number

tronic components that will be removed with the cylinder head. Remove the rocker cover. On turbocharged models, remove the air intake tube from the turbo.

6. Turn the crankshaft until the TDC timing marks align and both No. 1 cylinder valves are closed, both rockers are off the cams. The engine will now be at top dead center with No. 1 piston on its compression stroke.

7. Remove the distributor cap and matchmark the rotor tip to the distributor housing and the housing to the engine. Now, remove the distributor.

➥With the distributor removed, do not crank the engine. If rotated with the distributor removed, the engine will have to be positioned with No. 1 cylinder at top dead center of its compression stroke prior to installing the distributor.

8. Remove the carburetor, if equipped. Remove the intake and the exhaust manifolds.

9. Remove the timing belt cover. Note the location of the camshaft sprocket timing mark. Loosen both timing belt tensioner mounting bolts and move tensioner toward the water pump as far as it will go. Retighten the adjusting bolt to hold the tensioner in this position. Pull the timing belt off the camshaft sprocket but leave it engaged with the other sprockets.

➥On 1498cc engines, a hex type socket is required to remove the head bolts.

10. Loosen the head bolts in the proper sequence. When all have been loosened, remove them. Then, pull the head off the engine block, rocking it slightly to break it loose.

11. Inspect the head with a straightedge and a flat feeler gauge of 0.002 in. (0.05mm) thickness. The tolerance for warping of a used head is 0.002 in. (0.05mm). The block deck must be flat within the same tolerance. The height of

the head should be 3.5 in. (89mm) with a maximum machining limit of 0.012 in. (0.3mm).

To install:

12. Clean the combustion chambers of carbon with a scraper that is not excessively sharp, being careful not to damage the aluminum surface. Sharp edges in the combustion chambers can cause detonation. Clean the gasket mating surfaces with a scraper and solvent.

13. The oil and water passages should be cleaned thoroughly. Also, blow compressed air through all the small oil passages to ensure that they are clear. Check that the EGR and air pump passages are also clear. Both gasket surfaces must be completely free of dirt.

14. Install a new head gasket, without sealant, and position the head on the cylinder block. Install all the bolts finger tight. Torque the bolts in sequence. First step to 15 ft. lbs. (20 Nm), 2nd step to 25 ft. lbs. (35 Nm). Then, torque again, in sequence, to 51–54 ft. lbs. (69–74 Nm).

15. Align the matchmarks and install the distributor to the engine.

16. Install the timing belt on the camshaft tensioner and rotate the camshaft sprocket backward so the belt is tight on what is normally the tension side. Make sure all the timing marks are now aligned. That is, timing marks on the crankshaft sprocket and front case must align; and the marks on the camshaft sprocket and the tab on the cylinder head must be simultaneously aligned with the side of the belt away from the tensioner under tension. Now, loosen the timing belt tensioner adjusting bolt and allow spring tension to tension the belt. Make sure all timing marks are still aligned. If not, the belt is out of time and must be shifted with the tensioner shifted back, toward the water pump and locked there. Now, torque the adjusting bolt on the right side, working through a slot, to 15–18 ft. lbs. (20–25 Nm). After the tensioner adjusting bolt is torqued, torque the hinged mounting bolt located on the opposite side. Don't torque the mounting bolt first or the tension on the belt will be too great.

17. Turn the crankshaft 1 full turn in the normal direction of rotation. Loosen first the tensioner pivot bolt and then the adjusting bolt. Now torque them exactly as before, adjusting bolt, working in the slot. This extra step is necessary to ensure the timing belt is properly seated before final tension is adjusted.

18. Install the cylinder head cover and tighten the bolts to 13–16 inch lbs. (1.5–2.0 Nm).

19. Install the timing belt cover.

20. Install the intake manifold using a new gasket and tighten the bolts and nut to 12–14 ft. lbs. (16–19 Nm).

21. Install the exhaust manifold using a new gasket and tighten the nuts to 12–14 ft. lbs. (16–19 Nm).

22. Install the carburetor or throttle body assembly.

23. Install the distributor. Connect all hoses, lines and the air cleaner.

24. Refill the cooling system. Operate the engine and check for leaks. After the engine has reached normal operating temperature, turn it off and remove the air cleaner and rocker cover. Retighten the cylinder head bolts to 58–61 ft. lbs. (78–83 Nm), in the sequence.

25. Reinstall the rocker cover and the air cleaner.

2351cc Engine

▶ **See Figures 75, 76 and 77**

1. Disconnect the negative battery cable. Drain the engine coolant.

2. Remove the intake and exhaust manifolds.

3. Remove the air cleaner. Detach and tag all vacuum hoses, heater hoses and gauge connectors which connect with the cylinder head or would obstruct its removal.

4. Remove the throttle air valve.

5. Remove the timing belt cover.

6. Remove the rocker cover.

7. Rotate the crankshaft until the timing marks are at TDC with No. 1 cylinder at the firing position, front valves closed fully. If the rockers are not all the way off the cams, turn the engine another 360 degrees.

8. Label and disconnect all spark plug wires at the plugs.

9. Remove the distributor.

10. Remove the timing belt.

11. Using an 8mm hex socket, loosen the head bolts, in order, in 3 stages, alternating from bolt to bolt. Rock the head to break it loose and then remove the head and the gasket from the block.

12. Inspect the head with a straightedge and a flat feeler gauge of 0.10mm thickness. Run the gauge in every direction. The tolerance for warping of a used head is 0.05mm across the entire length. The block deck must be flat within the

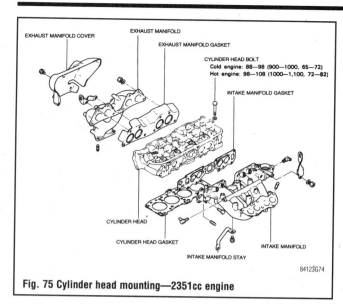

Fig. 75 Cylinder head mounting—2351cc engine

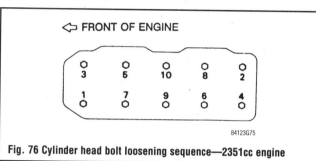

Fig. 76 Cylinder head bolt loosening sequence—2351cc engine

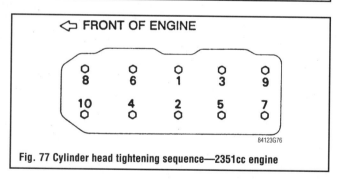

Fig. 77 Cylinder head tightening sequence—2351cc engine

same tolerance. The refacing limit is 0.2mm. The overall head height should be 89.9—90.1mm.

To install:

13. Clean the combustion chambers of carbon with a scraper that is not excessively sharp and use it carefully to avoid damaging the relatively soft aluminum surface. Clean the gasket mating surfaces with a scraper and solvent.

14. The oil and water passages should be cleaned thoroughly, Blow compressed air through all the small oil passages to ensure that they are clear. Check that the EGR and air pump passages are also clear. Both gasket surfaces must be completely free of dirt.

15. Apply sealant around the 4 oil drain holes on the cylinder head gasket. Install the head gasket on the block deck, with the identification mark facing upward toward the cylinder head.

16. Put the head into position and install the head bolts. The bolts must be torqued to a cold specification, which is 65—72 ft. lbs. (88—98 Nm), in 3 stages. Using the proper sequence, torque the bolts, in order, to 25 ft. lbs. (34 Nm), 33-36 ft. lbs. (45—48 Nm). Then, repeat the operation, tightening them to the full torque of 72 ft. lbs. (98 Nm).

17. Perform the remaining steps in reverse of the removal procedure.

18. Connect the negative battery cable.

19. Start the engine, check for leaks and run the engine to normal operating temperature. Stop the engine. Remove the valve cover and torque the head bolts, warm, in sequence, to 72—80 ft. lbs. (96—108 Nm). Replace the valve cover.

1596cc, 1796cc and 1997cc Engines

♦ **See Figures 78, 79 and 80**

1. Release the fuel system pressure. Disconnect the negative battery cable and drain the cooling system.

2. Disconnect the accelerator cable, PCV hoses, breather hoses, spark plug cables and remove the valve cover.

3. Rotate the crankshaft clockwise and align the timing marks so No. 1 piston will be at TDC of the compression stroke. At this time the timing marks on the camshaft sprocket and the upper surface of the cylinder head should coincide, and the dowel pin of the camshaft sprocket should be at the upper side.

➡**Always rotate the crankshaft in a clockwise direction. Make a mark on the back of the timing belt indicating the direction of rotation so it may be reassembled in the same direction if it is to be reused.**

4. Remove the timing belt upper and lower covers.

5. Remove the timing belt.

6. Remove the crank angle sensor.

7. Loosen the cylinder head mounting bolts in 3 steps, starting from the outside and working inward. Lift off the cylinder head assembly and remove the head gasket.

To install:

8. Thoroughly clean and dry the mating surfaces of the head and block. Check the cylinder head for cracks, damage or engine coolant leakage. Remove scale, sealing compound and carbon. Clean oil passages thoroughly. Check the head for flatness. End to end, the head should be within 0.002 in. normally, with 0.008 in. the maximum allowed out of true. The total thickness allowed to be removed from the head and block is 0.008 in. maximum.

9. Place a new head gasket on the cylinder block with the identification marks at the front top (upward) position. Make sure the gasket has the proper identification mark for the engine. Do not use sealer on the gasket.

10. Carefully install the cylinder head on the block. Using 3 even steps, torque the head bolts in sequence to 76—83 ft. lbs. (105—115 Nm) on 1997cc engine. On 1596cc and 1796cc engines, torque the head bolts in sequence to 65—72 ft. lbs. (90—100 Nm) using 3 even steps. These torques apply to a cold engine.

11. Install the timing belt and all related items.

12. Align the punch mark on the crank angle sensor housing with the notch on the plate. Install the crank angle sensor into the cylinder head.

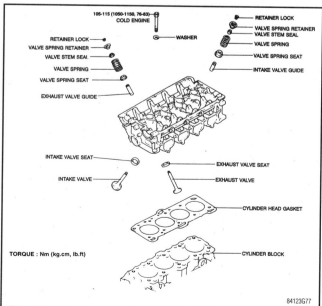

Fig. 78 Cylinder head mounting—1596cc, 1796cc and 1997cc engines

➡️ **The crank angle sensor can be installed even when the punch mark is positioned opposite the notch; however, the position results in incorrect fuel injection and ignition timing.**

13. Apply sealer to the perimeter of the half-round seal and to the lower edges of the half-round portions of the belt-side of the new gasket. Install the valve cover.

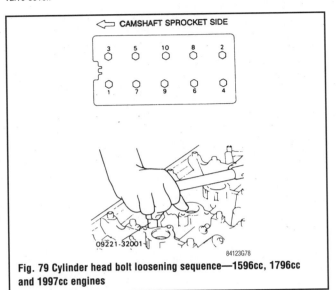

Fig. 79 Cylinder head bolt loosening sequence—1596cc, 1796cc and 1997cc engines

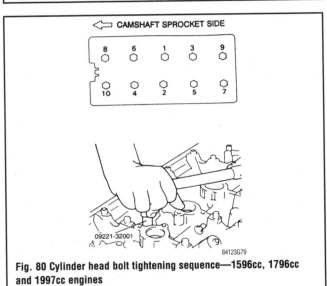

Fig. 80 Cylinder head bolt tightening sequence—1596cc, 1796cc and 1997cc engines

14. Connect or install all previously disconnected hoses, cables and electrical connections. Adjust the throttle cable(s).
15. Install the spark plug cable center cover.
16. Replace the O-rings and connect the fuel lines.
17. Install the air cleaner and intake hose. Connect the breather hose.
18. Change the engine oil and oil filter.
19. Fill the system with coolant. Connect the negative battery cable, run the vehicle until the thermostat opens and fill the radiator completely.
20. Check and adjust the idle speed and ignition timing.
21. Once the vehicle has cooled, recheck the coolant level.

2972cc Engine

♦ **See Figures 81, 82 and 83**

1. Relieve the fuel pressure. Disconnect the negative battery cable. Drain the cooling system.
2. Remove the compressor drive belt and the air conditioning compressor from its mount and support it aside. Using a ½ in. drive breaker bar, insert it into the square hole of the serpentine drive belt tensioner, rotate it counterclockwise to reduce the belt tension and remove the belt. Remove the alternator and power steering pump from the brackets and move them aside.
3. Raise the vehicle and support safely. Remove the right front wheel and the inner splash shield.
4. Remove the crankshaft pulleys and the torsional damper.
5. Lower the vehicle. Using a floor jack and a block of wood positioned under the oil pan, raise the engine slightly. Remove the engine mount bracket from the timing cover end of the engine and the timing belt covers.
6. To remove the timing belt, perform the following procedures:
   a. Rotate the crankshaft to position the No. 1 cylinder on TDC of its compression stroke; the crankshaft sprocket timing mark should align with the oil pan timing indicator and the camshaft sprocket timing marks (triangles) should align with the rear timing belt cover timing marks.
   b. Mark the timing belt in the direction of rotation for reinstallation purposes.
   c. Loosen the timing belt tensioner and remove the timing belt.

➡️ **When removing the timing belt from the camshaft sprocket, make sure the belt does not slip off of the other camshaft sprocket. Support the belt so it cannot slip off of the crankshaft sprocket and opposite side camshaft sprocket.**

7. Remove the air cleaner assembly. Label and disconnect the spark plug wires and the vacuum hoses.
8. Remove the valve cover.
9. Install auto lash adjuster retainer tools MD998443 or equivalent, on the rocker arms.
10. If removing the front cylinder head, matchmark the distributor rotor to the distributor housing and the housing to distributor extension locations. Remove the distributor and the distributor extension.
11. Remove the camshaft bearing assembly to cylinder head bolts but do not remove the bolts from the assembly. Remove the rocker arms, rocker shafts and bearing caps as an assembly, as required. Remove the camshafts from the cylinder head and inspect them for damage.
12. Remove the intake manifold assembly.

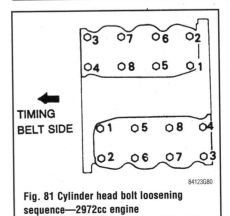

Fig. 81 Cylinder head bolt loosening sequence—2972cc engine

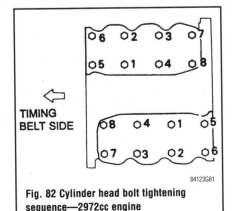

Fig. 82 Cylinder head bolt tightening sequence—2972cc engine

Fig. 83 On the 2972cc engine, install the cylinder head gasket so that the identification mark is UP

13. Remove the exhaust manifold.

14. Remove the cylinder head bolts, starting from the outside and working inward. Remove the cylinder head from the engine.

15. Clean the gasket mounting surfaces and check the heads for warpage; maximum warpage is 0.008 in. (0.20mm).

To install:

16. Install the new cylinder head gasket over the dowels on the engine block.

17. Install the cylinder head(s) on the engine and torque the cylinder head bolts, in sequence, using 3 even steps, to 70 ft. lbs. (95 Nm).

18. Install or connect all items that were removed or disconnected during the removal procedure.

19. When installing the timing belt on the camshaft sprocket, use care not to allow the belt to slip off the opposite camshaft sprocket.

20. Make sure the timing belt is installed on the camshaft sprocket in the same position as when removed.

21. Refill the cooling system. Connect the negative battery cable. Start the engine and check for leaks using the DRB I or II to activate the fuel pump.

22. Adjust the timing, as required.

Jet Valves

Jet valves are used on 1986–89 Excels and Sonatas with 4-cylinder engines.

REMOVAL & INSTALLATION

♦ **See Figures 84, 85, 86, 87 and 88**

1. Remove the rocker arm assemblies.

2. Using special socket tool MD998310 (09222–21300), remove the jet valve. Care must be taken not to twist the socket while removing the valve, it can be easily broken.

3. The valve may be disassembled using special tool MD998309 (90222–21400). Using the tool, compress the spring and remove the valve retainer lock. Remove the spring retainer and spring. Don't separate the jet valve from the

valve body or leakage and improper operation will result. Using pliers, pull off the valve stem seal and discard them.

4. Make sure that the valve slides smoothly in the valve body. If any roughness or sticking is noted or any other damage is found, replace the valve and valve body as a unit.

5. Check the valve head and seat for wear, damage and binding. The valve stem diameter should be 4.30 mm. The angle of the valve face and seat is 45 . The jet valve spring free length should be 29.600mm for both Excel and Sonata and its load at length should be 5½ lbs. @21.5mm for Excel and 7.7 lbs. @ 21.5mm for Sonata.

6. Using special jet valve seal installer MD998308 (09222–21400) drive the new seal onto the valve body. If this tool is not used, the seal could become deformed and oil will leak into the combustion chamber.

7. Using MD998309 (09222–21500), compress the valve spring and reinstall the retainer locks.

8. Apply a coat of clean engine oil to a new O-ring and install it in the groove in the jet valve body.

9. Apply a coat of clean engine oil to the threaded portion of the valve body and seating surface and thread the assembly into place in the head using finger pressure only.

10. When the valve body is seated in the head, tighten it, with tool MD998310 (09222–21300), to 13–16 ft. lbs. Be very careful to keep the tool perfectly straight on the valve body to prevent distortion or damage to the valve assembly.

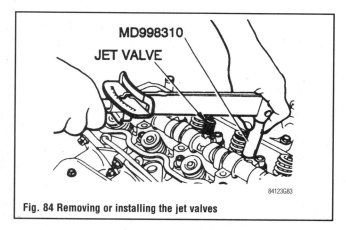

Fig. 84 Removing or installing the jet valves

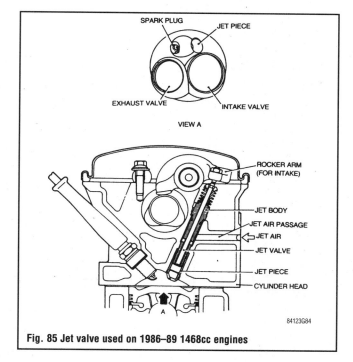

Fig. 85 Jet valve used on 1986–89 1468cc engines

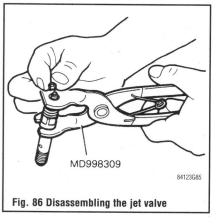

Fig. 86 Disassembling the jet valve

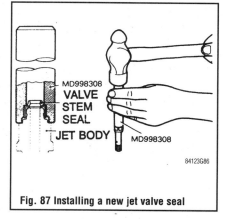

Fig. 87 Installing a new jet valve seal

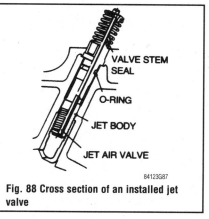

Fig. 88 Cross section of an installed jet valve

Oil Pan

REMOVAL & INSTALLATION

1468cc, 1495cc, 1596cc, 1796cc and 1997cc Engines

♦ **See Figures 89, 90, 91 and 92**

1. Disconnect the negative battery cable. Raise the vehicle and support it safely.
2. Drain the oil.
3. Remove the underbody splash shield.
4. Remove the oil pan bolts, drop the pan and slide it out from under the vehicle.
5. Clean the mating surfaces of the oil pan and the engine block.
6. Apply a ⅛ in. (3mm) bead of RTV sealer along the groove in the oil pan.

To install:

7. Using non-hardening sealer, glue a new gasket to the oil pan.
8. Install the oil pan. Hand tighten the retaining bolts.
9. Starting at one end of the pan, gradually tighten the retaining bolts to 6–11 ft. lbs. (7–15 Nm), in a crisscross pattern.
10. Lower the engine and tighten the mount retaining nuts.
11. Install the oil pan drain plug.
12. Install the splash shield and lower the vehicle.
13. Refill the crankcase with oil. Start the engine and check for leaks.

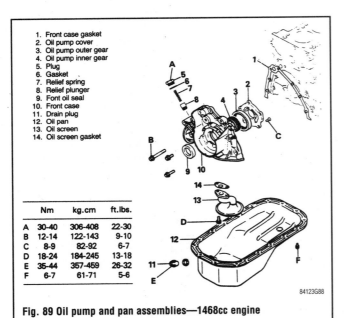

1. Front case gasket
2. Oil pump cover
3. Oil pump outer gear
4. Oil pump inner gear
5. Plug
6. Gasket
7. Relief spring
8. Relief plunger
9. Font oil seal
10. Front case
11. Drain plug
12. Oil pan
13. Oil screen
14. Oil screen gasket

	Nm	kg.cm	ft.lbs.
A	30-40	306-408	22-30
B	12-14	122-143	9-10
C	8-9	82-92	6-7
D	18-24	184-245	13-18
E	35-44	357-459	26-32
F	6-7	61-71	5-6

Fig. 89 Oil pump and pan assemblies—1468cc engine

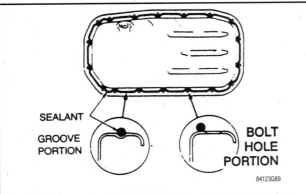

Fig. 90 Oil pan sealant application points—all 4 cylinder engines

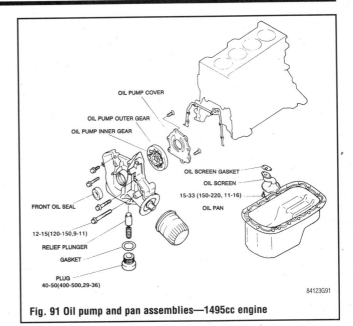

Fig. 91 Oil pump and pan assemblies—1495cc engine

OIL PUMP COVER
OIL PUMP OUTER GEAR
OIL PUMP INNER GEAR
FRONT OIL SEAL
12-15(120-150,9-11)
RELIEF PLUNGER
GASKET
PLUG 40-50(400-500,29-36)
OIL SCREEN GASKET
OIL SCREEN
15-33 (150-220, 11-16)
OIL PAN

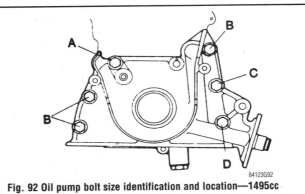

Fig. 92 Oil pump bolt size identification and location—1495cc engine

2351cc Engine

1. Disconnect the negative battery cable. Raise the vehicle and support it safely.
2. Drain the oil.
3. Remove the underbody splash shield.
4. Remove the oil pan bolts, drop the pan and slide it out from under the vehicle.
5. Clean the mating surfaces of the oil pan and the engine block.

To install:

6. Apply sealer to the engine block at the block-to-chain case and block-to-rear oil seal case joint faces.
7. Use a non-hardening sealer and secure a new gasket to the oil pan.
8. Install the oil pan. Hand-tighten the retaining bolts.
9. Starting at one end of the pan, tighten the pan bolts to 48–72 inch lbs. in a crisscross pattern.
10. Install the oil pan drain plug.
11. Install the splash shield and lower the vehicle.
12. Fill the crankcase with the proper amount of oil. Connect the negative battery cable. Start the engine and check for leaks.

2972cc Engine

♦ **See Figure 93**

1. Disconnect the negative battery cable.
2. Raise the vehicle and support safely.
3. Remove the torque converter bolt access cover.

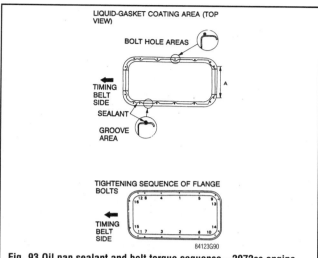

Fig. 93 Oil pan sealant and bolt torque sequence—2972cc engine. DO NOT apply sealant in the "A" range

4. Drain the engine oil.
5. Remove the oil pan retaining screws and remove the oil pan and gasket.

To install:

6. Thoroughly clean and dry all sealing surfaces, bolts and bolt holes.
7. Apply silicone sealer to the chain cover to block mating seam and the rear main seal retainer to block seam, if equipped.
8. Install a new pan gasket or apply silicone sealer to the sealing surface of the pan and install it to the engine.
9. Install the retaining screws and torque to 50 inch lbs. (6 Nm).
10. Install the torque converter bolt access cover, if equipped. Lower the vehicle.
11. Install the dipstick. Fill the engine with the proper amount of oil.
12. Connect the negative battery cable and check for leaks.

Oil Pump

REMOVAL & INSTALLATION

➡️**Whenever the oil pump is disassembled or the cover removed, the gear cavity must be filled with petroleum jelly for priming purposes. Do not use grease.**

1468cc and 1495cc Engines

♦ **See Figures 91 and 92**

1. Disconnect the negative battery cable. Remove the timing belt.
2. Remove the oil pan.
3. Remove the oil screen.
4. Unbolt and remove the front case assembly.
5. Remove the oil pump cover.
6. Remove the inner and outer gears from the front case.

➡️**The outer gear has no identifying marks to indicate direction of rotation. Clean the gear and mark it with an indelible marker.**

7. Remove the plug, relief valve spring and relief valve from the case.

To install:

8. Check the front case for damage or cracks. Replace the front seal. Replace the oil screen O-ring. Clean all parts thoroughly with a safe solvent.
9. Check the pump gears for wear or damage. Clean the gears thoroughly and place them in position in the case to check the clearances. There is a crescent-shaped piece between the 2 gears.
10. Check that the relief valve can slide freely in the case.
11. Check the relief valve spring for damage. The relief valve free length should be 1.8 in. (47mm). Load length should be 13.4 lbs. at 1.6 in. (40mm).
12. Thoroughly coat both oil pump gears with clean engine oil and install them in the correct direction of rotation.

13. Install the pump cover and torque the bolts to 6–8 ft. lbs. (8–12 Nm).
14. Coat the relief valve and spring with clean engine oil, install them and tighten the plug to 30–36 ft. lbs. (39–49 Nm).
15. Position a new front case gasket, coated with sealer, on the engine and install the front case. Torque the bolts to 8–11 ft. lbs. (12–15 Nm). Note that the bolts have different shank lengths. Use the following guide to determine which bolts go where. Bolts marked:

1468cc Engine
- A: 0.08 in. (20mm)
- B: 1.2 in. (30mm)
- C: 2.4 in. (60mm)

1495cc Engine
- A: 0.98 in. (25mm)
- B: 1.18 in. (30mm)
- C: 1.77 in. (45mm)
- D: 2.36 in. (60mm)

16. Coat the lips of a new seal with clean engine oil and slide it along the crankshaft until it touches the front case. Drive it into place with a seal driver.
17. Install the sprocket, timing belt and pulley.
18. Install the oil screen.
19. Thoroughly clean both the oil pan and engine mating surfaces. Apply a ⅛ in. (3mm) wide bead of RTV sealer in the groove of the oil pan mating surface.
20. Tighten the oil pan bolts to 60–72 inch lbs. Connect the negative battery cable.

1596cc, 1796cc and 1997cc Engines

♦ **See Figure 94**

1. Disconnect the negative battery cable.
2. Remove the front engine mount bracket and accessory drive belts.
3. Remove timing belt upper and lower covers.
4. Remove the timing belt and crankshaft sprocket.
5. Remove the oil pan.
6. Remove the oil screen and gasket.
7. Remove and tag the front cover mounting bolts. Note the lengths of the mounting bolts as they are removed for proper installation.
8. On 1596cc and 1796cc engines, remove the plug cap using tool MD998162 or equivalent, and remove the oil pressure switch.
9. Remove the front case cover and oil pump assembly. If necessary, the silent shaft can come out with the assembly. Disassemble as required.

To install:

10. Thoroughly clean all gasket material from all mounting surfaces.
11. Apply engine oil to the entire surface of the gears or rotors.
12. On engines with silent shaft, install the drive/driven gears with the 2 timing marks aligned.

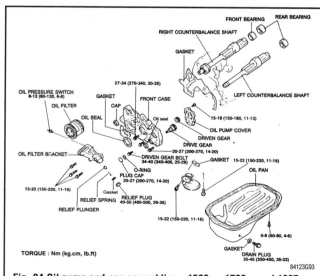

Fig. 94 Oil pump and pan assemblies—1596cc, 1796cc and 1997cc engines

13. Assemble the front case cover and oil pump assembly to the engine block using a new gasket. On 1596cc and 1796cc engines, assemble the front case cover and oil pump assembly using tool MD998285 or equivalent, on the front end of the crankshaft. Tighten the bolts to specification.

14. Install the oil screen with new gasket.

15. Install the oil pan and timing belts.

16. Connect the negative battery cable and check for adequate oil pressure.

2351cc Engine

▶ **See Figures 95 thru 101**

1. Disconnect the negative battery cable. Remove the timing belt.
2. Remove the oil pump cover and gears.
3. Remove the relief valve plug, spring and plunger.
4. Thoroughly clean all parts in a safe solvent and check for wear and damage.
5. Clean all orifices and passages.

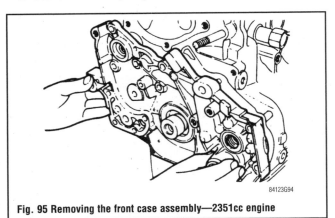

Fig. 95 Removing the front case assembly—2351cc engine

6. Place the gear back in the pump body and check clearances.
- Gear teeth-to-body—0.10–0.15mm
- Driven gear end-play—0.06–0.12mm
- Drive gear-to-bearing (front end)—0.020–0.045mm
- Drive gear-to-bearing (rear end)—0.043–0.066mm.

➡ **If gear replacement is necessary, the entire pump body must be replaced.**

7. Check the relief valve spring for wear or damage. Free length should be 47mm; load/length should be 9.5 lbs. at 40mm.

To install:

8. Assemble the pump components. Make sure the gears are installed with the mating marks aligned.

9. Install the timing belt. Connect the negative battery cable.

2972cc Engine

▶ **See Figures 102, 103 and 104**

1. Disconnect the negative battery cable. Remove the dipstick.
2. Raise the vehicle and support safely. Remove the timing belt, drain the engine oil and remove the oil pan from the engine. Remove the oil pickup.
3. Remove the oil pump mounting bolts and remove the pump from the front of the engine. Note the different length bolts and their position in the pump for installation.

To install:

4. Clean the gasket mounting surfaces of the pump and engine block.
5. Prime the pump by pouring fresh oil into the pump and turning the rotors. Using a new gasket, install the oil pump on the engine and torque all bolts to 11 ft. lbs. (15 Nm).
6. Install the balancer and crankshaft sprocket to the end of the crankshaft.
7. Clean out the oil pickup or replace, if necessary. Replace the oil pickup gasket ring and install the pickup to the pump.
8. Install the timing belt, oil pan and all related parts.
9. Install the dipstick. Fill the engine with the proper amount of oil.
10. Connect the negative battery cable and check the oil pressure.

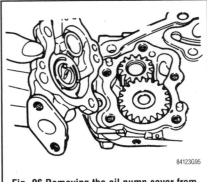

Fig. 96 Removing the oil pump cover from the front case—2351cc engine

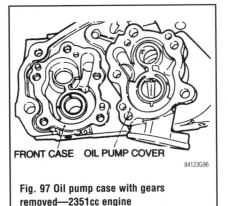

Fig. 97 Oil pump case with gears removed—2351cc engine

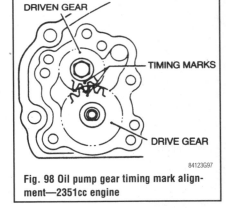

Fig. 98 Oil pump gear timing mark alignment—2351cc engine

Fig. 99 Oil seal guide tool installation—2351cc engine

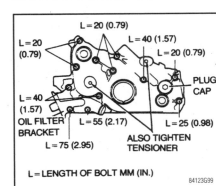

Fig. 100 Front case bolt lengths and identification—2351cc engine

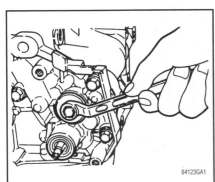

Fig. 101 Tightening the relief plug—2351cc engine

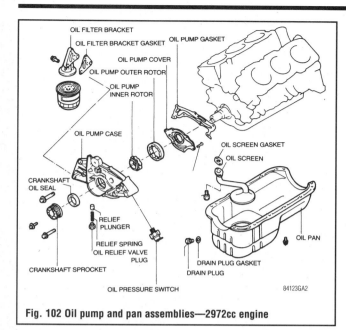

Fig. 102 Oil pump and pan assemblies—2972cc engine

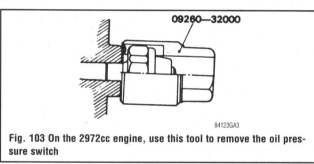

Fig. 103 On the 2972cc engine, use this tool to remove the oil pressure switch

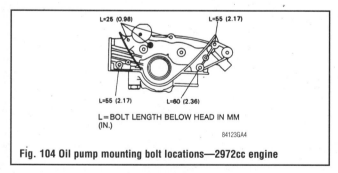

Fig. 104 Oil pump mounting bolt locations—2972cc engine

Timing Belt Front Cover

♦ **See Figures 105, 106 and 107**

REMOVAL & INSTALLATION

Except 2972cc Engine

1. Disconnect the negative battery cable.
2. Remove the engine undercover.
3. Using the proper equipment, slightly raise the engine to take the weight off of the side engine mount. Remove the engine mount bracket.
4. Remove the accessory drive belts, tension pulley brackets, water pump pulley and crankshaft pulley.
5. Remove all attaching screws and remove the upper and lower timing belt covers.
6. Installation is the reverse of the removal procedure. Make sure all pieces of packing are positioned in the inner grooves of the covers when installing.

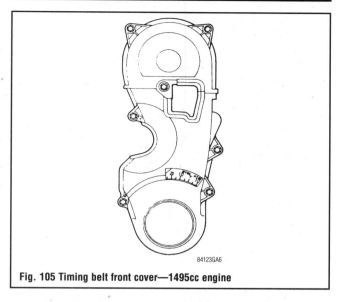

Fig. 105 Timing belt front cover—1495cc engine

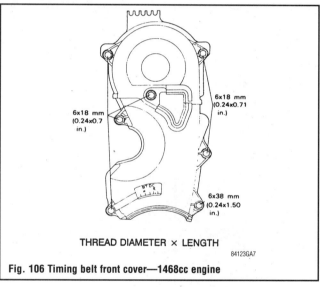

THREAD DIAMETER × LENGTH

Fig. 106 Timing belt front cover—1468cc engine

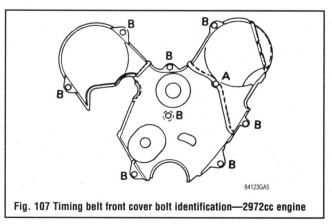

Fig. 107 Timing belt front cover bolt identification—2972cc engine

2972cc Engine

1. Disconnect the negative battery cable.
2. Remove the engine undercover.
3. Remove the accessory drive belts.
4. Remove the air conditioner compressor tension pulley assembly.

5. Remove the tension pulley bracket.

6. Using the proper equipment, slightly raise the engine to take the weight off of the side engine mount.

7. Disconnect the power steering pump pressure switch connector. Remove the power steering pump and wire aside.

8. Remove the engine support bracket.

9. Remove the crankshaft pulley.

10. Remove the timing belt cover cap.

11. Remove the timing belt upper and lower covers.

To install:

12. Install the timing covers. Make sure all pieces of packing are positioned in the inner grooves of the covers when installing.

13. Install the crankshaft pulley. Torque the bolt to 108–116 ft. lbs. (150–160 Nm).

14. Install the engine support bracket.

15. Install the power steering pump and reconnect wire harness at the power steering pump pressure switch.

16. Install the engine mounting bracket and remove the engine support fixture.

17. Install the tension pulleys and drive belts.

18. Install the cruise control actuator.

19. Install the engine undercover.

20. Connect the negative battery cable.

Timing Belt and Tensioner

ADJUSTMENT

1468cc and 1495cc Engines

▶ **See Figures 108 and 109**

1. Rotate the crankshaft clockwise and align the timing marks so No. 1 piston will be at TDC of the compression stroke. Disconnect the negative battery cable.

2. Remove the timing belt covers.

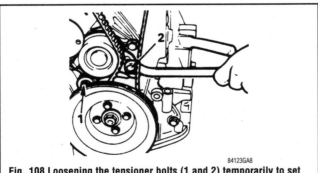

Fig. 108 Loosening the tensioner bolts (1 and 2) temporarily to set the belt tension. Tighten the No. 2 bolt first then the No. 1, otherwise the tensioner will move

3. Loosen the tensioner lower mounting bolt first, then the uppermost bolt.

4. Check to insure that the timing marks are in correct alignment and secure, tightening the uppermost bolt first.

5. Rotate the crankshaft 1 revolution in operating direction (clockwise), and realign the timing marks. Loosen the tensioner lower mounting bolt first, then the uppermost bolt.

6. Retighten the attaching bolts, uppermost first, to 14–20 ft. lbs. (20–27 Nm).

7. Apply a moderate pressure to the tension side of the timing belt and measure the belt deflection. The inner (cog) side of the belt should be depressed to the center of the tensioner mounting bolt head. If the deflection point is correct, the tension adjustment of the timing belt is correct.

8. If a tension gauge is used, measure the tension in the middle of the tension side span. The desired reading is 32–47 lbs.

9. Install the timing belt covers and all related components.

10. Reconnect the negative battery cable.

2351cc Engine

▶ **See Figures 110, 111 and 112**

1. Disconnect the negative battery cable.

2. Remove the upper and lower timing belt covers.

3. Check the tensioners for a smooth rate of movement and leaking seal. Replace any tensioner that binds or shows grease leakage through the seal.

4. Rotate the crankshaft clockwise and align the timing marks so No. 1 piston will be at TDC of the compression stroke. Do not rotate the crankshaft in a counterclockwise direction as this can cause improper timing belt tension.

5. Loosen the timing belt tensioner bolt and nut, using a 14mm socket wrench.

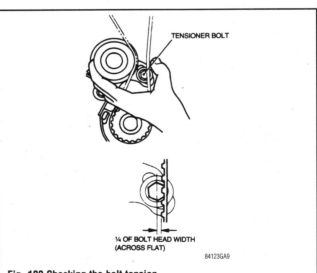

Fig. 109 Checking the belt tension

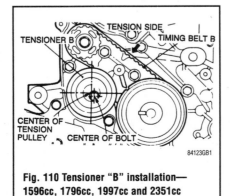

Fig. 110 Tensioner "B" installation—1596cc, 1796cc, 1997cc and 2351cc engines

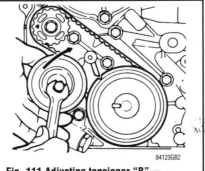

Fig. 111 Adjusting tensioner "B"—1596cc, 1796cc, 1997cc and 2351cc engines

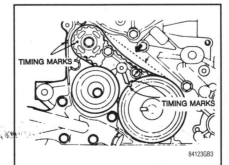

Fig. 112 Checking the deflection of timing belt "B"—1596cc, 1796cc, 1997cc and 2351cc engines

6. Rotate the crankshaft and camshaft sprocket clockwise 2 teeth. Do not turn the engine counterclockwise. Momentarily apply slight pressure behind the tensioner to assure tensioner is not sticking and then release pressure. After tension has equalized, tighten the tensioner mounting bolt (lower side) first, and then tighten the upper mounting nut. Be sure to tighten the mounting hardware in that order. If the nut it tightened first, the tensioner will rotate with the nut and the belt will be loose.

7. Check to ensure proper tension of the belt by measuring its deflection. The standard value is 0.200–0.276 in. (5–7mm) with moderate pressure applied to the center of the timing belt.

8. Install the upper and lower timing belt covers.

9. Install the crankshaft pulley.

10. Install the water pump drive belt and pulley. Connect the negative battery cable.

1596cc, 1796cc and 1997cc Engines

1. Disconnect the negative battery cable.

2. Remove the timing belt covers.

3. Adjust the silent shaft (inner) belt tension first. Loosen the idler pulley center bolt so the pulley can be moved.

4. Move the pulley by hand so the long side of the belt deflects about ¼ in.

5. Hold the pulley tightly so the pulley cannot rotate when the bolt is tightened. Tighten the bolt to 15 ft. lbs. (20 Nm) and recheck the amount of deflection.

6. To adjust the timing (outer) belt, turn the crankshaft ¼ turn counterclockwise, then turn it clockwise to move No. 1 cylinder to TDC.

7. Loosen the center bolt. Using tool MD998752 or equivalent and a torque wrench, apply a torque of 1.88–2.03 ft. lbs. (2.6–2.8 Nm). If the body of the vehicle interferes with the special tool and the torque wrench, use a jack and slightly raise the engine assembly. Holding the tensioner pulley, tighten the center bolt.

8. Screw special tool MD998738 or exact equivalent into the engine left support bracket until its end makes contact with the tensioner arm. At this point, screw the special tool in some more and remove the set wire attached to the auto tensioner, if wire was not previously removed. Then remove the special tool.

9. Rotate the crankshaft 2 complete turns clockwise and let it sit for approximately 15 minutes. Then, measure the auto tensioner protrusion (the distance between the tensioner arm and auto tensioner body) to ensure that it is within 0.15–0.18 in. (3.8–4.5mm). If out of specification, repeat Step 1–4 until the specified value is obtained.

10. If the timing belt tension adjustment is being performed with the engine mounted in the vehicle, and clearance between the tensioner arm and the auto tensioner body cannot be measured, the following alternative method can be used:

   a. Screw in special tool MD998738 or equivalent, until its end makes contact with the tensioner arm.

   b. After the special tool makes contact with the arm, screw it in some more to retract the auto tensioner pushrod while counting the number of turns the tool makes until the tensioner arm is brought into contact with the auto tensioner body. Make sure the number of turns the special tool makes conforms with the standard value of 2½–3 turns.

   c. Install the rubber plug to the timing belt rear cover.

11. Install the timing belt covers and all related items.

12. Connect the negative battery cable.

2972cc Engine

1. Disconnect the negative battery cable.

2. If equipped with air conditioning, remove the compressor drive belt.

3. Remove the access cover located in the lower timing belt cover.

4. Loosen the timing belt tensioner mounting bolt 1–2 turns.

5. Rotate the engine clockwise 2 revolutions.

6. Tighten the timing belt tensioner mounting bolt.

7. Install the access cover and the air compressor drive belt.

8. Reconnect the negative battery cable.

REMOVAL & INSTALLATION

1468cc and 1495cc Engines

▶ See Figures 113 and 114

1. Disconnect the negative battery cable. Remove the timing belt cover.

2. Rotate the crankshaft clockwise and align the timing marks so No. 1 pis-

ton will be at TDC of the compression stroke. Loosen the tensioning bolt, it runs in the slotted portion of the tensioner, and the pivot bolt on the timing belt tensioner. Move the tensioner as far as it will go toward the water pump. Tighten the adjusting bolt. Mark the timing belt with an arrow showing direction of rotation if the belt is to be reused.

3. Remove the timing belt.

4. Remove the camshaft sprocket as required.

5. Remove the crankshaft sprocket bolts and remove the crankshaft sprocket and flange, noting the direction of installation for each. Remove the timing belt tensioner.

6. Inspect the belt thoroughly. The back surface must be pliable and rough. If it is hard and glossy, the belt should be replaced. Any cracks in the belt backing or teeth or missing teeth mean the belt must be replaced. The canvas cover should be intact on all the teeth. If rubber is exposed anywhere, the belt should be replaced.

7. Inspect the tensioner for grease leaking from the grease seal and any roughness in rotation. Replace a tensioner for either defect.

8. The sprockets should be inspected and replaced, if there is any sign of damaged teeth or cracking. Do not immerse sprockets in solvent, as solvent that has soaked into the metal may cause deterioration of the timing belt later. Do not clean the tensioner in solvent either, as this may wash the grease out of the bearing.

To install:

9. Install the flange and crankshaft sprocket. The flange must go on first with the chamfered area outward. The sprocket is installed with the boss forward and the studs for the fan belt pulley outward. Install and torque the crankshaft sprocket bolt to 51–72 ft. lbs. (69–98 Nm). Install the camshaft sprocket and bolt, torquing it to 47–54 ft. lbs. (64–74 Nm) on 1468cc engines and 58–72 ft. lbs. (80–100 Nm) on 1495cc engines.

10. Align the timing marks of the camshaft sprocket. Check that the crankshaft timing marks are still in alignment (the locating pin on the front of the crankshaft sprocket is aligned with a mark on the front case).

11. Mount the tensioner, spring and spacer with the bottom end of the spring free. Then, install the bolts and tighten the adjusting bolt slightly with the tensioner moved as far as possible away from the water pump. Install the free end of the spring into the locating tang on the front case. Position the belt over the crankshaft sprocket and then over the camshaft sprocket. Slip the back of the belt over the tensioner wheel. Turn the camshaft sprocket in the opposite of its normal direction of rotation until the straight side of the belt is tight and make sure the timing marks align. If not, shift the belt 1 tooth at a time in the appropriate direction until this occurs.

12. Loosen the tensioner mounting bolts so the tensioner works, without the interference of any friction, under spring pressure. Make sure the belt follows the curve of the camshaft pulley so the teeth are engaged all the way around.

13. Correct the path of the belt, if necessary. Torque the tensioner adjusting bolt to 15–18 ft. lbs. (20–26 Nm). Then, torque the tensioner pivot bolt to the same figure. Bolts must be torqued, in order, or tension won't be correct.

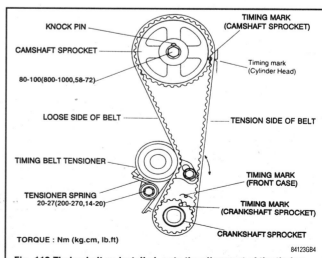

TORQUE : Nm (kg.cm, lb.ft)

84123GB4

Fig. 113 Timing belt as installed, note the alignment of the timing marks—1468cc and 1495cc engines

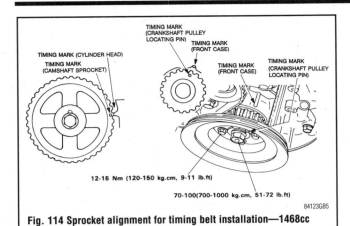

Fig. 114 Sprocket alignment for timing belt installation—1468cc and 1495cc engines

14. Turn the crankshaft 1 turn clockwise until timing marks again align to seat the belt. Loosen both tensioner attaching bolts and let the tensioner position itself under spring tension as before. Torque the bolts in order. Check belt tension by putting a finger on the water pump side of the tensioner wheel and pull the belt toward it. The belt should move toward the pump until the teeth are about ¼ of the way across the head of the tensioner adjusting bolt. Retension the belt, if necessary.

15. Install the timing belt covers.

16. Install the crankshaft pulley, making sure the pin on the crankshaft

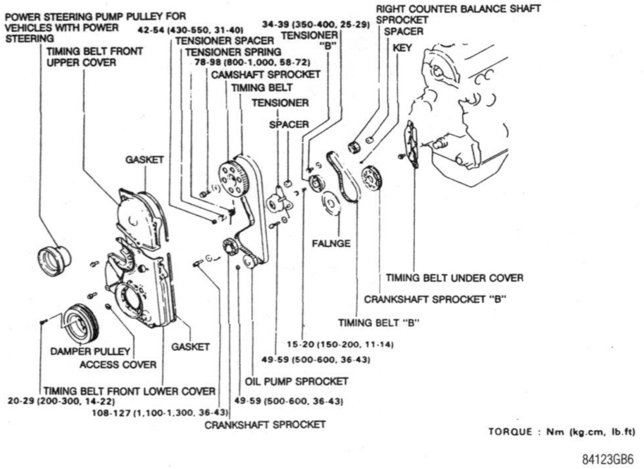

Fig. 115 Timing covers and timing belt assemblies—2351cc engine

sprocket fits through the hole in the rear surface of the pulley. Install the bolts and torque to 7.5–8.5 ft. lbs. (9–12 Nm). Connect the negative battery cable.

2351cc Engine

▶ **See Figures 115 thru 120**

➡**An 8mm diameter metal bar is needed for this procedure.**

1. Disconnect the negative battery cable. Remove the water pump drive belt and pulley.
2. Remove the crank adapter and crankshaft pulley.
3. Remove the upper and lower timing belt covers.
4. Move the tensioner fully in the direction of the water pump and temporarily secure it there.
5. If the timing belt is to be reused, make a paint mark on the belt to indicate the direction of rotation. Slip the belt from the sprockets.
6. Remove the camshaft sprocket bolt and pull the sprocket from the camshaft.
7. Remove the crankshaft sprocket bolt and pull the crankshaft sprocket and flange from the crankshaft.
8. Remove the plug on the left side of the block and insert an 8mm diameter metal bar in the opening to keep the silent shaft in position.
9. Remove the oil pump sprocket retaining nut and remove the oil pump sprocket.
10. Loosen the right silent shaft sprocket mounting bolt until it can be turned by hand.
11. Remove the belt tensioner and remove the timing belt.

➡**Do not attempt to turn the silent shaft sprocket or loosen its bolt while the belt is off.**

12. Remove the silent shaft belt sprocket from the crankshaft.
13. Check the belt for wear, damage or glossing. Replace it if any cracks, damage, brittleness or excessive wear are found.
14. Check the tensioners for a smooth rate of movement.
15. Replace any tensioner that shows grease leakage through the seal.

To install:

16. Install the silent shaft belt sprocket on the crankshaft, with the flat face toward the engine.
17. Apply light engine oil on the outer face of the spacer and install the spacer on the right silent shaft. The side with the rounded shoulder faces the engine.
18. Install the sprocket on the right silent shaft and install the bolt but do not tighten completely at this time.

➡**Align the silent shaft and oil pump sprockets using the timing marks. If the 8mm metal bar can not be inserted into the hole 2.36 inch (60mm), the oil pump sprocket will have to turned 1 full rotation until the bar can be inserted to the full length. The above step assures that the oil pump sprocket and silent shafts are in correct orientation. This step must not be skipped or a vibration may develop during engine operation.**

19. Install the silent shaft belt and adjust the tension, by moving the tensioner into contact with the belt, tight enough to remove all slack. Tighten the tensioner bolt to 21 ft. lbs. (28 Nm).

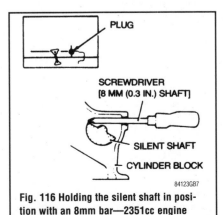

Fig. 116 Holding the silent shaft in position with an 8mm bar—2351cc engine

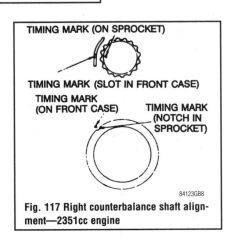

Fig. 117 Right counterbalance shaft alignment—2351cc engine

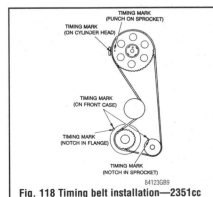

Fig. 118 Timing belt installation—2351cc engine

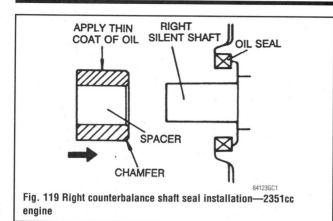

Fig. 119 Right counterbalance shaft seal installation—2351cc engine

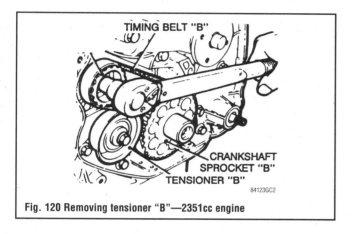

Fig. 120 Removing tensioner "B"—2351cc engine

➡ **Always rotate the crankshaft in a clockwise direction. Make a mark on the back of the timing belt indicating the direction of rotation so it may be reassembled in the same direction if it is to be reused.**

4. Remove the auto tensioner and remove the outermost timing belt.

5. Remove the timing belt tensioner pulley, tensioner arm, idler pulley, oil pump sprocket, special washer, flange and spacer.

6. Remove the silent shaft (inner) belt tensioner and remove the inner belt.

To install:

7. Align the timing marks on the crankshaft sprocket and the silent shaft sprocket. Fit the inner timing belt over the crankshaft and silent shaft sprocket. Ensure that there is no slack in the belt.

8. While holding the inner timing belt tensioner with your fingers, adjust the timing belt tension by applying a force towards the center of the belt, until the tension side of the belt is taut. Tighten the tensioner bolt.

➡ **When tightening the bolt of the tensioner, ensure that the tensioner pulley shaft does not rotate with the bolt. Allowing it to rotate with the bolt can cause excessive tension on the belt.**

9. Check belt for proper tension by depressing the belt on its long side with your finger and noting the belt deflection. The desired reading is 0.20–0.28 in. (5–7mm). If tension is not correct, readjust and check belt deflection.

10. Install the flange, crankshaft and washer to the crankshaft. The flange on the crankshaft sprocket must be installed towards the inner timing belt sprocket. Tighten bolt to 80–94 ft. lbs. (110–130 Nm).

11. To install the oil pump sprocket, insert a Phillips screwdriver with a shaft 0.31 in. (8mm) in diameter into the plug hole in the left side of the cylinder block to hold the left silent shaft. Tighten the nut to 36–43 ft. lbs. (50–60 Nm).

12. Using a wrench, hold the camshaft at its hexagon between journal No. 2 and 3 and tighten bolt to 58–72 ft. lbs. (80–100 Nm). If no hexagon is present between journal No. 2 and 3, hold the sprocket stationary with a spanner wrench while tightening the retainer bolt.

13. Carefully push the auto tensioner rod in until the set hole in the rod is aligned with the hole in the cylinder. Place a wire into the hole to retain the rod.

20. Tighten the silent shaft sprocket bolt to 28 ft. lbs. (36 Nm).

21. Install the flange and crankshaft sprocket on the crankshaft. The flange conforms to the front of the silent shaft sprocket and the timing belt sprocket is installed with the flat face toward the engine.

➡ **The flange must be installed correctly or a broken belt will result.**

22. Install the washer and bolt in the crankshaft and torque it to 94 ft. lbs. (130 Nm).

23. Install the camshaft sprocket and bolt and torque the bolt to 72 ft. lbs. (96 Nm).

24. Install the timing belt tensioner, spacer and spring.

25. Align the timing mark on each sprocket with the corresponding mark on the front case.

26. Install the timing belt on the sprockets and move the tensioner against the belt with sufficient force to allow a deflection of 5–7mm along its longest straight run.

27. Tighten the tensioner bolt to 21 ft. lbs. (28 Nm).

28. Install the upper and lower covers, the crankshaft pulley and the crank adapter. Tighten the bolts to 21 ft. lbs. (28 Nm).

29. Remove the 8mm bar and install the plug. Connect the negative battery cable.

1596cc, 1796cc and 1997cc Engines

▶ **See Figures 121 thru 127**

➡ **The 1596cc engine is not equipped with silent shafts. Disregard all instructions pertaining to silent shafts if working on that engine.**

1. Disconnect the negative battery cable.

2. Remove the timing belt upper and lower covers.

3. Rotate the crankshaft clockwise and align the timing marks so No. 1 piston will be at TDC of the compression stroke. At this time the timing marks on the camshaft sprocket and the upper surface of the cylinder head should coincide, and the dowel pin of the camshaft sprocket should be at the upper side.

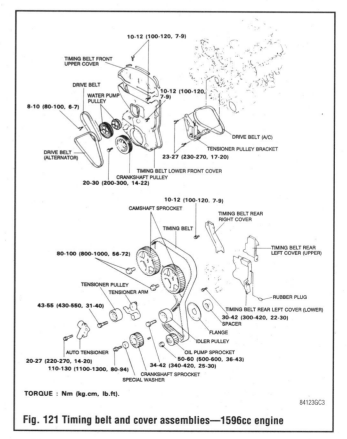

Fig. 121 Timing belt and cover assemblies—1596cc engine

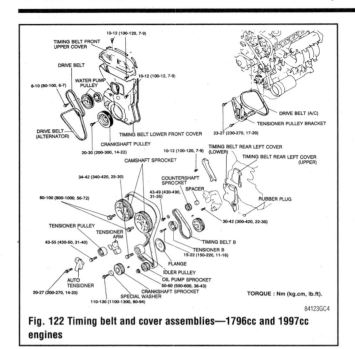

Fig. 122 Timing belt and cover assemblies—1796cc and 1997cc engines

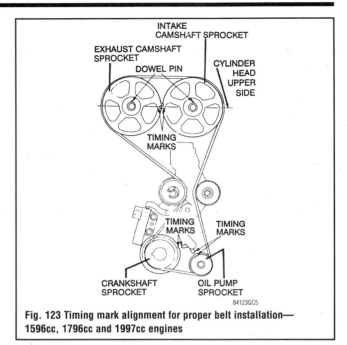

Fig. 123 Timing mark alignment for proper belt installation— 1596cc, 1796cc and 1997cc engines

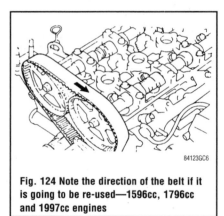

Fig. 124 Note the direction of the belt if it is going to be re-used—1596cc, 1796cc and 1997cc engines

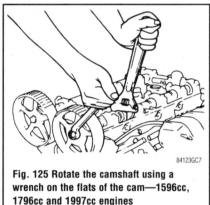

Fig. 125 Rotate the camshaft using a wrench on the flats of the cam—1596cc, 1796cc and 1997cc engines

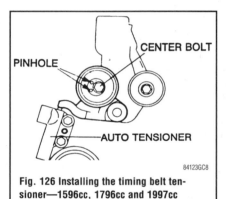

Fig. 126 Installing the timing belt tensioner—1596cc, 1796cc and 1997cc engines

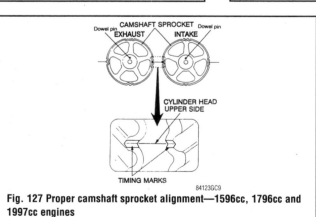

Fig. 127 Proper camshaft sprocket alignment—1596cc, 1796cc and 1997cc engines

14. Install the tensioner pulley onto the tensioner arm. Locate the pinhole in the tensioner pulley shaft to the left of the center bolt. Then, tighten the center bolt finger-tight.

15. When installing the timing belt, turn the 2 camshaft sprockets so their dowel pins are located on top. Align the timing marks facing each other with the top surface of the cylinder head. When you let go of the exhaust camshaft sprocket, it will rotate 1 tooth in the counterclockwise direction. This should be taken into account when installing the timing belts on the sprocket.

➡Both camshaft sprockets are used for the intake and exhaust camshafts and are provided with 2 timing marks. When the sprocket is mounted on the exhaust camshaft, use the timing mark on the right with the dowel pin hole on top. For the intake camshaft sprocket, use the 1 on the left with the dowel pin hole on top.

16. Align the crankshaft sprocket and oil pump sprocket timing marks.

17. After alignment of the oil pump sprocket timing marks, remove the plug on the cylinder block and insert a Phillips screw driver with a shaft diameter of 0.31 in. (8mm) through the hole. If the shaft can be inserted 2.4 in. deep, the silent shaft is in the correct position. If the shaft of the tool can only be inserted 0.8—1.0 in. (20—25mm) deep, turn the oil pump sprocket 1 turn and realign the marks. Reinsert the tool making sure it is inserted 2.4 in. deep. Keep the tool inserted in hole for the remainder of this procedure.

➡The above step assures that the oil pump socket is in correct orientation to the silent shafts. This step must not be skipped or a vibration may develop during engine operation.

18. Install the timing belt as follows:

a. Install the timing belt around the intake camshaft sprocket and retain it with 2 spring clips or binder clips.

b. Install the timing belt around the exhaust sprocket, aligning the timing marks with the cylinder head top surface using 2 wrenches. Retain the belt with 2 spring clips.

c. Install the timing belt around the idler pulley, oil pump sprocket, crankshaft sprocket and the tensioner pulley. Remove the 2 spring clips.

d. Lift upward on the tensioner pulley in a clockwise direction and tighten the center bolt. Make sure all timing marks are aligned.

e. Rotate the crankshaft ¼ turn counterclockwise. Then, turn in clockwise until the timing marks are aligned again.

19. To adjust the timing (outer) belt, turn the crankshaft ¼ turn counterclockwise, then turn it clockwise to move No. 1 cylinder to TDC.

20. Loosen the center bolt. Using tool MD998738 or equivalent and a torque wrench, apply a torque of 1.88–2.03 ft. lbs. (2.6–2.8 Nm). Tighten the center bolt.

21. Screw the special tool into the engine left support bracket until its end makes contact with the tensioner arm. At this point, screw the special tool in some more and remove the set wire attached to the auto tensioner, if the wire was not previously removed. Then remove the special tool.

22. Rotate the crankshaft 2 complete turns clockwise and let it sit for approximately 15 minutes. Then, measure the auto tensioner protrusion (the distance between the tensioner arm and auto tensioner body) to ensure that it is within 0.15–0.18 in. (3.8–4.5mm). If out of specification, repeat Step 1–4 until the specified value is obtained.

23. If the timing belt tension adjustment is being performed with the engine mounted in the vehicle, and clearance between the tensioner arm and the auto tensioner body cannot be measured, the following alternative method can be used:

a. Screw in special tool MD998738 or equivalent, until its end makes contact with the tensioner arm.

b. After the special tool makes contact with the arm, screw it in some more to retract the auto tensioner pushrod while counting the number of turns the tool makes until the tensioner arm is brought into contact with the auto tensioner body. Make sure the number of turns the special tool makes conforms with the standard value of 2½–3 turns.

c. Install the rubber plug to the timing belt rear cover.

24. Install the timing belt covers and all related items.

25. Connect the negative battery cable.

2972cc Engine

♦ **See Figures 128 and 129**

1. Disconnect the negative battery cable.

2. To remove the air conditioning compressor belt, loosen the adjustment pulley locknut, turn the screw counterclockwise to reduce the drive belt tension and remove the belt.

3. To remove the serpentine drive belt, insert a ½ in. breaker bar into the square hole of the tensioner pulley, rotate it counterclockwise to reduce the drive belt tension and remove the belt.

4. Remove the air conditioning compressor and the air compressor bracket, power steering pump and alternator from the mounts and support them to the side. Remove power steering pump/alternator automatic belt tensioner bolt and the tensioner.

5. Raise the vehicle and support safely. Remove the right inner fender splash shield.

6. Remove the crankshaft pulley bolt and the pulley/damper assembly from the crankshaft.

7. Lower the vehicle and place a floor jack under the engine to support it.

8. Separate the front engine mount insulator from the bracket. Raise the engine slightly and remove the mount bracket.

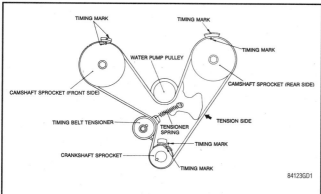

Fig. 128 Timing belt components and arrangement—2972cc engine

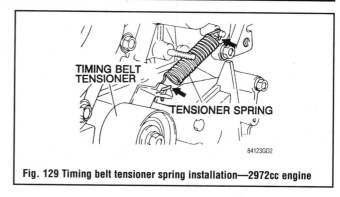

Fig. 129 Timing belt tensioner spring installation—2972cc engine

9. Remove the timing belt cover bolts and the upper and lower covers from the engine.

10. Turn the crankshaft until the timing marks on the camshaft sprocket and cylinder head are aligned.

11. Loosen the tensioning bolt, it runs in the slotted portion of the tensioner, and the pivot bolt on the timing belt tensioner.

12. Move the tensioner counterclockwise as far as it will go. Tighten the adjusting bolt.

13. Mark the timing belt with an arrow showing direction of rotation.

14. Remove the timing belt from the camshaft sprocket.

15. Remove the crankshaft pulley. Then, remove the timing belt. Remove the timing belt tensioner. Remove the retainer bolts from the timing sprockets and remove as required.

16. Inspect the belt thoroughly. The back surface must be pliable and rough. If it is hard and glossy, the belt should be replaced. Any cracks in the belt backing or teeth or missing teeth mean the belt must be replaced. The canvas cover should be intact on all the teeth. If rubber is exposed anywhere, the belt should be replaced.

17. Inspect the tensioner for grease leaking from the grease seal and any roughness in rotation. Replace a tensioner for either defect.

18. The sprockets should be inspected and replaced if there is any sign of damaged teeth or cracking anywhere.

19. Do not immerse sprockets in solvent, as solvent that has soaked into the metal may cause deterioration of the timing belt later.

20. Do not clean the tensioner in solvent either, as this may wash the grease out of the bearing.

To install:

21. Align the timing marks of the camshaft sprocket. Check that the crankshaft timing marks are still in alignment, the locating pin on the front of the crankshaft sprocket is aligned with a mark on the front case.

22. Mount the tensioner, spring and spacer with the bottom end of the spring free. Then, install the bolts and tighten the adjusting bolt slightly with the tensioner moved as far as possible away from the water pump. Install the free end of the spring into the locating tang on the front case. Position the belt over the crankshaft sprocket and then over the camshaft sprocket. Slip the back of the belt over the tensioner wheel. Turn the camshaft sprocket in the opposite of its normal direction of rotation until the straight side of the belt is tight and make sure the timing marks align. If not, shift the belt 1 tooth at a time in the appropriate direction until this occurs.

23. Loosen the tensioner mounting bolts so the tensioner works, without the interference of any friction, under spring pressure. Make sure the belt follows the curve of the camshaft pulley so the teeth are engaged all the way around.

24. Correct the path of the belt, if necessary. Torque the tensioner adjusting bolt to 16–21 ft. lbs. (22–29 Nm). Then, torque the tensioner pivot bolt to the same figure. Bolts must be torqued in that order, or tension won't be correct.

25. Turn the crankshaft 1 turn clockwise until timing marks again align to seat the belt. Then loosen both tensioner attaching bolts and let the tensioner position itself under spring tension as before. Finally, torque the bolts in the proper order exactly as before. Check belt tension by putting a finger on the water pump side of the tensioner wheel and pull the belt toward it. The belt should move toward the pump until the teeth are about ¼ of the way across the head of the tensioner adjusting bolt. Retension the belt, if necessary.

26. Install the timing belt covers.

27. Install the crankshaft pulley, making sure the pin on the crankshaft sprocket fits through the hole in the rear surface of the pulley. Install the retaining bolt and torque to 108–116 ft. lbs. (147–157 Nm).

28. Install the engine mount bracket and secure with the mounting hardware.

29. Install the pulley damper assembly to the crankshaft. Torque the bolt to 110 ft. lbs. (149 Nm). Install the splash shield.

30. Install the power steering pump/alternator automatic belt tensioner.

31. Install the air conditioning compressor bracket, compressor, power steering pump and alternator.

32. Install the accessory drive belt.

33. Connect the negative battery cable and check all disturbed components for proper operation.

Timing Sprockets and Oil Seals

REMOVAL & INSTALLATION

1. Disconnect the negative battery cable.
2. Remove the valve cover(s) and timing belt(s).
3. Remove the crankshaft pulley retainer bolts and remove the pulley.
4. Remove the crankshaft sprocket retainer bolt and washer from the sprocket, if used, and remove sprocket. If sprocket is difficult to remove or there are no bolts on the puller, the appropriate puller should be used to facilitate remove.
5. Hold the camshaft stationary using the hexagon cast between journals No. 2 and 3 and remove the retainer bolt. Remove the sprocket from the camshaft. If the camshaft does not have a hexagon cast between journals No. 2 and 3, use the appropriate spanner wrench to hold the shaft in position while removing the bolt.
6. Pry the seals from the bores and replace using the proper installation tools.
7. The sprockets should be inspected and replaced if there is any sign of damaged teeth or cracking. Do not immerse sprockets in solvent, as solvent that has soaked into the metal may cause deterioration of the timing belt later.

To install:

8. Install the sprockets to their shafts. Install the retainer bolts and torque the camshaft sprocket as follows:
- 1468cc Engine—54 ft. lbs. (75 Nm)
- 1495cc Engine—58–72 ft. lbs. (80– (100 Nm)
- 1596cc Engine—58–72 ft. lbs. (80– (100 Nm)
- 1796cc Engine—58–72 ft. lbs. (80– (100 Nm)
- 1997cc Engine—58–72 ft. lbs. (80– (100 Nm)
- 2351cc Engine—72 ft. lbs. (98 Nm)
- 2972cc Engine—72 ft. lbs. (98 Nm)

9. Install the flange and crankshaft sprocket. The flange must go on first with the chamfered area outward. The sprocket is installed with the boss forward and the studs for the fan belt pulley outward. Torque the crankshaft sprocket retaining bolt as follows:
- 1468cc Engine—72 ft. lbs. (98 Nm)
- 1495cc Engine—140–147 ft. lbs. (190–200 Nm)
- 1596cc Engine—80–94 ft. lbs. (110–130 Nm)
- 1796cc Engine—80–94 ft. lbs. (110–130 Nm)
- 1997cc Engine—80–94 ft. lbs. (110–130 Nm)
- 2351cc Engine—94 ft. lbs. (127 Nm)
- 2972cc Engine—116 ft. lbs. (157 Nm).

10. Install the timing belt(s) and valve cover(s).
11. Connect the negative battery cable and check for leaks.

Camshaft

REMOVAL & INSTALLATION

1468cc Engine

▶ See Figures 130, 131, 132, 133, and 134

1. Disconnect the negative battery cable. Remove the rocker cover. Remove the timing belt cover. Remove the distributor.
2. Loosen the 2 bolts and move the timing belt tensioner toward the water pump as far as it will go, then retighten the timing belt tensioner adjusting bolt. Disengage the timing belt from the camshaft sprocket and unbolt and remove the sprocket. The timing belt may be left engaged with the crankshaft sprocket and tensioner.
3. Remove the rocker shaft assembly. Remove the small, square cover that sits directly behind the camshaft on the transaxle side of the head. Remove the camshaft thrust case tightening bolt that sits on the top of the head right near that cover.
4. Carefully, slide the camshaft out of the head through the hole in the transaxle side of the head, being careful that the cam lobes do not strike the bearing bores in the head.

To install:

5. Lubricate all journal and thrust surfaces with clean engine oil.
6. Carefully insert the camshaft into the engine. Make sure the camshaft goes in with the threaded hole in the top of the thrust case straight upward.
7. Align the bolt hole in the thrust case and the cylinder head surface.
8. Install the thrust case bolt and tighten firmly.
9. Install the rear cover with a new gasket and install and tighten the bolts to 5.8–7.2 ft. lbs. (8–10 Nm).
10. Coat the external surface of the front oil seal with engine oil.
11. Using special installer tool MD 998306-01 or equivalent, drive a new front camshaft oil seal into the clearance between the cam and head at the forward end, making sure the seal seats fully.
12. Install the camshaft sprocket and torque the bolt to 47–54 ft. lbs. (64–74 Nm).
13. Reconnect the timing belt, check the timing and adjust the belt tension.
14. Reinstall the rocker shaft assembly. Adjust the valves and install the rocker and timing belt covers.

1495cc Engine

▶ See Figures 135 and 136

1. Disconnect the negative battery cable. Remove the rocker cover. Remove the air intake tube on turbocharged models. Remove the timing belt cover. Remove the distributor.
2. Loosen the 2 bolts and move the timing belt tensioner toward the water pump as far as it will go, then retighten the timing belt tensioner adjusting bolt. Disengage the timing belt from the camshaft sprocket and unbolt and remove

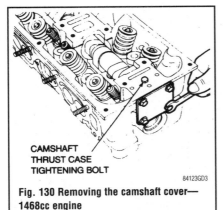

CAMSHAFT THRUST CASE TIGHTENING BOLT

84123GD3

Fig. 130 Removing the camshaft cover— 1468cc engine

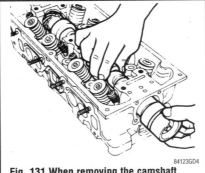

84123GD4

Fig. 131 When removing the camshaft, use care not to damage the bearings— 1468cc engine

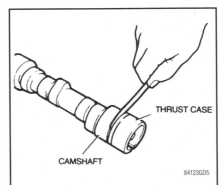

THRUST CASE

CAMSHAFT

84123GD5

Fig. 132 Measuring the camshaft end-play—1468cc engine

Fig. 133 Camshaft seal installation—1468cc engine

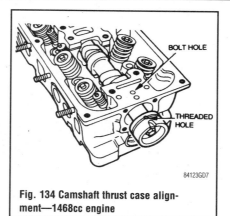

Fig. 134 Camshaft thrust case alignment—1468cc engine

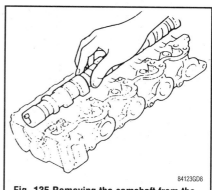

Fig. 135 Removing the camshaft from the cylinder head—1495cc engine

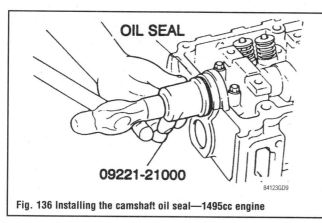

Fig. 136 Installing the camshaft oil seal—1495cc engine

the sprocket. The timing belt may be left engaged with the crankshaft sprocket and tensioner.

3. Remove the rocker shaft assembly.

4. Remove the camshaft bearing caps, making sure to note the original location of each cap.

5. Remove the camshaft from the cylinder head.

To install:

6. Check the camshaft journals for wear, if the journals are worn or shown signs of damage, replace the camshaft.

7. Check each part of the camshaft bearings, if the bearings are excessively worn, replace the bearing cap or the cylinder head as needed.

8. Check the camshaft oil seal and replace it if needed.

9. Lubricate the camshaft journals with clean engine oil and install the camshaft into the cylinder head.

10. Install the camshaft bearing caps and tighten the bolts to 14–20 ft. lbs. (20–27 Nm). Tighten the camshaft bearing caps starting from the center and working outward to the end caps.

11. Install the rocker arm shaft assembly.

12. Install a new camshaft oil seal, using tool 09221–21000 or equivalent. Install the distributor.

13. Install the camshaft sprocket. Align the camshaft sprocket and the crankshaft sprocket timing marks and install the timing belt.

14. Adjust the valve clearance to the proper specification for a cold engine. Install the rocker cover, using a new gasket. Install the air intake tube on turbocharged models.

15. Install the timing belt cover and the accessory drive belts. Connect the negative battery cable. Run the engine to normal operating temperature, then recheck the valve clearance once the engine has been warmed, adjust it if needed.

2351cc Engine

▶ See Figures 137, 138 and 139

➡A special tool 09246-32000 (MD998443) or equivalent, is required to retain the automatic lash adjusters in this procedure.

1. Remove the rocker cover and gasket and the timing belt cover.

2. Turn the crankshaft so the No. 1 piston is at TDC compression. At this point, the timing mark on the camshaft sprocket and the timing mark on the head to the left of the sprocket will be aligned.

3. Remove the timing belt and camshaft sprocket.

4. Remove the camshaft bearing cap bolts.

5. Install the automatic lash adjuster retainer tool 09246-32000 or equivalent, to keep the adjuster from falling out of the rocker arms.

6. Lift off the bearing caps and rocker arm assemblies.

7. Lift out the camshaft.

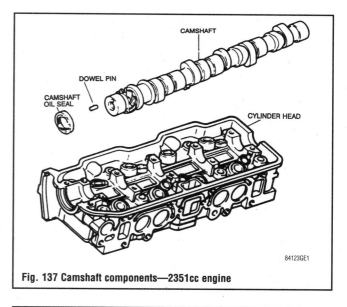

Fig. 137 Camshaft components—2351cc engine

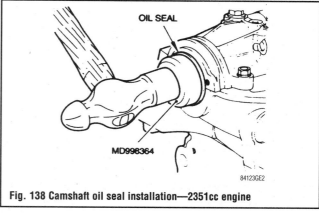

Fig. 138 Camshaft oil seal installation—2351cc engine

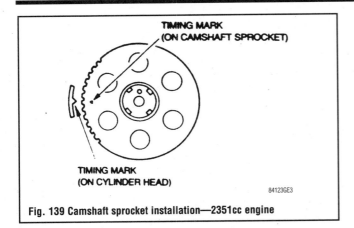

Fig. 139 Camshaft sprocket installation—2351cc engine

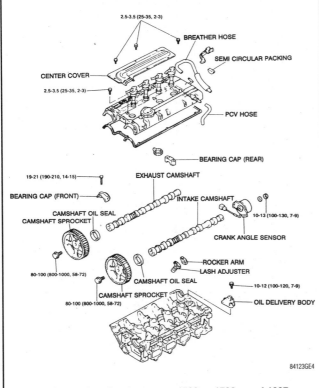

Fig. 140 Camshaft and rocker arms—1596cc, 1796cc and 1997cc engines

➡Keep all parts in the order in which they were removed. None of the parts are interchangeable. The lash adjusters are filled with diesel fuel, which will spill out if they are inverted. If any diesel fuel is spilled, the adjusters must be bled.

To install:

8. Check all parts for wear or damage. Replace any damaged or excessively worn part.

9. Coat the camshaft with clean engine oil and place it on the head.

10. Assemble all parts. Note the following:

a. The rocker shafts are installed with the notches in the ends facing up.

b. The left rocker shaft is longer than the right.

c. The wave washers are installed on the left shaft.

d. Coat all parts with clean engine oil prior to assembly.

e. Insert the lash adjuster from under the rocker arm and install the special holding tool. If any of the diesel fuel is spilled, the adjuster must be bled.

f. Tighten the bearing cap bolts, working from the center towards the ends, to 15 ft. lbs. (20 Nm) in 3 progressions.

g. Check the operation of each lash adjuster by positioning the camshaft so the rocker arm bears on the low or round portion of the cam, pointed part of the cam facing straight down. Insert a thin steel wire, or tool MD998442 or equivalent, in the hole in the top of the rocker arm, over the lash adjuster and depress the check ball at the top of the adjuster. While holding the check ball depressed, move the arm up and down. Looseness should be felt. Full plunger stroke should be 2.2mm. If not, remove, clean and bleed the lash adjusters.

1596cc, 1796cc and 1997cc Engines

▶ **See Figures 140 thru 145**

1. Relieve the fuel system pressure.
2. Disconnect battery negative cable.
3. Disconnect the accelerator cable.
4. Remove the timing belt cover and timing belt.
5. Remove the center cover, breather and PCV hoses, and spark plug cables.
6. Remove the rocker cover, semi-circular packing, throttle body stay, crankshaft angle sensor, both camshaft sprockets, and oil seals.
7. Loosen the bearing cap bolts in 2–3 steps. Label and remove all camshaft bearing caps.

➡If the bearing caps are difficult to remove, use a plastic hammer to gently tap the rear part of the camshaft.

8. Remove the intake and exhaust camshafts.
9. Check the camshaft journals for wear or damage. Check the cam lobes for damage. Also, check the cylinder head oil holes for clogging.

To install:

10. Lubricate the camshafts with heavy engine oil and position the camshafts on the cylinder head.

➡Do not confuse the intake camshaft with the exhaust camshaft. The intake camshaft has a split on its rear end for driving the crank angle sensor.

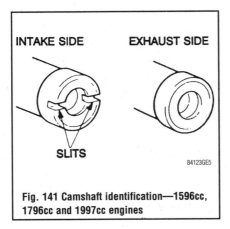

Fig. 141 Camshaft identification—1596cc, 1796cc and 1997cc engines

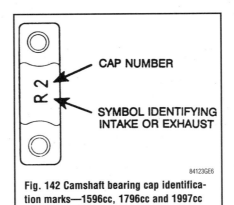

Fig. 142 Camshaft bearing cap identification marks—1596cc, 1796cc and 1997cc engines

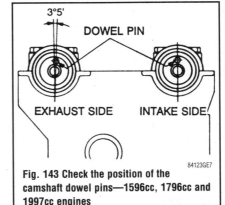

Fig. 143 Check the position of the camshaft dowel pins—1596cc, 1796cc and 1997cc engines

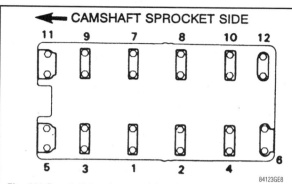

Fig. 144 Camshaft bearing cap tightening sequence—1596cc, 1796cc and 1997cc engines

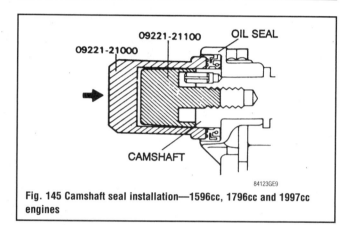

Fig. 145 Camshaft seal installation—1596cc, 1796cc and 1997cc engines

11. Make sure the dowel pin on both camshaft sprocket ends are located on the top.

12. Install the bearing caps. Tighten the caps in sequence and in 2 or 3 steps. No. 2 and 5 caps are of the same shape. Check the markings on the caps to identify the cap number and intake/exhaust symbol. Only **L** (intake) or **R** (exhaust) is stamped on No. 1 bearing cap. Also, make sure the rocker arm is correctly mounted on the lash adjuster and the valve stem end. Torque the retaining bolts to 15 ft. lbs. (20 Nm).

13. Apply a coating of engine oil to the oil seal. Using tool MD998307 or equivalent, press-fit the seal into the cylinder head.

14. Align the punch mark on the crank angle sensor housing with the notch in the plate. With the dowel pin on the sprocket side of the intake camshaft at top, install the crank angle sensor on the cylinder head.

➡Do not position the crank angle sensor with the punch mark positioned opposite the notch; this position will result in incorrect fuel injection and ignition timing.

15. Install the timing belt, valve cover and all related parts.
16. Connect the negative battery cable and check for leaks.

2972cc Engine

▸ See Figures 146, 147, 148 and 149

1. Disconnect the negative battery cable. Remove the air cleaner assembly and valve covers.

2. Install auto lash adjuster retainer tools MD998443 or equivalent on the rocker arms.

3. If removing the right side (front) camshaft, remove the distributor extension.

4. Remove the camshaft bearing caps but do not remove the bolts from the caps.

5. Remove the rocker arms, rocker shafts and bearing caps, as an assembly.

6. Remove the camshaft from the cylinder head.

7. Inspect the bearing journals on the camshaft, cylinder head and bearing caps.

To install:

8. Lubricate the camshaft journals and camshaft with clean engine oil and install the camshaft in the cylinder head.

9. Align the camshaft bearing caps with the arrow mark depending on cylinder numbers and install in numerical order.

10. Apply sealer at the ends of the bearing caps and install the assembly.

11. Torque the rocker arm and shaft assembly bolts to 15 ft. lbs. (21 Nm).

12. Install the distributor extension, if removed.

13. Install the valve cover and all related parts. Torque the valve cover retaining bolts to 7 ft. lbs. (10 Nm).

14. Connect the negative battery cable and road test the vehicle.

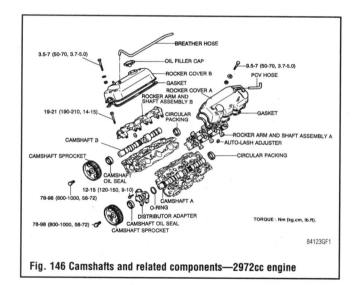

Fig. 146 Camshafts and related components—2972cc engine

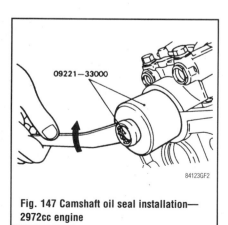

Fig. 147 Camshaft oil seal installation—2972cc engine

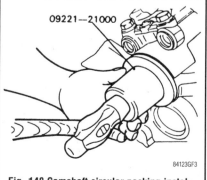

Fig. 148 Camshaft circular packing installation—2972cc engine

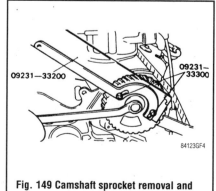

Fig. 149 Camshaft sprocket removal and installation—2972cc engine

Counterbalance Shafts and Bearings

REMOVAL & INSTALLATION

1997cc, 1796cc and 2351cc Engines

◆ **See Figures 150 thru 162**

You'll need a number of special tools to perform this operation. They are listed as follows:

- Bearing puller 09212–32000—to remove right countershaft front bearing.
- Bearing puller 09212–32100 and holding fixture 09212–32300—to remove left counter shaft rear bearing.
- Bearing installer 09212–32200—to install left and right countershaft rear bearings.
- Seal installer 90214–32100—to install the crankshaft front seal

1. Disconnect the negative battery cable.
2. Remove the oil filter, oil pressure switch, oil gauge sending unit, oil filter mounting bracket and gasket.
3. Raise and safely support the vehicle. Drain engine oil. Remove engine oil pan.
4. Lower the vehicle. Remove the timing belts.
5. Remove the crankshaft sprocket (inner) and counterbalance shaft sprocket.
6. Remove the front engine cover which is also the oil pump cover. Different length bolts are used. Take note of their locations. Discard the shaft seal and gasket.

7. Remove the oil pump driven gear flange bolt. When loosening this bolt, first remove the plug at the bottom of the left side of the cylinder block and insert a tool approximately ⅜ in. in diameter into the hole. The tool will hold the silent shaft in position. The tool must be inserted at least 2.4 in. into the hole. If depth of insertion is not correct, rotate the oil pump sprocket 1 revolution, and align the timing marks. Insert the tool shaft again, and watch the amount of insertion, which should be at least 2.4 in.
8. Remove the oil pump gears and remove the front case assembly. Remove the threaded plug, the oil pressure relief spring and plunger.
9. Remove the shaft alignment tool, front cover and oil pump as a unit, with the left countershaft attached.
10. Remove the oil pump gear and left counterbalance shaft.

➡️To aid in removal of the front cover, a driver groove is provided on the cover, above the oil pump housing. Avoid prying on the thinner parts of the housing flange or hammering on it to remove the case.

11. Remove the right counterbalance shaft from the engine block.
To replace the counterbalance shaft bearings:
12. Using special bearing puller tool 09212 32000 or equivalent, remove the right counterbalance shaft bearing from the cylinder block.
13. Using special bearing puller tool 09212 32100 and holding fixture 09212–32300 (to hold the puller) or equivalents, remove the left countershaft rear bearing from the cylinder block.
14. Coat the inner surfaces of the new bearings and the block bores with clean engine oil.
15. Install the left rear countershaft bearing into the cylinder block bore and install it using special bearing installer tool 09212–32200 and the special holding fixture 09212–32300 used before to remove the bearing. The fixture serves as a guide for the bearing installer tool.
16. Using special bearing installer tool 09212 32200 or equivalent, install the right countershaft front bearing into the block.
To install the counterbalance shafts:
17. Install a new front seal in the cover. Install the oil pump drive and driven gears in the front case, aligning the timing marks on the pump gears.
18. Install the left counterbalance shaft in the driven gear and temporarily tighten the bolt.
19. Install the right counterbalance shaft into the cylinder block.
20. Install an oil seal guide on the end of the crankshaft and install a new gasket on the front of the engine block for the front cover.
21. Install a new front case packing.
22. Insert the left counterbalance shaft into the engine block and at the same time, guide the front cover into place on the front of the engine block.
23. Install an O-ring on the oil pump cover and install it on the front cover.
24. Tighten the oil pump cover bolts and the front cover bolts to 11–13 ft. lbs. (15–18 Nm).
25. Install the upper and lower under covers.
26. Install the spacer on the end of the right counterbalance shaft, with the chamfered edge toward the rear of the engine.
27. Install the counterbalance shaft sprocket and temporarily tighten the bolt.
28. Install the inner crankshaft sprocket and align the timing marks on the sprockets with those on the front case.
29. Install the inner tensioner (B) with the center of the pulley on the left

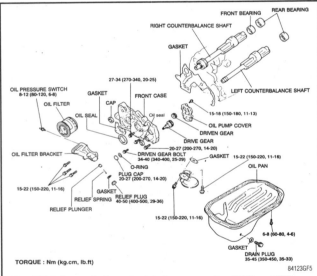

Fig. 150 Balance shafts and related components—1796cc, 1997cc and 2351cc engines

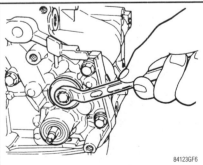

Fig. 151 Removing the plug cap from the oil pump portion of the front case—1796cc, 1997cc and 2351cc engines

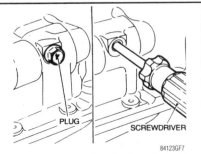

Fig. 152 Removing the plug from the left side of the cylinder block and inserting an 8mm bar to hold the counterbalance shaft—1796cc, 1997cc and 2351cc engines

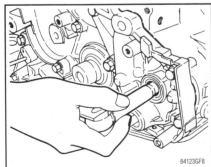

Fig. 153 Removing the oil pump driven gear and left silent shaft retaining bolt—1796cc, 1997cc and 2351cc engines

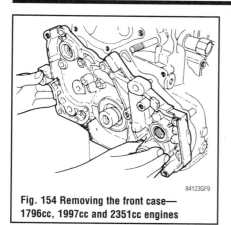

Fig. 154 Removing the front case—1796cc, 1997cc and 2351cc engines

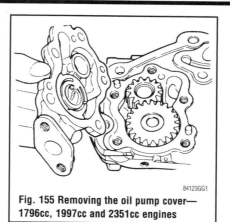

Fig. 155 Removing the oil pump cover—1796cc, 1997cc and 2351cc engines

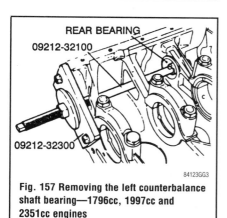

Fig. 156 Removing the right counterbalance shaft bearing—1796cc, 1997cc and 2351cc engines

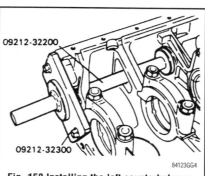

Fig. 157 Removing the left counterbalance shaft bearing—1796cc, 1997cc and 2351cc engines

Fig. 158 Installing the left counterbalance shaft rear bearing—1796cc, 1997cc and 2351cc engines

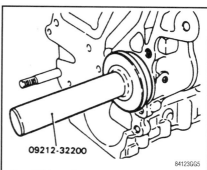

Fig. 159 Installing the right counterbalance shaft front bearing—1796cc, 1997cc and 2351cc engines

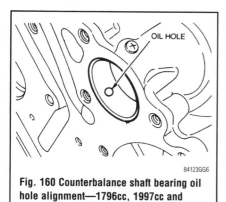

Fig. 160 Counterbalance shaft bearing oil hole alignment—1796cc, 1997cc and 2351cc engines

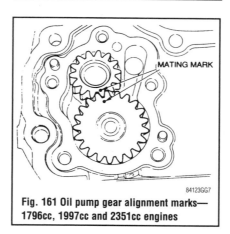

Fig. 161 Oil pump gear alignment marks—1796cc, 1997cc and 2351cc engines

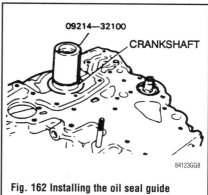

Fig. 162 Installing the oil seal guide tool—1796cc, 1997cc and 2351cc engines

side of the mounting bolt and with the pulley flange toward the front of the engine.

30. Lift the tensioner by hand, clockwise, to apply tension to the belt. Tighten the bolt to secure the tensioner.

31. Check that all alignment marks are in their proper places and the belt deflection is approximately ¼–½ in. on the tension side.

➡When the tensioner bolt is tightened, make sure the shaft of the tensioner does not turn with the bolt. If the belt is too tight there will be noise and if the belt is too loose, the belt and sprocket may come out of mesh.

32. Tighten the counterbalance shaft sprocket bolt to 22–28.5 ft. lbs. (29–40 Nm).

33. Install the flange and crankshaft sprocket. Tighten the bolt to 43–50 ft. lbs. (58–67 Nm).

34. Install the camshaft spacer and sprocket. Tighten the bolt to 44–57 ft. lbs. (61–75 Nm).

35. Align the camshaft sprocket timing mark with the timing mark on the upper inner cover.

36. Install the oil pump sprocket, tightening the nut to 25–28 ft. lbs. (34–39 Nm). Align the timing mark on the sprocket with the mark on the case.

➡To be assured that the phasing of the oil pump sprocket and the left counterbalance shaft is correct, a metal rod should be inserted in the plugged hole on the left side of the cylinder block. If it can be inserted more than 2.4 in., the phasing is correct. If the tool can only be inserted approximately 1.0 in., turn the oil pump sprocket through 1 turn and realign the timing marks. Keep the metal rod inserted until the installation of the timing belt is completed. Remove the tool from the hole and install the plug, before starting the engine.

37. Install the tensioner spring and tensioner. Temporarily tighten the nut. Install the front end of the tensioner spring (bent at right angles) on the projection of the tensioner and the other end (straight) on the water pump body.

38. If the timing belt is correctly tensioned, there should be about 12mm clearance between the outside of the belt and the edge of the belt cover. This is measured about halfway down the side of the belt opposite the tensioner.

39. Complete the assembly by installing the oil screen, gasket and oil pan.

40. Install the crankshaft pulley, alternator and accessory belts and adjust to specifications.

41. Install the radiator, fill the cooling system with antifreeze and the crankcase with clean engine oil. Connect the negative battery cable and start the engine.

Rear Main Oil Seal

REPLACEMENT

The rear main seal is located in a housing on the rear of the block. To replace the seal, it is necessary to remove the engine and perform the work on an engine stand or work bench.

1468cc and 1495cc Engines

▶ See Figure 163

1. Remove the engine from the vehicle and position on a suitable holding fixture.

2. Unscrew the retaining bolts and remove the housing from the block.

3. Remove the separator from the housing.

4. Using a small prybar, pry out the old seal.

5. Clean the housing and the separator.

To install:

6. Lightly oil the replacement seal. Tap the seal into the housing using a canister top or other circular piece of metal. The oil seal should be installed so that the seal plate fits into the inner contact surface of the seal case.

7. Install the separator into the housing so that the oil hole faces down.

8. Oil the lips of the seal and install the housing on the rear of the engine block.

9. Remove the engine from the holding fixture and install in vehicle.

1596cc, 1796cc, 1997cc, 2351cc and 2972cc Engines

▶ See Figures 164, 165, 166 and 167

1. Remove the transaxle and clutch from the car as described in Section 7. Remove the flywheel or driveplate and adapter plate.

2. Unbolt and remove the lower bell housing cover from the rear of the engine. Remove the rear plate from the upper portion of the rear of the block.

3. The lower surface of the oil seal case seals against the oil pan gasket or sealer at the rear. On engines with a gasket, carefully separate the gasket from the bottom of the seal case with a moderately sharp instrument. You may want to loosen the oil pan bolts slightly at the rear to make it easier to separate the two surfaces. If the gasket is damaged, the oil pan will have to be removed and the gasket replaced. On vehicles employing sealer, you'll have to unbolt and lower the oil pan now, and then clean both surfaces, apply new sealer, and reinstall the oil pan after Step 7 is completed.

4. Remove the oil seal case bolts, and pull it straight off the rear of the crankshaft. Remove the case gasket.

5. Remove the seal retainer or oil separator from the case, and then pry out the seal. Inspect the sealing surface at the rear of the crankshaft. If a deep groove is worn into the surface, the crankshaft will have to be replaced. Lubricate the sealing surface with clean engine oil.

6. Using a seal installer, install the new seal into the bore of rear oil seal case in such a way that the flat side of the seal will face outward when the case is installed on the engine. The inside of the seal must be flush with the inside surface of the seal case.

7. On all engines except the 2972cc, install the retainer directly over the seal with the small hole located at the bottom. On 2972cc engine, after cleaning the oil case mating surface thoroughly, apply a suitable sealing agent to the oil seal case shaded areas as shown in the figure. Then, install a new gasket onto the block surface and install the seal case to the rear of the block. Torque the seal case bolts to 7–9 ft. lbs. Retorque pan bolts, as necessary. Refill the oil pan if necessary.

8. Install the rear plate and bell housing cover. Install the flywheel or drive plate and the transaxle in reverse of the removal procedure.

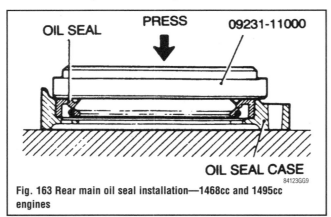

Fig. 163 Rear main oil seal installation—1468cc and 1495cc engines

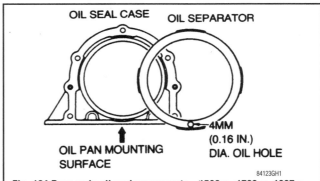

Fig. 164 Rear main oil seal components—1596cc, 1796cc, 1997cc and 2351cc engines

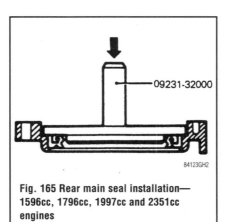

Fig. 165 Rear main seal installation—1596cc, 1796cc, 1997cc and 2351cc engines

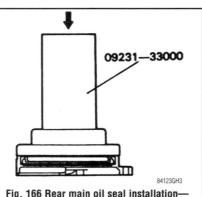

Fig. 166 Rear main oil seal installation—2972cc engine

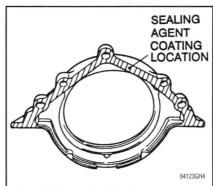

Fig. 167 Rear main oil seal case sealant application points

Flywheel and Ring Gear

REMOVAL & INSTALLATION

♦ **See Figures 168 and 169**

➡ **The ring gear is replaceable only on 1468cc, 1495cc and 2351cc engines mated with a manual transaxle. Engines with automatic transaxles have ring gears which are welded to the flex plate.**

1. Remove the transmission.
2. Remove the clutch, if equipped, or torque converter from the flywheel. The flywheel bolts should be loosened a little at a time in a cross pattern to avoid warping the flywheel. On vehicles with manual transaxle, replace the pilot bearing in the end of the crankshaft if removing the flywheel.

➡ **On 1495cc engines with a manual transaxle, there is a crank angle sensor ring bolted to the flywheel. This ring must be removed before any repairs are done on the flywheel or ring gear.**

3. The flywheel should be checked for cracks and glazing. It can be resurfaced by a machine shop.
4. If the ring gear is to be replaced, drill a hole in the gear between two teeth, being careful not to contact the flywheel surface. Using a cold chisel at this point, crack the ring gear and remove it.
5. Polish the inner surface of the new ring gear and heat it in an oven to about 316°C. Quickly place the ring gear on the flywheel and tap it into place, making sure that it is fully seated. Use proper hand protection when handling the flywheel.

➡ **Never heat the ring gear past 426°C, or the tempering will be destroyed.**

6. Position the flywheel on the end of the crankshaft. Torque the bolts a little at a time, in a cross pattern, to the torque figure shown in the Torque Specifications Chart. On 1495cc engines with a manual transaxle, install the crank angle sensor ring and tighten the mounting bolts to 8.6–10.8 ft. lbs. (12–15 Nm).
7. Install the clutch or torque converter.
8. Install the transmission and transfer case.

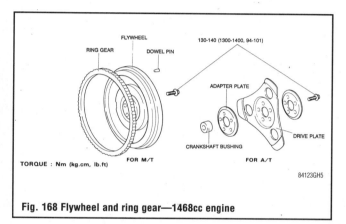

Fig. 168 Flywheel and ring gear—1468cc engine

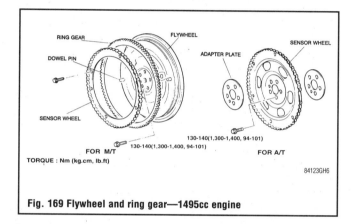

Fig. 169 Flywheel and ring gear—1495cc engine

EXHAUST SYSTEM

♦ **See Figures 170 thru 175**

Main (Rear) Muffler

➡ **On all cars, the tail pipe is one piece with the main muffler.**

REMOVAL & INSTALLATION

1. Raise and support the rear end on jackstands, placed under the frame, so that the wheels hang freely.
2. Unbolt the muffler inlet pipe from the catalytic converter. It may be necessary to spray the joint liberally with a penetrant/rust dissolver compound such as Liquid Wrench, WD-40, or equivalent.
3. Remove the muffler from the rubber hangers.
4. When installing the new muffler, make sure that the muffler and pipe are properly aligned and not in contact with any body or suspension part before tightening the joint. Use new flange gaskets. Torque the nuts to the specifications given in the illustrations.
5. Start the engine and check for exhaust leaks.

Exhaust (Intermediate) Pipe

REMOVAL & INSTALLATION

1. Raise and support the rear end on jackstands.
2. Unhook the exhaust pipe support ring from the bracket located towards the rear of the vehicle and just forward of the muffler.
3. Unbolt the main support bracket from the underside of the floor.

4. Remove the clamp securing the exhaust pipe to the front muffler and remove the hanger bracket from the catalytic converter joint. It may be necessary to spray the joint liberally with a penetrant/rust dissolver compound such as Liquid Wrench®, WD-40®, or equivalent.
5. Separate the pipe from the catalytic converter and the muffler. It may be necessary to use a chisel to open the muffler outlet pipe end. In this case, the muffler will have to be replaced.
6. When installing the new intermediate exhaust pipe, make certain that all parts are properly aligned before tightening any fasteners. Torque the nuts to the specifications given in the illustrations. Start the engine and check for exhaust leaks.

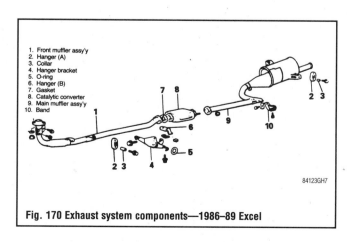

1. Front muffler assy'y
2. Hanger (A)
3. Collar
4. Hanger bracket
5. O-ring
6. Hanger (B)
7. Gasket
8. Catalytic converter
9. Main muffler assy'y
10. Band

Fig. 170 Exhaust system components—1986–89 Excel

Front Exhaust Pipe and Front Muffler Assembly (Head Pipe)

REMOVAL & INSTALLATION

1. Raise and support the car on jackstands.
2. Remove the engine undercover.
3. Disconnect the front pipe at the converter.
4. Remove the rubber supporter from the hanger bracket.

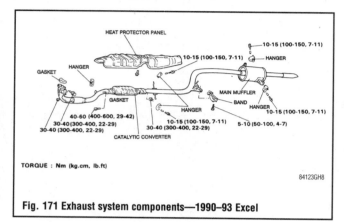

Fig. 171 Exhaust system components—1990–93 Excel

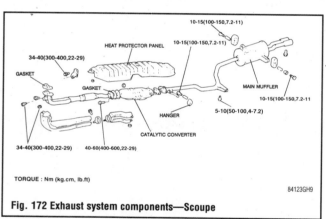

Fig. 172 Exhaust system components—Scoupe

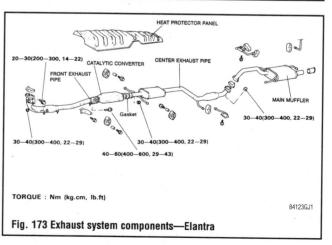

Fig. 173 Exhaust system components—Elantra

5. Remove the head pipe support clamp.
6. Disconnect the front pipe at the manifold(s).
7. To install, raise the pipe into position on the manifold and converter and install the attaching hardware. Make sure the pipe is properly aligned. Torque the nuts to the specifications given in the illustrations.
8. Start the engine and check for exhaust leaks.

Catalytic Converter

REMOVAL & INSTALLATION

1. Raise and support the rear end on jackstands.
2. Unbolt the muffler inlet pipe from the catalytic converter. It may be necessary to spray the joint liberally with a penetrant/rust dissolver compound such as Liquid Wrench®, WD-40®, or equivalent.
3. Support the front (head) pipe and remove the rubber support ring from the hanger bracket.
4. Unbolt the converter from the front pipe. On Sonata, remove the hanger bracket first.
5. Position the replacement converter in the system and connect it to the muffler inlet pipe.
6. Connect it to the head pipe, make sure that the converter is properly positioned and tighten converter-to-exhaust pipe nuts. On Sonata, torque the hanger bracket bolts
7. Lower the car. Start the engine and check for exhaust leaks.

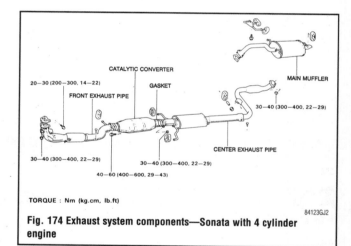

Fig. 174 Exhaust system components—Sonata with 4 cylinder engine

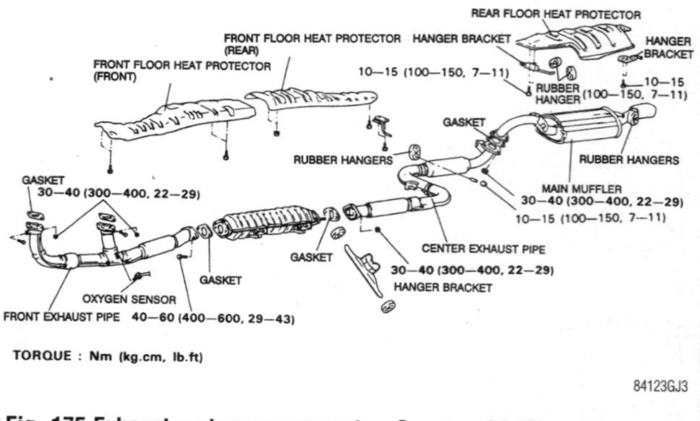

Fig. 175 Exhaust system components—Sonata with V6 engine

ENGINE RECONDITIONING

Determining Engine Condition

Anything that generates heat and/or friction will eventually burn or wear out (for example, a light bulb generates heat, therefore its life span is limited). With this in mind, a running engine generates tremendous amounts of both; friction is encountered by the moving and rotating parts inside the engine and heat is created by friction and combustion of the fuel. However, the engine has systems designed to help reduce the effects of heat and friction and provide added longevity. The oiling system reduces the amount of friction encountered by the moving parts inside the engine, while the cooling system reduces heat created by friction and combustion. If either system is not maintained, a break-down will be inevitable. Therefore, you can see how regular maintenance can affect the service life of your vehicle. If you do not drain, flush and refill your cooling system at the proper intervals, deposits will begin to accumulate in the radiator, thereby reducing the amount of heat it can extract from the coolant. The same applies to your oil and filter; if it is not changed often enough it becomes laden with contaminates and is unable to properly lubricate the engine. This increases friction and wear.

There are a number of methods for evaluating the condition of your engine. A compression test can reveal the condition of your pistons, piston rings, cylinder bores, head gasket(s), valves and valve seats. An oil pressure test can warn you of possible engine bearing, or oil pump failures. Excessive oil consumption, evidence of oil in the engine air intake area and/or bluish smoke from the tailpipe may indicate worn piston rings, worn valve guides and/or valve seals. As a general rule, an engine that uses no more than one quart of oil every 1000 miles is in good condition. Engines that use one quart of oil or more in less than 1000 miles should first be checked for oil leaks. If any oil leaks are present, have them fixed before determining how much oil is consumed by the engine, especially if blue smoke is not visible at the tailpipe.

COMPRESSION TEST

▶ **See Figure 176**

A noticeable lack of engine power, excessive oil consumption and/or poor fuel mileage measured over an extended period are all indicators of internal engine wear. Worn piston rings, scored or worn cylinder bores, blown head gaskets, sticking or burnt valves, and worn valve seats are all possible culprits. A check of each cylinder's compression will help locate the problem.

➡**A screw-in type compression gauge is more accurate than the type you simply hold against the spark plug hole. Although it takes slightly longer to use, it's worth the effort to obtain a more accurate reading.**

1. Make sure that the proper amount and viscosity of engine oil is in the crankcase, then ensure the battery is fully charged.
2. Warm-up the engine to normal operating temperature, then shut the engine **OFF**.
3. Disable the ignition system.
4. Label and disconnect all of the spark plug wires from the plugs.
5. Thoroughly clean the cylinder head area around the spark plug ports, then remove the spark plugs.

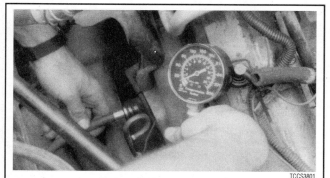

Fig. 176 A screw-in type compression gauge is more accurate and easier to use without an assistant

TCCS3801

6. Set the throttle plate to the fully open (wide-open throttle) position. You can block the accelerator linkage open for this, or you can have an assistant fully depress the accelerator pedal.
7. Install a screw-in type compression gauge into the No. 1 spark plug hole until the fitting is snug.

✳✳ WARNING

Be careful not to crossthread the spark plug hole.

8. According to the tool manufacturer's instructions, connect a remote starting switch to the starting circuit.
9. With the ignition switch in the **OFF** position, use the remote starting switch to crank the engine through at least five compression strokes (approximately 5 seconds of cranking) and record the highest reading on the gauge.
10. Repeat the test on each cylinder, cranking the engine approximately the same number of compression strokes and/or time as the first.
11. Compare the highest readings from each cylinder to that of the others. The indicated compression pressures are considered within specifications if the lowest reading cylinder is within 75 percent of the pressure recorded for the highest reading cylinder. For example, if your highest reading cylinder pressure was 150 psi (1034 kPa), then 75 percent of that would be 113 psi (779 kPa). So the lowest reading cylinder should be no less than 113 psi (779 kPa).
12. If a cylinder exhibits an unusually low compression reading, pour a tablespoon of clean engine oil into the cylinder through the spark plug hole and repeat the compression test. If the compression rises after adding oil, it means that the cylinder's piston rings and/or cylinder bore are damaged or worn. If the pressure remains low, the valves may not be seating properly (a valve job is needed), or the head gasket may be blown near that cylinder. If compression in any two adjacent cylinders is low, and if the addition of oil doesn't help raise compression, there is leakage past the head gasket. Oil and coolant in the combustion chamber, combined with blue or constant white smoke from the tailpipe, are symptoms of this problem. However, don't be alarmed by the normal white smoke emitted from the tailpipe during engine warm-up or from cold weather driving. There may be evidence of water droplets on the engine dipstick and/or oil droplets in the cooling system if a head gasket is blown.

OIL PRESSURE TEST

Check for proper oil pressure at the sending unit passage with an externally mounted mechanical oil pressure gauge (as opposed to relying on a factory installed dash-mounted gauge). A tachometer may also be needed, as some specifications may require running the engine at a specific rpm.

1. With the engine cold, locate and remove the oil pressure sending unit.
2. Following the manufacturer's instructions, connect a mechanical oil pressure gauge and, if necessary, a tachometer to the engine.
3. Start the engine and allow it to idle.
4. Check the oil pressure reading when cold and record the number. You may need to run the engine at a specified rpm, so check the specifications.
5. Run the engine until normal operating temperature is reached (upper radiator hose will feel warm).
6. Check the oil pressure reading again with the engine hot and record the number. Turn the engine **OFF**.
7. Compare your hot oil pressure reading to specification. If the reading is low, check the cold pressure reading against the chart. If the cold pressure is well above the specification, and the hot reading was lower than the specification, you may have the wrong viscosity oil in the engine. Change the oil, making sure to use the proper grade and quantity, then repeat the test.

Low oil pressure readings could be attributed to internal component wear, pump related problems, a low oil level, or oil viscosity that is too low. High oil pressure readings could be caused by an overfilled crankcase, too high of an oil viscosity or a faulty pressure relief valve.

Buy or Rebuild?

Now if you have determined that your engine is worn out, you must make some decisions. The question of whether or not an engine is worth rebuilding is largely a subjective matter and one of personal worth. Is the engine a popular one, or is it an obsolete model? Are parts available? Will it get acceptable gas mileage once it is rebuilt? Is the car it's being put into worth keeping? Would it be less expensive to buy a new engine, have your engine rebuilt by a pro, rebuild it yourself or buy a used engine from a salvage yard? Or would it be simpler and less expensive to buy another car? If you have considered all these matters, and have still decided to rebuild the engine, then it is time to decide how you will rebuild it.

➡️**The editors at Chilton feel that most engine machining should be performed by a professional machine shop. Think of it as an assurance that the job has been done right the first time. There are many expensive and specialized tools required to perform such tasks as boring and honing an engine block or having a valve job done on a cylinder head. Even inspecting the parts requires expensive micrometers and gauges to properly measure wear and clearances. A machine shop can deliver to you clean, and ready to assemble parts, saving you time and aggravation. Your maximum savings will come from performing the removal, disassembly, assembly and installation of the engine and purchasing or renting only the tools required to perform these tasks.**

A complete rebuild or overhaul of an engine involves replacing all of the moving parts (pistons, rods, crankshaft, camshaft, etc.) with new ones and machining the non-moving wearing surfaces of the block and heads. Unfortunately, this may not be cost effective. For instance, your crankshaft may have been damaged or worn, but it can be machined undersize for a minimal fee.

So although you can replace everything inside the engine, it is usually wiser to replace only those parts which are really needed, and, if possible, repair the more expensive ones. Later in this section, we will break the engine down into its two main components: the cylinder head and the engine block. We will discuss each component, and the recommended parts to replace during a rebuild on each.

Engine Overhaul Tips

Most engine overhaul procedures are fairly standard. In addition to specific parts replacement procedures and specifications for your individual engine, this section is also a guide to acceptable rebuilding procedures. Examples of standard rebuilding practice are given and should be used along with specific details concerning your particular engine.

Competent and accurate machine shop services will ensure maximum performance, reliability and engine life. In most instances it is more profitable for the do-it-yourself mechanic to remove, clean and inspect the component, buy the necessary parts and deliver these to a shop for actual machine work.

Much of the assembly work (crankshaft, bearings, piston rods, and other components) is well within the scope of the do-it-yourself mechanic's tools and abilities. You will have to decide for yourself the depth of involvement you desire in an engine repair or rebuild.

TOOLS

The tools required for an engine overhaul or parts replacement will depend on the depth of your involvement. With a few exceptions, they will be the tools found in a mechanic's tool kit (see Section 1 of this manual). More in-depth work will require some or all of the following:

- A dial indicator (reading in thousandths) mounted on a universal base
- Micrometers and telescope gauges
- Jaw and screw-type pullers
- Scraper
- Valve spring compressor
- Ring groove cleaner
- Piston ring expander and compressor
- Ridge reamer
- Cylinder hone or glaze breaker
- Plastigage®
- Engine stand

The use of most of these tools is illustrated in this section. Many can be rented for a one-time use from a local parts jobber or tool supply house specializing in automotive work.

Occasionally, the use of special tools is called for. See the information on Special Tools and the Safety Notice in the front of this book before substituting another tool.

OVERHAUL TIPS

Aluminum has become extremely popular for use in engines, due to its low weight. Observe the following precautions when handling aluminum parts:
- Never hot tank aluminum parts (the caustic hot tank solution will eat the aluminum.)
- Remove all aluminum parts (identification tag, etc.) from engine parts prior to the tanking.
- Always coat threads lightly with engine oil or anti-seize compounds before installation, to prevent seizure.
- Never overtighten bolts or spark plugs especially in aluminum threads.

When assembling the engine, any parts that will be exposed to frictional contact must be prelubed to provide lubrication at initial start-up. Any product specifically formulated for this purpose can be used, but engine oil is not recommended as a prelube in most cases.

When semi-permanent (locked, but removable) installation of bolts or nuts is desired, threads should be cleaned and coated with Loctite® or another similar, commercial non-hardening sealant.

CLEANING

♦ **See Figures 177, 178, 179 and 180**

Before the engine and its components are inspected, they must be thoroughly cleaned. You will need to remove any engine varnish, oil sludge and/or carbon deposits from all of the components to insure an accurate inspection. A crack in the engine block or cylinder head can easily become overlooked if hidden by a layer of sludge or carbon.

Most of the cleaning process can be carried out with common hand tools and readily available solvents or solutions. Carbon deposits can be chipped away using a hammer and a hard wooden chisel. Old gasket material and varnish or sludge can usually be removed using a scraper and/or cleaning solvent. Extremely stubborn deposits may require the use of a power drill with a wire brush. If using a wire brush, use extreme care around any critical machined surfaces (such as the gasket surfaces, bearing saddles, cylinder bores, etc.). USE OF A WIRE BRUSH IS NOT RECOMMENDED ON ANY ALUMINUM COMPONENTS. Always follow any safety recommendations given by the manufacturer of the tool and/or solvent.

❊❊ CAUTION

Always wear eye protection during any cleaning process involving scraping, chipping or spraying of solvents.

An alternative to the mess and hassle of cleaning the parts yourself is to drop them off at a local garage or machine shop. They should have the necessary equipment to properly clean all of the parts for a nominal fee.

Remove any oil galley plugs, freeze plugs and/or pressed-in bearings and carefully wash and degrease all of the engine components including the fasteners and bolts. Small parts such as the valves, springs, etc., should be placed in a metal basket and allowed to soak. Use pipe cleaner type brushes, and clean all passageways in the components.

Use a ring expander and remove the rings from the pistons. Clean the piston ring grooves with a special tool or a piece of broken ring. Scrape the carbon off of the top of the piston. You should never use a wire brush on the pistons. After preparing all of the piston assemblies in this manner, wash and degrease them again.

❊❊ WARNING

Use extreme care when cleaning around the cylinder head valve seats. A mistake or slip may cost you a new seat.

When cleaning the cylinder head, remove carbon from the combustion chamber with the valves installed. This will avoid damaging the valve seats.

REPAIRING DAMAGED THREADS

♦ **See Figures 181, 182, 183, 184 and 185**

Several methods of repairing damaged threads are available. Heli-Coil® (shown here), Keenserts® and Microdot® are among the most widely used. All involve basically the same principle—drilling out stripped threads, tapping the

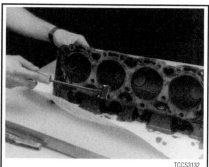
Fig. 177 Use a gasket scraper to remove the old gasket material from the mating surfaces

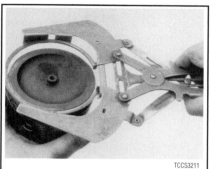
Fig. 178 Before cleaning and inspection, use a ring expander tool to remove the piston rings

Fig. 179 Clean the piston ring grooves using a ring groove cleaner tool, or . . .

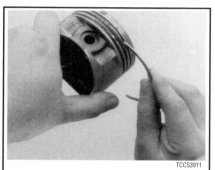
Fig. 180 . . . use a piece of an old ring to clean the grooves. Be careful, the ring can be quite sharp

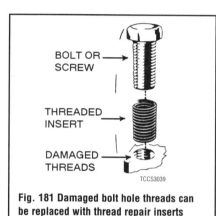
Fig. 181 Damaged bolt hole threads can be replaced with thread repair inserts

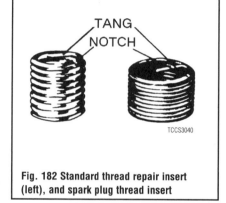
Fig. 182 Standard thread repair insert (left), and spark plug thread insert

Fig. 183 Drill out the damaged threads with the specified size bit. Be sure to drill completely through the hole or to the bottom of a blind hole

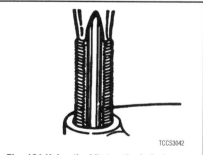
Fig. 184 Using the kit, tap the hole in order to receive the thread insert. Keep the tap well oiled and back it out frequently to avoid clogging the threads

Fig. 185 Screw the insert onto the installer tool until the tang engages the slot. Thread the insert into the hole until it is ¼–½ turn below the top surface, then remove the tool and break off the tang using a punch

hole and installing a prewound insert—making welding, plugging and oversize fasteners unnecessary.

Two types of thread repair inserts are usually supplied: a standard type for most inch coarse, inch fine, metric course and metric fine thread sizes and a spark lug type to fit most spark plug port sizes. Consult the individual tool manufacturer's catalog to determine exact applications. Typical thread repair kits will contain a selection of prewound threaded inserts, a tap (corresponding to the outside diameter threads of the insert) and an installation tool. Spark plug inserts usually differ because they require a tap equipped with pilot threads and a combined reamer/tap section. Most manufacturers also supply blister-packed thread repair inserts separately in addition to a master kit containing a variety of taps and inserts plus installation tools.

Before attempting to repair a threaded hole, remove any snapped, broken or damaged bolts or studs. Penetrating oil can be used to free frozen threads. The offending item can usually be removed with locking pliers or using a screw/stud extractor. After the hole is clear, the thread can be repaired as shown in the kit manufacturer's instructions.

Engine Preparation

To properly rebuild an engine, you must first remove it from the vehicle, then disassemble and diagnose it. Ideally you should place your engine on an engine stand. This affords you the best access to the engine components. Remove the flywheel or flexplate before installing the engine to the stand.

Now that you have the engine on a stand, and assuming that you have drained the oil and coolant from the engine, it's time to strip it of all but the necessary components. Before you start disassembling the engine, you may want to take a moment to draw some pictures, or fabricate some labels or containers to mark the locations of various components and the bolts and/or studs which fasten them. Modern day engines use a lot of little brackets and clips which hold wiring harnesses and such, and these holders are often mounted on studs and/or bolts that can be easily mixed up. The manufacturer spent a lot of time and money designing your vehicle, and they wouldn't have wasted any of it by haphazardly placing brackets, clips or fasteners on the vehicle. If it's present when you disassemble it, put it back when you assemble, you will regret not remembering that little bracket which holds a wire harness out of the path of a rotating part.

You should begin by unbolting any accessories still attached to the engine, such as the water pump, power steering pump, alternator, etc. Then, unfasten any manifolds (intake or exhaust) which were not removed during the engine removal procedure. Finally, remove any covers remaining on the engine such as the rocker arm, front or timing cover and oil pan. Some front covers may require the vibration damper and/or crank pulley to be removed beforehand. The idea is to reduce the engine to the bare necessities of cylinder head(s), valve train, engine block, crankshaft, pistons and connecting rods, plus any other `in block' components such as oil pumps, balance shafts and auxiliary shafts.

Finally, remove the cylinder head(s) from the engine block and carefully place on a bench. Disassembly instructions for each component follow later in this section.

Cylinder Head

There are two basic types of cylinder heads used on today's automobiles: the Overhead Valve (OHV) and the Overhead Camshaft (OHC). The latter can also be broken down into two subgroups: the Single Overhead Camshaft (SOHC) and the Dual Overhead Camshaft (DOHC). Generally, if there is only a single camshaft on a head, it is just referred to as an OHC head. Also, an engine with an OHV cylinder head is also known as a pushrod engine.

Most cylinder heads these days are made of an aluminum alloy due to its light weight, durability and heat transfer qualities. However, cast iron was the material of choice in the past, and is still used on many vehicles. Whether made from aluminum or iron, all cylinder heads have valves and seats. Some use two valves per cylinder, while the more hi-tech engines will utilize a multi-valve configuration using 3, 4 and even 5 valves per cylinder. When the valve contacts the seat, it does so on precision machined surfaces, which seals the combustion chamber. All cylinder heads have a valve guide for each valve. The guide centers the valve to the seat and allows it to move up and down within it. The clearance between the valve and guide can be critical. Too much clearance and the engine may consume oil, lose vacuum and/or damage the seat. Too little, and the valve can stick in the guide causing the engine to run poorly if at all,

and possibly causing severe damage. The last component all automotive cylinder heads have are valve springs. The spring holds the valve against its seat. It also returns the valve to this position when the valve has been opened by the valve train or camshaft. The spring is fastened to the valve by a retainer and valve locks (sometimes called keepers). Aluminum heads will also have a valve spring shim to keep the spring from wearing away the aluminum.

An ideal method of rebuilding the cylinder head would involve replacing all of the valves, guides, seats, springs, etc. with new ones. However, depending on how the engine was maintained, often this is not necessary. A major cause of valve, guide and seat wear is an improperly tuned engine. An engine that is running too rich, will often wash the lubricating oil out of the guide with gasoline, causing it to wear rapidly. Conversely, an engine which is running too lean will place higher combustion temperatures on the valves and seats allowing them to wear or even burn. Springs fall victim to the driving habits of the individual. A driver who often runs the engine rpm to the redline will wear out or break the springs faster then one that stays well below it. Unfortunately, mileage takes it toll on all of the parts. Generally, the valves, guides, springs and seats in a cylinder head can be machined and re-used, saving you money. However, if a valve is burnt, it may be wise to replace all of the valves, since they were all operating in the same environment. The same goes for any other component on the cylinder head. Think of it as an insurance policy against future problems related to that component.

Unfortunately, the only way to find out which components need replacing, is to disassemble and carefully check each piece. After the cylinder head(s) are disassembled, thoroughly clean all of the components.

DISASSEMBLY

OHV Heads

▶ See Figures 186 thru 191

Before disassembling the cylinder head, you may want to fabricate some containers to hold the various parts, as some of them can be quite small (such as keepers) and easily lost. Also keeping yourself and the components organized will aid in assembly and reduce confusion. Where possible, try to main-

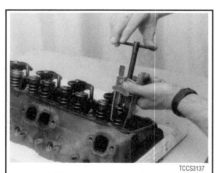

Fig. 186 When removing an OHV valve spring, use a compressor tool to relieve the tension from the retainer

Fig. 187 A small magnet will help in removal of the valve locks

Fig. 188 Be careful not to lose the small valve locks (keepers)

Fig. 189 Remove the valve seal from the valve stem—O-ring type seal shown

Fig. 190 Removing an umbrella/positive type seal

Fig. 191 Invert the cylinder head and withdraw the valve from the valve guide bore

tain a components original location; this is especially important if there is not going to be any machine work performed on the components.

1. If you haven't already removed the rocker arms and/or shafts, do so now.

2. Position the head so that the springs are easily accessed.

3. Use a valve spring compressor tool, and relieve spring tension from the retainer.

➡**Due to engine varnish, the retainer may stick to the valve locks. A gentle tap with a hammer may help to break it loose.**

4. Remove the valve locks from the valve tip and/or retainer. A small magnet may help in removing the locks.

5. Lift the valve spring, tool and all, off of the valve stem.

6. If equipped, remove the valve seal. If the seal is difficult to remove with the valve in place, try removing the valve first, then the seal. Follow the steps below for valve removal.

7. Position the head to allow access for withdrawing the valve.

➡**Cylinder heads that have seen a lot of miles and/or abuse may have mushroomed the valve lock grove and/or tip, causing difficulty in removal of the valve. If this has happened, use a metal file to carefully remove the high spots around the lock grooves and/or tip. Only file it enough to allow removal.**

8. Remove the valve from the cylinder head.

9. If equipped, remove the valve spring shim. A small magnetic tool or screwdriver will aid in removal.

10. Repeat Steps 3 though 9 until all of the valves have been removed.

OHC Heads

▸ **See Figures 192 and 193**

Whether it is a single or dual overhead camshaft cylinder head, the disassembly procedure is relatively unchanged. One aspect to pay attention to is careful labeling of the parts on the dual camshaft cylinder head. There will be an intake camshaft and followers as well as an exhaust camshaft and followers and they must be labeled as such. In some cases, the components are identical and could easily be installed incorrectly. DO NOT MIX THEM UP! Determining which is which is very simple; the intake camshaft and components are on the same side of the head as was the intake manifold. Conversely, the exhaust

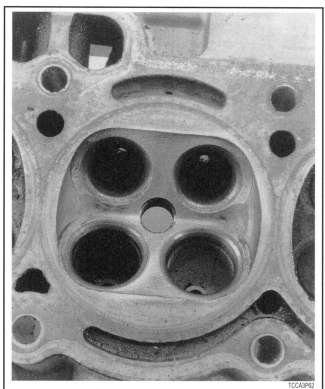

Fig. 193 Example of a multi-valve cylinder head. Note how it has 2 intake and 2 exhaust valve ports

camshaft and components are on the same side of the head as was the exhaust manifold.

CUP TYPE CAMSHAFT FOLLOWERS

▸ **See Figures 194, 195 and 196**

Most cylinder heads with cup type camshaft followers will have the valve spring, retainer and locks recessed within the follower's bore. You will need a C-clamp style valve spring compressor tool, an OHC spring removal tool (or equivalent) and a small magnet to disassemble the head.

1. If not already removed, remove the camshaft(s) and/or followers. Mark their positions for assembly.

2. Position the cylinder head to allow use of a C-clamp style valve spring compressor tool.

➡**It is preferred to position the cylinder head gasket surface facing you with the valve springs facing the opposite direction and the head laying horizontal.**

Fig. 192 Exploded view of a valve, seal, spring, retainer and locks from an OHC cylinder head

Fig. 194 C-clamp type spring compressor and an OHC spring removal tool (center) for cup type followers

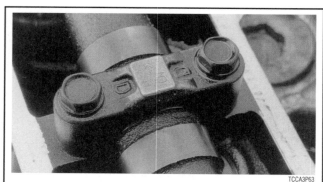

Fig. 195 Most cup type follower cylinder heads retain the camshaft using bolt-on bearing caps

Fig. 196 Position the OHC spring tool in the follower bore, then compress the spring with a C-clamp type tool

3. With the OHC spring removal adapter tool positioned inside of the follower bore, compress the valve spring using the C-clamp style valve spring compressor.

4. Remove the valve locks. A small magnetic tool or screwdriver will aid in removal.

5. Release the compressor tool and remove the spring assembly.

6. Withdraw the valve from the cylinder head.

7. If equipped, remove the valve seal.

➡**Special valve seal removal tools are available. Regular or needlenose type pliers, if used with care, will work just as well. If using ordinary pliers, be sure not to damage the follower bore. The follower and its bore are machined to close tolerances and any damage to the bore will effect this relationship.**

8. If equipped, remove the valve spring shim. A small magnetic tool or screwdriver will aid in removal.

9. Repeat Steps 3 through 8 until all of the valves have been removed.

ROCKER ARM TYPE CAMSHAFT FOLLOWERS

▶ **See Figures 197 thru 205**

Most cylinder heads with rocker arm-type camshaft followers are easily disassembled using a standard valve spring compressor. However, certain models may not have enough open space around the spring for the standard tool and may require you to use a C-clamp style compressor tool instead.

1. If not already removed, remove the rocker arms and/or shafts and the camshaft. If applicable, also remove the hydraulic lash adjusters. Mark their positions for assembly.

2. Position the cylinder head to allow access to the valve spring.

3. Use a valve spring compressor tool to relieve the spring tension from the retainer.

➡**Due to engine varnish, the retainer may stick to the valve locks. A gentle tap with a hammer may help to break it loose.**

4. Remove the valve locks from the valve tip and/or retainer. A small magnet may help in removing the small locks.

5. Lift the valve spring, tool and all, off of the valve stem.

6. If equipped, remove the valve seal. If the seal is difficult to remove with the valve in place, try removing the valve first, then the seal. Follow the steps below for valve removal.

7. Position the head to allow access for withdrawing the valve.

➡**Cylinder heads that have seen a lot of miles and/or abuse may have mushroomed the valve lock grove and/or tip, causing difficulty in removal of the valve. If this has happened, use a metal file to carefully remove the high spots around the lock grooves and/or tip. Only file it enough to allow removal.**

8. Remove the valve from the cylinder head.

9. If equipped, remove the valve spring shim. A small magnetic tool or screwdriver will aid in removal.

10. Repeat Steps 3 though 9 until all of the valves have been removed.

Fig. 197 Example of the shaft mounted rocker arms on some OHC heads

Fig. 198 Another example of the rocker arm type OHC head. This model uses a follower under the camshaft

Fig. 199 Before the camshaft can be removed, all of the followers must first be removed . . .

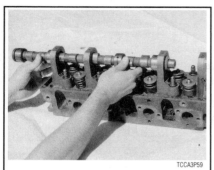

Fig. 200 . . . then the camshaft can be removed by sliding it out (shown), or unbolting a bearing cap (not shown)

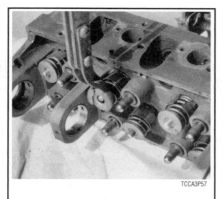

Fig. 201 Compress the valve spring . . .

Fig. 202 . . . then remove the valve locks from the valve stem and spring retainer

Fig. 203 Remove the valve spring and retainer from the cylinder head

Fig. 204 Remove the valve seal from the guide. Some gentle prying or pliers may help to remove stubborn ones

Fig. 205 All aluminum and some cast iron heads will have these valve spring shims. Remove all of them as well

INSPECTION

Now that all of the cylinder head components are clean, it's time to inspect them for wear and/or damage. To accurately inspect them, you will need some specialized tools:

- A 0–1 in. micrometer for the valves
- A dial indicator or inside diameter gauge for the valve guides
- A spring pressure test gauge

If you do not have access to the proper tools, you may want to bring the components to a shop that does.

Valves

♦ See Figures 206 and 207

The first thing to inspect are the valve heads. Look closely at the head, margin and face for any cracks, excessive wear or burning. The margin is the best place to look for burning. It should have a squared edge with an even width all around the diameter. When a valve burns, the margin will look melted and the edges rounded. Also inspect the valve head for any signs of tulipping. This will show as a lifting of the edges or dishing in the center of the head and will usually not occur to all of the valves. All of the heads should look the same, any that seem dished more than others are probably bad. Next, inspect the valve lock grooves and valve tips. Check for any burrs around the lock grooves, especially if you had to file them to remove the valve. Valve tips should appear flat, although slight rounding with high mileage engines is normal. Slightly worn valve tips will need to be machined flat. Last, measure the valve stem diameter with the micrometer. Measure the area that rides within the guide, especially towards the tip where most of the wear occurs. Take several measurements along its length and compare them to each other. Wear should be even along the length with little to no taper. If no minimum diameter is given in the specifications, then the stem should not read more than 0.001 in. (0.025mm) below the unworn portion of the stem. Any valves that fail these inspections should be replaced.

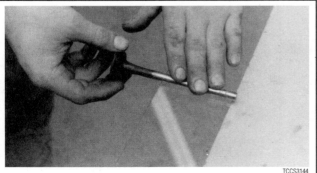

Fig. 206 Valve stems may be rolled on a flat surface to check for bends

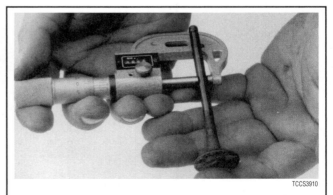

Fig. 207 Use a micrometer to check the valve stem diameter

Springs, Retainers and Valve Locks

▶ See Figures 208 and 209

The first thing to check is the most obvious, broken springs. Next check the free length and squareness of each spring. If applicable, insure to distinguish between intake and exhaust springs. Use a ruler and/or carpenter's square to measure the length. A carpenter's square should be used to check the springs for squareness. If a spring pressure test gauge is available, check each springs rating and compare to the specifications chart. Check the readings against the specifications given. Any springs that fail these inspections should be replaced.

The spring retainers rarely need replacing, however they should still be checked as a precaution. Inspect the spring mating surface and the valve lock retention area for any signs of excessive wear. Also check for any signs of cracking. Replace any retainers that are questionable.

Valve locks should be inspected for excessive wear on the outside contact area as well as on the inner notched surface. Any locks which appear worn or broken and its respective valve should be replaced.

Cylinder Head

There are several things to check on the cylinder head: valve guides, seats, cylinder head surface flatness, cracks and physical damage.

VALVE GUIDES

▶ See Figure 210

Now that you know the valves are good, you can use them to check the guides, although a new valve, if available, is preferred. Before you measure anything, look at the guides carefully and inspect them for any cracks, chips or breakage. Also if the guide is a removable style (as in most aluminum heads), check them for any looseness or evidence of movement. All of the guides should appear to be at the same height from the spring seat. If any seem lower (or higher) from another, the guide has moved. Mount a dial indicator onto the spring side of the cylinder head. Lightly oil the valve stem and insert it into the cylinder head. Position the dial indicator against the valve stem near the tip and

zero the gauge. Grasp the valve stem and wiggle towards and away from the dial indicator and observe the readings. Mount the dial indicator 90 degrees from the initial point and zero the gauge and again take a reading. Compare the two readings for an out of round condition. Check the readings against the specifications given. An Inside Diameter (I.D.) gauge designed for valve guides will give you an accurate valve guide bore measurement. If the I.D. gauge is used, compare the readings with the specifications given. Any guides that fail these inspections should be replaced or machined.

VALVE SEATS

A visual inspection of the valve seats should show a slightly worn and pitted surface where the valve face contacts the seat. Inspect the seat carefully for severe pitting or cracks. Also, a seat that is badly worn will be recessed into the cylinder head. A severely worn or recessed seat may need to be replaced. All cracked seats must be replaced. A seat concentricity gauge, if available, should be used to check the seat run-out. If run-out exceeds specifications the seat must be machined (if no specification is available given use 0.002 in. or 0.051mm).

CYLINDER HEAD SURFACE FLATNESS

▶ See Figures 211 and 212

After you have cleaned the gasket surface of the cylinder head of any old gasket material, check the head for flatness.

Place a straightedge across the gasket surface. Using feeler gauges, determine the clearance at the center of the straightedge and across the cylinder head at several points. Check along the centerline and diagonally on the head surface. If the warpage exceeds 0.003 in. (0.076mm) within a 6.0 in. (15.2cm) span, or 0.006 in. (0.152mm) over the total length of the head, the cylinder head must be resurfaced. After resurfacing the heads of a V-type engine, the intake manifold flange surface should be checked, and if necessary, milled proportionally to allow for the change in its mounting position.

CRACKS AND PHYSICAL DAMAGE

Generally, cracks are limited to the combustion chamber, however, it is not uncommon for the head to crack in a spark plug hole, port, outside of the head

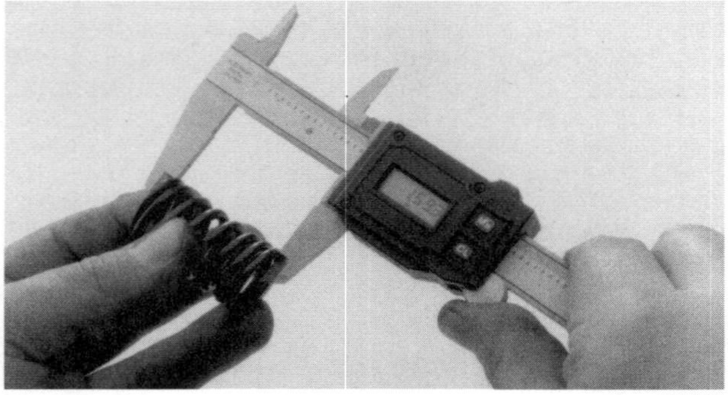

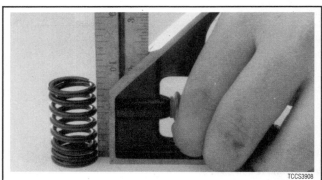
Fig. 209 Check the valve spring for squareness on a flat surface; a carpenter's square can be used

Fig. 208 Use a caliper to check the valve spring free-length

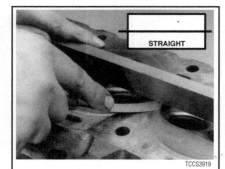
Fig. 211 Check the head for flatness across the center of the head surface using a straightedge and feeler gauge

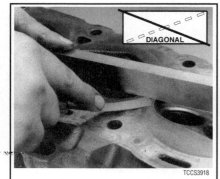
Fig. 212 Checks should also be made along both diagonals of the head surface

Fig. 210 A dial gauge may be used to check valve stem-to-guide clearance; read the gauge while moving the valve stem

or in the valve spring/rocker arm area. The first area to inspect is always the hottest: the exhaust seat/port area.

A visual inspection should be performed, but just because you don't see a crack does not mean it is not there. Some more reliable methods for inspecting for cracks include Magnaflux®, a magnetic process or Zyglo®, a dye penetrant. Magnaflux® is used only on ferrous metal (cast iron) heads. Zyglo® uses a spray on fluorescent mixture along with a black light to reveal the cracks. It is strongly recommended to have your cylinder head checked professionally for cracks, especially if the engine was known to have overheated and/or leaked or consumed coolant. Contact a local shop for availability and pricing of these services.

Physical damage is usually very evident. For example, a broken mounting ear from dropping the head or a bent or broken stud and/or bolt. All of these defects should be fixed or, if unrepairable, the head should be replaced.

Camshaft and Followers

Inspect the camshaft(s) and followers as described earlier in this section.

REFINISHING & REPAIRING

Many of the procedures given for refinishing and repairing the cylinder head components must be performed by a machine shop. Certain steps, if the inspected part is not worn, can be performed yourself inexpensively. However, you spent a lot of time and effort so far, why risk trying to save a couple bucks if you might have to do it all over again?

Valves

Any valves that were not replaced should be refaced and the tips ground flat. Unless you have access to a valve grinding machine, this should be done by a machine shop. If the valves are in extremely good condition, as well as the valve seats and guides, they may be lapped in without performing machine work.

It is a recommended practice to lap the valves even after machine work has been performed and/or new valves have been purchased. This insures a positive seal between the valve and seat.

LAPPING THE VALVES

➡️ Before lapping the valves to the seats, read the rest of the cylinder head section to insure that any related parts are in acceptable enough condition to continue. Also, remember that before any valve seat machining and/or lapping can be performed, the guides must be within factory recommended specifications.

1. Invert the cylinder head.
2. Lightly lubricate the valve stems and insert them into the cylinder head in their numbered order.
3. Raise the valve from the seat and apply a small amount of fine lapping compound to the seat.
4. Moisten the suction head of a hand-lapping tool and attach it to the head of the valve.
5. Rotate the tool between the palms of both hands, changing the position of the valve on the valve seat and lifting the tool often to prevent grooving.
6. Lap the valve until a smooth, polished circle is evident on the valve and seat.
7. Remove the tool and the valve. Wipe away all traces of the grinding compound and store the valve to maintain its lapped location.

✳✳ WARNING

Do not get the valves out of order after they have been lapped. They must be put back with the same valve seat with which they were lapped.

Springs, Retainers and Valve Locks

There is no repair or refinishing possible with the springs, retainers and valve locks. If they are found to be worn or defective, they must be replaced with new (or known good) parts.

Cylinder Head

Most refinishing procedures dealing with the cylinder head must be performed by a machine shop. Read the sections below and review your inspection data to determine whether or not machining is necessary.

VALVE GUIDE

➡️ **If any machining or replacements are made to the valve guides, the seats must be machined.**

Unless the valve guides need machining or replacing, the only service to perform is to thoroughly clean them of any dirt or oil residue.

There are only two types of valve guides used on automobile engines: the replaceable-type (all aluminum heads) and the cast-in integral-type (most cast iron heads). There are four recommended methods for repairing worn guides.
- Knurling
- Inserts
- Reaming oversize
- Replacing

Knurling is a process in which metal is displaced and raised, thereby reducing clearance, giving a true center, and providing oil control. It is the least expensive way of repairing the valve guides. However, it is not necessarily the best, and in some cases, a knurled valve guide will not stand up for more than a short time. It requires a special knurlizer and precision reaming tools to obtain proper clearances. It would not be cost effective to purchase these tools, unless you plan on rebuilding several of the same cylinder head.

Installing a guide insert involves machining the guide to accept a bronze insert. One style is the coil-type which is installed into a threaded guide. Another is the thin-walled insert where the guide is reamed oversize to accept a split-sleeve insert. After the insert is installed, a special tool is then run through the guide to expand the insert, locking it to the guide. The insert is then reamed to the standard size for proper valve clearance.

Reaming for oversize valves restores normal clearances and provides a true valve seat. Most cast-in type guides can be reamed to accept an valve with an oversize stem. The cost factor for this can become quite high as you will need to purchase the reamer and new, oversize stem valves for all guides which were reamed. Oversizes are generally 0.003–0.030 in. (0.076–0.762mm), with 0.015 in. (0.381mm) being the most common.

To replace cast-in type valve guides, they must be drilled out, then reamed to accept replacement guides. This must be done on a fixture which will allow centering and leveling off of the original valve seat or guide, otherwise a serious guide-to-seat misalignment may occur making it impossible to properly machine the seat.

Replaceable-type guides are pressed into the cylinder head. A hammer and a stepped drift or punch may be used to install and remove the guides. Before removing the guides, measure the protrusion on the spring side of the head and record it for installation. Use the stepped drift to hammer out the old guide from the combustion chamber side of the head. When installing, determine whether or not the guide also seals a water jacket in the head, and if it does, use the recommended sealing agent. If there is no water jacket, grease the valve guide and its bore. Use the stepped drift, and hammer the new guide into the cylinder head from the spring side of the cylinder head. A stack of washers the same thickness as the measured protrusion may help the installation process.

VALVE SEATS

➡️ **Before any valve seat machining can be performed, the guides must be within factory recommended specifications. If any machining occurred or if replacements were made to the valve guides, the seats must be machined.**

If the seats are in good condition, the valves can be lapped to the seats, and the cylinder head assembled. See the valves section for instructions on lapping.

If the valve seats are worn, cracked or damaged, they must be serviced by a machine shop. The valve seat must be perfectly centered to the valve guide, which requires very accurate machining.

CYLINDER HEAD SURFACE

If the cylinder head is warped, it must be machined flat. If the warpage is extremely severe, the head may need to be replaced. In some instances, it may be possible to straighten a warped head enough to allow machining. In either case, contact a professional machine shop for service.

➡Any OHC cylinder head that shows excessive warpage should have the camshaft bearing journals align bored after the cylinder head has been resurfaced.

✳✳✳ WARNING

Failure to align bore the camshaft bearing journals could result in severe engine damage including but not limited to: valve and piston damage, connecting rod damage, camshaft and/or crankshaft breakage.

CRACKS AND PHYSICAL DAMAGE

Certain cracks can be repaired in both cast iron and aluminum heads. For cast iron, a tapered threaded insert is installed along the length of the crack. Aluminum can also use the tapered inserts, however welding is the preferred method. Some physical damage can be repaired through brazing or welding. Contact a machine shop to get expert advice for your particular dilemma.

ASSEMBLY

The first step for any assembly job is to have a clean area in which to work. Next, thoroughly clean all of the parts and components that are to be assembled. Finally, place all of the components onto a suitable work space and, if necessary, arrange the parts to their respective positions.

OHV Engines

1. Lightly lubricate the valve stems and insert all of the valves into the cylinder head. If possible, maintain their original locations.
2. If equipped, install any valve spring shims which were removed.
3. If equipped, install the new valve seals, keeping the following in mind:
• If the valve seal presses over the guide, lightly lubricate the outer guide surfaces.
• If the seal is an O-ring type, it is installed just after compressing the spring but before the valve locks.
4. Place the valve spring and retainer over the stem.
5. Position the spring compressor tool and compress the spring.
6. Assemble the valve locks to the stem.
7. Relieve the spring pressure slowly and insure that neither valve lock becomes dislodged by the retainer.
8. Remove the spring compressor tool.
9. Repeat Steps 2 through 8 until all of the springs have been installed.

OHC Engines

▶ See Figure 213

CUP TYPE CAMSHAFT FOLLOWERS

To install the springs, retainers and valve locks on heads which have these components recessed into the camshaft follower's bore, you will need a small screwdriver-type tool, some clean white grease and a lot of patience. You will also need the C-clamp style spring compressor and the OHC tool used to disassemble the head.

1. Lightly lubricate the valve stems and insert all of the valves into the cylinder head. If possible, maintain their original locations.
2. If equipped, install any valve spring shims which were removed.
3. If equipped, install the new valve seals, keeping the following in mind:
• If the valve seal presses over the guide, lightly lubricate the outer guide surfaces.
• If the seal is an O-ring type, it is installed just after compressing the spring but before the valve locks.
4. Place the valve spring and retainer over the stem.
5. Position the spring compressor and the OHC tool, then compress the spring.
6. Using a small screwdriver as a spatula, fill the valve stem side of the lock with white grease. Use the excess grease on the screwdriver to fasten the lock to the driver.
7. Carefully install the valve lock, which is stuck to the end of the screwdriver, to the valve stem then press on it with the screwdriver until the grease squeezes out. The valve lock should now be stuck to the stem.
8. Repeat Steps 6 and 7 for the remaining valve lock.

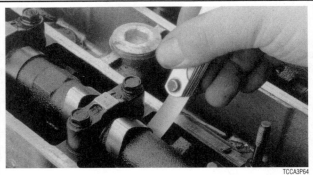

Fig. 213 Once assembled, check the valve clearance and correct as needed

9. Relieve the spring pressure slowly and insure that neither valve lock becomes dislodged by the retainer.
10. Remove the spring compressor tool.
11. Repeat Steps 2 through 10 until all of the springs have been installed.
12. Install the followers, camshaft(s) and any other components that were removed for disassembly.

ROCKER ARM TYPE CAMSHAFT FOLLOWERS

1. Lightly lubricate the valve stems and insert all of the valves into the cylinder head. If possible, maintain their original locations.
2. If equipped, install any valve spring shims which were removed.
3. If equipped, install the new valve seals, keeping the following in mind:
• If the valve seal presses over the guide, lightly lubricate the outer guide surfaces.
• If the seal is an O-ring type, it is installed just after compressing the spring but before the valve locks.
4. Place the valve spring and retainer over the stem.
5. Position the spring compressor tool and compress the spring.
6. Assemble the valve locks to the stem.
7. Relieve the spring pressure slowly and insure that neither valve lock becomes dislodged by the retainer.
8. Remove the spring compressor tool.
9. Repeat Steps 2 through 8 until all of the springs have been installed.
10. Install the camshaft(s), rockers, shafts and any other components that were removed for disassembly.

Engine Block

GENERAL INFORMATION

A thorough overhaul or rebuild of an engine block would include replacing the pistons, rings, bearings, timing belt/chain assembly and oil pump. For OHV engines also include a new camshaft and lifters. The block would then have the cylinders bored and honed oversize (or if using removable cylinder sleeves, new sleeves installed) and the crankshaft would be cut undersize to provide new wearing surfaces and perfect clearances. However, your particular engine may not have everything worn out. What if only the piston rings have worn out and the clearances on everything else are still within factory specifications? Well, you could just replace the rings and put it back together, but this would be a very rare example. Chances are, if one component in your engine is worn, other components are sure to follow, and soon. At the very least, you should always replace the rings, bearings and oil pump. This is what is commonly called a "freshen up".

Cylinder Ridge Removal

Because the top piston ring does not travel to the very top of the cylinder, a ridge is built up between the end of the travel and the top of the cylinder bore.

Pushing the piston and connecting rod assembly past the ridge can be difficult, and damage to the piston ring lands could occur. If the ridge is not removed before installing a new piston or not removed at all, piston ring breakage and piston damage may occur.

➡It is always recommended that you remove any cylinder ridges before removing the piston and connecting rod assemblies. If you know that new pistons are going to be installed and the engine block will be bored oversize, you may be able to forego this step. However, some ridges may actually prevent the assemblies from being removed, necessitating its removal.

There are several different types of ridge reamers on the market, none of which are inexpensive. Unless a great deal of engine rebuilding is anticipated, borrow or rent a reamer.
1. Turn the crankshaft until the piston is at the bottom of its travel.
2. Cover the head of the piston with a rag.
3. Follow the tool manufacturers instructions and cut away the ridge, exercising extreme care to avoid cutting too deeply.
4. Remove the ridge reamer, the rag and as many of the cuttings as possible. Continue until all of the cylinder ridges have been removed.

DISASSEMBLY

▶ See Figures 214 and 215

The engine disassembly instructions following assume that you have the engine mounted on an engine stand. If not, it is easiest to disassemble the engine on a bench or the floor with it resting on the bell housing or transmission mounting surface. You must be able to access the connecting rod fasteners and turn the crankshaft during disassembly. Also, all engine covers (timing, front, side, oil pan, whatever) should have already been removed. Engines which are seized or locked up may not be able to be completely disassembled, and a core (salvage yard) engine should be purchased.

OHV Engines

If not done during the cylinder head removal, remove the pushrods and lifters, keeping them in order for assembly. Remove the timing gears and/or timing chain assembly, then remove the oil pump drive assembly and withdraw the camshaft from the engine block. Remove the oil pick-up and pump assembly. If equipped, remove any balance or auxiliary shafts. If necessary, remove the cylinder ridge from the top of the bore. See the cylinder ridge removal procedure earlier in this section.

OHC Engines

If not done during the cylinder head removal, remove the timing chain/belt and/or gear/sprocket assembly. Remove the oil pick-up and pump assembly and, if necessary, the pump drive. If equipped, remove any balance or auxiliary shafts. If necessary, remove the cylinder ridge from the top of the bore. See the cylinder ridge removal procedure earlier in this section.

All Engines

Rotate the engine over so that the crankshaft is exposed. Use a number punch or scribe and mark each connecting rod with its respective cylinder number. The cylinder closest to the front of the engine is always number 1. However, depending on the engine placement, the front of the engine could either be the

Fig. 214 Place rubber hose over the connecting rod studs to protect the crankshaft and cylinder bores from damage

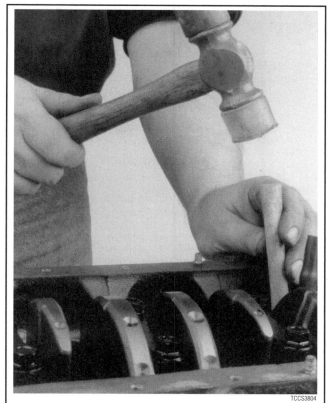

Fig. 215 Carefully tap the piston out of the bore using a wooden dowel

flywheel or damper/pulley end. Generally the front of the engine faces the front of the vehicle. Use a number punch or scribe and also mark the main bearing caps from front to rear with the front most cap being number 1 (if there are five caps, mark them 1 through 5, front to rear).

✳✳ WARNING

Take special care when pushing the connecting rod up from the crankshaft because the sharp threads of the rod bolts/studs will score the crankshaft journal. Insure that special plastic caps are installed over them, or cut two pieces of rubber hose to do the same.

Again, rotate the engine, this time to position the number one cylinder bore (head surface) up. Turn the crankshaft until the number one piston is at the bottom of its travel, this should allow the maximum access to its connecting rod. Remove the number one connecting rods fasteners and cap and place two lengths of rubber hose over the rod bolts/studs to protect the crankshaft from damage. Using a sturdy wooden dowel and a hammer, push the connecting rod up about 1 in. (25mm) from the crankshaft and remove the upper bearing insert. Continue pushing or tapping the connecting rod up until the piston rings are out of the cylinder bore. Remove the piston and rod by hand, put the upper half of the bearing insert back into the rod, install the cap with its bearing insert installed, and hand-tighten the cap fasteners. If the parts are kept in order in this manner, they will not get lost and you will be able to tell which bearings came form what cylinder if any problems are discovered and diagnosis is necessary. Remove all the other piston assemblies in the same manner. On V-style engines, remove all of the pistons from one bank, then reposition the engine with the other cylinder bank head surface up, and remove that banks piston assemblies.

The only remaining component in the engine block should now be the crankshaft. Loosen the main bearing caps evenly until the fasteners can be turned by hand, then remove them and the caps. Remove the crankshaft from the engine block. Thoroughly clean all of the components.

INSPECTION

Now that the engine block and all of its components are clean, it's time to inspect them for wear and/or damage. To accurately inspect them, you will need some specialized tools:
- Two or three separate micrometers to measure the pistons and crankshaft journals
  - A dial indicator
  - Telescoping gauges for the cylinder bores
  - A rod alignment fixture to check for bent connecting rods

If you do not have access to the proper tools, you may want to bring the components to a shop that does.

Generally, you shouldn't expect cracks in the engine block or its components unless it was known to leak, consume or mix engine fluids, it was severely overheated, or there was evidence of bad bearings and/or crankshaft damage. A visual inspection should be performed on all of the components, but just because you don't see a crack does not mean it is not there. Some more reliable methods for inspecting for cracks include Magnaflux®, a magnetic process or Zyglo®, a dye penetrant. Magnaflux® is used only on ferrous metal (cast iron). Zyglo® uses a spray on fluorescent mixture along with a black light to reveal the cracks. It is strongly recommended to have your engine block checked professionally for cracks, especially if the engine was known to have overheated and/or leaked or consumed coolant. Contact a local shop for availability and pricing of these services.

Engine Block

ENGINE BLOCK BEARING ALIGNMENT

Remove the main bearing caps and, if still installed, the main bearing inserts. Inspect all of the main bearing saddles and caps for damage, burrs or high spots. If damage is found, and it is caused from a spun main bearing, the block will need to be align-bored or, if severe enough, replacement. Any burrs or high spots should be carefully removed with a metal file.

Place a straightedge on the bearing saddles, in the engine block, along the centerline of the crankshaft. If any clearance exists between the straightedge and the saddles, the block must be align-bored.

Align-boring consists of machining the main bearing saddles and caps by means of a flycutter that runs through the bearing saddles.

DECK FLATNESS

The top of the engine block where the cylinder head mounts is called the deck. Insure that the deck surface is clean of dirt, carbon deposits and old gasket material. Place a straightedge across the surface of the deck along its centerline and, using feeler gauges, check the clearance along several points. Repeat the checking procedure with the straightedge placed along both diagonals of the deck surface. If the reading exceeds 0.003 in. (0.076mm) within a 6.0 in. (15.2cm) span, or 0.006 in. (0.152mm) over the total length of the deck, it must be machined.

CYLINDER BORES

▶ See Figure 216

The cylinder bores house the pistons and are slightly larger than the pistons themselves. A common piston-to-bore clearance is 0.0015–0.0025 in. (0.0381mm–0.0635mm). Inspect and measure the cylinder bores. The bore should be checked for out-of-roundness, taper and size. The results of this inspection will determine whether the cylinder can be used in its existing size and condition, or a rebore to the next oversize is required (or in the case of removable sleeves, have replacements installed).

The amount of cylinder wall wear is always greater at the top of the cylinder than at the bottom. This wear is known as taper. Any cylinder that has a taper of 0.0012 in. (0.305mm) or more, must be rebored. Measurements are taken at a number of positions in each cylinder: at the top, middle and bottom and at two points at each position; that is, at a point 90 degrees from the crankshaft centerline, as well as a point parallel to the crankshaft centerline. The measurements are made with either a special dial indicator or a telescopic gauge and micrometer. If the necessary precision tools to check the bore are not available, take the block to a machine shop and have them mike it. Also if you don't have the tools to check the cylinder bores, chances are you will not have the necessary devices to check the pistons, connecting rods and crankshaft. Take these components with you and save yourself an extra trip.

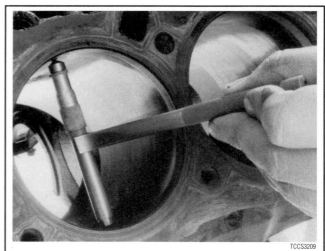
TCCS3209

Fig. 216 Use a telescoping gauge to measure the cylinder bore diameter—take several readings within the same bore

For our procedures, we will use a telescopic gauge and a micrometer. You will need one of each, with a measuring range which covers your cylinder bore size.

1. Position the telescopic gauge in the cylinder bore, loosen the gauges lock and allow it to expand.

➡**Your first two readings will be at the top of the cylinder bore, then proceed to the middle and finally the bottom, making a total of six measurements.**

2. Hold the gauge square in the bore, 90 degrees from the crankshaft centerline, and gently tighten the lock. Tilt the gauge back to remove it from the bore.
3. Measure the gauge with the micrometer and record the reading.
4. Again, hold the gauge square in the bore, this time parallel to the crankshaft centerline, and gently tighten the lock. Again, you will tilt the gauge back to remove it from the bore.
5. Measure the gauge with the micrometer and record this reading. The difference between these two readings is the out-of-round measurement of the cylinder.
6. Repeat steps 1 through 5, each time going to the next lower position, until you reach the bottom of the cylinder. Then go to the next cylinder, and continue until all of the cylinders have been measured.

The difference between these measurements will tell you all about the wear in your cylinders. The measurements which were taken 90 degrees from the crankshaft centerline will always reflect the most wear. That is because at this position is where the engine power presses the piston against the cylinder bore the hardest. This is known as thrust wear. Take your top, 90 degree measurement and compare it to your bottom, 90 degree measurement. The difference between them is the taper. When you measure your pistons, you will compare these readings to your piston sizes and determine piston-to-wall clearance.

Crankshaft

Inspect the crankshaft for visible signs of wear or damage. All of the journals should be perfectly round and smooth. Slight scores are normal for a used crankshaft, but you should hardly feel them with your fingernail. When measuring the crankshaft with a micrometer, you will take readings at the front and rear of each journal, then turn the micrometer 90 degrees and take two more readings, front and rear. The difference between the front-to-rear readings is the journal taper and the first-to-90 degree reading is the out-of-round measurement. Generally, there should be no taper or out-of-roundness found, however, up to 0.0005 in. (0.0127mm) for either can be overlooked. Also, the readings should fall within the factory specifications for journal diameters.

If the crankshaft journals fall within specifications, it is recommended that it be polished before being returned to service. Polishing the crankshaft insures that any minor burrs or high spots are smoothed, thereby reducing the chance of scoring the new bearings.

Pistons and Connecting Rods

PISTONS

▶ See Figure 217

The piston should be visually inspected for any signs of cracking or burning (caused by hot spots or detonation), and scuffing or excessive wear on the skirts. The wrist pin attaches the piston to the connecting rod. The piston should move freely on the wrist pin, both sliding and pivoting. Grasp the connecting rod securely, or mount it in a vise, and try to rock the piston back and forth along the centerline of the wrist pin. There should not be any excessive play evident between the piston and the pin. If there are C-clips retaining the pin in the piston then you have wrist pin bushings in the rods. There should not be any excessive play between the wrist pin and the rod bushing. Normal clearance for the wrist pin is approx. 0.001–0.002 in. (0.025mm–0.051mm).

Use a micrometer and measure the diameter of the piston, perpendicular to the wrist pin, on the skirt. Compare the reading to its original cylinder measurement obtained earlier. The difference between the two readings is the piston-to-wall clearance. If the clearance is within specifications, the piston may be used as is. If the piston is out of specification, but the bore is not, you will need a new piston. If both are out of specification, you will need the cylinder rebored and oversize pistons installed. Generally if two or more pistons/bores are out of specification, it is best to rebore the entire block and purchase a complete set of oversize pistons.

CONNECTING ROD

You should have the connecting rod checked for straightness at a machine shop. If the connecting rod is bent, it will unevenly wear the bearing and piston, as well as place greater stress on these components. Any bent or twisted connecting rods must be replaced. If the rods are straight and the wrist pin clearance is within specifications, then only the bearing end of the rod need be checked. Place the connecting rod into a vice, with the bearing inserts in place, install the cap to the rod and torque the fasteners to specifications. Use a telescoping gauge and carefully measure the inside diameter of the bearings. Compare this reading to the rods original crankshaft journal diameter measurement. The difference is the oil clearance. If the oil clearance is not within specifications, install new bearings in the rod and take another measurement. If the clearance is still out of specifications, and the crankshaft is not, the rod will need to be reconditioned by a machine shop.

➡**You can also use Plastigage® to check the bearing clearances. The assembling section has complete instructions on its use.**

Camshaft

Inspect the camshaft and lifters/followers as described earlier in this section.

Bearings

All of the engine bearings should be visually inspected for wear and/or damage. The bearing should look evenly worn all around with no deep scores or pits. If the bearing is severely worn, scored, pitted or heat blued, then the bearing, and the components that use it, should be brought to a machine shop for inspection. Full-circle bearings (used on most camshafts, auxiliary shafts, bal-

ance shafts, etc.) require specialized tools for removal and installation, and should be brought to a machine shop for service.

Oil Pump

➡**The oil pump is responsible for providing constant lubrication to the whole engine and so it is recommended that a new oil pump be installed when rebuilding the engine.**

Completely disassemble the oil pump and thoroughly clean all of the components. Inspect the oil pump gears and housing for wear and/or damage. Insure that the pressure relief valve operates properly and there is no binding or sticking due to varnish or debris. If all of the parts are in proper working condition, lubricate the gears and relief valve, and assemble the pump.

REFINISHING

▶ See Figure 218

Almost all engine block refinishing must be performed by a machine shop. If the cylinders are not to be rebored, then the cylinder glaze can be removed with a ball hone. When removing cylinder glaze with a ball hone, use a light or penetrating type oil to lubricate the hone. Do not allow the hone to run dry as this may cause excessive scoring of the cylinder bores and wear on the hone. If new pistons are required, they will need to be installed to the connecting rods. This should be performed by a machine shop as the pistons must be installed in the correct relationship to the rod or engine damage can occur.

Pistons and Connecting Rods

▶ See Figure 219

Only pistons with the wrist pin retained by C-clips are serviceable by the home-mechanic. Press fit pistons require special presses and/or heaters to remove/install the connecting rod and should only be performed by a machine shop.

All pistons will have a mark indicating the direction to the front of the engine and the must be installed into the engine in that manner. Usually it is a notch or arrow on the top of the piston, or it may be the letter F cast or stamped into the piston.

C-CLIP TYPE PISTONS

1. Note the location of the forward mark on the piston and mark the connecting rod in relation.
2. Remove the C-clips from the piston and withdraw the wrist pin.

➡**Varnish build-up or C-clip groove burrs may increase the difficulty of removing the wrist pin. If necessary, use a punch or drift to carefully tap the wrist pin out.**

3. Insure that the wrist pin bushing in the connecting rod is usable, and lubricate it with assembly lube.
4. Remove the wrist pin from the new piston and lubricate the pin bores on the piston.
5. Align the forward marks on the piston and the connecting rod and install the wrist pin.

Fig. 217 Measure the piston's outer diameter, perpendicular to the wrist pin, with a micrometer

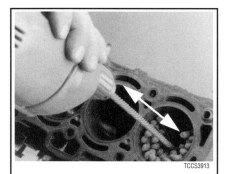

Fig. 218 Use a ball type cylinder hone to remove any glaze and provide a new surface for seating the piston rings

Fig. 219 Most pistons are marked to indicate positioning in the engine (usually a mark means the side facing the front)

6. The new C-clips will have a flat and a rounded side to them. Install both C-clips with the flat side facing out.

7. Repeat all of the steps for each piston being replaced.

ASSEMBLY

Before you begin assembling the engine, first give yourself a clean, dirt free work area. Next, clean every engine component again. The key to a good assembly is cleanliness.

Mount the engine block into the engine stand and wash it one last time using water and detergent (dishwashing detergent works well). While washing it, scrub the cylinder bores with a soft bristle brush and thoroughly clean all of the oil passages. Completely dry the engine and spray the entire assembly down with an anti-rust solution such as WD-40® or similar product. Take a clean lint-free

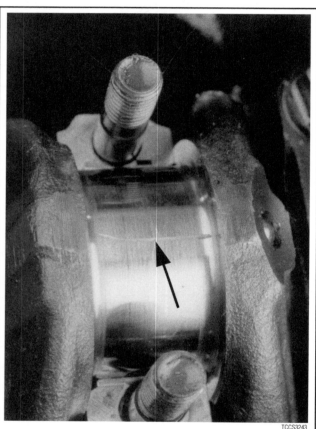

Fig. 220 Apply a strip of gauging material to the bearing journal, then install and torque the cap

rag and wipe up any excess anti-rust solution from the bores, bearing saddles, etc. Repeat the final cleaning process on the crankshaft. Replace any freeze or oil galley plugs which were removed during disassembly.

Crankshaft

♦ See Figures 220, 221, 222 and 223

1. Remove the main bearing inserts from the block and bearing caps.

2. If the crankshaft main bearing journals have been refinished to a definite undersize, install the correct undersize bearing. Be sure that the bearing inserts and bearing bores are clean. Foreign material under inserts will distort bearing and cause failure.

3. Place the upper main bearing inserts in bores with tang in slot.

➡ **The oil holes in the bearing inserts must be aligned with the oil holes in the cylinder block.**

4. Install the lower main bearing inserts in bearing caps.

5. Clean the mating surfaces of block and rear main bearing cap.

6. Carefully lower the crankshaft into place. Be careful not to damage bearing surfaces.

7. Check the clearance of each main bearing by using the following procedure:

a. Place a piece of Plastigage® or its equivalent, on bearing surface across full width of bearing cap and about ¼ in. off center.

b. Install cap and tighten bolts to specifications. Do not turn crankshaft while Plastigage® is in place.

c. Remove the cap. Using the supplied Plastigage® scale, check width of Plastigage® at widest point to get maximum clearance. Difference between readings is taper of journal.

d. If clearance exceeds specified limits, try a 0.001 in. or 0.002 in. undersize bearing in combination with the standard bearing. Bearing clearance must be within specified limits. If standard and 0.002 in. undersize bearing does not bring clearance within desired limits, refinish crankshaft journal, then install undersize bearings.

8. Install the rear main seal.

9. After the bearings have been fitted, apply a light coat of engine oil to the journals and bearings. Install the rear main bearing cap. Install all bearing caps except the thrust bearing cap. Be sure that main bearing caps are installed in original locations. Tighten the bearing cap bolts to specifications.

10. Install the thrust bearing cap with bolts finger-tight.

11. Pry the crankshaft forward against the thrust surface of upper half of bearing.

12. Hold the crankshaft forward and pry the thrust bearing cap to the rear. This aligns the thrust surfaces of both halves of the bearing.

13. Retain the forward pressure on the crankshaft. Tighten the cap bolts to specifications.

14. Measure the crankshaft end-play as follows:

a. Mount a dial gauge to the engine block and position the tip of the gauge to read from the crankshaft end.

b. Carefully pry the crankshaft toward the rear of the engine and hold it there while you zero the gauge.

c. Carefully pry the crankshaft toward the front of the engine and read the gauge.

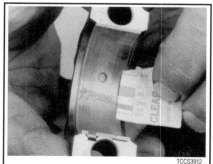

Fig. 221 After the cap is removed again, use the scale supplied with the gauging material to check the clearance

Fig. 222 A dial gauge may be used to check crankshaft end-play

Fig. 223 Carefully pry the crankshaft back and forth while reading the dial gauge for end-play

d. Confirm that the reading is within specifications. If not, install a new thrust bearing and repeat the procedure. If the reading is still out of specifications with a new bearing, have a machine shop inspect the thrust surfaces of the crankshaft, and if possible, repair it.

15. Rotate the crankshaft so as to position the first rod journal to the bottom of its stroke.

Pistons and Connecting Rods

◆ See Figures 224, 225, 226 and 227

1. Before installing the piston/connecting rod assembly, oil the pistons, piston rings and the cylinder walls with light engine oil. Install connecting rod bolt protectors or rubber hose onto the connecting rod bolts/studs. Also perform the following:

a. Select the proper ring set for the size cylinder bore.

b. Position the ring in the bore in which it is going to be used.

c. Push the ring down into the bore area where normal ring wear is not encountered.

d. Use the head of the piston to position the ring in the bore so that the ring is square with the cylinder wall. Use caution to avoid damage to the ring or cylinder bore.

e. Measure the gap between the ends of the ring with a feeler gauge. Ring gap in a worn cylinder is normally greater than specification. If the ring gap is greater than the specified limits, try an oversize ring set.

f. Check the ring side clearance of the compression rings with a feeler gauge inserted between the ring and its lower land according to specification. The gauge should slide freely around the entire ring circumference without binding. Any wear that occurs will form a step at the inner portion of the lower land. If the lower lands have high steps, the piston should be replaced.

2. Unless new pistons are installed, be sure to install the pistons in the cylinders from which they were removed. The numbers on the connecting rod

Fig. 224 Checking the piston ring-to-ring groove side clearance using the ring and a feeler gauge

and bearing cap must be on the same side when installed in the cylinder bore. If a connecting rod is ever transposed from one engine or cylinder to another, new bearings should be fitted and the connecting rod should be numbered to correspond with the new cylinder number. The notch on the piston head goes toward the front of the engine.

3. Install all of the rod bearing inserts into the rods and caps.

4. Install the rings to the pistons. Install the oil control ring first, then the second compression ring and finally the top compression ring. Use a piston ring expander tool to aid in installation and to help reduce the chance of breakage.

5. Make sure the ring gaps are properly spaced around the circumference of the piston. Fit a piston ring compressor around the piston and slide the piston and connecting rod assembly down into the cylinder bore, pushing it in with the wooden hammer handle. Push the piston down until it is only slightly below the top of the cylinder bore. Guide the connecting rod onto the crankshaft bearing journal carefully, to avoid damaging the crankshaft.

6. Check the bearing clearance of all the rod bearings, fitting them to the crankshaft bearing journals. Follow the procedure in the crankshaft installation above.

7. After the bearings have been fitted, apply a light coating of assembly oil to the journals and bearings.

8. Turn the crankshaft until the appropriate bearing journal is at the bottom of its stroke, then push the piston assembly all the way down until the connecting rod bearing seats on the crankshaft journal. Be careful not to allow the bearing cap screws to strike the crankshaft bearing journals and damage them.

9. After the piston and connecting rod assemblies have been installed, check the connecting rod side clearance on each crankshaft journal.

10. Prime and install the oil pump and the oil pump intake tube.

11. Install the auxiliary/balance shaft(s)/assembly(ies).

OHV Engines

CAMSHAFT, LIFTERS AND TIMING ASSEMBLY

1. Install the camshaft.
2. Install the lifters/followers into their bores.
3. Install the timing gears/chain assembly.

CYLINDER HEAD(S)

1. Install the cylinder head(s) using new gaskets.
2. Assemble the rest of the valve train (pushrods and rocker arms and/or shafts).

OHC Engines

CYLINDER HEAD(S)

1. Install the cylinder head(s) using new gaskets.
2. Install the timing sprockets/gears and the belt/chain assemblies.

Engine Covers and Components

Install the timing cover(s) and oil pan. Refer to your notes and drawings made prior to disassembly and install all of the components that were removed. Install the engine into the vehicle.

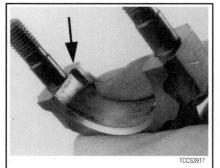
Fig. 225 The notch on the side of the bearing cap matches the tang on the bearing insert

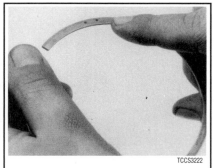
Fig. 226 Most rings are marked to show which side of the ring should face up when installed to the piston

Fig. 227 Install the piston and rod assembly into the block using a ring compressor and the handle of a hammer

Engine Start-up and Break-in

STARTING THE ENGINE

Now that the engine is installed and every wire and hose is properly connected, go back and double check that all coolant and vacuum hoses are connected. Check that your oil drain plug is installed and properly tightened. If not already done, install a new oil filter onto the engine. Fill the crankcase with the proper amount and grade of engine oil. Fill the cooling system with a 50/50 mixture of coolant/water.

1. Connect the vehicle battery.
2. Start the engine. Keep your eye on your oil pressure indicator; if it does not indicate oil pressure within 10 seconds of starting, turn the vehicle **OFF**.

✳✳ WARNING

Damage to the engine can result if it is allowed to run with no oil pressure. Check the engine oil level to make sure that it is full. Check for any leaks and if found, repair the leaks before continuing. If there is still no indication of oil pressure, you may need to prime the system.

3. Confirm that there are no fluid leaks (oil or other).

4. Allow the engine to reach normal operating temperature (the upper radiator hose will be hot to the touch).
5. At this point any necessary checks or adjustments can be performed, such as ignition timing.
6. Install any remaining components or body panels which were removed.

BREAKING IT IN

Make the first miles on the new engine, easy ones. Vary the speed but do not accelerate hard. Most importantly, do not lug the engine, and avoid sustained high speeds until at least 100 miles. Check the engine oil and coolant levels frequently. Expect the engine to use a little oil until the rings seat. Change the oil and filter at 500 miles, 1500 miles, then every 3000 miles past that.

KEEP IT MAINTAINED

Now that you have just gone through all of that hard work, keep yourself from doing it all over again by thoroughly maintaining it. Not that you may not have maintained it before, heck you could have had one to two hundred thousand miles on it before doing this. However, you may have bought the vehicle used, and the previous owner did not keep up on maintenance. Which is why you just went through all of that hard work. See?

CAMSHAFT SPECIFICATIONS

All measurements given in inches.

Year	Engine ID/VIN	Engine Displacement Liters (cc)	Journal Diameter 1	2	3	4	5	Elevation In.	Ex.	Bearing Clearance	Camshaft End Play
1986	M	1.5 (1468)	1.338	1.338	1.338	1.338	—	1.532	1.522	0.0020–0.0035	0.004–0.008
1987	M	1.5 (1468)	1.338	1.338	1.338	1.338	—	1.532	1.522	0.0020–0.0035	0.004–0.008
1988	M	1.5 (1468)	1.338	1.338	1.338	1.338	—	1.532	1.522	0.0020–0.0035	0.004–0.008
1989	M	1.5 (1468)	1.338	1.338	1.338	1.338	—	1.532	1.522	0.0020–0.0035	0.004–0.008
	S	2.4 (2351)	1.336–1.337	1.336–1.337	1.336–1.337	1.336–1.337	1.336–1.337	1.753	1.753	0.0020–0.0035	0.004–0.008
1990	M	1.5 (1468)	1.338	1.338	1.338	1.338	—	1.532	1.522	0.0020–0.0035	0.004–0.008
	J	1.5 (1468)	1.338	1.338	1.338	1.338	—	1.532	1.534	0.0020–0.0035	0.004–0.008
	S	2.4 (2351)	1.336–1.337	1.336–1.337	1.336–1.337	1.336–1.337	1.336–1.337	1.753	1.753	0.0020–0.0035	0.004–0.008
	T	3.0 (2972)	1.336–1.337	1.336–1.337	1.336–1.337	1.336–1.337	—	1.620–1.628	1.620–1.628	0.0020–0.0035	0.004–0.008
1991	M	1.5 (1468)	1.338	1.338	1.338	1.338	—	1.532	1.522	0.0020–0.0035	0.004–0.008
	J	1.5 (1468)	1.338	1.338	1.338	1.338	—	1.532	1.534	0.0020–0.0035	0.004–0.008
	S	2.4 (2351)	1.336–1.337	1.336–1.337	1.336–1.337	1.336–1.337	1.336–1.337	1.753	1.753	0.0020–0.0035	0.004–0.008
	T	3.0 (2972)	1.336–1.337	1.336–1.337	1.336–1.337	1.336–1.337	—	1.620–1.628	1.620–1.628	0.0020–0.0035	0.004–0.008
1992	M	1.5 (1468)	1.338	1.338	1.338	1.338	—	1.532	1.522	0.0020–0.0035	0.004–0.008
	J	1.5 (1468)	1.338	1.338	1.338	1.338	—	1.532	1.534	0.0020–0.0035	0.004–0.008
	F	2.0 (1997)	1.020	1.020	1.020	1.020	1.020	1.753	1.753	0.0020–0.0035	0.004–0.008
	T	3.0 (2972)	1.336–1.337	1.336–1.337	1.336–1.337	1.336–1.337	—	1.620–1.628	1.620–1.628	0.0020–0.0035	0.004–0.008
	R	1.6 (1596)	1.020	1.020	1.020	1.020	1.020	1.386	1.374	0.0020–0.0035	0.004–0.008
1993	M	1.5 (1468)	1.338	1.338	1.338	1.338	—	1.532	1.522	0.0020–0.0035	0.004–0.008
	J	1.5 (1468)	1.338	1.338	1.338	1.338	—	1.532	1.534	0.0020–0.0035	0.004–0.008
	N	1.5 (1468)	1.338	1.338	1.338	1.338	—	⊙	1.625	0.0020–0.0035	0.004–0.008
	F	2.0 (1997)	1.020	1.020	1.020	1.020	1.020	1.753	1.753	0.0020–0.0035	0.004–0.008
	T	3.0 (2972)	1.336–1.337	1.336–1.337	1.336–1.337	1.336–1.337	—	1.620–1.628	1.620–1.628	0.0020–0.0035	0.004–0.008
	R	1.6 (1596)	1.020	1.020	1.020	1.020	1.020	1.386	1.374	0.0020–0.0035	0.004–0.008
	M	1.8 (1796)	1.020	1.020	1.020	1.020	1.020	1.386	1.374	0.0020–0.0035	0.004–0.008

⊙ 1.617 on Non-Turbo Models
  1.625 on Turbocharged Models

84123C03

VALVE SPECIFICATIONS

Year	Engine ID/VIN	Engine Displacement Liters (cc)	Seat Angle (deg.)	Face Angle (deg.)	Spring Test Pressure (lbs. @ in.)	Spring Installed Height (in.)	Stem-to-Guide Clearance (in.) Intake	Exhaust	Stem Diameter (in.) Intake	Exhaust
1986	M	1.5 (1468)	45	45	53 @ 1.07①	1.42②	0.0012–0.0024	0.0020–0.0035	0.2598	0.2598
1987	M	1.5 (1468)	45	45	53 @ 1.07①	1.42②	0.0012–0.0024	0.0020–0.0035	0.2598	0.2598
1988	M	1.5 (1468)	45	45	53 @ 1.07①	1.42②	0.0012–0.0024	0.0020–0.0035	0.2598	0.2598
1989	M	1.5 (1468)	45	45	53 @ 1.07①	1.42②	0.0012–0.0024	0.0020–0.0035	0.2598	0.2598
	S	2.4 (2351)	45	45	73 @ 1.591①	1.591①	0.0012–0.0024	0.0020–0.0035	0.3150	0.3150
1990	M	1.5 (1468)	45	45	53 @ 1.07①	1.42②	0.0012–0.0024	0.0020–0.0035	0.2598	0.2598
	J	1.5 (1468)	45	45	53 @ 1.07①	1.42②	0.0012–0.0024	0.0020–0.0035	0.2598	0.2598
	S	2.4 (2351)	45	45	73 @ 1.591①	1.591①	0.0012–0.0024	0.0020–0.0035	0.3150	0.3150
	T	3.0 (2972)	44–44.5	45	74 @ 1.591①	1.59	0.0012–0.0024	0.0020–0.0035	0.3150	0.3134
1991	M	1.5 (1468)	45	45	53 @ 1.07①	1.42②	0.0012–0.0024	0.0020–0.0035	0.2598	0.2598
	J	1.5 (1468)	45	45	53 @ 1.07①	1.42②	0.0012–0.0024	0.0020–0.0035	0.2598	0.2598
	S	2.4 (2351)	45	45	73 @ 1.591①	1.591①	0.0012–0.0024	0.0020–0.0035	0.3150	0.3150
	T	3.0 (2972)	44–44.5	45	74 @ 1.591①	1.59	0.0012–0.0024	0.0020–0.0035	0.3150	0.3134
1992	M	1.5 (1468)	45	45	53 @ 1.07①	1.42②	0.0012–0.0024	0.0020–0.0035	0.2598	0.2598
	J	1.5 (1468)	45	45	53 @ 1.07①	1.42②	0.0012–0.0024	0.0020–0.0035	0.2598	0.2598
	F	2.0 (1997)	44–44.5	45–45.5	66 @ 1.575	③	0.0012–0.0024	0.0020–0.0035	0.2585	0.2591
	T	3.0 (2972)	44–44.5	45–45.5	74 @ 1.591①	1.59	0.0012–0.0024	0.0020–0.0035	0.3150	0.3134
	R	1.6 (1596)	44–44.5	45–45.5	66 @ 1.575	③	0.0008–0.0019	0.0020–0.0033	0.2585	0.2591
1993	M	1.5 (1468)	45	45	53 @ 1.07①	1.42②	0.0012–0.0024	0.0020–0.0035	0.2598	0.2598
	J	1.5 (1468)	45	45	53 @ 1.07①	1.42②	0.0012–0.0024	0.0020–0.0035	0.2598	0.2598
	N	1.5 (1495)	45	45	53 @ 1.07	1.42	0.0012–0.0024	0.0020–0.0035	0.2598	0.2598
	F	2.0 (1997)	44–44.5	45–45.5	66 @ 1.575	③	0.0008–0.0019	0.0020–0.0031	0.2585	0.2591
	T	3.0 (2972)	44–44.5	45–45.5	74 @ 1.591①	1.59	0.0012–0.0024	0.0020–0.0035	0.3150	0.3134
	R	1.6 (1596)	44–44.5	45–45.5	66 @ 1.575	③	0.0008–0.0019	0.0020–0.0033	0.2585	0.2591
	M	1.8 (1796)	44–44.5	45–45.5	66 @ 1.575	③	0.0008–0.0019	0.0020–0.0033	0.2591	0.2579

① Jet Valve—7.7 @ 0.846   ② Jet Valve—0.846   ③ Free Length—1.902

84123C02

CRANKSHAFT AND CONNECTING ROD SPECIFICATIONS

All measurements are given in inches.

Year	Engine ID/VIN	Engine Displacement Liters (cc)	Main Brg. Journal Dia.	Crankshaft Main Brg. Oil Clearance	Shaft End-play	Thrust on No.	Connecting Rod Journal Diameter	Oil Clearance	Side Clearance
1986	M	1.5 (1468)	1.8898	0.0008–0.0020	0.002–0.007	3	1.6535	0.0006–0.0017	0.004–0.010
1987	M	1.5 (1468)	1.8898	0.0008–0.0020	0.002–0.007	3	1.6535	0.0006–0.0017	0.004–0.010
1988	M	1.5 (1468)	1.8898	0.0008–0.0020	0.002–0.007	3	1.6535	0.0006–0.0017	0.004–0.010
1989	M	1.5 (1468)	1.8898	0.0008–0.0020	0.002–0.007	3	1.6535	0.0006–0.0017	0.004–0.010
	S	2.4 (2351)	2.2436	0.0008–0.0020	0.002–0.007	3	1.7709–1.7715	0.0006–0.0017	0.004–0.010
1990	M	1.5 (1468)	1.8898	0.0008–0.0020	0.002–0.007	3	1.6535	0.0006–0.0017	0.004–0.010
	J	1.5 (1468)	1.8898	0.0008–0.0020	0.002–0.007	3	1.6535	0.0006–0.0017	0.004–0.010
	S	2.4 (2351)	2.2436	0.0008–0.0020	0.002–0.007	3	1.7709–1.7715	0.0006–0.0017	0.004–0.010
	T	3.0 (2972)	2.3622	0.0008–0.0020	0.002–0.007	3	1.9685	0.0006–0.0017	0.004–0.010
1991	M	1.5 (1468)	1.8898	0.0008–0.0020	0.002–0.007	3	1.6535	0.0006–0.0017	0.004–0.010
	J	1.5 (1468)	1.8898	0.0008–0.0020	0.002–0.007	3	1.6535	0.0006–0.0017	0.004–0.010
	S	2.4 (2351)	2.2436	0.0008–0.0020	0.002–0.007	3	1.7709–1.7715	0.0008–0.0020	0.004–0.010
	T	3.0 (2972)	2.3622	0.0008–0.0020	0.002–0.007	3	1.9685	0.0006–0.0017	0.004–0.010
1992	M	1.5 (1468)	1.8898	0.0008–0.0020	0.002–0.007	3	1.6535	0.0006–0.0017	0.004–0.010
	J	1.5 (1468)	1.8898	0.0008–0.0020	0.002–0.007	3	1.6535	0.0006–0.0017	0.004–0.010
	F	2.0 (1997)	2.2433–2.2439	0.0008–0.0020	0.002–0.007	3	1.7709–1.7715	0.0008–0.0020	0.004–0.010
	T	3.0 (2972)	2.3622	0.0008–0.0020	0.002–0.007	3	1.9685	0.0006–0.0017	0.004–0.010
	R	1.6 (1596)	2.2400	0.0008–0.0020	0.002–0.007	3	1.770	0.0008–0.0020	0.004–0.010
1993	M	1.5 (1468)	1.8898	0.0008–0.0020	0.002–0.007	3	1.6535	0.0006–0.0017	0.004–0.010
	J	1.5 (1468)	1.8898	0.0008–0.0020	0.002–0.007	3	1.6535	0.0006–0.0017	0.004–0.010
	N	1.5 (1495)	1.9685	0.0013–0.0020	0.002–0.007	3	1.6535	0.0013–0.0022	0.004–0.010
	F	2.0 (1997)	2.2433–2.2439	0.0008–0.0020	0.002–0.007	3	1.7709–1.7715	0.0008–0.0020	0.004–0.010
	T	3.0 (2972)	2.3622	0.0008–0.0020	0.002–0.007	3	1.9685	0.0006–0.0017	0.004–0.010
	R	1.6 (1596)	2.2400	0.0008–0.0020	0.002–0.007	3	1.770	0.0008–0.0020	0.004–0.010
	M	1.8 (1796)	2.2400	0.0008–0.0020	0.002–0.007	3	1.770	0.0008–0.0020	0.004–0.010

84123C04

PISTON AND RING SPECIFICATIONS

All measurements are given in inches.

Year	Engine ID/VIN	Engine Displacement Liters (cc)	Piston Clearance	Ring Gap Top Compression	Ring Gap Bottom Compression	Ring Gap Oil Control	Ring Side Clearance Top Compression	Ring Side Clearance Bottom Compression	Ring Side Clearance Oil Control
1986	M	1.5 (1468)	0.0008–0.0016	0.008–0.014	0.008–0.014	0.008–0.028	0.0012–0.0028	0.0008–0.0024	NA
1987	M	1.5 (1468)	0.0008–0.0016	0.008–0.014	0.008–0.014	0.008–0.028	0.0012–0.0028	0.0008–0.0024	NA
1988	M	1.5 (1468)	0.0008–0.0016	0.008–0.014	0.008–0.014	0.008–0.028	0.0012–0.0028	0.0008–0.0024	NA
1989	M	1.5 (1468)	0.0008–0.0016	0.008–0.014	0.008–0.014	0.008–0.028	0.0012–0.0028	0.0008–0.0024	NA
	S	2.4 (2351)	0.0004–0.0012	0.010–0.016	0.008–0.014	0.008–0.028	0.0012–0.0028	0.0008–0.0024	NA
1990	M	1.5 (1468)	0.0008–0.0016	0.008–0.014	0.008–0.014	0.008–0.028	0.0012–0.0028	0.0008–0.0024	NA
	J	1.5 (1468)	0.0008–0.0016	0.008–0.014	0.008–0.014	0.008–0.028	0.0012–0.0028	0.0008–0.0024	NA
	S	2.4 (2351)	0.0004–0.0012	0.010–0.016	0.008–0.014	0.008–0.028	0.0012–0.0028	0.0008–0.0024	NA
	T	3.0 (2972)	0.0008–0.0016	0.012–0.018	0.010–0.016	0.008–0.028	0.0012–0.0035	0.0012–0.0028	NA
1991	M	1.5 (1468)	0.0008–0.0016	0.008–0.014	0.008–0.014	0.008–0.028	0.0012–0.0028	0.0008–0.0024	NA
	J	1.5 (1468)	0.0008–0.0016	0.008–0.014	0.008–0.014	0.008–0.028	0.0012–0.0028	0.0008–0.0024	NA
	S	2.4 (2351)	0.0004–0.0012	0.010–0.016	0.008–0.014	0.008–0.028	0.0012–0.0028	0.0008–0.0024	NA
	T	3.0 (2972)	0.0008–0.0016	0.012–0.018	0.010–0.016	0.008–0.028	0.0012–0.0035	0.0012–0.0028	NA
1992	M	1.5 (1468)	0.0008–0.0016	0.008–0.014	0.008–0.014	0.008–0.028	0.0012–0.0028	0.0008–0.0024	NA
	J	1.5 (1468)	0.0008–0.0016	0.008–0.014	0.008–0.014	0.008–0.028	0.0012–0.0028	0.0008–0.0024	NA
	F	2.0 (1997)	0.0004–0.0012	0.010–0.018	0.014–0.020	0.008–0.028	0.0012–0.0028	0.0012–0.0028	NA
	T	3.0 (2972)	0.0008–0.0016	0.012–0.018	0.010–0.016	0.008–0.028	0.0012–0.0035	0.0012–0.0028	NA
	R	1.6 (1596)	0.0008–0.0016	0.010–0.016	0.010–0.020	0.008–0.028	0.0012–0.0028	0.0012–0.0028	NA
1993	M	1.5 (1468)	0.0008–0.0016	0.008–0.014	0.008–0.014	0.008–0.028	0.0012–0.0028	0.0008–0.0024	NA
	J	1.5 (1468)	0.0008–0.0016	0.008–0.014	0.008–0.014	0.008–0.028	0.0012–0.0028	0.0008–0.0024	NA
	Y	1.5 (1468)	0.0008–0.0016	0.012–0.020	0.012–0.020	0.010–0.030	0.0016–0.0031	0.0016–0.0031	NA
	F	2.0 (1997)	0.0004–0.0012	0.010–0.018	0.014–0.020	0.008–0.028	0.0012–0.0028	0.0012–0.0028	NA
	T	3.0 (2972)	0.0008–0.0016	0.012–0.018	0.010–0.016	0.008–0.028	0.0012–0.0035	0.0012–0.0028	NA
	R	1.6 (1596)	0.0008–0.0016	0.010–0.016	0.010–0.020	0.008–0.028	0.0012–0.0028	0.0012–0.0028	NA
	M	1.8 (1796)	0.0008–0.0016	0.010–0.016	0.018–0.024	0.008–0.028	0.0012–0.0028	0.0012–0.0028	NA

NA—Not available

84123C05

ENGINE MECHANICAL SPECIFICATIONS—1468cc ENGINE

Component	U.S.	Metric
All measurements are SERVICE LIMITS, unless otherwise specified		
CAMSHAFT		
Endplay	0.016 in.	0.04mm
Camshaft lobe height:		
Intake	1.5118 in.	38.409 mm
Exhaust:		
Carbureted engine	1.5016 in.	38.448mm
Fuel injected engine	1.5144 in.	38.474mm
CONNECTING ROD		
Bend	0.0020 in.	0.05mm
Bearing oil clearance	0.0006–0.0017 in.	0.014–0.044mm
Bearing undersize	0.01–0.03 in.	0.25–0.75mm
Side clearance	0.016 in.	0.4mm
Twist	0.0039 in.	0.10mm
CRANKSHAFT		
Bend	0.0012 in.	0.03mm
Endplay	0.0098 in.	0.25mm
Journal O.D.	1.8898 in.	48mm
Out-of-roundness (journal/pin taper)	0.0004 in.	0.01mm
Pin O.D.	1.6535 in.	42mm
CYLINDER BLOCK		
Cylinder bore	2.9724–2.9736 in.	75.50–75.53mm
Out-of-roundness and taper of bore	within 0.0008 in.	0.02mm
Piston clearance	0.0008–0.0016 in.	0.02–0.04mm

84123C07

TORQUE SPECIFICATIONS

All readings in ft. lbs.

Year	Engine ID/VIN	Engine Displacement Liters (cc)	Cylinder Head Bolts	Main Bearing Bolts	Rod Bearing Bolts	Crankshaft Damper Bolts	Flywheel Bolts	Manifold Intake	Manifold Exhaust	Spark Plugs	Lug Nut
1986	M	1.5 (1468)	①	36-39	23-25	72	94-101	12-14	12-14	18	80
1987	M	1.5 (1468)	①	36-39	23-25	72	94-101	12-14	12-14	18	80
1988	M	1.5 (1468)	①	36-39	23-25	72	94-101	12-14	12-14	18	80
1989	M	1.5 (1468)	①	36-39	23-25	72	94-101	12-14	12-14	18	80
	S	2.4 (2351)	②	36-40	38	94	94-101	12-14	12-14	18	80
1990	M	1.5 (1468)	①	36-39	23-25	72	94-101	12-14	12-14	18	80
	J	1.5 (1468)	①	36-39	23-25	72	94-101	12-14	12-14	18	80
	S	2.4 (2351)	②	36-40	38	94	94-101	11-14	12-14	18	80
	T	3.0 (2972)	②	55-61	36-38	109-115	65-70	11-14	11-16	18	80
1991	M	1.5 (1468)	①	36-39	23-25	72	94-101	12-14	12-14	18	80
	S	2.4 (2351)	②	36-40	38	94	94-101	11-14	12-14	18	80
	T	3.0 (2972)	②	55-61	36-38	109-115	65-70	11-14	11-16	18	80
1992	M	1.5 (1468)	①	36-39	23-25	72	94-101	12-14	12-14	18	80
	J	1.5 (1468)	①	36-39	23-25	72	94-101	12-14	12-14	18	80
	F	2.0 (1997)	76-83	47-51	38	80-94	94-101	22	18-22	14-22	80
	T	3.0 (2972)	②	55-61	36-38	109-115	65-70	11-14	11-16	18	80
	R	1.6 (1596)	②	47-51	36-38	80-94	94-101	⑤	18-22	15-21	80
1993	M	1.5 (1468)	①	36-39	23-25	72	94-101	12-14	12-14	18	80
	J	1.5 (1468)	①	36-39	23-25	72	94-101	12-14	12-14	18	80
	N	1.5 (1495)	①	39-43	25-27	137-145	94-101	12-14	12-14	18	80
	F	2.0 (1997)	76-83	47-51	38	80-94	94-101	22	18-22	14-22	80
	T	3.0 (2972)	②	55-61	36-38	109-115	65-70	11-14	11-16	18	80
	R	1.6 (1596)	②	47-51	36-38	80-94	94-101	⑤	18-22	15-21	80
	M	1.8 (1796)	76-83④	47-51	36-38	80-94	94-101	⑤	18-22	15-21	80

① Cold: 51-54 ft. lbs.; Warm: 58-61 ft. lbs.
② Cold: 65-72 ft. lbs.; Warm: 72-80 ft. lbs.
③ M8 bolt: 11-14 ft. lbs.
④ Except M8 bolt: 22-30 ft. lbs.
⑤ Cold Engine

8412C06

ENGINE MECHANICAL SPECIFICATIONS—1495cc ENGINE

Component	U.S.	Metric
CRANKSHAFT		
Bend	0.0012 in.	0.03mm
Endplay	0.0020–0.0069 in.	0.05–0.175mm
Journal O.D.	1.9685 in.	50mm
Out-of-roundness (journal/pin taper)	0.0004 in.	0.01mm
Pin O.D.	1.7717 in.	45mm
CYLINDER BLOCK		
Cylinder bore	2.9724–2.9736 in.	75.50–75.53mm
Out-of-roundness and taper of bore	0.0004 in.	0.01mm
Piston clearance:		
Non-Turbocharged engine	0.0008–0.0016 in.	0.02–0.04mm
Turbocharged engine	0.0010–0.0018 in.	0.025–0.045mm
CYLINDER HEAD		
Warpage of head surface	0.002 in.	0.05mm
PISTON		
O.D.:		
Non-Turbocharged engine	2.9713–2.9724 in.	75.470–75.500mm
Turbocharged engine	2.9710–2.9722 in.	45.465–75.495mm
Oversize	0.010–0.039 in.	0.25mm–1.0mm
Rings:		
End gap		
No. 1 and No. 2	0.012–0.020 in.	0.30–0.50mm
Oil ring	0.010–0.039	0.25–1.0mm
Side clearance		
No. 1	0.0016–0.0031 in.	0.04–0.08mm
No. 2	0.0016–0.0031 in.	0.04–0.08mm
VALVES		
Clearance (hot engine):		
Intake	0.01 in.	0.25mm
Exhaust	0.12 in.	0.3mm
Guide-to-steam clearance:		
Intake	0.0012–0.0024 in.	0.03–0.06mm
Exhaust	0.0020–0.0031 in.	0.05–0.08mm
Stem O.D.:		
Intake	0.2 in.	6mm
Exhaust	0.2 in.	6mm
Valve head thickness:		
Intake	0.043 in.	1.1mm
Exhaust	0.55 in.	1.4mm
Valve guide:		
Installed dimension	0.433 in.	11.0mm
Oversize	0.002–0.020 in.	0.05–0.50mm
Valve seat:		
Width of contant:		
Intake	0.043–0.059 in.	1.1–1.5mm
Exhaust	0.059–0.075 in.	1.5–1.9mm
Angle	45 degrees	45 degrees
Valve spring:		
Free length	1.575 in.	40mm
Load		20kg @ 32.0mm
Squareness (limit)	1.5 degrees	1.5 degrees

84123C10

ENGINE MECHANICAL SPECIFICATIONS—1468cc ENGINE

Component	U.S.	Metric
CYLINDER HEAD		
Camshaft clearance	0.002–0.0035 in.	0.05–0.09mm
Warpage of head surface	within 0.002 in.	0.05mm
PISTON		
O.D.	2.9713–2.9724 in.	75.47–75.50mm
Oversize	0.010–0.039 in.	0.25–1.00mm
Rings:		
End gap		
No. 1 and No. 2	0.031 in.	0.8mm
Oil ring	0.031 in.	0.8mm
Side clearance		
No. 1	0.006 in.	0.15mm
No. 2	0.005 in.	0.12mm
VALVES		
Clearance (hot engine):		
Intake	0.006 in.	0.15mm
Exhaust	0.010 in.	0.25mm
Jet valve (carbureted engine)	0.010 in.	0.25mm
Guide-to-stam clearance:		
Intake	0.004 in.	0.10mm
Exhaust	0.006 in.	0.15mm
Stem O.D.:		
Intake	0.26 in.	6.6mm
Exhaust	0.26 in.	6.6mm
Jet valve	0.1693 in.	4.3mm
Valve head thickness:		
Intake	0.028 in.	0.7mm
Exhaust	0.039 in.	1.0mm
Valve guide:		
Installed dimension	0.5394–0.5630 in.	13.7–14.3mm
Oversize	0.002–0.020 in.	0.05–0.5mm
Valve seat:		
Width of contact	0.035–0.051 in.	0.9–1.3mm
Angle	45 degrees	45 degrees
Valve spring:		
Free length	1.756 in.	44.6mm
Load	53 lbs. @ 1.075 in.	24kg @ 27.3mm
Squareness (limit)	3 degrees	3 degrees

84123C08

ENGINE MECHANICAL SPECIFICATIONS—1495cc ENGINE

All measurements are SERVICE STANDARDS, unless otherwise specified

Component	U.S.	Metric
CAMSHAFT		
Camshaft lobe height:		
Intake:		
Non-Turbo engine		41.0837mm
Turbocharged engine		41.2689mm
Exhaust		41.2698mm
CONNECTING ROD		
Bend	0.0020 in.	0.05mm
Bearing oil clearance	0.0013–0.0022 in.	0.032–0.056mm
Bearing undersize	0.01–0.03 in.	0.25–0.75mm
Side clearance	0.04–0.010 in.	0.10–0.25mm
Twist	0.004 in.	0.10mm

84123C09

ENGINE MECHANICAL SPECIFICATIONS—1596cc/1796cc/1997cc ENGINES

All measurements are SERVICE LIMITS, unless otherwise specified

Component	U.S.	Metric
CAMSHAFT		
Endplay:		
1596cc engine	0.004–0.008 in.	0.1–0.2mm
1796cc engine	0.004–0.008 in.	0.1–0.2mm
1997cc engine	0.004–0.008 in.	0.1–0.2mm
Camshaft lobe height:		
Intake:		
1596cc engine	1.3661 in.	34.700mm
1796cc engine	1.3777 in.	34.993mm
1997cc engine	1.3777 in.	34.993mm
Exhaust:		
1596cc engine	1.3546 in.	34.407mm
1796cc engine	1.3661 in.	34.700mm
1997cc engine	1.3661 in.	34.700mm
CONNECTING ROD		
Bend	0.0020 in.	0.05mm
Bearing oil clearance	0.004 in.	0.1mm
Side clearance	0.0157 in.	0.4mm
Twist	0.004 in.	0.1mm
COUNTERSHAFT		
Right counterbalance shaft:		
Front journal diameter	1.6519–1.6526 in.	41.959–41.975mm
Rear journal diameter	1.6122–1.6129 in.	40.951–40.967mm
Oil clearance:		
Front	0.0008–0.0024 in.	0.020–0.0061mm
Rear	0.0020–0.0036 in.	0.050–0.091mm
Left counterbalance shaft:		
Front journal diameter	0.7270–0.7276 in.	18.467–18.480mm
Rear journal diameter	1.6126–1.6132 in.	40.959–40.975mm
Oil Clearance:		
Front	0.0008–0.0021 in.	0.020–0.054mm
Rear	0.0017–0.0033 in.	0.042–0.083mm
CRANKSHAFT		
Endplay	0.0098 in.	0.25mm
Journal O.D.	2.24 in.	57.00mm
Out-of-roundness (journal/pin taper)	0.006 in.	0.015mm
Pin O.D.	1.77 in.	45mm
CYLINDER BLOCK		
Cylinder bore:		
1596cc engine	3.2402–3.2413 in.	82.30–82.33mm
1796cc engine	3.2087–3.2098 in.	81.50–81.53mm
1997cc engine	3.3465–3.3476 in.	85.00–85.03mm
Out-of-roundness and taper of bore	0.0004 in.	0.01mm
Flatness of deck	0.0020 in.	0.05mm
CYLINDER HEAD		
Flatness of manifold mounting surface	0.008 in.	0.2mm
Warpage of head surface	0.0039 in.	0.1mm

8412C11

ENGINE MECHANICAL SPECIFICATIONS—1596cc/1796cc/1997cc ENGINES

Component	U.S.	Metric
PISTON		
O.D.:		
1596cc engine	3.2390–2.2402 in.	82.27–82.30mm
1796cc engine	3.2075–3.2087 in.	81.47–81.50mm
1997cc engine	3.3453–3.3465 in.	84.97–85.00mm
Oversize	0.010–0.039 in.	0.25–1.0mm
Rings:		
End gap		
No. 1:		
1596cc engine	0.031 in.	0.8mm
1796cc engine	0.031 in.	0.8mm
1997cc engine	0.031 in.	0.8mm
No. 2:		
1596cc engine	0.031 in.	0.8mm
1796cc engine	0.031 in.	0.8mm
1997cc engine	0.031 in.	0.8mm
Oil ring:		
1596cc engine	0.039 in.	1.0mm
1796cc engine	0.039 in.	1.0mm
1997cc engine	0.039 in.	1.0mm
Side clearance		
No. 1	0.004 in.	0.1mm
No. 2	0.004 in.	0.1mm
VALVES		
Guide-to-stem clearance:		
Intake	0.0039 in.	0.10mm
Exhaust	0.0059 in.	0.15mm
Stem O.D.:		
Intake	0.2585–0.2591 in.	6.565–6.580mm
Exhaust	0.2571–0.2579 in.	6.530–6.550mm
Valve head thickness:		
Intake	0.028 in.	0.7mm
Exhaust	0.039 in.	1.0mm
Valve guide:		
Length:		
Intake	1.791 in.	45.5mm
Exhaust	1.988 in.	50.5mm
Oversize	0.002–0.020 in.	0.05–0.50mm
Valve length:		
Intake	4.311 in.	109.5mm
Exhaust	4.319 in.	109.7mm
Valve seat:		
Width of contact	0.0035–0.051 in.	0.9–1.3mm
Angle	44–44.5 degrees	44–44.5 degrees
Valve spring:		
Free length	1.862 in.	47.3mm
Load	66 lbs. @ 1.575 in.	300N @ 40mm
Squareness (limit)	4 degrees	4 degrees

8412C12

ENGINE MECHANICAL SPECIFICATIONS—2351cc ENGINE

Component	U.S.	Metric
All measurements are SERVICE STANDARDS, unless otherwise specified		
CAMSHAFT		
Endplay	0.004–0.008 in.	0.1–0.2mm
Camshaft lobe height:		
Intake	1.3777 in.	34.993mm
Exhaust	1.3661 in.	34.700mm
CONNECTING ROD		
Bend	0.0020 in.	0.05mm
Bearing oil clearance	0.0008 in.	0.02mm
Twist	0.004 in.	0.1mm
COUNTERSHAFT		
Right counterbalance shaft:		
Front journal diameter	1.6519–1.6526 in.	41.959–41.975mm
Rear journal diameter	1.6122–1.6129 in.	40.951–40.967mm
Oil clearance:		
Front	0.0008–0.0024 in.	0.020–0.0061mm
Rear	0.0020–0.0036 in.	0.050–0.091mm
Left counterbalance shaft:		
Front journal diameter	0.7270–0.7276 in.	18.467–18.480mm
Rear journal diameter	1.6126–1.6132 in.	40.959–40.975mm
Oil clearance:		
Front	0.0008–0.0021 in.	0.020–0.054mm
Rear	0.0017–0.0033 in.	0.042–0.083mm
CRANKSHAFT		
Endplay	0.0020–0.0071 in.	0.05–0.18mm
Journal O.D.	2.2433–2.2439 in.	56.980–56.995mm
Out-of-roundness (journal/pin taper)	0.006 in.	0.015mm
Pin O.D.	1.7709–1.7715 in.	44.980–44.995mm
CYLINDER BLOCK		
Cylinder bore	3.4051–3.4067 in.	86.49–86.53mm
Out-of-roundness and taper of bore	0.0004 in.	0.01mm
Flatness of deck	0.0020 in.	0.05mm
CYLINDER HEAD		
Flatness of manifold mounting surface	0.008 in.	0.2mm
Warpage of head surface	0.0039 in.	0.1mm
PISTON		
O.D.	3.4043–3.4055 in.	86.47–86.50mm
Oversize	0.010–0.039 in.	0.25–1.0mm
Rings:		
End gap		
No. 1	0.031 in.	0.8mm
No. 2	0.031 in.	0.8mm
Oil ring	0.039 in.	1.0mm
Side clearance		
No. 1	0.004 in.	0.1mm
No. 2	0.004 in.	0.1mm
VALVES		
Guide-to-stem clearance:		
Intake	0.0039 in.	0.10mm
Exhaust	0.0059 in.	0.015mm
Stem O.D.:		
Intake	0.315 in.	8.0mm
Exhust	0.315 in.	8.0mm
Jet valve	0.169 in.	4.3mm

84123C13

ENGINE MECHANICAL SPECIFICATIONS—2351cc ENGINE

Component	U.S.	Metric
VALVES		
Valve guide:		
Length:		
Intake	1.791 in.	45.5mm
Exhaust	1.988 in.	50.5mm
Oversize	0.002–0.020 in.	0.05–0.50mm
Valve length:		
Intake	4.197 in.	106.6mm
Exhaust	4.142 in.	105.2mm
Valve seat:		
Width of cohntact	0.0035–0.051 in.	0.9–1.3mm
Angle	45 degrees	45 degrees
Valve spring:		
Free length:		
Intake and exhaust	1.961 in.	49.8mm
Jet valve	1.165 in.	29.60mm
Load:		
Intake and exhaust	72 lbs. @ 1.591 in.	32.9kg @ 40.4mm
Jet valve	7.7 lbs. @ 0.846 in.	3.5kg @ 21.5mm
Squareness (limit)	4 degrees	4 degrees

84123C14

ENGINE MECHANICAL SPECIFICATIONS—2972cc ENGINE

Component	U.S.	Metric
All measurements are SERVICE STANDARDS, unless otherwise specified		
CAMSHAFT		
Endplay	0.004–0.008 in.	0.1–0.2mm
Camshaft lobe height:		
Intake	1.600 in.	40.65mm
Exhaust	1.600 in.	40.65mm
CONNECTING ROD		
Bend	0.0020 in.	0.05mm
Bearing oil clearance	0.004 in.	0.1mm
Bearing undersize	0.010–0.030 in.	0.25–0.75mm
Side clearance	0.016 in.	0.4mm
Twist	0.0039 in.	0.1mm
CRANKSHAFT		
Endplay	0.012 in.	0.3mm
Journal O.D.	2.3614–2.3622 in.	59.980–60.000mm
Out-of-roundness (journal/pin taper)	0.0012 in.	0.03mm
Pin O.D.	1.9677–1.9685 in.	49.980–50.000mm
CYLINDER BLOCK		
Cylinder bore	3.5866–3.5882 in.	91.10–91.14mm
Out-of-roundness and taper of bore	0.0008 in.	0.02mm
Flatness of gasket surface	0.0020 in.	0.05mm
CYLINDER HEAD		
Flatness of manifold mounting surface:		
Intake	0.008 in.	0.2mm
Exhaust	0.012 in.	0.3mm
Warpage of head surface	0.008 in.	0.2mm

84123C15

ENGINE MECHANICAL SPECIFICATIONS—2972cc ENGINE

Component	U.S.	Metric
PISTON		
O.D.	3.5854–3.5866 in.	91.07–91.10mm
Oversize	0.010–0.020 in.	0.25–1.00mm
Rings:		
End gap		
No. 1 and No. 2	0.031 in.	0.8mm
Oil ring	0.039 in.	1.0mm
Side clearance		
No. 1	0.004 in.	0.1mm
No. 2	0.004 in.	0.1mm
ROCKER ARMS		
Oil clearance	0.0039 in.	0.1mm
Shaft O.D.	0.7435–0.7440 in.	18.885–18.898mm
Shaft Spring free length	2.173 in.	55.2mm
VALVES		
Face angle	45–45.5 degrees	45–45.5 degrees
Guide-to-stem clearance:		
Intake	0.0039 in.	0.10mm
Exhaust	0.0059 in.	0.15mm
Overall length:		
Intake	4.047 in.	102.97mm
Exhaust	4.042 in.	102.67mm
Stem O.D.:		
Intake	0.3148–0.3143 in.	7.995–7.982mm
Exhaust	0.3134–0.3126 in.	7.960–7.940mm
Valve spring:		
Free length	1.988 in.	50.5mm
Load	74 lbs. @ 1.591 in.	32.9kg @ 40.4mm
Squareness (limit)	4 degrees	4 degrees

84123C16

TORQUE SPECIFICATIONS

Component	U.S.	Metric
Connecting rod cap bolts		
1468cc engine	25 ft. lbs.	35 Nm
1495cc engine	25–27 ft. lbs.	35–38 Nm
1596cc engine	38 ft. lbs.	53 Nm
1796cc engine	38 ft. lbs.	53 Nm
1997cc engine	38 ft. lbs.	53 Nm
2351cc engine	38 ft. lbs.	53 Nm
2972cc engine	38 ft. lbs.	53 Nm
Crankshaft bearing cap bolts		
1468cc engine	39 ft. lbs.	54 Nm
1495cc engine	39 ft. lbs.	54 Nm
1596cc engine	51 ft. lbs.	70 Nm
1796cc engine	51 ft. lbs.	70 Nm
1997cc engine	51 ft. lbs.	70 Nm
2351cc engine	40 ft. lbs.	54 Nm
2972cc engine	61 ft. lbs.	85 Nm
Crankshaft sprocket bolt		
1468cc engine	72 ft. lbs.	100 Nm
1495cc engine	140–147 ft. lbs.	190–200 Nm
1596cc engine	94 ft. lbs.	127 Nm
1796cc engine	94 ft. lbs.	127 Nm
1997cc engine	94 ft. lbs.	127 Nm
2351cc engine	94 ft. lbs.	127 Nm
2972cc engine	115 ft. lbs.	160 Nm
Crankshaft pulley to sprocket		
1468cc engine	11 ft. lbs.	15 Nm
1495cc engine	9–10 ft. lbs.	13–14 Nm
1596cc engine	18 ft. lbs.	24 Nm
1796cc engine	18 ft. lbs.	24 Nm
1977cc engine	22 ft. lbs.	30 Nm
2351cc engine	18 ft. lbs.	24 Nm
2972cc engine	18 ft. lbs.	24 Nm
Crankshaft pulley bolt		
2972cc engine	116 ft. lbs.	160 Nm
Cylinder head bolts		
1468cc engine		
Step 1:	15 ft. lbs.	20 Nm
Step 2:	25 ft. lbs.	35 Nm
Step 3 (cold):	54 ft. lbs.	74 Nm
Step 4 (warm):	61 ft. lbs.	83 Nm
1495cc engine	51–54 ft. lbs.	70–75 Nm
1596cc engine		
Step 1:	25 ft. lbs.	34 Nm
Step 2:	36 ft. lbs.	48 Nm
Step 3:	72 ft. lbs.	100 Nm
1796cc engine		
Step 1:	25 ft. lbs.	34 Nm
Step 2:	36 ft. lbs.	48 Nm
Step 3 (cold):	83 ft. lbs.	115 Nm
1997cc engine		
Step 1:	25 ft. lbs.	34 Nm
Step 2:	36 ft. lbs.	48 Nm
Step 3 (cold):	83 ft. lbs.	115 Nm
2351cc engine		
Step 1:	25 ft. lbs.	34 Nm
Step 2:	36 ft. lbs.	48 Nm
Step 3 (cold):	72 ft. lbs.	98 Nm
Step 4 (warm):	80 ft. lbs.	108 Nm
2972cc engine		
Step 1:	25 ft. lbs.	34 Nm
Step 2:	36 ft. lbs.	48 Nm
Step 3 (cold):	76 ft. lbs.	105 Nm

84123C18

TORQUE SPECIFICATIONS

Component	U.S.	Metric
Camshaft bearing cap bolts		
1596cc engine		
Step 1:	5 ft. lbs.	7 Nm
Step 2:	10 ft. lbs.	15 Nm
Step 3:	15 ft. lbs.	21 Nm
1796cc engine		
Step 1:	5 ft. lbs.	7 Nm
Step 2:	10 ft. lbs.	15 Nm
Step 3:	14 ft. lbs.	19 Nm
1997cc engine		
Step 1:	5 ft. lbs.	7 Nm
Step 2:	10 ft. lbs.	15 Nm
Step 3:	14 ft. lbs.	19 Nm
Camshaft sprocket bolt		
1468cc engine	54 ft. lbs.	75 Nm
1495cc engine	58–72 ft. lbs.	80–100 Nm
1596cc engine	72 ft. lbs.	100 Nm
1796cc engine	72 ft. lbs.	100 Nm
1997cc engine	72 ft. lbs.	100 Nm
2351cc engine	72 ft. lbs.	100 Nm
2972cc engine	72 ft. lbs.	100 Nm

84123C17

TORQUE SPECIFICATIONS

Component	U.S.	Metric
Cylinder head cover		
1468cc engine	1.4 ft. lbs.	2.0 Nm
1495cc engine	3 ft. lbs.	3.5 Nm
1596cc engine	3 ft. lbs.	3.5 Nm
1796cc engine	3 ft. lbs.	3.5 Nm
1997cc engine	3 ft. lbs.	3.5 Nm
2351cc engine	5 ft. lbs.	7 Nm
2972cc engine	7 ft. lbs.	10 Nm
Exhaust manifold bolts/nuts	14 ft. lbs.	19 Nm
Flywheel bolts		
1468cc engine	101 ft. lbs.	137 Nm
1495cc engine	101 ft. lbs.	137 Nm
1596cc engine	101 ft. lbs.	137 Nm
1796cc engine	101 ft. lbs.	137 Nm
1997cc engine	101 ft. lbs.	137 Nm
2351cc engine	101 ft. lbs.	137 Nm
2972cc engine	65 ft. lbs.	88 Nm
Front case bolt		
1468cc engine	9 ft. lbs.	12 Nm
1495cc engine	8–11 ft. lbs.	12–15 Nm
1596cc engine		
M8 x 30	25 ft. lbs.	34 Nm
Except M8 x 30	20 ft. lbs.	27 Nm
1796cc engine		
M8 x 30	25 ft. lbs.	34 Nm
Except M8 x 30	20 ft. lbs.	27 Nm
1997cc engine		
M8 x 30	25 ft. lbs.	34 Nm
Except M8 x 30	20 ft. lbs.	27 Nm
2351cc engine	20 ft. lbs.	27 Nm
Intake manifold bolts/nuts	14 ft. lbs.	19 Nm
Intake manifold stay	18 ft. lbs.	25 Nm
Oil pan bolts		
1468cc engine	6 ft. lbs.	8 Nm
1495cc engine	4–6 ft. lbs.	6–8 Nm
1596cc engine	6 ft. lbs.	8 Nm
1796cc engine	6 ft. lbs.	8 Nm
1997cc engine	6 ft. lbs.	8 Nm
2351cc engine	6 ft. lbs.	8 Nm
2972cc engine	5 ft. lbs.	7 Nm
Oil pan drain plug		
1468cc engine	33 ft. lbs.	45 Nm
1495cc engine	25–33 ft. lbs.	35–45 Nm
1596cc engine	25 ft. lbs.	35 Nm
1796cc engine	25 ft. lbs.	35 Nm
1997cc engine	25 ft. lbs.	35 Nm
2351cc engine	33 ft. lbs.	45 Nm
2972cc engine	32 ft. lbs.	45 Nm
Oil pressure switch		
1468cc engine	11 ft. lbs.	15 Nm
1495cc engine	11 ft. lbs.	15 Nm
1596cc engine	9 ft. lbs.	12 Nm
1796cc engine	9 ft. lbs.	12 Nm
1997cc engine	6 ft. lbs.	8 Nm
2351cc engine	6 ft. lbs.	8 Nm
2972cc engine	9 ft. lbs.	12 Nm
Oil pump cover		
1596cc engine	13 ft. lbs.	18 Nm
1796cc engine	11 ft. lbs.	15 Nm
2351cc engine	11 ft. lbs.	15 Nm
2972cc engine	9 ft. lbs.	12 Nm

TORQUE SPECIFICATIONS

Component	U.S.	Metric
Oil pump sprocket nut		
2351cc engine	36 ft. lbs.	49 Nm
Rocker arm shaft bolt		
1468cc engine	20 ft. lbs.	27 Nm
1495cc engine	14–20 ft. lbs.	20–27 Nm
2351cc engine		
Large	15 ft. lbs.	21 Nm
Small	20 ft. lbs.	26 Nm
2972cc engine	15 ft. lbs.	21 Nm
Timing belt cover		
1468cc engine	7 ft. lbs.	10 Nm
1495cc engine	7 ft. lbs.	10 Nm
1596cc engine	7 ft. lbs.	10 Nm
1796cc engine	7 ft. lbs.	10 Nm
1997cc engine	7 ft. lbs.	10 Nm
2972cc engine	9 ft. lbs.	12 Nm
Water pump mounting bolt		
1468cc engine	11 ft. lbs.	15 Nm
1495cc engine	11 ft. lbs.	15 Nm
1596cc engine	11 ft. lbs.	15 Nm
1796cc engine	11 ft. lbs.	15 Nm
2351cc engine		
Head mark 4	15 ft. lbs.	21 Nm
Head mark 7	20 ft. lbs.	27 Nm
2972cc engine		
Head mark 4	15 ft. lbs.	21 Nm
Head mark 7	20 ft. lbs.	27 Nm
Water pump pulley bolt		
1468cc engine	6 ft. lbs.	8 Nm
1495cc engine	6 ft. lbs.	8 Nm
1596cc engine	7 ft. lbs.	10 Nm
1796cc engine	7 ft. lbs.	10 Nm
2351cc engine	7 ft. lbs.	10 Nm
2972cc engine	7 ft. lbs.	10 Nm
Spark plugs		
1468cc engine	18 ft. lbs.	24 Nm
1495cc engine	18 ft. lbs.	24 Nm
1596cc engine	18 ft. lbs.	24 Nm
1796cc engine	18 ft. lbs.	24 Nm
1997cc engine	19 ft. lbs.	26 Nm
2351cc engine	18 ft. lbs.	24 Nm
2973cc engine	18 ft. lbs.	24 Nm

84123C19

84123C20

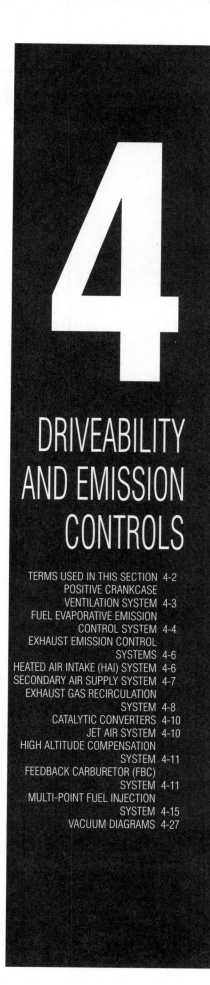

4

DRIVEABILITY AND EMISSION CONTROLS

TERMS USED IN THIS SECTION

The following is a list of the abbreviations used in this section and their meaning. These will help you to better understand the descriptions of the emission systems and components used in your Hyundai.

AFS: Air Flow Sensor
BTDC: Before Top Dead Center
BVV: Bowl Vent Valve
CO: Carbon Monoxide
DOHC: Double Overhead Camshaft
ECU: Electronic Control Unit
EGR: Exhaust Gas Recirculation
FBC: Feedback Carburetor
FBSV: Feedback Solenoid Valve
HAC: High Altitude Compensator
HAI: Heated Air Intake
HC: Hydrocarbon

ISC: Idle Speed Control Servo
MCV: Mixture Control Valve
MPI: Multi-Point Injection
MPS: Motor Position Switch
N/A: Natural Aspiration
NOx: Oxides of Nitrogen
OHC: Overhead Camshaft
PCV: Positive Crankcase Ventilation
SCSV: Slowcut Solenoid Valve
TPS: Throttle Position Switch
T/C: Turbocharged
UCC: Underfloor Catalytic Converter
VRV: Vacuum Regulating Valve
WOT: Wide Open Throttle

EMISSION COMPONENTS MAINTENANCE INTERVALS — TYPE A: NORMAL SERVICE
MODEL: ELANTRA, EXCEL, SCOUPE, SONATA

TO BE SERVICED	TYPE OF SERVICE	VEHICLE MILEAGE INTERVAL							
		7500	15,000	22,500	30,000	37,500	45,000	52,500	60,000
Ignition Timing	I			✔			✔		
Ignition Wires	R								✔
Spark Plugs	R				✔				✔
Engine Oil and Filter	R	✔	✔	✔	✔	✔	✔	✔	✔
Engine Air Cleaner Element	R				✔				✔
PCV Valve	①		✔		✔		✔		✔
Fuel Filter	R							✔	
Fuel/Vapor Return Lines	I							✔	
Fuel Tank Cap and Restrictor	I							✔	
Coolant System	②								✔
Exhaust Pipe and Muffler	I				✔				✔
Catalytic Converter and Shield	I								✔
EGR System	I				✔				✔
Timing Belt	R								✔
Drive Belts	①				✔				✔

FOR COMPLETE EMISSION WARRANTY COVERAGE CONSULT INDIVIDUAL VEHICLE MANUFACTURER'S WARRANTY MAINTENANCE GUIDE.

NOTE: Normal driving conditions:
- Normal driving with little Stop/Go driving
- No prolonged idling (vehicle NOT used in police, taxi or delivery service)
- Most trips at least 10 miles or more
- No driving in excessively dusty conditions
- No short trips in severe cold weather
- No sustained high speed driving in hot weather
- No driving in areas using road salt or other corrosive materials
- No driving on rough and/or muddy roads
- No towing a trailer
- No using rooftop carrier or camper

I—Inspect
R—Replace
① Inspect and replace if necessary
② Flush & Refill

84124C01

EMISSION COMPONENTS MAINTENANCE INTERVALS—TYPE B: SEVERE SERVICE
MODEL: ELANTRA, EXCEL, SCOUPE, SONATA

TO BE SERVICED	TYPE OF SERVICE	VEHICLE MILEAGE INTERVAL								
		3000	7500	15,000	22,500	30,000	37,500	45,000	52,500	60,000
Ignition Timing	I				✔			✔		
Vacuum Lines and Hoses	I									✔
Ignition Wires	R									✔
Spark Plugs	R									✔
Engine Oil and Filter	R	✔	✔	✔	✔	✔	✔	✔	✔	✔
Engine Air Cleaner Element	R			✔		✔		✔		
PCV Valve	①			✔		✔		✔		✔
Fuel Filter	R			✔				✔		
Fuel/Vapor Return Lines	I								✔	
Fuel Tank Cap and Restrictor	I								✔	
Coolant System	②					✔				✔
Exhaust Pipe and Muffler	I			✔		✔		✔		✔
Catalytic Converter and Shield	I					✔				✔
EGR System	I					✔				✔
Timing Belt	R									✔
Idle Speed System	I					✔				✔
Throttle Body	I					✔				✔
Drive Belts	①			✔		✔		✔		✔

FOR COMPLETE EMISSION WARRANTY COVERAGE CONSULT INDIVIDUAL VEHICLE MANUFACTURER'S WARRANTY MAINTENANCE GUIDE.

NOTE: Severe driving conditions:
- Stop/Go driving
- Prolonged idling (vehicle used in police, taxi or delivery service)
- Most trips less than 10 miles
- Driving in excessively dusty conditions
- Short trips in severe cold weather
- Sustained high speed driving in hot weather
- Driving in areas using road salt or other corrosive materials
- Driving on rough and/or muddy roads
- Towing a trailer
- Using rooftop carrier or camper

I—Inspect
R—Replace
① Inspect and replace if necessary
② Flush & Refill

84124C02

POSITIVE CRANKCASE VENTILATION SYSTEM

General Information

♦ **See Figures 1 and 2**

All vehicles are equipped with a closed crankcase ventilation system. The system is composed of a Positive Crankcase Ventilation (PCV) valve and related hoses. This system prevents blowby gases, burned gases which pass the piston rings during combustion, from escaping into the atmosphere. The exhaust gases include Hydrocarbon (HC), Carbon Monoxide (CO) and Oxides of Nitrogen (NOx).

The system supplies fresh air to the crankcase through the air cleaner. Inside the crankcase, the fresh air is mixed with blowby gases, which pass through the PCV valve into the induction system.

The PCV valve has a metered orifice through which the mixture of fresh air and blowby gases are drawn into the intake manifold in response to the manifold vacuum. Under low vacuum conditions (heavy acceleration) the mixture is backed up into the air cleaner.

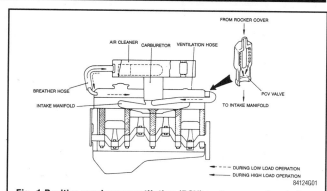

Fig. 1 Positive crankcase ventilation (PCV) system on carbureted vehicles

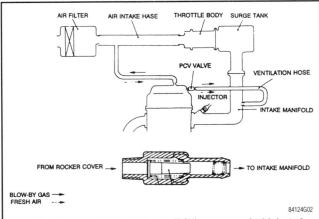

Fig. 2 Positive crankcase ventilation (PCV) system on fuel injected vehicles

FUEL EVAPORATIVE EMISSION CONTROL SYSTEM

General Information

♦ See Figures 3 and 4

The function of the evaporation control system is to prevent the emission of gas vapors from escaping into the atmosphere. When fuel evaporates, the vapors pass through vent hoses to the charcoal canister where they are stored until they can be drawn into the intake manifold. All vehicles are equipped with the charcoal canister for the storage of fuel vapors.

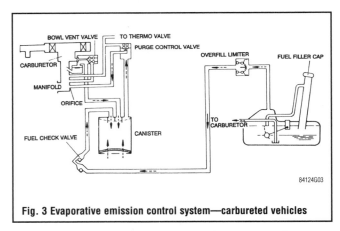

Fig. 3 Evaporative emission control system—carbureted vehicles

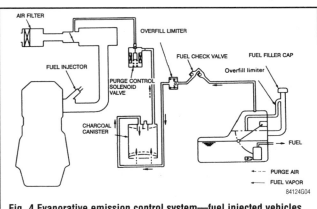

Fig. 4 Evaporative emission control system—fuel injected vehicles

TESTING

PCV Valve

➡The PCV valve should be checked every 15,000 miles and cleaned or replaced as required. Refer to Section 1 for PVC valve removal procedures.

1. Disconnect the ventilation hose from the PCV valve and remove the valve.
2. Insert a thin stick into the PCV valve from the threaded end and push to check if the plunger moves.
3. If the plunger does not move, the valve is clogged and should be cleaned or replaced.

The evaporative emission system for feedback carburetor engines consists of a charcoal canister, a bowl vent valve, a vacuum operated purge control valve, a thermo valve, an overfill limiter, a fuel check valve and a fuel filler cap equipped with a relief valve to prevent the escape of fuel vapor into the atmosphere.

The evaporative emission system for multi-point injection engines consists of a charcoal canister, a computer controlled purge control valve, an overfill limiter, a fuel check valve and a fuel filler cap equipped with a relief valve to prevent the escape of fuel vapor into the atmosphere. On multi-point fuel injection engines, the valve is opened when the Electronic Control Unit (ECU) determines that the conditions are correct.

Charcoal Canister

♦ See Figure 5

All vehicles are equipped with charcoal canisters. While the engine is inoperative, fuel vapors generated inside the fuel tank are absorbed and stored in the canister. When the engine is running, the vapors are drawn through the electronically controlled purge control valve and into the intake manifold. The vapors enter the air/fuel mixture and are burned in the combustion process.

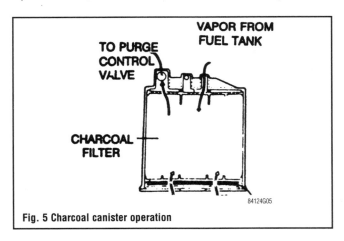

Fig. 5 Charcoal canister operation

CANISTER SERVICE

The only service required for the charcoal canister is to replace the filter pad on the bottom of the canister. The filter requires replacement every 12 months or 12,000 miles. If the vehicle is driven under severe conditions, the filter should be replaced more often.

Bowl Vent Valve

The bowl vent valve controls vapor in the feedback carburetor bowl. While the engine is running, the intake manifold vacuum acts on the diaphragm to close the bowl vent valve so the carburetor bowl opens the air vent. When the engine stops, the bowl vent valve opens to connect the carburetor to the canister, causing fuel vapor to be absorbed by the canister.

TESTING

♦ **See Figure 6**

Feedback Carburetor

1. Perform this test with the engine cold.
2. Remove the air cleaner.
3. Disconnect the bowl vapor hose from the Bowl Vent Valve (BVV).
4. Apply a vacuum of 6 in. Hg to the bowl vent valve.
5. With the engine OFF, the valve should not hold vacuum.
6. Start the engine and reapply the vacuum. With the engine running, the valve should hold vacuum.

Purge Control Valve

The purge control valve is kept closed during idling in order to prevent vaporized fuel from entering into the intake manifold. This ensures positive control of high idle CO emission, which is a particular problem under high ambient temperatures. On feedback carburetor engines, the valve is opened when vacuum working on the diaphragm exceeds the preset value. On fuel injected vehicles, the purge system is controlled electronically.

TESTING

♦ **See Figures 7**

Feedback Carburetor

1. Remove the purge control valve from the vehicle.
2. Connect a hand vacuum pump to the purge control valve nipple and apply a vacuum of 1.4 in. Hg to the valve.
3. Blow air into the canister side nipple and make sure the air exits through the intake manifold nipple with vacuum applied.
4. Replace the valve if defective.

Multi-Point Injection

1. Disconnect the vacuum hose (red and black striped) from the purge solenoid valve.
2. Disconnect the electrical terminal harness connector from the valve.
3. Connect the vacuum pump to the nipple on the valve from which the red and black striped hose was disconnected.

4. Connect the 12 volt power source to the valve terminals.
5. Apply vacuum to the valve with the vacuum pump and alternately apply and remove battery voltage at the valve terminals. When battery voltage is applied, vacuum should be released from the valve. When voltage is removed, the valve should hold a steady vacuum.
6. Remove the vacuum pump and voltage source. Connect an ohmmeter to the valve terminals to measure the coil resistance. The resistance should be 36–44 ohms at 68°F (20°C).
7. If the valve does not operate as described or if the solenoid coil resistance is not as specified, replace the valve.

Overfill Limiter (Two Way Valve)

The overfill limiter is used on all vehicles and consists of a pressure valve and a vacuum valve. The pressure valve is designed to open when the fuel tank's internal pressure has increased over the preset pressure limit. The vacuum valve opens when a vacuum has been produced in the tank.

TESTING

Remove the overfill limiter by loosening the clamps attaching the fuel line. Lightly breathe into the inlet and outlet. If the air passes through after slight resistance, then the valve is functioning properly.

Thermo Valve

Thermo valves are used on feedback carburetor equipped vehicles only. Multi-point fuel injection equipped vehicles use the ECU to activate the purge control solenoid valve. The valve, which is incorporated in the EGR system, is used for sensing the coolant temperature at the intake manifold. It closes the purge control valve when the coolant temperature is lower than a preset value, its function is to reduce CO and HC emissions under warm up conditions and to open the purge control valve when the coolant temperature rises above the preset temperature.

TESTING

♦ **See Figures 8, 9 and 10**

Feedback Carburetor

➠**When removing and installing the thermo valve, do not attempt to loosen the resin portion of the valve with a wrench. When disconnecting the vacuum hoses, make sure they are labeled for proper reassembly.**

1. Disconnect vacuum hose A from its nipple on the valve.
2. Connect a suitable hand vacuum pump to nipple A and apply vacuum to the valve.
3. At engine coolant temperatures below 56–66°F (13–19°C), the valve

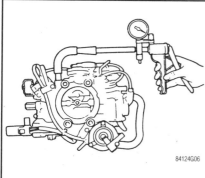

Fig. 6 Bowl vent valve test on 1986–89 Excel

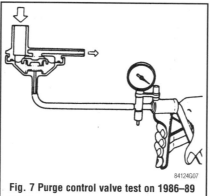

Fig. 7 Purge control valve test on 1986–89 Excel

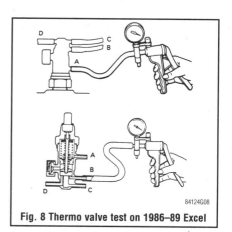

Fig. 8 Thermo valve test on 1986–89 Excel

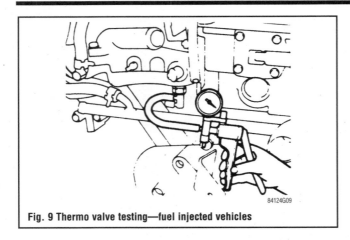

Fig. 9 Thermo valve testing—fuel injected vehicles

should not hold vacuum. At temperatures above 60–68°F (16–20°C), the valve should hold vacuum.

4. Disconnect the remaining 3 hoses from the valve.

5. Connect the vacuum pump to either nipple B, C or D of the valve. Plug the valve nipples that are not being used. Apply a vacuum to the nipple.

6. At engine coolant temperatures below 140–150°F (60–66°C), the valve should not hold vacuum. At temperatures above 145–153°F (63–67°C), the valve should hold vacuum.

7. If the valve does not function as described, replace the valve.

Fuel Check Valve

The fuel check valve is used on all vehicles to prevent fuel leakage should the vehicle roll over. The valve is connected in the fuel vapor line between canister and overfill limiter. The fuel check valve contains 2 balls and under normal conditions the gasoline vapor passage in the valve is open; if a vehicle roll over occurs, one of the balls closes the fuel passage thus preventing fuel leaks.

Fuel Filler Cap

The fuel filler cap is equipped with a vacuum relief valve to prevent the escape of fuel vapor into the atmosphere.

TESTING

Check the gasket for the cap and check the cap itself for damage or deformation. Replace the fuel cap if necessary.

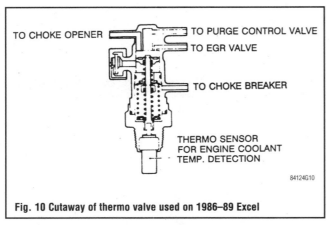

Fig. 10 Cutaway of thermo valve used on 1986–89 Excel

EXHAUST EMISSION CONTROL SYSTEMS

The exhaust emission control system encompasses the engine from the entrance of air into the induction system, until the exhaust by-product emerges from the tailpipe.

The exhaust emission system will usually include one or more of the following sub-systems: Thermostatically controlled air cleaner, Air injection systems, Ignition timing controls, Exhaust gas recirculation, Catalytic converter, Feedback carburetor, Fuel injection and Electronic control unit.

HEATED AIR INTAKE (HAI) SYSTEM

General Information

♦ See Figure 11

All feedback carburetor engines are equipped with a temperature regulated air cleaner. This allows the carburetor to be calibrated leaner to reduce CO and HC emissions, to provide improved engine warm-up characteristics and prevent carburetor icing. The air cleaner is provided with an air control valve, inside the snorkel, to modulate the temperature of intake air. The air can flow through 2 routes, through the front of the air cleaner (cold air) or through the heat cowl at the exhaust manifold (hot air). The air control valve is operated by a sensor which reads ambient air temperature under the hood and increases or decreases manifold vacuum to open and close the control valve.

TESTING

1. Remove the air cleaner cover and air duct.

2. Run the engine at idle and using a mirror to check to see if the air control valve is functioning properly. The valve should be open (cold air) at temperatures above 113°F (45°C) or closed at temperatures below 80°F (30°C).

3. If the system fails this test, proceed to the individual component tests.

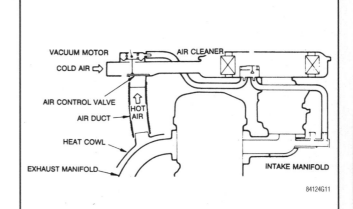

Fig. 11 Heated air intake (HAI) system—carbureted vehicles only

Air Control Valve

TESTING

▶ **See Figure 12**

1. Remove the air cleaner.
2. Disconnect the vacuum hose from the air control valve and connect a hand vacuum pump to the valve nipple.
3. Apply a vacuum of 2.8 in. Hg or less; the air control valve should be fully open (cold air).
4. Apply a vacuum of 7.5 in. Hg or more; the air control valve should be fully closed (hot air).
5. Replace the air control valve if it fails either test.

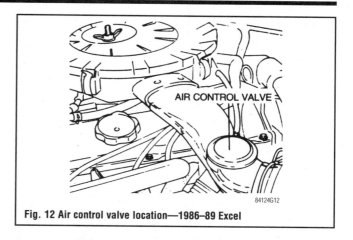

Fig. 12 Air control valve location—1986–89 Excel

SECONDARY AIR SUPPLY SYSTEM

General Information

▶ **See Figures 13 and 14**

The secondary air supply system is used on feedback carburetor engines only. It consists of a reed valve, a secondary air control valve, a secondary air control solenoid valve, an ECU and a sensor.

The reed valve supplies secondary air into the exhaust manifold for the purpose of promoting oxidation of exhaust emissions during the engine warm-up, deceleration and hot start operation. The reed valve is actuated by exhaust from pulsations in the exhaust manifold. Additional air is supplied into the exhaust manifold through the secondary air control valve.

The secondary air control valve is opened by the intake manifold vacuum when the solenoid valve is energized by the ECU, based on information on coolant temperature, engine speed, time and idle position.

Secondary Air Control Valve

TESTING

Feedback Carburetor

▶ **See Figure 15**

1. Disconnect the air supply hose from the air cleaner and check for vacuum by placing your thumb over the end of the air supply hose.
2. With engine coolant temperature between 64–145°F (18–63°C) and the engine idling, the hose should draw vacuum.
3. With the engine coolant temperature at 145°F (63°C) or more, the hose should draw vacuum for 70 seconds after start-up. The hose should not draw vacuum after 70 seconds.
4. With the engine coolant temperature at 145°F (63°C) or more, and the engine decelerating from 4000 rpm, the hose should draw vacuum.

➡ **If the secondary air control valve is not functioning properly, emission may blow back.**

5. Remove the secondary air control valve.
6. Blow in the air cleaner side of the valve to check that air does not flow through the valve.
7. Connect a hand vacuum pump to the secondary air control valve nipple and apply 5.9 in. Hg of vacuum.
8. Air should flow from the air cleaner side to the exhaust manifold side. Air should not flow from the exhaust side to the air cleaner side.
9. Replace the air control valve if it fails any of the above tests.
10. Tighten the air control valve to 51–61 ft. lbs. (69–82 Nm).

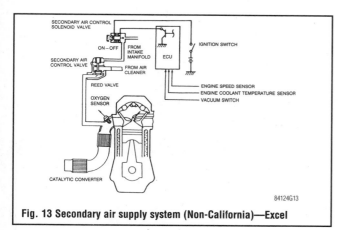

Fig. 13 Secondary air supply system (Non-California)—Excel

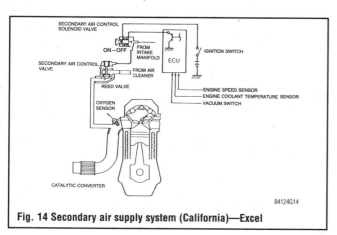

Fig. 14 Secondary air supply system (California)—Excel

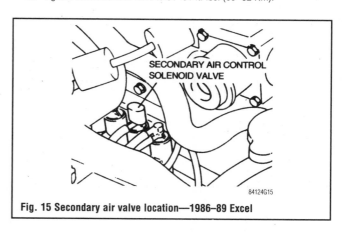

Fig. 15 Secondary air valve location—1986–89 Excel

Vacuum Regulator Valve (VRV)

▶ **See Figure 16**

The vacuum regulator valve, used on feedback carburetor engines only, modulates the vacuum signal to the EGR valve. It reduces the signal by air bleed when the pressure applied to the regulator valve under low engine load operation.

TESTING

Feedback Carburetor

1. Disconnect the vacuum hose (white stripe) from the VRV and connect a hand vacuum pump to the VRV.
2. Apply vacuum of 7.7 in. Hg and check the condition of the VRV valve.
3. With the engine OFF, the vacuum should bleed off.
4. With the engine running at 3500 rpm, the valve should hold vacuum.
5. Replace the valve if defective.

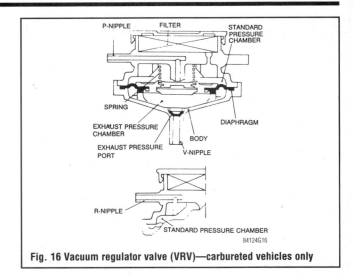

Fig. 16 Vacuum regulator valve (VRV)—carbureted vehicles only

EXHAUST GAS RECIRCULATION SYSTEM

General Information

▶ **See Figures 17 and 18**

The Exhaust Gas Recirculation (EGR) system recycles part of the exhaust gases into the combustion chamber to lower the peak temperatures. By lowering peak temperatures, a reduction in Oxides of Nitrogen (NOx) is obtained. The system consists of an EGR valve, thermo valve and a catalytic converter. California models use an EGR Control Solenoid Valve and an EGR Temperature Sensor.

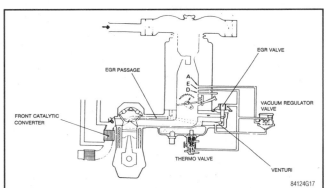

Fig. 17 Exhaust gas recirculation (EGR) system—feedback carburetor equipped vehicles

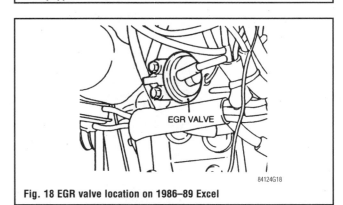

Fig. 18 EGR valve location on 1986–89 Excel

EGR Valve

TESTING

▶ **See Figure 19**

1. Remove the EGR valve and check it for sticking or carbon deposits. Clean the valve with solvent and ensure that the valve is fully seated on the contact surface.
2. Connect a hand vacuum pump to the valve and apply 19.4 in. HG of vacuum. Check that vacuum is held.
3. Release the vacuum and apply 1.7 in. Hg of vacuum. Blow air into one passage of the valve. Air should not blow through.
4. Increase the vacuum to 7.5 in. Hg and blow air into the passage again. Air should blow through.
5. Replace the EGR valve if it fails to function properly.
6. Install the EGR valve using a new gasket. Tighten the bolts to 11–16 ft. lbs. (15–22 Nm) on 4 cylinder engines or 14–20 ft. lbs. (19–28 Nm) on V6 engines.

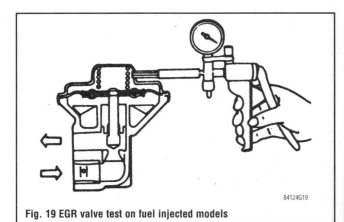

Fig. 19 EGR valve test on fuel injected models

Thermo Valve

The thermo valve is installed into the EGR vacuum supply line and is threaded into the intake manifold. The valve functions as a temperature switch to stop the vacuum signal to the EGR valve.

TESTING

▶ See Figure 20

1. Connect a hand vacuum pump to the thermo valve nipple.
2. Apply a vacuum with a hand vacuum pump.
3. At coolant temperatures below 122°F (50°C), the vacuum should not hold.
4. At coolant temperatures above 176°F (80°C), the vacuum should hold.
5. Replace the thermo valve if not functioning properly.

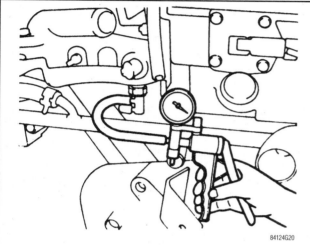

Fig. 20 Thermo valve resistance test—Fuel injected California vehicles

EGR Control Solenoid Valve (California)

TESTING

▶ See Figures 21, 22, 23 and 24

1. Tag and disconnect the vacuum lines and harness connector from the valve.
2. Connect a hand vacuum pump to the nipple where the green striped hose was connected and draw vacuum.
3. Connect a 12 volt source to the solenoid and check as follows:
   a. With voltage applied, vacuum should hold.
   b. With voltage disconnected, vacuum should bleed off.
   c. Measure the resistance between the terminals of the solenoid valve.
   d. Resistance should be 33–44 ohms at 68°F (20°C).

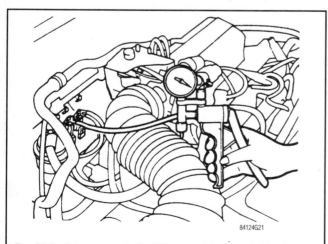

Fig. 21 Applying vacuum to the EGR solenoid valve—California Excel (with fuel injection)

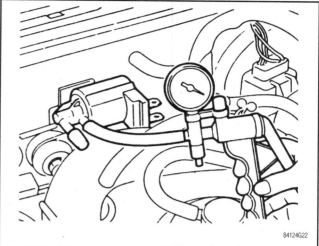

Fig. 22 Applying vacuum to the EGR solenoid valve—California Sonata

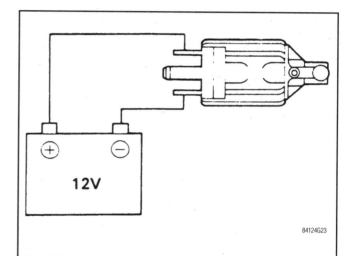

Fig. 23 Applying battery voltage to the EGR Solenoid valve—California vehicles

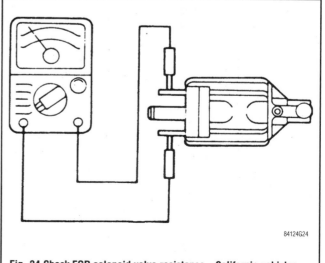

Fig. 24 Check EGR solenoid valve resistance—California vehicles

EGR Temperature Sensor (California)

TESTING

▶ See Figure 25

1. Remove the EGR temperature sensor from the EGR valve and place in a bucket of water with a thermometer.
2. Heat the water to 122°F (50°C) and measure the resistance across the sensor terminals. Resistance should be 60–83 ohms.
3. Raise the temperature of the water to 212°F (100°C) and measure the resistance again. Resistance should drop to 11–14 ohms.
4. Replace the EGR temperature sensor if defective.

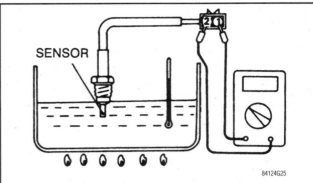

Fig. 25 EGR temperature sensor test—Fuel injected California vehicles

CATALYTIC CONVERTERS

General Information

▶ See Figures 26 and 27

A monolithic type 3-way catalytic converter is used to reduce vehicle emissions. The converter, working in combination with the air/fuel ratio, controls the CO, HC and reduces NOx.

Under normal operating conditions, the catalytic converter does not require maintenance. However, it is important to keep the engine properly tuned. If the engine is not kept properly tuned, the catalytic converter may overheat and the converter could be damaged. This situation can also occur during diagnostic testing if any spark plug cables are removed and the engine is allowed to run for an extended period of time.

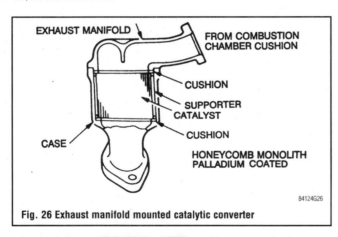

Fig. 26 Exhaust manifold mounted catalytic converter

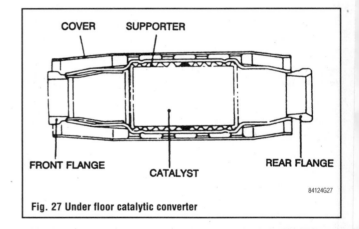

Fig. 27 Under floor catalytic converter

JET AIR SYSTEM

General Information

▶ See Figure 28

In addition to the intake valve and the exhaust valve, a jet valve has been added to draw air (super lean mixture or air) into the combustion chamber. The jet valve assembly consists of a valve, body and spring which are all screwed into the jet assembly and pressed into the cylinder head with the jet opening directed towards the spark plug. The jet valve draws its air from a passage in the carburetor, intake manifold and cylinder head. The air flows through the intake openings near the primary throttle valve of the carburetor and into the intake manifold and cylinder head, it then flows through the jet valve opening and into the combustion chamber. The jet valve is operated by the same cam as the intake valve and is attached by a common rocker arm so the jet valve and intake valve open and close at the same time.

On the intake stroke, the air/fuel mixture flows through the intake valve port and into the combustion chamber. At the same time, jet air is forced into the combustion chamber as the piston moves down. The jet air running out of the jet opening scavenges the residual gasses around the spark plug and creates a good secondary ignition condition. This also produces a strong air flow in the

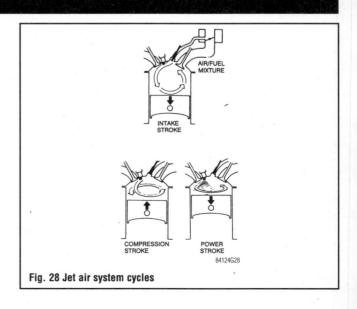

Fig. 28 Jet air system cycles

combustion chamber which continues throughout the compression stroke and improves the flame spread after ignition thus assuring a high combustion efficiency. The jet air flow dwindles with the increase of the throttle valve opening but the intensified inflow of normal intake air mixture can properly promote combustion.

➡An incorrect jet valve clearance would affect the emission levels and could also cause engine malfunction. Adjust the jet valve clearance before adjusting the intake valve clearance. Furthermore, the cylinder head bolts should be tightened before making this adjustment. The jet valve clearance should be adjusted with the adjusting screw on the intake valve side fully loosened.

HIGH ALTITUDE COMPENSATION SYSTEM

Federal Vehicles

So all Federal vehicles will meet the federal requirements at high altitude, all vehicles using a carburetor are equipped with a high altitude compensation system, in addition to the feedback carburetor system. The high altitude compensation system is made up of the following components: a High Altitude Compensator (HAC), vacuum switching valve and a distributor equipped with a high altitude advance system.

Air/fuel ratio at a high altitude is controlled by the HAC to be approximately the same value as the one at sea level. By supplying additional bleed air into the primary and secondary main wells through HAC and vacuum switching valves, the correct air/fuel ratio is obtained. In order to reduce hydrocarbon and carbon monoxide emissions and to get better performance at higher altitudes, the ignition timing is advanced by specific degrees at specific altitudes. The spark advance signal is sent to the sub-diaphragm chamber of the distributor, through the high altitude compensator. On California models, instead of using the vacuum switching valve, a check valve is used in its place.

California Vehicles

▶ **See Figures 29 and 30**

All vehicles are equipped with a high altitude compensation system in addition to the feedback carburetor system. This system consists of a high altitude

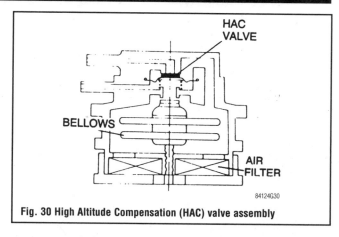

Fig. 30 High Altitude Compensation (HAC) valve assembly

compensator, a check valve and a distributor equipped with a high altitude advance system.

Air/fuel ratio at high altitude is controlled by the high altitude system to be about the same value as the one at sea level, by supplying additional air into the primary main well through the HAC. The air to fuel ratio is controlled precisely by the feedback carburetor system to comply with the California high altitude requirements.

In order to reduce HC and CO emissions and to get better driveability at high altitude, ignition timing is advanced by specified degrees at high altitude. Spark advance vacuum signal is sent to the sub diaphragm chamber of the distributor via the HAC.

High Altitude Compensation (HAC) Valve

TESTING

1. Remove the HAC and inspect for deformation or cracks.
2. Clean the air filter in the valve.
3. At altitudes below 3900 ft., the valve should leak vacuum at the lower nipple and hold vacuum at the upper nipple.
4. At altitudes above 3900 ft., the valve should hold vacuum at the lower nipple.

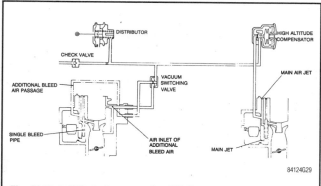

Fig. 29 High Altitude Compensation (HAC) system schematic—carbureted vehicles

FEEDBACK CARBURETOR (FBC) SYSTEM

General Information

The feedback carburetor system provides positive air/fuel ratio control for maximum reduction of emissions. The electronic control unit receives signals from various sensors and then modulates 2 solenoid valves installed on the carburetor to control the air/fuel ratio.

The ECU also controls the ignition timing, electric choke and the idle up solenoid by switching the solenoid valves ON and OFF.

SYSTEM OPERATION

▶ **See Figures 31, 32 and 33**

The air/fuel ratio control is maintained by the ECU in 1 of 2 operating modes.

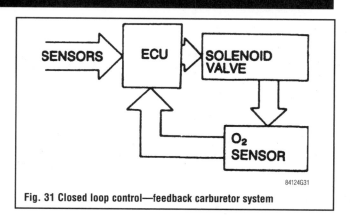

Fig. 31 Closed loop control—feedback carburetor system

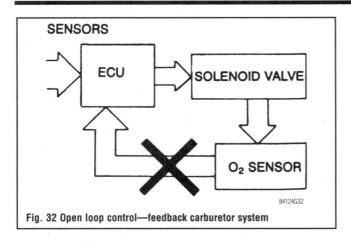

Fig. 32 Open loop control—feedback carburetor system

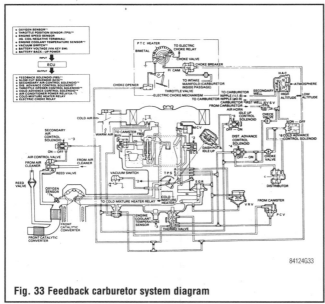

Fig. 33 Feedback carburetor system diagram

Closed Loop Control (Feedback Control)

Closed loop control is used after engine warm-up. The air/fuel mixture is determined by the feedback control, based on the oxygen sensor signal.

Oxygen sensor output voltage changes sharply at the stoichiometric ratio (14.7:1). The control unit senses this signal and uses the feedback solenoid valve to regulate the ratio. By providing a stoichiometric ratio, the best purification rate of the 3-catalyst converter may be kept. In this state, the slow cut solenoid valve is kept wide open (100 percent duty).

Open Loop Control

During engine start, warm-up, high load operation and deceleration, the air/fuel ratio is in open loop. Control is based on preset values contained in the ECU. These values are set by the factory and cannot be changed.

During deceleration, the slow cut solenoid valve limits fuel flow for better fuel economy and for prevention of overheating of the catalysts.

SYSTEM COMPONENTS

Electronic Control Unit (ECU)

The electronic control unit is mounted in the passenger compartment and consists of a printed circuit board mounted in a protective metal box. It receives analog inputs from sensors and converts them into digital signals. These signals and various inputs are processed and used by the ECU in controlling the fuel delivery, secondary air, deceleration spark and throttle opener management.

Coolant Temperature Sensor

The coolant temperature sensor is installed in the intake manifold. This sensor provides data to the ECU for use in controlling fuel delivery and secondary air management.

Throttle Position Sensor

The Throttle Position Sensor (TPS) is a potentiometer mounted to the carburetor. The TPS provides throttle angle information to the ECU to be used in controlling the fuel delivery and secondary management.

Engine Speed Sensor

The engine speed sensor signal comes from the negative terminal voltage of the ignition coil. Electric signals are sent to the ECU, where the time between these pulses is used to calculate engine speed, which is used in controlling fuel delivery, secondary air management, deceleration spark and throttle opener management.

Oxygen Sensor (Federal)

The oxygen sensor is mounted in the exhaust manifold. The output signal from the sensor, which varies with the oxygen content of the exhaust gas stream, is provided to the ECU for use in controlling closed loop compensation of fuel delivery.

Oxygen Sensor (California)

The oxygen sensor is mounted in the exhaust manifold. The oxygen sensor used in California models contains a heater element to obtain closed loop in a shorter amount of time. The output signal from the sensor, which varies with the oxygen content of the exhaust gas stream, is provided to the ECU for use in controlling closed loop compensation of fuel delivery.

Vacuum Switch

The switch is installed on the floor board or the fender and is electronically turned ON (switch closed) when the throttle valve is in the closed (idling) position. Information to this switch is provided from the ECU for use in controlling fuel delivery and secondary air management.

Feedback Solenoid Valve

The feedback solenoid valve is installed in the carburetor float chamber cover. The ECU controls the air to fuel ratio by controlling the duty cycle of the valve. As the duty ratio increases, the mixture becomes leaner.

Slow Cut Solenoid Valve

The slow cut solenoid valve is located in the carburetor float bowl chamber cover. The ECU controls the carburetor slow system fuel flow by controlling the duty cycle of the valve.

Idle Up Solenoid

When the tail switch or the blower motor switch is ON, the engine idle speed is increased by changing the throttle valve opening. In order to decrease HC emissions emitted during vehicle deceleration and to improve engine performance under a load, the ECU de-energizes the solenoid valve which supplies the manifold vacuum to the throttle opener at or above the preset engine speed and then the throttle opener operation is suspended.

Mixture Control Valve (MCV)

When the throttle is closed suddenly during deceleration or shifting, the fuel remaining in the intake manifold causes an over rich mixture temporarily. In order to prevent this, air is supplied from another passage to correct the air/fuel ratio and reduce HC emission. The increased manifold vacuum acts so air is supplied to the intake manifold. The vacuum is also supplied to chamber **B** but with some delay due to an orifice. When the vacuum is supplied to both chambers **B** and **A**, the spring causes the valve to close, stopping the supply of air. The check valve located at the diaphragm prevents high vacuum from remaining in chamber **B** during acceleration or deceleration. If a high vacuum remains in chamber **B**, the valve may fail to operate when vacuum acts on chamber **A**.

Diagnosis And Testing

♦ See Figures 34 and 35

If the FBC system components (sensors, carburetor control unit computer, solenoid, etc.) fail, interruption of the fuel supply or failure to supply the proper amount of fuel for engine operating conditions will result.

This condition will have several effects on the system: The engine will be hard to start or will not start at all, The engine idle will be unstable or poor performance will occur. If any of the above conditions are noted, first perform basic engine checks (ignition system malfunctions, incorrect engine adjustment, etc.).

If the basic engine checks show no faults, the FBC system can be checked by the use of FBC checker as follows:

➡**Before disconnecting the battery terminals, make sure the ignition switch is in the OFF position. If the battery terminals are disconnected while engine is running or when ignition switch is in the ON position, malfunction or damage of the ECU could result. Disconnect the battery cables before charging the battery. When battery is connected, be sure not to reverse polarity. Make sure all electrical harness connectors are securely connected. Be careful not to allow entry of water or oil into connectors.**

1. Turn ignition switch to the **OFF** position.
2. Remove the harness connector **A** (13 poles) and connector **B** (7 poles) from carburetor computer control unit.
3. Set the check switch of the FBC checker to the **OFF** position. Set the select switch of checker tool to the **A** position.
4. Connect the FBC harness connector to the connectors of FBC checker tool. Connect the FBC harness connectors and place FBC checker tool on front seat of the vehicle.
5. If the checker tool shows any departure from specifications, check the corresponding sensor and related electrical wiring. Repair or replace defective components as required.

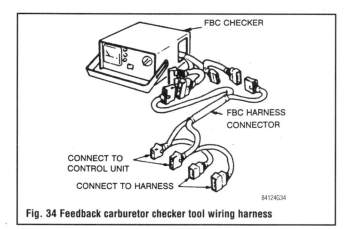

Fig. 34 Feedback carburetor checker tool wiring harness

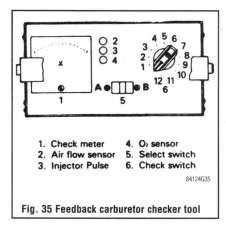

1. Check meter
2. Air flow sensor
3. Injector Pulse
4. O₂ sensor
5. Select switch
6. Check switch

Fig. 35 Feedback carburetor checker tool

6. After repair or replacement, check the system to confirm that repaired or replaced part is performing properly.
7. If the problem is still not corrected and the control unit appears to be at fault, perform all checker tests and individual sensor tests again. If everything is in order, replace the carburetor control unit.

Component Testing

ELECTRONIC CONTROL UNIT (ECU)

♦ See Figures 36

Testing

The only way to test the ECU is to replace if with a known-good unit and check to see if symptom persists.

REMOVAL & INSTALLATION

1. Disconnect the negative battery cable.
2. Disconnect the electrical connectors to the ECU.
3. Remove the 2 screws that secure the ECU and remove the ECU.
4. Installation is the reverse of the removal procedure.

COOLANT TEMPERATURE SENSOR

♦ See Figure 37

Testing

1. Disconnect the electrical connectors from the coolant temperature sensor.
2. Remove the coolant temperature sensor from the intake manifold.
3. Stick the sensing portion of the sensor in water and connect an ohmmeter to the terminals and check resistance.
4. With the water temperature at 32°F (0°C), the resistance should be 5.9 kilo-ohms. With the water temperature at 68°F (20°C), the resistance should be 2.5 kilo-ohms. With the water temperature at 104°F (40°C), the resistance should be 1.1 kilo-ohms. With the water temperature at 176°F (80°C), the resistance should be 0.3 kilo-ohms.
5. If the resistance is not within specifications, replace the sensor.
6. Install the coolant sensor and connect the electrical connectors. Connect the negative battery cable.

THROTTLE POSITION SENSOR

♦ See Figure 38

Testing

1. Loosen the accelerator cable.
2. Loosen speed adjusting screw No. 1 and No. 2 enough to close the throttle valve completely. Record the number of turns to loosen.

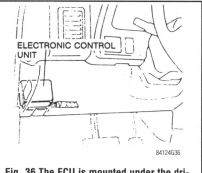

Fig. 36 The ECU is mounted under the drivers side of the instrument panel—Scoupe shown, others similar

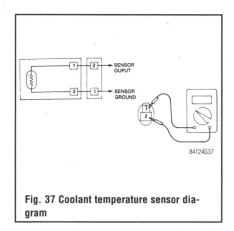

Fig. 37 Coolant temperature sensor diagram

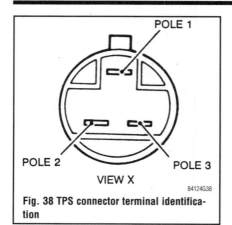

Fig. 38 TPS connector terminal identification

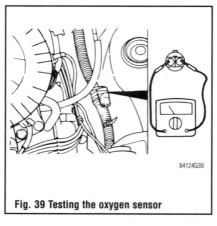

Fig. 39 Testing the oxygen sensor

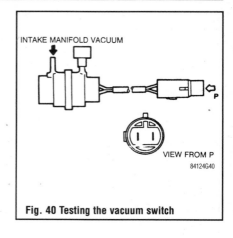

Fig. 40 Testing the vacuum switch

3. Connect voltmeter (digital type) between terminals No. **2** and No. **3** of the TPS connector pins.

➡**Do not disconnect the TPS connector from the chassis harness.**

4. Turn the ignition switch **ON** (engine will not start) and measure the TPS voltage. The voltage should read 250 millivolts.
5. If the output voltage is not correct, turn the TPS body to adjust to specification. Turning the TPS body clockwise increases the output voltage
6. Turn the ignition switch **OFF**.
7. Tighten speed adjusting screws the same number of turns as loosened.
8. Adjust the accelerator cable free-play.
9. Start the engine and check that the idle speed is correct.

OXYGEN SENSOR (FEDERAL)

Testing

▶ **See Figure 39**

1. Warm the engine to normal operating temperature.
2. Disconnect the oxygen sensor connector and connect a voltmeter to the sensor connector terminal of the oxygen sensor.
3. While increasing the engine rpm, measure the sensor output voltage.
4. As the rpm increase, the voltage should read approximately 0.6 volts. If not within specifications, replace the oxygen sensor.

Removal and Installation

1. Disconnect the electrical connector to the oxygen sensor.
2. Remove the oxygen sensor from the exhaust manifold.
3. To install, replace sensor and tighten to 29–36 ft. lbs. (40–50 Nm). Connect connector to sensor.

OXYGEN SENSOR (CALIFORNIA)

Testing

1. Warm the engine to normal operating temperature.
2. Disconnect the oxygen sensor connector and measure the resistance between terminals No. **3** and No. **4**. The resistance should measure 30 ohms or more at 752°F (400°C).
3. While increasing the engine rpm, measure the sensor output voltage between terminals No. **1** and No. **2**.
4. As the rpm increase, the voltage should read approximately 0.6 volts. If not within specifications, replace the oxygen sensor.

Removal and Installation

1. Disconnect the electrical connector to the oxygen sensor.
2. Remove the oxygen sensor from the exhaust manifold.
3. To install, replace sensor and tighten to 29–36 ft. lbs. (40–50 Nm). Connect connector to sensor.

VACUUM SWITCH

Testing

▶ **See Figure 40**

The vacuum switch can only be checked using the Hyundai FBC tester.
1. Connect FBC tester to the ECU harness connector at terminal No. **13**.
2. Set the select switch to the **A** mode and check switch to **6**.
3. With the ignition turned to the **ON** position and the engine not running, the meter should read 9–13 volts.
4. With the engine warm and at idle, the reading should be 0–0.6 volts.

FEEDBACK SOLENOID VALVE

Testing

The Feedback solenoid valve can only be checked using the Hyundai FBC tester.
1. Connect FBC tester to the ECU harness connector at terminal No. **1**.
2. Set the select switch to the **B** mode and check switch to **2**.
3. With the ignition turned to the **ON** position and the engine not running, the meter should read 11–13 volts.
4. With the engine warm and at idle, the reading should be 2–12 volts.

SLOW CUT SOLENOID VALVE

Testing

The Slow cut solenoid valve can only be checked using the Hyundai FBC tester.
1. Connect FBC tester to the ECU harness connector at terminal No. **9**.
2. Set the select switch to the **B** mode and check switch to **7**.
3. With the engine idling, the meter should read 0–0.6 volts.
4. Upon quick deceleration from above 4000 rpm to idle, the reading should momentarily be 13–15 volts.

IDLE UP SOLENOID

Testing

The idle up solenoid valve can only be checked using the Hyundai FBC tester.
1. Connect FBC tester to the ECU harness connector at terminal No. **2**.
2. Set the select switch to the **A** mode and check switch to **7**.
3. With the engine at idle and electrical accessories turned **ON**, the meter should read 0–0.6 volts.
4. With the engine running at 2000 rpm and the electrical accessories **ON**, the reading should be 9–15 volts.

CHOKE HEATER

Testing

♦ **See Figure 41**

1. Disconnect the electric choke heater connector and check the resistance of the heater.
2. The resistance should be approx. 6 ohms at 68°F.
3. If the resistance is a great deal out of range or the circuit is open, replace the choke mechanism.

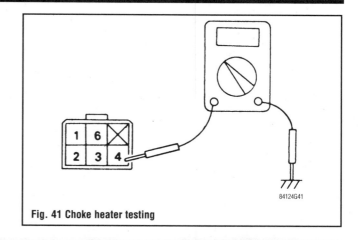

Fig. 41 Choke heater testing

MULTI-POINT FUEL INJECTION SYSTEM

General Information

♦ **See Figures 42, 43 and 44**

The fuel injection system used on Hyundai vehicles is classified as a Multi-point Fuel Injection (MPI) system. The basic function of the system is to control the air/fuel ratio, based on input signals from various engine sensors. The air/fuel ratio is controlled by varying the injector driving time. The system is controlled by an Electronic Control Unit (ECU), which monitors the engine conditions, then calculates the injection timing and air/fuel ratio according to the signals from the sensors. The ECU consists of an 8-bit microprocessor, Random Access Memory (RAM), Read Only Memory (ROM) and input and output signal interface system.

The MPI system consists of 2 operating modes:
• Open Loop—air/fuel ratio is controlled by information programmed into the ECU by the manufacturer.
• Closed Loop—air/fuel ratio is varied by the ECU based on information supplied by the oxygen sensor.

An electric fuel pump supplies sufficient fuel to the injection system and the pressure regulator maintains a constant pressure to the injectors. These injectors inject a metered quantity of fuel into the intake manifold in accordance with signals from the Electronic Control Unit (ECU) or engine computer. After pressure regulation excess fuel is returned to the fuel tank.

The injectors have 2 modes (Injector Drive Timing) of operation:
• Non-synchronous Injection (Simultaneous Injection)
• Synchronous Injection (Sequential Injection)

Non-synchronous injection is activated during engine starting (cranking). There are 2 fuel injections, for each engine rpm, to all 4 cylinders. Also, during acceleration, fuel proportionate to the magnitude of acceleration, is injected to 2 selected cylinders during the intake and exhaust strokes.

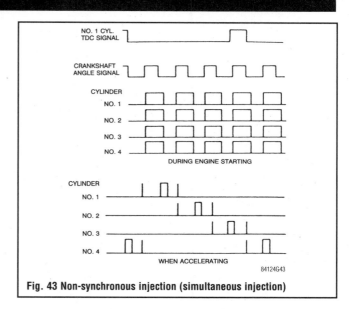

Fig. 43 Non-synchronous injection (simultaneous injection)

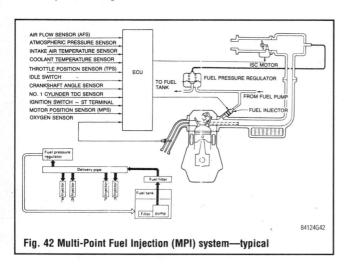

Fig. 42 Multi-Point Fuel Injection (MPI) system—typical

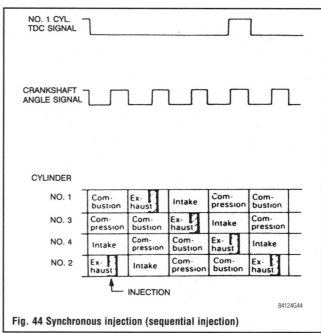

Fig. 44 Synchronous injection (sequential injection)

Synchronous Injection is activated after the engine has started. The injectors are activated at the exhaust stroke of each cylinder in a sequential manner, according to crankshaft angle sensor signal. There is 1 injection per cylinder for every 2 crankshaft revolution, according to firing order.

DATA SENSORS

Air Flow Sensor (AFS)

The AFS measures the intake air volume. The ECU uses this intake air volume signal to decide the basic fuel injection duration. The AFS on all models except the Turbo Scoupe is a hot film type, the Turbo Scoupe uses a hot wire type. The results that are obtained by the 2 types of sensor, however, are the same.

Atmosphere Pressure Sensor

The atmosphere pressure sensor signal is used by the ECU to compute the altitude of the vehicle so the ECU can correct the ignition timing and air/fuel ratio. The atmosphere pressure sensor is contain in the AFS.

Intake Air Temperature Sensor

The air temperature sensor is a resistor based sensor for detecting the intake air temperature. The ECU provides fuel injection control based on this information. The air temperature sensor is located on the AFS.

Engine Coolant Temperature Sensor

The coolant temperature sensor is located in the coolant passage of the intake manifold. The ECU uses this signal to determine the base fuel enrichment for cold and warm engine operation.

Throttle Position Sensor (TPS)

The TPS is a rotating type variable resistor that rotates with the throttle body shaft to sense the throttle valve opening. Based on TPS voltage signals, the ECU computes the throttle valve opening and accordingly corrects fuel for engine acceleration.

Idle Switch

♦ See Figure 45

The idle switch is a contact type switch. The switch is installed at the tip of the ISC. This switch provides the ECU with idle or off idle signal.

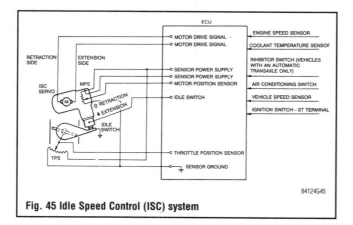

Fig. 45 Idle Speed Control (ISC) system

Motor Position Sensor (MPS)

The MPS is a variable resistor type sensor and is installed in the ISC servo. The MPS senses the ISC servo plunger position and sends the signal to the ECU. The ECU controls the valve opening, and consequently the idle speed by

using the MPS signal, idle signal, engine coolant temperature signal, load signals and vehicle speed sensor.

Cylinder TDC and Crankshaft Angle Sensor

The No. 1 TDC sensor and the crankshaft angle sensor are composed of a disc and unit assembly in the distributor. The No. 1 cylinder TDC is detected by the signal obtained through the single inner slit of the disc. The ECU, based upon this signal, determines the fuel injection cylinder. The crankshaft angle sensor signal comes from the 4 slits at the outer circumference of the disc serve to detect the position of the crankshaft. The ECU, based on this signal, determines the fuel injection timing, and also calculates the amount of intake air, the ignition timing, etc. for each stroke of engine.

Phase Sensor

1993 SCOUPE

The Phase Sensor is built into the distributor. It senses the TDC point of the No. 1 cylinder in its compression stroke. These signals are fed to the ECU to be used in determining fuel injection sequence.

Crankshaft Position Sensor

1993 SCOUPE

The crankshaft position sensor consists of a magnetic coil which is installed in the transaxle housing. The sensor gets its signal from a sensor ring mounted to the flywheel. The voltage signal is fed to the ECU for detecting engine rpm and crankshaft position.

Oxygen Sensor

The oxygen sensor, by detecting the oxygen content in the exhaust gas, maintains the stoichiometric air/fuel ratio. In operation, the ECU receives the signals from the sensor and changes the duration during which fuel is injected. The oxygen sensor is located in the exhaust manifold.

Vehicle Speed Sensor

The vehicle speed sensor uses a reed type switch. The speed sensor is built into the speedometer and converts the speedometer gear revolution into pulse signals, which are sent to the ECU.

Neutral (Inhibitor) Switch

The ECU, based on this signal, senses when the automatic transaxle is in **NEUTRAL** or **PARK** and operates the ISC servo to keep the idle speed correct.

Idle Speed Control (ISC) Servo

The ISC servo consists of a motor, worm gear, worm wheel and plunger. The MPS is used to detect plunger position and an idle switch to detect closed throttle position.

As the motor rotates, according to signals from the ECU, the plunger extends or retracts depending on direction of the motor rotation. This actuates the throttle valve via the ISC lever. The ECU controls the idle speed by changing the throttle opening through this function.

Knock Sensor

1993 SCOUPE

The Knock Sensor is attached to the cylinder block and senses engine knock. The sensor functions by reading the knocking vibration from the engine and converts this into a voltage signal delivered as output to the ECU. The ECU uses this signal to adjust the ignition timing.

Waste Gate Control Solenoid Valve

1993 SCOUPE TURBO

The waste gate control solenoid valve controls the turbo boost pressure. This valve is integrated with the rest of the engine sensors to ensure proper engine operating conditions under varying boost conditions. It also helps to reduce turbo lag and engine knock.

FUEL DELIVERY SYSTEM

Fuel Pump

The fuel pump is a compact impeller design and is installed inside the fuel tank. The pump assembly consists of the impeller (driven by the motor), the pump casing (which forms the pumping chamber), and cover of the pump. This pump is called a wet-type pump, because the inside is also filled with fuel. Never operate this type of pump when removed from the vehicle or explosion will result, due to fuel fumes, electric sparks and fresh air, which is not available in the fuel tank.

Fuel Injectors

The injectors are solenoid valves. When the solenoid coil is energized, the plunger is retracted. The needle valve that is attached to the plunger is pulled to the full open position.

Diagnosis and Testing

SERVICE PRECAUTIONS

- Do not operate the fuel pump if the fuel system is empty.
- Do not operate the fuel pump when removed from the fuel tank.
- Do not reuse fuel hose clamps.
- Make sure all ECU harness connectors are fastened securely. A poor connection can cause an extremely high surge voltage in the coil and condenser and result in damage to integrated circuits.
- Keep all ECU parts and harnesses dry during service.
- Do not attempt to disconnect the battery cables with the engine running.
- Do not disconnect wiring connector with the engine running, unless instructed to do so.
- Do not depress the accelerator pedal when starting.
- Do not rev up the engine immediately after starting or just prior to shutdown.
- Do not apply battery power directly to injectors.
- To avoid damage to the ECU, always turn the ignition switch **OFF** before disconnecting the battery cable.
- The control harnesses between the ECU and oxygen sensor are shielded wires with the shield grounded to the body in order to prevent the influence of ignition noises and radio interference. When the shielded wire is faulty, the control harness must be replaced.
- Before removing or installing any part(s), always check the self-diagnosis system.

SELF-DIAGNOSIS SYSTEM

Except 1993 Scoupe

The Engine Control Unit (ECU) is capable of monitoring both input and output signals. When the ECU notices that an irregularity has continued for a specified time or longer, it memorizes a trouble code and outputs the signal to the self-diagnosis output terminal. There are 14 diagnosis items, including the normal state. The trouble codes can be read out with a voltmeter or multi-tester.

Among the self-diagnosis items, a Malfunction Indicator Light (MIL) comes ON to notify the driver of the emission control items when an irregularity is detected.

Generally, the MIL will come ON for 5 seconds when the ignition switch is turned **ON**.

➡**Always check that the MIL illuminates for approximately 5 seconds, when the ignition switch is turned ON. If the light does not illuminate, check for an open circuit harness, blown fuse or blown bulb.**

1993 Scoupe

The Engine Control Unit (ECU) is capable of monitoring both input and output signals. When the ECU notices that an irregularity has continued for a spec-

ified time or longer, it memorizes a trouble code and outputs the signal to the self-diagnosis output terminal. There are 29 diagnosis items, including the normal state. The trouble codes can be read out with the On-Board Diagnostics (OBD) lamp or multi-tester.

Among the self-diagnosis items, the On-Board Diagnostics (OBD) lamp comes ON to notify the driver of the emission control items when an irregularity is detected.

Generally, the OBD will come ON for 5 seconds when the ignition switch is turned **ON**.

➡**Always check that the OBD illuminates for approximately 5 seconds, when the ignition switch is turned ON. If the light does not illuminate, check for an open circuit harness, blown fuse or blown bulb.**

READING CODES

◆ **See Figures 46 thru 52**

➡**The trouble codes for the 1993 Scoupe cannot be read using a voltmeter.**

Using Voltmeter

EXCEPT 1993 SCOUPE

1. Connect the voltmeter to the self-diagnostic connector, across the MPI diagnosis and ground terminals.
2. Turn the ignition switch **ON**. The ECU diagnostics memory will immediately start.
3. If the voltmeter displays a steady needle sweep, the system is normal and no codes are in the memory.
4. If the voltmeter displays a steady **HIGH** signal, the ECU is damaged.
5. If the ECU has detected a malfunction, the voltmeter will deflect, indicating the diagnostic code.
6. Record the codes displayed by the voltmeter needle deflections.
7. The ECU will continue to send any memorized trouble codes to the self-diagnostic for as long as the ignition is **ON**, or until the codes have been cleared from memory.

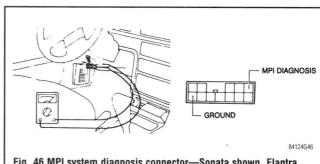

Fig. 46 MPI system diagnosis connector—Sonata shown, Elantra similar

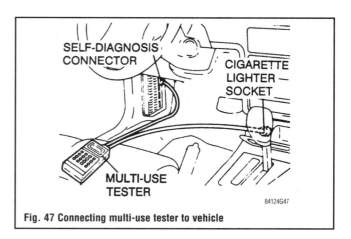

Fig. 47 Connecting multi-use tester to vehicle

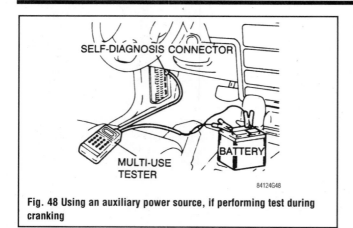

SELF-DIAGNOSIS CONNECTOR

MULTI-USE TESTER

BATTERY

84124G48

Fig. 48 Using an auxiliary power source, if performing test during cranking

Trouble code	Diagnosis item	Trouble code	Diagnosis item
11	Oxygen sensor	23	No.1 cylinder top dead center sensor
12	Air-flow sensor	24	Vehicle-speed reed switch
13	Air temperature sensor	25	Atmospheric pressure sensor
14	Throttle position sensor	41	Injector
15	Motor position sensor	42	Fuel pump
21	Engine coolant temperature sensor	43	EGR temperature sensor (For California Vehicles)
22	Crank angle sensor		

84124G49

Fig. 49 Diagnostic trouble code list—Except 1993 Scoupe

Output preference order	Diagnosis item	Trouble code			Check item (Remedy)
		Output signal pattern	No.	Memory	
1	Engine control unit		—	—	(Replace engine control unit)
2	Oxygen sensor		11	Retained	o Harness and connector o Fuel pressure o Injectors (Replace if defective.) o Intake air leaks o Oxygen sensor
3	Air flow sensor		12	Retained	o Harness and connector (If harness and connector are normal, replace air flow sensor assembly.)

84124G50

Fig. 50 Diagnostic trouble code pattern list—Except 1993 Scoupe

Using Multi-Use Tester (MUT)

1. Turn the ignition switch **OFF**.
2. Connect the Multi-Use Tester (MUT), (Tool 09391—33200 or equivalent), to the diagnosis connector in the fuse box.
3. Connect the power-source terminal of the MUT to the cigarette lighter switch.
4. Turn the ignition switch **ON** and the ECU memory contents will immediately start.
5. Read the self-diagnosis output and check output of correct code.
6. After recording the fault codes, check and repair each part according to the check items in the Diagnosis Charts.

➡**If the battery voltage is too low, trouble codes cannot be read. If the battery or the ECU connector is disconnected, the diagnosis memory will be erased.**

When the ignition key is in the **START** position, the cigarette lighter power is OFF. If it is necessary to perform tests, using the MUT in the crank mode, an auxiliary power supply will be necessary. Use the battery clamp harness provided.

Output preference order	Diagnosis item	Malfunction code			Check item (Remedy)
		Output signal pattern	No.	Memory	
4	Air temperature sensor		13	Retained	o Harness and connector o Air temperature sensor
5	Throttle position sensor		14	Retained	o Harness and connector o Throttle position sensor o Idle position switch
6	Motor position sensor		15	Retained	o Harness and connector o Motor position sensor
7	Engine coolant temperature sensor		21	Retained	o Harness and connector o Engine coolant temperature sensor
8	Crank angle sensor		22	Retained	o Harness and connector If harness and connector are normal, replace distributor assembly.)
9	No.1 cylinder top dead center sensor		23	Retained	o Harness and connector If harness and connector are normal, replace distributor assembly.)
10	Vehicle-speed sensor (reed switch)		24	Retained	o Harness and connector o Vehicle-speed sensor (reed switch)

84124G51

Fig. 51 Diagnostic trouble code pattern list (continued)—Except 1993 Scoupe

Output preference order	Diagnosis item	Trouble code			Check item (Remedy)
		Output signal pattern	No.	Memory	
11	Barometric pressure sensor		25	Retained	o Harness and connector If harness and connector are normal, replace barometric pressure sensor assembly.)
12	Injector		41	Retained	o Harness and connector o Injector coil resistance
13	Fuel pump		42	Retained	o Harness and connector o Control relay
14	EGR*		43	Retained	o Harness and connector o EGR temperature sensor o EGR valve o EGR control solenoid valve o EGR valve control vacuum
15	Normal state		—	—	

84124G52

Fig. 52 Diagnostic trouble code pattern list (continued)—Except 1993 Scoupe

Using On-Board Diagnostic (OBD) Lamp

1993 SCOUPE

▶ **See Figures 53, 54, 55 and 56**

1. Turn the ignition switch to the **ON** position (do not start the engine).
2. Ground the L wire (No. 10 pin) of the diagnostic connector, for 2.5 seconds, then remove the ground.
3. The first output is the fault code stored or the "NO FAULT DETECTED CODE" 4444.

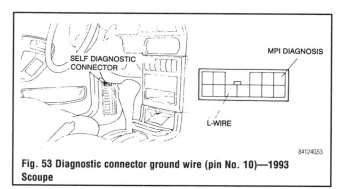

Fig. 53 Diagnostic connector ground wire (pin No. 10)—1993 Scoupe

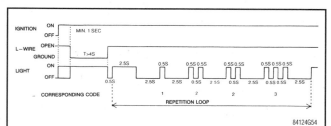

Fig. 54 Trouble code display pattern using On-Board Diagnostic lamp—1993 Scoupe

| Diagnosis item | Trouble code | | N/A | | T/C | Description |
	M.U.T. Display	Check engine lamp	UL	L		
Electronic Control Unit	13. ECU-ROM		O	O	-	ECU Failure-ROM
	14. ECU-RAM		O	O	-	ECU Failure-RAM
	16. ECU-ROM/RAM		-	-	O	ECU Failure-ROM/RAM
	17. ECU-KNOCK EVA		-	-	O	ECU Failure-Knock control
	19. ECU-KNOCK		O	O	O	ECU Failure-Knock evaluation circuit
	61. INJ./PURGE V		O	O	-	ECU Failure-injector or Purge control sol. valve
	62. ISA./AC RLY		O	O	-	ECU Failure idle speed actuator or air con. relay
	63. ECU-DRIVE (A)		O	O	-	ECU Failure-Driving circuit (A)
	65. ACTUATORS		-	-	O	ECU-Failure inj. or PCV or ISA ro AC/relay
	69. ECU-DRIVE (B)		O	O	-	ECU Failure-Driving circuit (B)
Oxygen sensor	21. O2 sensor		O	-	O	O2 sensor failure
Air flow sensor	22. AFS		O	O	O	Air flow sensor failure
Coolant temperature sensor	23. WTS		O	O	O	Coolant temperature sensor failure
Phase sensor	24. PHASE SENSOR		O	O	O	Phase sensor failure
Crankshaft position sensor	25. CRANK P.SNSR		O	O	O	Crankshaft position sensor failure
Throttle position sensor	26. TPS		O	O	O	Throttle position sensor failure
Knock sensor	27. KNOCK SNSR		O	O	O	Knock sensor failure
Vehicle speed sensor	29. VEH. SPD. SNSR		O	O	O	Vehicle speed sensor failure
Battery	31. BATTERY		O	O	O	Battery voltage & alternator failure
Air conditioning compressor	33. A/C COMPRESR		O	O	O	Air conditioning compressor failure

Fig. 55 Diagnostic trouble code pattern list—1993 Scoupe

| Diagnosis item | Trouble code | | N/A | | T/C | Description |
	M.U.T. Display	Check engine lamp	UL	L		
Boost sensor	36. BOOST-HIGH		-	-	O	Turbo boost-too high failure
	37. BOOST-CNTL		-	-	O	Turbo boost-control deviation failure
	38. BOOST-C. VLV.		-	-	O	Turbo boost-control valve failure
	39. BOOST-P. SNSR		-	-	O	Turbo boost-Pressure sensor failure
injector	41. NO.1 INJECTOR		O	O	O	No.1 Injector failure
	42. NO.2 INJECTOR		O	O	O	No.2 Injector failure
	43. NO.3 INJECTOR		O	O	O	No.3 Injector failure
	44. NO.4 INJECTOR		O	O	O	No.4 Injector failure
Purge control solenoid	45. PURGE VALVE		O	-	-	Purge control solenoid valve failure
Idle speed actuator	47. ISA-OPEN'G		O	O	O	Idle speed actuator-opening failure
	48. ISA-CLOS'G		O	O	O	Idle speed actuator-closing failure
Fuel pump relay	53. FUEL PUMP RLY		O	O		Fuel pump relay failure
Air/Fuel ratio	81. A/F CTRL-INTG.		O	-	O	Air/Fuel control failure
	82. A/F ADAP.-MUL		O	-	O	Air/Fuel adaptive failure-multiplicative
	83. A/F ADAP.-A/N		O	-	O	Air/Fuel adaptive failure-A/N
	84. A/F ADAP.-ADD		O	-	O	Air/Fue adaptive failure-additive

Fig. 56 Diagnostic trouble code pattern list (continued)—1993 Scoupe

4. Each blink code is repeated continuously until the next step is ordered.
5. The next code can be read by grounding the L wire (No. 10 pin) again for 2.5 seconds. After that the next code will follow. Continue this until all codes are displayed.
6. The last code displayed will be the end of output code (3333).

CLEARING CODES

After completion of the repair or correction of the problem:
1. Turn the ignition switch **OFF**.
2. Disconnect the negative battery cable for approximately 15 seconds.
3. Reconnect the negative battery cable.
4. Check that no trouble codes are displayed by the MUT.
5. Remove the Multi-Use Tester (MUT).

FUEL PUMP

▶ **See Figures 57, 58, 59 and 60**

Operational Check

1. Turn the ignition switch **OFF**.
2. Apply battery voltage to the fuel pump drive connector and check that the fuel pump operates. The fuel pump is located inside the fuel tank and can be heard without removing the fuel tank cap.
3. Pinch the high pressure hose and note if fuel pressure is felt.

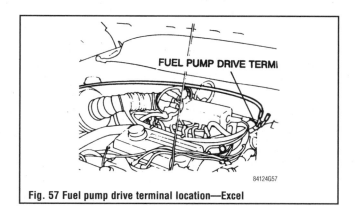

Fig. 57 Fuel pump drive terminal location—Excel

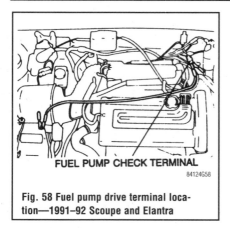

Fig. 58 Fuel pump drive terminal location—1991–92 Scoupe and Elantra

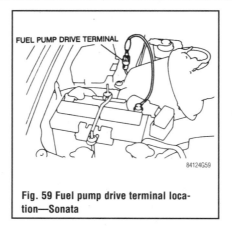

Fig. 59 Fuel pump drive terminal location—Sonata

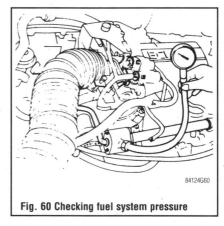

Fig. 60 Checking fuel system pressure

FUEL PRESSURE

Relieving

1. Disconnect the fuel pump harness at the rear of the tank.
2. Start engine and allow to idle.
3. After engine stalls, fuel pressure is reduced.
4. Disconnect the negative battery cable and reconnect the fuel pump wiring.
5. Remove the fuel tank cap.

➡**When disconnecting any fuel system hoses, always place a shop towel to prevent residual fuel from spraying.**

Testing

1. Relieve fuel system pressure.
2. Turn ignition switch **OFF** and disconnect the negative battery cable.

➡**When disconnecting any fuel system hoses, always place a shop towel to prevent residual fuel from spaying.**

3. Disconnect the high pressure hose at the delivery side. Using a fuel pressure gauge and adapter (09353-24000 or equivalent), install the adapter to the delivery pipe.
4. Connect the negative battery cable.
5. Activate the fuel pump, by applying battery voltage to the fuel pump drive terminal. Check that there is no leakage from pressure gauge or connections.
6. Disconnect the vacuum hose from the pressure regulator and plug.
7. Operate the engine at idle and check the fuel pressure. Fuel pressure should be 47–50 psi (330–350 kPa).
8. Reconnect the vacuum hose to the pressure regulator. With the engine idling, fuel pressure should be 39 psi (270 kPa).
9. If the specified values are not met, make the necessary repairs, as indicated in the diagnosis chart.
10. Shut the engine OFF. Check that the fuel pressure is maintained at the value indicated in Step 8, for approximately 5 minutes.
11. Relieve the fuel pressure.
12. Remove the fuel pressure gauge and reconnect the high pressure hose, using a new O-ring.
13. Start the engine and check for leaks.

IDLE SPEED CONTROL MOTOR

Testing

SONATA

▶ **See Figure 61**

1. Disconnect the ISC motor connector.
2. Check the continuity of the ISC motor coil between terminal 1 and 2. Reading should be 5–35 ohms at 68°F (20°C).

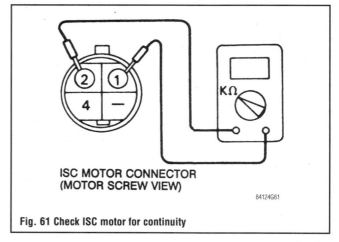

ISC MOTOR CONNECTOR
(MOTOR SCREW VIEW)

Fig. 61 Check ISC motor for continuity

3. Connect a 6 volt DC power supply (4 dry cells) between terminal 1 and 2. Check that the servo operates.

➡**Do not apply voltages higher than 6 volts DC or locking of the servo gears can result.**

4. If the servo does not operate, replace it as an assembly.

CONTROL RELAY

Failure of the control relay will interrupt power supply to the fuel pump, injectors and the ECU, resulting in a No Start condition.

Testing

ELANTRA

▶ **See Figure 62**

1. Apply 12 volts (+) power supply to terminal 6 of the control relay. Note the voltage at terminal 2 and at terminal 1 when the negative (−) lead is connected and disconnected from terminal 8. Should indicated 12 volts when connected and 0 volt when disconnected.
2. Apply 12 volts (+) power supply to terminal 3 of the control relay. Note the voltage at terminal 4 when the negative (−) lead is connected and disconnected from terminal 9. Should indicated 12 volts when connected and 0 volt when disconnected.
3. Connect the negative lead (−) of the power supply to terminal 10 of the control relay. Check for continuity between terminals 3 and 4 when the positive (+) terminal is connected and disconnected to terminal 7. Should indicate continuity when connected.
4. If the results are not satisfactory, replace the control relay.

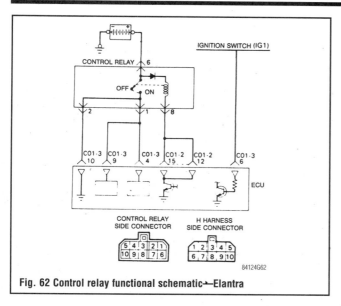

Fig. 62 Control relay functional schematic—Elantra

EXCEL

♦ See Figures 63 and 64

1. Check for continuity between the terminals when the relay coil is not energized, as follow:

   a. Terminals 1 and 4. Should be infinity (non-conductive).
   b. Terminals 2 and 8. Should indicate a value of approximately 95 ohms.
   c. Terminals 3 and 8. Should indicate a value of approximately 95 ohms.
   d. Terminals 6 and 7. Should indicate a value of approximately 35 ohms.
   e. Terminals 1 and 2. Should be infinity (non-conductive).

2. Connect the ohmmeter across terminals 1 and 4. Jumper terminal 6 to

ground and momentarily apply battery voltage to terminal 7 (Relay energized). Should indicate a value of 0 ohm.

3. Connect the ohmmeter across terminals 1 and 2. Jumper terminal 5 to ground and momentarily apply battery voltage to terminal 7 (Relay energized). Should indicate a value of 0 ohm.

4. If the results are not satisfactory, replace the control relay.

1991–92 SCOUPE

♦ See Figure 65

1. Check for continuity between the terminals when the relay coil is not energized, as follow:

   a. Terminals 2 and 8. Should indicate a value of approximately 95 ohms.
   b. Terminals 3 and 8. Should indicate a value of approximately 35 ohms.
   c. Terminals 5 and 7. Should indicate continuity, but only in one direction.

2. Connect the ohmmeter across terminals 1 and 4. Jumper terminal 6 to ground and momentarily apply battery voltage to terminal 7 (Relay energized). Should indicate a value of 0 ohm. When the relay is de-energized it should indicate infinity.

3. Connect the ohmmeter across terminals 1 and 3. Jumper terminal 5 to ground and momentarily apply battery voltage to terminal 7 (Relay energized). Should indicate a value of 0 ohm. When the relay is de-energized it should indicate infinity.

4. If the results are not satisfactory, replace the control relay.

SONATA

♦ See Figures 66 and 67

1. Check for continuity between the terminals when the relay coil is not energized, as follow:

   a. Terminals 1 and 4. Should be infinity (non-conductive).
   b. Terminals 2 and 8. Should indicate a value of approximately 95 ohms.
   c. Terminals 3 and 8. Should indicate a value of approximately 95 ohms.
   d. Terminals 6 and 7. Should indicate a value of approximately 35 ohms.

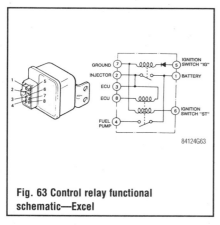

Fig. 63 Control relay functional schematic—Excel

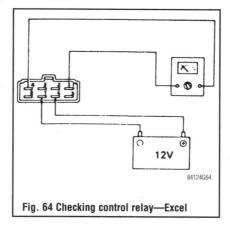

Fig. 64 Checking control relay—Excel

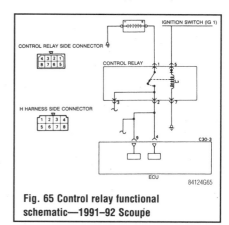

Fig. 65 Control relay functional schematic—1991–92 Scoupe

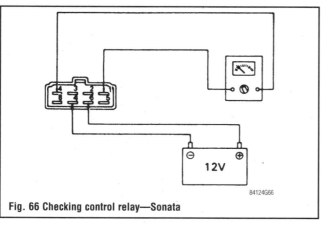

Fig. 66 Checking control relay—Sonata

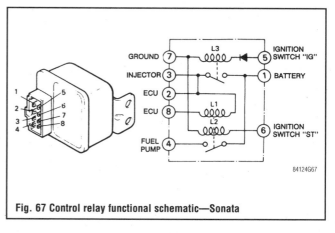

Fig. 67 Control relay functional schematic—Sonata

e. Terminals 1 and 3. Should be infinity (non-conductive).

2. Connect the ohmmeter across terminals 1 and 4. Jumper terminal 6 to ground and momentarily apply battery voltage to terminal 7 (Relay energized). Should indicate a value of 0 ohm.

3. Connect the ohmmeter across terminals 1 and 3. Jumper terminal 5 to ground and momentarily apply battery voltage to terminal 7 (Relay energized). Should indicate a value of 0 ohm.

4. If the results are not satisfactory, replace the control relay.

IDLE SPEED CONTROL SERVO

▶ See Figure 68

Testing

ELANTRA—STEPPER MOTOR TYPE

1. Connect a 6 volt power supply source to the indicated terminals and check if stepper motor movement occurs, as follows:
   a. Positive (+) lead to terminal 2 and 5 of the connector.
   b. Negative (−) lead to terminal 1 and 4.
   c. Negative (−) lead to terminal 3 and 4.
   d. Negative (−) lead to terminal 3 and 6.
   e. Negative (−) lead to terminal 1 and 6.
2. Measure the resistance between the respective terminals, as follows:
   a. Terminals 2–3 and 1—28–33 ohms at 68°F (20°C)
   b. Terminals 5–4 and 6—28–33 ohms at 68°F (20°C)
3. If the results are not as indicated in Step 1 and 2, replace the idle speed control servo.

SCOUPE—DC MOTOR TYPE

1. Check for an open-circuit or short-circuit to ground between the ECU terminals 1 and 2 to the ISC servo.
2. Disconnect the ISC servo connector.
3. Check for continuity across the terminals of the ISC. Should indicate a reading of 5–35 ohms at 68°F (20°C).
4. Connect a 6 volt DC power source across the ISC and check that the ISC servo operates.

➡**Do not apply more than 6 volts DC. A higher voltage may cause the servo gears to lock.**

5. If the results are not as indicated, replace the ISC servo.

IDLE SPEED ACTUATOR (ISA)

Testing

1993 SCOUPE

▶ See Figure 69

1. Disconnect the connector at the ISA.
2. Measure the resistance between the terminals at the ISA side of the connector. Resistance should be:

a. Between terminals 1 and 2: 13 ohms at 68°F
b. Between terminals 2 and 3: 14 ohms at 68°F
3. Reconnect the ISA connector.

INJECTOR

Testing

The easiest way to test the operation of the fuel injectors is to listen for a clicking sound coming from the injectors while the engine is running. This is accomplished using a mechanic's stethoscope, or a long screwdriver. Place the end of the stethoscope or the screwdriver (tip end, not handle) onto the body of the injector. Place the ear pieces of the stethoscope in your ears, or if using a screwdriver, place your ear on top of the handle. An audible clicking noise should be heard; this is the solenoid operating. If the injector makes this noise, the injector driver circuit and computer are operating as designed. Continue testing all the injectors this way.

✳✳ CAUTION

Be extremely careful while working on an operating engine, make sure you have no dangling jewelry, extremely loose clothes, power tool cords or other items that might get caught in a moving part of the engine.

All Injectors Clicking

If all the injectors are clicking, but you have determined that the fuel system is the cause of your driveability problem, continue diagnostics. Make sure that you have checked fuel pump pressure as outlined earlier in this section. An easy way to determine a weak or unproductive cylinder is a cylinder drop test. This is accomplished by removing one spark plug wire at a time, and seeing which cylinder causes the least difference in the idle. The one that causes the least change is the weak cylinder.

If the injectors were all clicking and the ignition system is functioning properly, remove the injector of the suspect cylinder and bench test it. This is accomplished by checking for a spray pattern from the injector itself. Install a fuel supply line to the injector (or rail if the injector is left attached to the rail) and momentarily apply 12 volts DC and a ground to the injector itself; a visible fuel spray should appear. If no spray is achieved, replace the injector and check the running condition of the engine.

One or More Injectors Are Not Clicking

▶ See Figures 70, 71, 72 and 73

If one or more injectors are found to be not operating, testing the injector driver circuit and computer can be accomplished using a "noid" light. First, with the engine not running and the ignition key in the **OFF** position, remove the connector from the injector you plan to test, then plug the "noid" light tool into the injector connector. Start the engine and the "noid" light should flash, signaling that the injector driver circuit is working. If the "noid" light flashes, but the injector does not click when plugged in, test the injector's resistance. resistance should be between 13–16 ohms at 68°F (20°C).

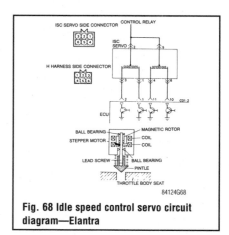

Fig. 68 Idle speed control servo circuit diagram—Elantra

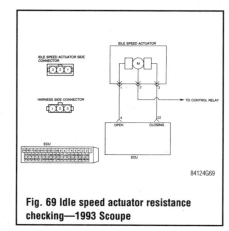

Fig. 69 Idle speed actuator resistance checking—1993 Scoupe

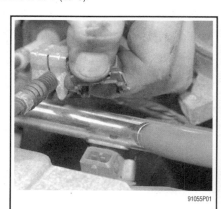

Fig. 70 Unplug the fuel injector connector

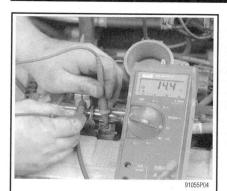

Fig. 71 Probe the two terminals of a fuel injector to check it's resistance

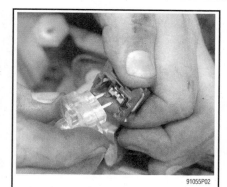

Fig. 72 Plug the correct "noid" light directly into the injector harness connector

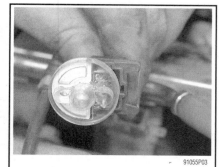

Fig. 73 If the correct "noid" light flashes while the engine is running, the injector driver circuit inside the PCM is working

If the "noid" light does not flash, the injector driver circuit is faulty. Disconnect the negative battery cable. Unplug the "noid" light from the injector connector and also unplug the PCM. Check the harness between the appropriate pins on the harness side of the PCM connector and the injector connector. Resistance should be less than 5.0 ohms; if not, repair the circuit. If resistance is within specifications, the injector driver inside the PCM is faulty and replacement of the PCM will be necessary.

AIR FLOW SENSOR (AFS)

Testing

EXCEPT 1993 SCOUPE

1. Disconnect the harness connector to the AFS.
2. Turn the ignition switch **ON**.
3. Measure the supply voltage at terminal 2.
4. If source volt is not indicated, repair the harness from the control relay or the control relay is faulty.
5. Measure the voltage to terminal 3. Should indicate 4.8–5.2 volts.
6. If not within specification, repair harness and/or connector, as follow:
    a. 1.5L engine—harness from the ECU terminal 3 (C30-1) or ECU is faulty.
    b. 1.6L and 2.0L engines—harness from the ECU terminal 3 (C01-1) or ECU is faulty.
    c. 3.0L engine—harness from the ECU terminal 15 (C81-1) or ECU is faulty.
7. If the harness is okay, its a faulty ECU connection or faulty ECU.
8. Check terminal 6 for continuity to ground. If continuity is not indicated, repair harness from ECU terminals 13 and 20 (except 3.0L engine) or terminal 13 only (3.0L engine).
9. If the harness is okay, substitute a known good ECU.
10. If problem still exist, replace the AFS.

1993 SCOUPE

1. Disconnect the harness connector to the AFS.
2. Turn the ignition switch **ON**.
3. Measure the supply voltage at terminal
4. If source volt is not indicated, repair the harness from the control relay or the control relay is faulty.
5. Measure the voltage to terminal 4. Should indicate 0.94–0.98 volts at 800 rpm.
6. If not within specification, repair harness from the ECU terminal 4 (H4-7) or ECU is faulty.
7. If the harness is okay, its a faulty ECU connection or faulty ECU.
8. Check terminal 2 for continuity to ground. If continuity is not indicated, repair harness from ECU terminals 2 and 26.
9. If the harness is okay, substitute a known good ECU.
10. If problem still exist, replace the AFS.

1993 SCOUPE TURBO

▶ See Figure 74

1. Disconnect the harness connector to the AFS.
2. Turn the ignition switch **ON**.
3. Measure the supply voltage at terminal
4. If source volt is not indicated, repair the harness from the control relay or the control relay is faulty.
5. Measure the voltage to terminal 3. Should indicate 2.0–2.6 volts at 800 rpm.
6. If not within specification, repair harness from the ECU terminal 3 (H3-7) or ECU is faulty.
7. If the harness is okay, its a faulty ECU connection or faulty ECU.
8. Check terminal 1 for continuity to ground. If continuity is not indicated, repair harness from ECU terminals 1 and 19.
9. If the harness is okay, substitute a known good ECU.
10. If problem still exist, replace the AFS.

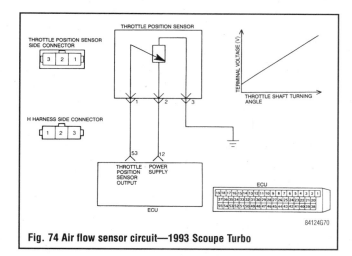

Fig. 74 Air flow sensor circuit—1993 Scoupe Turbo

INTAKE AIR TEMPERATURE SENSOR

Testing

1990 EXCEL

1. Disconnect the harness connector to the air flow sensor.
2. Measure the resistance between terminals 4 and 6 (AFS side connector). Resistance values should be as follow:
    • 32°F (0°C)—5.4–6.6 ohms

- 68°F (20°C)—2.3–2.9.0 ohms
- 176°F (80°C)—0.3–0.4 ohms

3. Measure the resistance while heating the sensor with a hair drier. As the temperature increases, the resistance should decrease.

4. If the readings deviate from these values, replace the air flow sensor.

EXCEPT 1990 EXCEL AND 1993 SCOUPE

1. Disconnect the harness connector to the air flow sensor.
2. Turn the ignition switch **ON**.
3. Measure the supply voltage at terminal 4 (harness side). Should indicate 4.5–4.9 volts.
4. If not okay, check the harness from ECU terminal 3 (2.0L and 3.0L engines) or ECU terminal 5 (1.5L and 1.6L engines).
5. If the harness is okay, its a faulty ECU connection or faulty ECU.
6. Check terminal 6 for continuity to ground (harness side). If continuity is not indicated, repair harness from ECU terminals 13 and 20 (2.0L engine), terminal 13 (3.0L engine) or ECU is faulty.
7. Measure the resistance across the air flow sensor terminals. Readings should be 2.7 ohms at 68°F (20°C).
8. If the specified values are not obtained, replace the air flow sensor.

COOLANT TEMPERATURE SENSOR

Testing

1990 1.5L ENGINE

1. Disconnect the harness connector from the coolant sensor and remove the sensor from the intake manifold.
2. Measure the resistance across the sensor terminals, with the sensing portion of the sensor immersed in hot water. The sensor housing should be 0.12 inch (3mm) above the surface of the water.
3. Resistance values should be as follow:
- 32°F (0°C)—5.9 ohms
- 68°F (20°C)—2.5 ohms
- 104°F (40°C)—1.1 ohms
- 176°F (80°C)—0.3 ohms
4. If the readings deviate from these values, replace the coolant sensor.

EXCEPT 1990 1.5L ENGINE

1. Disconnect the harness connector to the sensor.
2. Turn the ignition switch **ON**.
3. Measure the supply voltage at terminal 2 (harness side). Should indicate 4.5–4.9 volts.
4. If not okay, check the harness from ECU terminal 17 or ECU is faulty.
5. If the harness is okay, its a faulty ECU connection or faulty ECU.
6. Check terminal 1 for continuity to ground (harness side). If continuity is not indicated, repair harness from ECU terminals 13 and 23 (1.5L engine), 13 and 20 (1.6L, 1.8L and 2.0L engine) or terminal 13 (3.0L engine).
7. If the harness is okay, its a faulty ECU connection or faulty ECU.

THROTTLE POSITION SENSOR

Testing

1990 1.5L ENGINES

1. Turn the ignition switch **OFF** and disconnect the harness connector to the TPS sensor.
2. Measure the resistance between terminals 1 and 3 of the TPS. Should indicate a reading between 3.5–6.5 kilo-ohms.
3. Connect an analog-type ohmmeter between terminals 1 and 2.
4. Slowly open the throttle valve form the idle position to the fully open position and check that the resistance value changes smoothly with the opening of the throttle valve. Should indicate a reading between 3.5–6.5 kilo-ohms.
5. If the specified values are not obtained, replace the TPS.

1.6L, 1.8L AND 1991–93 1.5L ENGINES—EXCEPT 1993 SCOUPE

1. Disconnect the harness connector to the TPS sensor.
2. Turn the ignition switch **ON**.

3. Measure the supply voltage at terminal 4 (harness side). Should indicate 4.8–5.2 volts.
4. If not okay, check the harness from ECU terminal 14.
5. If the harness is okay, its a faulty ECU connection or faulty ECU.
6. Check terminal 1 for continuity to ground (harness side). If continuity is not indicated, repair harness from ECU terminals 13 and 23 (1.5L engine), 13 and 20 (1.6L engine).
7. If the harness is okay, its a faulty ECU connection or faulty ECU.
8. Check for an open-circuit or short-circuit to ground between the ECU terminal 18 and the TPS terminal 3.
9. If the supply voltage is obtained and the harness is okay, replace the TPS.

1993 SCOUPE

▶ **See Figure 75**

1. Disconnect the harness connector to the TPS sensor.
2. Turn the ignition switch **ON**.
3. Measure the supply voltage at terminal 2 (harness side). Should indicate 4.8–5.2 volts.
4. If not okay, check the harness from ECU terminal 12.
5. If the harness is okay, its a faulty ECU connection or faulty ECU.
6. Check terminal 3 for continuity to ground (harness side). If continuity is not indicated, repair harness from ECU terminals 12 and 53.
7. If the harness is okay, its a faulty ECU connection or faulty ECU.
8. Check for an open-circuit or short-circuit to ground between the ECU terminal 53 and the TPS terminal 1.
9. If the supply voltage is obtained and the harness is okay, replace the TPS.

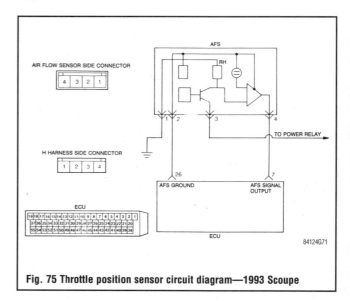

Fig. 75 Throttle position sensor circuit diagram—1993 Scoupe

2.0L AND 3.0L ENGINES

1. Disconnect the harness connector to the TPS sensor.
2. Turn the ignition switch **ON**.
3. Measure the supply voltage at terminal 3 (harness side). Should indicate 4.8–5.2 volts.
4. If not okay, check the harness from ECU terminal 16.
5. If the harness is okay, its a faulty ECU connection or faulty ECU.
6. Check terminal 2 for continuity to ground (harness side). If continuity is not indicated, repair harness from ECU terminals 13 and 20 (2.0L engine) or terminal 13 only (3.0L engine).
7. If the harness is okay, its a faulty ECU connection or faulty ECU.
8. Check for an open-circuit or short-circuit to ground between the ECU terminal 18 and the TPS terminal 4.
9. If the supply voltage is obtained and the harness is okay, replace the TPS.

PHASE SENSOR

Testing

1993 SCOUPE

▶ See Figure 76

1. Disconnect the connector from the phase sensor. Turn the ignition switch to the **ON** position.
2. At the harness side of the connector, check the supply voltage at connector terminal 3. The voltage reading should be 4.8–5.2 volts. If not repair the harness between connector terminal 3 and ECU terminal 12.
3. At the harness side of the connector, check for continuity between terminal 1 and ground. If there is no continuity, check the harness at terminal connector 1.
4. Check for an open or short circuit to ground between the ECU and phase sensor by checking the harness connector terminal 2 to ground and the ECU connector 8 to ground. Repair the harness to ECU terminal 8 if a short is found.

WASTE GATE CONTROL SOLENOID VALVE

Testing

1992 SCOUPE TURBO

1. Disconnect the waste gate solenoid connector.
2. Measure the resistance between the terminals of the valve. The resistance should be approximately 1 mega-ohm at 68°F.

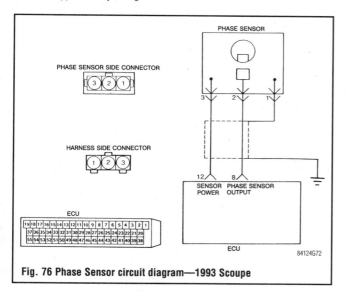

Fig. 76 Phase Sensor circuit diagram—1993 Scoupe

3. If the resistance is far out of specification, the waste gate control solenoid valve should be replaced.

CURB IDLE RPM

Checking

1. Operate the engine until operating temperature is reached.
2. Turn OFF all accessories. Place the gear selector in **P** (automatic transaxle) or **N** (manual transaxle).
3. Set the steering wheel in straight ahead position. Apply the parking brake and block the drive wheels.
4. Check that the electric cooling fan is OFF.
5. Stop the engine and connect a tachometer and timing light. If available, the Multi-Use Tester (MUT) (Tool 09391-33200 or equivalent) may be used (Press Code 22 and read the idle rpm).
6. Operate the engine at curb idle.
7. Check basic ignition timing and adjust, if necessary. Timing should be 5–7 degrees BTDC.
8. Operate the engine for more than 5 seconds between 2000–3000 rpm.
9. Operate the engine at idle for 2 minutes; then check the curb idle rpm. Should be 600–700 rpm.

➡**Idle speed adjustment is usually unnecessary, since the ECU controls the idle speed.**

10. If the curb idle rpm is not within specifications, use the following procedures:
   a. 1.5L and 2.4L Engines—go to Idle Speed Control and TPS system adjustment.
   b. 1.6L, 2.0L and 3.0L Engines—go to Basic Idle Speed Adjustment.

IDLE SPEED CONTROL (ISC) AND THROTTLE POSITION SENSOR (TPS)

▶ See Figures 77, 78 and 79

1.5L AND 2.4L ENGINES

1. Operate the engine until operating temperature is reached.
2. Turn OFF all accessories. Place the gear selector in **P** (automatic transaxle) or **N** (manual transaxle)
3. Set the steering wheel in straight ahead position. Apply the parking brake and block the drive wheels.
4. Loosen the accelerator cable.
5. Connect a digital type voltmeter between terminals 1 and 2 of the TPS. Insert the voltmeter probes at rear of the TPS connector. Do not disconnect the TPS connector from the throttle body.
6. Turn the ignition switch to the **ON** position for approximately 15 seconds; then check to be sure the idle speed control servo if fully retracted to the curb idle position. Do not start the engine.

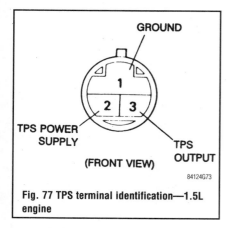

Fig. 77 TPS terminal identification—1.5L engine

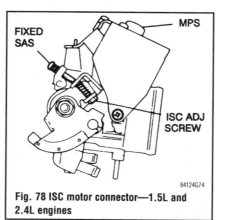

Fig. 78 ISC motor connector—1.5L and 2.4L engines

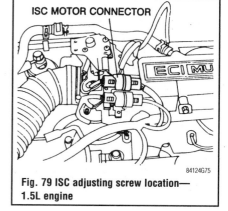

Fig. 79 ISC adjusting screw location—1.5L engine

➡When the ignition switch is first turned ON, the ISC plunger extends to the fast idle position; then after 15 seconds, it retracts to curb idle position.

7. Turn the ignition switch OFF.

8. Disconnect the ISC motor connector and secure the ISC motor at the fully retracted position.

9. In order to prevent the throttle valve from sticking, open it 2 or 3 times; then release it to let it click shut, and sufficiently loosen the fixed Speed Adjusting Screw (SAS).

10. Start the engine and let it run at idle speed.

11. Check that the curb idle speed is within specifications.

12. If the curb idle speed is not within specifications, adjust the ISC adjusting screw to obtain the specified value.

➡The curb idle speed on a new vehicle driven less than 300 miles (500 Km) may be 20–100 rpm lower than specifications, but no adjustment is necessary. If the engine stalls or the engine speed is too low, clean the throttle valve area.

13. Tighten the fixed Speed Adjusting Screw (SAS) until the engine speed starts to increase; then loosen it until the engine speed ceases to drop (touch point) and then loosen a half turn from the touch point.

14. Stop the engine.

15. Turn the ignition switch to the **ON** and check that the TPS output voltage is within specifications. Should be 0.48–0.52 volts.

16. If adjustment is necessary, loosen the TPS mounting screws and turn the TPS until the specified value is obtained. Tighten the TPS mounting screws.

17. Turn the ignition switch OFF.

18. Adjust the accelerator cable play: Automatic transmission—0.12–0.2 in. (3–5mm). All others—0.04–0.08 in. (1–2mm).

19. Connect the ISC motor connector.

20. Disconnect the voltmeter, and connect the TPS connector.

21. Start the engine and check that the idle speed is correct.

22. Turn the ignition switch **OFF** and erase any fault code stored in the system memory.

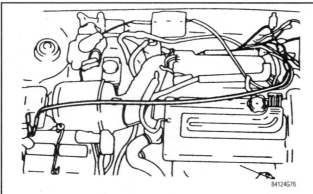

Fig. 80 Ignition timing adjustment terminal—1.6L and 1.8L engines

BASIC IDLE SPEED

▶ See Figures 80, 81, 82 and 83

1.6L, 1.8L AND 2.0L ENGINES

1. Operate the engine until operating temperature is reached.

2. Turn OFF all accessories. Place the gear selector in **P** (automatic transaxle) or **N** (manual transaxle).

3. Set the steering wheel in straight ahead position. Apply the parking brake and block the drive wheels.

4. Loosen the accelerator cable.

5. Connect the Multi-Use Tester (MUT) to the diagnostic connector in the fuse box. If the MUT is not used, connect a tachometer to the engine and ground the self-diagnostic terminal.

6. Ground the ignition timing adjustment terminal.

7. Operate the engine for more than 5 seconds between 2000–3000 rpm.

8. Operate the engine at idle for 2 minutes; then check the curb idle speed. Should be 700–800 rpm.

9. If the curb idle speed is not within specifications, turn the Speed Adjusting Screw (SAS) until the specified value is obtained.

➡If the idle speed is higher than specified, even with the SAS fully closed, check whether the idle switch (fixed SAS) moving mark exists or not. If it is found that the switch has moved, repair as required.

10. Turn the ignition switch **OFF**.

11. Disconnect the ground lead from the ignition timing adjusting terminal and remove the test equipment.

12. Operate the engine for approximately 10 minutes and check that the engine is in normal idling condition.

3.0L ENGINE

1. Run the engine until operating temperature is reached.

2. Turn OFF all accessories. Place the gear selector in **P** (automatic transaxle) or **N** (manual transaxle).

3. Set the steering wheel in straight ahead position. Apply the parking brake and block the drive wheels.

4. Loosen the accelerator cable.

5. Connect the Multi-Use Tester (MUT) to the diagnostic connector in the fuse box. If the MUT is not used, connect a tachometer to the engine and ground the ignition timing adjustment terminal.

6. Operate the engine at idle and check ignition timing. Timing should be 3–7 degrees BTDC.

7. Turn the ignition switch **OFF** and ground the self-diagnostic check terminal.

8. Operate the engine for more than 5 seconds between 2000–3000 rpm.

9. Operate the engine at idle for 2 minutes; then check the curb idle speed. Should be 650–750 rpm.

10. If the curb idle speed is not within specifications, turn the Speed Adjusting Screw (SAS) until the specified value is obtained.

➡If the idle speed is higher than specified, even with the SAS fully closed, check whether the idle switch (fixed SAS) moving mark exists or not. If it is found that the switch has moved, repair as required.

11. Turn the ignition switch **OFF**.

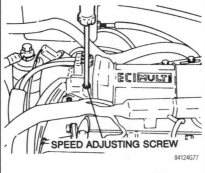

Fig. 81 Speed Adjusting Screw (SAS) location—1.6L, 1.8L and 2.0L engines

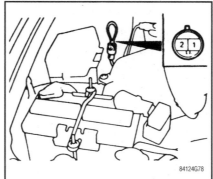

Fig. 82 Ignition timing adjustment terminal—2.0L and 3.0L engines

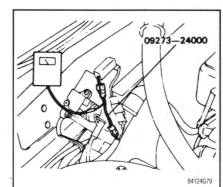

Fig. 83 Checking engine rpm, with tachometer—3.0L engine

12. Disconnect the ground lead from the ignition timing adjusting terminal and self-diagnosis check terminal. Remove the test equipment.

13. Clear the diagnostic memory.

14. Adjust the tension of the acceleration cable.

15. Operate the engine for approximately 10 minutes and check that the engine is in normal idling condition.

THROTTLE POSITION SENSOR (TPS)

Adjustment

2.0L ENGINE

1. Connect the MUT to the diagnostic connector in the fuse box. If the MUT is not used, connect a digital-type voltmeter, using special service tool (09351-33000 or equivalent).

➡**Do not disconnect the ECU connector from the ECU.**

2. Turn the ignition switch **ON**. Do not start the engine.

3. Check the TPS output voltage. If the MUT is used, press code No. 14 and read the voltage. Voltage should be 0.480–0.520.

4. If not within specifications, loosen the TPS mounting screws and adjust by turning the TPS. Tighten the TPS mounting screws.

5. Turn the ignition switch **OFF**.

6. Erase the ECU memory.

3.0L ENGINE

1. Loosen the acceleration cable tension.

2. Connect the MUT to the diagnostic connector in the fuse box. If the MUT is not used, connect a digital-type voltmeter between terminals 2 and 4 of the TPS.

➡**Do not disconnect the TPS.**

3. Turn the ignition switch **ON**. Do not start the engine.

4. Check the TPS output voltage. Voltage should be 0.48–0.56. volts.

5. If not within specifications, loosen the TPS mounting screws and adjust by turning the TPS. Tighten the TPS mounting screw.

6. Turn the ignition switch **OFF**.

7. Start the engine and check the idle speed.

8. Erase the ECU memory.

9. Adjust the accelerator cable.

IDLE POSITION SWITCH (FIXED SAS)

Adjustment

2.0L AND 3.0L ENGINES

1. Loosen the accelerator cable tension.

2. Disconnect the idle switch (fixed SAS) harness connector.

3. Loosen the idle switch (fixed SAS) locknut.

4. Turn the idle switch counterclockwise until the throttle valve closes.

5. Connect an ohmmeter between the terminal of the switch and body.

6. Adjust the idle switch until continuity is indicated. Then turn the idle switch the amount of additional turns indicated:

    a. 2.0L engine—turn the idle switch an additional 1¼ turns.

    b. 3.0L engine—Then turn the idle switch and additional 1¼ turns.

7. Tighten the locknut, while keeping the switch from moving. Reconnect the harness connector.

8. Adjust the accelerator cable.

9. Adjust the curb idle speed and TPS.

VACUUM DIAGRAMS

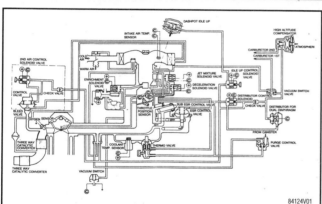

84124V01

Fig. 84 Emission control system schematic—1986–87 Excel (Non-California)

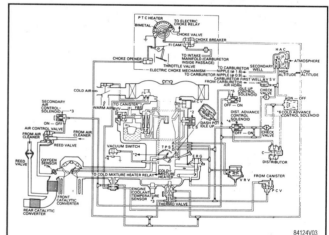

84124V03

Fig. 86 Emission control system schematic—1988–89 Excel (Non-California)

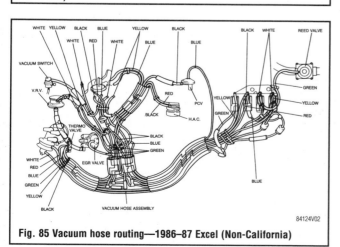

84124V02

Fig. 85 Vacuum hose routing—1986–87 Excel (Non-California)

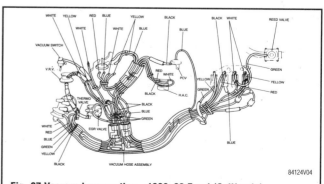

84124V04

Fig. 87 Vacuum hose routing—1988–89 Excel (California)

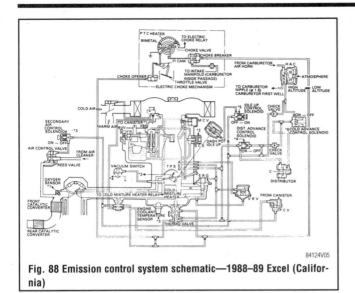

Fig. 88 Emission control system schematic—1988–89 Excel (California)

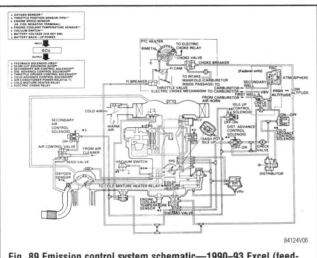

Fig. 89 Emission control system schematic—1990–93 Excel (feedback carburetor)

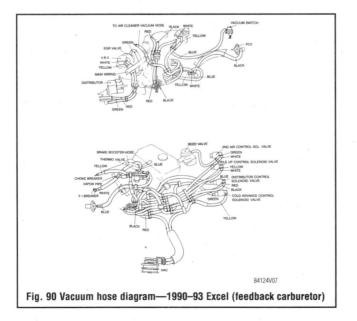

Fig. 90 Vacuum hose diagram—1990–93 Excel (feedback carburetor)

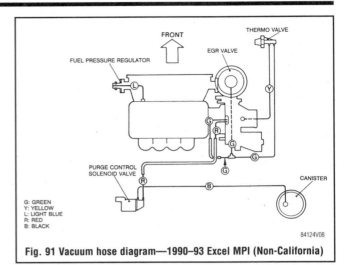

G: GREEN
Y: YELLOW
L: LIGHT BLUE
R: RED
B: BLACK

Fig. 91 Vacuum hose diagram—1990–93 Excel MPI (Non-California)

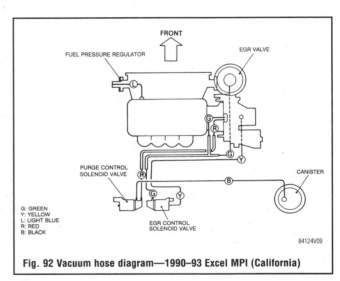

G: GREEN
Y: YELLOW
L: LIGHT BLUE
R: RED
B: BLACK

Fig. 92 Vacuum hose diagram—1990–93 Excel MPI (California)

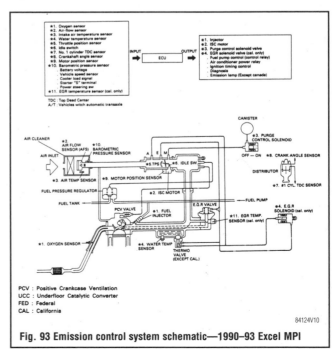

PCV : Positive Crankcase Ventilation
UCC : Underfloor Catalytic Converter
FED : Federal
CAL : California

Fig. 93 Emission control system schematic—1990–93 Excel MPI

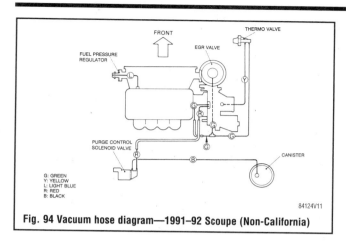

Fig. 94 Vacuum hose diagram—1991–92 Scoupe (Non-California)

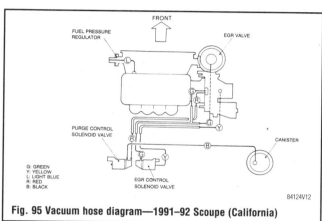

Fig. 95 Vacuum hose diagram—1991–92 Scoupe (California)

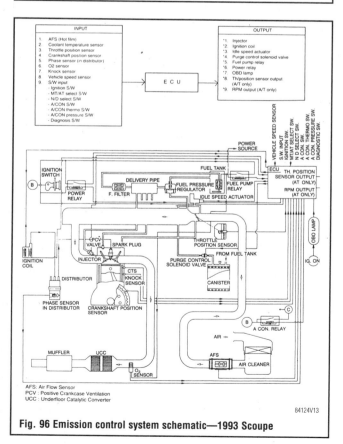

Fig. 96 Emission control system schematic—1993 Scoupe

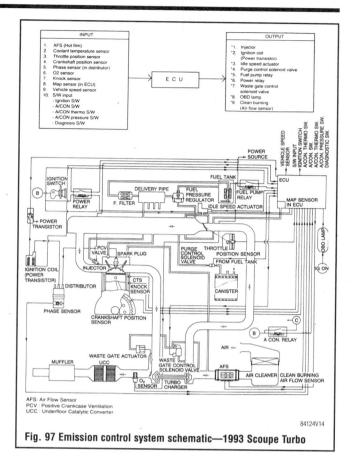

Fig. 97 Emission control system schematic—1993 Scoupe Turbo

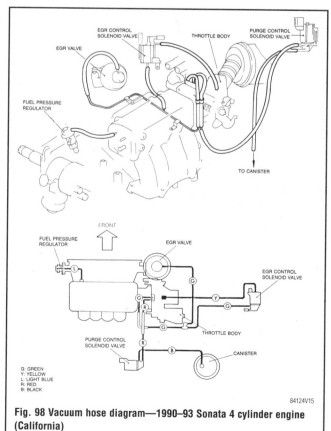

Fig. 98 Vacuum hose diagram—1990–93 Sonata 4 cylinder engine (California)

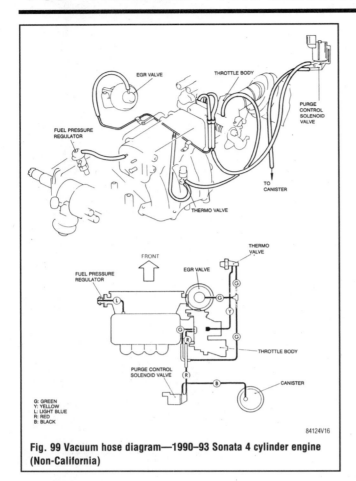

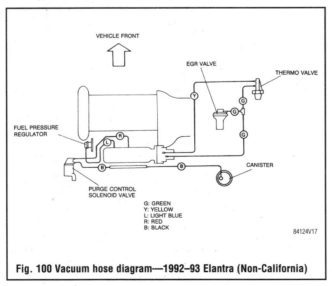

Fig. 99 Vacuum hose diagram—1990–93 Sonata 4 cylinder engine (Non-California)

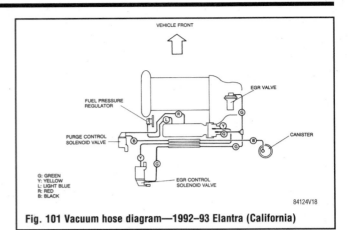

Fig. 100 Vacuum hose diagram—1992–93 Elantra (Non-California)

Fig. 101 Vacuum hose diagram—1992–93 Elantra (California)

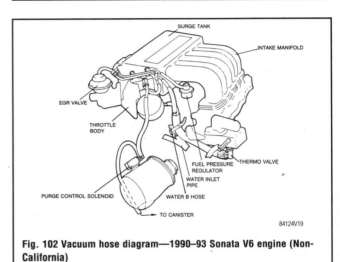

Fig. 102 Vacuum hose diagram—1990–93 Sonata V6 engine (Non-California)

Fig. 103 Vacuum hose diagram—1990–93 Sonata V6 engine (California)

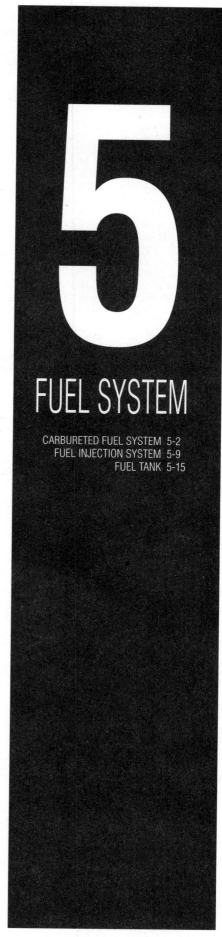

5

FUEL SYSTEM

CARBURETED FUEL SYSTEM

General Description

The feedback carburetor (FBC) system used on the Excel provides the capability to perform closed loop fuel control. It also provides the capability to control the secondary air system, the deceleration spark control system and the throttle opener system. The basic functions of this system are described below.

Input signals from a variety of sensors are fed to a microprocessor based Electronic Control Unit (ECU). The ECU then generates output signals for all of the controlled functions. The feedback carburetor is a 2-barrel, downdraft carburetor designed for closed loop system. When used with the closed loop system of mixture control, this carburetor includes special design features for optimum air/fuel mixtures during all ranges of engine operation. Fuel metering is accomplished through the use of three solenoid-operated on/off valves (jet mixture, enrichment and deceleration solenoids), adding or reducing fuel to the engine. The activation of the on/off valve is controlled by the length of the time current is supplied to the solenoid. The solenoid operates at a fixed frequency. By varying the amount of time the solenoid is energized during each cycle (defined as duty cycle), the air/fuel mixture delivered to the engine can be precisely controlled, The duty cycle to the solenoid is controlled by the ECU in response to the signals from the exhaust oxygen sensor, throttle position sensor. For more information on FBC systems refer to Section 4.

Fuel Filter

REPLACEMENT

All models use an inline filter which should be replaced every 12,000 miles (19,000km). See Section 1 for details.

Mechanical Fuel Pump

The mechanical fuel pump operates directly off of a camshaft eccentric. A fuel return valve is located in the upper body of the pump. If the fuel temperature rises above 122°F (50°C), the valve opens and routes fuel back to the tank, preventing percolation.

REMOVAL & INSTALLATION

♦ See Figure 1

1. Remove the two screws and remove the plastic heat shield.
2. Disconnect the three fuel pump lines.
3. Unscrew the two retaining nuts and remove the fuel pump and fuel pump pushrod.

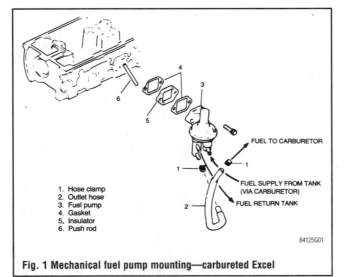

1. Hose clamp
2. Outlet hose
3. Fuel pump
4. Gasket
5. Insulator
6. Push rod

FUEL TO CARBURETOR

FUEL SUPPLY FROM TANK (VIA CARBURETOR)

FUEL RETURN TANK

84125G01

Fig. 1 Mechanical fuel pump mounting—carbureted Excel

4. Remove the gasket, insulator, and gasket.
5. Clean the fuel pump gasket mating surface. If the fuel pump pushrod is bent, replace it.
6. To make fuel pump installation a little easier, engage the crankshaft pulley nut with a socket and turn the engine over until the No. 1 piston is at TDC. This is done to minimize the pressure that the cam exerts on the fuel pump actuating lever, thus reducing the effort it takes to position the pump onto the head studs.
7. Apply non-hardening sealer to both sides of the gaskets. Position a gasket, the insulator and the other gasket on the head studs.
8. Insert the pushrod into the cylinder head.
9. Install the pump and torque the nuts to 25 ft. lbs.
10. Connect the fuel pump lines, with hose clamps and install the plastic heat shield.
11. Start the engine and check for fuel and oil leaks.

TESTING

♦ See Figures 2 and 3

Inlet Valve Test

1. Disconnect the fuel supply line from the bottom of the pump. Connect a vacuum gauge of known calibration to the pump where the hose was connected.
2. Have an assistant bump the engine over using the starter motor or a remote starter device. You should notice a vacuum on the gauge. If fuel blows back out of the supply nipple or no vacuum is shown at all, then the relief valve is not seating properly and the fuel pump should be replaced.

Pressure Test

Disconnect the fuel line from the carburetor and attach a pressure tester to the end of the line. Crank the engine. The tester should show 2.7–3.7 psi.

Volume Test

♦ See Figures 4 and 5

1. Disconnect the fuel pump outlet hose and insert the end of the hose into a graduated beaker with a one quart capacity.
2. Disconnect the fuel return hose from the pump and plug the end or direct the hose into a container to collect the return fuel.
3. Start the engine and run it for one minute.
4. At the end of one minute, stop the engine and measure the amount of fuel collected in the beaker. There should be approximately 0.85 quart (0.8L) of fuel.
5. If the volume is not approximately 0.85 quart (0.8L), replace the pump. The actual volume may vary due to wear of the pump. If the pump is fairly new, the volume will be close to 0.85 quart (0.8L). If the pump has been in service for awhile, it will be slightly less.

Leak Test

At the base of the fuel pump diaphragm housing there is a small breather hole, more commonly known as a tell-tale hole. This hole enables you to determine the internal condition of the fuel pump oil seal which separates the pump lubrication and drive section from the fuel system. Check the hole for the presence of engine oil or fuel. If oil or fuel leakage is evident from the breather hole, then the fuel pump's oil seal or diaphragm is defective and the fuel pump will have to be replaced.

Carburetor

SERVICE ADJUSTMENTS

Throttle Linkage

♦ See Figures 6 and 7

1. Run the engine to operating temperature and allow it to idle at curb idle speed.

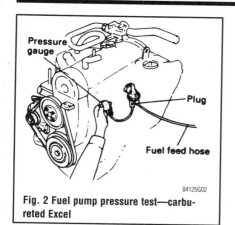

Fig. 2 Fuel pump pressure test—carbureted Excel

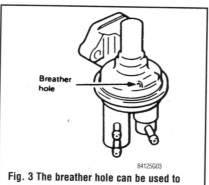

Fig. 3 The breather hole can be used to determine the internal condition of the fuel pump

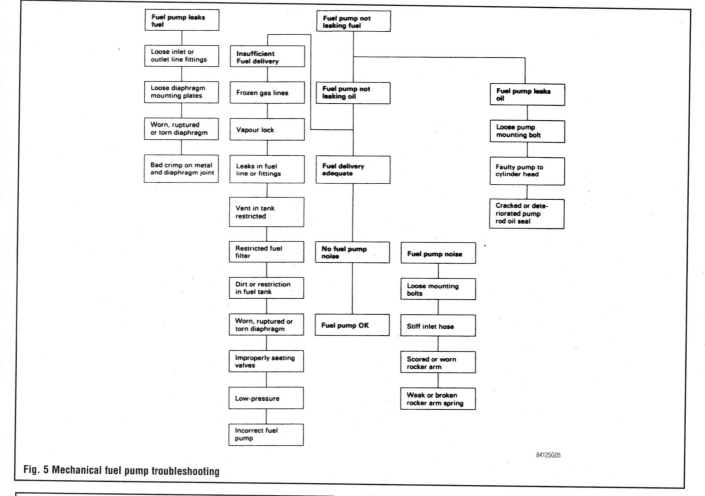

Fig. 5 Mechanical fuel pump troubleshooting

Fig 4. Fuel pump volume test—carbureted Excel

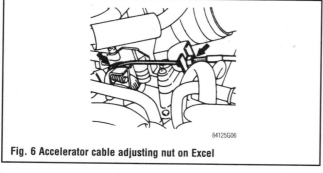

Fig. 6 Accelerator cable adjusting nut on Excel

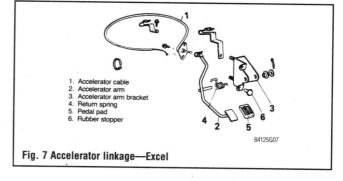

1. Accelerator cable
2. Accelerator arm
3. Accelerator arm bracket
4. Return spring
5. Pedal pad
6. Rubber stopper

Fig. 7 Accelerator linkage—Excel

2. There should be no slack in the exposed part of the throttle cable near the carburetor.

3. Make sure that there are no sharp bends in the cable.

4. Loosen the cable adjusting nut locknut and turn the adjusting nut until the throttle just starts to open.

5. At this point, back off the adjusting nut one full turn and lock it with the locknut.

Fuel and Float Level Adjustment

▶ See Figure 8

➡ Float and fuel level adjustments are possible only on 1986-87 Excels

FUEL LEVEL

A sight glass is fitted in the float chamber and the fuel level can be checked without disassembling the carburetor. Normal fuel level is within the level mark on the sight glass. The fuel level adjustment is corrected by increasing or decreasing the number of needle valve packings (shims) between the valve and top cover.

FLOAT LEVEL

▶ See Figure 9

1. Remove the carburetor air horn.

2. Turn it upside-down and measure the distance between the float bottom (which, inverted, is now the top), and the gasket surface of the air horn. The distance should be 20.0mm plus or minus 1.0mm.

3. Adjust the distance, as necessary, adding or deleting shims under the needle seat. Shim kits are available with shims in three thicknesses: 0.3mm, 0.4mm and 0.5mm. Each shim change will change the float setting by three times the thickness of the shim.

Fast Idle Adjustment

1986–87 EXCEL

▶ See Figure 10

1. Start the engine and open the throttle valve about 45°. Manually close the choke valve and slowly return the throttle valve to the stop position.

2. With a tachometer connected, check that the fast idle speed is 2000 rpm or lower. (Not less than 1700 rpm). Adjust the speed as necessary with the fast idle speed screw.

3. Cold start the engine and check the automatic choke and fast idle operation.

1988–93 EXCEL

▶ See Figures 11, 12 and 13

Before attempting the fast idle adjustment, make sure the following conditions are met:

- Warm up car to normal operating temperature
- Lights, cooling fan, electrical accessories set to OFF position
- Transaxle in Neutral or Park
- Steering wheel in straight ahead position (if equipped with power steering)

1. Remove the air cleaner and connect a tachometer to the engine.

2. Disconnect the vacuum hose (with the white stripe) from the choke opener.

3. Set the throttle lever to the second highest step on the fast idle cam.

4. Start the engine and check the fast idle speed. On manual transaxles, the fast idle speed should be 2800 rpm and on automatic transaxles it should be 2700 rpm.

5. If the fast idle speed is not within specification, adjust it with the fast idle adjusting screw.

6. Connect the choke opener vacuum hose, remove the tachometer and install the air cleaner.

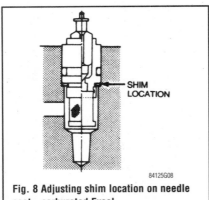

Fig. 8 Adjusting shim location on needle seat—carbureted Excel

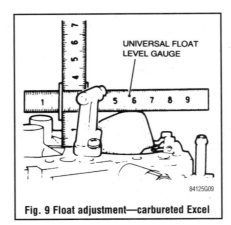

Fig. 9 Float adjustment—carbureted Excel

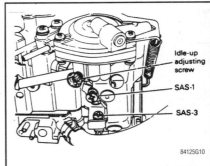

Fig. 10 Carburetor adjustment screws on Excel; SAS-1 is the curb idle screw; SAS-3 is the fast idle screw

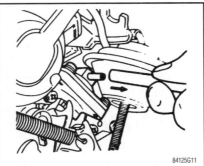

Fig. 11 Disconnecting the choke opener vacuum hose for fast idle adjustment— carbureted Excel

Fig. 12 Set the throttle lever to the second step on the fast idle cam for fast idle adjustment—carbureted Excel

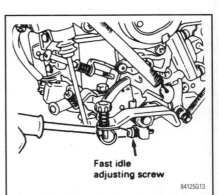

Fig. 13 Fast idle adjusting screw—carbureted Excel

Idle Mixture Adjustment

▶ See Figure 14

➡This adjustment is preset at the factory and is not a normal adjustment. Mixture adjustment is necessary only after unscheduled major maintenance has been performed on the carburetor. A CO meter is absolutely necessary for this procedure.

1. Remove the carburetor from the engine.
2. Secure the carburetor in a soft-jawed vise, without touching the gasket surface, and with the mixture adjusting screw (on the bottom) facing up.
3. Using a 2mm drill bit, drill a pilot hole in the casting surrounding the mixture adjusting screw at a 45° angle. Then, redrill the hole with a 3mm (⅛ in.) bit.
4. Using a blunt punch in the hole, drive out the plug.

➡Make sure all metal filings from drilling are completely removed before installing the carburetor on the engine.

5. Install the carburetor on the engine.
6. Run the engine to normal operating temperature.
7. Make sure that the lights, electric cooling fan and all accessories are OFF. Place the transmission in neutral. Block the wheels and set the parking brake.
8. Run the engine for 5 seconds at 2000–3000 rpm.
9. Return the engine to idle and let it idle at normal curb idle speed for 2 minutes.
10. Make sure that the idle speed is correct. If not, adjust it with the idle speed screw.
11. Using a CO meter, adjust the idle CO by turning the mixture screw. CO level should meet state or local requirements.

Secondary Throttle Plate Adjustment

The secondary throttle plate stop screw is adjusted to keep the throttle plate from closing too tightly. This adjustment is only made with the carburetor off of the engine. The screw is set at the factory and doesn't normally need adjustment.

Automatic Choke Adjustment

➡All carburetors are equipped with a tamper-proof choke that has been pre-adjusted at the factory. Choke adjustment should only be performed as part of major carburetor overhaul or choke calibration as required by state or local inspections.

1986–87 EXCEL

▶ See Figures 15, 16, 17 and 18

1. Remove the air cleaner, and choke mechanism cover.

➡These models have headless, tamper proof screws securing the choke mechanism cover. These have to be drilled out. In that case, it's easier to remove the carburetor.

2. Remove the bracket bridging the choke spring gear and choke actuating cam.
3. Slip the choke strangler spring from the choke lever. Align the scribed black line on the choke gear with the mark below the teeth on the actuating cam and reassemble all parts.
4. Temporarily tighten the lower bracket screw.
5. Move the arm at the upper screw to align the center line scribed in the notch on the arm with the punch mark on the float chamber.
6. Tighten the screws.
7. Install the cover with new screws.

1988–93 EXCEL

▶ See Figures 19, 20 and 21

➡This check must be performed when the coolant temperature is at or lower than 50°F (10°C).

1. Remove the air cleaner.
2. Check that the marks on the choke and bi-metal assembly are aligned properly. If not, rotate the bi-metal assembly until the marks are aligned. If the marks were in fact misaligned, you may have experienced the following symptoms:

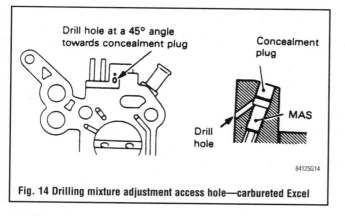

Fig. 14 Drilling mixture adjustment access hole—carbureted Excel

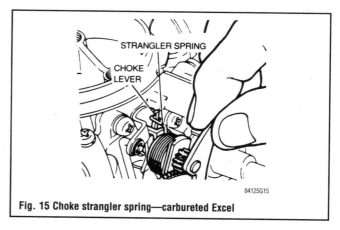

Fig. 15 Choke strangler spring—carbureted Excel

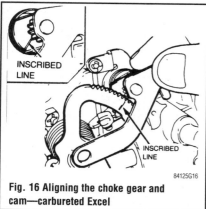

Fig. 16 Aligning the choke gear and cam—carbureted Excel

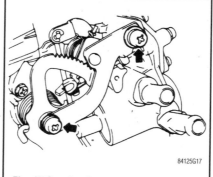

Fig. 17 Cam bracket attaching screws—carbureted Excel

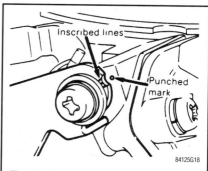

Fig. 18 Aligning the upper bracket arm and carburetor body marks—carbureted Excel

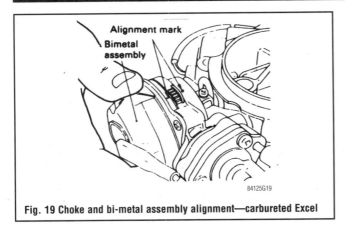

Fig. 19 Choke and bi-metal assembly alignment—carbureted Excel

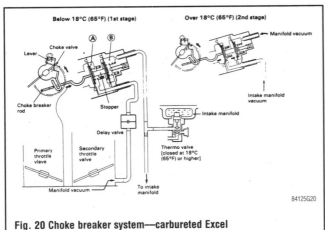

Fig. 20 Choke breaker system—carbureted Excel

Step	Engine coolant temperature	Checking condition	Normal choke valve operation	Probable cause of trouble
1	Lower than 10°C (50°F)	Before engine start	Closes fully	Faulty bimetal assembly o: linkage operation
2	Lower than 10°C (50°F)	Start engine and run idle (fully depress accelerator pedal and then start)	Opens slowly and slightly (immediately after starting) [gap approx. 1.5 mm (0.059 in.)]	o Clogged delay valve o Broken diaphragm (chamber A)
3	Lower than 10°C (50°F)	Disconnect vacuum hose (yellow stripe) from choke breaker during idling	Stationary	o Faulty thermo valve
4	Higher than 25°C (77°F)	Connect vacuum hose (yellow stripe) and run engine idle	When closed lightly with finger, stops at larger opening than step 2 [gap arrrox. 3 mm (0.118 in.)]	o Faulty thermo valve o Broken diaphragm (chamber B)

Fig. 21 Use this table to inspect the condition of the choke valve—carbureted Excel

- Clockwise misalignment: will result in good cold weather startability, but will cause carbon deposits on the plugs.
- Counterclockwise misalignment: will result in poor startability and stalling.
3. Make sure the coolant temperature is at or lower than 50°F.
4. Start the engine and place your hand on the body of the choke. Check the operation of the choke, choke valve and fast idle cam as follows:
   a. Choke: As the engine warms up, the choke body should get hotter.
   b. Choke valve: The choke valve will open at the bi-metal temperature rises.
   c. Fast idle cam: The fast idle engine speed should stop after the engine warms up and the coolant temperature rises.
5. If the choke body remains cool even after the engine is warm, then the electric choke breaker system must be checked out and adjusted as described in the procedure that immediately follows.

Choke Breaker System Inspection And Adjustment

♦ **See Figures 22, 23 and 24**

1988–93 EXCEL

♦ **See Figures 25, 26, 27 and 28**

If the choke breaker system is suspect of malfunctioning, use the accompanying chart to check the operation of the choke valve and breaker system, then proceed to the adjustment section.
1. Remove the air cleaner.
2. Disconnect the yellow striped vacuum hose from the choke breaker.
3. Start the engine and run at idle.
4. Lightly close the choke valve with your finger until it stops. DO NOT force it! With a feeler gauge, measure the clearance between the choke valve and the choke bore. The clearance should be 0.055–0.063 in.
5. If the choke valve clearance is not as specified, stop the engine and matchmark the bi-metal assembly to the choke body. Remove the bi-metal end cover from the choke valve lever. Then, adjust the choke breaker rod end opening until the 0.055–0.063 in. clearance is obtained. Install the bi-metal assembly, using new screws and rivets.

➥These models have headless, tamper proof screws securing the choke mechanism cover. These have to be drilled out. In that case, it's easier to remove the carburetor.

6. Reconnect the yellow striped vacuum hose to the choke breaker and recheck the choke valve to choke bore clearance again with the engine running. This time the clearance should be 0.114–0.122 in.
7. If the clearance is not as specified, turn the choke breaker adjusting screw until the 0.114–0.122 in. clearance is obtained.
8. Stop the engine and install the air cleaner.

Throttle Opener (Idle-Up) Actuator Test

The throttle opener controls the idle speed when heavy electrical loads or power steering loads are placed upon the engine.
1. Check that all vacuum hoses and wires at the actuator are connected.
2. Disconnect the vacuum hose at the actuator nipple.
3. Connect a tachometer to the engine.

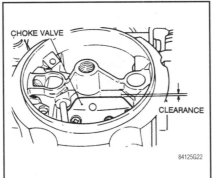

Fig. 22 Measuring choke valve clearance—carbureted Excel

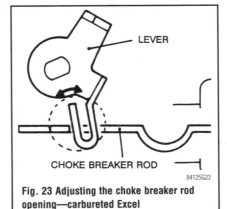

Fig. 23 Adjusting the choke breaker rod opening—carbureted Excel

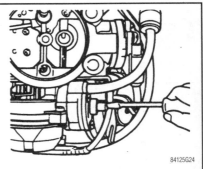

Fig. 24 Using the choke breaker adjusting screw to adjust the choke valve clearance—carbureted Excel

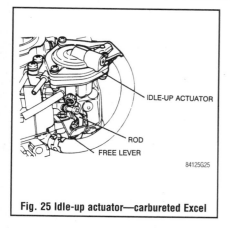

Fig. 25 Idle-up actuator—carbureted Excel

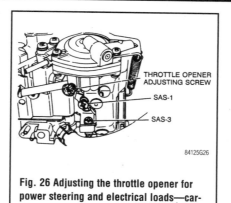

Fig. 26 Adjusting the throttle opener for power steering and electrical loads—carbureted Excel

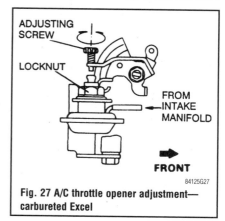

Fig. 27 A/C throttle opener adjustment—carbureted Excel

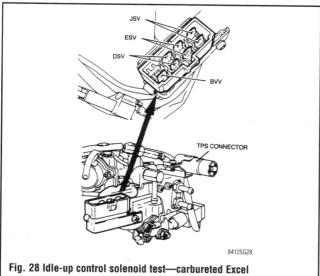

Fig. 28 Idle-up control solenoid test—carbureted Excel

4. Start the engine and allow it to reach normal operating temperature at curb idle speed. If the idle speed is not correct, adjust it.

5. Using a hand-held vacuum pump connected at the actuator nipple, apply 300mm Hg vacuum. The idle speed should increase. If not, replace the actuator.

Throttle Opener (Idle-Up) Actuator Adjustment

1. Remove the air cleaner assembly.
2. Connect a tachometer to the engine.
3. Start the engine and allow it to reach normal operating temperature at curb idle speed. If the idle speed is not correct, adjust it.
4. Apply an electrical load, such as the blower motor.
5. Disconnect the wiring from the idle-up solenoid valve and connect a jumper wire across the connector terminals on the valve. This will activate the valve and apply vacuum to and activate the idle-up actuator.
6. Now, open the throttle slightly until the engine speed reaches 2000 rpm. Then, let up on the throttle slowly.
7. Adjust the engine idle speed to 750–950 rpm by turning the throttle opener adjusting screw.
8. Repeat Step 5, and check the idle speed again. It should be 750–950 rpm.
9. Stop the engine and remove the idle-up solenoid jumper wire, remove the tachometer and install the air cleaner assembly.

Throttle Opener (Idle-Up) Adjustment
For Operation Under Air Conditioning Loads

1988–1993 EXCEL ONLY

This procedure is used to check and adjust the idle speed control function of the throttle opener when an air conditioning load is applied to the engine.

1. Start the engine and connect a tachometer.
2. Turn the air conditioner on. The A/C solenoid will open and allow intake manifold vacuum to actuate the throttle opener.
3. Check the idle speed. If the idle speed is not within 850–900 rpm, adjust it by turning the A/C throttle adjusting screw.

Throttle Opener (Idle-Up) Control Solenoid Valve Test

1. With the ignition switch off, unplug the connector from the idle-up solenoid valve.
2. Using an ohmmeter, check continuity across the terminal. If an open or short is detected, replace the solenoid valve. Solenoid valve coil resistance should be about 40 ohms.

Throttle Position Sensor Testing

♦ See Figures 29, 30, 31 and 32

➥A digital ohmmeter is necessary for this adjustment.

1. Disconnect the TPS connector.
2. Check the resistance with an ohmmeter between terminals 2 and 3 (the bottom, adjacent terminals in the connector) on 1986–87 Excel and terminals 1 and 3 on 1988–89 Excel. With the throttle closed, resistance should be 1.2 ohms on 1986–87 Excel and 3.5k ohms on 1988–89 Excel. Resistance should slowly increase to 4.9 ohms on 1986–87 Excel and 6.5k ohms on 1988–89 Excel at wide open throttle.

Throttle Position Sensor Adjustment

➥A digital voltmeter is necessary for this adjustment.

1. Run the engine to normal operating temperature. Make sure that the fast idle cam is released.
2. Shut off the engine and loosen the throttle cable a small amount.
3. Back off SAS-1 and SAS-2, the two idle speed adjustment screws, until the throttle is fully closed. Record the exact number of turns that you backed each off.

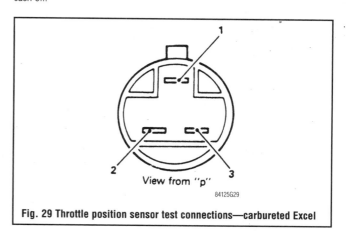

Fig. 29 Throttle position sensor test connections—carbureted Excel

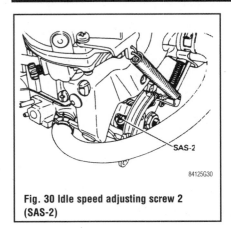

Fig. 30 Idle speed adjusting screw 2 (SAS-2)

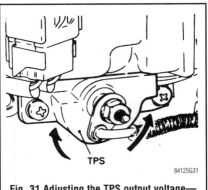

Fig. 31 Adjusting the TPS output voltage— carbureted Excel

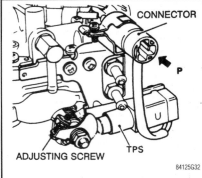

Fig. 32 TPS adjustment points—carbureted Excel

4. Connect a digital voltmeter between terminals 2 and 3 (the two bottom ones) of the TPS connector.

➡**Do not disconnect the TPS connector from the chassis harness.**

5. Turn on the ignition switch and adjust the TPS output voltage to 250mV with the adjustment screw by turning the body of the TPS in either the clockwise or counterclockwise direction. Turning the TPS in the CLOCKWISE direction increases the output voltage.

6. Turn off the ignition switch.

7. Return the two idle speed adjustment screws to their exact positions.

8. Adjust the accelerator cable free-play, start the engine and check the idle speed.

Jet Mixture Solenoid Test

1986–87 EXCEL

▶ **See Figure 33**

1. With the ignition switch ON but the engine not running, the voltage at the JMS checker should be 11–13v.

2. With the engine running at normal operating temperature at curb idle, the voltage at the checker should be 5–12v. If not, replace the JMS valve.

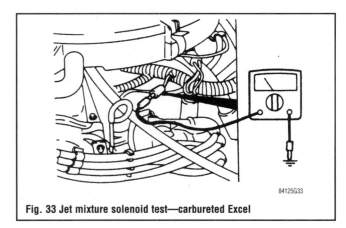

Fig. 33 Jet mixture solenoid test—carbureted Excel

REMOVAL & INSTALLATION

USA Vehicles

1. Disconnect the negative battery cable. Drain the coolant down to below the level of the intake manifold.

2. Remove the air cleaner. Disconnect the throttle cable at the carburetor.

3. Disconnect and label all vacuum hoses.

4. Disconnect the connectors for the solenoid valves and the Throttle Position Sensor (TPS).

5. Place a pan under the fuel connections and then disconnect them. Remove the container, avoiding the spilling of fuel.

6. Remove the mounting bolts, lift the carburetor off the engine and remove it to a workbench, keeping it level to avoid the spilling of fuel from the float bowl.

To install:

7. Inspect the mating surfaces of the carburetor and manifold. They should be clean and free of nicks or burrs. Clean and, if necessary, remove any slight imperfections with crocus cloth. Put a new carburetor gasket on the surface of the manifold.

8. Position the carburetor on top of the gasket with all holes aligned. Install the carburetor bolts and tighten them alternately and evenly.

9. Connect the throttle linkage. Depress the accelerator pedal and make sure the throttle blade opens all the way. Adjust, if necessary.

10. Connect the vacuum hoses. Make sure all are soft and free of cracks to make a good seal. Replace hoses that are hard and cracked. Reconnect the fuel hoses.

11. Install the remaining parts in reverse order. Connect the negative battery cable. To start the engine, set the choke and operate the starter. Do not attempt to prime the engine by pouring gas into the carburetor inlet. Check for leaks with the engine running.

Canadian Vehicles

1. Disconnect the negative battery cable.

2. Drain the coolant to a level just below the intake manifold.

3. Remove the air cleaner.

4. Disconnect the wiring from the fuel cutoff solenoid.

5. Disconnect the accelerator rod and, if equipped with automatic transaxle, the shift rod.

6. Tag and disconnect the vacuum hoses from the carburetor.

7. Place a container under the fuel inlet and return hoses to catch any leaking fuel and disconnect the hoses.

8. Disconnect the water hose which runs between the carburetor and the cylinder head.

9. Unscrew the 4 retaining nuts and remove the carburetor. Hold the carburetor level to avoid a fuel spill.

To install:

10. Mount the carburetor on the intake manifold and install nuts. Attach the choke water hose to the carburetor.

11. Reconnect the fuel lines and vacuum hoses to the carburetor.

12. Connect the accelerator or shift rod.

13. Reconnect the fuel cut-off solenoid and replace the air cleaner.

14. Refill the system with coolant. Connect the negative battery cable.

FUEL INJECTION SYSTEM

General Description

➡️**For a complete description of the fuel injection system and its operation, as well as diagnosis and testing, refer to Section 4 of this manual.**

The fuel injection system used on Hyundai vehicles, is classified as a Multipoint Fuel Injection (MPI) system. The basic function of the system is to control the air/fuel ratio, based on input signals from various engine sensors. The air/fuel ratio is controlled by varying the injector driving time. The system is controlled by an Electronic Control Unit (ECU), which monitors the engine conditions, then calculates the injection timing and air/fuel ratio according to the signals from the sensors. The ECU consists of an 8-bit microprocessor, Random Access Memory (RAM), Read Only Memory (ROM) and input and output signal interface system.

The MPI system consists of 2 operating modes:
• Open Loop—air/fuel ratio is controlled by information programmed into the ECU by the manufacturer.
• Closed Loop—air/fuel ratio is varied by the ECU based on information supplied by the oxygen sensor.

An electric fuel pump supplies sufficient fuel to the injection system and the pressure regulator maintains a constant pressure to the injectors. These injectors inject a metered quantity of fuel into the intake manifold in accordance with signals from the Electronic Control Unit (ECU) or engine computer. After pressure regulation excess fuel is returned to the fuel tank.

The injectors have 2 modes (Injector Drive Timing) of operation:
• Non-synchronous Injection (Simultaneous Injection)
• Synchronous Injection (Sequential Injection)

Non-synchronous injection is activated during engine starting (cranking). There are 2 fuel injections, for each engine rpm, to all 4 cylinders. Also, during acceleration, fuel proportionate to the magnitude of acceleration, is injected to 2 selected cylinders during the intake and exhaust strokes.

Synchronous Injection is activated after the engine has started. The injectors are activated at the exhaust stroke of each cylinder in a sequential manner, according to crankshaft angle sensor signal. There is 1 injection per cylinder for every 2 crankshaft revolution, according to firing order.

DATA SENSORS

Air Flow Sensor (AFS)

The AFS measures the intake air volume. The ECU uses this intake air volume signal to decide the basic fuel injection duration. The AFS on all models except the Turbo Scoupe is a hot film type, the Turbo Scoupe uses a hot wire type. The results that are obtained by the 2 types of sensor, however, are the same.

Atmosphere Pressure Sensor

The atmosphere pressure sensor signal is used by the ECU to compute the altitude of the vehicle and so the ECU can correct the ignition timing and air/fuel ratio. The atmosphere pressure sensor is contain in the AFS.

Intake Air Temperature Sensor

The air temperature sensor is a resistor based sensor for detecting the intake air temperature. The ECU provides fuel injection control based on this information. The air temperature sensor is located on the AFS.

Engine Coolant Temperature Sensor

The coolant temperature sensor is located in the coolant passage of the intake manifold. The ECU uses this signal to determine the base fuel enrichment for cold and warm engine operation.

Throttle Position Sensor (TPS)

The TPS is a rotating type variable resistor that rotates with the throttle body shaft to sense the throttle valve opening. Based on TPS voltage signals, the ECU computes the throttle valve opening and accordingly corrects fuel for engine acceleration.

Idle Switch

The idle switch is a contact type switch. The switch is installed at the tip of the ISC. This switch provides the ECU with idle or off idle signal.

Motor Position Sensor (MPS)

The MPS is a variable resistor type sensor and is installed in the ISC servo. The MPS senses the ISC servo plunger position and sends the signal to the ECU. The ECU controls the valve opening, and consequently the idle speed by using the MPS signal, idle signal, engine coolant temperature signal, load signals and vehicle speed sensor.

Cylinder TDC and Crankshaft Angle Sensor

The No. 1 TDC sensor and the crankshaft angle sensor are composed of a disc and unit assembly in the distributor. The No. 1 cylinder TDC is detected by the signal obtained through the single inner slit of the disc. The ECU, based upon this signal, determines the fuel injection cylinder. The crankshaft angle sensor signal that comes from the 4 slits at the outer circumference of the disc, serves to detect the position of the crankshaft. The ECU, based on this signal, determines the fuel injection timing, and also calculates the amount of intake air, the ignition timing, etc. for each stroke of engine.

Phase Sensor

1993 SCOUPE

The Phase Sensor is built into the distributor. It senses the TDC point of the No. 1 cylinder in its compression stroke. These signals are fed to the ECU to be used in determining fuel injection sequence.

Crankshaft Position Sensor

1993 SCOUPE

The crankshaft position sensor consists of a magnetic coil which is installed in the transaxle housing. The sensor gets its signal from a sensor ring mounted to the flywheel. The voltage signal is fed to the ECU for detecting engine rpm and crankshaft position.

Oxygen Sensor

The oxygen sensor, by detecting the oxygen content in the exhaust gas, maintains the stoichiometric air/fuel ratio. In operation, the ECU receives the signals from the sensor and changes the duration during which fuel is injected. The oxygen sensor is located in the exhaust manifold.

Vehicle Speed Sensor

The vehicle speed sensor uses a reed type switch. The speed sensor is built into the speedometer and converts the speedometer gear revolution into pulse signals, which are sent to the ECU.

Neutral (Inhibitor) Switch

The ECU, based on this signal, senses when the automatic transaxle is in **NEUTRAL** or **PARK** and operates the ISC servo to keep the idle speed correct.

Idle Speed Control (ISC) Servo

The ISC servo consists of a motor, worm gear, worm wheel and plunger. The MPS is used to detect plunger position and an idle switch to detect closed throttle position.

As the motor rotates, according to signals from the ECU, the plunger extends or retracts depending on direction of the motor rotation. This actuates the throttle valve via the ISC lever. The idle speed is controlled by the ECU through this function.

Knock Sensor

1993 SCOUPE

The Knock Sensor is attached to the cylinder block and senses engine knock. The sensor functions by reading the knocking vibration from the engine and converting this into a voltage signal delivered as output to the ECU. The ECU uses this signal to adjust the ignition timing.

Waste Gate Control Solenoid Valve

1993 SCOUPE TURBO

The waste gate control solenoid valve controls the turbo boost pressure. This valve is integrated with the rest of the engine sensors to ensure proper engine operating conditions under varying boost conditions. It also helps to reduce turbo lag and engine knock.

FUEL DELIVERY SYSTEM

Fuel Pump

The fuel pump is a compact impeller design and is installed inside the fuel tank. The pump assembly consists of the impeller (driven by the motor), the pump casing (which forms the pumping chamber), and cover of the pump. This pump is called a wet-type pump, because the inside is also filled with fuel. Never operate this type of pump when removed from the vehicle or explosion will result, due to fuel fumes, electric sparks and fresh air, which is not available in the fuel tank.

Fuel Injectors

The injectors are solenoid valves. When the solenoid coil is energized, the plunger is retracted. The needle valve that is attached to the plunger is pulled to the full open position.

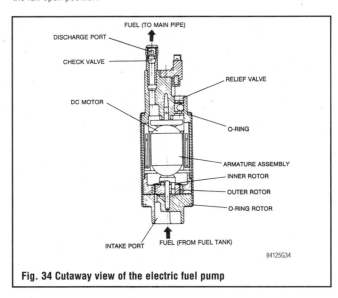

Fig. 34 Cutaway view of the electric fuel pump

Relieving Fuel System Pressure

1. Turn the ignition to the **OFF** position.
2. Loosen the fuel filler cap to release fuel tank pressure.
3. Disconnect the fuel pump harness connector which is located under the rear seat cushion on Elantra or in the area of the fuel tank on the remaining models.
4. Start the vehicle and allow it to run until engine stalls from lack of fuel. Turn the key to the **OFF** position.
5. Disconnect the negative battery cable, then reconnect the fuel pump connector.
6. Service the fuel system as required.

Fuel Filter

The fuel filter should be replaced about every 12,000 miles. Fuel filter service is outlined in Section 1 of this manual.

Electric Fuel Pump

♦ See Figures 34 and 35

The fuel pump's job is to draw fuel from the fuel tank, pressurize it and deliver the fuel to the fuel injectors for combustion in the cylinders. The fuel pump is located inside the fuel tank and is usually completely submerged in fuel, depending on the level of fuel in the tank. The pump is considered a wet-type pump because the inside of the pump is filled with fuel at all times. The pump and motor are cooled by the fuel passing through it. The pump is comprised of a DC motor directly coupled to an impeller type pump. The pump itself is made up of an impeller, casing and a cover with O-ring seals. Additional pump components include a relief valve and a check valve. Fuel pressurization is accomplished when the motor turns the impeller and creates a pressure differential between the bottom and the top of the impeller due to grooves in the outer circumference of the impeller. As soon as the pressure difference is created, the fuel swirling inside the pump is pressurized and flows through the motor, cooling it along the way. Fuel then flows from the motor, opens the check valve and is expelled from the discharge port.

The relief valve acts as a safety device to prevent over-pressurization of the fuel pump for any reason. In such a situation, the relief valve ball overcomes its spring pressure and lifts in response to the increase in pump pressure. The fuel is then diverted back to the suction side of the pump. The relief valve will stay open as long as the over-pressure situation exists. The check valve is a device that permits one way flow of a fluid. When the fuel pump stops, a back pressure is exerted on the check valve causing it to seal off fuel system pressure. By keeping constant pressure in the fuel system, the engine is able to be re-started more easily and vapor lock at high temperatures is prevented.

OPERATION TEST

♦ See Figures 36, 37, 38, 39 and 40

If the fuel pump does not work:
1. Check the fuse.
2. Check all wiring connections.
3. Check the control relay which is located in the engine compartment, next to the ignition coil. If the engine starts when the ignition switch is turned

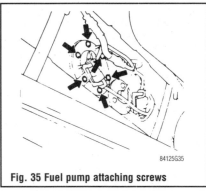

Fig. 35 Fuel pump attaching screws

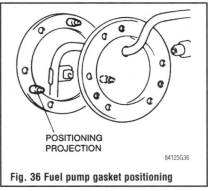

Fig. 36 Fuel pump gasket positioning

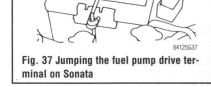

Fig. 37 Jumping the fuel pump drive terminal on Sonata

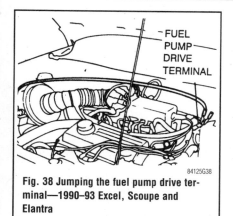

Fig. 38 Jumping the fuel pump drive terminal—1990–93 Excel, Scoupe and Elantra

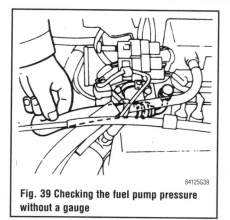

Fig. 39 Checking the fuel pump pressure without a gauge

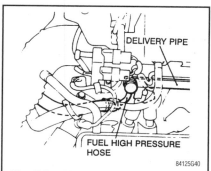

Fig. 40 Location of the high pressure fuel connection on Sonata. This is where the fuel pressure gauge is connected

to **START**, but stops when it is turned to **ON**, the relay is defective. Jumper terminals 1 and 2 of the test connector; the fuel pump should operate. If the pump fails to operate when the jumper is connected, the pump is probably defective.

PRESSURE TESTING

▶ **See Figures 41, 42, 43 and 44**

1. Relieve fuel system pressure. Disconnect the battery negative cable.
2. Hold the upper fuel filter nut securely with a backup or spanner wrench. Cover the hoses with shop towels and remove the upper eye bolt. Discard the gaskets.
3. Using a fuel pressure gauge with the appropriate adapters, install the pressure gauge to the fuel filter.
4. Connect the negative battery terminal. Apply battery voltage to the fuel pump test connector located in the engine compartment, which will energize the

fuel pump. With pressure applied, check for fuel leakage at the gauge. If no leaks are present, continue with the test procedure.

5. Start the engine and run at curb idle speed.
6. Measure the fuel pressure and compare to specifications.
7. Locate and disconnect the vacuum hose running to the fuel pressure regulator. Plug the end of the hose and record the fuel pressure again. The fuel pressure should have increased approximately 10 psi.
8. If the pressure readings were not at the desired specifications, perform the following diagnostic procedure:

   a. If fuel pressure is too low, check for a clogged fuel filter, a defective fuel pressure regulator or a defective fuel pump, any of which will require replacement.

   b. If fuel pressure is too high, the fuel pressure regulator is defective and will have to be replaced, or the fuel return is bent or clogged. If the fuel pressure reading does not change when the vacuum hose is disconnected, the hose is clogged or the valve is stuck in the fuel pressure regulator and it will have to be replaced.

   c. Stop the engine and check for changes in the fuel pressure gauge. It should not drop. If the gauge reading does drop, watch the rate of drop. If fuel pressure drops slowly, the likely cause is a leaking injector which will require replacement. If the fuel pressure drops immediately after the engine is stopped, the check valve in the fuel pump isn't closing and the fuel pump will have to be replaced.

9. Relieve fuel system pressure.
10. Remove the fuel pressure gauge.
11. Install a new O-ring and the pressure hose to the filter. After installation, apply battery voltage to the terminal for fuel pump activation to run the fuel pump. Check for leaks.

REMOVAL & INSTALLATION

1. Reduce pressure in the fuel lines as follows:
   a. Turn the ignition to the **OFF** position.
   b. Loosen the fuel filler cap to release fuel tank pressure.

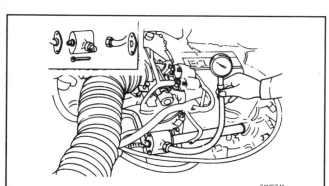

Fig. 41 Connecting the fuel pressure gauge—Excel, Elantra and Scoupe

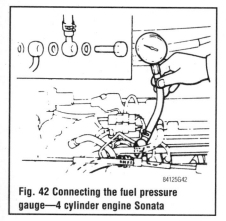

Fig. 42 Connecting the fuel pressure gauge—4 cylinder engine Sonata

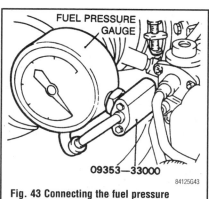

Fig. 43 Connecting the fuel pressure gauge—Sonata V6 engine

Fig. 44 Disconnecting the fuel pressure regulator hose

c. Disconnect the fuel pump harness connector located under the rear seat cushion on Elantra or in the area of the fuel tank on the remaining models.

d. Start the vehicle and allow it to run until it stalls from lack of fuel. Turn the key to the **OFF** position.

e. Disconnect the negative battery cable, then reconnect the fuel pump connector.

2. Raise the vehicle and support it safely.

3. Remove the fuel tank from the vehicle. Disconnect the hoses at the pump.

4. Unbolt and remove the pump from the tank.

To install:

5. Install the new pump with new gasket in place into the fuel tank and secure.

6. Install the fuel tank into the vehicle.

7. Connect the fuel lines and the electrical connectors to the fuel pump and sending unit.

8. Connect the negative battery cable, pressurize the fuel system and check for leaks.

Throttle Body

REMOVAL & INSTALLATION

▶ **See Figures 45, 46, 47 and 48**

1. Release the fuel system pressure as described previously in this section.

2. Disconnect the air intake hose from the throttle body.

3. Disconnect the accelerator and cruise control (if so equipped) from the throttle lever.

4. Drain the engine coolant to a level just below the intake manifold.

5. Remove the water hoses from the throttle body.

6. Label, then disconnect all electrical wiring and vacuum hoses from the throttle body.

7. Remove the four retaining bolts and separate the throttle body from the surge tank. Remove the throttle body gasket and cover the surge tank opening with masking tape to prevent anything from falling into the engine. Purchase a new gasket.

To install:

8. Make sure all the gasket mating surfaces are clean.

9. Position the throttle body and gasket onto the surge tank and install the four retaining bolts. Torque the bolts evenly in a diagonal pattern to 7–9 ft. lbs. To ensure uniform compression of the gasket, DO NOT overtighten the bolts or the gasket will be over-compressed and not seal properly.

10. Connect the vacuum hoses, electrical wiring and water hoses to the throttle body. Make sure all connections are tight.

11. Connect the accelerator and cruise control cables to the throttle lever and adjust them as described in this section.

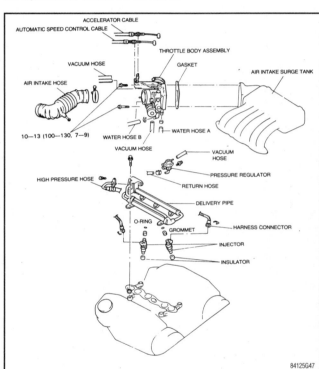

Fig. 47 Throttle body and related components—Sonata V6 engine

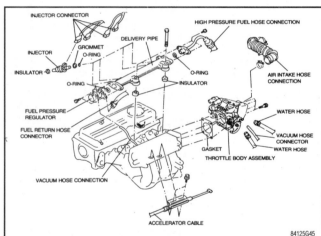

Fig. 45 Throttle body and related fuel system components—1990–93 Excel

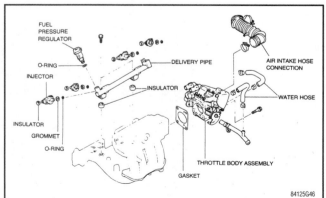

Fig. 46 Throttle body and related components—4 cylinder engine Sonata

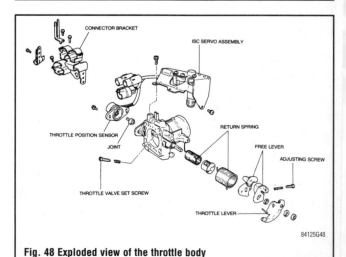

Fig. 48 Exploded view of the throttle body

12. Connect the air intake hose to the throttle body and tighten the hose clamp.
13. Fill the cooling system to the proper level with a 50% mix of antifreeze.
14. Start the engine and adjust the idle speed.

ADJUSTMENTS

▶ **See Figures 49 thru 55**

Accelerator Cable

VEHICLES WITHOUT CRUISE CONTROL

On Excel and Sonata without cruise control, the throttle cable is adjusted by loosening the two screws on the slotted throttle cable bracket(s) attached to the surge tank. Move the bracket(s) as required until a slight tension in the cable is obtained. To check the cable tension, lightly press the cable with the tip of your finger. There should be 0–1mm of slack in the cable. Once the cable is properly tensioned, hold the bracket in place and tighten the two screws. Coat the cable and throttle lever with multipurpose grease.

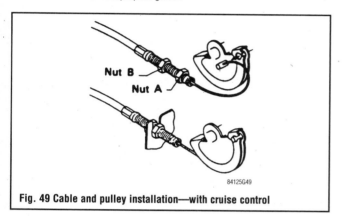

Fig. 49 Cable and pulley installation—with cruise control

VEHICLES WITH CRUISE CONTROL

On Sonata, if the throttle and cruise control cables were disconnected for any reason, there is a four part adjustment sequence to adjust cable tension. The four parts are as follows:
- Accelerator cable (pedal side)
- Accelerator cable (throttle valve side)
- Actuator cable
- Final accelerator cable adjustment

To perform the accelerator cable (pedal side) adjustment:
1. Connect the accelerator cable to the pulley. Then, position the cable in the cable bracket and make the two locknuts A and B finger tight.
2. Pull the cable tight so that the pulley rests against the stop and tighten locknut B until it is flush against the bracket. Then, back locknut B off one complete turn.

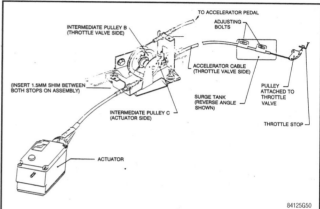

Fig. 50 Cruise control and accelerator cable arrangement—with cruise control

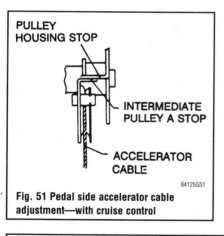

Fig. 51 Pedal side accelerator cable adjustment—with cruise control

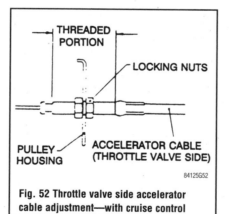

Fig. 52 Throttle valve side accelerator cable adjustment—with cruise control

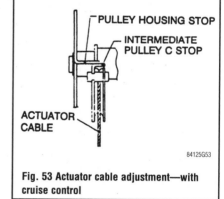

Fig. 53 Actuator cable adjustment—with cruise control

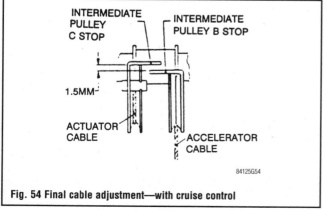

Fig. 54 Final cable adjustment—with cruise control

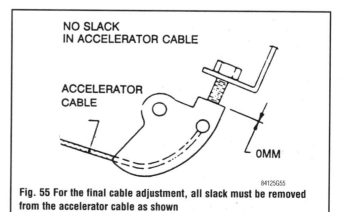

Fig. 55 For the final cable adjustment, all slack must be removed from the accelerator cable as shown

3. Tighten locknut A. The cable should have approximately 1mm of slack.

To perform the accelerator cable (throttle valve side) adjustment:

1. Connect the throttle valve side accelerator cable to intermediate pulley B. Then, adjust and tighten the cable locknuts so that there are just about equal lengths of the cable threaded portion on both sides of the cable housing bracket.

To perform the actuator cable adjustment:

1. Connect the actuator cable to intermediate pulley C.

2. Position the cable in the cable bracket and make the two locknuts A and B finger tight.

3. Pull the cable tight so that the pulley rests against the stop and tighten locknut B until it is flush against the bracket, then back locknut B off one complete turn.

4. Tighten locknut A. The cable should have approximately 1.5mm of slack with the pulley flush against the stop.

To perform the final cable adjustment:

1. If not already completed, connect the accelerator cable to the throttle valve pulley and attach the cable and slotted bracket to the rear side of the surge tank. DO NOT tighten the two bracket mounting screws at this time.

➡**Before proceeding with any further adjustments, make sure the throttle valve pulley is in the NORMAL idle position.** .

2. Insert a 1.5mm shim or feeler gauge between intermediate pulley stops B and C and hold it there.

3. Adjust the cable casing at the rear side of the surge tank until all slack is removed from the cable. If all slack is removed, the throttle stop bolt should be contacting the throttle valve lever. Make sure the throttle valve pulley does not deviate from the normal idle position during the adjustment.

4. Once all slack is removed from the accelerator cable, tighten the two bracket mounting screws at this time.

5. Remove the shim installed between the intermediate pulleys.

Fuel Injectors

▶ **See Figures 56, 57, 58, 59 and 60**

Fuel injectors are injection nozzles with solenoid valves. They're responsible for injecting fuel into the intake manifold at precisely the right instant based on signals from the engine's electronic control unit (ECU).

REMOVAL & INSTALLATION

1596cc, 1796cc and 1997cc Engines

1. Relieve the fuel system pressure.

2. Disconnect the negative battery cable.

3. Wrap the connection with a shop towel and disconnect the high pressure fuel line at the fuel rail.

4. Disconnect the fuel return hose.

5. Disconnect the vacuum hose from the fuel pressure regulator. Remove the fuel pressure regulator and O-ring.

6. Disconnect and remove the PCV hose.

7. Label and disconnect the electrical connectors from each injector.

8. Remove the injector rail retaining bolts. Make sure the rubber mounting bushings do not get lost.

9. Lift the rail assembly up and away from the engine.

10. Remove the injectors from the rail by pulling gently. Discard the lower insulator. Check the resistance through the injector. The specification is 13–16 ohms at 70°F (20°C). If resistance is out of desired reading, replace the injector.

To install:

11. Install a new grommet and O-ring to the injector. Coat the O-ring with light oil.

12. Install the injector to the fuel rail turning to the left and right during installation.

13. Install the fuel rail and injectors to the manifold. Make sure the rubber bushings are in place before tightening the mounting bolts.

14. Tighten the retaining bolts to 72 inch lbs. (11 Nm).

15. Connect the electrical harness connectors to the injectors. Install and connect the PCV hose.

16. Replace the O-ring, lightly lubricate it and connect the fuel pressure regulator.

17. Connect the fuel return hose.

18. Replace the O-ring, lightly lubricate it and connect the high pressure fuel line.

19. Connect the negative battery cable and check the entire system for proper operation and leaks.

1468cc, 1495cc and 2351cc Engines

1. Relieve the fuel system pressure.

2. Disconnect the negative battery cable.

3. Disconnect and remove the air intake hoses as required.

4. Wrap the connection with a shop towel and disconnect the high pressure fuel line at the fuel rail.

5. Disconnect the fuel return hose.

6. Disconnect the accelerator cable connection from the throttle body and position aside.

7. Disconnect the vacuum connection from the fuel pressure regulator.

8. Disconnect the electrical harness connector from each fuel injector.

9. Remove the injector rail retaining bolts. Make sure the rubber mounting insulators do not get lost.

10. Lift the rail assembly up and away from engine.

11. Remove the injectors from the rail by pulling gently. Discard the lower insulator. Check the resistance through the injector. The specification is 13–16 ohms at 70°F (20°C).

To install:

12. Install a new grommet and O-ring to the injector. Coat the O-ring with light weight oil.

13. Install the injector to the fuel rail.

14. Install the fuel rail and injectors to the manifold. Make sure the rubber bushings are in place before tightening the mounting bolts.

15. Tighten the retaining bolts to 9 ft. lbs. (12 Nm).

16. Connect the electrical connectors to the injectors.

17. Replace the O-ring on the fuel pressure regulator, lightly lubricate and install on the delivery pipe. Connect the vacuum hose to the fuel pressure regulator.

18. Connect the fuel return hose.

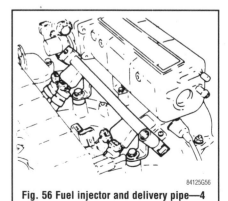

Fig. 56 Fuel injector and delivery pipe—4 cylinder engine Sonata

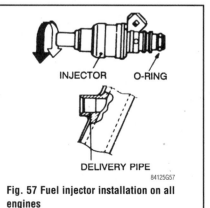

Fig. 57 Fuel injector installation on all engines

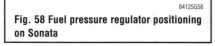

Fig. 58 Fuel pressure regulator positioning on Sonata

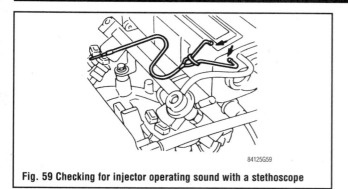

Fig. 59 Checking for injector operating sound with a stethoscope

19. Replace the O-ring on high pressure fuel line, lightly lubricate it and connect to delivery pipe.
20. Reconnect the accelerator cable to the throttle body and adjust to specifications.
21. Connect the negative battery cable and check the entire system for proper operation and leaks.

2972cc Engine

1. Relieve the fuel system pressure.
2. Disconnect the negative battery cable.
3. Drain the cooling system.
4. Disconnect all components from the air intake plenum and remove the plenum from the intake manifold. Discard the gaskets.
5. Wrap the connection with a shop towel and disconnect the high pressure fuel line at the fuel rail.
6. Disconnect the fuel return hose and remove the O-ring.
7. Disconnect the vacuum hose from the fuel pressure regulator. Remove the fuel pressure regulator and O-ring.
8. Disconnect the electrical connectors from each injector.
9. Remove the injector rail retaining bolts. Make sure the rubber mounting bushings do not get lost.
10. Lift the rail assemblies up and away from the engine.
11. Remove the injectors from the rail by pulling gently. Discard the lower insulator. Check the resistance through the injector. The specification is 13–16 ohms at 68°F (20°C).
   To install:
12. Install a new grommet and O-ring to the injector. Coat the O-ring with light oil.
13. Install the injector to the fuel rail.
14. Replace the seats in the intake manifold, if equipped. Install the fuel rails and injectors to the manifold. Make sure the rubber bushings are in place before tightening the mounting bolts.
15. Tighten the retaining bolts to 72 inch lbs. (11 Nm). Install the fuel pipe with new gasket.
16. Connect the electrical connectors to the injectors.
17. Replace the O-ring, lightly lubricate it and connect the fuel pressure regulator.
18. Connect the fuel return hose.

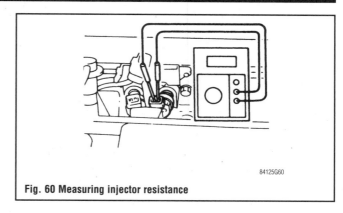

Fig. 60 Measuring injector resistance

19. Replace the O-ring, lightly lubricate it and connect the high pressure fuel line.
20. Using new gaskets, install the intake plenum and all related items. Torque the plenum mounting bolts to 13 ft. lbs. (18 Nm).
21. Fill the cooling system.
22. Connect the negative battery cable and check the entire system for proper operation and leaks.

TESTING

Removal of the fuel injectors is not necessary to test them. To test the injectors you will need an engineer's stethoscope and an ohmmeter.

Operating Sound Check

The sound check is performed to check for an injector(s) that is not working. To check operating sound, have an assistant start the engine and operate the gas pedal. With an engineer's stethoscope touching the injector body, listen for the operating sound at idle speed. You should hear a distinct "ticking" sound at a steady interval as the solenoid valve opens and closes. Listen to all four injectors. Have the assistant increase the engine speed and listen again. The ticking interval should increase in proportion to the increase in engine speed. Again, perform this test on all injectors.

➡**Sometimes the sound from an adjacent injector will be transmitted to another injector across the delivery pipe. In this case a bad injector will appear to be working fine. To avoid this, make sure the tip of the stethoscope is placed directly on the injector body and does not bridge the delivery pipe.**

Resistance Check

To measure injector resistance, disconnect the electrical connector from the injector and place the probes of the ohmmeter across the injector terminals. Set the ohmmeter to the x1 range and check the resistance. It should be 13–16 ohms. Connect the injector connector and move on to the next injector. If the resistance reading is not as specified, replace the injector.

FUEL TANK

Tank Assembly

REMOVAL & INSTALLATION

✳✳ CAUTION

When working on fuel tanks, be sure to disconnect the battery ground (negative) cable.

1986–89 Excel

1. Disconnect the negative battery cable. Remove the drain plug and drain the fuel into a suitable waste container.

2. Loosen the fuel hose (main and return) clamps and disconnect the fuel lines.
3. Disconnect the filler hose and breather hose from the filler neck.
4. Remove the fuel tank mounting band while supporting the tank. Lower the fuel tank slightly and disconnect the fuel gauge wiring connector.
5. Remove the fuel tank.
   To install:
6. Raise the fuel tank into position and connect the fuel level gauge connector. Make sure the band is bonded fully to the tank and tighten the band until the end touches the ground. Torque the strap nuts to 14 ft. lbs.
7. Connect the breather and filler hoses to the filler neck.
8. Connect the fuel lines to their respective tank connections.
9. Install and tighten the drain plug to 58–72 ft. lbs. (78–98 Nm).
10. Fill the tank to the proper level and connect the negative battery cable.

1990–93 Excel, Elantra And Scoupe

▶ See Figures 61

1. Release the fuel system pressure as described earlier in this section. Leave the fuel pump connector disconnected.
2. Disconnect the negative battery cable.
3. Remove the fuel tank cap.
4. Raise the rear of the vehicle and support safely.
5. Position a suitable drain pan under the fuel tank. Remove the drain plug and drain all the fuel from the tank.
6. Disconnect the fuel return and vapor hoses from the fuel tank. Make sure that you label which is which.
7. Disconnect the electrical connector from the fuel sending unit.
8. Loosen the flare nut fitting and disconnect the high pressure hose from the fuel tank.
9. Disconnect the fuel filler and leveling hoses from the fuel tank.
10. Loosen the two self-locking nuts that hold the tank bands to the tank. Support the fuel tank from underneath and swing the tank bands down away from the tank. Disconnect the fuel vapor hose, lower and remove the tank.

To install:

11. Raise the fuel tank into position and connect the vapor hose. Make sure the band is bonded fully to the tank and tighten the band until the end of the band contacts the body.
12. Connect the leveling hose to the tank and the filler neck. Make sure the hose is pushed at least 40mm (1.6 in.) onto the filler neck.
13. Connect the filler hose so that the end of the hose with the shorter straight pipe is connected to the tank side.
14. Connect the fuel vapor and return hoses. Make sure the hoses are pushed at least 1.0–1.2 in. (25–30mm) onto their connections.
15. Loosen connect the high pressure hose to the tank by making the flare nut hand tight. Hold the stationary nut with a wrench and torque the flare nut to 23–30 ft. lbs. Make sure that the fuel hose does not twist when the flare fitting is being tightened.
16. Connect the fuel pump and sending unit wires.
17. Install the drain plug and tighten to 11–18 ft. lbs.
18. Lower the vehicle.
19. Fill the tank to the proper level and connect the negative battery cable.

Sonata

▶ See Figure 62

1. Relieve the pressure from the fuel system.
2. Disconnect the negative battery cable and raise the rear of the vehicle.
3. Remove the fuel tank cap.
4. Remove the drain plug and drain the fuel into a suitable waste container.
5. Label and disconnect the fuel return and vapor hoses.
6. Disconnect the fuel gauge and fuel pump connectors.

7. Disconnect the fuel tank high pressure hose by loosening the union fitting while holding the other fitting stationary.
8. Label and disconnect the fuel filler and leveling hoses from the filler neck.
9. Support the fuel tank from the bottom.
10. Loosen and remove the two self-locking nuts that hold the tank bands in place.
11. Swing the two tank bands down, disconnect the vapor hose and lower the fuel tank to the ground to remove it. After removal, make sure the pad is fully bonded to the tank.

To install:

12. Raise the fuel tank into position and lift the two tank bands into place. Install the tank band self-locking nuts and torque them to 11–18 ft. lbs. until the rear end of the tank makes contact with the body.
13. Push the leveling hose onto the tank so that the hose covers 1.6 in. (40mm) of the connection.
14. Connect the filler hose so that the end having the shorter straight pipe attaches to the tank side.
15. Connect the vapor and return hoses making sure that the hose covers 1.0–1.2 in. (25–30mm) of each connection.
16. Connect the high pressure hose fitting to the fuel pump hose and make hand tight. Hold the other fitting with an open end wrench and torque the fuel tank high pressure fitting to 22–29 ft. lbs.

➡**When tightening the high pressure fitting, make sure that the hose is not allowed to become twisted or bent.**

17. Connect the fuel pump and fuel gauge connectors.
18. Install and torque the drain plug to 11–18 ft. lbs. Fill the fuel tank to the proper level.

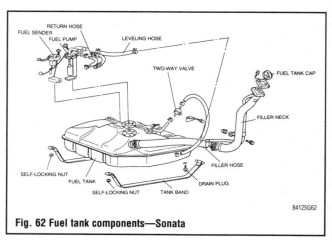

Fig. 62 Fuel tank components—Sonata

84125G62

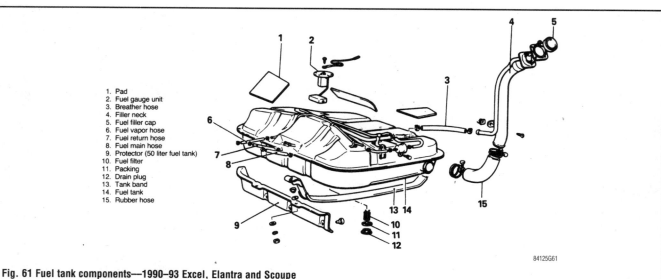

1. Pad
2. Fuel gauge unit
3. Breather hose
4. Filler neck
5. Fuel filler cap
6. Fuel vapor hose
7. Fuel return hose
8. Fuel main hose
9. Protector (50 liter fuel tank)
10. Fuel filter
11. Packing
12. Drain plug
13. Tank band
14. Fuel tank
15. Rubber hose

Fig. 61 Fuel tank components—1990–93 Excel, Elantra and Scoupe

84125G61

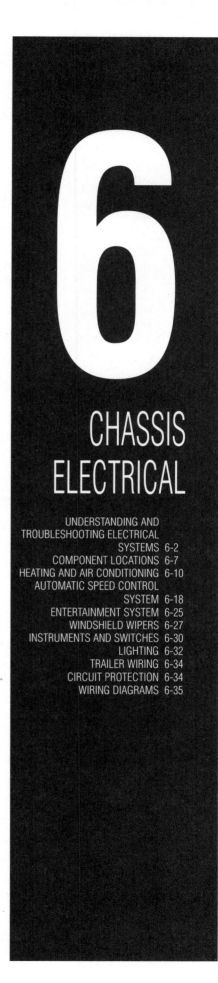

6

CHASSIS ELECTRICAL

UNDERSTANDING AND TROUBLESHOOTING ELECTRICAL SYSTEMS

Basic Electrical Theory

▶ See Figure 1

For any 12 volt, negative ground, electrical system to operate, the electricity must travel in a complete circuit. This simply means that current (power) from the positive (+) terminal of the battery must eventually return to the negative (-) terminal of the battery. Along the way, this current will travel through wires, fuses, switches and components. If, for any reason, the flow of current through the circuit is interrupted, the component fed by that circuit will cease to function properly.

Perhaps the easiest way to visualize a circuit is to think of connecting a light bulb (with two wires attached to it) to the battery—one wire attached to the negative (-) terminal of the battery and the other wire to the positive (+) terminal. With the two wires touching the battery terminals, the circuit would be complete and the light bulb would illuminate. Electricity would follow a path from the battery to the bulb and back to the battery. It's easy to see that with longer wires on our light bulb, it could be mounted anywhere. Further, one wire could be fitted with a switch so that the light could be turned on and off.

The normal automotive circuit differs from this simple example in two ways. First, instead of having a return wire from the bulb to the battery, the current travels through the frame of the vehicle. Since the negative (-) battery cable is attached to the frame (made of electrically conductive metal), the frame of the vehicle can serve as a ground wire to complete the circuit. Secondly, most automotive circuits contain multiple components which receive power from a single circuit. This lessens the amount of wire needed to power components on the vehicle.

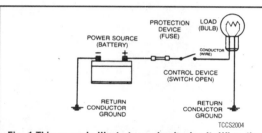

Fig. 1 This example illustrates a simple circuit. When the switch is closed, power from the positive (+) battery terminal flows through the fuse and the switch, and then to the light bulb. The light illuminates and the circuit is completed through the ground wire back to the negative (-) battery terminal. In reality, the two ground points shown in the illustration are attached to the metal frame of the vehicle, which completes the circuit back to the battery

HOW DOES ELECTRICITY WORK: THE WATER ANALOGY

Electricity is the flow of electrons—the subatomic particles that constitute the outer shell of an atom. Electrons spin in an orbit around the center core of an atom. The center core is comprised of protons (positive charge) and neutrons (neutral charge). Electrons have a negative charge and balance out the positive charge of the protons. When an outside force causes the number of electrons to unbalance the charge of the protons, the electrons will split off the atom and look for another atom to balance out. If this imbalance is kept up, electrons will continue to move and an electrical flow will exist.

Many people have been taught electrical theory using an analogy with water. In a comparison with water flowing through a pipe, the electrons would be the water and the wire is the pipe.

The flow of electricity can be measured much like the flow of water through a pipe. The unit of measurement used is amperes, frequently abbreviated as amps (a). You can compare amperage to the volume of water flowing through a pipe. When connected to a circuit, an ammeter will measure the actual amount of current flowing through the circuit. When relatively few electrons flow through a circuit, the amperage is low. When many electrons flow, the amperage is high.

Water pressure is measured in units such as pounds per square inch (psi); The electrical pressure is measured in units called volts (v). When a voltmeter is connected to a circuit, it is measuring the electrical pressure.

The actual flow of electricity depends not only on voltage and amperage, but also on the resistance of the circuit. The higher the resistance, the higher the force necessary to push the current through the circuit. The standard unit for measuring resistance is an ohm. Resistance in a circuit varies depending on the amount and type of components used in the circuit. The main factors which determine resistance are:

- Material—some materials have more resistance than others. Those with high resistance are said to be insulators. Rubber materials (or rubber-like plastics) are some of the most common insulators used in vehicles as they have a very high resistance to electricity. Very low resistance materials are said to be conductors. Copper wire is among the best conductors. Silver is actually a superior conductor to copper and is used in some relay contacts, but its high cost prohibits its use as common wiring. Most automotive wiring is made of copper.
- Size—the larger the wire size being used, the less resistance the wire will have. This is why components which use large amounts of electricity usually have large wires supplying current to them.
- Length—for a given thickness of wire, the longer the wire, the greater the resistance. The shorter the wire, the less the resistance. When determining the proper wire for a circuit, both size and length must be considered to design a circuit that can handle the current needs of the component.
- Temperature—with many materials, the higher the temperature, the greater the resistance (positive temperature coefficient). Some materials exhibit the opposite trait of lower resistance with higher temperatures (negative temperature coefficient). These principles are used in many of the sensors on the engine.

OHM'S LAW

There is a direct relationship between current, voltage and resistance. The relationship between current, voltage and resistance can be summed up by a statement known as Ohm's law.

Voltage (E) is equal to amperage (I) times resistance (R): $E = I \times R$

Other forms of the formula are $R = E/I$ and $I = E/R$

In each of these formulas, E is the voltage in volts, I is the current in amps and R is the resistance in ohms. The basic point to remember is that as the resistance of a circuit goes up, the amount of current that flows in the circuit will go down, if voltage remains the same.

The amount of work that the electricity can perform is expressed as power. The unit of power is the watt (w). The relationship between power, voltage and current is expressed as:

Power (w) is equal to amperage (I) times voltage (E): $W = I \times E$

This is only true for direct current (DC) circuits; The alternating current formula is a tad different, but since the electrical circuits in most vehicles are DC type, we need not get into AC circuit theory.

Electrical Components

POWER SOURCE

Power is supplied to the vehicle by two devices: The battery and the alternator. The battery supplies electrical power during starting or during periods when the current demand of the vehicle's electrical system exceeds the output capacity of the alternator. The alternator supplies electrical current when the engine is running. Just not does the alternator supply the current needs of the vehicle, but it recharges the battery.

The Battery

In most modern vehicles, the battery is a lead/acid electrochemical device consisting of six 2 volt subsections (cells) connected in series, so that the unit is capable of producing approximately 12 volts of electrical pressure. Each subsection consists of a series of positive and negative plates held a short distance apart in a solution of sulfuric acid and water.

The two types of plates are of dissimilar metals. This sets up a chemical reaction, and it is this reaction which produces current flow from the battery when its positive and negative terminals are connected to an electrical load. The power removed from the battery is replaced by the alternator, restoring the battery to its original chemical state.

The Alternator

On some vehicles there isn't an alternator, but a generator. The difference is that an alternator supplies alternating current which is then changed to direct current for use on the vehicle, while a generator produces direct current. Alternators tend to be more efficient and that is why they are used.

Alternators and generators are devices that consist of coils of wires wound together making big electromagnets. One group of coils spins within another set and the interaction of the magnetic fields causes a current to flow. This current is then drawn off the coils and fed into the vehicles electrical system.

GROUND

Two types of grounds are used in automotive electric circuits. Direct ground components are grounded to the frame through their mounting points. All other components use some sort of ground wire which is attached to the frame or chassis of the vehicle. The electrical current runs through the chassis of the vehicle and returns to the battery through the ground (-) cable; if you look, you'll see that the battery ground cable connects between the battery and the frame or chassis of the vehicle.

➡ **It should be noted that a good percentage of electrical problems can be traced to bad grounds.**

PROTECTIVE DEVICES

♦ See Figure 2

It is possible for large surges of current to pass through the electrical system of your vehicle. If this surge of current were to reach the load in the circuit, the surge could burn it out or severely damage it. It can also overload the wiring, causing the harness to get hot and melt the insulation. To prevent this, fuses, circuit breakers and/or fusible links are connected into the supply wires of the electrical system. These items are nothing more than a built-in weak spot in the system. When an abnormal amount of current flows through the system, these protective devices work as follows to protect the circuit:

• Fuse—when an excessive electrical current passes through a fuse, the fuse "blows" (the conductor melts) and opens the circuit, preventing the passage of current.

• Circuit Breaker—a circuit breaker is basically a self-repairing fuse. It will open the circuit in the same fashion as a fuse, but when the surge subsides, the circuit breaker can be reset and does not need replacement.

• Fusible Link—a fusible link (fuse link or main link) is a short length of special, high temperature insulated wire that acts as a fuse. When an excessive electrical current passes through a fusible link, the thin gauge wire inside the link melts, creating an intentional open to protect the circuit. To repair the circuit, the link must be replaced. Some newer type fusible links are housed in plug-in modules, which are simply replaced like a fuse, while older type fusible links must be cut and spliced if they melt. Since this link is very early in the

electrical path, it's the first place to look if nothing on the vehicle works, yet the battery seems to be charged and is properly connected.

❊❊ CAUTION

Always replace fuses, circuit breakers and fusible links with identically rated components. Under no circumstances should a component of higher or lower amperage rating be substituted.

SWITCHES & RELAYS

♦ See Figures 3 and 4

Switches are used in electrical circuits to control the passage of current. The most common use is to open and close circuits between the battery and the various electric devices in the system. Switches are rated according to the amount of amperage they can handle. If a sufficient amperage rated switch is not used in a circuit, the switch could overload and cause damage.

Some electrical components which require a large amount of current to operate use a special switch called a relay. Since these circuits carry a large amount of current, the thickness of the wire in the circuit is also greater. If this large wire were connected from the load to the control switch, the switch would have to carry the high amperage load and the fairing or dash would be twice as large to accommodate the increased size of the wiring harness. To prevent these problems, a relay is used.

Relays are composed of a coil and a set of contacts. When the coil has a current passed though it, a magnetic field is formed and this field causes the contacts to move together, completing the circuit. Most relays are normally open, preventing current from passing through the circuit, but they can take any electrical form depending on the job they are intended to do. Relays can be considered "remote control switches." They allow a smaller current to operate devices that require higher amperages. When a small current operates the coil, a larger current is allowed to pass by the contacts. Some common circuits which may use relays are the horn, headlights, starter, electric fuel pump and other high draw circuits.

LOAD

Every electrical circuit must include a "load" (something to use the electricity coming from the source). Without this load, the battery would attempt to deliver its entire power supply from one pole to another. This is called a "short circuit." All this electricity would take a short cut to ground and cause a great amount of damage to other components in the circuit by developing a tremendous amount of heat. This condition could develop sufficient heat to melt the insulation on all the surrounding wires and reduce a multiple wire cable to a lump of plastic and copper.

WIRING & HARNESSES

The average vehicle contains meters and meters of wiring, with hundreds of individual connections. To protect the many wires from damage and to keep

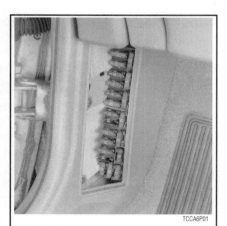

Fig. 2 Most vehicles use one or more fuse panels. This one is located on the driver's side kick panel

TCCA6P01

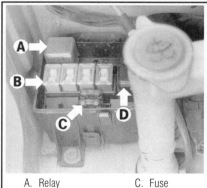

A. Relay   C. Fuse
B. Fusible link   D. Flasher

TCCA6P02

Fig. 3 The underhood fuse and relay panel usually contains fuses, relays, flashers and fusible links

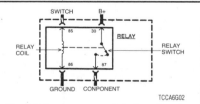

TCCA6G02

Fig. 4 Relays are composed of a coil and a switch. These two components are linked together so that when one operates, the other operates at the same time. The large wires in the circuit are connected from the battery to one side of the relay switch (B+) and from the opposite side of the relay switch to the load (component). Smaller wires are connected from the relay coil to the control switch for the circuit and from the opposite side of the relay coil to ground

them from becoming a confusing tangle, they are organized into bundles, enclosed in plastic or taped together and called wiring harnesses. Different harnesses serve different parts of the vehicle. Individual wires are color coded to help trace them through a harness where sections are hidden from view.

Automotive wiring or circuit conductors can be either single strand wire, multi-strand wire or printed circuitry. Single strand wire has a solid metal core and is usually used inside such components as alternators, motors, relays and other devices. Multi-strand wire has a core made of many small strands of wire twisted together into a single conductor. Most of the wiring in an automotive electrical system is made up of multi-strand wire, either as a single conductor or grouped together in a harness. All wiring is color coded on the insulator, either as a solid color or as a colored wire with an identification stripe. A printed circuit is a thin film of copper or other conductor that is printed on an insulator backing. Occasionally, a printed circuit is sandwiched between two sheets of plastic for more protection and flexibility. A complete printed circuit, consisting of conductors, insulating material and connectors for lamps or other components is called a printed circuit board. Printed circuitry is used in place of individual wires or harnesses in places where space is limited, such as behind instrument panels.

Since automotive electrical systems are very sensitive to changes in resistance, the selection of properly sized wires is critical when systems are repaired. A loose or corroded connection or a replacement wire that is too small for the circuit will add extra resistance and an additional voltage drop to the circuit.

The wire gauge number is an expression of the cross-section area of the conductor. Vehicles from countries that use the metric system will typically describe the wire size as its cross-sectional area in square millimeters. In this method, the larger the wire, the greater the number. Another common system for expressing wire size is the American Wire Gauge (AWG) system. As gauge number increases, area decreases and the wire becomes smaller. An 18 gauge wire is smaller than a 4 gauge wire. A wire with a higher gauge number will carry less current than a wire with a lower gauge number. Gauge wire size refers to the size of the strands of the conductor, not the size of the complete wire with insulator. It is possible, therefore, to have two wires of the same gauge with different diameters because one may have thicker insulation than the other.

It is essential to understand how a circuit works before trying to figure out why it doesn't. An electrical schematic shows the electrical current paths when a circuit is operating properly. Schematics break the entire electrical system down into individual circuits. In a schematic, usually no attempt is made to represent wiring and components as they physically appear on the vehicle; switches and other components are shown as simply as possible. Face views of harness connectors show the cavity or terminal locations in all multi-pin connectors to help locate test points.

CONNECTORS

♦ See Figures 5 and 6

Three types of connectors are commonly used in automotive applications—weatherproof, molded and hard shell.

• Weatherproof—these connectors are most commonly used where the connector is exposed to the elements. Terminals are protected against moisture and dirt by sealing rings which provide a weathertight seal. All repairs require the use of a special terminal and the tool required to service it. Unlike standard blade type terminals, these weatherproof terminals cannot be straightened once they are bent. Make certain that the connectors are properly seated and all of the sealing rings are in place when connecting leads.

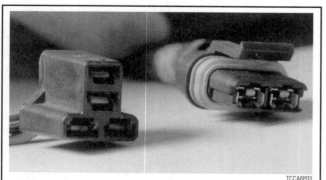
TCCA6P03
Fig. 5 Hard shell (left) and weatherproof (right) connectors have replaceable terminals

TCCA6P04
Fig. 6 Weatherproof connectors are most commonly used in the engine compartment or where the connector is exposed to the elements

• Molded—these connectors require complete replacement of the connector if found to be defective. This means splicing a new connector assembly into the harness. All splices should be soldered to insure proper contact. Use care when probing the connections or replacing terminals in them, as it is possible to create a short circuit between opposite terminals. If this happens to the wrong terminal pair, it is possible to damage certain components. Always use jumper wires between connectors for circuit checking and NEVER probe through weatherproof seals.

• Hard Shell—unlike molded connectors, the terminal contacts in hard-shell connectors can be replaced. Replacement usually involves the use of a special terminal removal tool that depresses the locking tangs (barbs) on the connector terminal and allows the connector to be removed from the rear of the shell. The connector shell should be replaced if it shows any evidence of burning, melting, cracks, or breaks. Replace individual terminals that are burnt, corroded, distorted or loose.

Test Equipment

Pinpointing the exact cause of trouble in an electrical circuit is most times accomplished by the use of special test equipment. The following describes different types of commonly used test equipment and briefly explains how to use them in diagnosis. In addition to the information covered below, the tool manufacturer's instructions booklet (provided with the tester) should be read and clearly understood before attempting any test procedures.

JUMPER WIRES

✳✳ CAUTION

Never use jumper wires made from a thinner gauge wire than the circuit being tested. If the jumper wire is of too small a gauge, it may overheat and possibly melt. Never use jumpers to bypass high resistance loads in a circuit. Bypassing resistances, in effect, creates a short circuit. This may, in turn, cause damage and fire. Jumper wires should only be used to bypass lengths of wire or to simulate switches.

Jumper wires are simple, yet extremely valuable, pieces of test equipment. They are basically test wires which are used to bypass sections of a circuit. Although jumper wires can be purchased, they are usually fabricated from lengths of standard automotive wire and whatever type of connector (alligator clip, spade connector or pin connector) that is required for the particular application being tested. In cramped, hard-to-reach areas, it is advisable to have insulated boots over the jumper wire terminals in order to prevent accidental grounding. It is also advisable to include a standard automotive fuse in any jumper wire. This is commonly referred to as a "fused jumper". By inserting an in-line fuse holder between a set of test leads, a fused jumper wire can be used for bypassing open circuits. Use a 5 amp fuse to provide protection against voltage spikes.

Jumper wires are used primarily to locate open electrical circuits, on either the ground (-) side of the circuit or on the power (+) side. If an electrical component fails to operate, connect the jumper wire between the component and a good ground. If the component operates only with the jumper installed, the ground circuit is open. If the ground circuit is good, but the component does not operate, the circuit between the power feed and component may be open. By moving the jumper wire successively back from the component toward the power source, you can isolate the area of the circuit where the open is located. When the component stops functioning, or the power is cut off, the open is in the segment of wire between the jumper and the point previously tested.

You can sometimes connect the jumper wire directly from the battery to the "hot" terminal of the component, but first make sure the component uses 12 volts in operation. Some electrical components, such as fuel injectors or sensors, are designed to operate on about 4 to 5 volts, and running 12 volts directly to these components will cause damage.

TEST LIGHTS

♦ See Figure 7

The test light is used to check circuits and components while electrical current is flowing through them. It is used for voltage and ground tests. To use a 12 volt test light, connect the ground clip to a good ground and probe wherever necessary with the pick. The test light will illuminate when voltage is detected. This does not necessarily mean that 12 volts (or any particular amount of voltage) is present; it only means that some voltage is present. It is advisable before using the test light to touch its ground clip and probe across the battery posts or terminals to make sure the light is operating properly.

✳✳ WARNING

Do not use a test light to probe electronic ignition, spark plug or coil wires. Never use a pick-type test light to probe wiring on computer controlled systems unless specifically instructed to do so. Any wire insulation that is pierced by the test light probe should be taped and sealed with silicone after testing.

Like the jumper wire, the 12 volt test light is used to isolate opens in circuits. But, whereas the jumper wire is used to bypass the open to operate the load, the 12 volt test light is used to locate the presence of voltage in a circuit. If the test light illuminates, there is power up to that point in the circuit; if the test light does not illuminate, there is an open circuit (no power). Move the test light in successive steps back toward the power source until the light in the handle illuminates. The open is between the probe and a point which was previously probed.

The self-powered test light is similar in design to the 12 volt test light, but contains a 1.5 volt penlight battery in the handle. It is most often used in place of a multimeter to check for open or short circuits when power is isolated from the circuit (continuity test).

The battery in a self-powered test light does not provide much current. A weak battery may not provide enough power to illuminate the test light even when a complete circuit is made (especially if there is high resistance in the circuit). Always make sure that the test battery is strong. To check the battery,

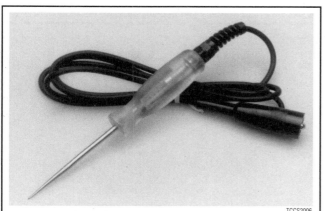

TCCS2006

Fig. 7 A 12 volt test light is used to detect the presence of voltage in a circuit

briefly touch the ground clip to the probe; if the light glows brightly, the battery is strong enough for testing.

➡**A self-powered test light should not be used on any computer controlled system or component. The small amount of electricity transmitted by the test light is enough to damage many electronic automotive components.**

MULTIMETERS

Multimeters are an extremely useful tool for troubleshooting electrical problems. They can be purchased in either analog or digital form and have a price range to suit any budget. A multimeter is a voltmeter, ammeter and ohmmeter (along with other features) combined into one instrument. It is often used when testing solid state circuits because of its high input impedance (usually 10 megaohms or more). A brief description of the multimeter main test functions follows:

• Voltmeter—the voltmeter is used to measure voltage at any point in a circuit, or to measure the voltage drop across any part of a circuit. Voltmeters usually have various scales and a selector switch to allow the reading of different voltage ranges. The voltmeter has a positive and a negative lead. To avoid damage to the meter, always connect the negative lead to the negative (-) side of the circuit (to ground or nearest the ground side of the circuit) and connect the positive lead to the positive (+) side of the circuit (to the power source or the nearest power source). Note that the negative voltmeter lead will always be black and that the positive voltmeter will always be some color other than black (usually red).

• Ohmmeter—the ohmmeter is designed to read resistance (measured in ohms) in a circuit or component. Most ohmmeters will have a selector switch which permits the measurement of different ranges of resistance (usually the selector switch allows the multiplication of the meter reading by 10, 100, 1,000 and 10,000). Some ohmmeters are "auto-ranging" which means the meter itself will determine which scale to use. Since the meters are powered by an internal battery, the ohmmeter can be used like a self-powered test light. When the ohmmeter is connected, current from the ohmmeter flows through the circuit or component being tested. Since the ohmmeter's internal resistance and voltage are known values, the amount of current flow through the meter depends on the resistance of the circuit or component being tested. The ohmmeter can also be used to perform a continuity test for suspected open circuits. In using the meter for making continuity checks, do not be concerned with the actual resistance readings. Zero resistance, or any ohm reading, indicates continuity in the circuit. Infinite resistance indicates an opening in the circuit. A high resistance reading where there should be none indicates a problem in the circuit. Checks for short circuits are made in the same manner as checks for open circuits, except that the circuit must be isolated from both power and normal ground. Infinite resistance indicates no continuity, while zero resistance indicates a dead short.

✳✳ WARNING

Never use an ohmmeter to check the resistance of a component or wire while there is voltage applied to the circuit.

• Ammeter—an ammeter measures the amount of current flowing through a circuit in units called amperes or amps. At normal operating voltage, most circuits have a characteristic amount of amperes, called "current draw" which can be measured using an ammeter. By referring to a specified current draw rating, then measuring the amperes and comparing the two values, one can determine what is happening within the circuit to aid in diagnosis. An open circuit, for example, will not allow any current to flow, so the ammeter reading will be zero. A damaged component or circuit will have an increased current draw, so the reading will be high. The ammeter is always connected in series with the circuit being tested. All of the current that normally flows through the circuit must also flow through the ammeter; if there is any other path for the current to follow, the ammeter reading will not be accurate. The ammeter itself has very little resistance to current flow and, therefore, will not affect the circuit, but it will measure current draw only when the circuit is closed and electricity is flowing. Excessive current draw can blow fuses and drain the battery, while a reduced current draw can cause motors to run slowly, lights to dim and other components to not operate properly.

Troubleshooting Electrical Systems

When diagnosing a specific problem, organized troubleshooting is a must. The complexity of a modern automotive vehicle demands that you approach any problem in a logical, organized manner. There are certain troubleshooting techniques, however, which are standard:

• Establish when the problem occurs. Does the problem appear only under certain conditions? Were there any noises, odors or other unusual symptoms? Isolate the problem area. To do this, make some simple tests and observations, then eliminate the systems that are working properly. Check for obvious problems, such as broken wires and loose or dirty connections. Always check the obvious before assuming something complicated is the cause.

• Test for problems systematically to determine the cause once the problem area is isolated. Are all the components functioning properly? Is there power going to electrical switches and motors? Performing careful, systematic checks will often turn up most causes on the first inspection, without wasting time checking components that have little or no relationship to the problem.

• Test all repairs after the work is done to make sure that the problem is fixed. Some causes can be traced to more than one component, so a careful verification of repair work is important in order to pick up additional malfunctions that may cause a problem to reappear or a different problem to arise. A blown fuse, for example, is a simple problem that may require more than another fuse to repair. If you don't look for a problem that caused a fuse to blow, a shorted wire (for example) may go undetected.

Experience has shown that most problems tend to be the result of a fairly simple and obvious cause, such as loose or corroded connectors, bad grounds or damaged wire insulation which causes a short. This makes careful visual inspection of components during testing essential to quick and accurate troubleshooting.

Testing

OPEN CIRCUITS

♦ See Figure 8

This test already assumes the existence of an open in the circuit and it is used to help locate the open portion.

1. Isolate the circuit from power and ground.
2. Connect the self-powered test light or ohmmeter ground clip to the ground side of the circuit and probe sections of the circuit sequentially.
3. If the light is out or there is infinite resistance, the open is between the probe and the circuit ground.
4. If the light is on or the meter shows continuity, the open is between the probe and the end of the circuit toward the power source.

SHORT CIRCUITS

➡Never use a self-powered test light to perform checks for opens or shorts when power is applied to the circuit under test. The test light can be damaged by outside power.

1. Isolate the circuit from power and ground.
2. Connect the self-powered test light or ohmmeter ground clip to a good ground and probe any easy-to-reach point in the circuit.
3. If the light comes on or there is continuity, there is a short somewhere in the circuit.
4. To isolate the short, probe a test point at either end of the isolated circuit (the light should be on or the meter should indicate continuity).

5. Leave the test light probe engaged and sequentially open connectors or switches, remove parts, etc. until the light goes out or continuity is broken.
6. When the light goes out, the short is between the last two circuit components which were opened.

VOLTAGE

This test determines voltage available from the battery and should be the first step in any electrical troubleshooting procedure after visual inspection. Many electrical problems, especially on computer controlled systems, can be caused by a low state of charge in the battery. Excessive corrosion at the battery cable terminals can cause poor contact that will prevent proper charging and full battery current flow.

1. Set the voltmeter selector switch to the 20V position.
2. Connect the multimeter negative lead to the battery's negative (-) post or terminal and the positive lead to the battery's positive (+) post or terminal.
3. Turn the ignition switch **ON** to provide a load.
4. A well charged battery should register over 12 volts. If the meter reads below 11.5 volts, the battery power may be insufficient to operate the electrical system properly.

VOLTAGE DROP

♦ See Figure 9

When current flows through a load, the voltage beyond the load drops. This voltage drop is due to the resistance created by the load and also by small resistances created by corrosion at the connectors and damaged insulation on the wires. The maximum allowable voltage drop under load is critical, especially if there is more than one load in the circuit, since all voltage drops are cumulative.

1. Set the voltmeter selector switch to the 20 volt position.
2. Connect the multimeter negative lead to a good ground.
3. Operate the circuit and check the voltage prior to the first component (load).
4. There should be little or no voltage drop in the circuit prior to the first component. If a voltage drop exists, the wire or connectors in the circuit are suspect.
5. While operating the first component in the circuit, probe the ground side of the component with the positive meter lead and observe the voltage readings. A small voltage drop should be noticed. This voltage drop is caused by the resistance of the component.
6. Repeat the test for each component (load) down the circuit.
7. If a large voltage drop is noticed, the preceding component, wire or connector is suspect.

RESISTANCE

♦ See Figures 10 and 11

✷✷ WARNING

Never use an ohmmeter with power applied to the circuit. The ohmmeter is designed to operate on its own power supply. The normal 12 volt electrical system voltage could damage the meter!

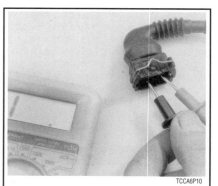

TCCA6P10

Fig. 8 The infinite reading on this multimeter indicates that the circuit is open

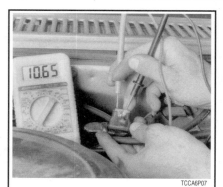

TCCA6P07

Fig. 9 This voltage drop test revealed high resistance (low voltage) in the circuit

TCCA6P08

Fig. 10 Checking the resistance of a coolant temperature sensor with an ohmmeter. Reading is 1.04 kilohms

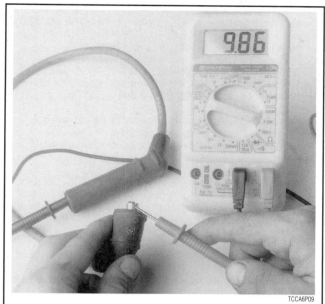

Fig. 11 Spark plug wires can be checked for excessive resistance using an ohmmeter

TCCA6P09

1. Isolate the circuit from the vehicle's power source.
2. Ensure that the ignition key is **OFF** when disconnecting any components or the battery.
3. Where necessary, also isolate at least one side of the circuit to be checked, in order to avoid reading parallel resistances. Parallel circuit resistances will always give a lower reading than the actual resistance of either of the branches.
4. Connect the meter leads to both sides of the circuit (wire or component) and read the actual measured ohms on the meter scale. Make sure the selector switch is set to the proper ohm scale for the circuit being tested, to avoid misreading the ohmmeter test value.

Wire and Connector Repair

Almost anyone can replace damaged wires, as long as the proper tools and parts are available. Wire and terminals are available to fit almost any need. Even the specialized weatherproof, molded and hard shell connectors are now available from aftermarket suppliers.

Be sure the ends of all the wires are fitted with the proper terminal hardware and connectors. Wrapping a wire around a stud is never a permanent solution and will only cause trouble later. Replace wires one at a time to avoid confusion. Always route wires exactly the same as the factory.

➡**If connector repair is necessary, only attempt it if you have the proper tools. Weatherproof and hard shell connectors require special tools to release the pins inside the connector. Attempting to repair these connectors with conventional hand tools will damage them.**

COMPONENT LOCATIONS

Circuit Breakers

The fuse box is located low on the left side of the dashboard behind a cover, or at the left side kick panel, behind a cover.

Fusible Links

Fusible links are located in a holder next to the battery.

Relay, Sensors And Computer Locations

LOCATIONS

1986–89 Excel

- **A/C Capacitor** —is located at the right rear of the engine compartment.
- **A/C Condenser Fan Relay** —is located at the left front of the engine compartment.
- **A/C Diode** —is located under the right side of the dash.
- **A/C Dual Pressure Switch** —is located on the side of the receiver drier.
- **A/C Fast Idle Control Device (carbureted)** —is located under the air cleaner at the base of the carburetor.
- **A/C Relay** —is located under the right side of the dash.
- **Air Control Solenoid Valve** —is located at the top of the engine on the transaxle side.
- **Back-Up Light Switch** —is located at the front of the transaxle, near the radiator.
- **Bowl Vent Valve** —is located on the top of the carburetor, on float chamber cover.
- **Brake Fluid Sensor** —is located in the master cylinder reservoir.
- **Brake/Stop Light Switch** —is located above the brake pedal.
- **Chime Bell** —is located under the center of the dash.
- **Cold Advance Solenoid Valve** —is located at the top of the engine on the transaxle side.
- **Cold Heater** —is located at the right rear of the engine compartment, near the wiring harness grommet on the firewall.
- **Coolant Temperature Switch** —is located on the intake manifold coolant passage.

- **Deceleration Solenoid** —is located on the float chamber of the carburetor.
- **Distributor Advance Solenoid Valve** —is located at the top of the engine on the transaxle side.
- **Door Warning Lamp Diode** —is located under the center of the dash.
- **Electric Choke Relay** —is located at the right rear of the engine compartment, on the firewall.
- **Enrichment Solenoid** —is located on the float chamber of the carburetor.
- **Feed Back Carburetor (FBC) Unit** —is located under the center of the dash.
- **Feedback Solenoid Valve** —is located at the carburetor.
- **Flasher Relay** —is located in the relay box under the left side of the dash.
- **Fuse Box** —is located at the lower left of the dash.
- **Fusible Link Box** —is located next to the battery.
- **Headlight Relay** —is located in the relay box under the left side of the dash.
- **Horn Relay** —is located in the relay box under the left side of the dash.
- **Idle-Up Relay** —is located in the relay box under the left side of the dash.
- **Idle-Up Solenoid** —is located at the top of the engine on the transaxle side.
- **In Manifold Heater Relay** —is located at the right rear of the engine compartment, on the firewall.
- **Inhibitor Switch (automatic transaxle)** —is located on the top of the transaxle, linked to the control cable.
- **Intermittent Wiper Relay** —is located under the dash, to the right of the steering column.
- **Jet Mixture Solenoid** —is located on the float chamber of the carburetor.
- **Lock-Up Control Unit** —is located under the right side of the dash, at the kick panel.
- **Lock-Up Solenoid (automatic transaxle)** —is located at the top of the transaxle.
- **Neutral Switch (manual transaxle)** —is located in the right side of the transaxle.
- **Oil Pressure Switch** —is located at the back of the block near the firewall, on the distributor side of the engine.
- **Oxygen Sensor Checker** —is located on the center right side of the engine compartment.

- **Parking Brake Switch** —is located in the center console at the base of the parking brake.
- **Power Steering Pump Switch** —is located at the left front of the engine compartment.
- **Pulse Generator** —is located at the top of the transaxle.
- **Radiator Thermo Switch** —is located at the bottom of the radiator.
- **Rear Defogger Timer** —is located under the left side of the dash.
- **Relay Box** —is located under the left side of the dash.
- **Seat Belt Switch** —is located at the base of driver's seat belt buckle.
- **Seat Belt Timer** —is located under the center of the dash.
- **Select Switch (manual transaxle)** —is located at the back of the block near the firewall, on the transaxle side of the engine.
- **Slow Cut Solenoid Valve** —is located at the carburetor.
- **Starter Solenoid** —is located on the rear bottom of the engine compartment.
- **Taillight Relay** —is located in the relay box under the left side of the dash.
- **Throttle Position Sensor** —is located at the base of the carburetor.
- **Vacuum Switch** —is located at the left rear of the engine compartment, on the firewall.
- **Water Temperature Sender** —is located at the top of the block on the distributor side.
- **Water Temperature Sensor** —is located on the intake manifold.

1990–93 Excel

- **A/C Diode** —is located under the right side of the dash.
- **A/C Dual Pressure Switch** —is located in the receiver drier.
- **A/C Relay** —is located at the right front of the engine compartment.
- **Accelerator Switch** —is located on the accelerator pedal bracket.
- **Air Flow Sensor** —is located in the air cleaner.
- **Automatic Transaxle Control Unit (TACU)** —is located under the left front seat.
- **Automatic Transaxle Solenoid Valve** —is located at the radiator side of the transaxle.
- **Back-Up Light Switch** —is located on top of the transaxle.
- **Bowl Vent Valve (carburetor)** —is located on the top of the carburetor, on float chamber cover.
- **Brake Fluid Sensor** —is located in the master cylinder.
- **Cold Mixture Heater (carburetor)** —is located under the carburetor.
- **Condenser Fan Relay** —is located at the left front of the engine compartment.
- **Coolant Temperature Sensor** —is located in the rear of the engine under the fresh air duct.
- **Crankshaft Angle Sensor** —is located in the distributor.
- **Daytime Running Light Unit (Canada)** —is located at the right front of the engine compartment.
- **Door Warning Switch** —is located at the ignition switch.
- **EGR Control Solenoid Valve (California)** —is located on the firewall in the engine compartment.
- **EGR Temperature Sensor (California)** —is located on the EGR valve.
- **Electronic Control Unit (ECU)** —is located under the dash on the left side.
- **Exhaust Gas Recirculation (EGR) Valve** —is located near the fuel injection unit mounted to the engine block.
- **Feedback Solenoid Valve (carbureted)** —is located at the carburetor.
- **Fuel Injection** —see Multi-Point Injection (MPI).
- **Fuse Box Relay (red)** —is located in the fusible link box, at the battery.
- **Fuse Box** —is located in the left kick panel.
- **Hazard Flasher** —is located in the relay box under the left side of the dash.
- **Headlight Relay (pink)** —is located in the fusible link box, at the battery.
- **Idle Speed Control Sensor** —is located on the fuel injection unit near the firewall.
- **Ignition Lock Switch (manual transaxle)** —is located on the clutch pedal bracket.
- **Ignition Relay (pink)** —is located in the fusible link box, at the battery.
- **Inhibitor Switch** —is located on the top of the transaxle.

- **Intake Air Temperature Sensor** —is located in the air cleaner.
- **Kick Down Switch** —is located is located on the radiator side of the transaxle.
- **Main Fuse Box** —is located on the side of the battery.
- **Main-Fusible Link Box** —is located at the battery.
- **MPI Diagnostic Connector** —is located at the left kick panel.
- **MPI Relay (blue)** —is located in the fusible link box, at the battery.
- **Multi-Point Injection (MPI) Control Unit** —is located to the left of the center console under the dash.
- **Noise Filter** —is located at the left front of the engine compartment.
- **Oil Pressure Switch** —is located behind the alternator.
- **Oil Temperature Sensor** —is located is located on the radiator side of the transaxle.
- **Oxygen Sensor** —is located in the exhaust manifold.
- **Oxygen Sensor Checker** —is located on the center right side of the engine compartment.
- **PCV Valve** —is located on the back of the valve cover, near the spark plug wires.
- **Power Steering Oil Pressure Switch** —is located on the power steering pump.
- **Power Transistor** —is located on the back of the valve cover near the injectors.
- **Power/Economy Switch** —is located in the transaxle shift lever on the console.
- **Pulse Generator** —is located on the top of the transaxle.
- **Purge Control Solenoid Valve** —is located on the firewall in the engine compartment.
- **Radiator Fan Motor Relay** —is located at the left front of the engine compartment.
- **Radiator Fan Resistor** —is located near the thermostat switch.
- **Relay Box** —is located under the left side of the dash.
- **Self Diagnosis Check Connector** —is located in the left kick panel.
- **Slow Cut Solenoid Valve (carbureted)** —is located at the carburetor.
- **Starter Relay** —is located in the relay box under the left side of the dash.
- **Sub-Fusible Link Box** —is located at the left front of the engine compartment.
- **Taillight Relay** —is located in the relay box under the left side of the dash.
- **Thermo Valve** —is located at the rear of the engine on the battery side.
- **Thermostat Switch** —is located at the injector side of the engine near the firewall.
- **Throttle Position Sensor** —is located on the front of the fuel injection unit, or on the carburetor.
- **Transaxle Control Unit (TCU)** —is located under the right front seat.
- **Two Way Valve** —is located in the fuel tank.
- **Vehicle Speed Sensor** —is located in the speedometer.

Elantra

- **A/C Diode** —is located under the right side of the dash.
- **A/C Dual Pressure Switch** —is located in the receiver drier.
- **A/C Relay** —is located at the right front of the engine compartment.
- **Accelerator Switch** —is located on the accelerator pedal bracket.
- **Air Flow Sensor** —is located in the air cleaner.
- **Automatic Transaxle Control Unit (TACU)** —is located under the left front seat.
- **Automatic Transaxle Solenoid Valve** —is located at the radiator side of the transaxle.
- **Back-Up Light Switch** —is located on top of the transaxle.
- **Brake Fluid Sensor** —is located in the master cylinder.
- **Condenser Fan Relay** —is located at the left front of the engine compartment.
- **Coolant Temperature Sensor** —is located in the rear of the engine under the fresh air duct.
- **Daytime Running Light Unit (Canada)** —is located at the right front of the engine compartment.
- **Door Warning Switch** —is located at the ignition switch.
- **EGR Control Solenoid Valve (California)** —is located on the firewall in the engine compartment.

- **EGR Temperature Sensor (California)** —is located on the EGR valve.
- **Electronic Control Unit (ECU)** —is located under the dash on the left side.
- **Exhaust Gas Recirculation (EGR) Valve** —is located near the fuel injection unit mounted to the engine block.
- **Fuse Box Relay (red)** —is located in the fusible link box, at the battery.
- **Fuse Box** —is located in the left kick panel.
- **Hazard Flasher** —is located in the relay box under the left side of the dash.
- **Headlight Relay (pink)** —is located in the fusible link box, at the battery.
- **Idle Speed Control Sensor** —is located on the fuel injection unit near the firewall.
- **Ignition Lock Switch (manual transaxle)** —is located on the clutch pedal bracket.
- **Ignition Relay (pink)** —is located in the fusible link box, at the battery.
- **Inhibitor Switch** —is located on the top of the transaxle.
- **Intake Air Temperature Sensor** —is located in the air cleaner.
- **Kick Down Switch** —is located is located on the radiator side of the transaxle.
- **Main Fuse Box** —is located on the side of the battery.
- **Main-Fusible Link Box** —is located at the battery.
- **MPI Diagnostic Connector** —is located at the left kick panel.
- **MPI Relay (blue)** —is located in the fusible link box, at the battery.
- **Multi-Point Injection (MPI) Control Unit** —is located to the left of the center console under the dash.
- **Oil Pressure Switch** —is located behind the alternator.
- **Oil Temperature Sensor** —is located is located on the radiator side of the transaxle.
- **Oxygen Sensor** —is located in the exhaust manifold.
- **Oxygen Sensor Checker** —is located on the center right side of the engine compartment.
- **PCV Valve** —is located on the back of the valve cover, near the spark plug wires.
- **Power Steering Oil Pressure Switch** —is located on the power steering pump.
- **Power Transistor** —is located on the back of the valve cover near the injectors.
- **Power/Economy Switch** —is located in the transaxle shift lever on the console.
- **Pulse Generator** —is located on the top of the transaxle.
- **Radiator Fan Motor Relay** —is located at the left front of the engine compartment.
- **Radiator Fan Resistor** —is located near the thermostat switch.
- **Relay Box** —is located under the left side of the dash.
- **Self Diagnosis Check Connector** —is located in the left kick panel.
- **Starter Relay** —is located in the relay box under the left side of the dash.
- **Sub-Fusible Link Box** —is located at the left front of the engine compartment.
- **Taillight Relay** —is located in the relay box under the left side of the dash.
- **Thermo Valve** —is located at the rear of the engine on the battery side.
- **Thermostat Switch** —is located at the injector side of the engine near the firewall.
- **Throttle Position Sensor** —is located on the front of the fuel injection unit.
- **Transaxle Control Unit (TCU)** —is located under the right front seat.
- **Two Way Valve** —is located in the fuel tank.
- **Vehicle Speed Sensor** —is located in the speedometer.

Scoupe

- **Accelerator Switch** —is located at the accelerator pedal bracket.
- **A/C Condenser Fan Relay** —is located at the right front of the engine compartment.
- **A/C Dual Pressure Switch** —is located in the receiver drier.
- **A/C Relay** —is located at the right front of the engine compartment in the sub-fusible link box.
- **Air Flow Sensor** —is located inside the air filter.
- **ASC Actuator** —is located at the right rear of the engine compartment, above the master cylinder.

- **ASC Control Unit** —is located under the left side of the dash.
- **Automatic Transaxle Control Unit** —is located under the left front seat.
- **Automatic Transaxle Solenoid Valve Connector** —is located on the front of the transaxle, near the dipstick.
- **Brake Fluid Switch** —is located in the master cylinder.
- **Clutch Switch** —is located on the clutch pedal bracket.
- **Control Relay** —is located under the left side of the dash, next to the relay box.
- **Coolant Temperature Sensor** —is located under the fresh air duct on the engine block.
- **Cooling System Resistor With Diode** —is located on the firewall.
- **Crank Angle Sensor** —is located inside the distributor.
- **Cruise Control** —see Automatic Speed Control (ASC).
- **Daytime Running Light Control Unit (Canada)** —is located at the right front of the engine compartment.
- **Diagnosis Terminal** —is located in the left kick panel.
- **EGR Control Solenoid Valve** —is located next to the purge control solenoid valve on the firewall.
- **EGR Temperature Sensor** —is located on the EGR valve.
- **Electronic Control Unit (ECU)** —is located under the left side of the dash.
- **Electronic Time and Alarm Control System** —see ETACS.
- **ETACS Control Unit** —is located under the left side of the dash.
- **Exhaust Gas Recirculation (EGR) Valve** —is located next to throttle body at the top of the engine.
- **Fuel Injection** —see Multi Point Injection (MPI).
- **Fuse Box** —is located at the left side kick panel.
- **Idle Speed Control (ISC) Servo** —is located at the throttle body.
- **Inhibitor Switch** —is located at the top of the transaxle.
- **Key Lock Control Unit** —is located at the left quarter panel, behind the trim panel.
- **Key Lock Solenoid** —is located at the ignition key in the steering column.
- **Kickdown Switch** —is located at the back of the transaxle, near the right inner fender well.
- **Main Fusible Link Box** —is located next to the battery.
- **MPI Control Relay** —is located under the left side of the dash.
- **MPI Control Unit** —is located at the right side kick panel.
- **Oil Temperature Sensor** —is located is located at the front of the transaxle, near the dipstick.
- **Oxygen Sensor** —is located in the exhaust manifold near the alternator.
- **PCV Valve** —is located on the valve cover.
- **Power Steering Oil Pressure Switch** —is located on the power steering pump.
- **Power Transistor** —is located at the valve cover near the injectors.
- **Pulse Generator** —is located at the top of the transaxle.
- **Purge Control Solenoid Valve** —is located on the firewall in the engine compartment.
- **Relay Box (engine compartment)** —is located at the left front of the engine compartment.
- **Relay Box (passenger compartment)** —is located under the left side of the dash.
- **Stop Light Switch** —is located on the brake pedal bracket.
- **Thermo Valve** —is located on the right side of the engine next to the fresh air duct.
- **Throttle Position Sensor (TPS)** —is located at the throttle body.
- **Transaxle Control Unit** —is located under the right front seat.
- **Two Way Valve** —is located at the fuel tank.
- **Vehicle Speed Sensor** —is located in the speedometer.

Sonata

- **Accelerator Switch** —is located at the accelerator pedal bracket.
- **A/C Relay** —is located at the right front of the engine compartment in the sub-fusible link box.
- **A/C Pressure Switches** —are located at the left front of the engine compartment and at the center of the firewall.
- **Air Flow Sensor** —is located inside the air filter.
- **ASC Actuator** —is located at the right rear of the engine compartment, above the master cylinder.
- **ASC Control Unit** —is located under the left side of the dash.

- **Automatic Transaxle Solenoid Valve Connector** —is located on the front of the transaxle, near the dipstick.
- **Blower Relay** —is located at the right front of the engine compartment.
- **Clutch Switch** —is located on the clutch pedal bracket.
- **Condenser Fan Relay** —is located at the left front of the engine compartment.
- **Control Relay** —is located under the left side of the dash, next to the relay box.
- **Control Relay** —is located under the right side of the dash, at the kick panel.
- **Coolant Temperature Sensor (except V6)** —is located next to the intake manifold on the engine block.
- **Coolant Temperature Sensor (V6)** —is located at the right front of the engine, next to the engine lifting tab.
- **Coolant Temperature Sensor** —is located at the front of the engine, near the radiator.
- **Cooling System Resistor With Diode** —is located on the firewall.
- **Crank Angle Sensor** —is located inside the distributor.
- **Cruise Control** —see Automatic Speed Control (ASC).
- **Daytime Running Light Control Unit (Canada)** —is located at the right front of the engine compartment.
- **Dedicated Fuse** —is located in the sub-fusible link box.
- **Diagnosis Terminal** —is located under the left side of the dash.
- **EGR Temperature Sensor** —is located on the EGR valve.
- **Electronic Time and Alarm Control System** —see ETACS.
- **ETACS Control Unit** —is located under the left side of the dash.
- **Exhaust Gas Recirculation (EGR) Valve** —is located next to the throttle body at the top of the engine.
- **Fuel Injection** —see Multi Point Injection (MPI).
- **Fuse Box** —is located at the left side of the dash, near the hood release latch or at the kick panel.
- **Idle Speed Control (ISC) Servo** —is located at the throttle body.
- **Inhibitor Switch** —is located at the top of the transaxle.
- **Key Lock Control Unit** —is located under the center of the dash, at the console.

- **Key Lock Solenoid (automatic transaxle)** —is located in the shift lever assembly.
- **Kickdown Switch** —is located at the back of the transaxle, near the right inner fender well.
- **Main Fusible Link Box** —is located next to the battery.
- **MPI Control Relay** —is located at the right kick panel.
- **MPI Control Unit** —is located at the right side kick panel.
- **Oil Temperature Sensor** —is located is located at the front of the transaxle, near the dipstick.
- **Oil Temperature Sensor** —is located is located at the front of the transaxle, near the dipstick.
- **Oxygen Sensor** —is located in the exhaust manifold.
- **Park Position Switch** —is located in the shift lever assembly.
- **Positive Crankcase Ventilation (PCV) Valve** —is located on the valve cover.
- **Power Transistor (except 3.0L)** —is located at the left rear of the engine compartment, on the firewall.
- **Power Transistor (3.0L)** —is located at the rear of the engine, near the injectors.
- **Pulse Generator** —is located at the top of the transaxle.
- **Purge Control Solenoid Valve** —is located at the right rear corner of the engine compartment.
- **Relay Box** —is located under the left side of the dash.
- **Stop Light Switch** —is located on the brake pedal bracket.
- **Sub-Fusible Link Box** —is located at the right front of the engine compartment.
- **Sunroof Relays** —are located at the sunroof motor.
- **Thermo Valve (except V6)** —is located on the right side of the engine next to the fresh air duct.
- **Thermo Valve (V6)** —is located near the throttle body at the front of the engine.
- **Throttle Position Sensor (TPS)** —is located at the throttle body.
- **Two Way Valve** —is located at the fuel tank.
- **Vehicle Speed Sensor** —is located in the speedometer.

HEATING AND AIR CONDITIONING

➡Before performing any procedures that require the air conditioning system to be discharged, refer to Section 1 of this manual for the correct procedures and precautions.

System

GENERAL INFORMATION

The heater unit is located in the center of the vehicle, along the firewall. The heater system is a bi-level system, designed to direct air through the vents to either the windshield or the floor and cool air to the panel vents. On Sonata this system also includes ducts that direct air to the rear seat passengers.

The air conditioning system is designed to be activated in combination with a separate air conditioning switch installed in the control assembly and the fan speed switch. Some Sonata models are equipped with an electronically controlled system.

The control assemblies used vary depending on year and model. Some models use cable operated control heads, that route cables from the control head to the various air doors in the heater/air conditioning case. Other models use a vacuum control system to operate the various air doors.

Blower Motor

TESTING

The blower motor can be tested by connecting it to the battery positive and negative terminals. It should run smoothly in both directions, this can be checked by reversing the wires on the battery. If the motor runs unevenly or fails to run, it should be replaced.

REMOVAL & INSTALLATION

1986–89 Excel

♦ See Figure 12

1. Disconnect the battery ground cable.
2. Set the heater control to HOT and drain the cooling system.
3. Disconnect the coolant hoses at the heater core tubes, in the engine compartment.

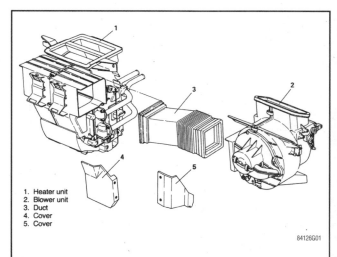

1. Heater unit
2. Blower unit
3. Duct
4. Cover
5. Cover

84126G01

Fig. 12 Blower unit and related components—1986–89 Excel

4. Remove the lower instrument panel section.

5. Remove the center console and on-board computer.

6. Loosen the heater duct mounting screw.

7. Pushing downward and pulling, remove the heater ducts.

8. Disconnect the heater control cable.

9. Disconnect the wiring at the motor.

10. Remove the five heater case mounting bolts and remove the heater case from under the dash.

11. Separate the case halves and remove the blower motor, blower wheel and gasket. Discard the gasket and purchase a new one. Inspect the blower wheel for damage and replace it as necessary.

To install:

12. Install the blower assembly with a new gasket.

13. Put the upper and lower case halves together using new gaskets and sealant as required.

14. Position the heater case under the dash and secure it with the five retaining bolts.

15. Connect the blower motor wiring.

16. Connect the heater control wire.

17. Install the heater ducts and secure with mounting screw.

18. Install the center console and computer assembly.

19. Install the lower instrument panel section.

20. Working from the engine compartment, connect the coolant hoses to the heater core tubes.

21. Fill the cooling system to the proper level with a 50% mix of anti-freeze.

22. Connect the negative battery cable.

1990–93 Excel, Elantra and Scoupe

♦ See Figure 13

The blower unit is located on the passenger's side of the vehicle to the right of the heater control panel.

1. Disconnect the negative battery cable.

2. Remove the glove box housing cover.

3. Remove the lower crash pad, crash pad center fascia and lower crash pad center skin.

4. Disconnect the blower motor and blower resistor connectors.

5. Disconnect the blower motor cooling tube.

6. Remove the three screws that attach the blower motor to the lower case and lower the blower motor far enough so that the FRESH/ RECIRC vacuum connector can be disconnected. Remove the blower motor from the car.

7. Inspect the blower wheel for damage and replace it as necessary. Replace the blower motor mounting seal.

8. Raise the blower motor and seal up onto the lower case half and connect the FRESH/ RECIRC vacuum connector. Mount the blower onto the lower case half and install the three retaining screws.

9. Connect the blower motor cooling tube.

10. Connect the blower motor and resistor wire connectors.

11. Install the lower crash pad center skin, crash pad center fascia and lower crash pad.

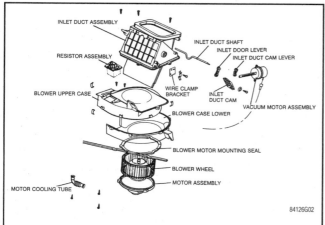

INLET DUCT ASSEMBLY
INLET DUCT SHAFT
INLET DOOR LEVER
RESISTOR ASSEMBLY
INLET DUCT CAM LEVER
WIRE CLAMP BRACKET
INLET DUCT CAM
BLOWER UPPER CASE
VACUUM MOTOR ASSEMBLY
BLOWER CASE LOWER
BLOWER MOTOR MOUNTING SEAL
BLOWER WHEEL
MOTOR ASSEMBLY
MOTOR COOLING TUBE

84126G02

Fig. 13 Blower unit and related components–1990–93 Excel

12. Install the glove box housing cover.

13. Connect the negative battery cable.

14. Check the blower for proper operation at all speeds.

Sonata

➡The heater core hoses use spring-lock type couplings that require the uses of special coupling tool 09977-33600 (A/B) to disconnect and connect. Spring lock coupling REMOVAL & INSTALLATION is detailed in Section 1.

1. Disconnect the negative battery cable and drain the coolant from the radiator.

2. From inside the engine compartment, disconnect the heater hoses and evaporator drain hose from the heater core tubes using the spring lock coupling tool described in Section 1. Disconnect the drain hose. These three hoses are located just above the fuel filter.

3. Remove the front and rear console assemblies.

4. Remove the left and right side covers by removing the two retaining screws on each side.

5. Remove the glove box, center crash pad cover, center crash pad and cassette assembly.

6. Remove the lower crash pad.

7. Remove the console and center support mounting brackets.

8. Disconnect the rear passenger heating duct assembly and rear heating duct Y-joint from the heater case.

9. Remove the heater control assembly from the dash by removing the four retaining screws.

10. Disconnect the blower motor wiring connector.

11. Remove the four retaining screws and pull the heater case down and out of the dash.

12. Separate the case halves and remove the blower motor, blower wheel and gasket from the lower case half. Discard the gasket. Inspect the blower wheel for damage and replace it as necessary.

To install:

13. Install the blower assembly into the lower heater case half with a new gasket.

14. Assemble the upper and lower case halves together using new gaskets and sealant as required.

15. Position the heater case under the dash and secure it with the four retaining screws.

16. Connect the blower motor wiring.

17. Install the heater control assembly into the dash and secure it with the four retaining screws.

18. Connect the rear heating Y-joint and left and right rear passenger heating ducts to the heater case openings.

19. Install the center and console support mounting brackets.

20. Install the lower crash pad.

21. Install the cassette assembly, center crash pad and cover and the glove box.

22. Install the left and right side covers.

23. Install the front and rear console assembly.

24. Connect the drain hose. Connect the hoses to the heater core tubes using the proper tool (see Section 1).

25. Fill the cooling system to the proper level with a 50% mix of anti-freeze and connect the negative battery cable. Start the engine and check for coolant leaks.

Heater Case and Core

REMOVAL & INSTALLATION

1986–89 Excel

♦ See Figures 14 and 15

1. Disconnect the negative battery cable.

2. Set the heater control to HOT and drain the cooling system.

3. Disconnect the coolant hoses at the heater core tubes, in the engine compartment.

4. Remove the lower instrument panel section.

5. Remove the center console and on-board computer.
6. Loosen the heater duct mounting screw.
7. Pushing downward and pull, remove the heater ducts.
8. Disconnect the heater control cable.
9. Disconnect the wiring at the motor.

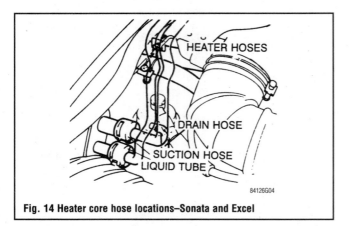

Fig. 14 Heater core hose locations—Sonata and Excel

10. Remove the five heater case mounting bolts and remove the heater case from under the dash.
11. Separate the case halves and remove the heater core.

To install:

12. Insert the heater core into the heater case. Assemble the case halves together using new gaskets and sealant as required.
13. Position the heater case under the dash and secure it with the five retaining bolts.
14. Connect the blower motor wiring.
15. Connect the heater control wire.
16. Install the heater ducts and secure with mounting screw.
17. Install the center console and computer assembly.
18. Install the lower instrument panel section.
19. Working from the engine compartment, connect the coolant hoses to the heater core tubes.
20. Fill the cooling system to the proper level with a 50% mix of anti-freeze.
21. Connect the negative battery cable.

1990–93 Excel

▶ **See Figures 16 and 17**

1. Disconnect the negative battery cable.
2. Set the heater control to **HOT** and drain the cooling system.

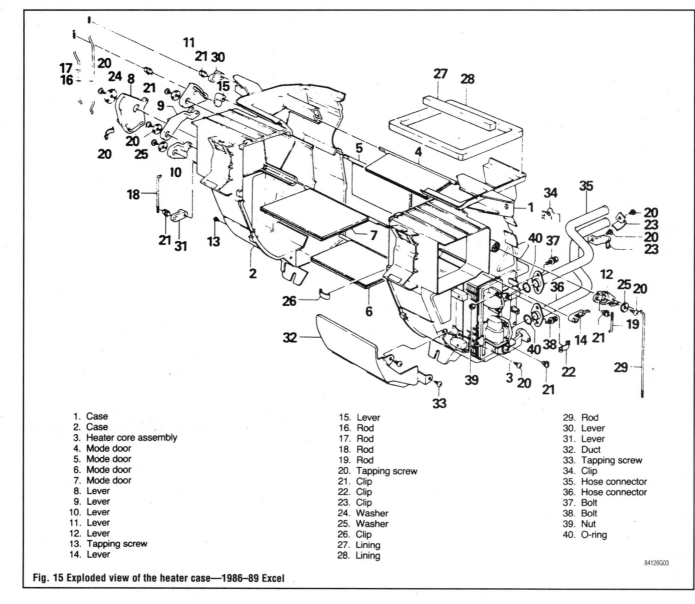

1. Case	15. Lever	29. Rod
2. Case	16. Rod	30. Lever
3. Heater core assembly	17. Rod	31. Lever
4. Mode door	18. Rod	32. Duct
5. Mode door	19. Rod	33. Tapping screw
6. Mode door	20. Tapping screw	34. Clip
7. Mode door	21. Clip	35. Hose connector
8. Lever	22. Clip	36. Hose connector
9. Lever	23. Clip	37. Bolt
10. Lever	24. Washer	38. Bolt
11. Lever	25. Washer	39. Nut
12. Lever	26. Clip	40. O-ring
13. Tapping screw	27. Lining	
14. Lever	28. Lining	

Fig. 15 Exploded view of the heater case—1986–89 Excel

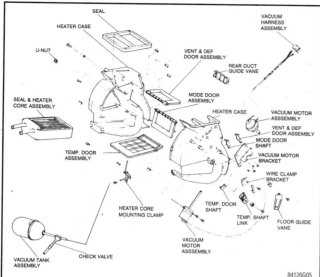

Fig. 16 Exploded view of the heater case—1990–93 Excel and Scoupe with vacuum controls

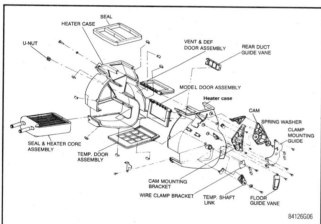

Fig. 17 Exploded view of the heater case—1990–93 Excel

3. Disconnect the coolant hoses at the heater core tubes, in the engine compartment.

4. Remove the lower instrument panel section.

5. Remove the center console and on-board computer.

6. Loosen the heater duct mounting screw.

7. While pushing downward and gently pulling, remove the heater ducts.

8. Disconnect the heater control cable.

9. Disconnect the wiring at the motor.

10. Remove the heater case mounting bolts and remove the heater case from under the dash.

11. Separate the case halves and remove the blower motor and the heater core assembly.

To install:

12. Install the heater core into the case and assemble the case halves. Install the blower.

13. Install the heater case into the vehicle and secure using the mounting bolts.

14. Connect the electrical harness at the motor.

15. Connect the heater control cable.

16. Install the heater ducts.

17. Tighten the heater duct mounting screw.

18. Install the center console and on-board computer.

19. Install the lower instrument panel section.

20. Connect the coolant hoses at the heater core tubes, in the engine compartment.

21. Set the heater control to **HOT** and refill the cooling system.

22. Connect the negative battery cable.

23. Start the vehicle and run until normal operating temperature is reached. Check the operation of the air conditioning and heating systems and inspect for leaks.

24. Shut the engine OFF and allow to cool. Carefully remove the radiator cap. Add coolant as required to fill the system to the appropriate level.

Elantra

▶ See Figure 18

1. Disconnect the negative battery cable.

2. Position the heater control to **HOT** and drain the cooling system.

3. Disconnect the heater hoses from the heater core tubes at the firewall.

4. Remove the evaporator drain hose.

5. Using the proper equipment, drain the air conditioning system.

6. Disconnect the suction and liquid line connections at the firewall and cap to prevent contamination of the system.

7. Remove the floor console assembly as follows:

   a. Remove the center console plate and then loosen 1 screw.

   b. Disconnect the outside mirror control switch connector and remove the switch.

   c. Remove the transaxle shift control lever knob.

   d. Remove the 4 screws securing the front console to the front and the center mounting brackets.

   e. Remove the remaining rear console mounting screws and remove the console assembly.

8. Remove the glove box assembly.

9. Remove the hood release handle and the side lower crash pads.

10. Remove the lower crash pad center fascia panel and disconnect the electrical harness connectors. Remove the radio making sure to disconnect all connectors.

11. Remove the mounting screws from the lower main crash pad and remove from the vehicle. Remove the lower crash pad support bracket assembly.

12. Disconnect and remove the air conditioning/heater control assembly. Disconnect the electrical harness at the blower motor.

13. Remove the evaporator mounting screws and the evaporator unit assembly.

14. Remove the rear heating joint duct assembly.

15. Remove the heater unit from the vehicle.

16. Separate the case halves and remove the heater core.

To install:

17. Install the heater unit into the vehicle.

18. Install the rear heating joint duct assembly.

19. Install the evaporator unit assembly and secure with the mounting screws.

20. Install the air conditioning/heater control assembly. Connect the electrical harness at the blower motor.

21. Install the lower crash pad support bracket assembly and lower crash pad on vehicle.

22. Install the radio connecting all harness connectors.

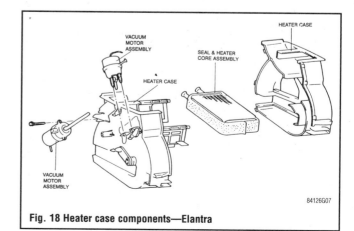

Fig. 18 Heater case components—Elantra

23. Connect the electrical harness connectors while installing the lower crash pad center fascia panel.

24. Install the lower side crash pads and the hood release handle.

25. Install the glove box assembly.

26. Install the floor console assembly.

27. Connect the suction and the liquid line connections at the firewall making sure to use new gaskets at all unions.

28. Connect the heater hoses to the heater core tubes at the firewall.

29. Refill the cooling system to the proper level.

30. Install the drain hose to the evaporator drain, evacuate and recharge the air conditioning system, if equipped.

31. Reconnect the negative battery cable.

32. Start the vehicle and run until normal operating temperature is reached. Check the operation of the air conditioning and heating systems and inspect for leaks.

33. Shut the engine OFF and allow to cool. Carefully remove the radiator cap. Add coolant as required to fill the system to the appropriate level.

Sonata

♦ **See Figure 19**

1. Disconnect the negative battery cable.

2. Place the control in the HOT position.

3. Drain the cooling system.

4. Remove the heater hoses from the core tubes.

5. Discharge the air conditioning system.

6. Disconnect the suction and liquid refrigerant lines at the firewall connectors. Always use back-up wrenches. Cap all openings at once.

7. Remove the front and rear center consoles.

8. Remove the heater side covers.

9. Remove the glove box, center crash pad cover, center crash pad and the radio.

10. Remove the lower crash pad.

11. Remove the console mounting bracket and center support.

12. Remove the left and right rear heat duct assemblies and the rear heating joint duct.

13. Remove the control unit.

14. Disconnect the blower speed actuator connector and, on Canadian vehicles, disconnect the blend door actuator connector.

15. Remove the heater/air conditioning unit.

16. Remove the blower motor from the case.

17. Separate the case halves and lift out the core.

To install:

18. Assemble the case halves.

19. Install the blower motor to the case.

20. Install the heater/air conditioning unit.

21. Connect the blower speed actuator connector and, on Canadian vehicles, connect the blend door actuator connector.

22. Install the control unit.

23. Install the left and right rear heat duct assemblies and the rear heating joint duct.

24. Install the console mounting bracket and center support.

25. Install the lower crash pad.

26. Install the glove box, center crash pad cover, center crash pad and the radio.

27. Install the heater side covers.

28. Install the front and rear center consoles.

29. Connect the suction and liquid refrigerant lines at the firewall connectors. Always use back-up wrenches.

30. Recharge the air conditioning system.

31. Install the heater hoses to the core tubes.

32. Refill the cooling system.

33. Connect the negative battery cable.

34. Start the vehicle and run until normal operating temperature is reached. Check the operation of the air conditioning and heating systems and inspect for leaks.

35. Shut the engine OFF and allow to cool. Carefully remove the radiator cap. Add coolant as required to fill the system to the appropriate level.

Scoupe

♦ **See Figures 20 thru 25**

1. Disconnect the negative battery cable.

2. Set the heater control to **HOT** and drain the cooling system.

3. Disconnect the coolant hoses at the heater core tubes, in the engine compartment.

4. Remove the console assembly, cluster fascia panel and lower crash pad center skin.

5. Loosen the heater duct mounting screw.

6. Remove the heater ducts.

7. Disconnect the heater control cable.

8. Disconnect the wiring at the motor.

9. Remove the heater case mounting bolts and remove the heater case from under the dash.

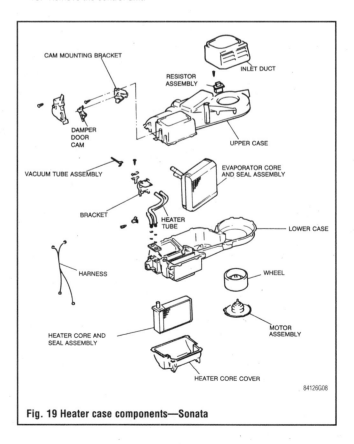

Fig. 19 Heater case components—Sonata

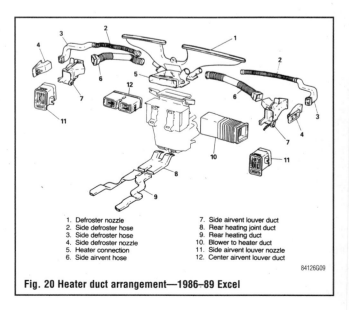

1. Defroster nozzle	7. Side airvent louver duct
2. Side defroster hose	8. Rear heating joint duct
3. Side defroster hose	9. Rear heating duct
4. Side defroster nozzle	10. Blower to heater duct
5. Heater connection	11. Side airvent louver nozzle
6. Side airvent hose	12. Center airvent louver duct

Fig. 20 Heater duct arrangement—1986–89 Excel

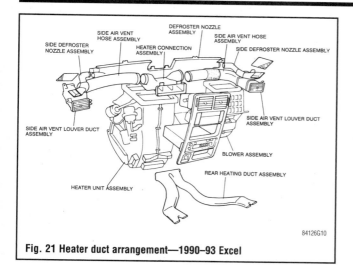

Fig. 21 Heater duct arrangement—1990–93 Excel

10. Separate the case halves and remove the blower.

To install:

11. Assemble the case halves.

12. Install the heater case and mounting bolts.

13. Connect the wiring at the motor.

14. Connect the heater-control cable.

15. Install the heater ducts.

16. Tighten the heater duct mounting screw.

17. Install the console assembly, cluster fascia panel and lower crash pad center skin.

18. Connect the coolant hoses at the heater core tubes, in the engine compartment.

19. Refill the cooling system.

20. Connect the negative battery cable.

21. Start the vehicle and run until normal operating temperature is reached. Check the operation of the air conditioning and heating systems and inspect for leaks.

22. Shut the engine OFF and allow to cool. Carefully remove the radiator cap. Add coolant as required to fill the system to the appropriate level.

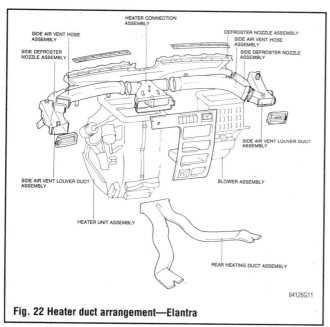

Fig. 22 Heater duct arrangement—Elantra

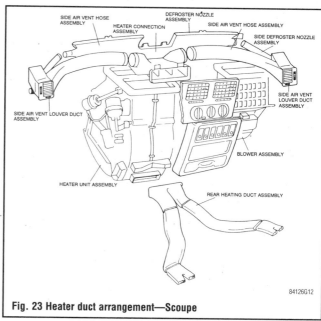

Fig. 23 Heater duct arrangement—Scoupe

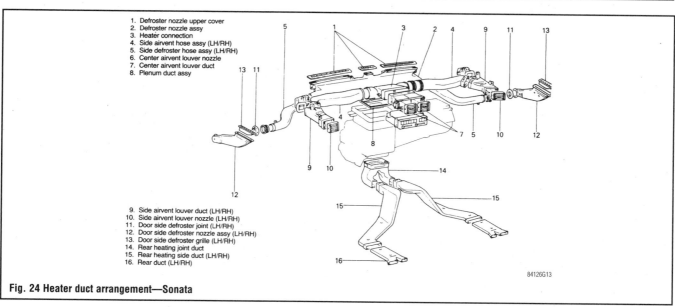

1. Defroster nozzle upper cover
2. Defroster nozzle assy
3. Heater connection
4. Side airvent hose assy (LH/RH)
5. Side defroster hose assy (LH/RH)
6. Center airvent louver nozzle
7. Center airvent louver duct
8. Plenum duct assy

9. Side airvent louver duct (LH/RH)
10. Side airvent louver nozzle (LH/RH)
11. Door side defroster joint
12. Door side defroster nozzle assy (LH/RH)
13. Door side defroster grille (LH/RH)
14. Rear heating joint duct
15. Rear heating side duct (LH/RH)
16. Rear duct (LH/RH)

Fig. 24 Heater duct arrangement—Sonata

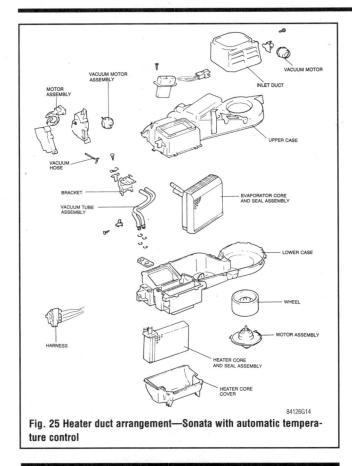

Fig. 25 Heater duct arrangement—Sonata with automatic temperature control

Control Panel

REMOVAL & INSTALLATION

1986–89 Excel

▶ See Figures 26, 27 and 28

1. Remove the lower dash pad section.
2. Remove the bolts securing the control head bracket to the dash pad.
3. Disconnect the control cables and wiring, and remove the control head.

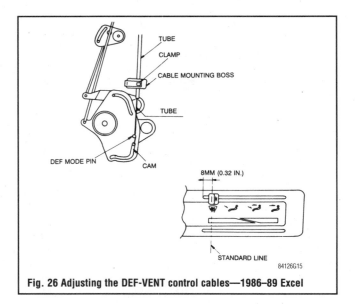

Fig. 26 Adjusting the DEF-VENT control cables—1986–89 Excel

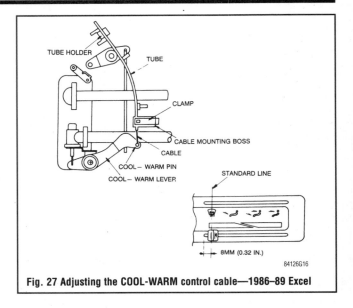

Fig. 27 Adjusting the COOL-WARM control cable—1986–89 Excel

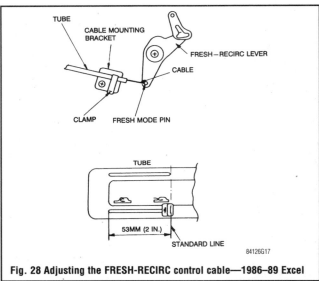

Fig. 28 Adjusting the FRESH-RECIRC control cable—1986–89 Excel

4. Installation is the reverse of removal. When connecting the cables, the DEF/VENT control should be in the DEF position; the COOL/WARM control should be in the WARM position; the FRESH/RECIRC control should be in the RECIRC position.

1990–93 Excel

▶ See Figure 29

1. Disconnect the negative battery cable. Pull the ashtray out and remove the bolt that attaches it to the fascia panel.
2. Remove the four screws and pull out the heater control panel far enough to disconnect the A/C switch, defroster and cigarette lighter connectors.
3. Remove the heater control panel mounting screws.
4. Pull out the heater control panel and disconnect the blower motor switch connector, vacuum connector or temperature control cable.
5. Installation is the reverse of the removal procedure. Check all the heater control panel functions for proper operation.

Elantra

▶ See Figures 30 and 31

1. Disconnect the negative battery cable.
2. Remove the ashtray.

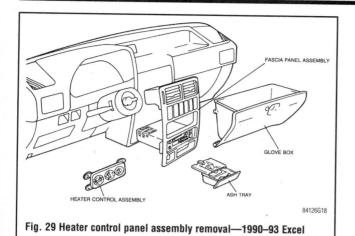

Fig. 29 Heater control panel assembly removal—1990–93 Excel

3. Remove the 2 screws from the ashtray opening.

4. Remove the screw from the left side of the center instrument panel console.

5. Using a small prybar, pry the left side of the center instrument panel out until the spring clip releases. Remove the center instrument panel trim.

6. Remove the 4 screws that retain the heater/air conditioning control head. Pull the control head forward and disconnect the connectors from it. Remove it from the vehicle.

To install:

7. Install the control head in position, connecting any wiring.

8. Install the center instrument panel trim and the ashtray.

9. Connect the negative battery cable and check the operation of the control head.

Scoupe

▶ **See Figures 32, 33 and 34**

1. Disconnect the negative battery cable.

2. Remove the transmission gearshift knob.

3. Remove the ashtray assembly.

4. Pry the rear of the center console upward and remove it.

5. Remove the 2 screws from inside the ashtray opening (the screws are in the top of the opening and can be reached with a small screwdriver).

6. Pry the center part of the trim around the radio off with a small prybar.

7. Remove the clock assembly by prying it away from the instrument panel. Disconnect the connector.

8. Remove the 6 screws that retain the trim panel around the instrument cluster. Remove the trim panel, use care not to damage it.

9. Remove the 4 screws retaining the control assembly and pull it from the instrument panel. Disconnect the connectors and the vacuum line.

To install:

10. Install the control assembly in position and connect the wiring.

11. Install the cluster trim panel.

12. Install the clock.

13. Install the remaining trim components and the clock.

14. Install the center console trim and the transmission gearshift knob.

15. Connect the negative battery cable and the check the operation of control assembly.

Sonata

▶ **See Figures 35 and 36**

1. Disconnect the negative battery cable. Remove the center crash pad cover, center crash pad and radio trim surround assemblies.

2. Remove the four screws and pull the control head assembly from the dash. Disconnect the electrical connector and/or vacuum line.

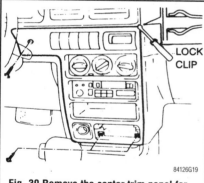

Fig. 30 Remove the center trim panel for heater control panel removal—Elantra

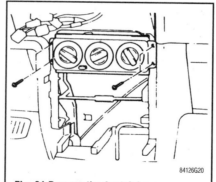

Fig. 31 Remove the 4 retaining screws then remove the control head—Elantra

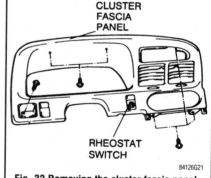

Fig. 32 Removing the cluster fascia panel for heater control removal—Scoupe

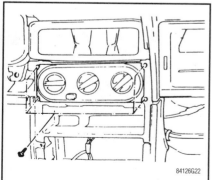

Fig. 33 Remove the 4 retaining screws then remove the control head—Scoupe

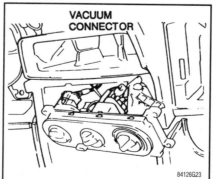

Fig. 34 Pull the control head out then disconnect the connectors—Scoupe

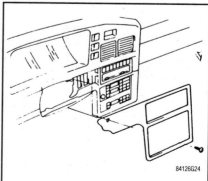

Fig. 35 Remove the center trim panel for heater control panel removal—Sonata

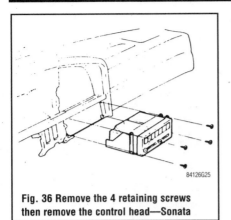

Fig. 36 Remove the 4 retaining screws then remove the control head—Sonata

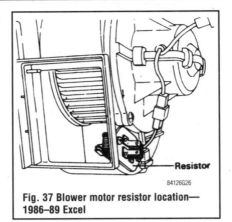

Fig. 37 Blower motor resistor location—1986–89 Excel

Fig. 38 Blower resistor location and removal—Sonata

3. Installation is the reverse of the removal procedure. Check all the heater control panel functions for proper operation.

Air Conditioning Components

REMOVAL & INSTALLATION

Repair or service of air conditioning components is not covered by this manual, because of the risk of personal injury or death, and because of the legal ramifications of servicing these components without the proper EPA certification and experience. Cost, personal injury or death, environmental damage, and legal considerations (such as the fact that it is a federal crime to vent refrigerant into the atmosphere), dictate that the A/C components on your vehicle should be serviced only by a Motor Vehicle Air Conditioning (MVAC) trained, and EPA certified automotive technician.

➡ **If your vehicle's A/C system uses R-12 refrigerant and is in need of recharging, the A/C system can be converted over to R-134a refrigerant (less environmentally harmful and expensive). Refer to Section 1 for additional information on R-12 to R-134a conversions, and for additional considerations dealing with your vehicle's A/C system.**

Blower Resistor

REMOVAL & INSTALLATION

1986-89 Excel

▶ **See Figure 37**

The blower resistor is attached to the outside of the blower case.
1. Disconnect the negative battery cable.
2. Disconnect the wiring from the resistor.

3. Remove the two screws that attach the blower resistor to the blower case and remove it.
4. Installation is the reverse of the removal procedure. Check the blower for proper operation at all speeds.

1990–93 Excel, Elantra and Scoupe

The blower resistor is located on top of the upper blower case.
1. Remove the glove box housing cover.
2. Remove the lower crash pad assembly.
3. Disconnect the wire from the blower resistor.
4. Remove the two retaining screws and withdraw the blower resistor from the blower upper case.
5. Install the blower resistor into the upper case half with the two retaining screws.
6. Connect the blower resistor wire.
7. Install the lower crash pad assembly.
8. Install the glove box housing cover.
9. Check the blower for proper operation at all speeds.

Sonata

▶ **See Figure 38**

The blower resistor is located inside the blower case to the left of the air inlet duct. The resistor is accessible by removing the glove box.
1. Open the glove box, release the glove box retainers and allow the glove box to swing down.
2. Disconnect the electrical connector from the resistor.
3. Remove the two attaching screws and remove the resistor from the heater case.

➡ **During installation, do not apply sealer of any kind to the resistor board mounting surface.**

4. Installation is the reverse of the removal procedure. Check the blower for proper operation at all speeds.

AUTOMATIC SPEED CONTROL SYSTEM

General Description

The cruise control system is used on the Elantra, Sonata and the Scoupe and may be purchased as an option of the Excel. This system is comprised of the following components:
• Vehicle speed sensor—this sensor is used to convert vehicle speed to the signal pulse.
• Electronic control unit (ECU)—this electronic control unit receives signals from the sensor and control switches and then uses all of this data to control the automatic cruise control functions.
• Actuator—the actuator is used to regulate the throttle valve to the set opening by signals from the ECU.
• Cruise main switch—this switch is used for the cruise control power supply.

• Set/Resume switch—this switch controls the cruise control functions by set (coast) and resume (accel.).
• Cruise main indicator switch—this switch illuminates when the cruise main switch in on (built into the cruise switch.
• Piezo alarm—When the set or resume switch is switched on, the alarm sounds to notify the driver that the control unit has received the on signal.
• Cancel switch—which incorporates the brake, inhibitor and clutch switches, sends the cancel signal to the ECU.
• ELC-4 speed automatic transaxle control unit—control the overdrive on and off, based on signals from the ECU and the ASC.
• Diagnostic connector—is used by connecting a voltmeter or multi-tester so as to retrieve the control unit diagnosis codes.

Control Unit Functions

♦ See Figures 39 and 40

EXPLANATION

Set (Fixed Speed Control)

With the main switch turned to the **ON** position, the set switch is switched from **ON** to **OFF** position while the vehicle is being driven within the speed range in which the speed settings are possible (approximately 25–90 mph). The vehicle speed at the moment the set switch was switched from **ON** to **OFF** is memorized as the set vehicle speed and there after the actuator is controlled so that fixed speed driving at that speed is possible.

Initial Pulse

The initial pulse opens the throttle valve to a degree of opening which approximately corresponds to the vehicle speed. This pulse is output when the cruise control system is set.

Trim Pulse

The trim pulse is a control pulse for correcting the vehicle speed which is output response to detect speed errors. The output pulse width is determined based on the amount of deviation between the current vehicle speed and the set vehicle speed and on throttle position.

Coast

During fixed speed driving, while the coast switch is **ON**, the actuator D.C. motor is caused to rotate to the rel (release) side. The vehicles speed when the switch is **OFF** as deceleration continues is entered in the memory, and thereafter controlled as a fixed speed.

Resume Speed

When (after the cruise control system is canceled by the cancel conditions) the resume switch is switched from **OFF** to **ON** , while driving at a vehicle speed which is the low speed limit (approximately 25 mph) or higher, the vehicle speed memorized before cancellation of the cruise control system will be controlled as the fixed speed.

Acceleration

During fixed speed driving or above the low speed limit, while the acceleration switch is **ON** , the actuator's D.C. motor is caused to rotate to the pull side. The vehicle speed when the switch is **OFF** as acceleration continues is entered in the memory and is thereafter controlled as the fixed speed.

Cancellation

When the signals below are input (during fixed speed driving), conductivity to the electromagentic clutch is interrupted, thus canceling the cruise control system:
1. Brake lamp switch **ON** (brake pedal depressed).
2. Inhibitor switch **ON** (selector lever at the **P** or **N** position).
3. Clutch switch **ON** (clutch pedal depressed).

➡When the brake pedal is depressed and the brake lamp switch is switched ON, the cruise control system will be canceled even if there is wiring damage or disconnection at the fuse for the brake lamp.

Low Speed Limit

There is automatic cancellation at or below the low speed limit (approximately 25 mph).

High Speed Limit

The vehicle cannot be driven at a fixed speed which is at or higher than the high speed limit (approximately 90 mph). Note that the vehicle speed memorized when the set switch is pressed while the vehicle is traveling at the high speed limit or higher will be the high speed limit vehicle speed.

Automatic Cancellation

When, during fixed speed driving, the signals described below are input, conductivity to the electromagnetic clutch is interrupted, thus canceling the cruise control system.
1. If the vehicle speed decreases to a speed which is approximately 12 mph or more below the memorized vehicle speed.
2. If there is no input of the vehicle speed signal for more than 0.5 second.
3. If there is damaged or disconnecting wiring of the input line (brake lamp switch load side) of the brake lamp switch.
4. If the cancel switches (brake lamp switch, inhibitor switch, and clutch switch) and command switches (set switch or resume switch) are switched on at the same time.

➡If the set and resume switches are ON at the same time, the cruise control will operate in the coast mode and the speed will decreases.

Piezo Alarm

When the cruise switch is **ON**, the set switch or resume switch **ON** signals are received, the alarm is activated for approximately 0.2 seconds. Be sure to note the power is supplied from fuse 13 (10 amp) on Excel and fuse 8 (10 amp) on Sonata, to the alarm.

Accelerator Switch

The accelerator switch is a switch that functions to detect the condition of the accelerator pedal and is one of the ELC 4 automatic transaxle sensors. Because the accelerator pedal is not used during fixed speed driving, the accelerator switch is **OFF** during this time only, so as not to adversely affect the functions of the ELC 4 automatic transaxle.

Overdrive Cancel Function

When, during fixed speed driving, the actual vehicle speed decreases to (or below) a speed which is below memorized vehicle speed and the actual vehicle speed continues at that reduced speed or during the resume operation or the acceleration operations that have already been described, it becomes necessary to return to the vehicle speed for a short period of time and to accelerate, the overdrive function of the ELC 4 automatic transaxle equipped vehicles is canceled for a certain time.

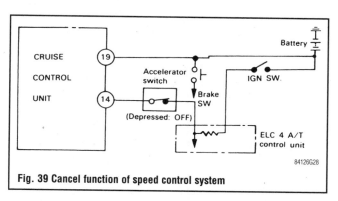

Fig. 39 Cancel function of speed control system

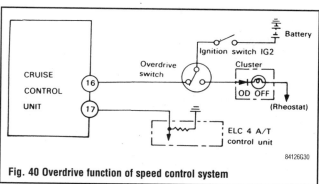

Fig. 40 Overdrive function of speed control system

Self Diagnosis Function

The cruise control system can display trouble codes from the cruise control unit through the diagnostic connector. The codes can be read by using a voltmeter or a multi-use tester. Be sure to turn the main switch **ON** before trying to read the codes.

➡ **The display of the trouble codes starts if the vehicle speed decreases to less than approximately 12 mph after the cancellation of the cruise control system function and stops if the vehicle speed increases to approximately 12 mph or higher.**

Input Switch Check

The unit has a check function for the input signal switch. The display starts when the main switch is turned **ON** while the set and resume switches are turned to the **ON** position.

1. Trouble codes are stored in memory and display in sequential order of priority.
2. Smaller code numbers shall be placed higher in priority.
3. Even when a input of higher priority is detected among check function items, an item currently in stored in memory shall be shown on display for one cycle (one cycle shall be an interval during which all checked functions stored in memory are shown on display).
4. Code number 24 and 25 should be checked while the vehicle is running.

Diagnosis and Testing

SERVICE PRECAUTIONS

- Never disconnect any electrical connection with the ignition switch **ON** unless instructed to do so in a test.
- Always wear a grounded wrist static strap when servicing any control module or component labeled with a Electrostatic Discharge (ESD) sensitive device symbol.
- Avoid touching module connector pins.
- Leave new components and modules in the shipping package until ready to install them.
- Always touch a vehicle ground after sliding across a vehicle seat or walking across vinyl or carpeted floors to avoid static charge damage.
- Never allow welding cables to lie on, near or across any vehicle electrical wiring.
- Do not allow extension cords for power tools or drop lights to lie on, near or across any vehicle electrical wiring.
- Do not operate the cruise control or the engine with the drive wheels off the ground unless specifically instructed to do so by a test procedure.

BEFORE TROUBLESHOOTING

The cruise control system performs control functions for the setting or cancellation of the fixed speed driving speed based upon the data provided by input signals. As a result, when the cruise control system is canceled, the cause of cancellation is memorized in a separate circuit by the ECU, regardless of whether or not the cruise control system condition is normal or abnormal, thus providing the ECU with the self diagnosis function by certain fixed patterns as well as the function of being able to check whether or not the ECU's input switches or sensor are normal. Thus, by effectively using these functions, the time required checking and repairing the system can be shortened.

➡ **When the ECU power supply (ignition switch and main switch) is switched OFF, the memorized trouble codes are erased, and so for this reason the power supply must be left ON until the checking is completed.**

SELF-DIAGNOSIS CHECKING

♦ **See Figures 41 and 42**

The self-diagnosis checking is performed when there has been an automatic cancellation, without cancel switch operation. The following 2 methods can be used for checking diagnosis. Note that the diagnosis check connector is located in the fuse box.

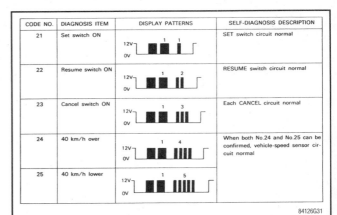

CODE NO.	DIAGNOSIS ITEM	DISPLAY PATTERNS	SELF-DIAGNOSIS DESCRIPTION
11	Clutch coil		1. Open transistor 2. Open brake circuit, blown fuse 3. Stop lamp switch closed. 4. Stop lamp circuit open.
12	Speed sensor		No vehicle speed signal input for more than 1 seconds
13	Low speed limit		Vehicle speed less than 40 km/h.
14	Redundant brake		Vehicle speed less than memory speed by 20 km/h.
15	Control switch		SET and RESUME switches on simultaneously.
16	Cancal signal		1. Open fuse or circuit in stop lamp switch. 2. Auto transaxle inhibit switch ON (closed). 3. Open circuit in stop lamp circuit. 4. Stop lamp switch ON.

84126G29

Fig. 41 Self-diagnostic codes—speed control system

CODE NO.	DIAGNOSIS ITEM	DISPLAY PATTERNS	SELF-DIAGNOSIS DESCRIPTION
21	Set switch ON		SET switch circuit normal
22	Resume switch ON		RESUME switch circuit normal
23	Cancel switch ON		Each CANCEL circuit normal
24	40 km/h over		When both No.24 and No.25 can be confirmed, vehicle-speed sensor circuit normal
25	40 km/h lower		

84126G31

Fig. 42 Self-diagnostic codes—speed control system (continued)

Multi-Use Tester Tool Method

♦ **See Figures 43 and 44**

1. Connect the multi-use tester's (09391–33000 or equivalent) socket and connector to the cigarette lighter socket and the self-diagnosis check connector and set the tester.
2. Use the tester according to its operation instructions; display the diagnosis code number and then check.

Voltmeter Method

Connect a voltmeter between the ground terminal and the terminal of for the cruise control of the diagnosis connector. It is possible to discover which circuit is the cause of the cancellation by verifying the indication shown on the voltmeter with the display patterns.

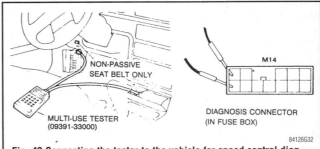

84126G32

Fig. 43 Connecting the tester to the vehicle for speed control diagnosis

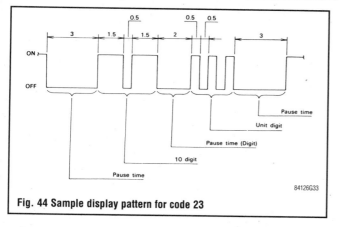

Fig. 44 Sample display pattern for code 23

When trouble codes number 11, 12, 15 or 16 are displayed, check the troubleshooting symptom applicable to that number.

➡Code number 16 is entered in the memory as cancel switch ON signal input if the system is canceled by depressing the brake pedal, and code number 13 or 14 is entered when there is an automatic cancellation because the vehicle speed drops when the vehicle is driven up a steep slope with the preset speed setting left set etc., when however, there is a cancellation not intentionally made by the driver, the cause might be a damaged or disconnected stop lamp switch input wiring, a malfunction of the stop lamp switch ON, etc., even though the same code number 16 is displayed.

Troubleshooting Procedures

First, select the applicable malfunction symptom from the trouble symptom charts. Conduct the self-diagnostic test following the directions on the charts. Determine the condition of all function circuits by making the following preliminary inspections:

➡Because the computer (self-diagnosis) memory data will be erased, when the system is unintentionally canceled during fixed speed driving, the ignition switch and/or the cruise main switch of the cruise control system should not switched OFF, and the battery should not be disconnected.

1. Check that the installation of actuator, accelerator cables are correct, and that the cables and links are securely connected.
2. Check that the accelerator pedal moves smoothly.
3. Adjust the cable so there is no excessive tension or excessive play on the accelerator cable.
4. Check that the ECU, actuator, cruise main and control switch and the connector of each cancel switch are connected securely.
5. Check in the sequence indicated in the trouble symptom chart.
6. If these checks indicate a normal condition, replace the cruise control unit.

➡Codes indicated by the * symbol are displayed, if the conditions are satisfied, even if the system is normal. In either case, the system is normal if can be reset. If there is an automatic cancellation not intentionally made by the driver, however, excluding cancellations explicitly made by a cancel procedure, there may be a temporary malfunction such as a poor contact of a harness connector even though the system can be reset, and for that reason it is necessary to check according to each individual check the chart that is applicable.

SPEED CONTROL TROUBLE DIAGNOSIS

Trouble Symptom 1

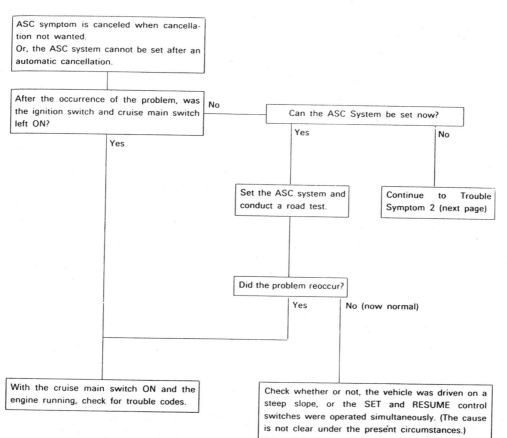

SPEED CONTROL TROUBLE DIAGNOSIS (CONTINUED)

Trouble Symptom 3

Trouble symptom	Probable cause	Remedy
o The set vehicle speed varies greatly upward or downward o "Surging" (repeated alternating acceleration and deceleration) occurs after setting	Malfunction of the vehicle speed sensor circuit	Repair the vehicle speed sensor system, or replace the part
	Malfunction of the speedometer cable or speedometer drive gear	
	Actuator circuit poor contact	Repair the actuator system, or replace the part
	Malfunction of the actuator	
	Malfunction of the ECU	Replace the ECU

Trouble Symptom 4

Trouble symptom	Probable cause	Remedy
The ASC system is not canceled when the brake pedal is depressed	Damaged or disconnected wiring of the stop lamp switch	Repair the harness or replace the stop lamp switch
	Actuator drive circuit short	Repair the harness or replace the actuator
	Malfunction of the ECU	Replace the ECU

Trouble Symptom 5

Trouble symptom	Probable cause	Remedy
The ASC system is not canceled when the shift lever is moved to the "N" position (It is canceled, however, when the brake pedal is depressed)	Damaged or disconnected wiring of inhibitor switch input circuit	Repair the harness or repair or replace the inhibitor switch
	Improper adjustment of inhibitor switch	
	Malfunction of the ECU	Replace the ECU

84126C03

SPEED CONTROL TROUBLE DIAGNOSIS (CONTINUED)

Trouble Symptom 2

[ASC system cannot be set]

↓

Check the ECU power supply circuit and SET or RESUME switch. Are they normal?

No → o Damaged or disconnected wiring of the ECU power-supply circuit
o Damaged or disconnected wiring of the SET or RESUME switch

Yes ↓

Check the input check items

Input check items

Check results	Probable cause	Remedy
Code 21 remains even though SET switch is set to OFF.	SET switch ON malfunction	Replace the control switch
	SET switch input line short-circuit	Repair the harness.
Code 22 remains even though RESUME switch is set to OFF.	RESUME switch ON malfunction	Replace the control switch.
	RESUME switch input line short-circuit	Repair the harness.
Code 23 remains even though CANCEL switch is set to OFF.	Malfunction of the CANCEL circuit (ON circuit malfunction)	Check or repair each CANCEL circuit.
Code 25 does not disappear, and code 24 does not appear, even though vehicle speed reaches approximately 40 km/h (25 mph) or higher.	Malfunction to the vehicle-speed sensor circuit (damaged or disconnected wiring, or short-circuit)	Check or repair the vehicle speed sensor circuit.

Normal ↓

Check the actuator circuit

NOTE
If the check results of the actuator circuit of the actuator itself reveal a normal condition, replace the electronic control unit (ECU)

84126C02

SPEED CONTROL TROUBLE DIAGNOSIS (CONTINUED)

Trouble Symptom 6

Trouble symptom		
Cannot decelerate (coast) by using the SET switch		

Probable cause	Remedy
Temporary damaged or disconnected wiring of SET switch input circuit	Repair the harness or replace the SET switch
Actuator circuit poor contact	Repair the harness or replace the actuator
Malfunction of the actuator	
Malfunction of the ECU	Replace the ECU

Trouble Symptom 7

Trouble symptom		
Cannot accelerate or resume speed by using the RESUME switch		

Probable cause	Remedy
Damaged or disconnected wiring, or short circuit, or RESUME switch input circuit	Repair the harness or replace the RESUME switch
Actuator circuit poor contact	Repair the harness or replace the actuator
Malfunction of the actuator	
Malfunction of the ECU	Replace the ECU

Trouble Symptom 8

Trouble symptom		
ASC system can be set while driving at a vehicle speed of less than 40 km/h (25 mph), or there is no automatic cancellation at that speed		

Probable cause	Remedy
Malfunction of the vehicle-speed sensor circuit	Repair the vehicle speed sensor system, or replace the part
Malfunction of the speedometer cable or the speedometer drive gear	
Malfunction of the ECU	Replace the ECU.

Trouble Symptom 9

Trouble symptom		
The cruise main switch indicator lamp does not illuminate (But ASC system is normal.)		

Probable cause	Remedy
Damaged or disconnected bulb of cruise main switch indicator lamp	Repair the harness or replace the part.
Harness damaged or disconnected	

84126C04

SPEED CONTROL TROUBLE DIAGNOSIS (CONTINUED)

Trouble Symptom 10

Trouble symptom		
No alarm sound when SET switch or RESUME switch is used. (But ASC system is normal.)		

Probable cause	Remedy
Malfunction of the alarm circuit	Repair the harness or replace the part
Malfunction of the ECU	

Trouble Symptom 11

Trouble symptom		
Malfunction of control function by ON/OFF switching of ELC 4 A/T accelerator switch		

Probable cause	Remedy
Malfunction of circuit related to accelerator switch OFF function	Repair the harness or replace the part
Malfunction of the ECU	

Trouble Symptom 12

Trouble symptom		
Overdrive is not canceled during fixed speed driving.		
No shift to overdrive during manual driving.		

Probable cause	Remedy
Malfunction of circuit related to overdrive cancelation, or malfunction of ECU	Repair the harness or replace the part

84126C05

Diagnosis codes are display when, after cancellation of the cruise control system, the vehicle speed decreases to less than approximately 12 mph, and are erased by switching OFF the ignition switch or the MAIN switch. After the diagnosis codes in memory are erased, if (when power supply of the electronic control unit is switched ON once again) the power supply of the electronic control unit is normal, the diagnosis output code display will be as follows; regardless of whether the system condition is normal or not.

If a multi-use tester is used, **NORMAL** will be displayed. If a voltmeter is used, continuous **ON/OFF** signals will be displayed at 0.5 second intervals.

Component Testing

BRAKE LIGHT SWITCH

▶ See Figures 45 and 46

Inspection

1. Using an ohmmeter, check for continuity between the terminals.
2. While depressing the brake pedal, there should be continuity between terminals **C** and **D** of the brake light switch connector.
3. While not depressing the brake pedal, there should be continuity between terminals **A** and **B** of the brake light switch connector.
4. If the brake light switch fails any portion of this test, replace it with a new one.

INHIBITOR SWITCH

▶ See Figures 47 and 48

Inspection

1. Disconnect the inhibitor switch connector.
2. Using a suitable ohmmeter, check that there is continuity between connector (E12) terminals 3 and 5, 3 and 4 when the shift lever is moved from the **N** range and the **P** range.
3. If the inhibitor switch fails any portion of this test, replace it with a new one.

ACTUATOR

Inspection

▶ See Figure 49

1. Disconnect the actuator connector.
2. Using a suitable ohmmeter, check the resistance value of the clutch coil.
3. The resistance of the clutch coil between connector terminals 3 and 4 should be approximately 55 ohms.
4. If the actuator fails any portion of this test, replace it with a new one.

CLUTCH SWITCH

Inspection

1. Using a suitable ohmmeter, check for continuity between the terminals.
2. While depressing the clutch pedal, there should be continuity between terminals of the clutch switch connector.
3. While not depressing the clutch pedal, there should be no continuity between the terminals of the clutch switch connector.
4. If the clutch switch fails any portion of this test, replace it with a new one.

Component Replacement

ACTUATOR CABLE

Installation and Adjustment

▶ See Figure 50

1. Accelerator pedal side—With the rear locknut (A) at the end of the cable, assemble the accelerator cable to the intermediate pulley.
2. Pull the cable tight in the bracket with the pulley against the stop. Tighten the front locknut (B) against the bracket. Back off the front locknut (B) 1 turn.

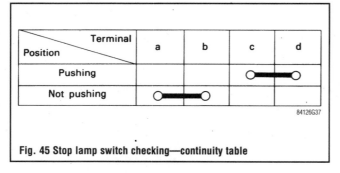

Position / Terminal	a	b	c	d
Pushing			⊙━━⊙	
Not pushing	⊙━━⊙			

84126G37

Fig. 45 Stop lamp switch checking—continuity table

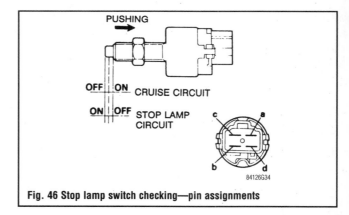

84126G34

Fig. 46 Stop lamp switch checking—pin assignments

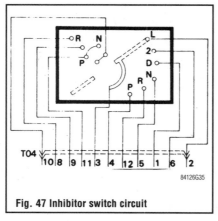

84126G35

Fig. 47 Inhibitor switch circuit

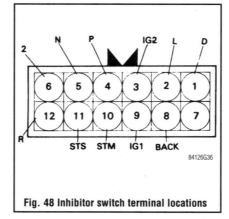

84126G36

Fig. 48 Inhibitor switch terminal locations

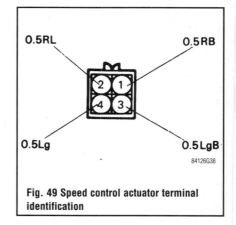

84126G38

Fig. 49 Speed control actuator terminal identification

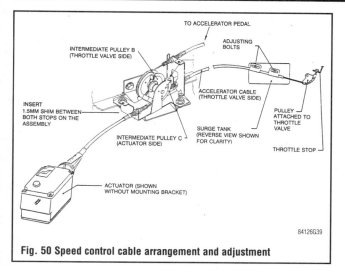

Fig. 50 Speed control cable arrangement and adjustment

3. Tighten the rear locknut (A).
4. The cable should have approximately 1mm of slack with the pulley against the stop.
5. Throttle valve side—assemble the accelerator cable to the intermediate pulley.

6. The locking nuts should be adjusted and tighten securely at approximately the mid point of the threaded area of the accelerator cable.
7. With the rear locking nut (A) at the end of the cable, assemble the actuator cable to the intermediate pulley.
8. Pull the cable tight in the bracket with the pulley against the stop. Tighten the front locknut (B) against the bracket. Back off the front locknut (B) 1 turn.
9. Tighten the rear locknut (A).
10. The cable should have approximately 1.5mm of slack with the pulley against the stop.

➡**Prior to proceeding with the final cable adjustment, make sure that the pulley attached to the throttle valve is in the NORMAL idle position.**

11. To make the final adjustment, use the following procedure:
   a. Assemble the accelerator cable to the throttle valve pulley (if not assembled).
   b. Attach the cable casing to the surge tank using the appropriate supplied adjusting bolts. Do not tighten the bolts at this time.
   c. Insert a shim or similar tool, 1.5mm thick, between the 2 pulley stops.
   d. Adjust the cable casing at the rear side of the surge tank to allow all the slack to be removed from the inner cable. Make sure the throttle valve pulley remains in the **NORMAL** idle position.
   e. Tighten the adjustment bolts. Remove the shim from between the 2 intermediate pulleys.

ENTERTAINMENT SYSTEM

Radio Head Unit

REMOVAL & INSTALLATION

▶ **See Figure 51**

1986–89 Excel

The radio head unit is retained by spring clips that use special hooked tools to release them. The removal tools are U-shaped, with a small 90 degree bend on each end. These tools can easily be fabricated by bending a heavy gauge paper clip into a U-shape and bending each end approximately 1/8 inch at a 90 degree angle. The tools are then inserted (2 required, one for each side) into the small holes at the side of the radio face plate and the radio can then be pulled out.
1. Disconnect the negative battery cable.
2. Remove the radio head unit surround trim by prying it off.
3. Insert the special removal tools into each side of the radio and pull the radio forward.
4. Disconnect the electrical leads from the radio. Disconnect the antenna wire.
5. To install the radio, plug in the connectors and antenna, and slide the radio into place until it latches.
6. Connect the negative battery cable and check the operation of the radio.

1990–93 Excel

▶ **See Figure 52**

1. Disconnect the negative battery cable.
2. Remove the ashtray and the 2 screws from the center panel.
3. Remove the four center lower crash pad fascia panel screws. Gently pull the fascia panel away from it's mounting.
4. Remove the screws that attach the radio to the radio mounting bracket. Disconnect the radio wiring and slide the radio from the mounting bracket. Make sure that all the wiring connections are clearly labeled to avoid confusion during installation.
5. Installation is the reverse of the removal procedure.

Elantra and Scoupe

▶ **See Figures 53, 54, 55 and 56**

1. Disconnect the negative battery cable.
2. Remove the ashtray and the screws from the center panel.
3. Tip the panel forward and disconnect the electrical connectors from the panel.
4. Remove the screws that attach the radio to the radio mounting bracket. Disconnect the radio wiring and slide the radio from the mounting bracket.

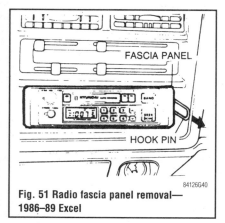

Fig. 51 Radio fascia panel removal—1986–89 Excel

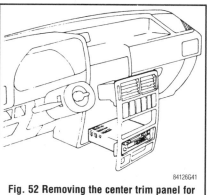

Fig. 52 Removing the center trim panel for radio removal—1990–93 Excel

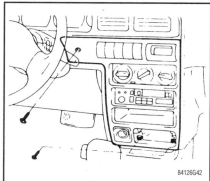

Fig. 53 Removing the center trim panel for radio removal—Elantra

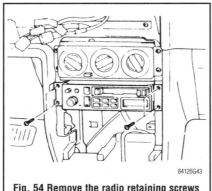

Fig. 54 Remove the radio retaining screws then the radio—Elantra

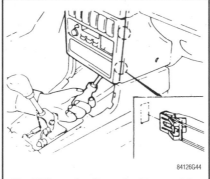

Fig. 55 Removing the center trim panel for radio removal—Scoupe

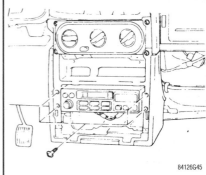

Fig. 56 Remove the radio retaining screws and then the radio—Scoupe

Make sure that all the wiring connections are clearly labeled to avoid confusion during installation.

  5. Installation is the reverse of the removal procedure.

Sonata

▶ **See Figures 57 and 58**

  1. Disconnect the negative battery cable.
  2. The fascia is retained by two screws. Once these screws are removed, the fascia can be lifted straight away from the crash pad.
  3. Remove the lower crash pad.
  4. Disconnect the radio wiring harness. Remove the nuts from behind the knobs, the screws from the bracket and remove the radio from the crash pad.
  5. Installation is the reverse of the removal procedure.

Compact Disc Player

REMOVAL & INSTALLATION

For vehicles equipped with a compact disc player, it is removed the same as the radio head unit. The CD player is mounted below the radio.

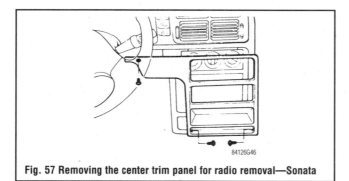

Fig. 57 Removing the center trim panel for radio removal—Sonata

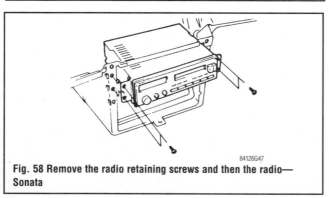

Fig. 58 Remove the radio retaining screws and then the radio—Sonata

Radio Speakers

REMOVAL & INSTALLATION

▶ **See Figures 59 thru 64**

While the location of the stereo speakers varies from vehicle to vehicle, the removal of those speakers is the same. The speaker can be removed by simply removing its grille cover (in most cases they just snap in position) and then removing the speaker mounting screws. The speaker can then be pulled from its opening and the wires disconnected.

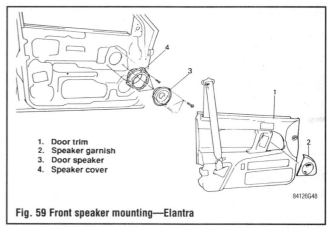

  1. Door trim
  2. Speaker garnish
  3. Door speaker
  4. Speaker cover

Fig. 59 Front speaker mounting—Elantra

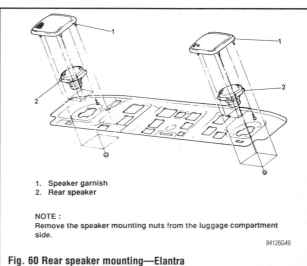

  1. Speaker garnish
  2. Rear speaker

NOTE :
Remove the speaker mounting nuts from the luggage compartment side.

Fig. 60 Rear speaker mounting—Elantra

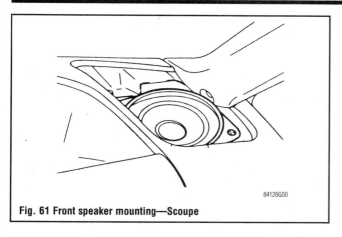

Fig. 61 Front speaker mounting—Scoupe

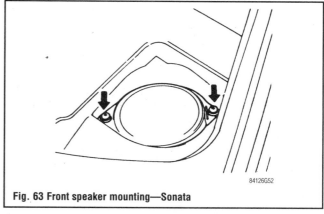

Fig. 63 Front speaker mounting—Sonata

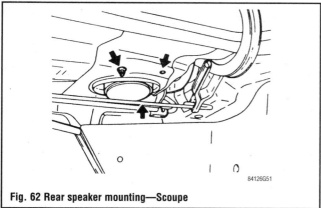

Fig. 62 Rear speaker mounting—Scoupe

Fig. 64 Rear speaker mounting—Sonata

WINDSHIELD WIPERS

Windshield Wiper Arms

REMOVAL & INSTALLATION

Front

♦ **See Figures 65, 66, 67 and 68**

1. Remove the wiper arm nut head cap and pivot it up on the wiper shaft. Remove the wiper arm nut. When removing the wiper arm nut, be careful not to scratch the hood.
2. Remove the wiper arm and blade assembly from the pivot housing.
To install:
3. Connect the wiper arm and blade assembly to the wiper pivot housing.

4. Position the wiper arm blade approximately 30mm from the edge of the windshield glass moulding on the passengers side and 50mm on the drivers side.
5. Once the blade is in position, install and tighten the wiper blade nut. Torque the nut to 7–11 ft. lbs. (10–16 Nm) on Excel and 12–15 ft. lbs. (17–21 Nm) on Elantra, Scoupe and Sonata.
6. Slide the wiper arm nut cap along the wiper shaft and press it firmly onto the nut.

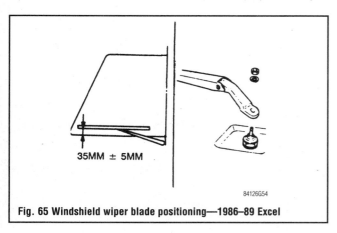

Fig. 65 Windshield wiper blade positioning—1986–89 Excel

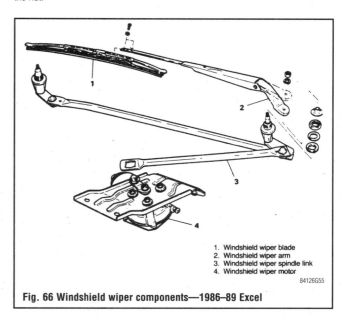

1. Windshield wiper blade
2. Windshield wiper arm
3. Windshield wiper spindle link
4. Windshield wiper motor

Fig. 66 Windshield wiper components—1986–89 Excel

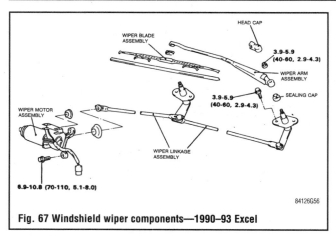

Fig. 67 Windshield wiper components—1990–93 Excel

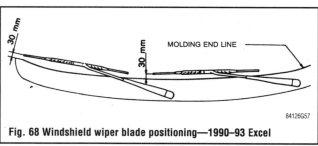

Fig. 68 Windshield wiper blade positioning—1990–93 Excel

Rear

EXCEL

♦ See Figures 69 and 70

1. Remove the wiper arm nut head cap and pivot it up on the wiper shaft. Remove the wiper arm nut. When removing the wiper arm nut, be careful not to scratch the hood.
2. Remove the wiper arm and blade assembly from the pivot housing.
To install:
3. Connect the wiper arm and blade assembly to the wiper pivot housing.
4. Position the wiper arm blade approximately 40mm from the edge of the windshield glass moulding.
5. Once the blade is in position, install and tighten the wiper blade nut. Torque the nut to 3–4 ft. lbs. (4–6 Nm).

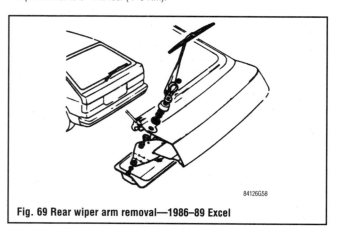

Fig. 69 Rear wiper arm removal—1986–89 Excel

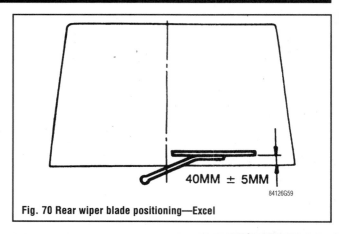

Fig. 70 Rear wiper blade positioning—Excel

Windshield Wiper Motor

REMOVAL & INSTALLATION

Front

♦ See Figures 71 and 72

1. Disconnect the negative battery cable. Remove the wiper arm and blade assemblies. Remove the air inlet and cowl front center trim panels. Remove the 3 pivot shaft mounting nuts and push the pivot shafts into the area under the cowl.
2. Remove the motor mounting bolts. Pull the motor into the best possible position for access and remove the linkage off the motor crank arm. Remove the motor and then the linkage as required.
3. If the motor is being replaced, matchmark the position of the crank arm of the motor shaft of the new motor and then remove the nut and crank arm, transferring both to the new motor.

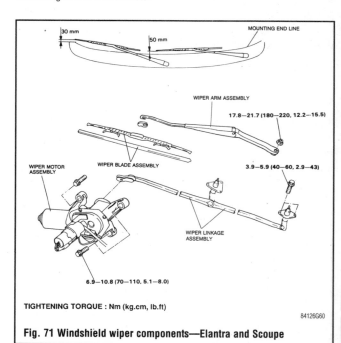

Fig. 71 Windshield wiper components—Elantra and Scoupe

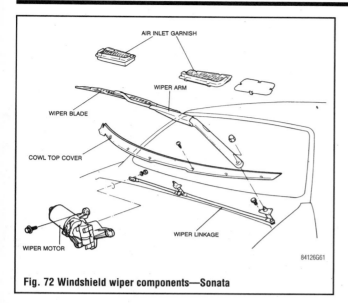

Fig. 72 Windshield wiper components—Sonata

To install:

4. Torque the pivot shaft nuts to 4.3–5.8 ft. lbs. (5–8 Nm).

5. Position the wiper arms so, on the Excel and Elantra, the blades are about 15mm above the lower windshield molding, on the driver's side and 20mm above it, on the passenger's side.

6. On the Sonata, each blade tip should be about 30mm above the molding. On Scoupe, the driver's side blade tip should be about 50mm above the lower

windshield molding and the passenger side blade tip should be about 30mm above the lower windshield molding. Torque the nut to 7–11 ft. lbs. (10–16 Nm) on Excel and 12–15 ft. lbs. (17–21 Nm) on Elantra, Scoupe and Sonata.

7. Make sure the wiper motor is securely grounded. Connect the negative battery cable.

Rear

♦ **See Figures 73, 74, 75 and 76**

1. Remove the wiper blade and arm by lifting the wiper blade locknut cover and removing the locknut. Then, pull the arm from the shaft.

2. Remove the lift gate trim panel and disconnect the wiring harness connector.

3. Matchmark the relationship of the crank arm to the motor and remove the crank arm.

4. Remove the inside and outside motor mounting nuts and remove the motor.

5. Installation is the reverse of the removal procedures.

➡ **When installing the wiper arm, the distance between the tip of the blade and the lower window molding should be 40mm.**

Washer Fluid Reservoir and Washer Pumps

REMOVAL & INSTALLATION

♦ **See Figures 77, 78 and 79**

The washer fluid reservoir can be removed through the engine compartment. The reservoir for all models includes the front and rear washer motors.

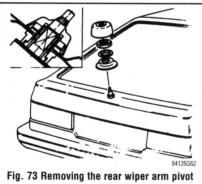

Fig. 73 Removing the rear wiper arm pivot shaft cap—Excel

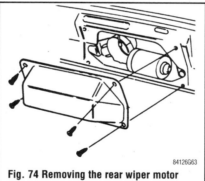
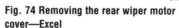

Fig. 74 Removing the rear wiper motor cover—Excel

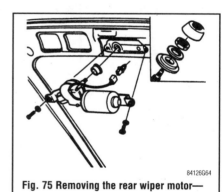

Fig. 75 Removing the rear wiper motor— Excel

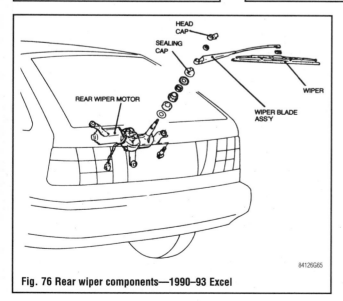

Fig. 76 Rear wiper components—1990–93 Excel

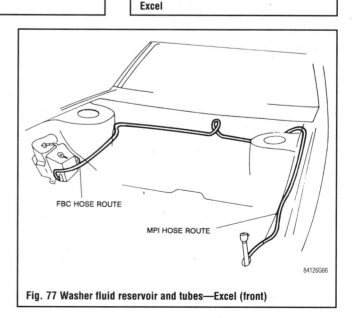

Fig. 77 Washer fluid reservoir and tubes—Excel (front)

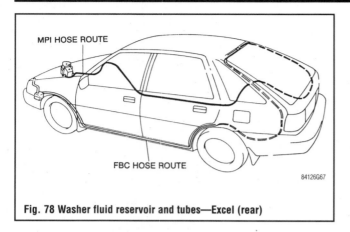

Fig. 78 Washer fluid reservoir and tubes—Excel (rear)

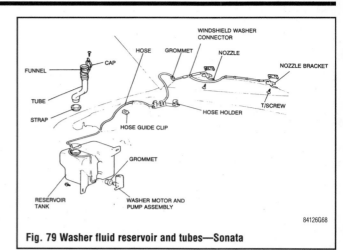

Fig. 79 Washer fluid reservoir and tubes—Sonata

1. Disconnect the negative battery cable.
2. On Excel with carbureted engine, the washer tank is on the passengers side.
3. Disconnect the electrical leads from the washer pump motors.
4. Disconnect 1 of the hoses and drain the washer fluid into a suitable container, for reuse.
5. Disconnect the other hose from the tank. Remove the tank retaining bolts.
6. Remove the tank from above, through the engine compartment.
7. The washer pumps can now be removed if needed.

To install:

8. Install the pumps in the tank, if removed.
9. Install the tank into the vehicle and install the mounting bolts. Tighten the mounting bolts to 7 ft. lbs. (10 Nm).
10. Connect the electrical lead and the hoses.
11. Connect the negative battery cable.
12. Refill the reservoir and test the operation of the system.

INSTRUMENTS AND SWITCHES

Instrument Cluster

REMOVAL & INSTALLATION

Excel

♦ **See Figures 80, 81, 82 and 83**

1. Disconnect the negative battery cable. Remove the meter hood attaching screws, located at the bottom and tilt the lower meter hood outward. Pull the hood downward to release the locking tangs at the top and remove it.

2. Remove the meter assembly mounting screws and pull the unit outward. Disconnect the speedometer cable and all connectors. Remove the unit.
3. Installation is the reverse order of the removal procedures.

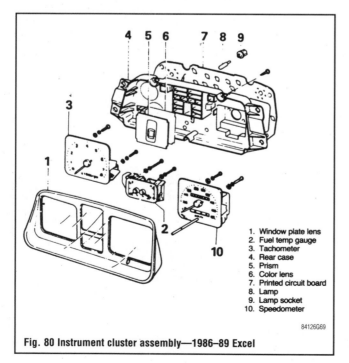

Fig. 80 Instrument cluster assembly—1986–89 Excel

1. Window plate lens
2. Fuel temp gauge
3. Tachometer
4. Rear case
5. Prism
6. Color lens
7. Printed circuit board
8. Lamp
9. Lamp socket
10. Speedometer

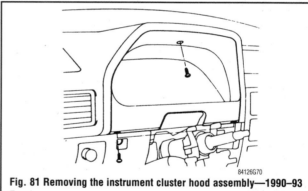

Fig. 81 Removing the instrument cluster hood assembly—1990–93 Excel

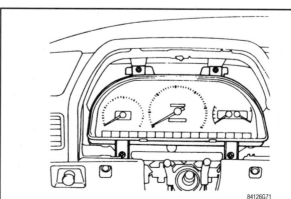

Fig. 82 Remove the 4 retaining screws and then the cluster—1990–93 Excel

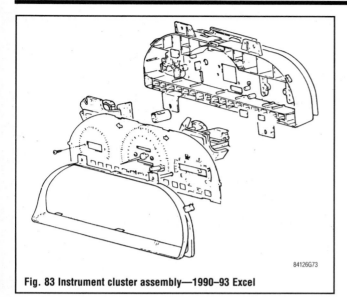

Fig. 83 Instrument cluster assembly—1990–93 Excel

Elantra

▶ See Figures 84 and 85

1. Disconnect the negative battery cable.
2. Remove the coin box, ash tray and lower crash pad center facial panel.
3. Separate the connectors from the clock, hazard switch, air conditioning switch, rear heater switch and the cruise control switch.
4. Remove the 3 screws at the cluster fascia panel. If the speedometer is to be removed, do so now.
5. Remove the 4 screws retaining the cluster and connectors to the instrument panel. Remove the cluster assembly from the vehicle.
6. Installation is the reverse of the removal procedure.

Scoupe

▶ See Figure 86

1. Disconnect the negative battery cable.
2. Remove the ashtray.
3. Remove the lower crash pad center fascia panel.
4. Remove the digital clock and remote mirror switch.
5. Remove the 7 screws at the cluster fascia panel.
6. Remove the 4 screws retaining the cluster and connectors
7. Install the instrument cluster by reversing the removal procedure.

Sonata

▶ See Figure 87

1. Disconnect the negative battery cable. Remove the steering column support bolts and carefully lower the column on the front seat.

2. Remove the cluster trim panel.
3. Remove the cluster mounting screws and slowly pull the cluster outward. Disconnect the wires.
4. Installation is the reverse of removal. Torque the steering column bolts to 20 ft. lbs. (27 Nm).

Speedometer

REMOVAL & INSTALLATION

1. Disconnect the negative battery cable.
2. Remove the instrument cluster from the instrument panel.
3. Place the instrument cluster on clean work area.
4. Remove the speedometer lens retaining screws from the side of the cluster and remove the lens.
5. From the rear side of the cluster, remove the speedometer retaining screws and carefully remove the speedometer from the cluster assembly.
   To install:
6. Install the speedometer into the cluster and install the retaining screws.
7. Position the cluster assembly to the dash, while inserting the speedometer cable into the speedometer, push in securely.
8. Install the instrument cluster face plate and lens to the panel.
9. Connect the negative battery cable.

Speedometer Cable

REMOVAL & INSTALLATION

1. Remove the instrument cluster far enough to disconnect the speedometer cable.
2. Raise and support the front end on jackstands.
3. Disconnect the speedometer cable at the transmission or transaxle.
4. Installation is the reverse of removal. Insert the cable into the speedometer until the stopper engages with the groove. Install the firewall grommet so that the attachment and projecting portions are horizontal. Route the cable in the engine compartment so that the radius of the cable bend does not exceed 150mm (6 in.). Use wire ties to control the bend of the cable as required.

➡**Improper installation or bend radius of the speedometer cable will cause a fluctuation of the pointer needle, noise or a damaged wiring harness inside the instrument panel.**

Windshield Wiper Switch

REMOVAL & INSTALLATION

The windshield wiper switch is part of a multi-function switch. For switch removal details, see "Multi-Function Switch, REMOVAL & INSTALLATION" in Section 8 of this manual.

Fig. 84 Remove the cluster hood retaining screws—Elantra

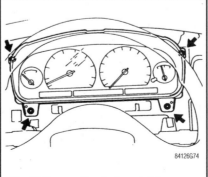

Fig. 85 Remove the cluster retaining screws and then the cluster—Elantra

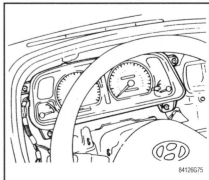

Fig. 86 Remove the cluster retaining screws and then the cluster—Scoupe

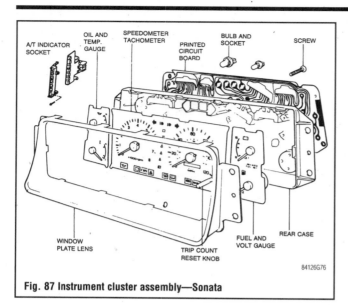

Fig. 87 Instrument cluster assembly—Sonata

Rear Window Wiper Switch

REMOVAL & INSTALLATION

1. Pry the switch bezel from the panel.
2. Reach behind the panel and disconnect the wiring from the switch.
3. Depress the two retainers and pull the switch from the panel.
4. Installation is the reverse of removal.

Headlight Switch

REMOVAL & INSTALLATION

The headlight switch is part of the multifunction switch. For switch removal details, see "Multi-Function Switch, REMOVAL & INSTALLATION" in Section 8 of this manual.

LIGHTING

Headlight, Signal And Marker Lights

REMOVAL & INSTALLATION

▶ **See Figure 88**

Headlights

▶ **See Figure 89**

➡**This procedure only applies to replaceable halogen headlight bulbs (such as Nos. 9004 and 9005); it does not pertain to sealed beam units.**

1. Open the vehicle's hood and secure it in an upright position.
2. Unfasten the locking ring which secures the bulb and socket assembly, then withdraw the assembly rearward.
3. If necessary, gently pry the socket's retaining clip over the projection on the bulb (use care not to break the clip.) Pull the bulb from the socket.
   To install:
4. Before installing a light bulb into the socket, ensure that all electrical contact surfaces are free of corrosion or dirt.

Fig. 89 Carefully pull the halogen headlight bulb from its socket. If applicable, release the retaining clip

5. Line up the replacement headlight bulb with the socket. Firmly push the bulb onto the socket until the spring clip latches over the bulb's projection.

❊❊ WARNING

Do not touch the glass bulb with your fingers. Oil from your fingers can severely shorten the life of the bulb. If necessary, wipe off any dirt or oil from the bulb with rubbing alcohol before completing installation.

6. To ensure that the replacement bulb functions properly, activate the applicable switch to illuminate the bulb which was just replaced. (If this is a combination low and high beam bulb, be sure to check both intensities.) If the replacement light bulb does not illuminate, either it too is faulty or there is a problem in the bulb circuit or switch. Correct if necessary.
7. Position the headlight bulb and secure it with the locking ring.
8. Close the vehicle's hood.

Turn Signal and Brake Lights

▶ **See Figure 90**

1. Depending on the vehicle and bulb application, either unscrew and remove the lens or disengage the bulb and socket assembly from the rear of the lens housing.

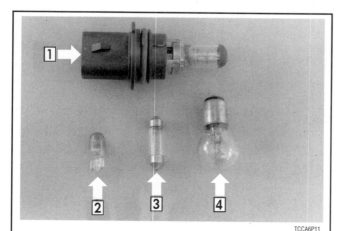

1. Halogen headlight bulb
2. Side marker light bulb
3. Dome light bulb
4. Turn signal/brake light bulb

Fig. 88 Examples of various types of automotive light bulbs

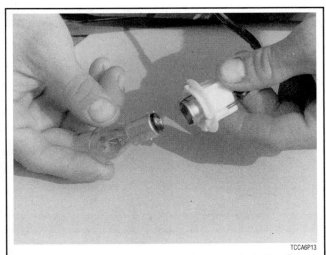

TCCA6P13

Fig. 90 Depress and twist this type of bulb counterclockwise, then pull the bulb straight from its socket

2. To remove a light bulb with retaining pins from its socket, grasp the bulb, then gently depress and twist it 1/8 turn counterclockwise, and pull it from the socket.

To install:

3. Before installing a light bulb into the socket, ensure that all electrical contact surfaces are free of corrosion or dirt.

➡**Before installing the light bulb, note the positions of the two retaining pins on the bulb. They will likely be at different heights on the bulb, to ensure that the bulb is installed correctly. If, when installing the bulb, it does not turn easily, do not force it. Remove the bulb and rotate it 180 degrees from its former position, then reinsert it into the bulb socket.**

4. Insert the light bulb into the socket and, while depressing the bulb, twist it 1/8 turn clockwise until the two pins on the light bulb are properly engaged in the socket.

5. To ensure that the replacement bulb functions properly, activate the applicable switch to illuminate the bulb which was just replaced. If the replacement light bulb does not illuminate, either it too is faulty or there is a problem in the bulb circuit or switch. Correct if necessary.

6. If applicable, install the socket and bulb assembly into the rear of the lens housing; otherwise, install the lens over the bulb.

Side Marker Light

▶ See Figure 91

1. Disengage the bulb and socket assembly from the lens housing.
2. Gently grasp the light bulb and pull it straight out of the socket.

To install:

3. Before installing the light bulb into the socket, ensure that all electrical contact surfaces are free of corrosion or dirt.

4. Line up the base of the light bulb with the socket, then insert the light bulb into the socket until it is fully seated.

5. To ensure that the replacement bulb functions properly, activate the applicable switch to illuminate the bulb which was just replaced. If the replacement light bulb does not illuminate, either it too is faulty or there is a problem in the bulb circuit or switch. Correct as necessary.

6. Install the socket and bulb assembly into the lens housing.

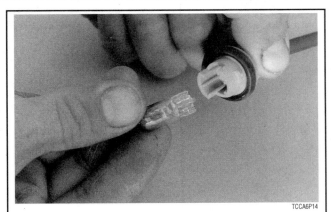

TCCA6P14

Fig. 91 Simply pull this side marker light bulb straight from its socket

Dome Light

▶ See Figure 92

1. Using a small prytool, carefully remove the cover lens from the lamp assembly.

2. Remove the bulb from its retaining clip contacts. If the bulb has tapered ends, gently depress the spring clip/metal contact and disengage the light bulb, then pull it free of the two metal contacts.

To install:

3. Before installing the light bulb into the metal contacts, ensure that all electrical conducting surfaces are free of corrosion or dirt.

4. Position the bulb between the two metal contacts. If the contacts have small holes, be sure that the tapered ends of the bulb are situated in them.

5. To ensure that the replacement bulb functions properly, activate the applicable switch to illuminate the bulb which was just replaced. If the replacement light bulb does not illuminate, either it is faulty or there is a problem in the bulb circuit or switch. Correct as necessary.

6. Install the cover lens until its retaining tabs are properly engaged.

TCCA6P15

Fig. 92 Disengage the spring clip which retains one tapered end of this dome light bulb, then withdraw the bulb

TRAILER WIRING

Wiring the vehicle for towing is fairly easy. There are a number of good wiring kits available and these should be used, rather than trying to design your own.

All trailers will need brake lights and turn signals as well as tail lights and side marker lights. Most areas require extra marker lights for overwide trailers. Also, most areas have recently required back-up lights for trailers, and most trailer manufacturers have been building trailers with back-up lights for several years.

Additionally, some Class I, most Class II and just about all Class III and IV trailers will have electric brakes. Add to this number an accessories wire, to operate trailer internal equipment or to charge the trailer's battery, and you can have as many as seven wires in the harness.

Determine the equipment on your trailer and buy the wiring kit necessary. The kit will contain all the wires needed, plus a plug adapter set which includes the female plug, mounted on the bumper or hitch, and the male plug, wired into, or plugged into the trailer harness.

When installing the kit, follow the manufacturer's instructions. The color coding of the wires is usually standard throughout the industry. One point to note: some domestic vehicles, and most imported vehicles, have separate turn signals. On most domestic vehicles, the brake lights and rear turn signals operate with the same bulb. For those vehicles without separate turn signals, you can purchase an isolation unit so that the brake lights won't blink whenever the turn signals are operated.

One, final point, the best kits are those with a spring loaded cover on the vehicle mounted socket. This cover prevents dirt and moisture from corroding the terminals. Never let the vehicle socket hang loosely; always mount it securely to the bumper or hitch.

CIRCUIT PROTECTION

➡**For complete locations of all important vehicle electrical components, computers, relays, fusible links and switches, refer to "Component Locations" at the beginning of this section.**

Fuses

The fuse panel is located behind a snap-off cover in front of the driver's left knee.

Fusible Links

Fusible links are sections of wire, with special insulation, designed to melt under electrical overload. Replacements are simply effected by removing the old unit and inserting the new into the block. Fusible links are identified by the color of their housing.

Turn Signal and Hazard Flashers

The flashers are located under the left side of the instrument panel. If the turn signals operate in only one direction, a bulb is probably burned out. If they operate in neither direction, a bulb on each side may be burned out, or the flasher may be defective.

REMOVAL & INSTALLATION

1. Pull the flasher from its spring clip mounting.
2. Unplug and discard the flasher. Plug in the new flasher.
3. Replace the flasher in the spring clip and check operation.

WIRING DIAGRAMS

INDEX OF WIRING DIAGRAMS

84126W01

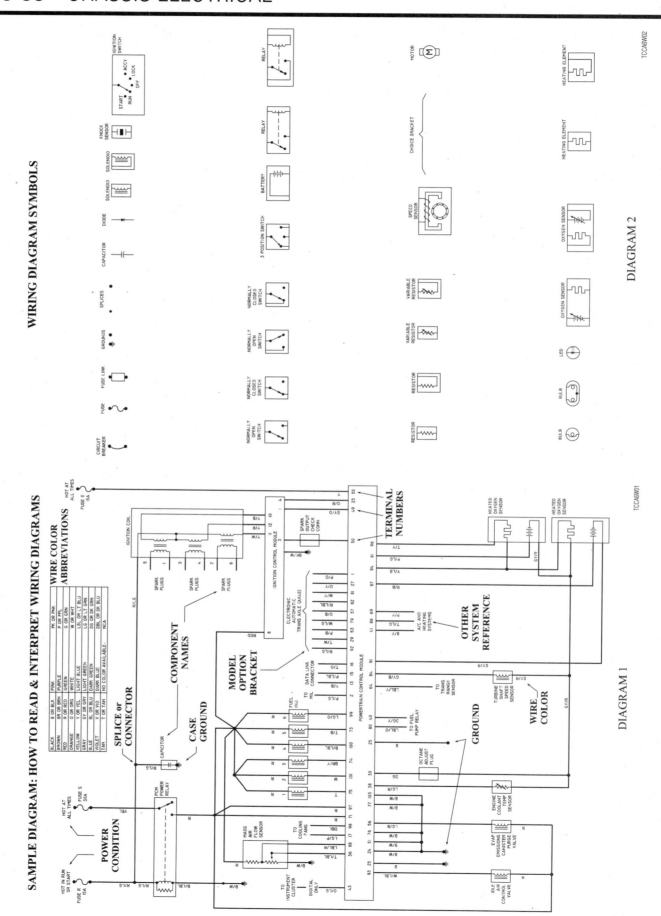

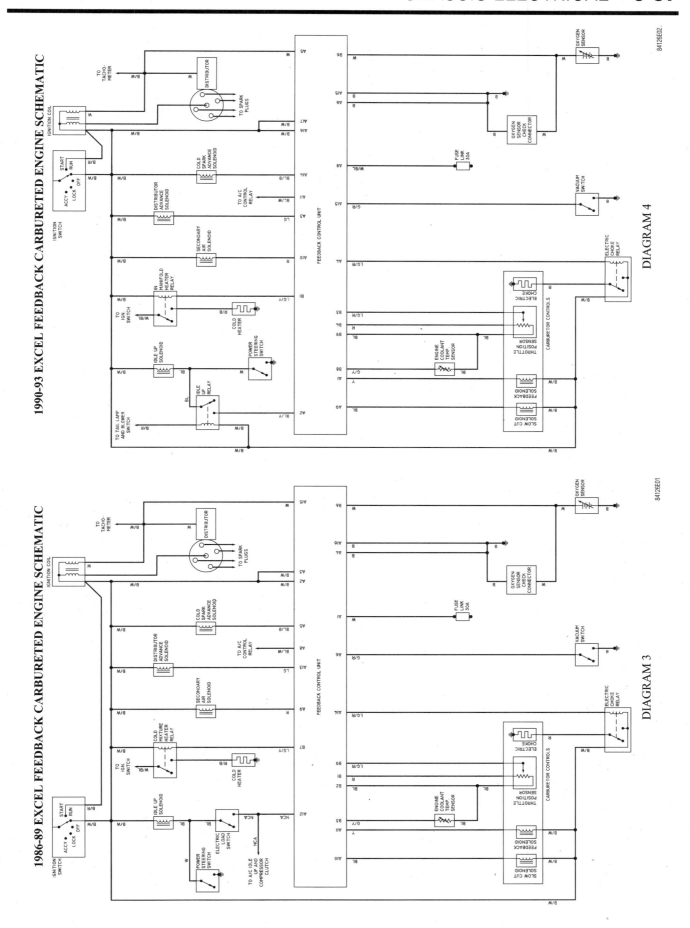

1990-93 EXCEL FEEDBACK CARBURETED ENGINE SCHEMATIC

DIAGRAM 4

1986-89 EXCEL FEEDBACK CARBURETED ENGINE SCHEMATIC

DIAGRAM 3

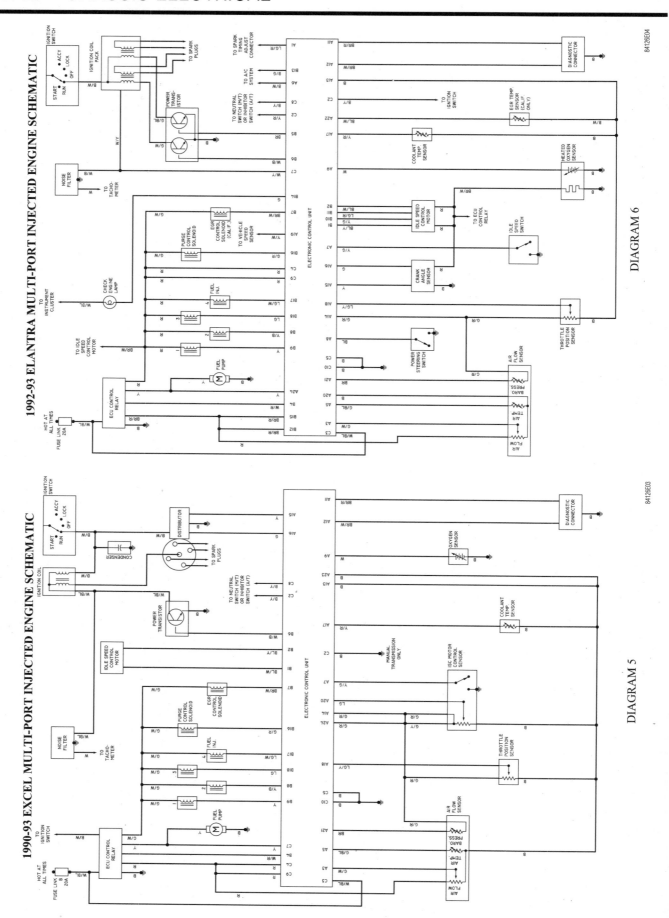

1992-93 ELANTRA MULTI-PORT INJECTED ENGINE SCHEMATIC

DIAGRAM 6

1990-93 EXCEL MULTI-PORT INJECTED ENGINE SCHEMATIC

DIAGRAM 5

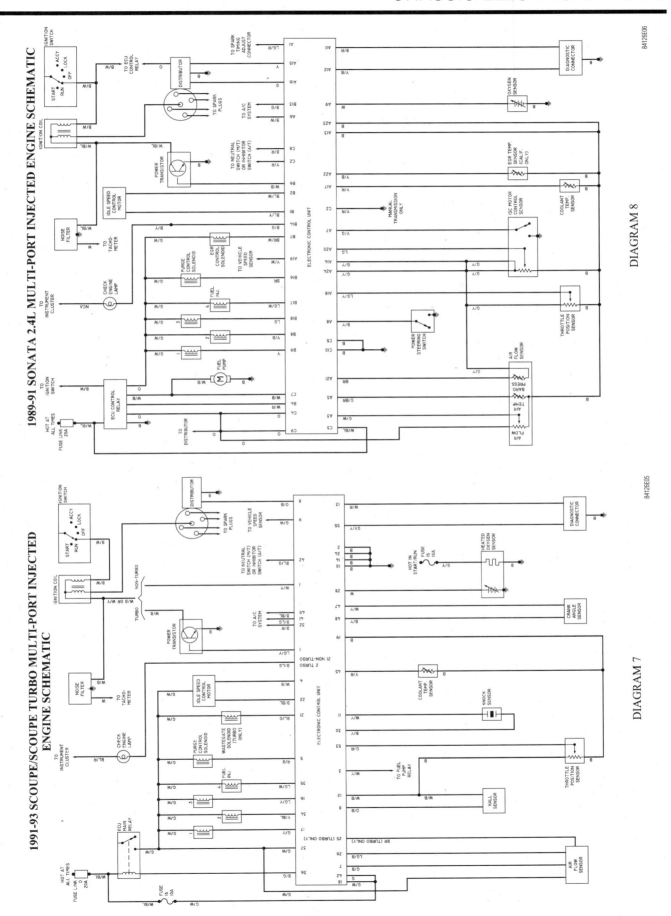

1989-91 SONATA 2.4L MULTI-PORT INJECTED ENGINE SCHEMATIC

DIAGRAM 8

1991-93 SCOUPE/SCOUPE TURBO MULTI-PORT INJECTED ENGINE SCHEMATIC

DIAGRAM 7

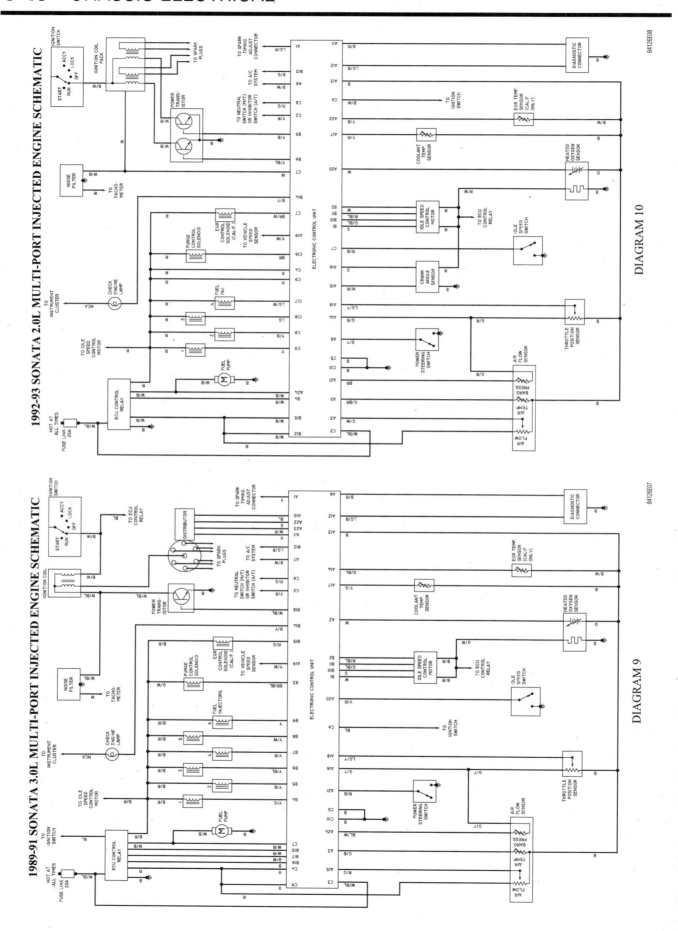

1992-93 SONATA 2.0L MULTI-PORT INJECTED ENGINE SCHEMATIC

DIAGRAM 10

1989-91 SONATA 3.0L MULTI-PORT INJECTED ENGINE SCHEMATIC

DIAGRAM 9

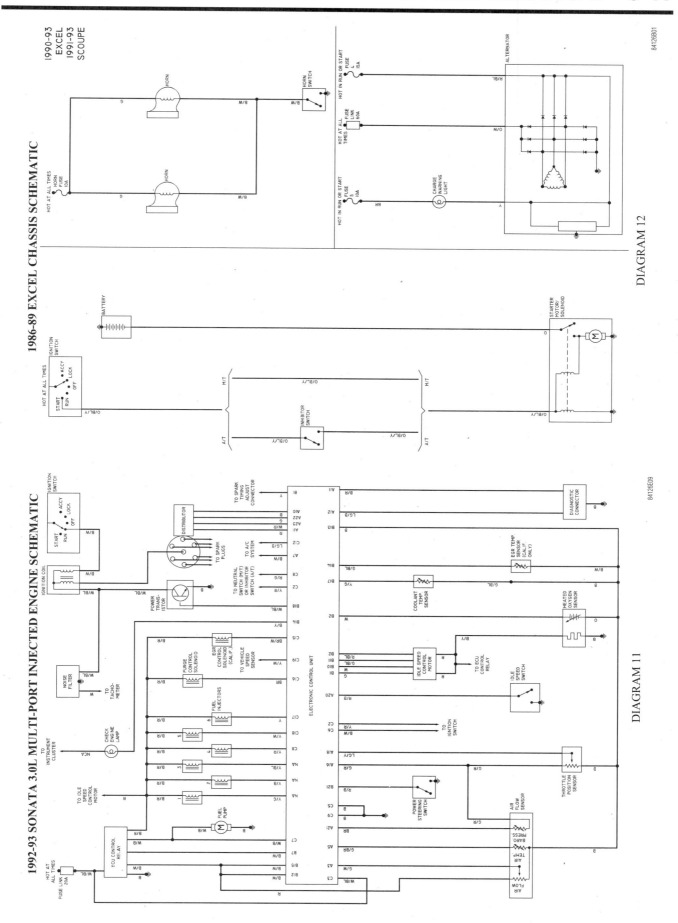

1986-89 EXCEL CHASSIS SCHEMATIC

1990-93 EXCEL
1991-93 SCOUPE

DIAGRAM 12

1992-93 SONATA 3.0L MULTI-PORT INJECTED ENGINE SCHEMATIC

DIAGRAM 11

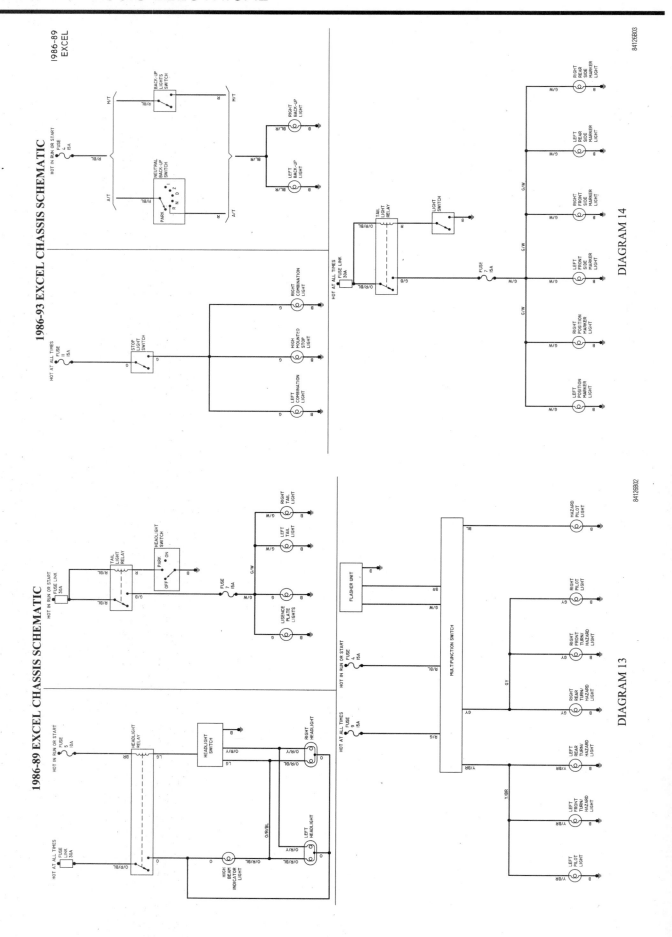

1986-89 EXCEL CHASSIS SCHEMATIC

1986-93 EXCEL CHASSIS SCHEMATIC

1986-89 EXCEL

DIAGRAM 14

DIAGRAM 13

1986-89 EXCEL CHASSIS SCHEMATIC

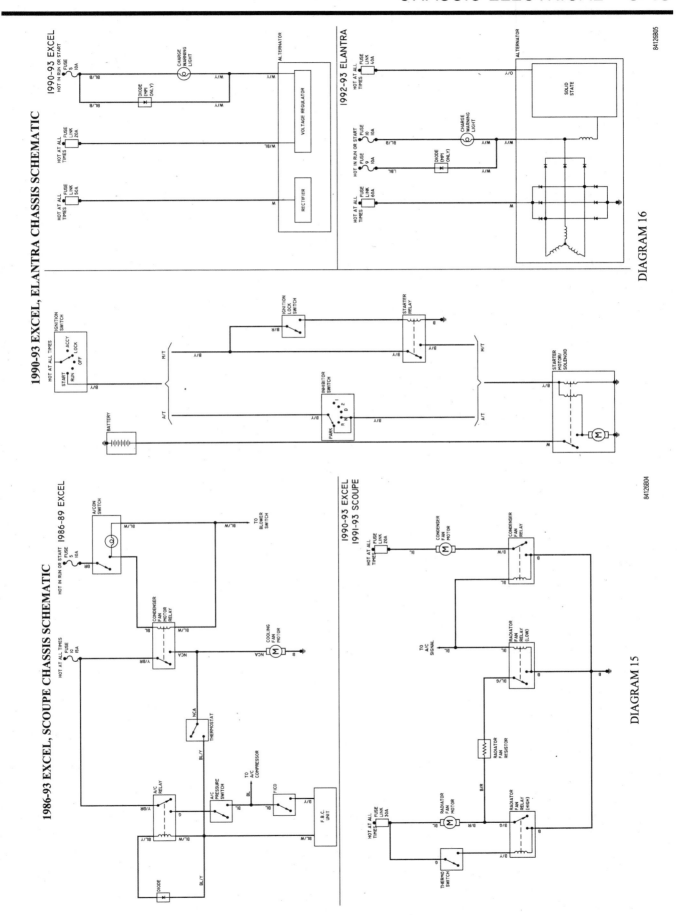

84126B05

DIAGRAM 16

84126B04

DIAGRAM 15

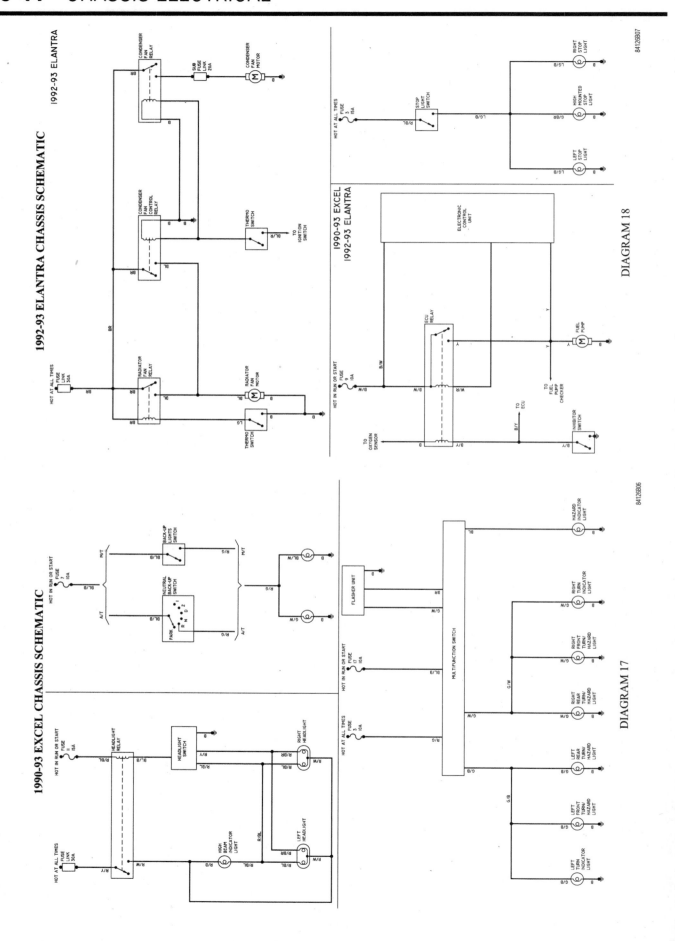

1992-93 ELANTRA

1992-93 ELANTRA CHASSIS SCHEMATIC

1990-93 EXCEL
1992-93 ELANTRA

DIAGRAM 18

1990-93 EXCEL CHASSIS SCHEMATIC

DIAGRAM 17

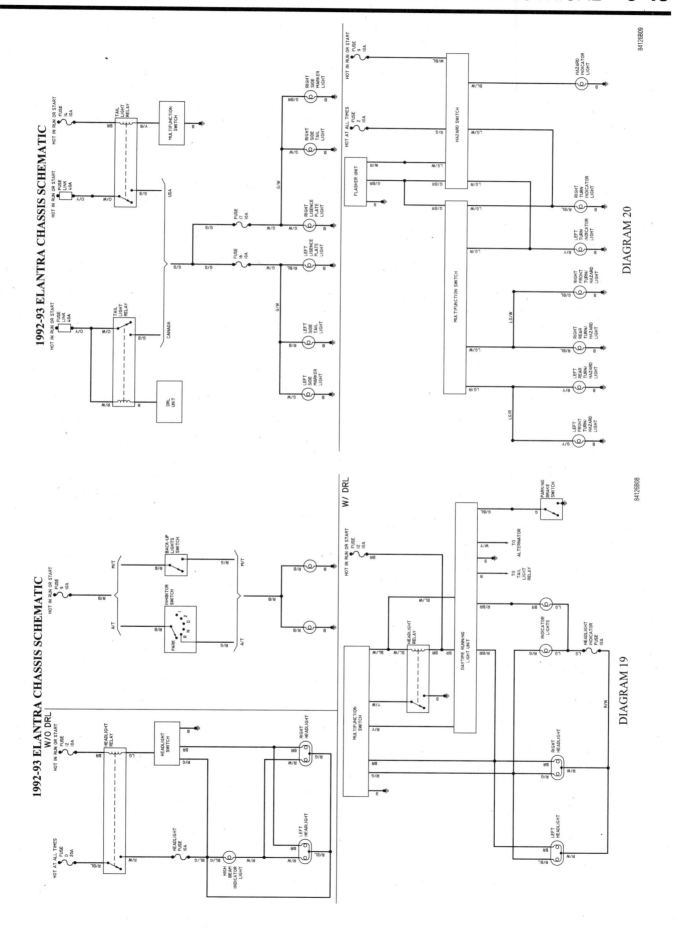

1992-93 ELANTRA CHASSIS SCHEMATIC

DIAGRAM 20

DIAGRAM 19

84126B09

84126B08

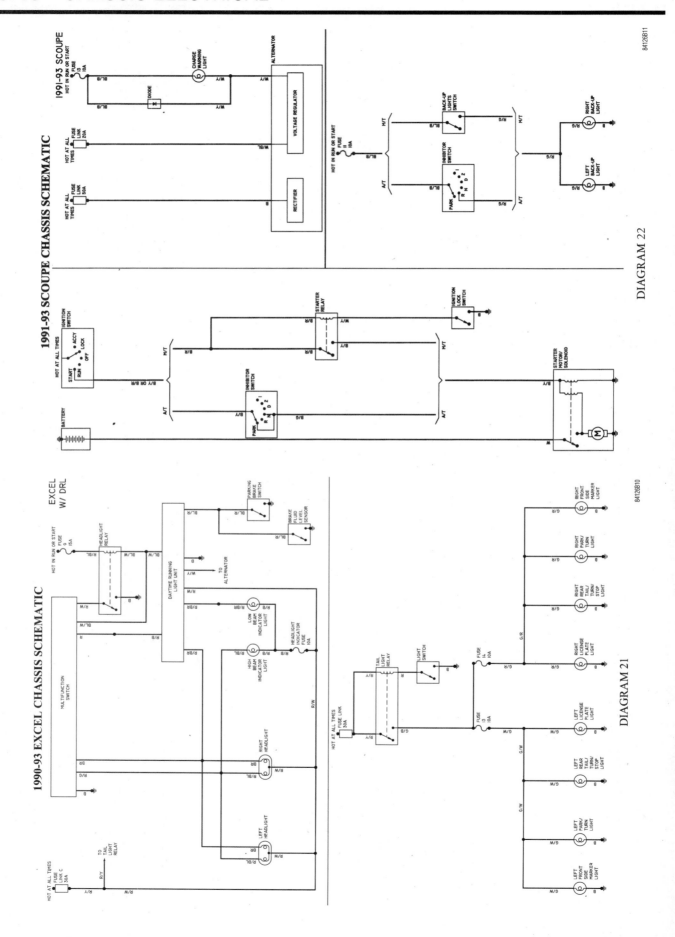

1991-93 SCOUPE CHASSIS SCHEMATIC

DIAGRAM 22

1990-93 EXCEL CHASSIS SCHEMATIC

DIAGRAM 21

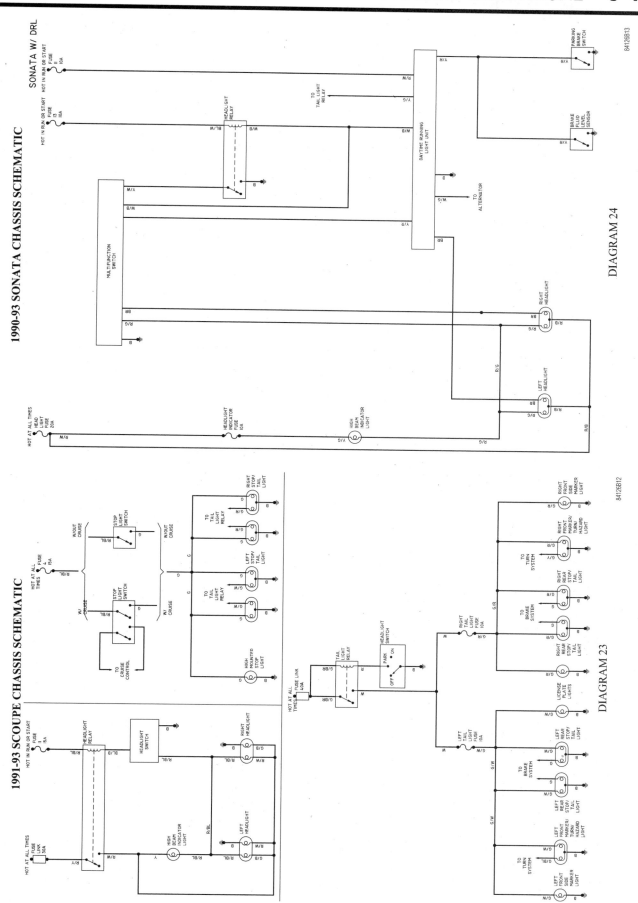

1990-93 SONATA CHASSIS SCHEMATIC

SONATA W/ DRL

DIAGRAM 24

84126B13

1991-93 SCOUPE CHASSIS SCHEMATIC

DIAGRAM 23

84126B12

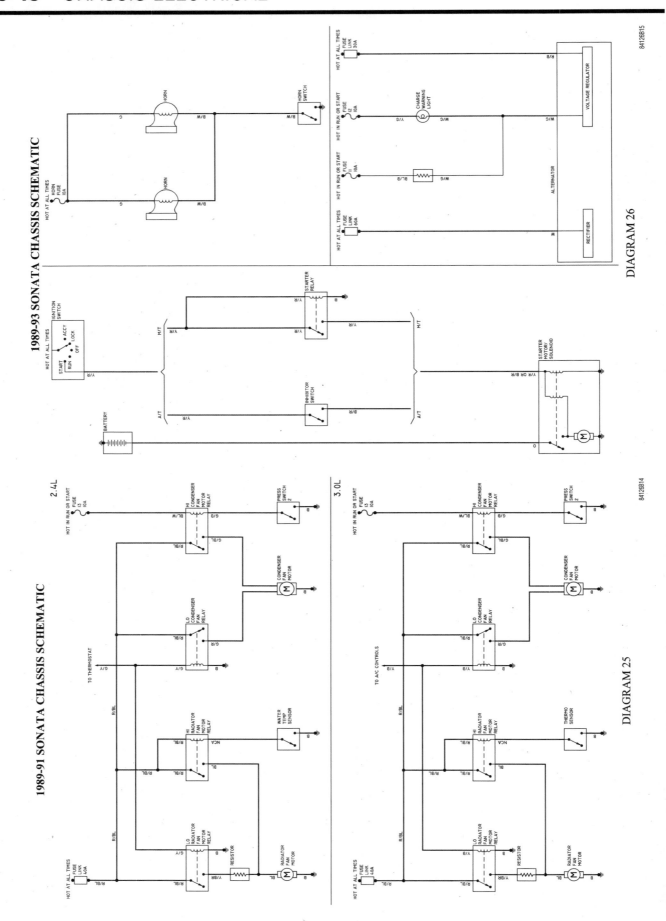

1989-93 SONATA CHASSIS SCHEMATIC

DIAGRAM 26

1989-91 SONATA CHASSIS SCHEMATIC

DIAGRAM 25

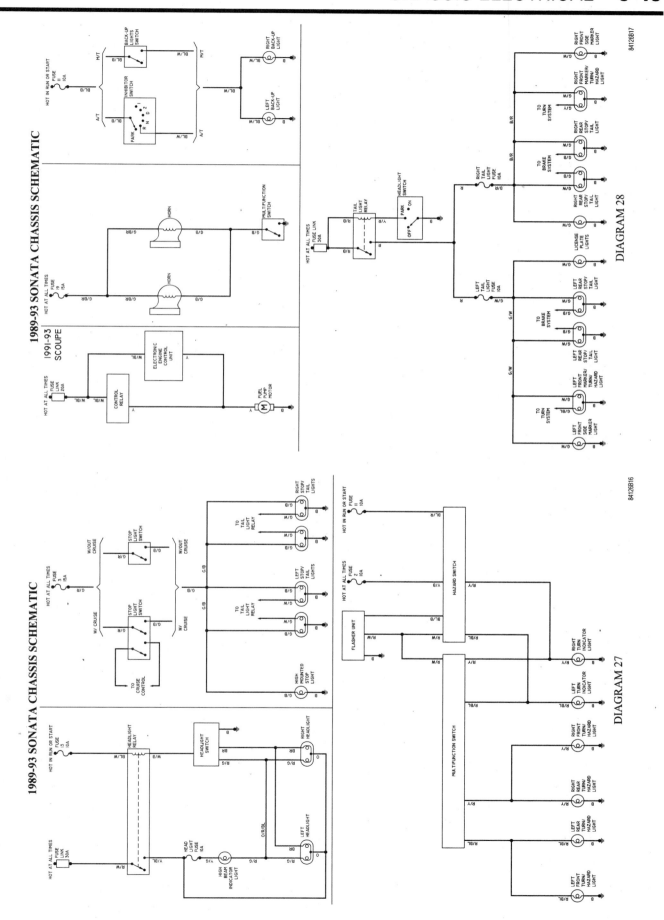

1989-93 SONATA CHASSIS SCHEMATIC

1991-93 SCOUPE

DIAGRAM 28

1989-93 SONATA CHASSIS SCHEMATIC

DIAGRAM 27

1991-93 SCOUPE CHASSIS SCHEMATIC

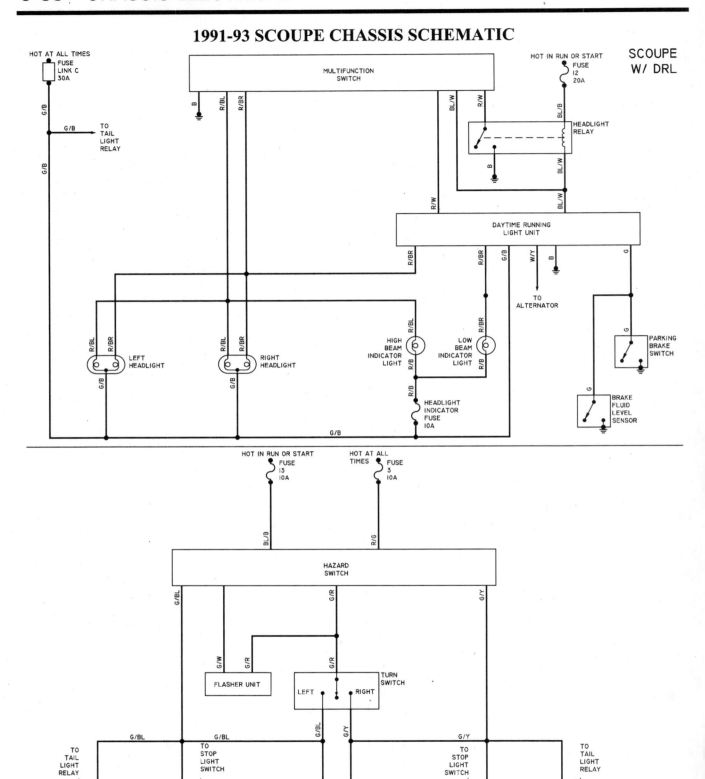

DIAGRAM 29

84126B18

7

DRIVE TRAIN

MANUAL TRANSAXLE

Identification

The transaxle can be identified by the vehicle information code plate which is riveted onto the bulkhead in the engine compartment. The plate shows model code, engine model, transaxle model and body color code.

The 1986–89 Excels use either a Mitsubishi KM-161, 4-speed transaxle or KM-162, 5-speed transaxle. The 1990–93 Excels use either a Mitsubishi KM-200, 4-speed transaxle or KM-201, 5-speed transaxle.

The Elantra and 1991–91 Scoupe are equipped with the Mitsubishi KM-201, 5-speed transaxle. The 1993 Scoupe is equipped with Hyundai's redesigned transaxle, the ALPHA-T/M, which is functionally similar to the Mitsubishi KM-201 transaxle.

The Sonata is equipped with the Mitsubishi KM-210, 5-speed transaxle. This transaxle is functionally similar to the Mitsubishi KM-201 transaxle.

Back-Up Light Switch

REMOVAL & INSTALLATION

The switch is screwed into the right side of the transaxle case and is replaceable, but not adjustable. To remove the switch, disconnect the wiring harness and unscrew the switch from the transaxle case. Do not remove the steel ball from the switch mounting bore. If it falls out, make sure that you retrieve it and put it back. Install the new switch in reverse of the removal procedure using a new gasket. Torque the switch to 22–25 ft. lbs. (29–33 Nm). Check the new switch for proper operation.

Transaxle

REMOVAL & INSTALLATION

➡️**If the vehicle is going to be rolled while the halfshafts are out of the vehicle, obtain 2 outer CV-joints or proper equivalent tools and install to the hubs. If the vehicle is rolled without the proper torque applied to the front wheel bearings, the bearings will no longer be usable.**

1986–89 Excel

▶ **See Figures 1, 2, 3, 4 and 5**

1. Disconnect the negative battery cable.
2. Disconnect or remove from the transaxle: the clutch cable, speedometer cable, back-up light harness, starter motor (remove) and the four upper bolts connecting the engine to the transaxle. On cars with a 5-speed transaxle, disconnect the selector control valve.
3. Raise the vehicle and support it safely on jackstands.
4. Remove the front wheels. Remove the splash shield. Drain the transaxle fluid into a suitable waste container.
5. Remove the shift rod and extension rod. It may be necessary to remove any heat shields that can interfere with your progress.
6. Remove the stabilizer bar from the lower arm and disconnect the lower arm from the body side.
7. Remove the right and left driveshafts from the transaxle case. See drive axle removal in this section.
8. Disconnect the range selector cable (if equipped). Remove the engine rear cover.

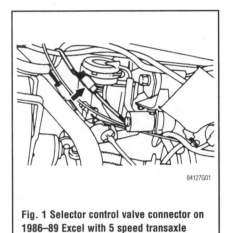

Fig. 1 Selector control valve connector on 1986–89 Excel with 5 speed transaxle

Fig. 2 Upper transaxle-to-engine bolts on 1986–89 Excel

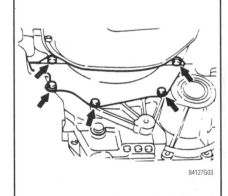

Fig. 3 Lower transaxle-to-engine bolts on 1986–89 Excel

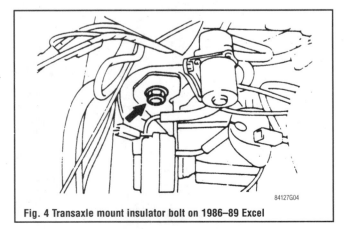

Fig. 4 Transaxle mount insulator bolt on 1986–89 Excel

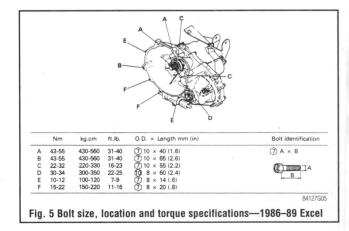

	Nm	kg.cm	ft.lb.	O.D. × Length mm (in)	Bolt identification
A	43-55	430-560	31-40	⑦ 10 × 40 (1.6)	⑦ A × B
B	43-55	430-560	31-40	⑦ 10 × 65 (2.6)	
C	22-32	220-330	16-23	⑦ 10 × 55 (2.2)	
D	30-34	300-350	22-25	⑩ 8 × 60 (2.4)	
E	10-12	100-120	7-9	⑦ 8 × 14 (.6)	
F	15-22	150-220	11-16	⑦ 8 × 20 (.8)	

Fig. 5 Bolt size, location and torque specifications—1986–89 Excel

9. Support the weight of the engine from above (chain hoist). Support the transaxle and remove the remaining lower mounting bolts.

10. Remove the transaxle mount insulator bolt.

11. Remove (slide back and away from the engine) and lower the transaxle on a suitable transmission jack.

To install:

12. Maneuver the transaxle into position under the engine and raise into place using the transmission jack. Make sure the weight of the engine is supported by the chain hoist.

13. Install the transaxle insulator and the lower transaxle mounting bolts. Tighten them enough to support the transaxle, then torque the bolts to specification (see fig5 for bolt location and torque values).

14. Install the engine rear cover and connect the range selector cable (if equipped).

15. Connect the driveshafts to the transaxle case. Use new retaining rings.

16. Connect the lower control arm. Connect the stabilizer bar to the lower arm. Torque the stabilizer bar bolts to 4 ft. lbs. (5.5 Nm) and the lower control arm bolts to 69–87 ft. lbs. (93–117 Nm).

17. Install any heat shield at this time. Connect the extension and shift rods.

18. Mount the front wheels and lower the vehicle.

19. If equipped with a 5-speed, connect the selector control valve mechanism.

20. Install the remaining four upper transaxle to engine bolts and torque to specification.

21. Install the starter motor.

22. Connect the back-up fight harness, speedometer cable and clutch cable to the transaxle.

23. Connect the negative battery cable.

24. Fill the transaxle to the proper level with the proper fluid. Move the shift lever through all the gears to make sure they engage properly.

1990–93 Excel, Elantra and Scoupe

▶ See Figures 6 thru 11

➡ **If the vehicle is going to be rolled while the halfshafts are out of the vehicle, obtain 2 outer CV-joints or proper equivalent tools and install to the hubs. If the vehicle is rolled without the proper torque applied to the front wheel bearings, the bearings will no longer be usable.**

7. Remove the transaxle mounting bolts accessible from the top side of the transaxle.

8. Unbolt and remove the starter motor.

9. Raise the vehicle and support it safely. Then, remove the splash shield from under the engine. Drain the transaxle fluid.

10. Disconnect the extension rod and the shift rod at the transaxle end and lower them.

11. Disconnect the stabilizer bar at the lower control arm.

12. Remove the halfshafts from the transaxle assembly.

13. Support the transaxle from below with a floor jack. Make sure the support is widely enough spread that the transaxle pan will not be damaged. Then, remove the attaching bolts and the bell housing cover.

14. Remove the lower bolts attaching the transaxle to the engine.

15. Remove the transaxle insulator mount bolt. Remove the cover from inside the right fender shield and remove the transaxle support bracket.

16. Remove the transaxle mount bracket.

17. Pull the assembly away from the engine and lower it from the vehicle.

To install:

18. Install the transaxle to the engine and install the mounting bolts. Tighten the mounting bolts as follows:

- M10–7T engine-to-transaxle bolts—35 ft. lbs. (48 Nm)
- M8–10T engine-to-transaxle bolts—25 ft. lbs. (34 Nm)

19. When installing the halfshafts, use new circlips on the axle ends. Take care to get the inboard joint parts straight, not bent relative to the axle. Care must be taken to ensure that the oil seal lip of the transaxle is not damaged by the serrated part of the driveshaft.

20. Install the undercover.

21. Install the mounting brackets and torque the mounting bracket bolt to 40 ft. lbs. (54 Nm).

22. Install the starter making sure to fasten the ground wire with the upper fastener and the harness fastener with the lower fastener.

23. Connect the back-up light switch connector and speedometer cable.

24. Install the clutch and shifter actuation components. If the hydraulic system was opened, it should be bled after installation.

25. Install the air cleaner and battery.

26. Make sure the vehicle is level when refilling the transaxle. Use Hypoid gear oil or equivalent, GL-4 or higher.

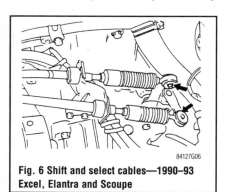

Fig. 6 Shift and select cables—1990–93 Excel, Elantra and Scoupe

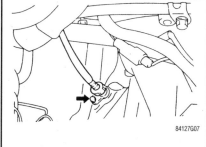

Fig. 7 Speedometer cable attaching bolt— 1990–93 Excel, Elantra and Scoupe

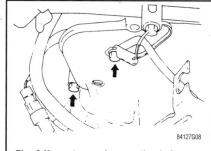

Fig. 8 Upper transaxle mounting bolts— 1990–93 Excel, Elantra and Scoupe

1. Disconnect the negative battery cable. Remove the air cleaner assembly, battery and battery tray as required.

2. On 5-speed transaxle, disconnect the electrical connector for the selector control valve.

➡ **The actuator-to-shaft coupling pin collar is not reusable; replace it.**

3. Disconnect and remove the speedometer cable.

4. If equipped with a cable operated clutch, disconnect the clutch cable from the transaxle assembly.

5. If equipped with a hydraulically operated clutch, remove the clevis pin connecting the slave cylinder to the release fork shaft and remove the slave cylinder mounting bolts. Remove the bolts attaching the hydraulic line support bracket to the transaxle. Remove and support the slave cylinder assembly out of the way with a length of mechanics wire.

6. Disconnect the back-up lamp electrical connector. Remove the starter motor electrical harness.

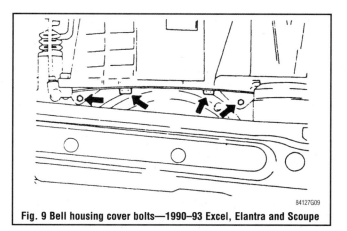

Fig. 9 Bell housing cover bolts—1990–93 Excel, Elantra and Scoupe

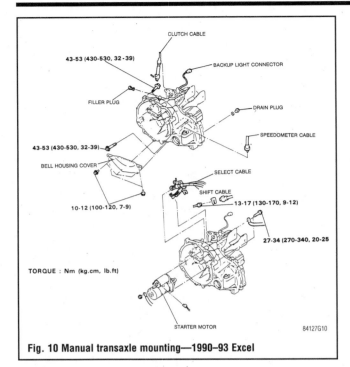

Fig. 10 Manual transaxle mounting—1990–93 Excel

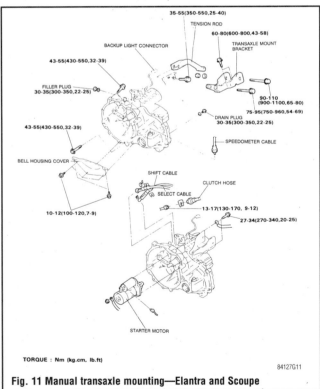

Fig. 11 Manual transaxle mounting—Elantra and Scoupe

27. Connect the negative battery cable and check the transaxle for proper operation. Make sure the reverse lights come on when in R.

Sonata

▶ **See Figure 12**

1. Disconnect the negative battery cable.
2. Remove the clutch release cylinder from the transaxle case as described later in this section.
3. Drain the transaxle oil into a suitable waste container.

4. Remove the air cleaner assembly.
5. Remove the pin clips and cotter pins and disconnect the select and shift cables from the control levers.
6. Disconnect the back-up lamp switch connector and route the wiring harness off to the side and out of the way.
7. Disconnect the speedometer cable from the transaxle.
8. Disconnect and label the starter wiring. Remove the starter.
9. Jack up the car, support on jackstands and remove the front wheels. Remove any interfering shield or undercover.
10. Remove the left and right driveshafts as described later in this section.
11. Unbolt and remove the bell housing cover.
12. Connect a chain hoist or equivalent to the engine lifting bracket. Tension the hoist to support the weight of the engine.
13. Support the bottom of the transaxle with a transmission jack.
14. Remove the 4 plastic mounting bracket bolt access caps and remove the 4 transaxle mounting bracket bolts.
15. Remove the upper and lower transaxle-to-engine and engine-to-transaxle mounting bolts.
16. Lower the transaxle away from the engine.

To install:

17. Raise the transaxle up and onto the engine. Align the bolt holes and install the upper and lower mounting bolts. Install the four transaxle bracket bolts. Make sure the weight of the engine is supported with the chain hoist. Torque all bolts to specification. Install the four plastic caps.
18. Install the bell housing cover.
19. Install the driveshafts using new clips.
20. Install any shield or under cover that was removed.
21. Mount the front wheels and lower the vehicle.
22. Install the starter and connect the starter wiring.
23. Connect the speedometer cable to the transaxle.
24. Plug in the back-up light switch harness.
25. Connect the shift and select cables to their respective control levers. Adjust the cable tension.
26. Install the air cleaner assembly.
27. Install the clutch release cylinder. Make sure the hose fittings are tight.
28. Connect the negative battery cable.
29. Fill the transaxle and clutch master cylinder to the proper level with the specified fluid. Move the shift lever through all the gears to make sure they engage and disengage properly.

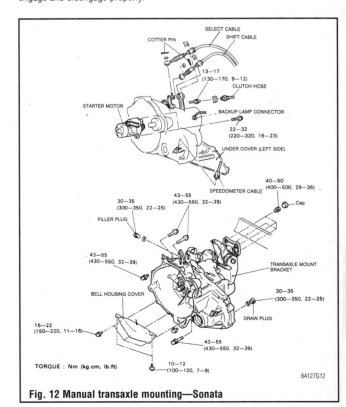

Fig. 12 Manual transaxle mounting—Sonata

CLUTCH

On 1986–89 Excel models, a mechanical clutch linkage system in which clutch actuation is controlled by a cable from the clutch pedal is used. On Elantra, Scoupe and Sonata, the clutch cables are actuated hydraulically. On the 1990–93 Excel, manual transaxles are available with both cable and hydraulic actuating systems.

✳✳ CAUTION

The clutch driven disc contains asbestos fibers, which has been determined to be a cancer causing agent. Never clean the clutch surfaces with compressed air! Avoid inhaling nasty dust from any clutch surface. When cleaning clutch surfaces, use a commercially available brake cleaning fluid.

The clutch assembly consists of a single dry disc and a diaphragm spring pressure plate. The throwout bearing is controlled by a shaft mounted horizontally in the clutch housing.

Adjustments

PEDAL HEIGHT AND FREE-PLAY

1986–89 Excel

♦ See Figures 13, 14 and 15

1. Measure the distance between the floor and the top of the clutch pedal (dimension "A"). This is clutch pedal height. The distance should be 185-193mm. If the clutch pedal height is not as specified, first disconnect the clutch switch connector. Then, loosen the clutch switch locknut and move the pedal stop bolt as necessary until the pedal height is as specified. After the adjustment is complete, tighten the locknut and connect the clutch switch connector.

2. Gently pull the cable out from the firewall and measure the distance between the clutch cable adjusting nut and the cable retainer. Turn the adjusting wheel on the cable until the play between the wheel and the cable retainer is 0.20-0.25 as checked with a feeler gauge. Release the cable and make sure that the end of the tension spring engages the adjusting wheel, so that it won't turn.

3. Check the clutch pedal free-play. Free-play is the distance that the pedal will travel before any resistance is felt. Free-play should be 20-30mm. If not, adjust it by means of the adjusting wheel on the cable as described above.

4. Check the clutch pedal stroke. It should be 145mm. If the stroke is greater than the specified value, suspect that the clutch is worn. Repair or replace the clutch as necessary.

1990–93 Excel with Cable Clutch

♦ See Figures 16, 17 and 18

1. Measure the distance between the floor and the top of the clutch pedal (dimension "A"). The distance should be 178mm.

➡**Clutch pedal height cannot be adjusted on the 1990 Excel with cable clutch. If the clutch pedal height is not within specs, check the pedal stopper of the pedal support member for deterioration.**

2. Check the clutch pedal free-play. Free-play is the distance that the pedal will travel before any resistance is felt. Free-play should be 20-30mm. If not, adjust it by means of the adjusting wheel on the cable. If the free-play is not as specified, gently pull the cable out from the firewall. Next, turn the adjusting wheel on the cable until the play between the wheel and the cable retainer is 0.20-0.25mm as checked with a feeler gauge. Release the cable and make sure that the end of the tension spring engages the adjusting wheel, so that it won't turn.

3. After making the free-play adjustment, depress the clutch pedal several times and measure the clutch pedal-to-floor board clearance. It should be 33mm. If the clearance is less than specified, the clutch may be worn. Repair or replace the clutch as necessary.

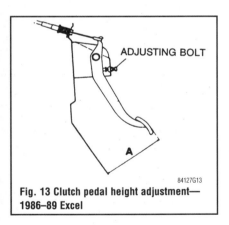

Fig. 13 Clutch pedal height adjustment—1986–89 Excel

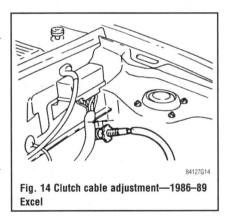

Fig. 14 Clutch cable adjustment—1986–89 Excel

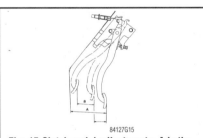

Fig. 15 Clutch pedal adjustments: A is the pedal height; the small measurement is the pedal free-play; B is the pedal stroke, which is found by subtracting the free-play from the pedal height

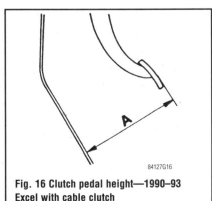

Fig. 16 Clutch pedal height—1990–93 Excel with cable clutch

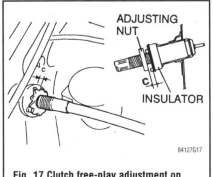

Fig. 17 Clutch free-play adjustment on 1990–93 Excel with cable clutch

Fig. 18 Clutch pedal-to-floor board clearance—1990–93 Excel with cable clutch

1990–93 Excel with Hydraulic Clutch

♦ **See Figures 19, 20 and 21**

1. Measure the distance between the floor and the top of the clutch pedal. This is clutch pedal height. The distance should be 178mm. If the clutch pedal height is not as specified, make the following adjustments depending on whether the pedal height is greater or less than the specified value:

a. If the pedal height is greater than the specified value, loosen the clutch switch locknut and move the pedal stop bolt as necessary until the pedal height is as specified. Tighten the locknut after the adjustment is complete.

b. If the pedal height is less than the specified value, first loosen pedal stop bolt locknut. Then, adjust the pedal height by turning the clutch release cylinder push rod. After the adjustment turn the adjusting bolt until it contacts the pedal stop and tighten the locknut.

2. Check the clutch pedal free-play and the distance between the clutch pedal and the toe board with the clutch disengaged. Free-play is the distance that the pedal will travel before any resistance is felt. Free-play should be 613mm. Clutch pedal-to-toe board distance should be 40mm. If the free-play or pedal-to-toe board distances are not as specified value, this may be a result of air in the hydraulic system or a bad master cylinder or clutch. In this case bleed the hydraulic system as described in this section or disassemble and inspect the master cylinder or clutch.

Elantra

Measure the pedal height from the top of the pedal pad to the closest point on the floor. The distance should be 7.0 in. (182mm). If incorrect and the vehicle is not equipped with cruise control, adjust the height by loosening the locknut on the pedal stop bolt and adjusting the bolt to the proper length. Secure

the pushrod locknut and connect the clutch switch connector. Lubricate the clevis pin with a small amount of wheel bearing or multi-purpose grease.

➡**When adjusting the clevis pin play, do not push the push rod into the master cylinder or damage will be result.**

Check the clutch pedal free-play and the distance between the clutch pedal and the firewall with the clutch disengaged. To check clutch pedal free-play, lightly depress the clutch pedal and visually approximate the amount of pedal travel until resistance is felt. Clutch pedal free-play should be 5.0-12.0mm. The clutch pedal-to-firewall distance should be 56mm. If the free-play or clevis pin play are not within the specified values, adjust the clevis pin play as described above. If, after the clevis pin adjustment, the free-play is still not within specs, this may be a result of air in the hydraulic system or a bad master cylinder or clutch. In this case bleed the hydraulic system as described in this section or disassemble and inspect the master cylinder or clutch.

Clutch Cable

REMOVAL & INSTALLATION

♦ **See Figure 22**

1. Back-off the cable adjusting wheel in the engine compartment.
2. Raise and support the vehicle safely.
3. Pull out the split pin from the end of the clutch control lever and disconnect the cable from the lever.
4. Disconnect the cable at the clutch pedal and remove the clutch cable from the vehicle.
5. Installation is the reverse of removal. Adjust the clutch.

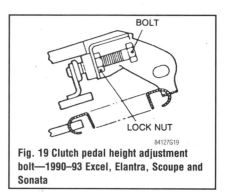

Fig. 19 Clutch pedal height adjustment bolt—1990–93 Excel, Elantra, Scoupe and Sonata

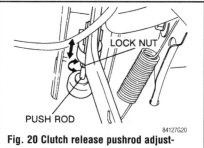
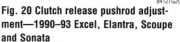

Fig. 20 Clutch release pushrod adjustment—1990–93 Excel, Elantra, Scoupe and Sonata

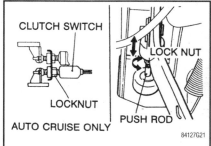

Fig. 21 Clevis pin adjustment—Elantra, Scoupe and Sonata

the adjustment by tightening the locknut. If the vehicle is equipped with cruise control, adjust as follows:

1. Disconnect the clutch switch wiring.
2. Loosen the locknut and turn the switch, as required.
3. Tighten the locknut.

Scoupe

Measure the pedal height from the top of the pedal pad to the closest point on the floor. The distance should be 7 in. (178mm). Loosen the clutch switch locknut and move the pedal stop bolt. Then, tighten the locknut.

Sonata

1. Measure the distance between the floor and the top of the clutch pedal. This is clutch pedal height. The distance should be 173–178mm. If the clutch pedal height is not within specs, the clevis pin play must be adjusted as described as follows:

a. To check clevis pin play, lightly depress the clutch pedal and visually approximate the amount of pedal travel until resistance is felt. Clevis pin play should be 1.0-3.0mm.

b. To adjust the clevis pin play, disconnect the clutch switch connector (cruise control only), loosen the master cylinder push rod locknut and rotate the pushrod until the clevis pin play is within the 1.0-3.0mm, then tighten

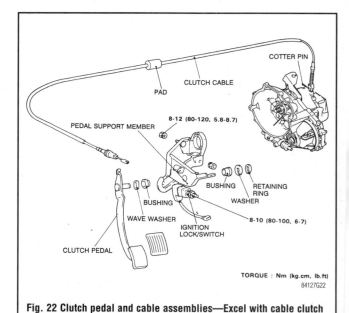

Fig. 22 Clutch pedal and cable assemblies—Excel with cable clutch

Driven Disc and Pressure Plate

REMOVAL & INSTALLATION

▶ **See Figures 23 and 24**

Cable Operated System

1. Remove the transaxle. Insert the forward end of an old transaxle input shaft or a clutch disc guide tool into the splined center of the clutch disc, pressure plate and the pilot bearing in the crankshaft. This will keep the disc from dropping when the pressure plate is removed from the flywheel.

2. Loosen the clutch mounting bolts alternately and diagonally in very small increments, no more than 2 turns at a time, so as to avoid warping the cover flange.

3. Remove the pressure plate and disc.

4. Remove the return clip and the clutch release bearing.

5. Insert tool 09414–24000 in the spring pin and attach the round nut to the end of the tool. While holding the shaft of the special tool, rotate the sleeve with a wrench to force the spring pin out.

6. Remove the clutch release shaft, packings, return spring and the release fork.

To install:

7. Apply a light coating of multi-purpose grease to the release fork shaft and the throw out bearing contact surfaces.

8. Align the lock pin holes of the release fork and shaft and drive 2 new spring pins into the holes. Make sure the spring pin slot is at right angles to the centerline of the control shaft.

9. Apply grease into the groove in the release bearing and install bearing into the front bearing retainer in the transaxle. Install the return clip to the release bearing and fork.

10. Make sure the surfaces of the pressure plate and flywheel are wiped clean of grease and lightly sand them with crocus cloth. Lightly grease the clutch disc and transaxle input shaft splines making sure not to allow any grease to contact the clutch disc material or clutch slip may result.

11. Locate the clutch disc on the flywheel with the stamped mark facing outward. Use a clutch disc guide or old input shaft to center the disc on the flywheel and then install the pressure plate over it. Install the bolts and tighten them evenly. Tighten them in increments of 2 turns or less to avoid warping the pressure plate. Torque to 11–15 ft. lbs. (15–21 Nm).

12. Remove the clutch disc centering tool. Install the transaxle. Adjust the clutch free-play.

Hydraulic System

▶ **See Figures 25, 26 and 27**

ELANTRA

1. Disconnect the negative battery cable. Raise and safely support the vehicle.

2. Remove the transaxle assembly from the vehicle.

3. Remove the pressure plate attaching bolts. If the pressure plate is to be reused, loosen the bolts in succession, 1 or 2 turns at a time to prevent warping the cover flange.

4. Remove the pressure plate release bearing assembly and the clutch disc. Do not use solvent to clean the bearing.

5. Inspect the condition of the clutch components and replace any worn parts.

To install:

6. Inspect the flywheel for heat damage or cracks. Resurface or replace the flywheel, as required. Install the flywheel using new bolts.

7. Using the proper alignment tool, install the clutch disc to the flywheel. Install the pressure plate assembly and tighten the pressure plate bolts evenly to 14 ft. lbs. (22 Nm). Remove the alignment tool.

8. Apply a very light coat of high temperature grease to the clutch fork at the ball pivot and where the fork contacts the bearing. Also a little bit of grease can be applied to the end of the release cylinder's pushrod and to the pushrod hole on the fork. Apply a light coat of grease on the transaxle input shaft splines.

9. Install a new clutch release bearing. Pack its inner surface with grease.

10. Install the transaxle assembly and check for proper clutch operation.

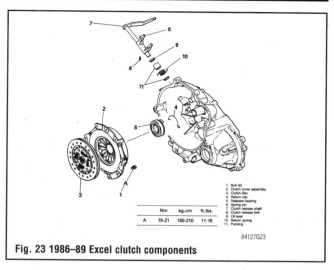

	Nm	kg.cm	ft.lbs.
A	15-21	150-210	11-15

1. Bolt (6)
2. Clutch cover assembly
3. Clutch disc
4. Return clip
5. Release bearing
6. Spring pin
7. Clutch release shaft
8. Clutch release fork
9. Oil seal
10. Return spring
11. Packing

84127G23

Fig. 23 1986–89 Excel clutch components

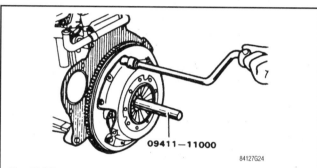

09411–11000

84127G24

Fig. 24 When removing the clutch disc, insert a pilot shaft to prevent the disc from falling

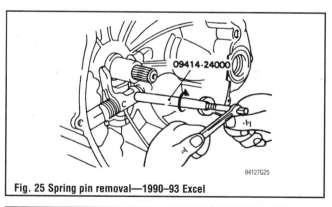

09414-24000

84127G25

Fig. 25 Spring pin removal—1990–93 Excel

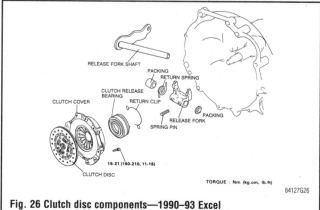

RELEASE FORK SHAFT

PACKING

RETURN SPRING

CLUTCH RELEASE BEARING

RETURN CLIP

CLUTCH COVER

PACKING

RELEASE FORK

SPRING PIN

15-21 (150-210, 11-15)

CLUTCH DISC

TORQUE : Nm (kg.cm, lb.ft)

84127G26

Fig. 26 Clutch disc components—1990–93 Excel

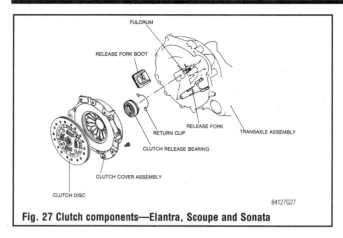

Fig. 27 Clutch components—Elantra, Scoupe and Sonata

EXCEPT ELANTRA

1. Disconnect the negative battery cable. Raise and safely support the vehicle.

2. Remove the transaxle assembly from the vehicle.

3. Remove the pressure plate attaching bolts. If the pressure plate is to be reused, loosen the bolts in succession, 1 or 2 turns at a time to prevent warping the cover flange.

4. Remove the pressure plate and disc.

5. Remove the return clip and the clutch release bearing.

6. Insert tool 09414–24000 in the spring pin and attach the round nut to the end of the tool. While holding the shaft of the special tool, rotate the sleeve with a wrench to force the spring pin out.

7. Remove the clutch release shaft, packings, return spring and the release fork.

To install:

8. Apply a light coating of multipurpose grease to the release fork shaft and the throw out bearing contact surfaces.

9. Align the lock pin holes of the release fork and shaft and drive 2 new spring pins into the holes. Make sure the spring pin slot is at right angles to the centerline of the control shaft.

10. Apply grease into the groove in the release bearing and install bearing into the front bearing retainer in the transaxle. Install the return clip to the release bearing and fork.

11. Make sure the surfaces of the pressure plate and flywheel are wiped clean of grease and lightly sand them with crocus cloth. Lightly grease the clutch disc and transaxle input shaft splines making sure not to allow any grease to contact the clutch disc material or clutch slip may result.

12. Locate the clutch disc on the flywheel with the stamped mark facing outward. Use a clutch disc guide or old input shaft to center the disc on the flywheel and then install the pressure plate over it. Install the bolts and tighten them evenly. Tighten them in increments of 2 turns or less to avoid warping the pressure plate. Torque to 11–15 ft. lbs. (15–21 Nm).

13. Remove the clutch disc centering tool. Install the transaxle. Adjust the clutch free-play.

Clutch Master Cylinder

REMOVAL & INSTALLATION

▶ See Figures 28, 29 and 30

1. Unscrew the reservoir cap. Loosen the bleeder plug and drain the clutch fluid into a suitable container. Disconnect the hydraulic tube from the bottom of the release cylinder.

2. From inside the vehicle, remove the split pin, clevis pin and washer from the clutch pedal to release the master cylinder pushrod.

3. Remove the clutch fluid reservoir tank mounting bolt.

4. Loosen the clutch tube clamps to permit movement of the clutch tube. Then, disconnect the clutch tube from the master cylinder.

5. Remove the two nuts and pull the master cylinder and gasket from the firewall.

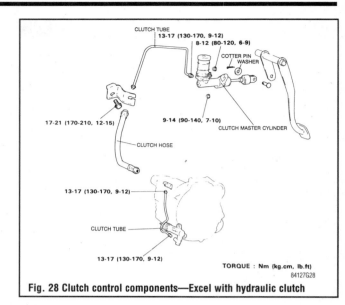

Fig. 28 Clutch control components—Excel with hydraulic clutch

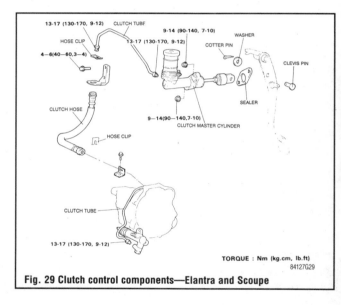

Fig. 29 Clutch control components—Elantra and Scoupe

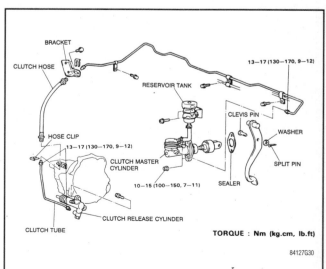

Fig. 30 Clutch control components—Sonata

6. Inspect the gasket for damage and replace as required.

To install:

7. Position the master cylinder assembly with gasket onto the fire wall and loosely install the fluid reservoir mounting bolt and the two master cylinder mounting nuts. Tighten the nuts and bolt to specifications.

8. Connect the clutch tube to the master cylinder and tighten the tube clamps.

9. Connect the pushrod to the clutch pedal and insert the clevis pin. Secure the clevis pin with the split pin.

10. Fill and bleed the system. Adjust the clutch as described above. When the pin play adjustment is complete, lubricate the clevis pin with a small amount of wheel bearing or multipurpose grease. Check the clutch for proper performance.

Clutch Release Cylinder

REMOVAL & INSTALLATION

1. Disconnect the clutch hose from the slave cylinder.
2. Unbolt the cylinder from the clutch housing and remove.
3. Inspect the cylinder for leakage or torn boots and repair or replace as required.

To install:

4. Apply a thin coating of grease to the contact points of the release fork and the cylinder and install the slave cylinder to the clutch housing. Tighten the cylinder retainer bolts to 11–16 ft. lbs. (15–22 Nm).

AUTOMATIC TRANSAXLE

Transaxle

Identification

The transaxle can be identified by the vehicle information code plate which is riveted onto the bulkhead in the engine compartment. The plate shows model code, engine model, transaxle model and body color code.

Fluid Pan

REMOVAL & INSTALLATION

▶ **See Figure 31**

1. Jack up the front of the car and support it safely on jackstands. Remove the splash shield.
2. Slide a drain pan under the differential drain plug. Loosen and remove the plug and drain the fluid. Move the drain pan under the transaxle oil pan, remove the plug and drain the fluid. The transmission fluid cannot all be drained by just draining the oil pan.
3. Remove the pan retaining bolts and remove the pan. Thoroughly clean the pan and transaxle gasket mating surfaces.
4. The filter may be serviced at this time. Remove the old filter and install then new one.

5. Connect the fluid line to the cylinder and tighten the fitting to 7–10 ft. lbs. (13–17 Nm).
6. Add clean DOT 3 brake fluid to the system and bleed.

Bleeding The Hydraulic Clutch System

Whenever a clutch system component is removed, a tube disconnected or the system is opened for any reason, the system must be bled to remove any air that may be trapped inside the system. To bleed the system you will need the following:

• A good supply of brake fluid that meets or exceeds DOT 3 specifications A small transparent plastic container A wrench to loosen and tighten the bleeder screw A small length of clear plastic hose to attach to the bleeder screw An assistant to work the clutch pedal

1. Unscrew the clutch fluid reservoir cap.
2. Loosen the bleeder screw just so fluid starts to leak out of the bleeder hole.
3. Fill the plastic container halfway with the brake fluid.
4. Connect the hose to the bleeder screw and place the other end of hose into the container of brake fluid.
5. Fill the reservoir to the MAX fill line and have the assistant pump the clutch pedal slowly. You will notice air bubbles rising to the top of the fluid container. Keep the reservoir full at all times.
6. Repeat Step 5 until all the air bubbles are gone.
7. Tighten the bleeder screw and check the fluid level. Add fluid as necessary until the proper level is reached.
8. Install the reservoir cap.

To install:

5. Use a new oil pan gasket and reinstall the pan in the reverse order of removal. Tighten the oil pan retaining bolts evenly in a crisscross pattern to 7–9 ft. lbs. (10–12 Nm).
6. Replace the drain plug and torque to 22–25 ft. lbs. (30–35 Nm). Lower the car. Refill the transmission to the proper level with Dexron®II fluid. Start the engine and allow to idle for at least two minutes. With the parking brake applied, move the selector to each position ending in N.
7. Add sufficient fluid to bring the level to the lower mark. Recheck the fluid level after the transmission is up to normal operating temperature.

Adjustments

CONTROL CABLE

Check

▶ **See Figures 32 and 33**

1. Apply parking and service brakes securely.
2. Place selector lever in R range.
3. Set ignition key to the START position.
4. Slowly move the selector lever upward until it clicks into the notch of the P range. If the starter motor operates when the lever clicks into place, then P position is correct.

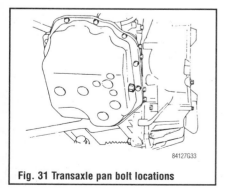

Fig. 31 Transaxle pan bolt locations

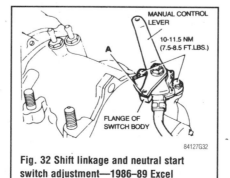

Fig. 32 Shift linkage and neutral start switch adjustment—1986–89 Excel

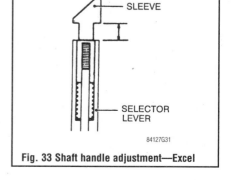

Fig. 33 Shaft handle adjustment—Excel

5. Next, slowly move the selector lever to N; if the starter operates in this gear, then N is also correct.

6. Also check to see that the vehicle does not move and the lever does not stop in between gears. If all of the above checks out, the cable is correctly adjusted.

7. Adjust the adjusting nuts where the cable is connected to the manual lever at the inhibitor switch to take up any slack in the control cable.

8. Recheck operation of the selector lever and inhibitor switch.

Adjustment

1986–89 EXCEL

1. Place the shift lever in the N position.

2. Open the hood. On top of the transaxle the control cable connects with a lever. In the lever is a hole which should index with a hole in the top of the transaxle case when the linkage is in the neutral position. If not, unlock and turn the adjusting nut on the linkage until alignment is achieved. Lock the adjusting nut.

3. Check that the car will start only in the N and P positions.

4. With the shift lever in the N position, remove the shift handle from the lever.

5. Measure the distance between the threaded sleeve and the top of the shift lever. The distance should be 17.2–17.9mm. If not, turn the sleeve as necessary.

6. Install the shift handle with the button on the driver's side.

1990–93 EXCEL, ELANTRA, SCOUPE AND SONATA

1. Open the hood.

2. On top of the transaxle the control cable connects to a lever. Where the control cable connects to the lever there are two locknuts.

3. To adjust the control cable, eliminate all the slack from the cable by tightening the two locknuts.

4. After the adjustment, from inside the vehicle operate the shifter lever to make sure everything works smoothly.

5. Check that the car will start only in the N and P positions.

6. Drive the vehicle and make sure that all gears shift properly.

THROTTLE CONTROL CABLE

♦ See Figures 34, 35 and 36

1986–89 Excel Only

➡**This adjustment is critical to transmission operation. If the adjustment is not correct, shift points will be altered and damage will result to the transmission.**

1. Make sure the engine is at normal operating temperature, with the throttle in normal idling position.

2. Loosen the lower cable bracket mounting bolt. Pull the small rubber cover located near the transaxle back toward the housing to expose the nipple. Now, move the cable bracket until the distance between the nipple and the outer end of the cover next to the bracket is 0.02–0.06 in. (0.5–1.5mm). Then, torque the bracket mounting bolt to 9–10.5 ft. lbs. (12–14 Nm).

3. With the engine **OFF**, open the throttle all the way and hold it there.

Then, pull the cable further upward to make sure it still has freedom of movement; that it has not bottomed out. If necessary, repeat the adjustment.

NEUTRAL SAFETY (INHIBITOR) SWITCH

The inhibitor switch is located on top of the transaxle case. This switch has the manual control lever attached to it and the selector cable attached to the lever. It is also a neutral safety switch that will prevent the vehicle from starting in any gear except P or N. The inhibitor switch also completes the reverse light circuit when backing up.

1986–89 Excel

1. Place the manual control lever in the NEUTRAL position.

2. Loosen the two switch attaching bolts. The switch is located on the side of transmission.

3. Turn the switch body until the flat end of the manual lever is centered over the square end of the switch body flange.

4. While keeping the switch body flange and manual lever aligned torque the two attaching bolts to 7.5–8.5 ft. lbs.

1990–93 Excel, Elantra, Scoupe and Sonata

1. Disconnect the negative battery cable.

2. Place the selector lever in the **N** position. Loosen the manual control lever flange nut to free up the cable and the lever.

3. Place the manual control lever in the **N** position.

4. Turn the inhibitor switch body until the 0.47 in. (12mm) wide end of the manual control lever aligns with the switch body flange. Tighten the mounting bolts to 7–9 ft. lbs. (10–12 Nm) torque.

➡**When setting up the switch body, be careful not to drop the O-ring from the switch body. Tighten the switch body carefully.**

Transaxle

REMOVAL & INSTALLATION

1986–89 Excel

♦ See Figure 37

➡**The transaxle and converter must be removed and installed as an assembly.**

1. Remove the battery and battery tray.

2. Disconnect the throttle control cable at the carburetor and the manual control cable at the transaxle.

3. Disconnect from the transaxle: the inhibitor switch (neutral safety) connector, fluid cooler hoses and the four upper bolts connecting the engine to the transaxle.

4. Jack up the car and support on jackstands.

5. Remove the front wheels. Remove the engine splash shield.

6. Drain the transaxle fluid.

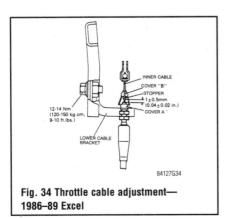

Fig. 34 Throttle cable adjustment—1986–89 Excel

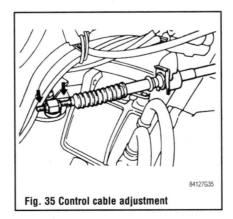

Fig. 35 Control cable adjustment

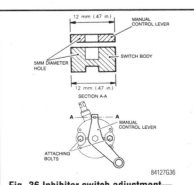

Fig. 36 Inhibitor switch adjustment—Elantra, Scoupe and Sonata

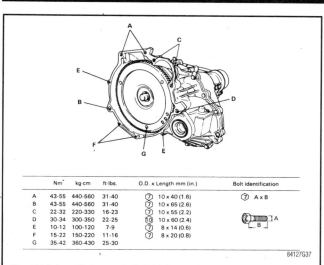

	Nm	kg·cm	ft-lbs.	O.D. x Length mm (in.)	Bolt identification
A	43-55	440-560	31-40	⑦ 10 x 40 (1.6)	⑦ A x B
B	43-55	440-560	31-40	⑦ 10 x 65 (2.6)	
C	22-32	220-330	16-23	⑦ 10 x 55 (2.2)	
D	30-34	300-350	22-25	⑩ 10 x 60 (2.4)	
E	10-12	100-120	7-9	⑦ 8 x 14 (0.6)	
F	15-22	150-220	11-16	⑦ 8 x 20 (0.8)	
G	35-42	360-430	25-30		

84127G37

Fig. 37 Automatic transaxle bolt torque and size specifications—1986–89 Excel

7. Disconnect the stabilizer bar at the lower arms, and disconnect the control arms from the body. Remove the right and left driveshafts from the transaxle case.

8. Disconnect the speedometer cable. Remove the starter motor.

9. Remove the lower cover from the converter housing. Remove the 3 bolts connecting the converter to the engine drive plate.

➡**Never support the full weight of the transaxle on the engine drive plate.**

10. Turn and force the converter back and away from the engine drive plate.

11. Support the weight of the engine from above (chain hoist). Support the transaxle and remove the remaining mounting bolts.

12. Remove the transaxle mount insulator bolt and remove the transaxle mounting bracket from the transaxle.

13. Remove (slide away from the engine to the right) and lower the transaxle and converter as an assembly.

To install:

14. Raise the transaxle and converter assembly into place and install the transaxle mounting bracket and insulator bolt. Torque the insulator bolt to 31–40 ft. lbs.

15. Tension the engine hoist and support the transaxle.

16. Install the bell housing bolts and torque them to specification. Use the illustration for bolt locations and corresponding torque values.

17. Install the 3 converter-to-drive plate bolts and torque them 25-30 ft. lbs.

18. Install the converter housing lower cover.

19. Install the starter motor.

20. Connect the speedometer cable to the transaxle.

21. Install the right and left driveshafts.

22. Connect the lower control arms to the body and stabilizer bar to control arms.

23. Install the engine splash shield and mount the front wheels.

24. Lower the car.

25. Install the 4 upper engine-to-transaxle bolts and torque to specification.

26. Connect the fluid cooler hoses and the inhibitor switch connector to the transaxle.

27. Connect the manual control cable to the control lever on the transaxle. Adjust the control cable and inhibitor switch as described in this section.

28. Connect the throttle cable to the carburetor.

29. Install the battery tray and battery.

30. Fill the transaxle to the proper level with Dexron®II automatic transmission fluid.

1990–93 Excel, Elantra and Scoupe

◆ **See Figures 38, 39, 40, 41 and 42**

1. Drain the fluid from the transaxle.

2. Remove the entire air cleaner assembly including the air intake and breather hoses. Disconnect the air flow sensor connector and the purge control solenoid valve connector and hoses. Label all the connections to avoid confusion during assembly.

3. Disconnect the cooler supply and return lines from the transaxle. Plug the line openings to prevent the entry of dirt and foreign matter.

4. Disconnect the control cable from the shift lever.

5. Disconnect the speedometer cable from the transaxle. Route the cable off to the side and out of the way.

6. Unplug the connectors to the solenoid valves, inhibitor switch, pulse generators, kickdown servo switch and oil temperature sensor.

7. Working from the top of the transaxle, remove the upper transaxle-to-engine mounting bolts.

8. Remove the transaxle mounting bracket.

9. Support the transaxle with a jack and remove the center member mounting bolts.

➡**To avoid placing excessive pressure on the oil pan, support the transaxle in a wide area.**

10. Raise the front of the vehicle and support on jackstands.

11. Remove both wheels and both axle-end cotter pins, nuts and washers.

12. Remove the ball joint nuts and separate the ball joints from the knuckles.

13. Remove the driveshaft from the transaxle.

➡**If desired, the axles may be left attached to the vehicle. Some prefer to have them out of the way. If left attached, be sure to suspend them with a strong rope or wire; if they hang free, the CV-joints or boots could get damaged.**

14. Unbolt and remove the bell housing cover.

15. Place the shifter lever in the N position. Remove the 3 special bolts attaching the torque converter to the drive plate. To remove these bolts, engage the crankshaft pulley nut with a socket and turn the crankshaft until each bolt comes into view. Remove each bolt with the proper size box end wrench by working through the bell housing cover access hole.

16. After the drive plate bolts are removed, reinstall the center member temporarily.

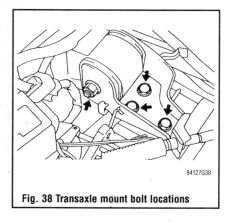

84127G38

Fig. 38 Transaxle mount bolt locations

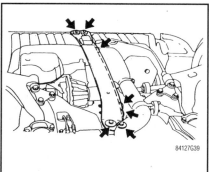

84127G39

Fig. 39 Remove the center member for transaxle removal

84127G40

Fig. 40 With the bell housing cover removed, rotate the converter to remove the converter bolts

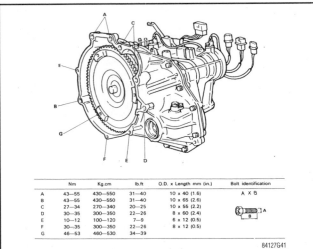

	Nm	Kg.cm	lb.ft	O.D. x Length mm (in.)	Bolt identification
A	43—55	430—550	31—40	10 x 40 (1.6)	A X B
B	43—55	430—550	31—40	10 x 65 (2.6)	
C	27—34	270—340	20—25	10 x 55 (2.2)	
D	30—35	300—350	22—26	8 x 60 (2.4)	
E	10—12	100—120	7—9	6 x 12 (0.5)	
F	30—35	300—350	22—26	8 x 12 (0.5)	
G	46—53	460—530	34—39		

84127G41

Fig. 41 Automatic transaxle bolt torque and size specifications—1990–93 Excel, Elantra and Scoupe

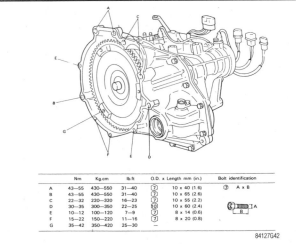

	Nm	Kg.cm	lb.ft	O.D. x Length mm (in.)	Bolt identification
A	43—55	430—550	31—40	7	10 x 40 (1.6)	7 A x B
B	43—55	430—550	31—40	7	10 x 65 (2.6)	
C	22—32	220—320	16—23	7	10 x 55 (2.2)	
D	30—35	300—350	22—25	10	10 x 60 (2.4)	
E	10—12	100—120	7—9	7	8 x 14 (0.6)	
F	15—22	150—220	11—16	7	8 x 20 (0.8)	
G	35—42	350—420	25—30		—	

84127G42

Fig. 42 Automatic transaxle bolt torque and size specifications—Sonata with KM-175 transaxle

17. Remove the lower engine-to-transaxle mounting bolts and lower the transaxle from the engine.

To install:

18. Place the transaxle on the transaxle jack securely and install onto the engine, using the dowels as guides. Make sure all heater tube clamps, wires, etc. are out of the way or it will not be possible to install the transaxle flush with the block.

19. Install the lower transaxle-to-engine bolts. Torque the bolts to specification (see illustration for bolt locations and torque values).

20. Remove the center member.

21. Install the torque converter-to-drive plate bolts and torque them to 34-39 ft. lbs.

22. Install the bell housing cover and torque the bolts to 7-9 ft. lbs.

23. Install the driveshafts.

24. Connect the ball joints to the steering knuckles.

25. Install the front axle, nuts and washers. Mount the front wheels.

26. Lower the vehicle.

27. Install the center member.

28. Install the transaxle mounting bracket and torque the bolts to 43-58 ft. lbs.

29. Install the upper transaxle mounting bolts (see illustration for bolt locations and torque values).

30. Plug in all the transaxle electrical connectors.

31. Connect the speedometer cable to the transaxle.

32. Connect the control cable to the shift lever. Adjust the control cable as described in this section.

33. Connect the cooler supply and return lines to the transaxle.

34. Install the air cleaner assembly.

35. Fill the transaxle to the proper level.

Sonata

♦ See Figure 43

1. Remove the drain plug and drain the transmission fluid.

2. Remove the entire air cleaner assembly including the air intake and breather hoses. Unplug the air flow sensor connector and the purge control solenoid valve connector and hoses.

3. Disconnect the manual control cable from the control lever.

4. Disconnect the speedometer cable from the transaxle.

5. Unplug the connectors to the solenoid valves, inhibitor switch, pulse generators, kickdown servo switch, oil temperature sensor and unplug the engine wiring harness.

6. Remove the starter motor.

7. Raise the front of the vehicle and support on jackstands.

8. Remove the left side under cover.

9. Remove the stabilizer bar.

10. Remove both wheels and both axle-end cotter pins, nuts and washers.

11. Remove the ball joint nuts and separate the ball joints from the knuckles.

12. Remove the driveshaft from the transaxle.

➡**If desired, the axles may be left attached to the vehicle. Some prefer to have them out of the way. If left attached, be sure to suspend them with a strong rope or wire; if they hang free, the CV-joints or boots could get damaged.**

13. Unbolt and remove the bell housing inspection cover.

14. Support the transaxle with a transmission jack and remove the center member from the crossmember.

15. Remove the lower cover from the converter housing. Remove the three bolts connecting the converter to the engine drive plate.

➡**Never support the full weight of the transaxle on the engine drive plate.**

16. Turn and force the converter back and away from the engine drive plate.

17. Remove and plug the oil cooler hoses.

18. Remove the plastic outer cover caps in the right fender shield. There are four of them. After removing the caps, remove the mounting bolts under them. These bolts attach the transmission mounting bracket to the body.

19. Support the engine and remove the upper engine-to-transaxle bolts. If it is necessary to remove heater hoses to gain access to the upper bolts, drain the radiator first.

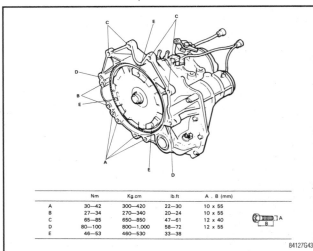

	Nm	Kg.cm	lb.ft	A . B (mm)
A	30—42	300—420	22—30	10 x 55
B	27—34	270—340	20—24	10 x 55
C	65—85	650—850	47—61	12 x 40
D	80—100	800—1,000	58—72	12 x 55
E	46—53	460—530	33—38	

84127G43

Fig. 43 Automatic transaxle bolt torque and size specifications—Sonata with KM-177 transaxle

20. Remove the remaining transaxle-to-engine bolts.

21. Slide the transaxle assembly to the right and tilt it down to remove it from the vehicle.

To install:

22. Install the torque converter to the transaxle. The converter is correctly installed when the distance from the ring gear to the bell housing surface is 12mm.

23. Place the transaxle on the transaxle jack securely and install the transaxle to the engine using the dowels as guides. Make sure all heater tube clamps, wires, etc. are out of the way or it will not be possible to install the transaxle flush with the block.

24. Install the lower transaxle-to-engine bolts. Torque the bolts to specification (see illustration for bolt locations and torque values).

25. Install the 4 transaxle-to-body mounting bolts and torque the to 43-57 ft. lbs. Install the 4 plastic caps.

26. Connect the oil cooler lines.

27. Turn and push the torque converter towards the drive plate.

28. Apply Loctite® to the threads and install the three torque converter bolts. Torque the bolts to specification (see illustration).

29. Install the torque converter inspection plate.

30. Install the transaxle center member onto the crossmember. Torque bolts to 58-71 ft. lbs.

31. Install the bell housing inspection cover and torque the retaining bolts to 7-9 ft. lbs.

32. Install the driveshafts. Make sure the shafts are completely seated in place and an circlips and snaprings are securely in place.

33. Install the ball joints to the knuckles and torque the locknuts to 43-52 ft. lbs.

34. If removed, install the axle-end washers, nuts and cotter pins. Torque the nuts to 145–188 ft. lbs.

35. Install the stabilizer bar.

36. Install the left side under cover. Lower the vehicle.

37. Install the starter motor.

38. Connect all the engine wiring harness connectors.

39. Install the speedometer cable.

40. Install the manual control cable and secure the cotter pin.

41. Install the air cleaner assembly.

42. Fill the transaxle to the proper level. Road test the vehicle.

DRIVELINE

Halfshafts

REMOVAL & INSTALLATION

Excel, Elantra and Scoupe

▶ See Figures 44, 45 and 46

1. Remove the hub center cap and loosen the driveshaft (axle) nut.
2. Loosen the wheel lug nuts.
3. Raise and support the front of the vehicle safely.
4. Remove the front wheels.
5. Remove the engine splash shield.
6. Remove the lower ball joint and strut bar from the lower control arm.

➡Place the lower arm ball joint on the lower arm to prevent damage to the ball joint dust boot.

7. Drain the transaxle fluid into a suitable waste container.

8. Insert a prybar between the transaxle case (on the raised rib) and the driveshaft inner joint case. Move the bar to the right to withdraw the left driveshaft; left, to remove the right driveshaft.

➡Do not insert the pry bar too deeply (7mm) or you will damage the oil seal.

9. Plug the transaxle case with a clean rag to prevent dirt from entering the case.

10. Use a puller/driver mounted on the wheel studs to push the driveshaft from the front hub. Take care to prevent the spacer shims from falling out of place.

To install:

11. To install, insert the driveshaft into the hub first, then install the transaxle end.

12. Install the hub nut washer. Torque the axle shaft hub nut to 144-187 ft. lbs.; the lower arm-to-ball joint nuts to 69-87 ft. lbs. on 1986–89 Excel models and 43–52 ft. lbs. on all other models; the lower arm-to-strut bar nuts to 68–87 ft. lbs. on 1986–89 Excel models and 54–65 ft. lbs. on all other models.

➡Always use a new inner joint retaining ring every time you remove the driveshaft.

Sonata with 4-cylinder Engine

1. Remove the hub center cap and loosen the driveshaft (axle) nut.
2. Loosen the wheel lug nuts.
3. Raise and support the front end on jackstands.
4. Remove the front wheels.
5. Remove the engine splash shield and drain the transaxle fluid.
6. Remove the split pin from the tie rod end and loosen the tie rod end nut but do not remove it.

7. Using special puller tool 09568-3100 or equivalent, disconnect the tie rod end from the steering knuckle. Tie the tool off to a suspension member component before using it. Remove the tie rod end nut.

8. Re-position the tool between the lower control arm and steering knuckle and disconnect the lower arm ball joint from the knuckle.

9. Insert a prybar between the transaxle case (on the raised rib) and the driveshaft inner joint case. Move the bar to the right to withdraw the left driveshaft; to the left to remove the right driveshaft.

➡Do not insert the pry bar too deeply (7mm) or you will puncture the oil seal.

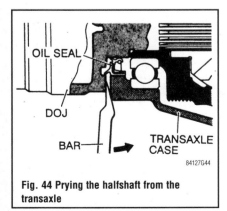

Fig. 44 Prying the halfshaft from the transaxle

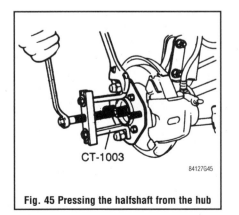

Fig. 45 Pressing the halfshaft from the hub

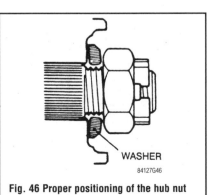

Fig. 46 Proper positioning of the hub nut washer on the Excel

10. Plug the transaxle case with a clean rag to prevent dirt from entering the case.

11. Use a puller/driver mounted on the wheel studs to push the driveshaft from the front hub. Take care to prevent the spacer shims from falling out of place.

12. To install, insert the driveshaft into the hub, first, then install the transaxle end. Install the hub nut washer as shown in the accompanying illustration. Observe the following torques:

    a. Axle shaft hub nut—145–188 ft. lbs.
    b. Lower arm ball joint-to-knuckle—42–50 ft. lbs.
    c. Tie rod end-to-knuckle—17–25 ft. lbs.

➡ **Always use a new inner joint retaining ring every time you remove the driveshaft.**

Sonata with V6 Engine

♦ **See Figures 47, 48, 49, 50 and 51**

LEFT HALFSHAFT

1. Remove the hub center cap and remove the split pin, driveshaft (axle) nut and washer. Make a mental note of how the washer is installed.
2. Loosen the wheel lug nuts.
3. Raise and support the front end on jackstands.
4. Remove the front wheels.
5. Remove the engine splash shield and drain the transaxle fluid.
6. Remove the split pin from the tie rod end and loosen the tie rod end nut but do not remove it.
7. Using special puller tool 09568-3100 or equivalent, disconnect the tie rod end from the steering knuckle. Tie the tool off to a suspension member component before using it. Remove the tie rod end nut.
8. Re-position the tool between the lower control arm and steering knuckle and disconnect the lower arm ball joint from the knuckle.
9. Using puller tool 09526-11001 or equivalent, pull the left driveshaft from the wheel hub.
10. Insert a prybar between the center bearing bracket and the driveshaft. Separate the driveshaft from the center bracket as shown.

➡ **Do not insert the pry bar any deeper than 7mm or you will puncture the oil seal and also damage the joint. When separating the driveshaft, do not allow the full weight of the vehicle to be placed on the wheel bearing. If the weight of the vehicle must be applied for any reason, support the wheel bearing with holding tool 09517-21500 or equivalent.**

11. Remove the oxygen sensor connector from the center bearing bracket. One screw holds the connector to the bracket.
12. Remove the two center bracket mounting bolts. Insert a pry bar between the center bearing bracket, inner shaft and cylinder block. Then, pull the center bracket and inner shaft assembly from the transaxle case. Plug the transaxle case with a clean rag to prevent dirt from entering the case.

To install:

➡ **Always use a new inner joint retaining ring every time you remove the driveshaft.**

13. Insert the inner shaft and bracket assembly into the transaxle case and install the center bracket mounting bolts. Torque the bolts to 26-33 ft. lbs.
14. Connect the oxygen sensor connector to the center mounting bracket with the mounting screw.
15. Insert the driveshaft into the center bearing, then into the wheel hub.
16. Connect the lower ball joint to the steering knuckle and torque the nut to 43-52 ft. lbs.
17. Connect the tie rod end to the steering knuckle and torque the tie rod end nut to 17-25 ft. lbs.
18. Install the splash shield.
19. Mount the front wheels, tighten the lug nuts, and lower the vehicle to the ground.
20. Install the axle washer and nut. Make sure the washer is installed properly. Torque the axle nut to 145-188 ft. lbs. and secure the nut with a new split pin.
21. Fill the transaxle to the proper level with the specified fluid.

RIGHT HALFSHAFT

1. Remove the hub center cap and loosen the driveshaft (axle) nut.
2. Loosen the wheel lug nuts.

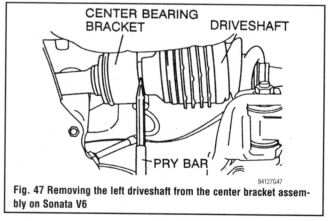

Fig. 47 Removing the left driveshaft from the center bracket assembly on Sonata V6

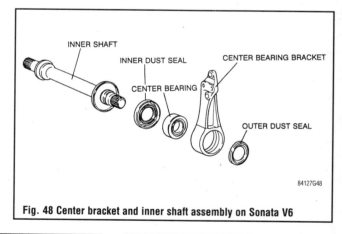

Fig. 48 Center bracket and inner shaft assembly on Sonata V6

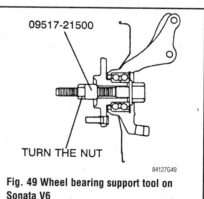

Fig. 49 Wheel bearing support tool on Sonata V6

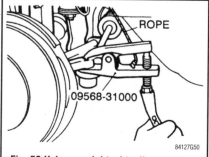

Fig. 50 Using special tool to disconnect the tie rod from the steering knuckle on Sonata. Note how the tool is tied off

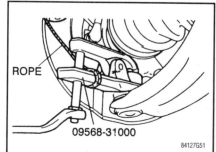

Fig. 51 Using special tool to separate the lower arm ball joint from the steering knuckle on Sonata

3. Raise and support the front end on jackstands.

4. Remove the front wheels.

5. Remove the engine splash shield and drain the transaxle fluid.

6. Remove the split pin from the tie rod end and loosen the tie rod end nut but do not remove it.

7. Using special puller tool 09568-3100 or equivalent, disconnect the tie rod end from the steering knuckle. Tie the tool off to a suspension member component before using it.

8. Remove the tie rod end nut.

9. Re-position the tool between the lower control arm and steering knuckle and disconnect the lower arm ball joint from the knuckle.

10. Insert a prybar between the transaxle case (on the raised rib) and the driveshaft inner joint case, Move the bar to the left to remove the right driveshaft.

➡ **Do not insert the pry bar any deeper than 7mm or you will puncture the oil seal.**

11. Plug the transaxle case with a clean rag to prevent dirt from entering the case.

12. Use a puller/driver mounted on the wheel studs to push the driveshaft from the front hub. Take care to prevent the spacer shims from falling out of place.

13. To install, insert the driveshaft into the hub, first, then install the transaxle end. Install the hub nut washer as shown in the accompanying illustration. Observe the following torques:

   a. Axle shaft hub nut—145–188 ft. lbs.

   b. Lower arm ball joint-to-knuckle—42–50 ft. lbs.

   c. Tie rod end-to-knuckle—17–25 ft. lbs.

➡ **Always use a new inner joint retaining ring every time you remove the driveshaft.**

CV-Joints

CV-JOINTS OVERHAUL

▶ **See Figures 52 thru 65**

These vehicles use several different types of joints. Engine size, transaxle type, whether the joint is an inboard or outboard joint, even which side of the vehicle is being serviced could make a difference in joint type. Be sure to properly identify the joint before attempting joint or boot replacement. Look for identification numbers at the large end of the boots and/or on the end of the metal retainer bands.

The 3 types of joints used are the Birfield Joint, (B.J.), the Tripod Joint (T.J.) and the Double Offset Joint (D.O.J.).

➡ **Do not disassemble a Birfield joint. Service with a new joint or clean and repack using a new boot kit.**

The distance between the large and small boot bands is important and should be checked prior to and after boot service. This is so the boot will not be installed either too loose or too tight, which could cause early wear and cracking, allowing the grease to get out and water and dirt in, leading to early joint failure.

➡ **The driveshaft joints use special grease; do not add any grease other than that supplied with the kit.**

Double Offset Joint

The Double Offset Joint (D.O.J.) is bigger than other joints and, in these applications, is normally used as an inboard joint.

1. Remove the halfshaft from the vehicle.

2. Side cutter pliers can be used to cut the metal retaining bands. Remove the boot from the joint outer race.

3. Locate and remove the large circlip at the base of the joint. Remove the outer race (the body of the joint).

4. Remove the small snapring and take off the inner race, cage and balls as an assembly. Clean the inner race, cage and balls without disassembling.

5. If the boot is to be reused, wipe the grease from the splines and wrap the splines in vinyl tape before sliding the boot from the shaft.

6. Remove the inner (D.O.J.) boot from the shaft. If the outer (B.J.) boot is to be replaced, remove the boot retainer rings and slide the boot down and off of the shaft at this time.

To install:

7. Be sure to tape the shaft splines before installing the boots. Fill the inside of the boot with the specified grease. Often the grease supplied in the replacement parts kit is meant to be divided in half, with half being used to lubricate the joint and half being used inside the boot.

8. Install the cage onto the halfshaft so the small diameter side of the cage is installed first. With a brass drift pin, tap lightly and evenly around the inner race to install the race until it comes into contact with the rib of the shaft. Apply the specified grease to the inner race and cage and fit them together. Insert the balls into the cage.

9. Install the outer race (the body of the joint) after filling with the specified grease. The outer race should be filled with this grease.

10. Tighten the boot bands securely. Make sure the distance between boot bands is correct.

11. Install the halfshaft to the vehicle.

Except Double Offset Joint

1. Disconnect the negative battery cable. Remove the halfshaft.

2. Use side cutter pliers to remove the metal retaining bands from the boot(s) that will be removed. Slide the boot from the T.J. case.

3. Remove the snapring and the tripod joint spider assembly from the half-shaft. Do not disassemble the spider and use care in handling.

4. If the boot is be reused, wrap vinyl tape around the spline part of the shaft so the boot(s) will not be damaged when removed. Remove the dynamic damper, if used, and the boots from the shaft.

To install:

5. Double check that the correct replacement parts are being installed. Wrap vinyl tape around the splines to protect the boot and install the boots and damper, if used, in the correct order.

6. Install the joint spider assembly to the shaft and install the snapring.

7. Fill the inside of the boot with the specified grease. Often the grease supplied in the replacement parts kit is meant to be divided in half, with half being used to lubricate the joint and half being used inside the boot. Keep grease off the rubber part of the dynamic damper (if used).

8. Secure the boot bands with the halfshaft in a horizontal position. Make sure distance between boot bands is correct.

9. Install the halfshaft to the vehicle and reconnect the negative battery cable.

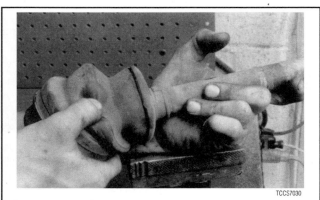

Fig. 52 Check the CV-boot for wear

TCCS7030

Fig. 53 Removing the outer band from the CV-boot

TCCS7031

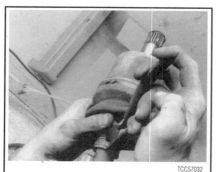

Fig. 54 Removing the inner band from the CV-boot

Fig. 55 Removing the CV-boot from the joint housing

Fig. 56 Clean the CV-joint housing prior to removing boot

Fig. 57 Removing the CV-joint housing assembly

Fig. 58 Removing the CV-joint

Fig. 59 Inspecting the CV-joint housing

Fig. 60 Removing the CV-joint outer snapring

Fig. 61 Checking the CV-joint snapring for wear

Fig. 62 CV-joint snapring (typical)

Fig. 63 Removing the CV-joint assembly

Fig. 64 Removing the CV-joint inner snapring

Fig. 65 Installing the CV-joint assembly (typical)

TORQUE SPECIFICATIONS

Component	U.S.	Metric
Automatic Transaxles:		
Bell housing cover to engine bolts	7–9 ft. lbs.	10–12 Nm
Drain plug	22–25 ft. lbs.	30–35 Nm
Fluid pan bolts	7–9 ft. lbs.	10–12 Nm
Neutral safety switch;		
Excel	7.5–8.5 ft. lbs.	9–12 Nm
Elantra	7.5–8.5 ft. lbs.	9–12 Nm
Scoupe	7.5–8.5 ft. lbs.	9–12 Nm
Sonata	20–25 ft. lbs.	27–34 Nm
Starter motor mounting bolts		
Throttle control cable bracket bolts;		
1986–89 Excel	9–10.5 ft. lbs.	12–14 Nm
Torque converter to driveplate;		
Excel	53–55 ft. lbs.	73–77 Nm
Elantra	53–55 ft. lbs.	73–77 Nm
Scoupe	53–55 ft. lbs.	73–77 Nm
Sonata	94–101 ft. lbs.	130–140 Nm
Transaxle mounting bolts;		
10mm	31–38 ft. lbs.	43–53 Nm
8mm	22–25 ft. lbs.	30–35 Nm
Transaxle mounting bracket to transaxle bolts	43–58 ft. lbs.	60–80 Nm
Clutch		
Clutch master cylinder to firewall bolts;		
Excel	6–9 ft. lbs.	8–12 Nm
Elantra	7–10 ft. lbs.	9–14 Nm
Scoupe	7–10 ft. lbs.	9–14 Nm
Sonata	9–12 ft. lbs.	13–17 Nm
Clutch release cylinder mounting bolts;		
Excel	11–16 ft. lbs.	15–22 Nm
Elantra	14–20 ft. lbs.	20–27 Nm
Scoupe	11–16 ft. lbs.	15–22 Nm
Sonata	14–20 ft. lbs.	20–27 Nm
Clutch cover bolts;		
Excel	11–16 ft. lbs.	15–22 Nm
Elantra	11–16 ft. lbs.	15–22 Nm
Scoupe	11–16 ft. lbs.	15–22 Nm
Sonata	11–16 ft. lbs.	15–22 Nm
Halfshafts		
Ball joint to knuckle;		
Excel	44–53 ft. lbs.	60–72 Nm
Elantra	44–53 ft. lbs.	60–72 Nm
Scoupe	44–53 ft. lbs.	60–72 Nm
Sonata	44–53 ft. lbs.	60–72 Nm
Driveshaft nut;		
Excel	145–188 ft. lbs.	200–260 Nm
Elantra	145–188 ft. lbs.	200–260 Nm
Scoupe	145–188 ft. lbs.	200–260 Nm
Sonata	145–188 ft. lbs.	200–260 Nm
Knuckle to strut bolts;		
Excel	65–76 ft. lbs.	90–105 Nm
Elantra	81–96 ft. lbs.	110–130 Nm
Scoupe	65–76 ft. lbs.	90–105 Nm
Sonata	65–76 ft. lbs.	90–105 Nm

84127C01

TORQUE SPECIFICATIONS

Component	U.S.	Metric
Manual Transaxles		
KM–161 and KM–162:		
Extension housing to transaxle	43–51 ft. lbs.	60–70 Nm
Shift rod set screw	24 ft. lbs.	33 Nm
Starter mounting bolts	16–23 ft. lbs.	22–32 Nm
Bell housing cover to transaxle;		
8 x 20mm	11–16 ft. lbs.	15–22 Nm
8 x 14mm	7–9 ft. lbs.	10–12 Nm
Transaxle mounting bolts;		
10mm	31–38 ft. lbs.	43–53 Nm
8mm	22–25 ft. lbs.	30–35 Nm
Front cover bolt	7–8 ft. lbs.	10–11 Nm
Oil filler plug	22–25 ft. lbs.	30–34 Nm
Oil drain plug	22–25 ft. lbs.	30–34 Nm
Housing to case tightening bolt	22–30 ft. lbs.	30–41 Nm
Front retainer bolt	11–15 ft. lbs.	15–21 Nm
Input shaft locking nut	65–79 ft. lbs.	89–107 Nm
Differential drive gear bolt	94–101 ft. lbs.	128–137 Nm
Speedometer sleeve plate bolt	2.5–3.5 ft. lbs.	3.0–4.5 Nm
Poppet plug bolt	20–24 ft. lbs.	27–33 Nm
Back-up lamp switch	22–25 ft. lbs.	30–35 Nm
KM–200 and KM–201:		
Shift cable and select cable to body bolts	9–11 ft. lbs.	12–15 Nm
Shift lever to body	9–11 ft. lbs.	12–15 Nm
Shift lever to lever A	13–20 ft. lbs.	19–28 Nm
Lever A to bracket assembly	13–20 ft. lbs.	19–28 Nm
Shift cable and select cable to transaxle		
Starter mounting bolts	11–16 ft. lbs.	15–22 Nm
Transaxle mount bracket to transaxle	20–25 ft. lbs.	27–34 Nm
Bell housing cover to transaxle	43–58 ft. lbs.	60–80 Nm
Transaxle mounting bolts	6–7 ft. lbs.	8–10 Nm
Rear cover bolt	11–15 ft. lbs.	15–22 Nm
Back-up light switch	22–25 ft. lbs.	30–35 Nm
Poppet spring plug	22–30 ft. lbs.	30–42 Nm
Speedometer sleeve bolt	2–4 ft. lbs.	3–5 Nm
Input shaft locknut	102–115 ft. lbs.	140–160 Nm
Intermediate gear locknut	102–115 ft. lbs.	140–160 Nm
Reverse idler gear shaft bolt	32–39 ft. lbs.	43–55 Nm
Transaxle case tightening bolt	26–30 ft. lbs.	35–42 Nm
Stopper bracket bolt	11–15 ft. lbs.	15–22 Nm
Restrict ball assembly	22–25 ft. lbs.	30–35 Nm
Reverse shift lever attaching bolt	11–15 ft. lbs.	15–22 Nm
Bearing retainer bolt	11–15 ft. lbs.	15–22 Nm
Differential drive gear bolt	94–101 ft. lbs.	130–140 Nm
Interlock plate bolt	15–19 ft. lbs.	20–27 Nm
Reverse brake cone mounting bolts	3–4 ft. lbs.	4–5.5 Nm

84127C02

TORQUE SPECIFICATIONS

Component	U.S.	Metric
KM–210 and ALPHA–M/T:		
Shift cable and select cable to body bolts	9–11 ft. lbs.	12–15 Nm
Shift lever to body	9–11 ft. lbs.	12–15 Nm
Shift lever to lever A	13–20 ft. lbs.	19–28 Nm
Lever A to bracket assembly	13–20 ft. lbs.	19–28 Nm
Shift cable and select cable to transaxle	11–16 ft. lbs.	15–22 Nm
Starter mounting bolts	20–25 ft. lbs.	27–34 Nm
Transaxle mount bracket to transaxle	43–58 ft. lbs.	60–80 Nm
Bell housing cover to transaxle	6–7 ft. lbs.	8–1 0 Nm
Transaxle mounting bolts	32–39 ft. lbs.	43–55 Nm
Rear cover bolt	6–8 ft. lbs.	8–11 Nm
Back-up light switch	22–25 ft. lbs.	30–35 Nm
Poppet spring plug	18–22 ft. lbs.	25–30 Nm
Speedometer sleeve bolt	2–4 ft. lbs.	3–5 Nm
Input shaft locknut	102–115 ft. lbs.	140–160 Nm
Intermediate gear locknut	102–115 ft. lbs.	140–160 Nm
Output gear locknut ALPHA–M/T	102–115 ft. lbs.	140–160 Nm
Reverse idler gear shaft bolt	32–39 ft. lbs.	43–55 Nm
Transaxle case tightening bolt	26–30 ft. lbs.	35–42 Nm
Stopper bracket bolt	11–15 ft. lbs.	15–22 Nm
Restrict ball assembly	22–25 ft. lbs.	30–35 Nm
Reverse shift lever attaching bolt	11–15 ft. lbs.	15–22 Nm
Bearing retainer bolt	11–15 ft. lbs.	15–22 Nm
Differential drive gear bolt	94–101 ft. lbs.	130–140 Nm
Interlock plate bolt	15–19 ft. lbs.	20–27 Nm

84127C03

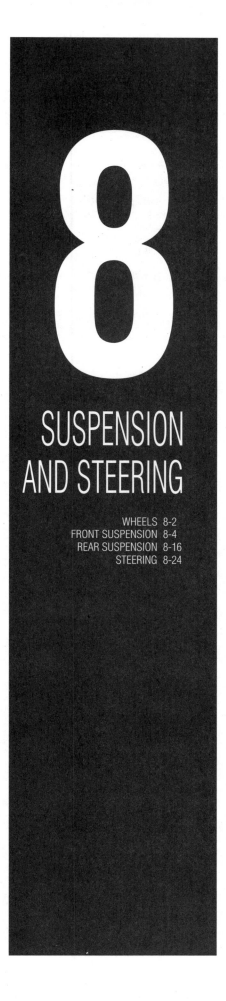

8

SUSPENSION AND STEERING

WHEELS

Wheel Assembly

REMOVAL & INSTALLATION

▶ **See Figures 1, 2 and 3**

1. Park the vehicle on a level surface.
2. Remove the jack, tire iron and, if necessary, the spare tire from their storage compartments.
3. Check the owner's manual or refer to Section 1 of this manual for the jacking points on your vehicle. Then, place the jack in the proper position.
4. If equipped with lug nut trim caps, remove them by either unscrewing or pulling them off the lug nuts, as appropriate. Consult the owner's manual, if necessary.
5. If equipped with a wheel cover or hub cap, insert the tapered end of the tire iron in the groove and pry off the cover.
6. Apply the parking brake and block the diagonally opposite wheel with a wheel chock or two.

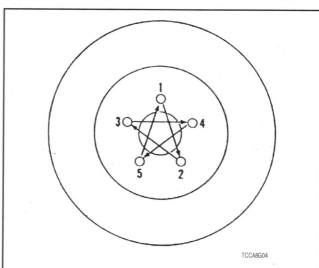

Fig. 3 Typical wheel lug tightening sequence

➡**Wheel chocks may be purchased at your local auto parts store, or a block of wood cut into wedges may be used. If possible, keep one or two of the chocks in your tire storage compartment, in case any of the tires has to be removed on the side of the road.**

7. If equipped with an automatic transmission/transaxle, place the selector lever in **P** or Park; with a manual transmission/transaxle, place the shifter in Reverse.
8. With the tires still on the ground, use the tire iron/wrench to break the lug nuts loose.

➡**If a nut is stuck, never use heat to loosen it or damage to the wheel and bearings may occur. If the nuts are seized, one or two heavy hammer blows directly on the end of the bolt usually loosens the rust. Be careful, as continued pounding will likely damage the brake drum or rotor.**

9. Using the jack, raise the vehicle until the tire is clear of the ground. Support the vehicle safely using jackstands.
10. Remove the lug nuts, then remove the tire and wheel assembly.

To install:

11. Make sure the wheel and hub mating surfaces, as well as the wheel lug studs, are clean and free of all foreign material. Always remove rust from the wheel mounting surface and the brake rotor or drum. Failure to do so may cause the lug nuts to loosen in service.
12. Install the tire and wheel assembly and hand-tighten the lug nuts.
13. Using the tire wrench, tighten all the lug nuts, in a crisscross pattern, until they are snug.
14. Raise the vehicle and withdraw the jackstand, then lower the vehicle.
15. Using a torque wrench, tighten the lug nuts in a crisscross pattern to 65–80 ft. lbs. (90–110 Nm). Check your owner's manual or refer to Section 1 of this manual for the proper tightening sequence.

✳✳ WARNING

Do not overtighten the lug nuts, as this may cause the wheel studs to stretch or the brake disc (rotor) to warp.

16. If so equipped, install the wheel cover or hub cap. Make sure the valve stem protrudes through the proper opening before tapping the wheel cover into position.
17. If equipped, install the lug nut trim caps by pushing them or screwing them on, as applicable.
18. Remove the jack from under the vehicle, and place the jack and tire iron/wrench in their storage compartments. Remove the wheel chock(s).
19. If you have removed a flat or damaged tire, place it in the storage com-

Fig. 1 Place the jack at the proper lifting point on your vehicle

Fig. 2 Before jacking the vehicle, block the diagonally opposite wheel with one or, preferably, two chocks

partment of the vehicle and take it to your local repair station to have it fixed or replaced as soon as possible.

INSPECTION

Inspect the tires for lacerations, puncture marks, nails and other sharp objects. Repair or replace as necessary. Also check the tires for treadwear and air pressure as outlined in Section 1 of this manual.

Check the wheel assemblies for dents, cracks, rust and metal fatigue. Repair or replace as necessary.

Wheel Lug Studs

REMOVAL & INSTALLATION

With Disc Brakes

▶ **See Figure 4**

1. Raise and support the appropriate end of the vehicle safely using jackstands, then remove the wheel.
2. Remove the brake pads and caliper. Support the caliper aside using wire or a coat hanger. For details, please refer to Section 9 of this manual.
3. Remove the outer wheel bearing and lift off the rotor. For details on wheel bearing removal, installation and adjustment, please refer to Section 1 of this manual.
4. Properly support the rotor using press bars, then drive the stud out using an arbor press.

➡**If a press is not available, CAREFULLY drive the old stud out using a blunt drift. MAKE SURE the rotor is properly and evenly supported or it may be damaged.**

To install:
5. Clean the stud hole with a wire brush and start the new stud with a hammer and drift pin. Do not use any lubricant or thread sealer.
6. Finish installing the stud with the press.

➡**If a press is not available, start the lug stud through the bore in the hub, then position about 4 flat washers over the stud and thread the lug nut. Hold the hub/rotor while tightening the lug nut, and the stud should be drawn into position. MAKE SURE THE STUD IS FULLY SEATED, then remove the lug nut and washers.**

7. Install the rotor and adjust the wheel bearings.
8. Install the brake caliper and pads.
9. Install the wheel, then remove the jackstands and carefully lower the vehicle.
10. Tighten the lug nuts to the proper torque.

With Drum Brakes

▶ **See Figures 5 and 6**

1. Raise the vehicle and safely support it with jackstands, then remove the wheel.
2. Remove the brake drum.
3. If necessary to provide clearance, remove the brake shoes, as outlined in Section 9 of this manual.
4. Using a large C-clamp and socket, press the stud from the axle flange.
5. Coat the serrated part of the stud with liquid soap and place it into the hole.

To install:
6. Position about 4 flat washers over the stud and thread the lug nut. Hold the flange while tightening the lug nut, and the stud should be drawn into position. MAKE SURE THE STUD IS FULLY SEATED, then remove the lug nut and washers.
7. If applicable, install the brake shoes.
8. Install the brake drum.
9. Install the wheel, then remove the jackstands and carefully lower the vehicle.
10. Tighten the lug nuts to the proper torque.

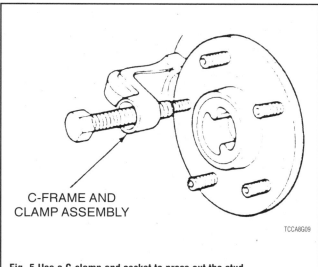

Fig. 5 Use a C-clamp and socket to press out the stud

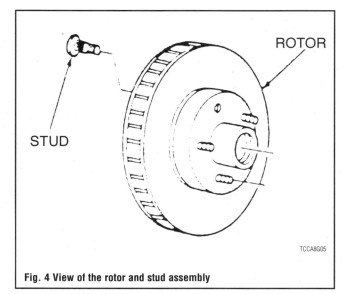

Fig. 4 View of the rotor and stud assembly

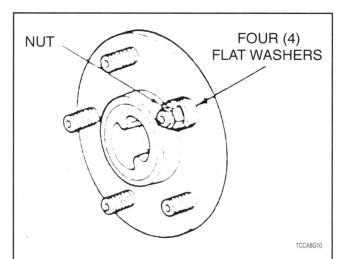

Fig. 6 Force the stud onto the axle flange using washers and a lug nut

FRONT SUSPENSION

SONATA FRONT SUSPENSION AND STEERING COMPONENTS

1. Lower ball joint
2. Outer tie rod end
3. Sway bar
4. Rack and pinion
5. Lower control arm
6. Strut assembly
7. Hub and steering knuckle

The front suspension consists of MacPherson struts, and lower control arms. The strut assembly performs several suspension functions: it provides the steering knuckle mounting, the concentric coil acts the springing medium, the integral shock absorber provides dampening and the strut assembly locates the wheel. The stabilizer bar minimizes body roll when cornering. The lower control arm acts to longitudinally locate the suspension/wheel.

MacPherson Struts

REMOVAL & INSTALLATION

▶ See Figures 7 thru 12

1. Raise and support the front end on jackstands.
2. Remove the front wheels.
3. Detach the brake hose from the clip on the strut.
4. Unbolt the strut from the knuckle.
5. Remove the four strut-to-fender apron nuts.
6. Pull the strut away from the steering knuckle and wheelhouse and out from the car.

➡On Sonata, after the strut is separated from the knuckle, raise the lower control arm with a jack and attach the brake hose, brake line, front speed sensor harness and drive shaft to the steering knuckle with a piece of rope or wire to prevent them from being removed with the strut.

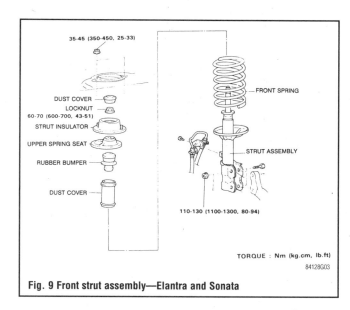

Fig. 9 Front strut assembly—Elantra and Sonata

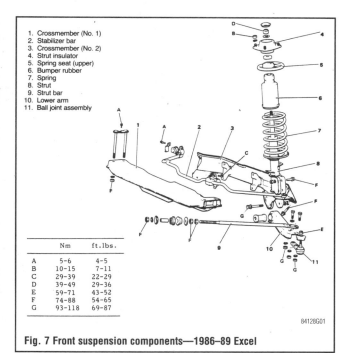

1. Crossmember (No. 1)
2. Stabilizer bar
3. Crossmember (No. 2)
4. Strut insulator
5. Spring seat (upper)
6. Bumper rubber
7. Spring
8. Strut
9. Strut bar
10. Lower arm
11. Ball joint assembly

	Nm	ft.lbs.
A	5-6	4-5
B	10-15	7-11
C	29-39	22-29
D	39-49	29-36
E	59-71	43-52
F	74-88	54-65
G	93-118	69-87

Fig. 7 Front suspension components—1986–89 Excel

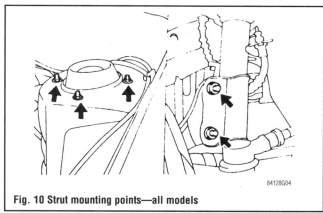

Fig. 10 Strut mounting points—all models

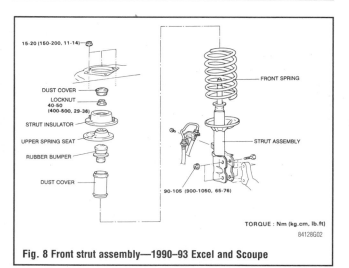

Fig. 8 Front strut assembly—1990–93 Excel and Scoupe

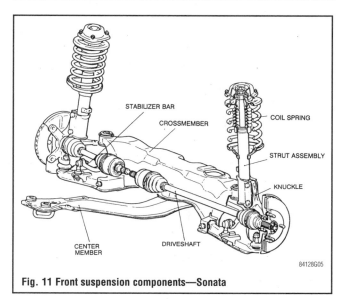

Fig. 11 Front suspension components—Sonata

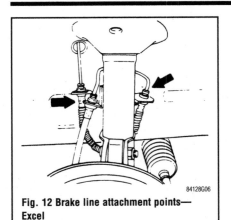

Fig. 12 Brake line attachment points—Excel

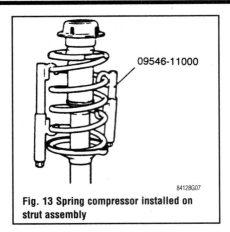

Fig. 13 Spring compressor installed on strut assembly

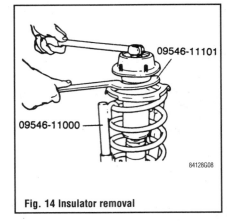

Fig. 14 Insulator removal

To install:

7. Before installing the strut, make sure the surface where the strut attaches to the knuckle is clean. This ensures a good connection.

8. Position the strut onto the knuckle and inside fender apron and install the upper and lower attaching hardware.

9. Observe the following torques:
- Strut-to-knuckle bolts—80–94 ft. lbs. (110–130 Nm) for Elantra.
- Strut-to-knuckle bolts—54–65 ft. lbs. (74–88 Nm) for 1986–89 Excel.
- Strut-to-knuckle bolts—65–76 ft. lbs. (95–105 Nm) for 1990–93 Excel.
- Strut-to-knuckle bolts—65–76 ft. lbs. (95–105 Nm) for Sonata.
- Strut-to-knuckle bolts—65–76 ft. lbs. (95–105 Nm) for Scoupe.
- Strut-to-fender well nuts—25–33 ft. lbs. (35–45 Nm) for Elantra.
- Strut-to-fender well nuts—7–11 ft. lbs. (10–15 Nm) for 1986–89 Excel.
- Strut-to-fender well nuts—11–14 ft. lbs. (15–20 Nm) for 1990–93 Excel.
- Strut-to-fender well nuts—18–25 ft. lbs. (25–34 Nm) for Sonata.
- Strut-to-fender well nuts—11–14 ft. lbs. (15–19 Nm) for Scoupe.

10. Install the tire and wheel and lower the vehicle.

STRUT OVERHAUL

➡**Hyundai does not recommend strut overhaul for late model vehicles. Instead the unit, if determined faulty, should be replaced as an assembly.**

1986–89 Excel

▶ **See Figures 13, 14, 15, 16 and 17**

1. Remove the strut from the car and clamp in a protected jaw vise.
2. Gently pry the dust cover from the strut insulator with a flat-blade screwdriver.

➡**Matchmark the upper end of the coil spring and bearing plate to avoid confusion during reassembly.**

3. Using a spring compressor, fully compress the spring.
4. Using the special tools shown, remove the self-locking gland nut.
5. Remove the rubber insulator, support, spring seat rubber bumper and the spring.
6. Using a brass drift, remove the bearing from the support.
7. Keep the upper mounting parts in order of their removal again to avoid confusion during reassembly.
8. Clean the outside of the strut body, especially around the top. Use the proper size wrench or a pipe wrench to loosen the top strut body nut.
9. Remove the body nut and discard if a new body nut came with the replacement cartridge. If not, save the nut.
10. Use a suitable tool and remove the O-ring from the top of the housing.
11. Grasp the piston rod and slowly pull the cartridge out of the housing. Remove the cartridge slowly to prevent the oil between the housing and the cartridge from splashing.
12. Pour all of the strut oil into a suitable container, clean the inside of the housing and inspect the cylinder for dents and to insure that all loose parts have been removed from the inside of the strut body.
13. Refill the strut cylinder with one ounce of the original or fresh oil. The oil helps dissipate internal heat during operation and results in a cooler running, longer lasting unit. Do not put too much oil in, otherwise the oil may leak at the body nut after expansion when heated.
14. Insert the replacement cartridge into the strut body. Push the piston rod all of the way down to avoid damage if the wrench slips when install the top nut. Install top body nut, take care not to cross-thread. Tighten the body nut to 100 ft. lbs.
15. Install the coil spring and top end parts, pay attention to the indexing marks you made when disassembling the strut. Make sure that both spring ends align with the groove in the spring seats. Tighten the gland nut to 29-36 ft. lbs.
16. Install the strut on the car.

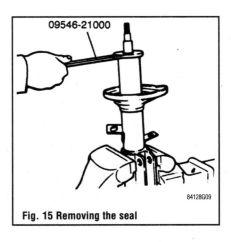

Fig. 15 Removing the seal

Fig. 16 Removing the O-ring

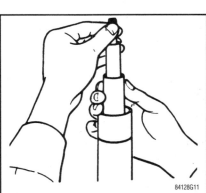

Fig. 17 Pulling the strut cartridge from the housing

Ball Joints

INSPECTION

▶ See Figure 18

Raise the vehicle and support it safely. Disconnect the ball joint at the lower end of the strut. Install the nut back onto the ball stud. Then, with an inch lbs. torque wrench, measure the torque required to start the ball joint rotating. The figures are 1.4–7.0 ft. lbs. (2.0–9.5 Nm). If the figures are within specification, the ball joint is satisfactory. If the figure is too high, the joint should be replaced. If the figure is too low, reuse the joint, provided its rotation is smooth and even. If there is roughness or play, it must be replaced. Inspect the dust cover for cracks and check all bolts for straightness and replace any damaged components.

REMOVAL & INSTALLATION

▶ See Figure 19

Excel and Scoupe

1. Raise the vehicle and support it safely.
2. Unbolt the ball joint from the control arm.
3. Remove the stud retaining nut.
4. Use a ball joint removing tool and separate the ball joint from the steering knuckle.
5. Replace the ball joint and tighten the ball joint to control arm nut to 69–87 ft. lbs. (99–118 Nm). Torque the ball joint stud nut 43–52 ft. lbs. (59–71 Nm).

Elantra

1. Raise the vehicle and support it safely.
2. Unbolt the ball joint from the control arm and using the special tool 09568-31000 or equivalent, disconnect the lower arm ball joint from the control arm.
3. Remove the stabilizer bar link self-locking nut and detach the stabilizer bar from the lower control arm.
4. Remove the ball joint mounting bolts and remove the joint from the arm.
5. Remove the dust cover from the ball joint.
   #### To install:
6. Park the specified grease in the new dust cover and press the cover to the ball joint using cup driver tool 09545-21100 or equivalent.
7. Install the joint to the lower arm. Tighten the ball joint mounting bolts.
8. Connect the ball joint to the steering knuckle and tighten the nut to 52 ft. lbs. (72 Nm).
9. Connect the stabilizer bar to the lower control arm and tighten the bar link self-locking nut to 40 ft. lbs. (55 Nm).
10. Install the tire and wheel assembly to the vehicle.

Sonata

▶ See Figure 20

1. Raise the vehicle and support it safely. Remove the tire and wheel assemblies.
2. Remove the lower control arm from the vehicle.
3. Remove the ball joint dust cover. Using a special tool, press the ball joint from the control arm.
   #### To install:
4. Apply grease to the lip of the control arm and to the ball joint contact surfaces.
5. Place the ball joint in the control arm. Using a special tool, press the ball joint into the control arm. The ball joint must be pressed evenly into the control arm.
6. Install a new dust cover on the ball joint. Install the control arm assembly into the vehicle. Torque the ball joint-to-steering knuckle retaining nut to 52 ft. lbs. (71 Nm).
7. Install the wheel and tire assembly. Lower the vehicle.

Stabilizer Bar

REMOVAL & INSTALLATION

Excel

▶ See Figures 21, 22 and 23

1. Raise the vehicle and support it safely.
2. Unbolt the stabilizer clamps from the crossmember.
3. Unbolt the stabilizer bar from the strut bar.
4. Examine the bushings for cracks and wear, if one is worn or cracked all the bushings must be replaced.
   #### To install:
5. Installation is the reverse order of the removal procedures. Reposition the stabilizer bar and tighten the chassis clamp bolts to 29 ft. lbs. (39 Nm); the strut bar clamps to 50 inch lbs. (6–7 Nm).

Elantra

▶ See Figure 24

1. Raise the vehicle and support it safely.
2. Disconnect and separate the tie rod end and the ball joint from the lower control arm and the steering knuckle.
3. Remove the stabilizer link self locking nut using a 14mm spanner wrench.
4. Remove the stabilizer bar through the access opening. Detach the upper and the lower fixtures; then remove the bushings.
   #### To install:
5. Install the bushings onto the bar. Align the upper and the lower fixtures with the bushings making sure the projections are securely in the space between the fixtures.

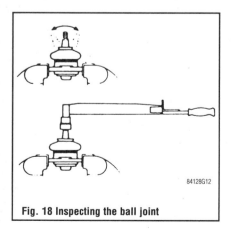

Fig. 18 Inspecting the ball joint

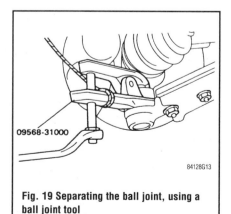

Fig. 19 Separating the ball joint, using a ball joint tool

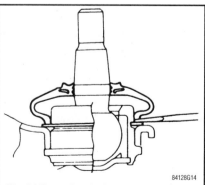

Fig. 20 Removing the ball joint snapring— Sonata

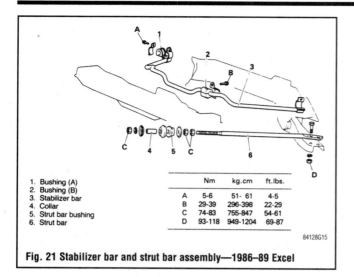

	Nm	kg.cm	ft.lbs.
A	5-6	51- 61	4-5
B	29-39	296-398	22-29
C	74-83	755-847	54-61
D	93-118	949-1204	69-87

1. Bushing (A)
2. Bushing (B)
3. Stabilizer bar
4. Collar
5. Strut bar bushing
6. Strut bar

84128G15

Fig. 21 Stabilizer bar and strut bar assembly—1986–89 Excel

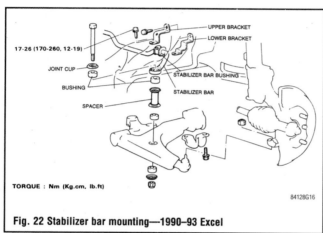

TORQUE : Nm (Kg.cm, lb.ft)

84128G16

Fig. 22 Stabilizer bar mounting—1990–93 Excel

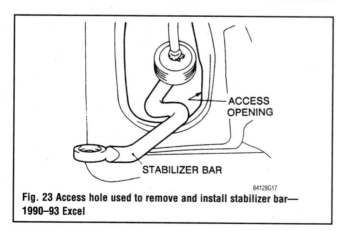

84128G17

Fig. 23 Access hole used to remove and install stabilizer bar—1990–93 Excel

➥**Distinguish the side the fixtures are to be installed by locating the identification marks stamped on each; R will denote the right side and L will denote the left side fixture. They are not the same and should be installed as labeled.**

6. Using the access opening, install the rod to the vehicle. Temporarily tighten the bushing fixtures.

7. Tighten the stabilizer bar link with a spanner wrench and install the self-locking nut tighten to 51 ft. lbs. (70 Nm).

8. Connect the tie rod end and the ball joint to the steering knuckle and control arm tightening the ball joint stud nut to 52 ft. lbs. (72 Nm).

9. Install the tire and wheel assembly and lower the vehicle.

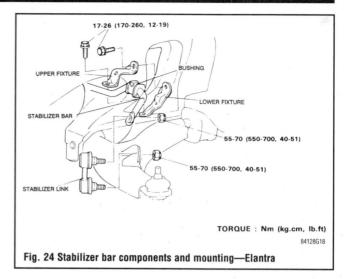

TORQUE : Nm (kg.cm, lb.ft)

84128G18

Fig. 24 Stabilizer bar components and mounting—Elantra

Sonata

▶ **See Figures 25 and 26**

1. Raise the vehicle and support it safely.
2. Remove the stabilizer bar brackets from the crossmember.
3. Lower the rear of the center member and lower the stabilizer bar.
4. Disconnect the end links and remove the stabilizer.
5. Installation is the reverse order of the removal procedures. Torque the end link nuts to 45 ft. lbs. (61 Nm); the bracket bolts to 30 ft. lbs. (41 Nm).

Scoupe

▶ **See Figure 27**

1. Raise and safely support the vehicle.
2. Remove the tire and wheel assembly.
3. Disconnect the tie rod end ball joint from the knuckle using special tool 09568–31000 or equivalent.
4. Remove the rear roll stopper mounting bolt and rear roll bracket assembly mounting bolt.
5. Pull the rear roll bracket assembly forward.
6. Loosen the stabilizer link bolt and nut, then separate the stabilizer bar from the lower arm.
7. Loosen the stabilizer bar mounting bolts through the steering gear box access opening provided on the vehicle body.
8. Remove the stabilizer through the access opening.
9. Detach the upper and lower bracket, then remove the bushing.

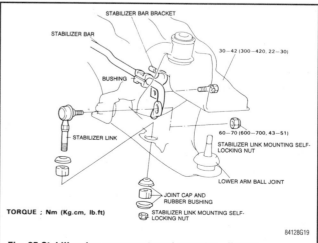

TORQUE ; Nm (Kg.cm, lb.ft)

84128G19

Fig. 25 Stabilizer bar components and mounting—Sonata

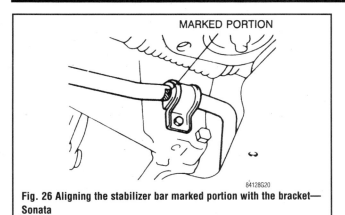

Fig. 26 Aligning the stabilizer bar marked portion with the bracket—Sonata

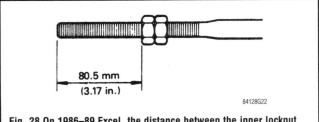

Fig. 27 Stabilizer bar components and mounting—Scoupe

10. Install the stabilizer bar by reversing the removal procedure, observing the following torque values:
- Stabilizer bar bracket bolts—12–19 ft. lbs. (15–26 Nm).
- Ball joint-to-knuckle—43–52 ft. lbs. (58–70 Nm).

Strut Bar

REMOVAL & INSTALLATION

1986–89 Excel Only

▶ See Figure 28

1. Raise and support the front end on jackstands.
2. Unbolt the stabilizer bar from the strut bar.
3. Remove the bolts securing the strut bar to the control arm.
4. Remove the strut bar-to-frame bracket outer nut and pull the bar from the bracket.

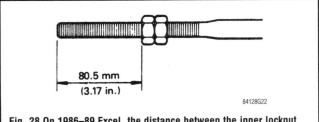

Fig. 28 On 1986–89 Excel, the distance between the inner locknut and the end of the bar should be as shown

5. Inspect all parts and replace any cracked, dry or deformed parts. The strut bar bend must not exceed 3mm over its entire length.

To install:

6. Install the strut bar into the strut bar bracket and install the bracket nut. Note that the left side bar is identified with a dab of white paint. When installing the strut bar at the strut bar bracket, the distance between the inner locknut and the end of the strut bar must be 80.5mm. Torque the strut bar-to-bracket nut to 60 ft. lbs. (81 Nm).

7. Install the strut bar-to-control arm bolts and torque them to 87 ft. lbs. (118 Nm).

8. Install the stabilizer bar-to-strut bar bolts and torque them to 50 inch lbs. (6–7 Nm).

Lower Control Arm

REMOVAL & INSTALLATION

1986–89 Excel

▶ See Figure 29

1. Raise the vehicle and support it safely. Remove the front wheel and tire assembly.
2. Remove the undercover.
3. Disconnect the stabilizer bar from the lower arm. Remove the nut from under the control arm and take off the washer and spacer.
4. Remove the ball joint stud nut and press the tool off with tool MB991113 or equivalent.
5. Remove the bolts which retain the spacer at the rear and the nut and washers on the front of the lower arm shaft (at the front). Slide the arm forward, off the shaft and out of the bushing.
6. Replace the dust cover on the ball joint. The new cover must be greased on the lip and inside with 2 EP multi-purpose grease or equivalent, and pressed on, with special tool MB990800 or equivalent, until it is fully seated.

To install:

7. When installing the control arm, the nut on the stabilizer bar bolt must be torqued until the link shows 0.8–0.9 in. (21–23mm) of threads below the bottom of the nut.
8. The washer for the lower arm must be installed as shown. The left side arm shaft has a left hand thread.
9. Torque the all fasteners with the vehicle on the ground. Observe the following torques:

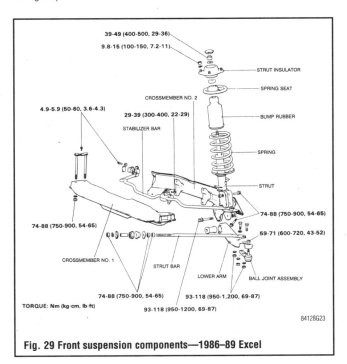

Fig. 29 Front suspension components—1986–89 Excel

- Knuckle-to-strut—54–65 ft. lbs. (75–88 Nm)
- Lower arm shaft-to-body—69–87 ft. lbs. (94–120 Nm)
- Stabilizer bar-to-body—22–29 ft. lbs. (29–38 Nm)
- Stabilizer bar-to-strut bar—48–60 inch lbs. (5–7 Nm)
- Ball joint-to-knuckle—44–53 ft. lbs. (60–73 Nm)
- Lower arm-to-strut bar—70–88 ft. lbs. (95–120 Nm)
- Strut bar-to-body—55–60 ft. lbs. (75–81 Nm)
- Strut bar inner locknut—55–60 ft. lbs. (75–81 Nm)

1990–93 Excel, Elantra and Scoupe

♦ See Figures 30, 31 and 32

1. Raise the front of the vehicle and support the frame on jackstands.
2. Remove the front wheels.
3. Using the proper tool, disconnect the lower arm ball joint from the lower control arm.
4. Remove the stabilizer bar locknut and bolt and disconnect the stabilizer bar from the lower control arm.
5. Remove the lower control arm mounting bracket.
6. Unbolt and remove the lower control arm from the frame.
7. Check all parts for wear and damage and replace any suspect part.

To install:

8. On Excel, install the lower control arm onto the frame and torque the mounting bolts to 116–137 ft. lbs. (160–190 Nm). On Elantra, tighten the through bolt to 69–87 ft. lbs. (95–120 Nm).
9. Install the lower control arm mounting bracket and torque the bolts to 43–58 ft. lbs. (60–80 Nm).
10. Connect the stabilizer link to the lower control arm making sure that the stabilizer bar mounting spacer, bushing and cup are aligned properly. Now the

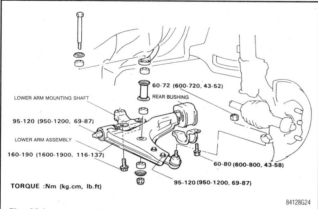

Fig. 30 Lower control arm assembly and mounting—1990–93 Excel and Scoupe

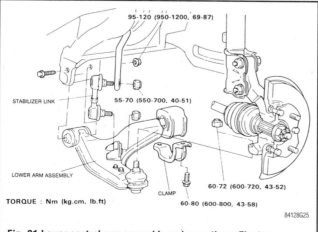

Fig. 31 Lower control arm assembly and mounting—Elantra

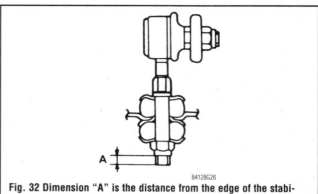

Fig. 32 Dimension "A" is the distance from the edge of the stabilizer link nut to the top of the stud

link must be fitted to the lower arm. To fit the link, tighten the link bolt lock nut until dimension "A" is within 22–26mm. Dimension "A" is the distance from the edge of the stabilizer link nut to the top of the stud.

11. Connect the tie rod end ball joint to the steering knuckle and torque the nut to 43–52 ft. lbs. (60–72 Nm).
12. Mount the front wheels and lower the vehicle.

Sonata

♦ See Figure 33

1. Raise the front end and support on jack stands.
2. Remove the front wheels.
3. Loosen the lower arm ball joint nut, but do not remove it at this time.
4. Using the special tool, disconnect the ball joint from the steering knuckle. Tie the tool off to a chassis member during use.
5. Disconnect the stabilizer link ball joint from the stabilizer bar.
6. Remove the lower arm shaft bolts and rod bushing clamp fasteners and remove the lower control arm.
7. Inspect all parts and replace any cracked, dry or deformed parts.

To install:

8. Bolt the lower control arm in place and snug all the fasteners. Final fastener torque will be applied with the full weight of the vehicle on the ground.
9. Connect the stabilizer bar to the stabilizer links. Engage the stabilizer link with a 5/8 in. open end wrench and install the self-locking nut. Torque the nut to 43–51 ft. lbs. (58–69 Nm). After tightening the nut, measure the distance

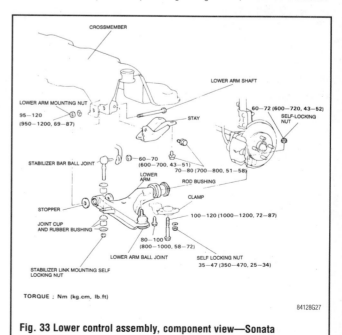

Fig. 33 Lower control assembly, component view—Sonata

from the edge of the stabilizer link self-locking nut to the top of the stabilizer link stud. If the distance is not 5–8mm, tighten the nut until the specified distance is obtained.

10. Reverse the special tool and press the ball joint into the steering knuckle. Install the ball joint attaching nut and snug it.

11. Mount the front wheels and lower the vehicle.

12. Tighten the fasteners with the vehicle on the ground. Observe the following torques:
- Lower arm shaft-to-body: 69–87 ft. lbs. (95–110 Nm)
- Ball joint-to-knuckle: 43–52 ft. lbs. (60–72 Nm)
- Rod bushing clamp nuts: 25–34 ft. lbs. (35–47 Nm)
- Rod bushing clamp center bolt: 72–87 ft. lbs. (100–118 Nm)
- Rod bushing clamp outside bolts: 58–72 ft. lbs. (80–100 Nm)

Front Wheel Hub, Knuckle and Bearings

REMOVAL & INSTALLATION

➡Sodium based grease is not compatible with lithium based grease. Read the package labels and be careful not to mix the two types. If there is any doubt as to the type of grease used, completely clean the old grease from the bearing and hub before replacing.

Before handling the bearings, there are a few things that you should remember to do and not to do.

Remember to DO the following:
- Remove all outside dirt from the housing before exposing the bearing.
- Treat a used bearing as gently as you would a new one.
- Work with clean tools in clean surroundings.
- Use clean, dry canvas gloves, or at least clean, dry hands.
- Clean solvents and flushing fluids are a must.
- Use clean paper when laying out the bearings to dry.
- Protect disassembled bearings from rust and dirt. Cover them up.
- Use clean rags to wipe bearings.

- Keep the bearings in oil-proof paper when they are to be stored or are not in use.
- Clean the inside of the housing before replacing the bearing.

Do NOT do the following:
- Don't work in dirty surroundings.
- Don't use dirty, chipped or damaged tools.
- Try not to work on wooden work benches or use wooden mallets.
- Don't handle bearings with dirty or moist hands.
- Do not use gasoline for cleaning. Use a safe solvent.
- Do not spin dry bearings with compressed air. It makes a nifty sound, but compressed air will damage the bearing.
- Do not spin dirty bearings.
- Avoid using cotton waste or dirty cloths to wipe bearings.
- Try not to scratch or nick bearing surfaces.
- Do not allow the bearing to come in contact with dirt or rust at any time.

Excel, Elantra and Scoupe

▶ See Figures 34 thru 47

➡The following procedure requires the use of several special tools.

1. Remove wheel ornaments then, remove the axle shaft nut.

2. Raise and support the car with jackstands positioned so that the front wheels hang freely.

3. Remove the front wheels.

4. Remove the caliper and suspend it out of the way without disconnecting the brake hose.

5. Disconnect the lower ball joint from the knuckle.

6. Disconnect the tie rod end from the knuckle using the proper tool.

7. Using a two-jawed puller, press the axle shaft from the hub.

8. Unbolt the strut from the knuckle. Remove the hub and knuckle assembly from the car.

9. Install first the arm, then the body of special tool 09517-21600 on the knuckle and tighten the nut.

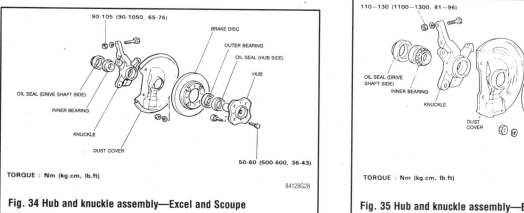

Fig. 34 Hub and knuckle assembly—Excel and Scoupe

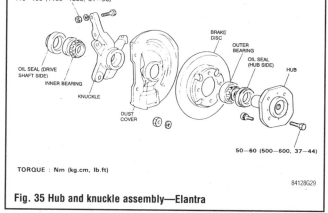

Fig. 35 Hub and knuckle assembly—Elantra

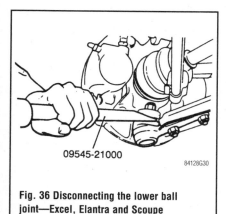

Fig. 36 Disconnecting the lower ball joint—Excel, Elantra and Scoupe

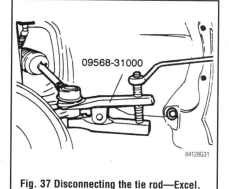

Fig. 37 Disconnecting the tie rod—Excel, Elantra and Scoupe

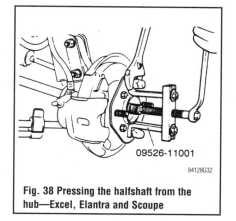

Fig. 38 Pressing the halfshaft from the hub—Excel, Elantra and Scoupe

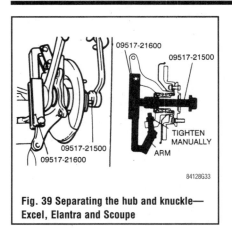

Fig. 39 Separating the hub and knuckle—Excel, Elantra and Scoupe

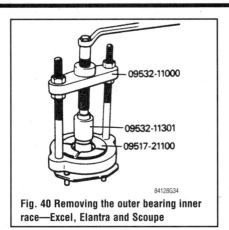

Fig. 40 Removing the outer bearing inner race—Excel, Elantra and Scoupe

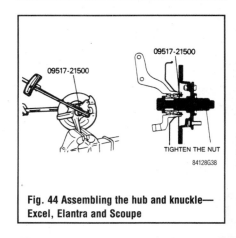

Fig. 41 Removing the oil seal and the inner bearing race—Excel, Elantra and Scoupe

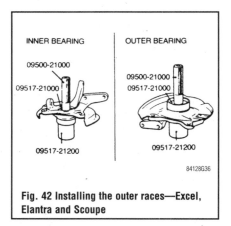

Fig. 42 Installing the outer races—Excel, Elantra and Scoupe

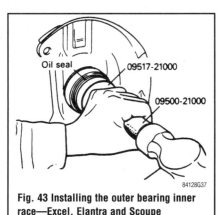

Fig. 43 Installing the outer bearing inner race—Excel, Elantra and Scoupe

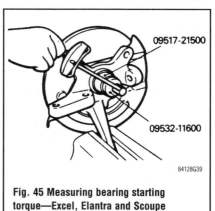

Fig. 44 Assembling the hub and knuckle—Excel, Elantra and Scoupe

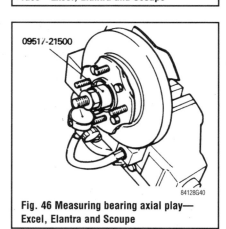

Fig. 45 Measuring bearing starting torque—Excel, Elantra and Scoupe

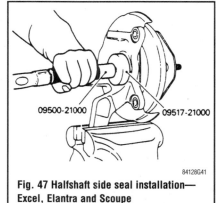

Fig. 46 Measuring bearing axial play—Excel, Elantra and Scoupe

Fig. 47 Halfshaft side seal installation—Excel, Elantra and Scoupe

10. Using special tool 09517-21500, separate the hub from the knuckle.

➡**Prying or hammering will damage the bearing. Use these special tools, or their equivalent to separate the hub and knuckle.**

11. Place the knuckle in a protected jaw vise and separate the rotor from the hub by removing the four attaching bolts.

12. Using special tools 09532-11000, 0953211301 and 09517-21100, remove the outer bearing inner race.

13. Drive the oil seal and inner bearing inner race from the knuckle with a brass drift .

14. Drive out both outer races in a similar fashion.

➡**Always replace bearings and races as a set. Never replace just an inner or outer bearing. If either is in need of replacement, both sets must be replaced.**

15. Thoroughly clean and inspect all parts. Any suspect part should be replaced.

To install:

16. Pack the wheel bearings with lithium based wheel bearing grease. Coat the inside of the knuckle with similar grease and pack the cavities in the knuckle.

➡**Apply a thin coating of grease to the outer surface of the race before installation.**

17. Using special tools 09500-21000, 09517- 21300, and 09517-21200, install the outer races.

18. Install the rotor on the hub and torque the bolts to 36–43 ft. lbs. (50–60 Nm).

19. Drive the outer bearing inner race into position.

20. Coat the out ring and lip of the oil seal and drive the hub side oil seal into place, using a seal driver.

21. Place the inner bearing in the knuckle.

22. Mount the knuckle in a vise. Position the hub and knuckle together. Install tool 0951721500 and tighten the tool to 145–188 ft. lbs. (200–260 Nm). Rotate the hub to seat the bearing.

23. With the knuckle still in the vise, measure the hub starting torque with an inch lbs. torque wrench and tool 09517-215000. Starting torque should be 11.5 inch lbs. If the starting torque is 0, measure the hub bearing axial play with a dial indicator. If axial play exceeds 0.11mm, while the nut is tightened to specification, the assembly has not been done correctly. Disassemble the knuckle and hub and start again.

24. Remove the special tool.

25. Place the outer bearing in the hub and drive the seal into place.

26. Position the knuckle and hub assembly onto the strut and install the attaching bolts. Torque the bolts to 54–65 ft. lbs. (74–88 Nm) on 1986–89 Excel, 65–76 ft. lbs. (90–105 Nm) on 1990–93 Excel and Scoupe, 81–96 ft. lbs. (110–130 Nm) on Elantra.

27. Using the proper tool, press the axle shaft into the hub.

28. Connect the tie rod end to the steering knuckle. Install the tie rod end nut and torque it to 11–25 ft. lbs. (15–34 Nm).

29. Connect the lower ball joint to the steering knuckle. Install the attaching bolt and snug it. The bolt will be torqued properly when the wheels are on the ground.

30. Mount the brake caliper assembly and brake hose.

31. Mount the front wheels and lower the vehicle to the ground. Now torque the lower ball joint bolt.

32. Install the axleshaft nut and torque it to 145–188 ft. lbs. (200–260 Nm). Secure the nut with a new cotter pin. Install the wheel.

Sonata

♦ **See Figures 48 thru 61**

➡ **The following procedure requires the use of several special tools.**

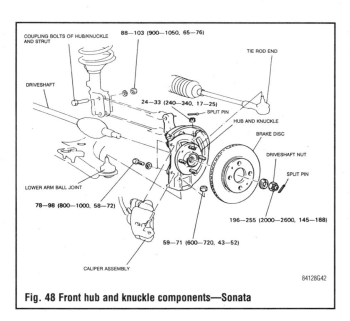

Fig. 48 Front hub and knuckle components—Sonata

1. Remove wheel ornaments.

2. Raise and support the car with jackstands positioned so that the front wheels hang freely.

3. Remove the front wheels.

4. Remove the caliper and suspend it out of the way without disconnecting the brake hose. Pull the rotor disc from the hub and set it aside.

5. Remove the axle shaft nut using a box end wrench and spanner 09517-21700.

6. Using special tool 09568-31000, disconnect the tie rod end from the knuckle. Tie the tool off to a chassis member during use.

7. Loosen but do not remove the lower arm ball joint nut. Using special tool 09568-31000, disconnect the ball joint from the steering knuckle, then remove the nut. Tie the tool off to a chassis member during use.

8. Press the driveshaft from the hub using special tool 09526-11001.

9. Unbolt and remove the knuckle/hub assembly from the strut.

10. Examine the hub and knuckle for cracks and check the spline for wear. Check the oil seal for deterioration. Replace any damaged component as required.

11. Install first the arm, then the body of special tool 09517-21600 on the knuckle and tighten the nut.

12. Mount the knuckle in a protected jaw vise.

13. Using special tool 09517-21500, separate the hub from the knuckle.

➡ **Prying or hammering will damage the bearing. Use special tools or their equivalents to separate the hub and knuckle.**

14. Using a drift punch, crush the hub oil seal in two places. This is done in preparation to install the bearing race removal tool. Then, install special puller tool 09455-21000 to separate the outside bearing inner race from the hub.

15. Pry the oil seal from the knuckle and discard it.

16. Remove the snapring from the knuckle and press the bearing out from the knuckle using the proper tools.

17. Examine the hub and brake disc for galling or any other surface imperfections. Check the bearing seating surface for cracks and galling. Check the bearing for damage. Replace any damaged component as required.

To install:

18. Pack the bearing and the cavities of the knuckle with multi-purpose grease. Press the bearing into the knuckle using the proper tools. Install the wheel bearing inner race.

19. Drive the new outer oil seal into the knuckle using the proper tools. The oil seal should be flush with the surface of the knuckle. After the oil seal is installed lubricate the seal lip and the areas where the seal contacts the hub with multi-purpose grease.

20. Mount the knuckle in a vise. Position the hub and knuckle together. Install tool 0951721500 and tighten the tool to 145–188 ft. lbs. (200–260 Nm). Rotate the hub to seat the bearing.

21. With the knuckle still in the vise, measure the hub starting torque with an inch lbs. torque wrench and tool 09532-11600. Starting torque should be 16.0 inch lbs. If the starting torque is 0, measure the hub bearing axial play with a dial indicator. If axial play exceeds 0.lmm, while the nut is tightened, the assembly has not been done correctly. Disassemble the knuckle and hub and start again.

22. Remove the special tool.

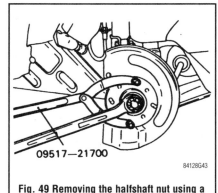

Fig. 49 Removing the halfshaft nut using a special tool—Sonata

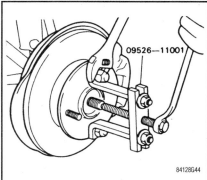

Fig. 50 Pressing the halfshaft from the hub—Sonata

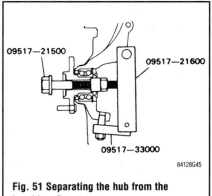

Fig. 51 Separating the hub from the knuckle—Sonata

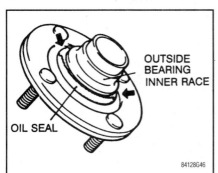

Fig. 52 Crush the hub oil seal in two places before installing the hub removal tool—Sonata

Fig. 53 Separating the outside bearing inner race from the hub using a puller—Sonata

Fig. 54 Removing the hub oil seal—Sonata

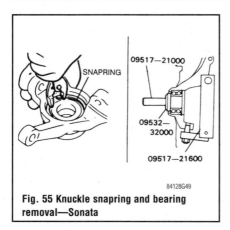

Fig. 55 Knuckle snapring and bearing removal—Sonata

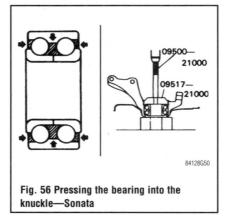

Fig. 56 Pressing the bearing into the knuckle—Sonata

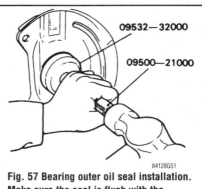

Fig. 57 Bearing outer oil seal installation. Make sure the seal is flush with the knuckle surface—Sonata

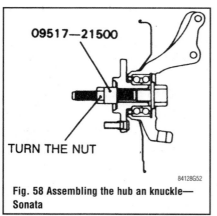

Fig. 58 Assembling the hub an knuckle—Sonata

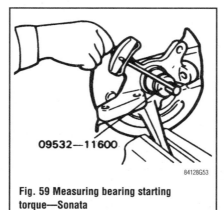

Fig. 59 Measuring bearing starting torque—Sonata

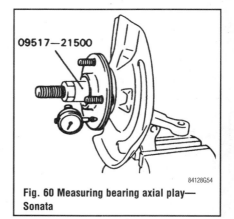

Fig. 60 Measuring bearing axial play—Sonata

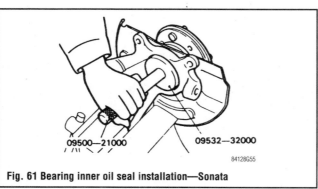

Fig. 61 Bearing inner oil seal installation—Sonata

23. Place the outer bearing in the hub and drive the seal into place. After the oil seal is installed lubricate the seal lip and the areas where the seal contacts the hub with multi-purpose grease.

24. Position the knuckle and hub assembly onto the strut and install the attaching bolts. Torque the bolts to 65–76 ft. lbs. (90–105 Nm).

25. Press the driveshaft into the hub using the proper tool.

26. Connect the ball joint to the steering knuckle and torque the nut to 43–52 ft. lbs. (60–72 Nm).

27. Connect the tie rod end to the steering knuckle and torque the nut to 17–25 ft. lbs. (24–34 Nm). Secure the nut with a new cotter pin.

28. Mount the rotor disc onto the hub and install the brake caliper assembly. Torque the caliper bolts to 58–72 ft. lbs. (80–100 Nm).

29. Mount the front wheels and lower the vehicle.

30. Install the wheel ornaments.

Wheel Alignment

If the tires are worn unevenly, if the vehicle is not stable on the highway or if the handling seems uneven in spirited driving, the wheel alignment should be checked. If an alignment problem is suspected, first check for improper tire inflation and other possible causes. These can be worn suspension or steering components, accident damage or even unmatched tires. If any worn or damaged components are found, they must be replaced before the wheels can be properly aligned. Wheel alignment requires very expensive equipment and involves minute adjustments which must be accurate; it should only be performed by a trained technician. Take your vehicle to a properly equipped shop.

Following is a description of the alignment angles which are adjustable on most vehicles and how they affect vehicle handling. Although these angles can apply to both the front and rear wheels, usually only the front suspension is adjustable.

CASTER

▶ **See Figure 62**

Looking at a vehicle from the side, caster angle describes the steering axis rather than a wheel angle. The steering knuckle is attached to a control arm or strut at the top and a control arm at the bottom. The wheel pivots around the line between these points to steer the vehicle. When the upper point is tilted back, this is described as positive caster. Having a positive caster tends to make the wheels self-centering, increasing directional stability. Excessive positive caster makes the wheels hard to steer, while an uneven caster will cause a pull to one side. Overloading the vehicle or sagging rear springs will affect caster, as will raising the rear of the vehicle. If the rear of the vehicle is lower than normal, the caster becomes more positive.

CAMBER

▶ **See Figure 63**

Looking from the front of the vehicle, camber is the inward or outward tilt of the top of wheels. When the tops of the wheels are tilted in, this is negative camber; if they are tilted out, it is positive. In a turn, a slight amount of negative camber helps maximize contact of the tire with the road. However, too much negative camber compromises straight-line stability, increases bump steer and torque steer.

TOE

▶ **See Figure 64**

Looking down at the wheels from above the vehicle, toe angle is the distance between the front of the wheels, relative to the distance between the back of the wheels. If the wheels are closer at the front, they are said to be toed-in or to have negative toe. A small amount of negative toe enhances directional stability and provides a smoother ride on the highway.

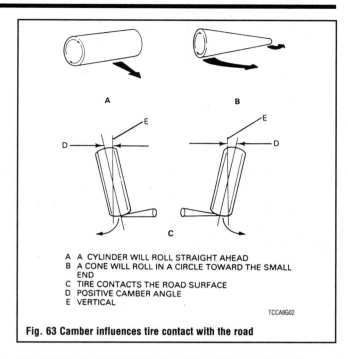

A A CYLINDER WILL ROLL STRAIGHT AHEAD
B A CONE WILL ROLL IN A CIRCLE TOWARD THE SMALL END
C TIRE CONTACTS THE ROAD SURFACE
D POSITIVE CAMBER ANGLE
E VERTICAL

TCCA8G02

Fig. 63 Camber influences tire contact with the road

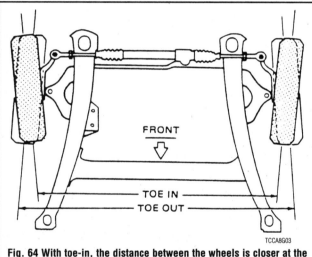
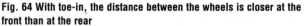

TCCA8G03

Fig. 64 With toe-in, the distance between the wheels is closer at the front than at the rear

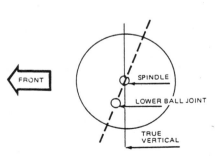

CASTER IS POSITIVE WHEN THE <u>LOAD</u>
(LOWER BALL JOINT) IS <u>AHEAD OR PULLING</u>
THE SPINDLE.

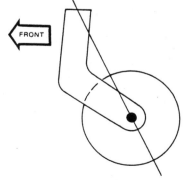

LOAD IS PULLING THE WHEEL.

TCCA8G01

Fig. 62 Caster affects straight-line stability. Caster wheels used on shopping carts, for example, employ positive caster

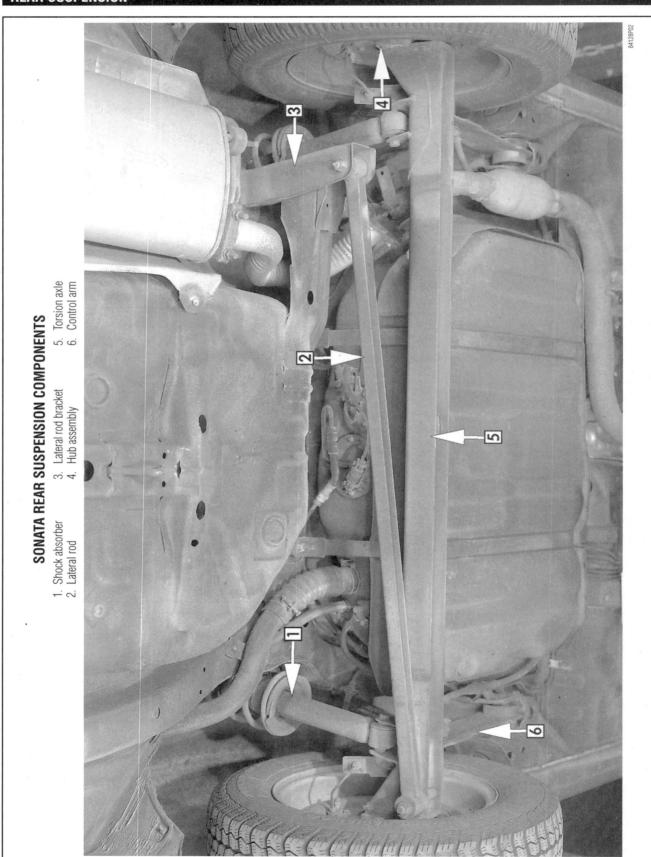

SONATA REAR SUSPENSION COMPONENTS

1. Shock absorber
2. Lateral rod
3. Lateral rod bracket
4. Hub assembly
5. Torsion axle
6. Control arm

Coil Springs

REMOVAL & INSTALLATION

Excel and Scoupe

1. Raise the vehicle and support it safely. Remove the rear wheels.
2. Support the rear suspension arm with a floor jack. Then, remove the lower shock absorber attaching bolt, nut and lock washer.
3. Slowly, lower the jack just to the point where the spring can be removed and remove the spring. If the spring is being replaced, transfer the spring seat to the new spring.
To install:
4. When installing the coil spring, make sure the smaller diameter is upward. Make sure the spring identification and load markings match up.
5. Torque the lower shock mounting nut/bolt to 47–58 ft. lbs. (64–78 Nm).

Elantra

1. Raise the vehicle and support it safely. Remove the wheel.
2. Remove the trim cover inside the rear compartment for access to the top mounting nuts.
3. Support the lower arm with a jack and compress the coil spring. Remove the lower mounting nut.
4. Remove the cap from the upper end of the shock.
5. Remove the upper mounting nut and the shock from the vehicle.
6. Compress the spring on the shock using spring compressor 09546-11000 or equivalent. Remove the piston rod tightening nut at the top of the strut while holding the piston rod with a wrench.
7. Disassemble the upped dust cover, bushing, pad, bracket and cup assembly taking note of positioning to assure correct installation. Remove the spring from the shock absorber.
To install:
8. Install the compressed spring to the shock absorber assembly and install the bump rubber, cup assembly, upper bushing, upper spring pad, collar, bracket assembly, upper bushing, washer and self-locking nut to the shock absorber in that order. Make sure the components are in the same orientation as was prior to removal.
9. Tighten the upper rod nut to 14–22 ft. lbs. (20–30 Nm).
10. Remove the spring compressor tool.
11. Install the shock absorber to the lower arm, install the lower mounting nut and tighten to 72 ft. lbs. (100 Nm).
12. Install the upper nut and torque to 33 ft. lbs. (45 Nm).
13. Install the cap and cover.
14. Lower the arm and remove the jack.

Shock Absorbers

REMOVAL & INSTALLATION

Excel And Scoupe

▶ **See Figures 65 and 66**

1. Remove the wheel cover. Loosen the lug nuts.
2. Raise the vehicle and support it safely. Remove the wheel.
3. Remove the upper mounting bolt/nut or nut.
4. While holding the bottom stud mount nut with one wrench, remove the locknut with another wrench, or on some vehicles, remove the nut and bolt from the mounting bracket.
5. Remove the shock absorber.
6. Check the shock for:
   a. Excessive oil leakage, some minor weeping is permissible;
   b. Bent center rod, damaged outer case, or other defects.
   c. Pump the shock absorber several times, if it offers even resistance on full strokes it may be considered serviceable.
To install:
7. Install the upper shock mounting nut and bolt. Hand-tighten the nut.

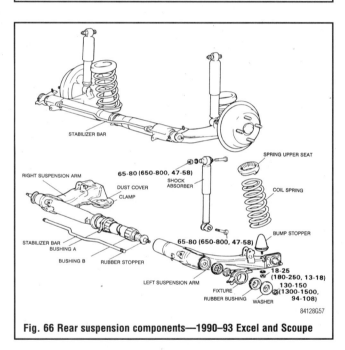

1. Shock absorber
2. Spring upper seat
3. Coil spring
4. Bump stopper
5. Suspension arm, right
6. Dust cover
7. Clamp
8. Bushing A
9. Bushing B
10. Rubber stopper
11. Suspension arm, left
12. Fixture
13. Rubber bushing
14. Washer
15. Stabilizer bar

	Nm	kg.cm	ft.lbs.
A	18-25	184-255	13-18
B	49-69	500-704	36-51
C	64-78	653-796	47-58

84128G56

Fig. 65 Rear suspension components—1986–89 Excel

STABILIZER BAR

RIGHT SUSPENSION ARM

DUST COVER

CLAMP

65-80 (650-800, 47-58)

SHOCK ABSORBER

SPRING UPPER SEAT

COIL SPRING

BUMP STOPPER

STABILIZER BAR BUSHING A

BUSHING B

RUBBER STOPPER

65-80 (650-800, 47-58)

LEFT SUSPENSION ARM

FIXTURE

RUBBER BUSHING

WASHER

18-25 (180-250, 13-18)

130-150 (1300-1500, 94-108)

84128G57

Fig. 66 Rear suspension components—1990–93 Excel and Scoupe

8. Install the bottom eye of the shock over the spring stud or into the mounting bracket and insert the bolt and nut. Tighten the nut to 47–58 ft. lbs. (64–78 Nm).
9. Tighten the upper fasteners to 47–58 ft. lbs. (64–78 Nm).

Elantra

▶ **See Figure 67**

1. Raise the vehicle and support it safely. Remove the wheel.
2. Remove the trim cover inside the rear compartment for access to the top mounting nuts.
3. Support the lower arm with a jack and compress the coil spring. Remove the lower mounting nut.
4. Remove the cap from the upper end of the shock.
5. Remove the upper mounting nut and the shock from the vehicle.
6. Install the shock absorber to the lower arm, install the lower nut and tighten to 72 ft. lbs. (100 Nm).
7. Install the upper nut and torque to 33 ft. lbs. (45 Nm).
8. Install the cap and cover.
9. Lower the arm and remove the jack.

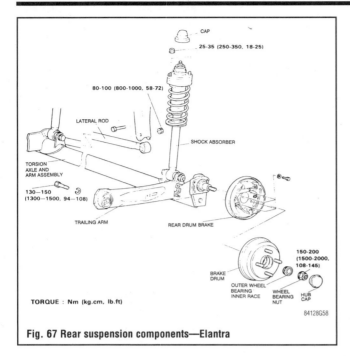

Fig. 67 Rear suspension components—Elantra

Sonata

♦ See Figure 68

1. Raise the vehicle and support it safely. Allow the lower arms and suspension to hang. Remove the wheels.

2. Place a block of wood on a floor jack and position the jack under the axle beam. Raise the axle slightly to relax the strut and to support the axle when the strut is removed. Position an additional support under the axle.

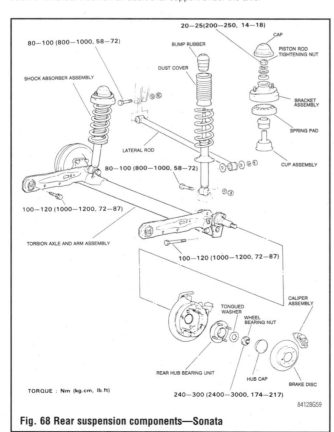

Fig. 68 Rear suspension components—Sonata

3. Take care in jacking that no contact is made on the lateral rod.
4. Remove the upper dust cover cap from the strut assembly.
5. Remove the upper mounting nuts. Remove the lower mounting bolt and nut.
6. Remove the strut.

To install:

7. Installation is the reverse order of the removal procedures. Torque the lower mounting bolt and nut to 58–72 ft. lbs. (79–96 Nm); The upper mounting nuts to 18–25 ft. lbs. (25–34 Nm).

Rear Control/Suspension Arm

REMOVAL & INSTALLATION

Excel And Scoupe

♦ See Figures 69 thru 79

1. Raise the vehicle and support it safely.
2. Remove the rear wheels.
3. Remove the brake drums and brake shoes.
4. Remove the muffler assembly.
5. Raise the suspension arm assembly slightly and keep in this position.
6. Disconnect the parking brake cable from the arm.
7. Remove the shock absorber.
8. Disconnect the brake hoses from their clips on the suspension members.
9. Lower the suspension slightly and carefully remove the coil spring.
10. Remove the rear suspension from the vehicle as an assembly.
11. Before removing any fixtures from the suspension arm matchmark all parts for assembly reference; this is extremely important! If equipped with stabilizer bars, make a mark on the bar in line with the punch mark on the bracket.
12. Remove the dust cover clamp.
13. Remove the nuts securing the control arms and pull them apart. Leave the dust cover attached to the right arm.
14. Remove the rubber stopper from the right arm.
15. Using a flat bladed chisel, drive bushing from right the arm.
16. Using a brass drift, drive bushing out from the left arm.

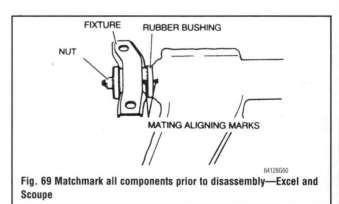

Fig. 69 Matchmark all components prior to disassembly—Excel and Scoupe

Fig. 70 Marking the rear stabilizer bar—Excel and Scoupe

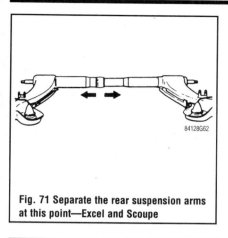

Fig. 71 Separate the rear suspension arms at this point—Excel and Scoupe

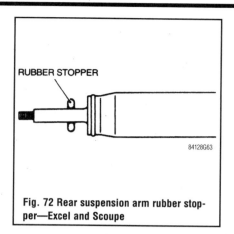

Fig. 72 Rear suspension arm rubber stopper—Excel and Scoupe

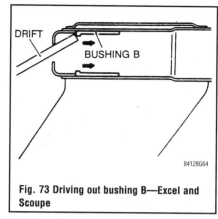

Fig. 73 Driving out bushing B—Excel and Scoupe

Fig. 74 Driving out bushing A—Excel and Scoupe

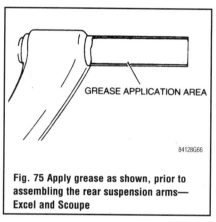

Fig. 75 Apply grease as shown, prior to assembling the rear suspension arms—Excel and Scoupe

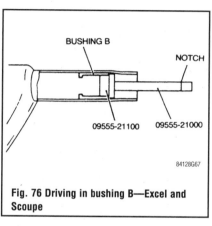

Fig. 76 Driving in bushing B—Excel and Scoupe

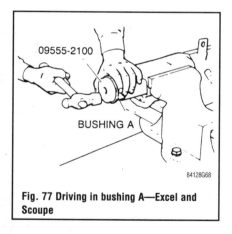

Fig. 77 Driving in bushing A—Excel and Scoupe

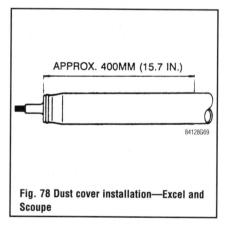

Fig. 78 Dust cover installation—Excel and Scoupe

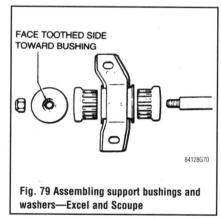

Fig. 79 Assembling support bushings and washers—Excel and Scoupe

17. Coat the inside of the left arm and the outside of the bushing with chassis lube and drive it into place with driver tools 09555-21100 and 09555-21000 or equivalent. Drive the bushing in until the notch on 09555-21000 or equivalent, reaches the end of the arm.

18. Coat the inside of the arm and the outside of the bushing with chassis lube and drive it into the arm until it is fully seated.

19. Install the dust cover to the center position of the right arm, about 400mm.

20. Apply chassis lube to the surface of the right arm and install the rubber stopper.

21. Align all matchmarks, including the stabilizer bar and slowly push the suspension halves together.

22. Install all remaining bushing, washers and attaching parts.

➡ **The toothed sides of the washers face the bushings.**

23. Install the end nuts and torque them loosely at this time.

To install:

24. Jack the assembly into position and torque the suspension-to-body bolts to 50 ft. lbs. (68 Nm).

25. Install the coil springs and loosely install the shock absorbers.

26. Install the rear brake assembly and related components.

27. Attach the parking brake cable and brake hoses to their clips on the suspension arm.

28. Install the tire and wheel assemblies.

29. Lower the vehicle and tighten the suspension arm end nuts to 65–80 ft. lbs. (88–108 Nm) for Scoupe, 36–51 ft. lbs. (49–69 Nm) for 1989 Excel, 65–80 ft. lbs. (88–108 Nm) for 1990–91 Excel and 94–108 ft. lbs. for 1992–93 Excel. Tighten the shock mounting bolts to 47–58 ft. lbs. (63–79 Nm).

30. Adjust the rear brake shoe clearance.

Elantra

1. Raise the vehicle and support it safely.
2. Support the rear torsion axle.
3. Remove the lateral rod assembly from the inner body mount and tie the rod to the axle beam using wire.
4. Remove the brake drums and brake shoes. Disconnect the brake line from the wheel cylinder and cap closed. Disconnect the parking brake cables and remove the brake backing plate from the rear hub.
5. Using a floor jack, slightly raise and support the rear torsion axle and arm assembly.
6. Remove the shock absorber lower mounting bolt. Using the floor jack, lower the arm enough to separate the shock from the trailing arm.
7. Remove the trailing arm mounting bolts and the arm from the vehicle.

To install:

8. Install the trailing arm to the vehicle and secure in place with mounting bolts. Tightened to 94–108 ft. lbs. (100–120 Nm) once weight of the vehicle is applied to the rear suspension. Install the shock absorber.
9. Attach the lateral rod to the inner mount and tighten bolt to 58–72 ft. lbs. (80–100 Nm).
10. Install the backing plate, brake lines and related components. Torque the rear wheel bearing nut to specifications and check the end-play of the bearing. Install the hub nut cap after filling with multi-purpose grease.
11. Install the tire and wheel assembly, adjust the rear brake shoes and bleed the brake system.

Sonata

1. Raise and safely support the vehicle.
2. Support the rear torsion axle assembly using floor jack or equivalent.
3. Disconnect the lateral rod at the axle and support aside. Remove the lower shock attaching bolts.
4. Remove the tire and wheel assemblies.
5. If equipped with drum brakes, remove the brake drums, brake shoes and hubs. Disconnect the brake fluid lines to the wheel cylinders and cap closed.
6. If equipped with rear disc brakes, remove the caliper assemblies and brake pads. Support the calipers out of the way using wire. Take care not to twist the brake hoses or lines.
7. Disconnect the parking brake cables.
8. Remove the trailing arm mounting bolts and lower the assembly from the vehicle.

To install:

9. Install the trailing arm assembly to the vehicle and secure using the mounting hardware. Once weight of the vehicle is on the rear suspension, torque the trailing arm-to-frame mounting bolts to 72–87 ft. lbs. (96–120 Nm), and the trailing arm-to-torsion axle to 72–87 ft. lbs. (100–120 Nm).
10. Connect the parking brake cables.
11. If equipped with rear disc brakes, install the caliper assemblies and brake pads. Take care not to twist the brake hoses or lines during installation.
12. If equipped with drum brakes, install the brake drums, brake shoes and hubs. Connect the brake fluid lines to the wheel cylinders.
13. Install the tire and wheel assemblies.
14. Connect the lateral rod to the axle and tighten fasteners to 58–72 ft. lbs. (80–100 Nm).
15. Install the lower shock attaching bolts and tighten to 58–72 ft. lbs. (80–100 Nm).
16. Bleed the brake system if any brake fluid lines were opened. Adjust the rear brake shoes, if equipped with drum brakes.

Lateral Rod

REMOVAL & INSTALLATION

Elantra and Sonata

1. Raise the vehicle and support it safely.
2. Disconnect the rod at each end and remove it from the vehicle.
3. Install the bar to the vehicle with the same orientation as prior to removal.

4. Install the bar retainer bolts and nuts at each end to hold bar in place. Do not apply final torque to the fasteners at this time.
5. Lower the vehicle so the weight of the car is resting on the suspension and torque the nuts to 58–72 ft. lbs. (78–97 Nm).

Rear Wheel Bearings

Before handling the bearings, there are a few things that you should remember to do and not to do.

Remember to DO the following:

- Remove all outside dirt from the housing before exposing the bearing.
- Treat a used bearing as gently as you would a new one.
- Work with clean tools in clean surroundings.
- Use clean, dry canvas gloves, or at least clean, dry hands.
- Clean solvents and flushing fluids are a must.
- Use clean paper when laying out the bearings to dry.
- Protect disassembled bearings from rust and dirt, Cover them up.
- Use clean rags to wipe bearings.
- Keep the bearings in oil-proof paper when they are to be stored or are not in use.
- Clean the inside of the housing before replacing the bearing.

Do NOT do the following:

- Don't work in dirty surroundings.
- Don't use dirty, chipped or damaged tools.
- Try not to work on wooden work benches or use wooden mallets.
- Don't handle bearings with dirty or moist hands.
- Do not use gasoline for cleaning. Use a safe solvent.
- Do not spin dry bearings with compressed air. They will be damaged.
- Do not spin dirty bearings.
- Avoid using cotton waste or dirty cloths to wipe bearings.
- Try not to scratch or nick bearing surfaces.
- Do not allow the bearing to come in contact with dirt or rust at any time.

REMOVAL & INSTALLATION

➡**Sodium-based grease is not compatible with lithium-based grease. If there is any doubt as to the type of grease used, completely clean the old grease from the bearing and hub before replacing.**

Excel

◆ **See Figures 80 thru 87**

1. Safely raise and support the rear of the vehicle. Remove the tire and wheel assembly.
2. Remove the grease cap, cotter pin, serrated nut cap, axle shaft nut and washer from the spindle as equipped.
3. Pull outward on the brake drum slightly to remove the outer wheel bearing.
4. Slide the drum down the spindle and remove assembly from the vehicle.
5. Pry the inner grease seal from the rear hub of the drum and discard.
6. Remove the inner wheel bearing. If the bearings are being replaced, drive the bearing races from the hub taking care not to damage the inner surface of the drum.

To install:

7. Coat the new races with EP lithium wheel bearing grease and drive them into the hub, making sure they are fully and squarely seated.
8. Pack the hub cavity with new EP lithium wheel bearing grease.
9. Install the inner bearing and drive a new grease seal into place. Make sure to pack the bearings completely with grease prior to installing into the drum.
10. Install the brake drum onto the spindle. Install the outer bearing, washer and shaft nut onto spindle.
11. On 1989–90 vehicles equipped with castellated nut and cotter pin, torque the bearing nut to 15 ft. lbs. (20 Nm) while turning the drum. Back off the nut until it is loose, then torque it to 48 inch lbs. Install the serrated nut cap and a new cotter pin. If the cotter pin holes have to be re-aligned, back off on the nut no more than 15 degrees; if not, repeat the adjustment procedure.
12. On 1991–93 vehicles equipped with bearing locknut, install and tighten bearing locknut as follows:

a. Prior to installation, inspect the rear bearing nut by threading the nut onto the spindle until the distance between the shoulder of the spindle and the inner flat on the nut is 0.07–0.11 in. (2.0–3.0mm).

b. Measure the torque required to rotate the rear wheel bearing locknut while turning counterclockwise. The limit is 48 ft. lbs. (5.5 Nm). If required torque is less than the limit, replace the nut.

c. Install the brake drum and outer bearing onto the spindle. Install and torque the nut to 108–145 ft. lbs. (147–196 Nm).

d. Check for correct bearing end-play by placing a dial indicator on the hub surface and moving the drum outward. Note the movement of the gauge and compare to the desired reading of 0.0043 in. or less (0.11mm or less). If end-play exceeds the desired reading, retighten the rear hub bearing nut and recheck end-play. If reading is still excessive, replace the hub assembly.

13. If end-play is correct, check the starting torque by attaching a spring balance to the hub lug bolts and pulling at a 90 degree angle while noting the required force to turn the hub. If the torque required is above the desired reading of 4.9 lbs. or less (22 N or less), loosen the nut and again tighten to the desired torque. Recheck the starting torque. If torque is still above the desired reading, replace the rear bearing.

14. After final tightening the wheel bearing nut, align with the spindle's indentation and crimp the edge of the nut to wedge in position.

15. Install the tire and wheel assembly and lower the vehicle. Prior to moving the vehicle, pump the brakes until a firm pedal is obtained.

Elantra

1. Safely raise and support the rear of the vehicle. Remove the tire and wheel assembly.

2. Remove the grease cap, axle shaft nut and washer.

3. Pull outward on the brake drum slightly to remove the outer wheel bearing.

4. Slide the drum down the spindle and remove from the vehicle.

5. Pry the inner grease seal from the rear hub of the drum and discard.

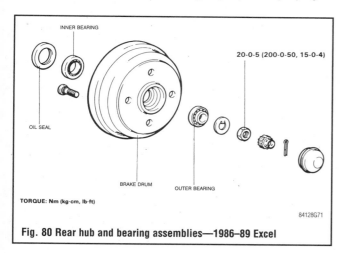

Fig. 80 Rear hub and bearing assemblies—1986–89 Excel

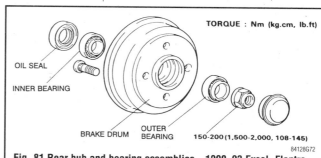

Fig. 81 Rear hub and bearing assemblies—1990–93 Excel, Elantra and Scoupe

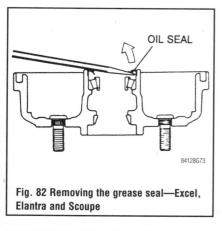

Fig. 82 Removing the grease seal—Excel, Elantra and Scoupe

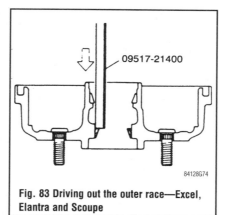

Fig. 83 Driving out the outer race—Excel, Elantra and Scoupe

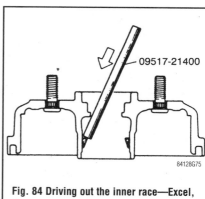

Fig. 84 Driving out the inner race—Excel, Elantra and Scoupe

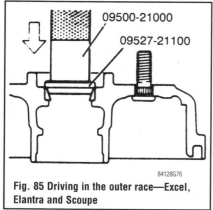

Fig. 85 Driving in the outer race—Excel, Elantra and Scoupe

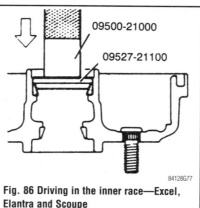

Fig. 86 Driving in the inner race—Excel, Elantra and Scoupe

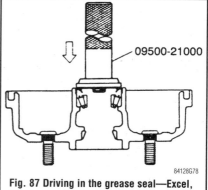

Fig. 87 Driving in the grease seal—Excel, Elantra and Scoupe

6. Remove the inner wheel bearing. If the bearings are being replaced, drive the bearing races from the hub taking care not to damage the inner surface of the drum.

To install:

7. Coat the new races with EP lithium wheel bearing grease and drive them into the hub, making sure they are fully and squarely seated.

8. Pack the hub cavity with new EP lithium wheel bearing grease.

9. Install the inner bearing and drive a new grease seal into place. Make sure to pack the bearings completely with grease prior to installing into the drum.

10. Before installing the rear drum assembly, inspect the rear bearing nut as follows:

    a. Thread the wheel nut onto the spindle until it gap between the shoulder of the spindle and the nut is 0.07–0.11 in. (2.0–3.0mm).

    b. Measure the torque required to rotate the rear wheel bearing nut while turning counterclockwise. The limit is 48 ft. lbs. (5.5 Nm). If torque is less than the limit, replace the nut.

11. Install the brake drum and bearing assembly onto the spindle and install the outer bearing and shaft nut. Tighten the nut to 108–145 ft. lbs. (150–200 Nm).

12. Check for correct bearing end-play by placing a dial indicator on the hub surface and moving the hub outward. Note the movement of the gauge and compare to the desired reading of 0.008 in. or less (0.2mm or less). If end-play exceeds the desired reading, retighten the rear hub bearing nut and recheck end-play. If reading is still excessive, replace the hub unit.

13. If end-play is correct, check the starting torque by attaching a spring balance to the hub lug bolts and pulling at a 90 degree angle while noting the required force to turn the hub. If the torque required is above the desired reading of 4.9 lbs. or less (22 N or less), loosen the nut and again tighten to the desired torque. Recheck the starting torque. If torque is still above the desired reading, replace the rear bearings.

14. Install the tire and wheel assembly and lower the vehicle. Prior to moving the vehicle, pump the brakes until a firm pedal is obtained.

Scoupe

1. Safely raise and support the rear of the vehicle. Remove the tire and wheel assembly.

2. Remove the grease cap, axle shaft nut and washer.

3. Pull outward on the brake drum slightly to remove the outer wheel bearing.

4. Slide the drum down the spindle and remove from the vehicle.

5. Pry the inner grease seal from the rear hub of the drum and discard.

6. Remove the inner wheel bearing. If the bearings are being replaced, drive the bearing races from the hub taking care not to damage the inner surface of the drum.

To install:

7. Coat the new races with EP lithium wheel bearing grease and drive them into the hub, making sure they are fully and squarely seated.

8. Pack the hub cavity with new EP lithium wheel bearing grease.

9. Install the inner bearing and drive a new grease seal into place. Make sure to pack the bearings completely with grease prior to installing into the drum.

10. Before installing the rear drum assembly, inspect the rear bearing nut as follows:

    a. Thread the wheel nut onto the spindle until it gap between the shoulder of the spindle and the nut is 0.07–0.11 in. (2.0–3.0mm).

    b. Measure the torque required to rotate the rear wheel bearing nut while turning counterclockwise. The limit is 48 ft. lbs. (5.5 Nm). If torque is less than the limit, replace the nut.

11. Install the brake drum and bearing assembly onto the spindle and install the outer bearing and shaft nut. Tighten the nut to 108–145 ft. lbs. (150–200 Nm).

12. Check for correct bearing end-play by placing a dial indicator on the hub surface and moving the hub outward. Note the movement of the gauge and compare to the desired reading of 0.0043 in. or less (0.11mm or less). If end-play exceeds the desired reading, retighten the rear bearing nut and recheck end-play. If reading is still excessive, replace the rear bearings.

13. Once end-play is correct, check the hub and drum starting force by attaching a spring balance to the lug bolts and pulling at a 90 degree angle while noting the required force to turn the drum assembly. If the torque required is above the desired reading of 4.8 lbs. or less (22 N or less), loosen the nut and again tighten to the desired torque. Recheck the starting torque. If torque is still above the desired reading, replace the rear bearings.

14. After final tightening the wheel bearing nut, align with the spindle's indentation and crimp the edge of the nut to wedge in position.

15. Install the tire and wheel assembly and lower the vehicle. Prior to moving the vehicle, pump the brakes until a firm pedal is obtained.

Sonata

1989–91

▶ See Figures 88 thru 95

1. Safely raise and support the rear of the vehicle. Remove the tire and wheel assembly.

2. If equipped with rear disc brakes, remove the brake caliper and support out of the way using wire. Do not disconnect the brake hose from the caliper.

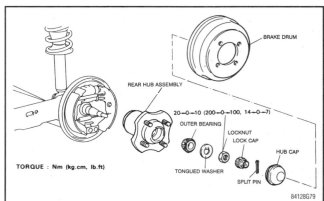

Fig. 88 Rear hub and bearing components—1989–91 Sonata with 4 cylinder engine

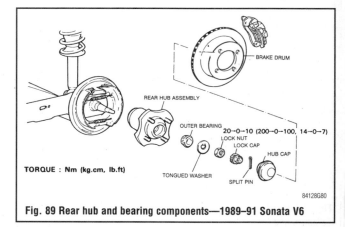

Fig. 89 Rear hub and bearing components—1989–91 Sonata V6

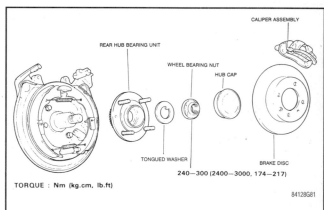

Fig. 90 Rear hub and bearing components—1992–93 Sonata

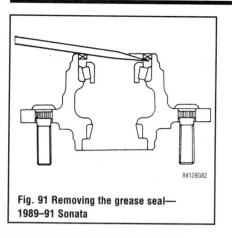

Fig. 91 Removing the grease seal—1989–91 Sonata

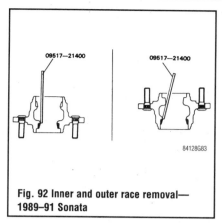

Fig. 92 Inner and outer race removal—1989–91 Sonata

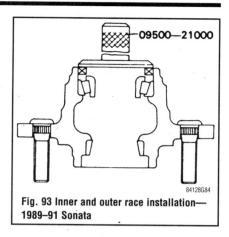

Fig. 93 Inner and outer race installation—1989–91 Sonata

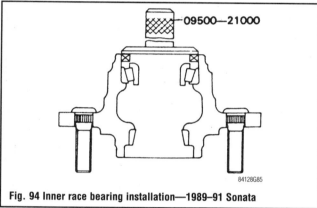

Fig. 94 Inner race bearing installation—1989–91 Sonata

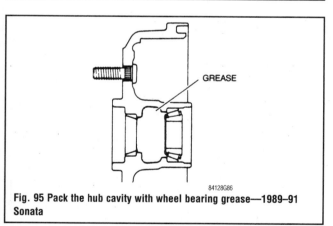

Fig. 95 Pack the hub cavity with wheel bearing grease—1989–91 Sonata

Remove the brake rotor. If equipped with drum brakes, remove the brake drum from the hub assembly.

3. Remove the grease cap, cotter pin, serrated nut cap, axle shaft nut and washer from the spindle as equipped.

4. Pull outward on the rear hub assembly slightly to remove the outer wheel bearing.

5. Slide the hub down the spindle and remove assembly from the vehicle.

6. Pry the inner grease seal from the hub and discard.

7. Remove the inner wheel bearing. If the bearings are being replaced, drive the bearing races from the hub taking care not to damage the inner surface of the hub.

To install:

8. Coat the new races with EP lithium wheel bearing grease and drive them into the hub, making sure they are fully and squarely seated.

9. Pack the hub cavity with new EP lithium wheel bearing grease.

10. Install the inner bearing and drive a new grease seal into place. Make

sure to pack both bearings completely with grease prior to installing into the hub.

11. Install the hub assembly onto the spindle. Install the outer bearing, washer and shaft nut onto spindle.

12. Torque the bearing nut to 14 ft. lbs. (20 Nm) while turning the hub or drum. Back off the nut until it is loose, then torque it to 7 ft. lbs. (10 Nm). Install the serrated nut cap and a new cotter pin. If the cotter pin holes have to be re-aligned, back off on the nut no more than 15 degrees; if not, repeat the adjustment procedure.

13. If equipped with drum brakes, install the brake drum to the hub assembly and adjust the brake shoes as required. If equipped with disc brakes, install the rotor and caliper.

14. Install the tire and wheel assembly and lower the vehicle. Pump the brake pedal to seat the brake pads against the rotors prior to moving the vehicle.

1992–93

➡The rear hub bearing unit can not be disassembled. If the hub shows signs of wear or damage, replacement of the unit is required.

1. Safely raise and support the rear of the vehicle. Remove the tire and wheel assembly.

2. If equipped with rear disc brakes, remove the brake caliper and support out of the way using wire. Do not disconnect the brake hose from the caliper. Remove the brake rotor. If equipped with drum brakes, remove the brake drum from the hub assembly.

3. Remove the grease cap, wheel bearing nut and washer from the center of the hub bearing unit. Remove the rear hub unit from the vehicle.

To install:

4. Install the rear bearing unit onto the spindle. Install the outer bearing and the tonged washer into the rear hub unit.

➡Press the inner race further until the inner race contacts with the spindle end.

5. Install and tighten the rear wheel bearing nut to 174–217 ft. lbs. (240–300 Nm).

6. Check for correct bearing end-play by placing a dial indicator on the hub surface and moving the hub outward. Note the movement of the gauge and compare to the desired reading of 0.004 in. or less (0.01mm or less). If end-play exceeds the desired reading, retighten the rear hub bearing nut and recheck end-play. If reading is still excessive, replace the hub unit.

7. If end-play is correct, check the starting torque by attaching a spring balance to the hub lug bolts and pulling at a 90 degree angle while noting the required force to turn the hub. If the torque required is above the desired reading of 7 lbs. or less (31 N or less), loosen the nut and again tighten to the desired torque. Recheck the starting torque. If torque is still above the desired reading, replace the rear hub bearing unit.

8. After final tightening the wheel bearing nut, align with the spindle's indentation and crimp the edge of the nut to wedge in position.

9. If equipped with rear disc brakes, install the brake disc and caliper to the vehicle. If equipped with drum brakes, install drum to hub assembly.

10. Install the tire and wheel assembly and lower the vehicle. Pump the brake pedal to assure correct brake operation, prior to moving the vehicle.

ADJUSTMENT

Excel

1. Raise the vehicle and support it safely. Remove the rear wheel assembly.
2. Remove dust cover from the hub.
3. On 1989–90 vehicles equipped with castellated nut and cotter pin, remove the cotter pin and nut cap. Torque the bearing nut to 15 ft. lbs. (20 Nm) while turning the drum. Back off the nut until it is loose, then torque it to 48 inch lbs. Install the serrated nut cap and a new cotter pin. If the cotter pin holes have to be re-aligned, back off on the nut no more than 15 degrees; if not, repeat the adjustment procedure.
4. On 1991–93 vehicles equipped with bearing locknut, adjust bearing locknut as follows:
    a. Loosen the nut and then torque nut to 108–145 ft. lbs. (147–196 Nm).
    b. Check for correct bearing end-play by placing a dial indicator on the hub surface and moving the drum outward. Note the movement of the gauge and compare to the desired reading of 0.0043 in. or less (0.11mm or less). If end-play exceeds the desired reading, retighten the rear hub bearing nut and recheck end-play. If reading is still excessive, replace the hub unit.
    c. If end-play is correct, check the starting torque by attaching a spring balance to the hub lug bolts and pulling at a 90 degree angle while noting the required force to turn the hub. If the torque required is above the desired reading of 4.9 lbs. or less (22 N or less), loosen the nut and again tighten to the desired torque. Recheck the starting torque. If torque is still above the desired reading, replace the rear bearings.
    d. After final tightening the wheel bearing nut, align with the spindle's indentation and crimp the edge of the nut to wedge in position.
5. Fill the dust cap with grease and install.
6. Install the tire and wheel assembly.

Sonata

1989–91

1. Safely raise and support the rear of the vehicle. Remove the tire and wheel assembly.
2. Remove the grease cap, cotter pin and serrated nut.
3. Torque the bearing nut to 14 ft. lbs. (20 Nm) while turning the hub or drum. Back off the nut until it is loose, then torque it to 7 ft. lbs. (10 Nm). Install the serrated nut cap and a new cotter pin. If the cotter pin holes have to be re-aligned, back off on the nut no more than 15 degrees; if not, repeat the adjustment procedure.
4. Install the nut lock and a new cotter pin.
5. Install the tire and wheel assembly and lower the vehicle. Pump the brake pedal to seat the brake pads against the rotors prior to moving the vehicle.

1992–93

1. Safely raise and support the rear of the vehicle. Remove the tire and wheel assembly.
2. If equipped with rear disc brakes, remove the brake caliper and support out of the way using wire. Do not disconnect the brake hose from the caliper. Remove the brake rotor. If equipped with drum brakes, remove the brake drum from the hub assembly.
3. Remove the grease cap and loosen the wheel bearing nut.
4. Tighten the rear wheel bearing nut to 174–217 ft. lbs. (240–300 Nm).
5. Check for correct bearing end-play by placing a dial indicator on the hub surface and moving the hub outward. Note the movement of the gauge and compare to the desired reading of 0.004 in. or less (0.01mm or less). If end-play exceeds the desired reading, retighten the rear hub bearing nut and recheck end-play. If reading is still excessive, replace the hub unit.
6. If end-play is correct, check the starting torque by attaching a spring balance to the hub lug bolts and pulling at a 90 degree angle while noting the required force to turn the hub. If the torque required is above the desired reading of 7 lbs. or less (31 N or less), loosen the nut and again tighten to the desired torque. Recheck the starting torque. If torque is still above the desired reading, replace the rear hub bearing unit.
7. After final tightening the wheel bearing nut, align with the spindle's indentation and crimp the edge of the nut to wedge in position.
8. If equipped with rear disc brakes, install the brake disc and caliper to the vehicle. If equipped with drum brakes, install drum to hub assembly.
9. Install the tire and wheel assembly and lower the vehicle. Pump the brake pedal to assure correct brake operation, prior to moving the vehicle.

Elantra

1. Safely raise and support the rear of the vehicle. Remove the tire and wheel assembly.
2. Remove the grease cap and loosen the axle shaft nut.
3. Tighten the nut to 108–145 ft. lbs. (150–200 Nm).
4. Check for correct bearing end-play by placing a dial indicator on the hub surface and moving the hub outward. Note the movement of the gauge and compare to the desired reading of 0.008 in. or less (0.2mm or less). If end-play exceeds the desired reading, retighten the rear hub bearing nut and recheck end-play. If reading is still excessive, replace the hub unit.
5. If end-play is correct, check the starting torque by attaching a spring balance to the hub lug bolts and pulling at a 90 degree angle while noting the required force to turn the hub. If the torque required is above the desired reading of 4.9 lbs. or less (22 N or less), loosen the nut and again tighten to the desired torque. Recheck the starting torque. If torque is still above the desired reading, replace the rear bearings.
6. Install the tire and wheel assembly and lower the vehicle. Prior to moving the vehicle, pump the brakes until a firm pedal is obtained.

Scoupe

1. Safely raise and support the rear of the vehicle. Remove the tire and wheel assembly.
2. Remove the grease cap and loosen the axle shaft nut.
3. Tighten the nut to 108–145 ft. lbs. (150–200 Nm).
4. Check for correct bearing end-play by placing a dial indicator on the hub surface and moving the hub outward. Note the movement of the gauge and compare to the desired reading of 0.0043 in. or less (0.11mm or less). If end-play exceeds the desired reading, retighten the rear bearing nut and recheck end-play. If reading is still excessive, replace the hub unit.
5. Once end-play is correct, check the hub and drum starting force by attaching a spring balance to the lug bolts and pulling at a 90 degree angle while noting the required force to turn the drum assembly. If the torque required is above the desired reading of 4.8 lbs. or less (22 N or less), loosen the nut and again tighten to the desired torque. Recheck the starting torque. If torque is still above the desired reading, replace the rear bearings.
6. After final tightening the wheel bearing nut, align with the spindle's indentation and crimp the edge of the nut to wedge in position.
7. Install the tire and wheel assembly and lower the vehicle. Prior to moving the vehicle, pump the brakes until a firm pedal is obtained.

STEERING

Steering Wheel

REMOVAL & INSTALLATION

▶ See Figures 96 and 97

Excel and Scoupe

1. Disconnect the negative battery cable. Pull off the horn cover at the center of the wheel by grasping the upper edge for Excel and prying off at the lower edge for Scoupe. Then, disconnect the horn wire connector.
2. Remove the steering wheel retaining nut. Matchmark the relationship between the wheel and shaft.
3. Remove the steering wheel dynamic dampener.
4. Screw the 2 bolts of a steering wheel puller into the wheel. Then, turn the bolt at the center of the puller to force the wheel off the steering shaft. Do not pound on the wheel to remove it or the collapsible steering shaft may be damaged.

To install:

5. The steering wheel can be pushed onto the shaft splines by hand far enough to start the retaining nut. Install the retaining nut and torque it to 26–32 ft. lbs. (34–44 Nm).

Fig. 96 Remove the 2 screws from behind to remove the horn cover

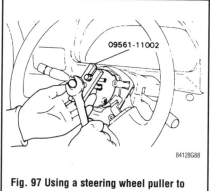

Fig. 97 Using a steering wheel puller to remove the steering wheel

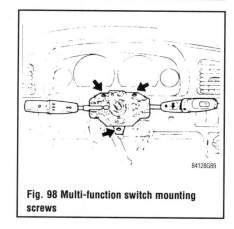

Fig. 98 Multi-function switch mounting screws

Elantra and Sonata

1. Disconnect the negative battery cable.
2. Remove the screws from the back of the horn pad and lift it off.
3. Disconnect the horn wire connector.
4. Pull the dynamic damper forward and off.
5. Remove the steering wheel retaining nut. Matchmark the relationship between the wheel and shaft.
6. Screw the 2 bolts of a steering wheel puller into the wheel. Then, turn the bolt at the center of the puller to force the wheel off the steering shaft. Do not pound on the wheel to remove it or the collapsible steering shaft may be damaged.

To install:

7. Install the steering wheel to the shaft aligning the matchmarks made during removal.
8. Install and tighten the retainer nut to 29–36 ft. lbs. (39–49 Nm).
9. Install the dynamic damper and horn pad to the steering shaft. Make sure to connect the horn wire to the pad prior to installation.
10. Fasten the horn pad to the wheel and reconnect the negative battery cable.

Combination Switch

➡The headlights, turn signals, dimmer switch, horn switch, windshield wiper/washer, intermittent wiper switch and the cruise control function are all built into 1 multi-function combination switch that is mounted on the steering column.

REMOVAL & INSTALLATION

▶ **See Figures 98 and 99**

1. Disconnect the negative battery cable. Remove the steering wheel. Remove the steering column covers.

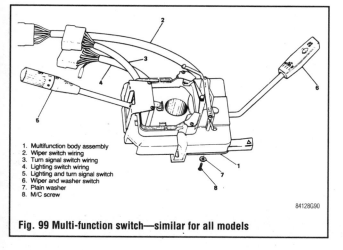

1. Multifunction body assembly
2. Wiper switch wiring
3. Turn signal switch wiring
4. Lighting switch wiring
5. Lighting and turn signal switch
6. Wiper and washer switch
7. Plain washer
8. M/C screw

Fig. 99 Multi-function switch—similar for all models

2. Unplug the electrical connectors and remove the electrical harness retainers.
3. Remove the retaining screws and slide the switch off the steering column.
4. Installation is the reverse order of the removal procedures.

Ignition Lock/Switch

REMOVAL & INSTALLATION

▶ **See Figures 100 and 101**

1. Disconnect the negative battery cable. Remove the steering wheel.

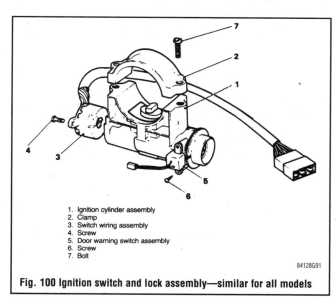

1. Ignition cylinder assembly
2. Clamp
3. Switch wiring assembly
4. Screw
5. Door warning switch assembly
6. Screw
7. Bolt

Fig. 100 Ignition switch and lock assembly—similar for all models

Fig. 101 Ignition switch steering lock removal

2. Remove the lower instrument panel knee protector, steering column covers and the clip that holds the wiring against the steering column.

3. Remove the combination switch and harness.

4. Unplug the electrical connector for the ignition lock.

5. Use a hacksaw to cut a slit in the top of each of the fastening bolts. Unscrew the bolts and remove the switch.

To install:

6. Installation is the reverse of the removal procedure. When installing the new switch, align the halves of the assembly around the steering column, align the assembly with the column boss and then install the special new installation bolts loosely.

7. Verify that the ignition switch works and tighten the bolts until their heads break off.

8. Install the steering wheel.

Steering Linkage

REMOVAL & INSTALLATION

Tie Rod Ends

EXCEL AND SCOUPE

▶ See Figures 102, 103, 104, 105 and 106

1. Loosen the lug nuts.

2. Raise and support the front end on jackstands under the frame.

3. Remove the front wheels.

4. Disconnect the tie rod ends with separator tool 09568-31000 or equivalent.

5. The tie rod ends can now be removed. Prior to removal, count the exact number of exposed threads on the tie rod ends, then loosen the locknut and

unscrew the tie rod end. When installing new tie rod ends, oil the threads and screw them into place so that the previously noted number of threads is visible with the locknut tight. Check the length of the tie rod after the locknut is tight. The correct length should be:

• 1986–89 Excel with manual steering—173.5mm
• 1986–89 Excel with power steering—155.5–157.5mm
• 1990–93 Excel and Scoupe with manual steering—179.3–181.3mm
• 1990–93 Excel and Scoupe with power steering—174.3–176.3mm

6. Connect the tie rods to the knuckle arms using new cotter pins. Torque the tie rod nuts to 11–25 ft. lbs. (15–34 Nm).

7. Mount the front wheels and lower the vehicle.

8. Have the front wheel alignment checked by an alignment specialist.

ELANTRA AND SONATA

▶ See Figures 107 and 108

1. Loosen the lug nuts.

2. Raise and support the front end on jackstands under the frame.

3. Remove the front wheels.

4. Disconnect the tie rod ends with separator tool 09568-31000.

5. The tie rod ends can now be removed. Prior to removal, count the exact number of exposed threads on the tie rod ends, then loosen the locknut and unscrew the tie rod end.

To install:

6. When installing new tie rod ends, oil the threads and screw them into place so that the previously noted number of threads is visible with the locknut tight. Check the length of the tie rod. On all 4-cylinder Sonata models and on V6 Sonata models with a Mando power steering box, the length should be 187.4mm. On V6 Sonata models with TRW power steering, the length should be 176.1mm. On Elantra the tie-rod length should be 181mm. Remember that the left and right tie rod ends should be equal.

7. Connect the tie rods to the knuckle arms using new cotter pins. Torque

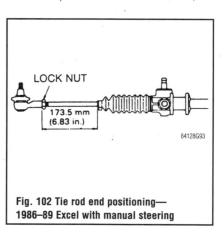

Fig. 102 Tie rod end positioning—1986–89 Excel with manual steering

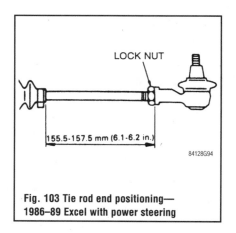

Fig. 103 Tie rod end positioning—1986–89 Excel with power steering

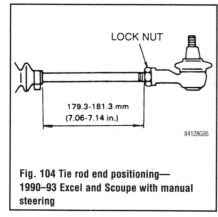

Fig. 104 Tie rod end positioning—1990–93 Excel and Scoupe with manual steering

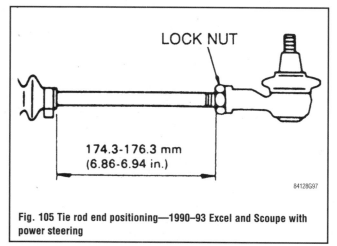

Fig. 105 Tie rod end positioning—1990–93 Excel and Scoupe with power steering

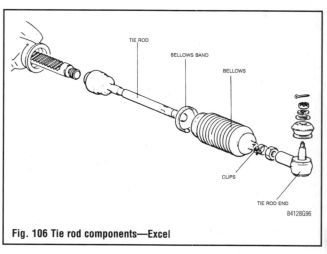

Fig. 106 Tie rod components—Excel

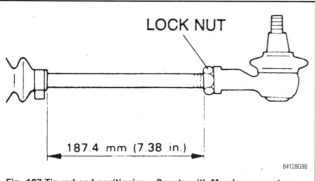

Fig. 107 Tie rod end positioning—Sonata with Mando power steering gear

187.4 mm (7.38 in.)

84128G98

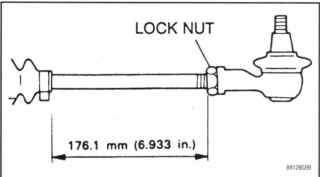

Fig. 108 Tie rod end positioning—Sonata with TRW power steering gear

176.1 mm (6.933 in.)

84128G99

the tie rod nuts to 17–25 ft. lbs. (24–34 Nm) on Sonata and 11–15 ft. lbs. (15–34 Nm) on Elantra.
8. Mount the front wheels and lower the vehicle.
9. Have the front wheel alignment checked by an alignment specialist.

Manual Steering Rack

➥Complete gear replacement with a new or reconditioned unit may be more cost and/or time efficient than repairing the original unit and may reduce the risk of damage or injury due to a part failure. Assessment of the situation may prove to be beneficial.

ADJUSTMENT

Excel and Scoupe

1. Mount the rack and pinion assembly in a soft jawed vise, clamping on the rack mounting area, only.
2. Using a spline adapter on an inch-pound torque wrench, turn the pinion shaft at the rate of 1 full turn every 4–6 seconds, turning the steering from lock-to-lock. Measure the total preload lock-to-lock. Preload should be 3.6–9.6 inch lbs.
3. Place a pull scale on each tie rod end, in turn and pull straight away. The rack starting force should be 11–66 lbs.
4. If the specifications in either Steps 2 or 3 are not met, the rubber cushion and yoke spring behind the pinion shaft nut will have to be replaced.

REMOVAL & INSTALLATION

Excel and Scoupe

1. Loosen the lug nuts.
2. Raise the vehicle and support it safely.
3. Remove the wheels.
4. Remove the steering shaft-to-pinion coupling bolt.

5. Disconnect the tie rod ends with a separator.
6. Removing the clamps securing the rack to the crossmember and remove the unit from the vehicle. The tie rod ends can now be removed. Prior to removal, count the exact number of exposed threads on the tie rod ends, then loosen the locknut and unscrew the tie rod end. When installing new tie rod ends, oil the threads and screw them into place so the previously noted number of threads is visible with the locknut tight. As a further reference, the distance between the end of the tie rod boot and the centerline of the tie rod ball stud should be 9.6 in. (243.5mm). Torque the locknut to 38 ft. lbs. (52 Nm).
   To install:
7. Install the rubber mount for the gear box with the slit on the downside.
8. Observe the following torques:
   • Rack-to-crossmember bolts—22–29 ft. lbs. (25–39 Nm) for 1986–1989 Excel models, 43–58 ft. lbs. (58–78 Nm) for 1990–93 Excel and Scoupe
   • Coupling bolt—11–14 ft. lbs. (15–19 Nm)
   • Tie rod end slotted nuts—11–25 ft. lbs. (15–34 Nm)

Power Steering Rack

➥Complete gear replacement with a new or reconditioned unit may be more cost and/or time efficient than repairing the original unit and may reduce the risk of damage or injury due to a part failure. assessment of the situation may prove to be beneficial.

ADJUSTMENT

Excel and Scoupe

1. Mount the rack in a soft jawed vise, clamping the vise on the rack mounting areas, only.
2. Using a spline adapter on an inch-pound torque wrench, rotate the pinion shaft several times, lock-to-lock and note the total pinion preload. Preload should be 5–11 inch lbs.
3. If the preload is note within specifications, adjust the position of the rack support cover and recheck the preload. If it does not work, the rack support cover components are defective.

REMOVAL & INSTALLATION

Excel and Scoupe

1. Loosen the lug nuts.
2. Raise the vehicle and support it safely.
3. Remove the wheels.
4. Remove the steering shaft-to-pinion coupling bolt.
5. Disconnect the tie rod ends with a separator.
6. Drain the fluid.
7. Disconnect the hoses from the steering gear.
8. Remove the band from the steering joint cover.
9. Unbolt and remove the stabilizer bar.
10. Remove the rear roll stopper-to-center member bolt and move the rear roll stopper forward, as required.
11. Remove the rack unit mounting clamp bolts and take the unit out the left side of the vehicle. The tie rod ends can now be removed. Prior to removal, count the exact number of exposed threads on the tie rod ends, then loosen the locknut and unscrew the tie rod end.
    To install:
12. When installing new tie rod ends, oil the threads and screw them into place so the previously noted number of threads is visible with the locknut tight. As a further reference, the distance between the end of the tie rod boot and the point at which the locknut touches the tie rod ball socket body should be 6.1–6.2 in. (155.5–157.5mm); 6.9–7.0 in. (174.3–176.3mm) for Scoupe. Torque the locknut to 38 ft. lbs. (52 Nm).
13. When installing the power steering rack, make sure the rubber isolators have their nubs aligned with the holes in the clamps.
14. Apply rubber cement to the slits in the gear mounting grommet.
15. Tighten the clamp bolt to 43–58 ft. lbs. (58–78 Nm), the tie rod end slotted nuts to 11–25 ft. lbs. (14–34 Nm) and the coupling bolt to 11–14 ft. lbs. (14–19 Nm).
16. Fill the system with Dexron®II ATF.

Elantra and Sonata

1. Raise the vehicle and support it safely.
2. Remove the wheels.
3. Drain the fluid from the power steering system.
4. Remove the steering shaft-to-pinion coupling bolt.
5. Remove the retainer nut and disconnect both tie rod ends using an appropriate puller.
6. Disconnect the left lower arm from the steering knuckle. This will increase clearance as the gear assembly will be removed from the left side of the vehicle.
7. Disconnect the fluid hoses from the gear box.
8. Remove the center member and temporarily retighten the front muffler.
9. Unbolt and remove the stabilizer bar.
10. Remove the rack unit mounting clamp bolts and move the rack towards the right and then take the unit out on the left side of the vehicle. The tie rod ends can now be removed. Prior to removal, count the exact number of exposed threads on the tie rod ends, then loosen the locknut and unscrew the tie rod end.

To install:

11. When installing new tie rod ends, oil the threads and screw them into place so the previously noted number of threads is visible with the locknut tight. As a further reference, the distance between the end of the tie rod boot and the point at which the locknut touches the tie rod ball socket body should be 187.4mm. Torque the locknut to 38 ft. lbs. (52 Nm).
12. When installing the power steering rack, make sure the rubber isolators have their nubs aligned with the holes in the clamps.
13. Apply rubber cement to the slits in the gear mounting grommet. Tighten the clamp bolt to 43–58 ft. lbs. (58–78 Nm), the tie rod nuts to 11–25 ft. lbs. (14–34 Nm) and the coupling bolt to 22–25 ft. lbs. (29–34 Nm).
14. Fill the system with Dexron®II ATF.

Power Steering Pump

REMOVAL & INSTALLATION

Excel and Scoupe

1. Place a drain pan under the pump.
2. Loosen the pump mounting bolts and remove the drive belt.
3. Disconnect the suction hose from the pump.
4. Disconnect the pressure hose from the pump and the return hose from the reservoir.
5. Remove the pump-to-mounting bracket bolts and lift out the pump. Unbolt and remove the pump reservoir.

To install:

6. Install the pump reservoir. Position the pump onto the mounting bracket and torque the mounting bolts to 15–20 ft. lbs. 20–27 Nm

7. Connect the suction hose to the pump. Install the hose so that the painted portion is toward the oil pump.
8. Connect the pressure hose to the pump and the return hose to the oil reservoir. When installing the return line, make sure you push it at least 25–30mm onto the return tube. The hoses should be twisted or allowed to come in contact with an other component in the engine compartment.
9. Install the drive belt and adjust the tension.
10. Fill the system with DEXRON®II ATF and bleed the system.

Elantra and Sonata

1. Place a drain pan under the pump.
2. Remove the pressure hose from the oil pump.
3. Disconnect the suction hose and drain the fluid in the container.
4. Loosen the pump mounting bolts and remove the drive belt.
5. Remove the pump-to-mounting bracket bolts and lift out the pump.

To install:

6. Position the pump onto the mounting bracket and torque the mounting bolts to 33–41 ft. lbs (45–55 Nm) on Elantra and 12–19 ft. lbs. (17–26 on Sonata models with V6 engine and 18–24 ft. lbs. (25–33 Nm) on Sonata models with 4 cylinder engines.
7. Connect the suction hose to the pump.
8. Install the drive belt and adjust the tension.
9. Connect the pressure hose to the pump and the return hose to the oil reservoir. When installing the return line, make sure you push it at least 30mm onto the return tube. The hoses should be twisted or allowed to come in contact with an other component in the engine compartment.
10. Fill the system with DEXRON®II ATF and bleed the system.

BLEEDING

1. Ensure that the reservoir is full of Dexron®II automatic transmission fluid.
2. Raise and safely support the front wheels of the vehicle.
3. Turn the steering wheel from lock to lock 5 or 6 times.
4. Disconnect the coil wire and connect to a solid ground. Operate the starter motor intermittently for 15 to 20 seconds and turn the steering wheel from lock to lock 5 or 6 times.

➡**Ensure that the reservoir is full during air bleeding to prevent the fluid level from falling below the lower position of the filter.**

5. Connect the coil wire and start the engine.
6. Turn the steering wheel from lock to lock until no more air bubbles are visible in the reservoir.
7. Confirm that the oil is not milky and that the fluid level is correct.
8. Confirm that there is little change in the fluid level when the steering wheel is turned to the left and right.

➡**An abrupt rise in the fluid level after stopping the engine is a sign of incomplete bleeding. If this occurs, repeat the bleeding procedure.**

TORQUE SPECIFICATIONS

Component	U.S.	Metric
Hub and Knuckle assembly;		
Caliper assembly to knuckle;		
Excel	47–54 ft. lbs.	65–75 Nm
Elantra	47–54 ft. lbs.	65–75 Nm
Scoupe	47–54 ft. lbs.	65–75 Nm
Sonata	47–54 ft. lbs.	65–75 Nm
Knuckle to strut assembly;		
Excel	65–76 ft. lbs.	90–105 Nm
Elantra	81–96 ft. lbs.	110–130 Nm
Scoupe	65–76 ft. lbs.	90–105 Nm
Sonata	65–76 ft. lbs.	90–105 Nm
Lower arm ball joint to knuckle;		
Excel	43–52 ft. lbs.	60–72 Nm
Elantra	43–52 ft. lbs.	60–72 Nm
Scoupe	43–52 ft. lbs.	60–72 Nm
Sonata	43–52 ft. lbs.	60–72 Nm
Tie rod end to knuckle;		
Excel	11-25 ft. lbs.	15–34 Nm
Elantra	11–25 ft. lbs.	15–34 Nm
Scoupe	11–25 ft. lbs.	15–34 Nm
Sonata	17–24 ft. lbs.	24–34 Nm
Front Suspension;		
Ball joint to lower arm assembly;		
Excel	69–87 ft. lbs.	95–120 Nm
Scoupe	69–87 ft. lbs.	95–120 Nm
Lower arm mounting shaft mounting nut;		
Excel	69–87 ft. lbs.	95–120 Nm
Elantra	69–87 ft. lbs.	95–120 Nm
Scoupe	69–87 ft. lbs.	95–120 Nm
Sonata	72–87 ft. lbs.	100–120 Nm
Lower arm mounting shaft bolt (to floor);		
Excel	16–137 ft. lbs.	160–190 Nm
Scoupe	16–137 ft. lbs.	160–190 Nm
Lower arm mounting bracket bolt;		
Excel	43–58 ft. lbs.	60–80 Nm
Elantra	43–58 ft. lbs.	60–80 Nm
Scoupe	43–58 ft. lbs.	60–80 Nm
Strut mounting self locking nut;		
Excel	29–36 ft. lbs.	40–50 Nm
Elantra	43–51 ft. lbs.	60–70 Nm
Scoupe	29–36 ft. lbs.	40–50 Nm
Sonata	43–51 ft. lbs.	60–70 Nm
Stabilizer bar bracket mounting bolt;		
Excel	12–19 ft. lbs.	17–26 Nm
Elantra	12–19 ft. lbs.	17–26 Nm
Scoupe	12–19 ft. lbs.	17–26 Nm
Sonata	22–30 ft. lbs.	30–42 Nm
Upper strut installation nut;		
Excel	11–14 ft. lbs.	15–20 Nm
Elantra	25–33 ft. lbs.	35–45 Nm
Scoupe	11–14 ft. lbs.	15–20 Nm
Sonata	18–25 ft. lbs.	25–35 Nm

84128C01

TORQUE SPECIFICATIONS

Component	U.S.	Metric
Wheel hub nut;		
Excel	145–188 ft. lbs.	200–260 Nm
Elantra	145–188 ft. lbs.	200–260 Nm
Scoupe	145–188 ft. lbs.	200–260 Nm
Sonata	145–188 ft. lbs.	200–260 Nm
Wheel lug nut;		
Excel	65–80 ft. lbs.	90–110 Nm
Elantra	65–80 ft. lbs.	90–110 Nm
Scoupe	65–80 ft. lbs.	90–110 Nm
Sonata	65–80 ft. lbs.	90–110 Nm
Rear Suspension;		
Lateral rod to body;		
Elantra	58–72 ft. lbs.	80–100 Nm
Sonata	58–72 ft. lbs.	80–100 Nm
Lateral rod to axle beam;		
Elantra	58–72 ft. lbs.	80–100 Nm
Sonata	72–87 ft. lbs.	100–120 Nm
Rear suspension arm assembly fixture mounting nuts;		
Excel	94–108 ft. lbs.	130–150 Nm
Scoupe	94–108 ft. lbs.	130–150 Nm
Rear Shock absorber mounting nuts;		
Excel	47–58 ft. lbs.	65–80 Nm
Elantra:		
Upper	18–25 ft. lbs.	25–35 Nm
Lower	58–72 ft. lbs.	80–100 Nm
Scoupe	47–58 ft. lbs.	65–80 Nm
Sonata:		
Upper	18–25 ft. lbs.	25–35 Nm
Lower	58–72 ft. lbs.	80–100 Nm
Spindle to backing plate bolts;		
Excel	36–43 ft. lbs.	50–60 Nm
Scoupe	36–43 ft. lbs.	50–60 Nm
Suspension arm mounting nuts;		
Excel	36–51 ft. lbs.	50–70 Nm
Scoupe	36–51 ft. lbs.	50–70 Nm
Trailing arm mounting bolt;		
Elantra	94–108 ft. lbs.	130–150 Nm
Sonata	72–87 ft. lbs.	100–120 Nm
Wheel bearing nut;		
Excel	108–145 ft. lbs.	150–200 Nm
Elantra	108–145 ft. lbs.	150–200 Nm
Scoupe	108–145 ft. lbs.	150–200 Nm
Sonata	174–217 ft. lbs.	240–300 Nm
Steering;		
Power steering pump mounting bracket bolt;		
Excel	14–20 ft. lbs.	20–27 Nm
Elantra	33–41 ft. lbs.	45–55 Nm
Scoupe	14–20 ft. lbs.	20–27 Nm
Sonata:		
V6 engine	12–19 ft. lbs.	17–26 Nm
4 cylinder engine	18–24 ft. lbs.	25–33 Nm
Power steering pump adjusting bolt;		
Excel	18–24 ft. lbs.	25–33 Nm
Elantra	18–24 ft. lbs.	25–33 Nm
Scoupe	18–24 ft. lbs.	25–33 Nm
Sonata	18–24 ft. lbs.	25–33 Nm
Rack support cover lock nut;		
Excel	36–51 ft. lbs.	50–70 Nm
Elantra	36–51 ft. lbs.	50–70 Nm
Scoupe	36–51 ft. lbs.	50–70 Nm
Sonata:		
Mando steering gear	36–51 ft. lbs.	50–70 Nm
TRW steering gear	43–65 ft. lbs.	60–90 Nm

84128C02

TORQUE SPECIFICATIONS

Component	U.S.	Metric
Steering wheel lock nut;		
Excel	25–33 ft. lbs.	35–45 Nm
Elantra	25–33 ft. lbs.	35–45 Nm
Scoupe	25–33 ft. lbs.	35–45 Nm
Sonata	29–36 ft. lbs.	40–50 Nm
Steering column and shaft assembly mounting bracket;		
Excel	9–13 ft. lbs.	13–18 Nm
Elantra	6–10 ft. lbs.	9–14 Nm
Scoupe	9–13 ft. lbs.	13–18 Nm
Sonata	9–13 ft. lbs.	13–18 Nm
Steering shaft and joint;		
Excel	11–14 ft. lbs.	15–20 Nm
Elantra	11–14 ft. lbs.	15–20 Nm
Scoupe	11–14 ft. lbs.	15–20 Nm
Sonata	22–29 ft. lbs.	30–40 Nm
Steering gearbox mounting clamp;		
Excel	43–58 ft. lbs.	60–80 Nm
Elantra	43–58 ft. lbs.	60–80 Nm
Scoupe	43–58 ft. lbs.	60–80 Nm
Sonata	43–58 ft. lbs.	60–80 Nm
Steering column dust cover mounting bolt;		
Excel	2.9–4.3 ft. lbs.	4–6 Nm
Elantra	2.9–4.3 ft. lbs.	4–6 Nm
Scoupe	2.9–4.3 ft. lbs.	4–6 Nm
Sonata	2.9–4.3 ft. lbs.	4–6 Nm

84128C03

9

BRAKES

BRAKE OPERATING SYSTEM

Basic Operating Principles

Hydraulic systems are used to actuate the brakes of all modern automobiles. The system transports the power required to force the frictional surfaces of the braking system together from the pedal to the individual brake units at each wheel. A hydraulic system is used for two reasons.

First, fluid under pressure can be carried to all parts of an automobile by small pipes and flexible hoses without taking up a significant amount of room or posing routing problems.

Second, a great mechanical advantage can be given to the brake pedal end of the system, and the foot pressure required to actuate the brakes can be reduced by making the surface area of the master cylinder pistons smaller than that of any of the pistons in the wheel cylinders or calipers.

The master cylinder consists of a fluid reservoir along with a double cylinder and piston assembly. Double type master cylinders are designed to separate the front and rear braking systems hydraulically in case of a leak. The master cylinder coverts mechanical motion from the pedal into hydraulic pressure within the lines. This pressure is translated back into mechanical motion at the wheels by either the wheel cylinder (drum brakes) or the caliper (disc brakes).

Steel lines carry the brake fluid to a point on the vehicle's frame near each of the vehicle's wheels. The fluid is then carried to the calipers and wheel cylinders by flexible tubes in order to allow for suspension and steering movements.

In drum brake systems, each wheel cylinder contains two pistons, one at either end, which push outward in opposite directions and force the brake shoe into contact with the drum.

In disc brake systems, the cylinders are part of the calipers. At least one cylinder in each caliper is used to force the brake pads against the disc.

All pistons employ some type of seal, usually made of rubber, to minimize fluid leakage. A rubber dust boot seals the outer end of the cylinder against dust and dirt. The boot fits around the outer end of the piston on disc brake calipers, and around the brake actuating rod on wheel cylinders.

The hydraulic system operates as follows: When at rest, the entire system, from the piston(s) in the master cylinder to those in the wheel cylinders or calipers, is full of brake fluid. Upon application of the brake pedal, fluid trapped in front of the master cylinder piston(s) is forced through the lines to the wheel cylinders. Here, it forces the pistons outward, in the case of drum brakes, and inward toward the disc, in the case of disc brakes. The motion of the pistons is opposed by return springs mounted outside the cylinders in drum brakes, and by spring seals, in disc brakes.

Upon release of the brake pedal, a spring located inside the master cylinder immediately returns the master cylinder pistons to the normal position. The pistons contain check valves and the master cylinder has compensating ports drilled in it. These are uncovered as the pistons reach their normal position. The piston check valves allow fluid to flow toward the wheel cylinders or calipers as the pistons withdraw. Then, as the return springs force the brake pads or shoes into the released position, the excess fluid reservoir through the compensating ports. It is during the time the pedal is in the released position that any fluid that has leaked out of the system will be replaced through the compensating ports.

Dual circuit master cylinders employ two pistons, located one behind the other, in the same cylinder. The primary piston is actuated directly by mechanical linkage from the brake pedal through the power booster. The secondary piston is actuated by fluid trapped between the two pistons. If a leak develops in front of the secondary piston, it moves forward until it bottoms against the front of the master cylinder, and the fluid trapped between the pistons will operate the rear brakes. If the rear brakes develop a leak, the primary piston will move forward until direct contact with the secondary piston takes place, and it will force the secondary piston to actuate the front brakes. In either case, the brake pedal moves farther when the brakes are applied, and less braking power is available.

All dual circuit systems use a switch to warn the driver when only half of the brake system is operational. This switch is usually located in a valve body which is mounted on the firewall or the frame below the master cylinder. A hydraulic piston receives pressure from both circuits, each circuit's pressure being applied to one end of the piston. When the pressures are in balance, the piston remains stationary. When one circuit has a leak, however, the greater pressure in that circuit during application of the brakes will push the piston to one side, closing the switch and activating the brake warning light.

In disc brake systems, this valve body also contains a metering valve and, in some cases, a proportioning valve. The metering valve keeps pressure from traveling to the disc brakes on the front wheels until the brake shoes on the rear wheels have contacted the drums, ensuring that the front brakes will never be used alone. The proportioning valve controls the pressure to the rear brakes to lessen the chance of rear wheel lock-up during very hard braking.

Warning lights may be tested by depressing the brake pedal and holding it while opening one of the wheel cylinder bleeder screws. If this does not cause the light to go on, substitute a new lamp, make continuity checks, and, finally, replace the switch as necessary.

The hydraulic system may be checked for leaks by applying pressure to the pedal gradually and steadily. If the pedal sinks very slowly to the floor, the system has a leak. This is not to be confused with a springy or spongy feel due to the compression of air within the lines. If the system leaks, there will be a gradual change in the position of the pedal with a constant pressure.

Check for leaks along all lines and at wheel cylinders. If no external leaks are apparent, the problem is inside the master cylinder.

DISC BRAKES

Instead of the traditional expanding brakes that press outward against a circular drum, disc brake systems utilize a disc (rotor) with brake pads positioned on either side of it. An easily-seen analogy is the hand brake arrangement on a bicycle. The pads squeeze onto the rim of the bike wheel, slowing its motion. Automobile disc brakes use the identical principle but apply the braking effort to a separate disc instead of the wheel.

The disc (rotor) is a casting, usually equipped with cooling fins between the two braking surfaces. This enables air to circulate between the braking surfaces making them less sensitive to heat buildup and more resistant to fade. Dirt and water do not drastically affect braking action since contaminants are thrown off by the centrifugal action of the rotor or scraped off the by the pads. Also, the equal clamping action of the two brake pads tends to ensure uniform, straight line stops. Disc brakes are inherently self-adjusting. There are three general types of disc brake:

- A fixed caliper.
- A floating caliper.
- A sliding caliper.

The fixed caliper design uses two pistons mounted on either side of the rotor (in each side of the caliper). The caliper is mounted rigidly and does not move.

The sliding and floating designs are quite similar. In fact, these two types are often lumped together. In both designs, the pad on the inside of the rotor is moved into contact with the rotor by hydraulic force. The caliper, which is not held in a fixed position, moves slightly, bringing the outside pad into contact with the rotor. There are various methods of attaching floating calipers. Some pivot at the bottom or top, and some slide on mounting bolts. In any event, the end result is the same.

DRUM BRAKES

Drum brakes employ two brake shoes mounted on a stationary backing plate. These shoes are positioned inside a circular drum which rotates with the wheel assembly. The shoes are held in place by springs. This allows them to slide toward the drums (when they are applied) while keeping the linings and drums in alignment. The shoes are actuated by a wheel cylinder which is mounted at the top of the backing plate. When the brakes are applied, hydraulic pressure forces the wheel cylinder's actuating links outward. Since these links bear directly against the top of the brake shoes, the tops of the shoes are then forced against the inner side of the drum. This action forces the bottoms of the two shoes to contact the brake drum by rotating the entire assembly slightly (known as servo action). When pressure within the wheel cylinder is relaxed, return springs pull the shoes back away from the drum.

Most modern drum brakes are designed to self-adjust themselves during application when the vehicle is moving in reverse. This motion causes both shoes to rotate very slightly with the drum, rocking an adjusting lever, thereby causing rotation of the adjusting screw. Some drum brake systems are designed to self-adjust during application whenever the brakes are applied. This on-board adjustment system reduces the need for maintenance adjustments and keeps both the brake function and pedal feel satisfactory.

Adjustments

The disc brakes require no adjustment. The rear drum and disc brakes are automatically adjusted by pulling and returning the parking brake lever, then stepping on the brake pedal.

BRAKE PEDAL HEIGHT ADJUSTMENT

▶ **See Figures 1, 2, 3 and 4**

1. Measure the distance from the top of the pedal pad to the firewall. The distance should be 183—188mm on 1986–89 Excel and 4–cylinder Sonata. On 1990–93 Excel and Scoupe it should be 165mm. On V6 Sonata and Elantra, it should be 178mm. If not, continue.
2. Back off the brake light switch, located above the pedal arm, until it no longer touches the pedal arm.
3. Loosen the locknut on the pedal pushrod and turn the pushrod with a pliers until the proper pedal height is reached. Tighten the locknut.
4. Adjust the brake light switch until the distance, B, between the outer case of the switch and the pedal arm is 0.5–l.0mm on all models. Tighten the locknut.

BRAKE PEDAL FREE-PLAY ADJUSTMENT

▶ **See Figures 5 and 6**

1. With the engine shut off, depress the brake pedal two or three times to release any vacuum pressure.
2. Depress the brake pedal by hand until resistance is felt. This motion before resistance is the pedal free-play. Proper free-play should be 10-15mm on Excel and 2.5-7.5mm on 4-cylinder Sonata and 5-10mm on V6 Sonata.
3. Free-play is adjusted at the stop light switch. Loosen the locknut and adjust the switch until the free-play is within specification.

STOP LIGHT SWITCH

The switch is located on a bracket above the brake pedal arm.

ADJUSTMENT

1. Disconnect the negative battery cable.
2. The stop light switch works off the brake pedal lever. To adjust, disconnect the electrical connection and loosen the switch locknut.
3. Screw the switch inward until it contacts the stop on the brake pedal arm. Back out the switch ½–1 full turn. The distance between the end of the switch plunger bore and the brake lever stop should be 0.020–0.040 in. (0.5–1.0mm).
4. Tighten the locknut and connect the wires.
5. Connect the negative battery cable.
6. Make sure the stop lights come on when the brake pedal is depressed and go out when the pedal is released. Also, make sure the cruise control system operates properly.

REMOVAL & INSTALLATION

1. Disconnect the negative battery cable.
2. Locate the stop light switch above the brake pedal lever.
3. Disconnect the wiring connectors from the switch and unscrew the switch.
4. Thread the stop light switch into the switch holding bracket. Adjust the switch to achieve correct operation.
5. Connect the stop light wires.
6. Connect the negative battery cable.
7. Make sure the stop lights come on when the brake pedal is depressed and go out when the pedal is released. Also, make sure the cruise control system operates properly.

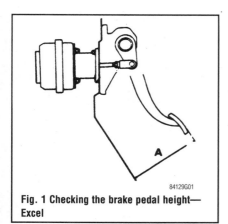

84129G01

Fig. 1 Checking the brake pedal height—Excel

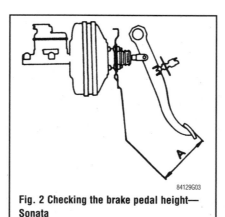

84129G03

Fig. 2 Checking the brake pedal height—Sonata

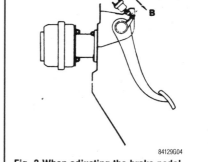

84129G04

Fig. 3 When adjusting the brake pedal height on 1986–89 Excel, set the stoplight switch clearance as shown

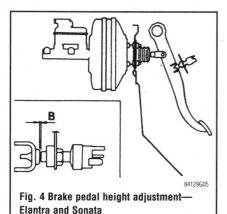

84129G05

Fig. 4 Brake pedal height adjustment—Elantra and Sonata

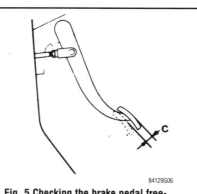

84129G06

Fig. 5 Checking the brake pedal free-play—Excel and Scoupe

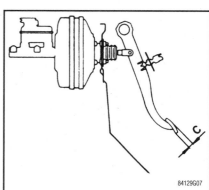

84129G07

Fig. 6 Checking the brake pedal free-play—Elantra and Sonata

Master Cylinder

✷✷ CAUTION

Be careful not to spill brake fluid on the painted surfaces of your car. The brake fluid will cause damage to the paint.

REMOVAL & INSTALLATION

▶ See Figure 7

1. Disconnect the fluid level sensor.
2. Disconnect the brake tubes from the master cylinder and cap them immediately to prevent the entry of moisture into the system. On V6 Sonata with rear disc brakes, disconnect the brake tubes without removing the proportioning valves.
3. Unbolt and remove the master cylinder and gasket from the booster. If the gaskets are worn, replace them. On V6 Sonata with rear disc brakes, there is a rubber O-ring located on the master cylinder cartridge that seals the unit to the brake booster. If this seal is worn or damaged in any way, replace it.
4. Before installing the master cylinder, check the pushrod-to-master cylinder clearance as follows:
   a. On 1986–89 Excel, measure the master cylinder pushrod clearance using the accompanying illustration and the following formula: A = B—C—D. A should be 0.4–0.8mm.
   b. On Sonata with rear drum brakes, with a Vernier caliper measure the distance from the booster front shell surface to the booster pushrod end (dimension "A"). It should be 37.35–37.65mm.

➡**Master cylinder pushrod clearance adjustment is not required on Sonata with rear disc brakes and the 1990–93 Excel, Elantra or Scoupe.**

5. If the pushrod-to-master cylinder clearance is not as specified, adjust by changing the pushrod length by turning the adjusting screw on the pushrod.
6. Position the master cylinder to the booster and install the mounting bolts. Torque the mounting bolts to 10–16 ft. lbs. (14–22 Nm) for Scoupe or 9 ft. lbs. (12 Nm) for remaining models.
7. Connect the brake tubes to the master cylinder. Torque the tubes to 9–12 ft. lbs. (13–17 Nm).
8. Bleed the brake system. Connect the negative battery cable. Road test the vehicle.

Power Brake Booster

LEAK TEST

To test the booster for a leak, proceed as follows:
1. Operate the engine at idle with the transmission in Neutral without touching the brake pedal for at least one or two minutes.
2. Turn off the engine, and wait one minute.

3. Test for the presence of assist vacuum by depressing the brake pedal and releasing it several times. Light application will produce less and less pedal travel, if vacuum was present. If there is no vacuum, air is leaking into the system somewhere.
4. Pump the brake pedal (with engine off) until the supply vacuum is entirely gone.
5. Put a light, steady pressure on the pedal.
6. Start the engine, and operate it at idle with the transmission in Neutral. If the system is operating, the brake pedal should fall toward the floor if constant pressure is maintained on the pedal. Power brake systems may be tested for hydraulic leaks just as ordinary systems are tested, except that the engine should be idling with the transmission in Neutral (manual) or Park (automatic) with the wheels blocked throughout the test.

REMOVAL & INSTALLATION

▶ See Figures 8, 9 and 10

1. Disconnect the negative battery cable. Slide back the clip and disconnect the vacuum supply line at the brake booster. Pull gently in order to avoid damaging the check valve.
2. Remove the master cylinder.
3. Disconnect the pushrod at the brake pedal. This requires pulling the lockpin out of the pedal clevis pin and then pulling the latter out of the pedal lever and clevis rod.
4. Remove the mounting bolts and nuts from the firewall and remove the booster.

To install:
5. Installation is the reverse of the removal procedures. Install the brake booster on the firewall and tighten the mounting nuts to 10–12 ft. lbs. (13–17 Nm) for Scoupe or 8 ft. lbs. (12 Nm) for the remaining models. Bleed the brake system.

Proportioning Valve

The valve performs one or more of the following functions:
1. Controls the amount of hydraulic pressure to the rear brakes.
2. Warns of failure in the brake system (warning light on dash).
3. Inactivates rear pressure control in case of failure in the front service brake system.

➡**On Excels with manual transmissions produced up to December of 1987 and on Excels with automatic transmissions produced up to February of 1987, a Sumitomo type proportioning valve is used. From January 1988 for manual transmissions and March 1987 for automatic transmissions, a Kelsey-Hayes type proportioning valve is used on Excel. All Sonatas with rear drum brakes use the Kelsey-Hayes type proportioning valve.**

REMOVAL & INSTALLATION

Except Sonata With Rear Disc Brakes

▶ See Figures 11 and 12

1. Disconnect the negative battery cable. Disconnect the brake lines at the valve.

➡**Use a flare nut wrench to avoid damage to the lines and fittings.**

2. Remove the mounting bolts and remove the valve.

➡**If the proportioning valve is found to be defective, it must be replaced.**

3. Install the proportioning valve and tighten the mounting bolts to 15 ft. lbs. (20 Nm).
4. Refill the system with fluid and bleed the brakes. Connect the negative battery cable.

Sonata With Rear Disc Brakes

▶ See Figure 13

These models use a Bendix master cylinder as opposed to the Mando master cylinder used on rear drum brake vehicles. On the Bendix master cylinder, the proportioning valves are screwed directly in the master cylinder.

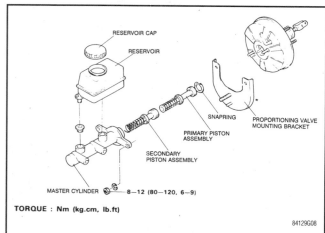

TORQUE : Nm (kg.cm, lb.ft)

84129G08

Fig. 7 Typical master cylinder assembly

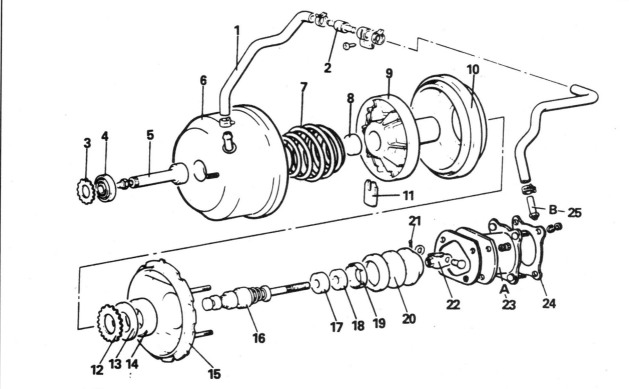

1. Vacuum hose
2. Check valve
3. Retainer
4. Plate and seal
5. Push rod
6. Front shell
7. Spring
8. Reaction disc
9. Diaphragm plate
10. Diaphragm
11. Valve plunger stop key
12. Retainer
13. Bearing
14. Seal
15. Rear shell
16. Valve rod and plunger
17. Air silencer filter
18. Silencer
19. Air silencer retainer
20. Boot
21. Clevis pin
22. Operating rod
23. Booster mounting bracket
24. Seal
25. Fitting

	Nm	kg.cm	ft.lbs.
A	8-12	82-122	6-9
B	15-18	153-184	11-13

84129G10

Fig. 8 Power booster assembly—1986—89 Excel

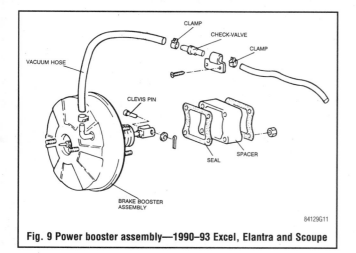

84129G11

Fig. 9 Power booster assembly—1990–93 Excel, Elantra and Scoupe

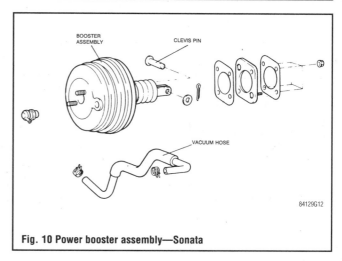

84129G12

Fig. 10 Power booster assembly—Sonata

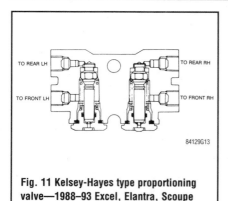

Fig. 11 Kelsey-Hayes type proportioning valve—1988–93 Excel, Elantra, Scoupe and Sonata with rear drum brakes

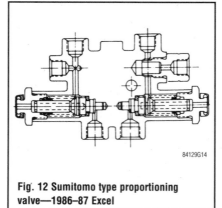

Fig. 12 Sumitomo type proportioning valve—1986–87 Excel

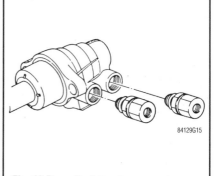

Fig. 13 Proportioning valve removal— Sonata with rear disc brakes

1. Unplug the fluid level sensor wire from the bottom of the fluid reservoir.
2. Using a line nut wrench, disconnect the fluid tubes from the proportioning valves. Plug the tube ends to prevent the loss of fluid.
3. Unscrew the valves from the master cylinder body.
4. Remove the valve O-rings. Discard them and install new ones. Before installation, lubricate the new O-rings with clean brake fluid.
5. Screw the valves into the master cylinder and torque them to 10–16 ft. lbs. DO NOT overtighten or the O-rings may be damaged.
6. Connect and tighten the fluid tubes to the valves.
7. Plug the fluid level sensor wire into the bottom of the fluid reservoir.
8. Fill the fluid reservoir to the proper level and bleed the brakes.

Brake Hoses and Lines

Metal lines and rubber brake hoses should be checked frequently for leaks and external damage. Metal lines are particularly prone to crushing and kinking under the vehicle. Any such deformation can restrict the proper flow of fluid and therefore impair braking at the wheels. Rubber hoses should be checked for cracking or scraping; such damage can create a weak spot in the hose and it could fail under pressure.

Any time the lines are removed or disconnected, extreme cleanliness must be observed. Clean all joints and connections before disassembly (use a stiff bristle brush and clean brake fluid); be sure to plug the lines and ports as soon as they are opened. New lines and hoses should be flushed clean with brake fluid before installation to remove any contamination.

REMOVAL & INSTALLATION

▶ **See Figures 14, 15, 16 and 17**

1. Disconnect the negative battery cable.
2. Raise and safely support the vehicle on jackstands.
3. Remove any wheel and tire assemblies necessary for access to the particular line you are removing.

4. Thoroughly clean the surrounding area at the joints to be disconnected.
5. Place a suitable catch pan under the joint to be disconnected.
6. Using two wrenches (one to hold the joint and one to turn the fitting), disconnect the hose or line to be replaced.
7. Disconnect the other end of the line or hose, moving the drain pan if necessary. Always use a back-up wrench to avoid damaging the fitting.
8. Disconnect any retaining clips or brackets holding the line and remove the line from the vehicle.

➡ **If the brake system is to remain open for more time than it takes to swap lines, tape or plug each remaining clip and port to keep contaminants out and fluid in.**

To install:
9. Install the new line or hose, starting with the end farthest from the master cylinder. Connect the other end, then confirm that both fittings are correctly threaded and turn smoothly using finger pressure. Make sure the new line will not rub against any other part. Brake lines must be at least 1/2 in. (13mm) from the steering column and other moving parts. Any protective shielding or insulators must be reinstalled in the original location.

✷✷ WARNING

Make sure the hose is NOT kinked or touching any part of the frame or suspension after installation. These conditions may cause the hose to fail prematurely.

10. Using two wrenches as before, tighten each fitting.
11. Install any retaining clips or brackets on the lines.
12. If removed, install the wheel and tire assemblies, then carefully lower the vehicle to the ground.
13. Refill the brake master cylinder reservoir with clean, fresh brake fluid, meeting DOT 3 specifications. Properly bleed the brake system.
14. Connect the negative battery cable.

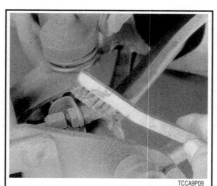

Fig. 14 Use a brush to clean the fittings of any debris

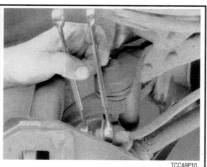

Fig. 15 Use two wrenches to loosen the fitting. If available, use flare nut type wrenches

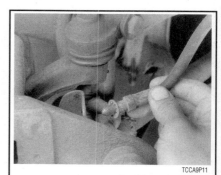

Fig. 16 Any gaskets/crush washers should be replaced with new ones during installation

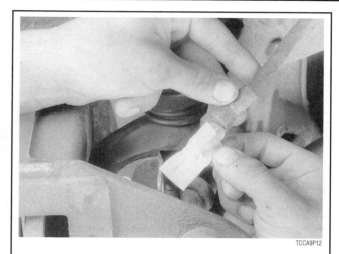

Fig. 17 Tape or plug the line to prevent contamination

Bleeding

▶ See Figures 18, 19 and 20

The brakes should be bled whenever a brake line, caliper, wheel cylinder, or master cylinder has been removed or when the brake pedal is low or soft.

➡️If using a pressure bleeder, follow the instructions furnished with the unit and choose the correct adapter for the application. Do not substitute an adapter that "almost fits" as it will not work and could be dangerous.

1. Fill the master cylinder with fresh brake fluid. Check the level often during the procedure.
2. Starting with the right rear wheel, remove the protective cap from the bleeder, if equipped, and place where it will not be lost. Clean the bleed screw.

✳✳ CAUTION

When bleeding the brakes, keep face away from the brake area. Spewing fluid may cause facial and/or visual injury. Do not allow brake fluid to spill on the vehicle's finish; it will remove the paint.

3. If the system is empty, the most efficient way to get fluid down to the wheel is to loosen the bleeder about ½–¾ turn, place a finger firmly over the bleeder and have a helper pump the brakes slowly until fluid comes out the bleeder. Once fluid is at the bleeder, close it before the pedal is released inside the vehicle.

➡️If the pedal is pumped rapidly, the fluid will churn and create small air bubbles, which are almost impossible to remove from the system. These air bubbles will eventually congregate and a spongy pedal will result.

4. Once fluid has been pumped to the caliper or wheel cylinder, open the bleed screw again, have an assistant press the brake pedal to the floor, lock the bleeder and have an assistant slowly release the pedal. Wait 15 seconds and repeat the procedure, including the 15 second wait, until no more air comes out of the bleeder upon application of the brake pedal. Remember to close the bleeder before the pedal is released inside the vehicle each time the bleeder is opened. If not, air will be induced into the system.
5. If a helper is not available, connect a small hose to the bleeder, place the end in a container of brake fluid and proceed to pump the pedal from inside the vehicle until no more air comes out the bleeder. The hose will prevent air from entering the system.
6. Repeat the procedure on remaining wheel cylinders in order:
   a. Left front caliper
   b. Left rear wheel cylinder or caliper
   c. Right front caliper
7. Hydraulic brake systems must be totally flushed, if the fluid becomes contaminated with water, dirt or other corrosive chemicals. To flush, bleed the entire system until all fluid has been replaced with the correct type of new fluid.
8. Install the bleeder cap(s) on the bleeder to keep dirt out. Always road test the vehicle.

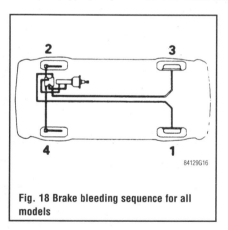

Fig. 18 Brake bleeding sequence for all models

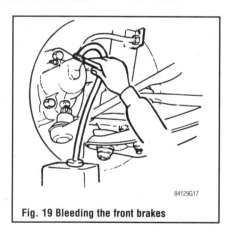

Fig. 19 Bleeding the front brakes

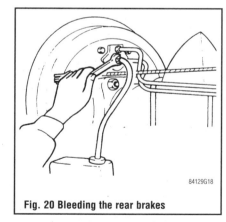

Fig. 20 Bleeding the rear brakes

FRONT DISC BRAKES

Disc Brake Pads

INSPECTION

▶ See Figures 21 and 22

The inner brake pads are equipped with metal wear indicators which act as warning devices to alert the driver to change the brake pads. When the brake pad wears to the minimum service limit, the indicator contacts the rotor and makes a noticeable "chirping" noise while the wheels are turning. When you here this sound, it's time to replace the front pads.

To perform a visual inspection, do the following:

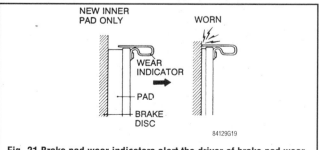

Fig. 21 Brake pad wear indicators alert the driver of brake pad wear

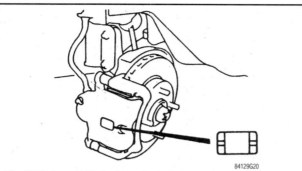

Fig. 22 To inspect the brake pads, look through the end of the caliper

1. Loosen the front lug nuts.
2. Raise the front end and support safely.
3. Remove the front wheels.
4. Check the brake lining thickness through the inspection window in the caliper with a 6 in. machinist's rule. After checking the brake lining thickness check the brake pads for oil deposits, and check the pad springs for wear and damage. Make replacements as necessary.

REMOVAL & INSTALLATION

❊❊ CAUTION

Brake linings contain asbestos. Asbestos is a known cancer-causing agent. When working on brakes, remember that the dust which accumulates on the brake parts and/or in the drum contains asbestos. Always wear a protective face covering, such as a painter's mask, when working on the brakes. NEVER blow the dust from the brakes or drum! There are solvents made for the purpose of cleaning brake parts.

1986–87 Excel

➡️**On Excels with manual transmissions produced up to December of 1987 and on Excels with automatic transmissions produced up to February of 1987, a Sumitomo type front disc system is used. On later models, a Tokico system is used.**

SUMITOMO FRONT DISC BRAKES

♦ See Figures 23, 24 and 25

1. Raise and support the front end on jackstands.
2. Remove the front wheels.
3. Pry off the dust shield from the caliper.
4. Depress the center of the outboard spring clip and remove the clip by slipping the ends from the pins.
5. Remove the inboard spring clip with pliers.

6. Using pliers, pull the retaining pins from the caliper.
7. Lift the pads and anti-squeal shims from the caliper.
8. Clean all caliper parts, especially the torque plate shafts, with a solvent made for brake parts.

❊❊ CAUTION

Replace all brake pads at the same time. Never replace the pads on one wheel only.

9. If the dust protector or spring clips are weak, damaged or deformed, replace them.
10. Remove the cap from the master cylinder reservoir and, using a clean suction gun, remove about 6mm of fluid.
11. Using a C-clamp, force the caliper piston back into the caliper as far as it will go.

➡️**If the anti-squeal shims are at all rusted or deformed, discard them and use an anti-squeal compound, available at most auto parts stores. Furthermore, the anti-squeal shims may not be usable with some after-market brake pads due to thicker linings. The shims may preclude the proper fit of these pads. In that case, discard the shims and use the anti-squeal compound.**

12. Install the inboard pad and anti-squeal shim.
13. Install the outboard pad and anti-squeal shim.
14. Install the pins.
15. Install the two spring clips.
16. Install the dust shield.
17. Install the wheels and lower the car. Get in the car and depress the brake pedal a few times. The first couple of strokes on the pedal will feel overly long. However, the pads will set themselves and the stroke will return to normal.

1988–93 Excel and Scoupe

1. Raise the vehicle and support it safely.
2. Remove the front wheels.
3. Pry off the dust shield from the caliper.
4. Depress the center of the outboard spring clip and remove the clip by slipping the ends from the pins.
5. Remove the inboard spring clip with pliers.
6. Using pliers, pull the retaining pins from the caliper.
7. Lift the pads and anti-squeal shims from the caliper.
8. Clean all caliper parts, especially the torque plate shafts, with a solvent made for brake parts.

➡️**Replace all brake pads at the same time. Never replace the pads on 1 wheel only.**

9. If the dust protector or spring clips are weak, damaged or deformed, replace them.
10. Remove the cap from the master cylinder reservoir and, using a clean suction gun, remove about 6mm of fluid.
To install:
11. Using a C-clamp, force the caliper piston back into the caliper as far as it will go.

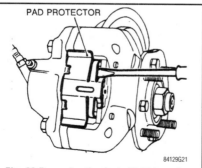

Fig. 23 Removing the dust shield from the caliper—early Excel with Sumitomo front caliper

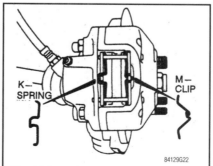

Fig. 24 Removing the spring clips from the caliper pins—early Excel with Sumitomo front caliper

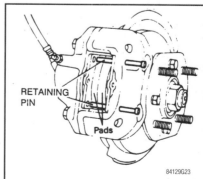

Fig. 25 Removing the caliper pins—early Excel with Sumitomo front caliper

12. Install the inboard pad and anti-squeal shim.
13. Install the outboard pad and anti-squeal shim.
14. Install the pins.
15. Install the spring clips.
16. Install the dust shield.
17. Install the wheels and lower the vehicle. Depress the brake pedal a few times. The first couple of strokes on the pedal will feel overly long. However, the pads will set themselves and the stroke will return to normal.

Elantra

1. Raise the vehicle and support it safely.
2. Remove the front wheel and tire assemblies.
3. Remove the 2 bolts from the torque plate and lift off the caliper. Suspend the caliper safely with wire. Don't stretch the brake hose.
4. Remove the pads and anti-rattle clips from the caliper.
5. Remove the cap from the master cylinder reservoir and siphon off about ⅓ of the fluid.
To install:
6. Using a large C-clamp, press the piston all the way back into the caliper.
7. Install the new pads and clips. Position the pad with the wear sensor on the piston side and upwards.
8. Position the caliper and install the bolts. Torque the bolts to 23 ft. lbs. (32 Nm).

Sonata

The Sonata is equipped with two types of front disc brakes: Mando and Bendix. Mando front disc brakes are used on 4 and 6 cylinder Sonatas equipped with rear drum brakes.

Bendix front disc brakes are used on V6 Sonatas equipped with rear disc brakes.

MANDO FRONT DISC BRAKES

1. Raise and support the front end on jackstands.
2. Remove the front wheels.
3. Remove the 2 caliper guide rod bolts and raise the caliper up and out of the way. Tie the caliper assembly off to a suspension member with a piece of string.
4. Lift the pads and anti-squeal shims from the caliper.
5. Depress the center of the outboard spring clip and remove the clip by slipping the ends from its anchors.
6. Remove the inboard spring clip with pliers.
7. Clean all caliper parts, especially the torque plate shafts, with a solvent made for brake parts.

✷✷ CAUTION

Replace all brake pads at the same time. Never replace the pads on one wheel only.

8. If the spring clips are weak, damaged or deformed, replace them.
9. Remove the cap from the master cylinder reservoir and, using a clean suction gun, remove about 6mm of fluid.
10. Install the pad clips.
11. Install the pads onto each clip.

➡**Position the inner pad so that the pad wear indicator is facing toward the piston side and up.**

12. Using a C-clamp or a piece of wood, force the caliper piston back into the caliper as far as it will go.
13. Untie the caliper and install the guide bolts. Torque the bolts to 16-23 ft. lbs.
14. Install the wheels and lower the car. Get in the car and depress the brake pedal a few times. The first couple of strokes on the pedal will feel overly long. However, the pads will set themselves and the stroke will return to normal.

BENDIX FRONT DISC BRAKES

1. Raise and support the front end on jackstands.
2. Remove the front wheels.
3. Remove the small retaining pin from the bottom of the caliper. This pin must be replaced whenever the front pads are replaced.

4. Rotate the caliper on the large locating pin until the brake pads are accessible.

✷✷ CAUTION

DO NOT remove the locating pin from the caliper. This pin is sealed for life and exposure to dust or dirt will cause it to fail prematurely.

5. Lift the pads and anti-squeal spring from the caliper.
6. Clean all caliper parts, especially the torque plate shafts, with a solvent made for brake parts.
7. Remove the cap from the master cylinder reservoir and, using a clean suction gun, remove about 6mm of fluid.
8. Using a C-clamp, a piece of wood, or special tool 09581-11000, force the caliper piston back into the caliper as far as it will go.
9. Install the pads and anti-rattle spring.

➡**Position the inner pad so that the pad wear indicator is facing toward the large caliper pin.**

10. Swing the caliper upward and install a new small retaining pin.
11. Add brake fluid to the fluid reservoir until the full line is reached.
12. Install the wheels and lower the car. Get in the car and depress the brake pedal a few times. The first couple of strokes on the pedal will feel overly long. However, the pads will set themselves and the stroke will return to normal. Replenish the master cylinder fluid reservoir as necessary.

Brake Calipers

REMOVAL & INSTALLATION

✷✷ CAUTION

Brake linings contain asbestos. Asbestos is a known cancer-causing agent. When working on brakes, remember that the dust which accumulates on the brake parts and/or in the drum contains asbestos. Always wear a protective face covering, such as a painter's mask, when working on the brakes. NEVER blow the dust from the brakes or drum.

1986–87 Excel

➡**On Excels with manual transmissions produced up to December of 1987 and on Excels with automatic transmissions produced up to February of 1987, a Sumitomo type front disc system is used. Later models use a Tokico system.**

SUMITOMO CALIPER

1. Raise and support the front end on jackstands.
2. Remove the wheels.
3. Remove the brake pads as described above.
4. Loosen the brake line at the caliper.

➡**Have some kind of capping device handy to plug the brake line once it is disconnected.**

5. Remove the caliper/torque plate mounting bolts. Lift off the caliper. Hold the brake line and unscrew the caliper. Plug the line to prevent the system from draining.
To install:
6. Support the brake line and connect it to the caliper. Position the caliper onto its mounting and install the mounting bolts. Use new lock tabs under the bolt heads. Torque the mounting bolts to 58 ft. lbs.; the brake hose to 11 ft. lbs.
7. Install the brake pads.
8. Bleed the system.
9. Install the front wheels. Lower the vehicle.

1988–93 Excel, Elantra and Scoupe

1. Raise and support the front end on jackstands.
2. Remove the front wheels.
3. Loosen the brake line at the caliper and disconnect it.

→**Have some kind of capping device handy to plug the brake line once it is disconnected.**

4. Remove the brake pads as described above.
5. Remove the pin and sleeve boots.
6. Remove the lower caliper bolt and raise the caliper up and out to remove it.

To install:

7. Position the caliper onto its mounting and install the lower mounting bolt. Torque the bolt to 16–23 ft. lbs. (22–32 Nm).
8. Install the pin boots, sleeve boots and brake pads.
9. Connect the brake line to the caliper with two new metal gaskets. Torque the brake line union bolt to 11 ft. lbs.
10. Bleed the system.
11. Mount the front wheels and lower the vehicle.

Sonata

MANDO CALIPER

1. Raise and support the front end on jackstands.
2. Remove the front wheels.
3. Loosen the brake line at the caliper and disconnect it.

→**Have some kind of capping device handy to plug the brake line once it is disconnected.**

4. Remove the two caliper guide rod bolts from the torque plate and raise the cylinder up and out to remove it.

To install:

5. Mount the caliper and install the two guide bolts. Torque the bolts to 16-23 ft. lbs.
6. Connect the brake line to the caliper and tighten the fitting to 9-12 ft. lbs.
7. Bleed the system.
8. Mount the front wheels and lower the vehicle.

BENDIX CALIPER

1. Raise and support the front end on jackstands.
2. Remove the front wheels.
3. Disconnect the brake tube from the brake hose. Release the brake hose clip and remove the brake hose from the strut.

→**Have some kind of capping device handy to plug the brake line once it is disconnected.**

4. Loosen and disconnect the brake line from the caliper.
5. Remove the small retaining pin from the lower part of the caliper.
6. Swing the caliper up until it clears the rotor and pads.
7. Slide the caliper inboard until the locating pin disengages from it's groove in the caliper. Pull the caliper from the locating pin.
8. Inspect the locating pin for wear and damage. Replace the pin as required. Protect the pin from exposure to dirt and dust, If the pin is contaminated it will wear prematurely and eventually fail. Inspect the anchor plate for wear and damage.

To install:

9. Lubricate the locating pin bore with white silicone compound. Mount the caliper onto the locating pin. Push the caliper firmly onto the pin making sure

that the pin snaps into the caliper groove. Lower the caliper until the small retaining pin holes are aligned. Install a new retaining pin into the lower part of the caliper. Tighten the pin.

Caliper

OVERHAUL

♦ **See Figures 26 thru 31**

→**Some vehicles may be equipped dual piston calipers. The procedure to overhaul the caliper is essentially the same with the exception of multiple pistons, O-rings and dust boots.**

1. Remove the caliper from the vehicle and place on a clean workbench.

⁙ CAUTION

NEVER place your fingers in front of the pistons in an attempt to catch or protect the pistons when applying compressed air. This could result in personal injury!

→**Depending upon the vehicle, there are two different ways to remove the piston from the caliper. Refer to the brake pad replacement procedure to make sure you have the correct procedure for your vehicle.**

2. The first method is as follows:
    a. Stuff a shop towel or a block of wood into the caliper to catch the piston.
    b. Remove the caliper piston using compressed air applied into the caliper inlet hole. Inspect the piston for scoring, nicks, corrosion and/or worn or damaged chrome plating. The piston must be replaced if any of these conditions are found.
3. For the second method, you must rotate the piston to retract it from the caliper.
4. If equipped, remove the anti-rattle clip.
5. Use a prytool to remove the caliper boot, being careful not to scratch the housing bore.
6. Remove the piston seals from the groove in the caliper bore.
7. Carefully loosen the brake bleeder valve cap and valve from the caliper housing.
8. Inspect the caliper bores, pistons and mounting threads for scoring or excessive wear.
9. Use crocus cloth to polish out light corrosion from the piston and bore.
10. Clean all parts with denatured alcohol and dry with compressed air.

To assemble:

11. Lubricate and install the bleeder valve and cap.
12. Install the new seals into the caliper bore grooves, making sure they are not twisted.
13. Lubricate the piston bore.
14. Install the pistons and boots into the bores of the calipers and push to the bottom of the bores.
15. Use a suitable driving tool to seat the boots in the housing.

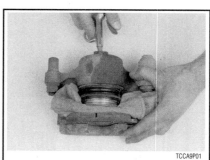

TCCA9P01

Fig. 26 For some types of calipers, use compressed air to drive the piston out of the caliper, but make sure to keep your fingers clear

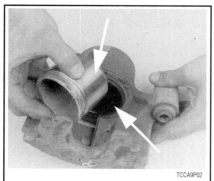

TCCA9P02

Fig. 27 Withdraw the piston from the caliper bore

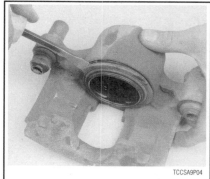

TCCSA9P04

Fig. 28 Use a prytool to carefully pry around the edge of the boot . . .

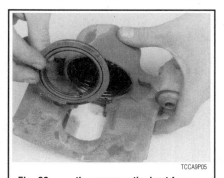

Fig. 29 . . . then remove the boot from the caliper housing, taking care not to score or damage the bore

Fig. 30 Use extreme caution when removing the piston seal; DO NOT scratch the caliper bore

Fig. 31 Use the proper size driving tool and a mallet to properly seal the boots in the caliper housing

16. Install the caliper in the vehicle.
17. Install the wheel and tire assembly, then carefully lower the vehicle.
18. Properly bleed the brake system.

Brake Disc (Rotor)

REMOVAL & INSTALLATION

Except 1989 Excel

▶ See Figure 32

1. Remove the center hub cap and halfshaft nut. Then raise the vehicle and support it safely. Allow the wheels to hang freely. Then remove the front wheel.
2. Remove the brake caliper without disconnecting the hydraulic line and suspend it out of the way with a piece of wire.
3. Disconnect the stabilizer bar and strut bar from the lower control arm.
4. Remove the halfshaft from the transaxle and press the halfshaft out of the hub using tool 09526-11001 or equivalent.
5. Unbolt and remove the hub and knuckle from the bottom of the strut and remove the hub and knuckle assembly from the vehicle.
6. Several special tools are required to press the hub and disc from the steering knuckle and to remount them. Use 09517–21600 or equivalent. Do not attempt to hammer the parts apart, or the bearing will be damaged. Install the arm of the special tool then the body onto the knuckle and tighten the nut manually. Using special tool 09517–21500, separate the hub from the knuckle. Pull the bearings out, noting their positions and direction of installation (smaller diameter inward).
7. Matchmark the relationship between the brake disc and hub. Then place the knuckle in a vise and separate the rotor from the hub by removing the attaching bolts.
To install:
8. Install the hub to the rotor and attaching bolts.
9. Install the hub and knuckle to the bottom of the strut.
10. Install the halfshaft to the transaxle.

11. Connect the stabilizer bar and strut bar to the lower control arm, if disconnected.
12. Install the brake caliper.
13. Install the halfshaft nut and center hub cap and halfshaft nut.
14. Install the front wheel and lower the vehicle.
15. Torque the hub nut to 145–188 ft. lbs. (200–260 Nm).

1989 Excel

1. Raise the vehicle and support safely.
2. Remove the wheel and tire assembly.
3. Remove the caliper and support aside. Do not disconnect the hydraulic lines.
4. Remove the disc retainer screw, if equipped, and remove the rotor from the hub.
5. Installation is the reverse of the removal procedure.

INSPECTION

▶ See Figure 33

1. Loosen the wheel nuts.
2. Raise the front end and support on jackstands.
3. Remove the front wheels.
4. Using a 0-1 inch micrometer or Vernier caliper measure the rotor thickness. Minimum allowable rotor thicknesses are as follows:
    a. 1986–87 Excel with Sumitomo brakes—13mm.
    b. 1988–93 Excel and Scoupe—19mm.
    c. Elantra—20mm.
    d. Sonata (Mando and Bendix)—20mm.
5. Mount a magnetic base dial indicator to the strut member and zero the indicator stylus on the face of the rotor. Rotate the rotor 360° by hand and record the run-out. Maximum rotor disc run-out for all Excel, Elantra and Scoupe models is 0.15mm and 0.10mm for Sonata.
6. If the thickness and run-out do not meet specifications, replace the rotor.

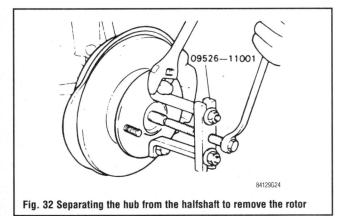

Fig. 32 Separating the hub from the halfshaft to remove the rotor

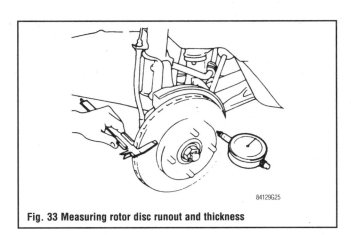

Fig. 33 Measuring rotor disc runout and thickness

REAR DRUM BRAKES

Brake Drums

REMOVAL & INSTALLATION

✱✱ CAUTION

Brake linings contain asbestos. Asbestos is a known cancer-causing agent. When working on brakes, remember that the dust which accumulates on the brake parts and/or in the drum contains asbestos. Always wear a protective face covering, such as a painter's mask, when working on the brakes. NEVER blow the dust from the brakes or drum.

1. Raise the vehicle and support safely.
2. Remove the wheel and tire assembly.
3. On vehicles without rear bearing hub, remove the dust cap, cotter pin, nut lock, wheel bearing nut and washer from the spindle. Remove the outer wheel bearing. Remove the drum with the inner wheel bearing from the spindle. If the drum is difficult to remove, remove the plug from the rear of the backing plate and push the self adjuster lever away from the star wheel. Rotate the star wheel to retract the shoes. Remove the grease seal.
4. If equipped with a rear bearing hub, remove the drum by removing the retainer screws from the drum and pulling the drum from the hub assembly. If the drum is difficult to remove, remove the plug from the rear of the backing plate and push the self adjuster lever away from the star wheel. Rotate the star wheel to retract the shoes.
   To install:
5. On vehicles equipped without rear bearing hub, lubricate and install the inner wheel bearing. Install a new grease seal. Install the drum to the spindle. Lubricate and install the outer wheel bearing, washer and nut. Adjust the bearing preload following the procedure outlined in the "Rear Wheel Bearing" of this section. When the bearing preload is properly set, install the nut lock and a new cotter pin. Install the grease cap.
6. On vehicles with rear bearing hub, install the brake drum to the hub assembly and install the retaining screws.
7. Install the wheel and tire assembly. Adjust the rear brakes as required.
8. Apply the brakes until a firm pedal is obtained, prior to moving the vehicle.

INSPECTION

▶ See Figures 34 and 35

1. Raise the rear end and remove the brake drum as previously described.
2. Thoroughly clean the drum with brake cleaning solvent and allow the drum to dry.
3. Measure the brake drum inside diameter with a outside Vernier caliper. The manufacturer's minimum allowable service specifications are as follows; Excel -182mm and Sonata—230mm.
4. Using a dial indicator, measure the brake drum for out-of-roundness. Maximum brake drum out-of-round for all vehicles is 0.15mm.
5. Check the brake linings for proper lining to drum contact.

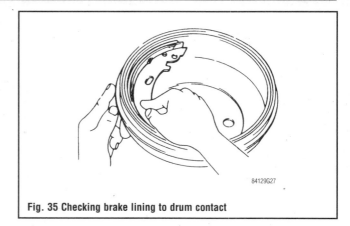

Fig. 35 Checking brake lining to drum contact

Brake Shoes

REMOVAL & INSTALLATION

✱✱ CAUTION

Brake linings contain asbestos. Asbestos is a known cancer-causing agent. When working on brakes, remember that the dust which accumulates on the brake parts and/or in the drum contains asbestos. Always wear a protective face covering, such as a painter's mask, when working on the brakes. NEVER blow the dust from the brakes or drum.

1986–88 Excel

▶ See Figures 36 and 37

1. Remove rear wheel and brake drum.
2. Remove the lower pressed metal spring clip, the shoe return spring (the large one piece spring between the two shoes), and the two shoe holddown springs.
3. Remove the shoes and adjuster as an assembly.
4. Disconnect the parking brake cable from the lever.
5. Remove the spring between the shoes and the lever from the rear (trailing) shoe.
6. Disconnect the adjuster retaining spring and remove the adjuster, turn the star wheel in to the adjuster body after cleaning and lubricating the threads.
   To install:
7. Clean the backing plate with solvent made for cleaning brakes.
8. Lubricate all contact points on the backing plate, anchor plate, wheel cylinder to shoe contact and parking brake strut joints and contacts with lithium based grease.
9. Transfer the lever to the new rear (trailing shoe).

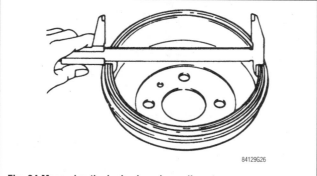

Fig. 34 Measuring the brake drum inner diameter

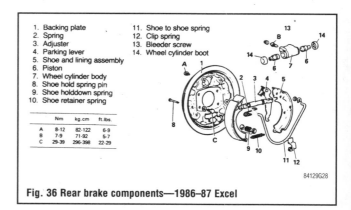

1. Backing plate
2. Spring
3. Adjuster
4. Parking lever
5. Shoe and lining assembly
6. Piston
7. Wheel cylinder body
8. Shoe hold spring pin
9. Shoe holddown spring
10. Shoe retainer spring
11. Shoe to shoe spring
12. Clip spring
13. Bleeder screw
14. Wheel cylinder boot

	Nm	kg.cm	ft.lbs.
A	8-12	82-122	6-9
B	7-9	71-92	5-7
C	29-39	296-398	22-29

Fig. 36 Rear brake components—1986–87 Excel

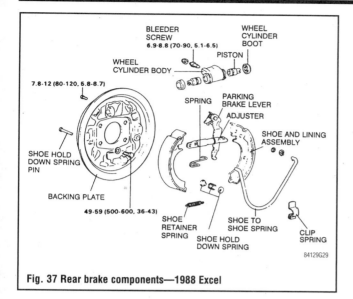

Fig. 37 Rear brake components—1988 Excel

10. Connect the adjuster and retaining spring to the shoes.
11. Connect the spring that spans the lever and the shoes.
12. Connect the parking brake lever.
13. Position the shoe and adjuster assembly onto the backing plate.
14. Install the two shoe hold-down springs, shoe return spring and spring clip.
15. Pre-adjustment of the brake shoe can be made by turning the adjuster star wheel out until the drum will just slide on over the brake shoes. Depending on the amount of wear on the drum, the outside diameter of the brake shoes should be 179.0-179.5mm to allow for the drum to slide over the shoes. Before installing the drum make sure the parking brake is not adjusted too tightly, if it is, loosen it, or the adjustment of the rear brakes will not be correct.
16. Install the drums and wheels.
17. The brakes shoes are adjusted by pumping the brake pedal and applying and releasing the parking brake. Adjust the parking brake stroke. Road test the car.

1989–93 Excel And Scoupe

♦ See Figures 38, 39 and 40

1. Raise the vehicle and support it safely.
2. Remove the rear wheels.
3. Remove the brake drum from the vehicle.
4. Thoroughly clean the spindle.
5. Remove the lower pressed metal spring clip, the shoe return spring, the large 1 piece spring between the 2 shoes, and the shoe hold-down springs.
6. Remove the shoes and adjuster as an assembly.

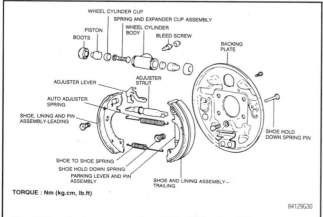

Fig. 38 Rear brake components—1990–93 Excel and Scoupe

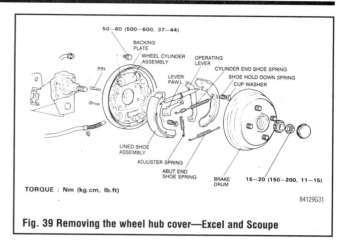

Fig. 39 Removing the wheel hub cover—Excel and Scoupe

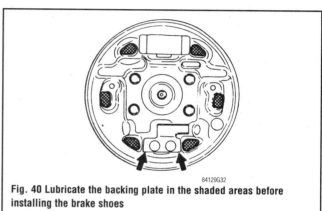

Fig. 40 Lubricate the backing plate in the shaded areas before installing the brake shoes

7. Disconnect the parking brake cable from the lever.
8. Remove the spring between the shoes and the lever from the rear (trailing) shoe.
9. Disconnect the adjuster retaining spring and remove the adjuster, turn the star wheel in to the adjuster body after cleaning and lubricating the threads.

To install:

10. Clean both backing plates and all brake components using the appropriate equipment.
11. Lubricate all contact points on the backing plate, anchor plate, wheel cylinder to shoe contact and parking brake strut joints and contacts with lithium based grease.
12. Install the parking brake lever to the new rear (trailing) shoe.
13. Install the brake shoes to the backing plates and install the hold down springs. Now that the shoes are fastened onto the backing plate, install the return springs and the adjuster to each brake shoe making sure the wheel cylinder pistons are correctly positioned on the brake shoe webbing. Reconnect the parking brake cable, if removed.
14. Pre-adjustment of the brake shoe can be made by turning the adjuster star wheel out until the drum will just slide on over the brake shoes. Before installing the drum make sure the parking brake is not adjusted too tightly, if it is, loosen it, or the adjustment of the rear brakes will not be correct.
15. Install the hub and drum assembly onto each spindle and set bearing preload, if equipped.
16. Install the tire and wheel assemblies. Check the fluid in the master cylinder reservoirs.
17. The brakes shoes are adjusted by pumping the brake pedal and applying and releasing the parking brake. Adjust the parking brake stroke. Road test the vehicle.

Elantra and Sonata

1. Raise the vehicle and support it safely.
2. Remove both tire and wheel assemblies.

3. Remove the hub nut, outer wheel bearing and brake drum.

4. Thoroughly clean the spindle.

5. Clean the brake shoes and backing plate using the appropriate equipment.

6. Remove the lower spring return springs.

7. Remove the upper spring return springs.

8. Remove the hold-down springs.

9. Remove the shoes and adjuster as an assembly.

10. Disconnect the parking brake cable from the adjuster arm.

To install:

11. Apply a thin coating of lithium based grease to the backing plate pads.

12. Connect the parking brake cable to the adjuster.

13. Position the shoes on the backing plate and install the hold-down springs and pins.

14. Install the upper spring, then the lower spring and lastly the adjuster spring.

15. Install the drum and adjust the wheel bearing.

Wheel Cylinders

REMOVAL & INSTALLATION

▶ **See Figure 41**

1. Remove the brake shoes.

2. Place a container or some old rags under the brake backing plate to catch the brake fluid that will run out of the wheel cylinder.

3. Disconnect the brake line(s) and remove the cylinder mounting bolts. Remove the cylinder from the backing plate.

4. Installation is the reverse of removal. Torque the wheel cylinder mounting bolts to 48-108 inch lbs.

5. Refill and bleed the system.

Wheel Cylinder

OVERHAUL

▶ **See Figures 42 thru 51**

Wheel cylinder overhaul kits may be available, but often at little or no savings over a reconditioned wheel cylinder. It often makes sense with these components to substitute a new or reconditioned part instead of attempting an overhaul.

If no replacement is available, or you would prefer to overhaul your wheel cylinders, the following procedure may be used. When rebuilding and installing wheel cylinders, avoid getting any contaminants into the system. Always use clean, new, high quality brake fluid. If dirty or improper fluid has been used, it will be necessary to drain the entire system, flush the system with proper brake fluid, replace all rubber components, then refill and bleed the system.

1. Remove the wheel cylinder from the vehicle and place on a clean workbench.

2. First remove and discard the old rubber boots, then withdraw the pistons. Piston cylinders are equipped with seals and a spring assembly, all located behind the pistons in the cylinder bore.

3. Remove the remaining inner components, seals and spring assembly. Compressed air may be useful in removing these components. If no compressed air is available, be VERY careful not to score the wheel cylinder bore when removing parts from it. Discard all components for which replacements were supplied in the rebuild kit.

4. Wash the cylinder and metal parts in denatured alcohol or clean brake fluid.

✳✳ WARNING

Never use a mineral-based solvent such as gasoline, kerosene or paint thinner for cleaning purposes. These solvents will swell rubber components and quickly deteriorate them.

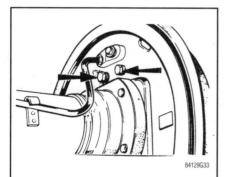

Fig. 41 Wheel cylinder retaining bolt location

Fig. 42 Remove the outer boots from the wheel cylinder

Fig. 43 Compressed air can be used to remove the pistons and seals

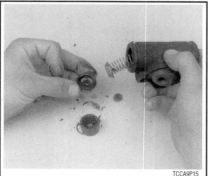

Fig. 44 Remove the pistons, cup seals and spring from the cylinder

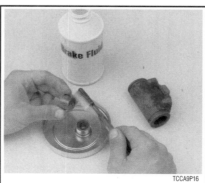

Fig. 45 Use brake fluid and a soft brush to clean the pistons . . .

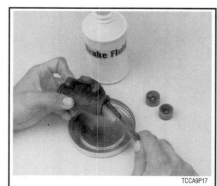

Fig. 46 . . . and the bore of the wheel cylinder

Fig. 47 Once cleaned and inspected, the wheel cylinder is ready for assembly

Fig. 48 Lubricate the cup seals with brake fluid

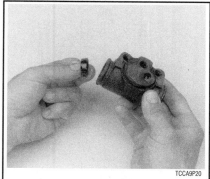

Fig. 49 Install the spring, then the cup seals in the bore

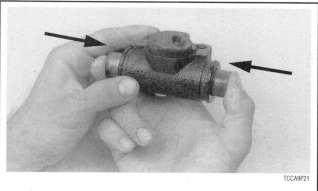

Fig. 50 Lightly lubricate the pistons, then install them

Fig. 51 The boots can now be installed over the wheel cylinder ends

5. Allow the parts to air dry or use compressed air. Do not use rags for cleaning, since lint will remain in the cylinder bore.

6. Inspect the piston and replace it if it shows scratches.

7. Lubricate the cylinder bore and seals using clean brake fluid.

8. Position the spring assembly.

9. Install the inner seals, then the pistons.

10. Insert the new boots into the counterbores by hand. Do not lubricate the boots.

11. Install the wheel cylinder.

REAR DISC BRAKES

➡**Rear disc brakes are available on Sonata V6 as an option. Rear disc brakes are standard on all Anti-lock Brake System (ABS) equipped Sonatas. For information on diagnosis and repair of the ABS system, refer to "Anti-lock Brake System" at the end of this section.**

Brake Pads

INSPECTION

▶ See Figure 52

The inner brake pads are equipped with metal wear indicators which act as warning devices to alert the driver to change the brake pads.

When the brake pad wears to the minimum service limit, the indicator contacts the rotor and makes a noticeable "chirping" noise while the wheels are turning. When you here this sound, it's time to replace the front pads.

To perform a visual inspection, do the following:

1. Loosen the rear lug nuts.

2. Raise the rear end and support safely.

3. Remove the rear wheels.

4. Check the brake lining thickness through the inspection window in the caliper with a six inch machinist's rule. Minimum pad thickness is 0.8mm.

After checking the brake lining thickness, check the brake pads for oil deposits, and check the pad springs for wear and damage. Make replacements as necessary.

5. Check the leading and trailing shoe keys and retaining screw for damage. If these components are damaged, replace them at the same time as the pads.

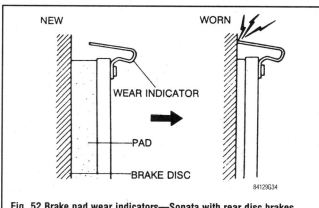

Fig. 52 Brake pad wear indicators—Sonata with rear disc brakes

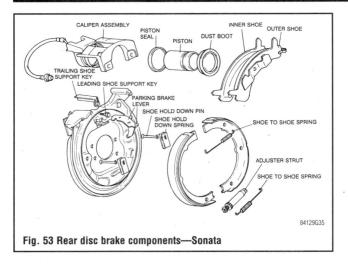

Fig. 53 Rear disc brake components—Sonata

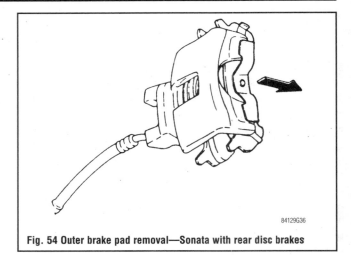

Fig. 54 Outer brake pad removal—Sonata with rear disc brakes

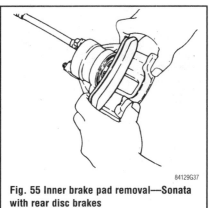

Fig. 55 Inner brake pad removal—Sonata with rear disc brakes

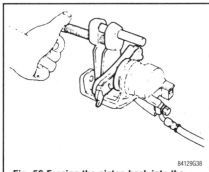
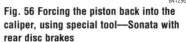

Fig. 56 Forcing the piston back into the caliper, using special tool—Sonata with rear disc brakes

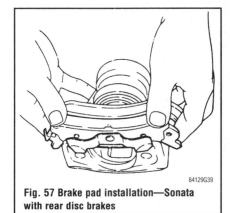

Fig. 57 Brake pad installation—Sonata with rear disc brakes

6. Check for worn or damaged dust boots. If mud or dirt has penetrated the piston seal, the caliper must be re-built or replaced.

7. Mount the rear wheels, tighten the lug nuts and lower the vehicle.

REMOVAL & INSTALLATION

♦ See Figures 53, 54, 55, 56 and 57

1. Raise the vehicle and support it safely.
2. Remove the tire and wheel assemblies.
3. Remove the screw which holds the trailing shoe key onto the anchor plate. Bias the caliper assembly against the thin key and slide the trailing shoe outward.
4. Remove both caliper support pins which holds the caliper to the anchor plate. While biasing the caliper assembly against the leading shoe key, swing the front end of the caliper up and past the anchor plate rail. The caliper should be free. Support the caliper using wire making sure not to twist the brake fluid hose during removal.
5. To remove the outer shoe, push the outer shoe inward off of the caliper legs. The locator buttons must clear the slots in the housing before the shoe can be removed. Remove the inner shoe by pulling the shoe outward until the shoe clears the piston.

To install:
6. Remove the cap from the master cylinder reservoir and, using a clean suction gun, remove about 6mm of fluid. Using a large C-clamp, press the piston all the way back into the caliper.
7. Install the new pads and clips. Position the pad with the wear sensor on the piston side and upwards.
8. Position the caliper and install the bolts. Torque the bolts to 25 ft. lbs. (34 Nm).
9. Refill the master cylinder, install the tire and wheel assemblies and pump the brake pedal until firm.

Rear Brake Caliper

REMOVAL & INSTALLATION

1. Loosen the rear wheel lug nuts.
2. Raise and support the rear end safely.
3. Remove the screw that attaches the trailing shoe key to the anchor plate.
4. Press the caliper assembly against the leading key (this is the thinner of the two keys) and slide the trailing shoe key outward. To remove the caliper, swing the front end of the caliper up and away from the anchor plate rail. After the keys are removed, the caliper should be free.
5. Once the caliper is free, disconnect the brake hose. Plug the end of the hose to prevent excess loss of fluid. The hose need not be disconnected if you are replacing the brakes. Support the caliper assembly with a piece of wire. Support in a manner that will allow you to work on the brake pads.
6. Remove the brake shoes.

To install:
7. Install the brake shoes and connect the brake hose.
8. Raise the caliper into position, and install the leading shoe key (the thinner key) on the anchor plate rail nearer the rear of the vehicle. Make sure the key is properly positioned and installed on the surface of the anchor plate rail.
9. Reposition the caliper so that the piston and hose are facing to the inboard side of the vehicle.
10. Seat the "V" of the shoes against the leading shoe key while both shoes are straddling the rotor disc. Position the assembly to compress the leading shoe key spring and swing the caliper down past the anchor plate rail. Align the "V"s of the shoes and the anchor plate rail. Then, slide the trailing shoe key inboard until it is fully seated. Install the trailing shoe key screw to hold it in place. Tighten the caliper mounting bolts to 25 ft. lbs. (34 Nm).

11. Mount the rear wheels and lower the vehicle.
12. Refill the master cylinder reservoir. Bleed the system. Pump the brake pedal several times to set the pads.

Caliper

OVERHAUL

▶ **See Figures 58 thru 63**

➡ **Some vehicles may be equipped dual piston calipers. The procedure to overhaul the caliper is essentially the same with the exception of multiple pistons, O-rings and dust boots.**

1. Remove the caliper from the vehicle and place on a clean workbench.

✳✳ CAUTION

NEVER place your fingers in front of the pistons in an attempt to catch or protect the pistons when applying compressed air. This could result in personal injury!

➡ **Depending upon the vehicle, there are two different ways to remove the piston from the caliper. Refer to the brake pad replacement procedure to make sure you have the correct procedure for your vehicle.**

2. The first method is as follows:
   a. Stuff a shop towel or a block of wood into the caliper to catch the piston.
   b. Remove the caliper piston using compressed air applied into the caliper inlet hole. Inspect the piston for scoring, nicks, corrosion and/or worn or damaged chrome plating. The piston must be replaced if any of these conditions are found.
3. For the second method, you must rotate the piston to retract it from the caliper.

4. If equipped, remove the anti-rattle clip.
5. Use a prytool to remove the caliper boot, being careful not to scratch the housing bore.
6. Remove the piston seals from the groove in the caliper bore.
7. Carefully loosen the brake bleeder valve cap and valve from the caliper housing.
8. Inspect the caliper bores, pistons and mounting threads for scoring or excessive wear.
9. Use crocus cloth to polish out light corrosion from the piston and bore.
10. Clean all parts with denatured alcohol and dry with compressed air.

To assemble:
11. Lubricate and install the bleeder valve and cap.
12. Install the new seals into the caliper bore grooves, making sure they are not twisted.
13. Lubricate the piston bore.
14. Install the pistons and boots into the bores of the calipers and push to the bottom of the bores.
15. Use a suitable driving tool to seat the boots in the housing.
16. Install the caliper in the vehicle.
17. Install the wheel and tire assembly, then carefully lower the vehicle.
18. Properly bleed the brake system.

Brake Disc (Rotor)

REMOVAL & INSTALLATION

▶ **See Figure 64**

1. Loosen the rear wheel lug nuts.
2. Raise the rear end and support safely.
3. Remove the rear wheels.
4. Remove the caliper assembly from the anchor plate and support it with wire. DO NOT disconnect the brake line from the caliper!

Fig. 58 For some types of calipers, use compressed air to drive the piston out of the caliper, but make sure to keep your fingers clear

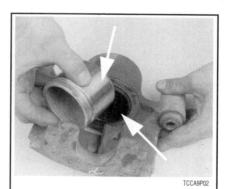

Fig. 59 Withdraw the piston from the caliper bore

Fig. 60 Use a prytool to carefully pry around the edge of the boot . . .

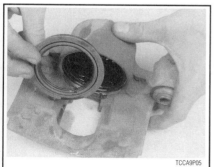

Fig. 61 . . . then remove the boot from the caliper housing, taking care not to score or damage the bore

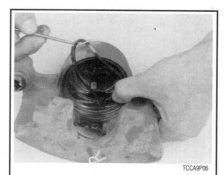

Fig. 62 Use extreme caution when removing the piston seal; DO NOT scratch the caliper bore

Fig. 63 Use the proper size driving tool and a mallet to properly seal the boots in the caliper housing

5. Remove the set screw from the face of the rotor and pull the rotor from the rear hub.

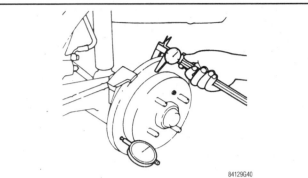

Fig. 64 Measuring rear brake disc thickness and runout—Sonata with rear disc brakes

6. Inspect the rotor as described below.
7. Position the rotor onto the hub and secure it with the setscrew.
8. Install the caliper assembly.
9. Mount the rear wheels and lower the vehicle.
10. Refill the master cylinder reservoir to the proper level. Pump the brake pedal several times to the set the rear pads.

INSPECTION

1. Loosen the wheel nuts.
2. Raise the rear end and support on jackstands.
3. Remove the rear wheels.
4. Using a micrometer or Vernier caliper measure the rotor thickness. Minimum allowable rotor thickness is 10.5mm.
5. Mount a magnetic base dial indicator to the strut member and zero the indicator stylus on the face of the rotor. Rotate the rotor 360 by hand and record the run-out. Maximum rotor disc run-out is 0.13mm.
6. If the thickness and run-out do not meet specifications, replace the rotor.

PARKING BRAKE

Cables

REMOVAL & INSTALLATION

1986–89 Excel

▶ **See Figures 65 and 66**

1. Block the front wheels, raise the rear of car and support it on jackstands.
2. Disconnect the brake cable at the parking brake lever (brakes released).
3. Remove the cable clamps inside the driver's compartment (two bolts).
4. Disconnect the clamps on the rear suspension arm.
5. Remove the rear brake drums and the brake shoes assemblies.
6. Disconnect the parking brake cable from the lever on the trailing (rear) brake shoe. Remove the brake cables.

To install:

7. Route, install and connect the new cables. Make certain the cables are routed flush with the floor and the cable protectors are properly positioned on the suspension arm.
8. Install the grommets as show in the illustration. Make certain that the grommets are facing in the right direction.
9. Install the rear suspension arm and driver's side cable clamps without twisting the cables.
10. On 1986–88 models, set the rear brake shoe outside diameter (dimension "A") to 179.0-179.5mm using the star wheel adjuster.

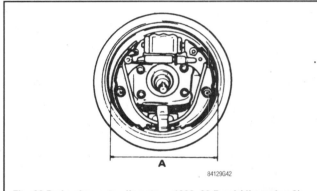

Fig. 66 Brake shoe outer diameter—1986–88 Excel (dimension A)

11. Adjust the parking brake and parking lever stroke. Check the operation of the parking brake and the parking brake switch.

1990–93 Excel And Scoupe

▶ **See Figure 67**

1. Raise the vehicle and support it safely. Remove the rear wheels and brake drums.

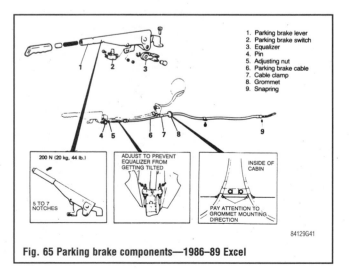

Fig. 65 Parking brake components—1986–89 Excel

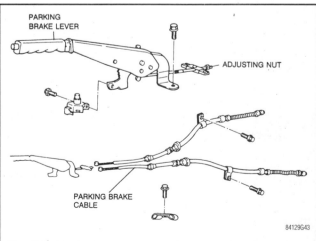

Fig. 67 Parking brake components—1990–93 Excel and Scoupe

2. Remove the console box and rear seat.

3. Release the hand brake and then disconnect the cable connectors at the equalizer. It may be necessary to loosen the cable adjusting nuts to do this.

4. Disconnect all cable clamps from the body. Remove the mounting bolts for the large mounting clamp located just forward of where the cables pass through the body grommets.

5. Pull the cables and grommets out of the body.

6. Disconnect the cables at the rear brakes.

To install:

7. When installing the cables, make sure the grommets are installed in the body completely and that the concave side faces to the rear. Adjust the hand brake mechanism. Adjust the switch for the indicator light so the light comes on when the lever is pulled 1 notch.

Elantra

▶ **See Figure 68**

1. Raise the vehicle and support it safely.

2. Remove the rear console.

3. Detach the adjusting nut and detach the parking brake cable.

4. Remove the tire and wheel assembly, brake drum and the brake shoes.

5. Detach the parking brake cable from the parking brake lever.

6. Remove the parking brake cable retainer ring in the rear of the backing plate.

7. Remove the ear seat cushion assembly and roll up the carpet.

8. Loosen the parking brake cable clamp and remove the cable assembly.

To install:

9. Check the parking brake cables for left and right identification marks and install accordingly.

10. Install the cable to the parking brake lever. Move the adjuster lever all the way to the back when installing the shoe—to—shoe spring. Install the brake shoes and the drum.

11. Install the parking brake retainer ring to the rear of the backing plate. Install the cable into the vehicle and secure using the cable clamp. Install the rear seat cushion.

12. Connect the parking brake cable to the actuator assembly and adjust the lever stroke. Apply a thin coating of specified grease to the sliding parts of the ratchet plate and the ratchet paw.

13. Install the tire and wheel assembly.

14. Raise and support the vehicle safely.

15. Apply and then release the hand brake and rotate each rear wheel to make sure the brakes are not dragging.

Sonata

WITH REAR DRUM BRAKES

▶ **See Figures 69, 70 and 71**

1. Remove the main console.

2. Remove the cable adjuster, pin, equalizer bracket and nut holder.

3. Disconnect the parking brake switch connector.

4. Remove the parking brake lever.

5. Remove the rear seat cushion and lift up the carpet.

6. Remove the parking brake cable clamp and grommet.

7. Raise the rear end and remove the tires, drums and hub assemblies.

8. Remove the brake shoe assemblies.

9. Remove the cable clip.

10. Disconnect the cable from the trailing shoe.

11. From underneath the vehicle pull the cable out to remove it. Check the cables for wear, cracks in the cable casing and fraying in the cable ends. Check

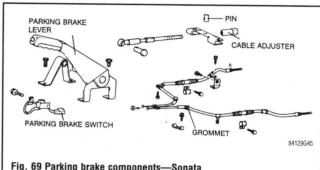

Fig. 69 Parking brake components—Sonata

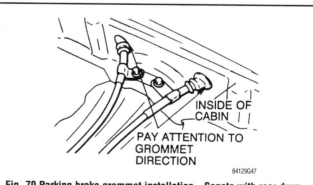

Fig. 70 Parking brake grommet installation—Sonata with rear drum brakes

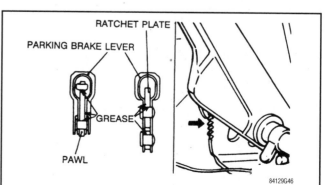

Fig. 71 Lubricate the parking brake ratchet plate and ratchet pawl sliding surfaces with multi-purpose grease

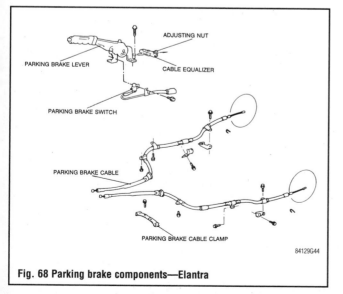

Fig. 68 Parking brake components—Elantra

the parking brake lever ratchet for wear. If the cable grommets are worn or cracked, replace them.

To install:

➡**The cables are marked right and left, so make sure they are installed on their respective sides.**

12. Route the cable up through the under body and connect the cable to the trailing shoe. Install the cable clip.

13. Install the brake shoe assemblies. Set the adjuster lever all the way back when installing the shoe-to-shoe spring.

14. Install the hub, drum and tire assemblies. Lower the rear end.

15. Install the grommets as show in the illustration. Make certain that the grommets are facing in the right direction.

16. Replace the carpet and the rear seat cushion.

17. Install the parking brake lever and connect the parking brake switch.

18. Install the nut holder, equalizer bracket, pin and cable adjuster. Lubricate the ratchet plate and ratchet pawl sliding surfaces with multi-purpose grease.

19. Adjust the parking brake lever stroke.

20. Install the main console. Check the parking brake and parking brake switch for proper operation.

WITH REAR DISC BRAKES

1. Raise the rear and support safely. Remove the rear wheels.

2. Remove the rear caliper, rotor disc, hub and bearing assemblies.

3. Remove the lower shoe-to-shoe spring.

4. Remove the parking brake lever adjusters.

5. Remove the upper shoe-to-shoe return spring.

6. Disconnect the shoe hold down pin and spring.

7. Disconnect the cable clevis from the adjusting lever. Be careful not to tear cable dust boot. Pull the lever and slider assembly out towards the outboard side of the brake and through the access window in the backing plate.

8. Remove the cable clips.

9. Unbolt the backing plate from the suspension arm.

10. Loosen the cable adjusting nut and remove the cables from the adjuster bracket.

11. Remove the cables. Check the cables for wear, cracks in the cable casing and fraying in the cable ends. Check the parking brake lever ratchet for wear. If the cable grommets are worn or cracked, replace them. Check the dust boots for rips and tears. Check the brake shoe linings for wear and oil contamination. Minimum brake lining thickness is 2mm. Check the shoe webs and adjusters for bending. Check the return springs for bent hooks, over-extension and breaks. Check the lever and slider assemblies for cracks, bending and wear. Check the drum surface for scoring, wear and oil contamination. Replace any worn or damaged component as necessary.

To install:

12. Mount the backing plate to the suspension flange and torque the bolts in a diagonal pattern to 45-60 ft. lbs.

13. Lubricate the area between the lever and slider and where the slider contacts the backing plate. Use multi-purpose grease.

14. Install the lever and slider assembly through the window in the backing plate. Be careful not damage the dust boot. The lever should be positioned with the long portion into the backing plate first and then the indent for the cable clevis facing toward the rear of the vehicle last. The slider should be positioned on top of the lever. Lubricate the slider with multipurpose grease for easy rotation. The long arm of the slider should be positioned on the rear of the backing plate. The assembly should slide and rotate freely. Connect the cable clevis to the lever indent.

15. Install the brake shoes and shoe holddown pin.

16. Shorten the adjuster assembly and install between the slots in the bottom portion of the shoes.

17. Install the upper and lower shoe-to-shoe springs. The upper portion of the shoe web should contact the anchor block. Adjust the cable as necessary to make this contact.

18. Check the lever function by pushing the end of the lever by the cable clevis and observe the movement of the brake shoes. The tab end of the lever should move against the shoe and the slider tab end should contact fully against the outer shoe.

19. Install the parking brake adjusters.

20. Install the rear hub and bearing, rotor disc and caliper assemblies.

21. Mount the rear wheels and lower the vehicle.

22. Adjust the parking brake lever stroke. Check the parking brake and parking brake switch for proper operation. Lubricate the ratchet plate and ratchet pawl sliding surfaces with multi-purpose grease.

LEVER STROKE ADJUSTMENT

1986–89 Excel

▶ **See Figure 72**

1. Fully release the brake lever.

2. Pull the parking brake upward with normal effort. Maximum travel should be 5-7 clicks. If not, proceed with the following steps:

3. Remove the floor console, pull back the carpeting and adjust the lever travel by turning the adjusting nuts on the cable ends. Adjust the right and left cables so that when the lever is pulled the cables are equal in length. If the cables are adjusted too tight, the adjuster lever will not engage the adjuster and the automatic shoe clearance adjuster mechanism will not work.

4. Loosen the parking brake switch mounting bolt. Adjust the switch so that when the lever is fully released, the switch lamp goes and out and when the lever is pulled one click, the switch lamp illuminates. If the switch does not operate as described check the switch lamp bulb. If the bulb is good, replace the switch.

5. After the adjustment, make sure that the rear brakes do not drag when the parking brake lever is released.

6. Install the main console.

1990–93 Excel, Elantra, Scoupe And Sonata

▶ **See Figures 73 and 74**

1. Fully release the brake lever.

2. Pull the parking brake upward with normal effort. Maximum travel should be 8-9 clicks on Sonata and 8-9 clicks on 1990 Excel.

3. If not, proceed with the following steps:

4. Remove the front console and adjust the cable length by turning the nut on the equalizer.

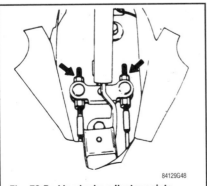

Fig. 72 Parking brake adjuster points— 1986–89 Excel

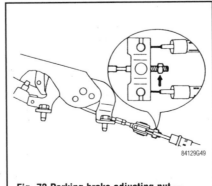

Fig. 73 Parking brake adjusting nut— 1990–93 Excel, Elantra and Scoupe

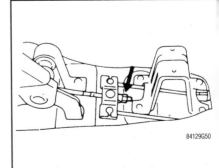

Fig. 74 Parking brake cable adjustment nut—Sonata

5. Loosen the parking brake switch mounting bolt. Adjust the switch so that when the lever is fully released, the switch lamp goes and out and when the lever is pulled one click, the switch lamp illuminates. If the switch does not operate as described check the switch lamp bulb. If the bulb is good, replace the switch.

6. After the adjustment, make sure that the rear brakes do not drag when the parking brake lever is released.

7. Install the main console.

Parking Brake Shoes

REMOVAL & INSTALLATION

Sonata

WITH REAR DISC BRAKES

1. Raise the rear and support safely.
2. Remove the rear wheels.
3. Remove the lower shoe-to-shoe spring.
4. Remove the parking brake lever adjuster.
5. Remove the upper shoe-to-shoe return spring.
6. Disconnect the shoe hold down pin and spring.

7. Remove the brake shoes.

8. Check the brake shoe linings for wear and oil contamination. Minimum brake lining thickness is 2mm. Check the shoe webs and adjusters for bending. Check the return springs for bent hooks, over-extension and breaks. Cheek the lever and slider assemblies for cracks, bending and wear. Check the drum surface for scoring, wear and oil contamination. Replace any worn or damaged component as necessary.

To install:

9. Lubricate the area between the lever and slider and where the slider contacts the backing plate. Use multi-purpose grease.

10. Install the brake shoes and shoe holddown pin.

11. Shorten the adjuster assembly and install between the slots in the bottom portion of the shoes.

12. Install the upper and lower shoe-to-shoe springs. The upper portion of the shoe web should contact the anchor block. Adjust the cable as necessary to make this contact.

13. Check the lever function by pushing the end of the lever by the cable clevis and observe the movement of the brake shoes. The tab end of the lever should move against the shoe and the slider tab end should contact fully against the outer shoe.

14. Mount the rear wheels and lower the vehicle.

15. Adjust the parking brake lever stroke. Check the parking brake and parking brake switch for proper operation. Lubricate the ratchet plate and ratchet pawl sliding surfaces with multi-purpose grease.

HYUNDAI FOUR WHEEL ANTI-LOCK BRAKE SYSTEMS

General Description

The 1992–93 Sonata uses a four channel ABS system which incorporates 6 solenoids (4 build/decay & 2 isolation valves) and 4 speed sensors (1 for each wheel).

Anti-lock braking systems are designed to prevent locked-wheel skidding during hard braking or during braking on slippery surfaces. The front wheels of a vehicle cannot apply steering force if they are locked and sliding; the vehicle will continue in its previous direction of travel. The four wheel anti-lock brake system found on the Sonata holds each wheel just below the point of locking, thereby allowing some steering response and preventing the rear of the vehicle from sliding sideways.

SYSTEM OPERATION

The system monitors and compares wheel speed based on the inputs from the wheel speed sensors. The brake pressure is controlled according to the impending lock-up computations of the ABS control unit.

As a wheel approaches lock-up, the controller actuates the appropriate build/decay or isolation solenoid. Depending on the inputs from each respective wheel speed sensor, the ECM may cycle one of the 2 isolation valve; thus stopping the flow of fluid from the master cylinder to either the LF/RR or RF/LR brake circuit or the ECM may cycle any combination of the 4 build/decay solenoids; thus allowing the system to build brake pressure at the caliper or release (decay) pressure to the modulator sump. This reduces the tendency of the vehicle to skid sideways under braking.

SYSTEM COMPONENTS

▶ **See Figure 75**

Modulator

▶ **See Figure 76**

The modulator is located in the engine compartment, just forward of the left forward area of the engine compartment.

The hydraulic unit contains the 6 solenoid valves, 4 shuttles, 2 sumps, release check valves, proportioning valves, accumulator and the pump/motor assembly which provides pressurized fluid for the anti-lock system when necessary.

Hydraulic units are not interchangeable between vehicles. The units are not serviceable; if any fault occurs within the hydraulic unit, the entire unit must be replaced.

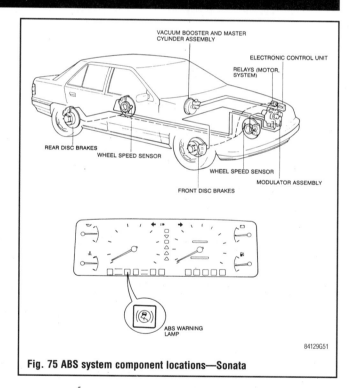

Fig. 75 ABS system component locations—Sonata

Electronic Control Unit (ECU)

The ECU is located in the left forward engine compartment above the modulator assembly. The ECU receives inputs from the 4 speed sensors, brake light switch and the diagnostic connector. The ECU outputs signals to the 6 solenoid valves, ABS warning light relay and pump motor relay if detecting an impending wheel lock-up.

It is a micro-processor capable of dealing with many inputs simultaneously and controls the function of the solenoid valves within the hydraulic unit.

Wheel Speed Sensors and Toothed Rings

Each wheel is equipped with a magnetic sensor which produces a small AC voltage linear to wheel speed (11 Hz/mph). The sensor is mounted a fixed dis-

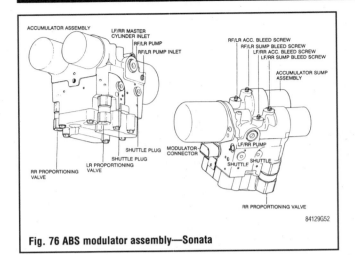

Fig. 76 ABS modulator assembly—Sonata

tance from a toothed ring which rotates with the wheel. The sensors are replaceable but not interchangeable; each must be fitted to its correct location. The toothed rings are replaceable although disassembly of the hub or axle shaft is required.

System Relays

▶ See Figure 77

Three separate relays aid the operation of the ABS system. The ABS system and the pump/motor relays are located together on the left inner fender well under the hood, near the modulator and ECU.

The ABS warning lamp relay is located in the underhood relay box.

Each of the relays may be replaced in the usual fashion, although care must be taken to release wiring or connector clips before removing the relay.

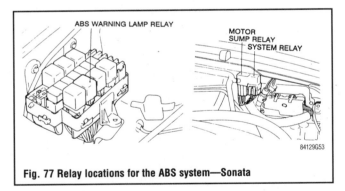

Fig. 77 Relay locations for the ABS system—Sonata

Warning Lamps

Both the amber ANTI-LOCK light and red BRAKE light are located on the instrument cluster. Each lamp warns the operator of a possible fault in the respective system. A fault in one system may cause the other lamp to illuminate depending on the nature and severity of the problem. The operation or behavior of the amber warning lamp is one of the prime diagnostic tools for the system.

At no time should the warning lamp be lit while the engine is running. Once the vehicle speed exceeds 3 mph, the system performs a self-check of the pump and solenoid function. Any failure in these circuits will cause the warning lamp to re-light, warning the operator of a problem.

Diagnosis and Testing

SERVICE PRECAUTIONS

• Certain components within the ABS system are not intended to be serviced or repaired individually. Only those components with removal & Installation procedures should be serviced.

• Do not use rubber hoses or other parts not specifically specified for the ABS system. When using repair kits, replace all parts included in the kit. Partial or incorrect repair may lead to functional problems and require the replacement of components.

• Lubricate rubber parts with clean, fresh brake fluid to ease assembly. Do not use lubricated shop air to clean parts; damage to rubber components may result.

• Use only DOT 3 brake fluid from an unopened container.

• If any hydraulic component or line is removed or replaced, it may be necessary to bleed the entire system.

• A clean repair area is essential. Always clean the reservoir and cap thoroughly before removing the cap. The slightest amount of dirt in the fluid may plug an orifice and impair the system function. Perform repairs after components have been thoroughly cleaned; use only denatured alcohol to clean components. Do not allow ABS components to come into contact with any substance containing mineral oil; this includes used shop rags.

• The Anti-Lock control unit is a microprocessor similar to other computer units in the vehicle. Ensure that the ignition switch is **OFF** and/or the negative battery cable is disconnected before removing or installing controller harnesses. Avoid static electricity discharge at or near the controller.

DEPRESSURIZING THE SYSTEM

The system operates on low hydraulic pressure and requires no special system depressurization prior to the opening of hydraulic lines or other system repairs. Simply verify the ignition switch is **OFF** and pump/motor is not running.

Wheel Speed Sensor

TESTING

1. Remove the wheel speed sensor from the vehicle.

➡**Handle the sensor carefully and protect the tip at all times. Do not subject the pole piece on the end to any impact or abrasion.**

2. The pole piece may become magnetized during operation. Check carefully for any metallic material clinging to the tip.

3. Inspect the pole piece carefully for any sign of cracking or contact with the toothed wheel. If any damage is found, replace the speed sensor.

4. Use an ohmmeter to measure resistance between the pins of the sensor. Correct resistance should be 2.25–2.75 kilo-ohms.

5. If resistance is outside the proper range, the sensor must be replaced.

6. With the ohmmeter still connected, manipulate and pull gently on the cable, trying to expose a hidden break in the line. Do not use excess force. Be suspicious of areas where the cable bends or turns during routing.

7. The toothed wheel should be inspected whenever the sensor is removed. Foreign matter should be removed without scratching or damaging the grooves. Inspect for any broken or chipped teeth; if any are found the toothed wheel must be replaced.

8. Reinstall the wheel speed sensor.

ABS System Relay

TESTING

1. Remove the relay from its mount and disconnect the harness.

2. Use an ohmmeter to check continuity. There should be no continuity between terminals 1 and 5. Continuity should exist between terminals 2 and 4.

3. Apply 12 volts to pin 2 and ground pin 4. With power applied, continuity should be found across terminals 1 and 5.

4. If any test condition is not met, the relay must be replaced.

Pump Motor Relay

TESTING

1. Remove the relay from its mount near the hydraulic unit.

2. Use an ohmmeter to check continuity. There should be no continuity between terminals 1 and 4. There should be continuity between terminals 2 and 3.

3. Apply 12 volts to terminal 2 and ground terminal 3. With power applied, there should be continuity between terminals 1 and 4.

4. If any test condition is not met, the relay must be replaced.

ABS Warning Lamp Relay

TESTING

1. Remove the relay from the relay box located in the engine compartment.

2. Use an ohmmeter to check continuity. There should be continuity between terminals 1 and 3. Continuity with approximately 0 ohms resistance should also exist between terminals 2 and 4.

3. Apply 12 volts to terminal 1 and ground terminal 3. With power applied, there should be no continuity between terminals 2 and 4.

4. If any test condition is not met, the relay must be replaced.

System Diagnostics

GENERAL INFORMATION

♦ See Figures 78 and 79

Diagnosis of the ABS system consists of 3 general steps, performed in order. First is the visual or preliminary inspection, including inspection of the basic brake system, it is always required before any other steps are taken. Next, diagnosis of the system is then made by a careful analysis of the ANTI-LOCK warning lamp display during start-up and operation. Third, the warning lamp diagnosis via the use of the Multi-Use Tester will direct the use of further charts.

The ABS systems may be checked with the Multi-Use Tester, allowing diagnostic codes to be output. Connect the tester properly; the system will enter diagnostic mode and prompt the operator through the diagnostic procedures.

Visual Inspection

Before diagnosing an apparent ABS problem, make absolutely certain that the normal braking system is in correct working order. Many common brake problems (dragging lining, seepage, etc.) will affect the ABS system. A visual check of specific system components may reveal problems creating an apparent ABS malfunction. Performing this inspection may reveal a simple failure, thus eliminating extended diagnostic time.

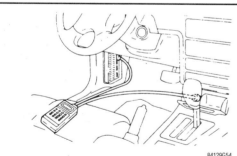

84129G54

Fig. 78 Connecting the multi-use tester for checking the ABS system—Sonata

Code	Diagnostic item	Code	Diagnostic item
11	ECU-FAIL	85	LF SENSOR
12	MODULATOR	86	RF SENSOR
13	EXCESS DECAY	87	LR SENSOR
22	WARNING LAMP	88	RR SENSOR
23	WARNING LAMP RELAY	95	LF SENSOR CONTINUITY
24	SYSTEM RELAY	96	RF SENSOR CONTINUITY
25	SOLENOID LOW VOLTAGE	97	LR SENSOR CONTINUITY
28	MOTOR PUMP	98	RR SENSOR CONTINUITY

84129G55

Fig. 79 ABS system diagnostic code list—Sonata

1. Inspect the brake fluid level in the reservoir.

2. Inspect brake lines, hoses, master cylinder assembly, and brake calipers for leakage.

3. Visually check brake lines and hoses for excessive wear, heat damage, punctures, contact with other parts, missing clips or holders, blockage or crimping.

4. Check the calipers for rust or corrosion. Check for proper sliding action if applicable.

5. Check the caliper pistons for freedom of motion during application and release.

6. Inspect the wheel speed sensors for proper mounting and connections. Make certain the sensor wiring is properly routed and retained in all clips.

7. Inspect the toothed wheels for broken teeth or poor mounting.

8. Inspect the wheels and tires on the vehicle. They must be of the same size and type to generate accurate speed signals. Check also for approximately equal tire pressures.

9. Confirm the fault occurrence with the operator. Certain driver induced faults may cause dash warning lamps to light. Excessive wheel spin on low-traction surfaces or high speed acceleration may also set fault codes and trigger a warning lamp. These induced faults are not system failures but examples of vehicle performance outside the parameters of the controller.

10. The most common cause of intermittent faults is not a failed sensor but a loose, corroded or dirty connector. Incorrect installation of the wheel speed sensor will cause a loss of wheel speed signal. Check harness and component connectors carefully.

READING CODES

Anti-Lock System

The diagnostic connector is located under the left side dashboard, in the kick panel. Stored diagnostic codes may be retrieved using a suitable scan tool as follows:

1. With the ignition **OFF**, connect the scan tool to the data link connector in the left side kick panel.

2. Turn the ignition **ON** and select the ABS diagnostics on the scan tool. Once in the diagnostic mode the anti-lock system becomes inoperative and the ABS light remains illuminated.

3. If the system does not enter into diagnostics, inspect the ECU power circuit and wire harness between the ECU and data link terminals.

4. Read the ECU memory stored codes.

5. Erase the codes stored in the ECU memory.

6. Turn the ignition **OFF** and disconnect the scan tool. Test drive the vehicle.

7. If the vehicle goes into the fail safe mode during the test drive and diagnostic codes are stored, refer to the trouble code diagnostic charts.

CLEARING CODES

➡**The anti-lock system memory codes can only be cleared using a scan tool. Disconnecting the negative battery cable or turning OFF the ignition switch will not clear the system memory.**

Refer to the manufacturers scan tool instructions. If the ECU is in the fail-safe mode and a component malfunction exists.

FILLING THE SYSTEM

The brake fluid reservoir is part of the normal brake system and is filled or checked in the usual manner. Always clean the reservoir cap and surrounding area thoroughly before removing the cap. Fill the reservoir only to the FULL or MAX mark; do not overfill. Use only fresh DOT 3 brake fluid from unopened containers. Do not use any fluid containing a petroleum base. Do not use any fluid which has been exposed to water or moisture. Failure to use the correct fluid will affect system function and component life.

BLEEDING THE SYSTEM

The brake system must be bled any time a line, hose or component is loosened or removed. Any air trapped within the system can affect pedal feel and system function. Bleeding the complete system including the modulator assembly requires the use of the Hyundai Multi-Use Tester (MUT) to cycle all of the build/decay and isolation valves of the hydraulic modulator. Make certain the fluid level in the reservoir is maintained at or near correct levels during bleeding operations. Use an inline filter when adding new brake fluid to the master cylinder reservoir. To bleed the system proceed as follows:

1. Bleed the normal brake system using the standard procedure. Bleed the wheel circuits in the following order: left rear, right front, right rear and left front.
2. Connect the MUT to the diagnostic connector located under the dash near the dash.
3. Turn the ignition switch **ON**, but do not start the engine.
4. Connect a clear vinyl tube to the bleeder screw to be opened and place the other end in a clear container partially filled with new brake fluid.
5. Depress the brake pedal lightly and use the MUT to actuate the appropriate valves. When each valve cycles, fluid from the respective fitting will emerge. Proceed with bleeding each of the 4 modulator circuits in the order shown.

☀☀ CAUTION

Fluid emerging from the modulator bleed ports will be at high pressure, ensure the vinyl tube is connected to each port prior to opening the corresponding bleeder to avoid personal injury and/or damage to the vehicle.

6. The pedal will drop slightly as the valve is cycled. If pedal drops completely, close the bleed valve and re-apply light pressure to the pedal.
7. When air bubbles no longer emerge from the bleed port, close the bleeder and proceed to the next port.
8. Check and add brake fluid to the reservoir as needed.

Modulator Unit

REMOVAL & INSTALLATION

1. Use a syringe or similar device to remove as much fluid as possible from the master cylinder reservoir. Some fluid will be spilled from lines during removal of the hydraulic unit; protect adjacent paint surfaces.
2. Disconnect the electrical harness to the hydraulic unit.
3. Disconnect the brake lines from the hydraulic unit. Correct re-assembly is critical. Label or identify the lines before removal. Plug each line and each port immediately after removal.
4. Remove the 4 bolts holding the modulator; remove the unit from the vehicle.
5. Set the unit upright supported by blocks on the workbench. The hydraulic unit must not be tilted or turned upside down. No component of the hydraulic unit should be loosened or disassembled.
6. The brackets may be removed if desired. Inspect the rubber grommets, washers and ferrules. Replace as required.
   To install:
7. Install the brackets if they were removed. Tighten the bracket bolts to 17–19 ft. lbs. (23–26 Nm).
8. Install the hydraulic unit into the vehicle, keeping it upright at all times.
9. Install the retaining bolts holding the brackets to the vehicle. Tighten the bolts to 7–9 ft. lbs. (13–16 Nm).
10. Connect each brake line loosely to the correct port and double check the placement. Tighten each line to 10–16 ft. lbs. (18–23 Nm).
11. Connect the hydraulic unit wire harness.
12. Fill the master cylinder reservoir to the MAX line with brake fluid.
13. Bleed the complete brake system.
14. Check ABS system function by turning the ignition **ON** and observing the dashboard warning lamp. Test drive the vehicle and confirm system operation.

Electronic Control Unit (ALCU)

REMOVAL & INSTALLATION

1. Ensure that the ignition switch is **OFF** throughout the procedure.
2. Disconnect the multi-pin connector from the control unit.
3. Remove the 4 retaining bolts and remove the control unit from the left fenderwell

To install:
4. Place the control unit in position and tighten the retaining bolts.
5. Connect the multi-pin connector and secure.
6. Turn ignition switch **ON** and verify operation of control unit.

Wheel Speed Sensors

REMOVAL & INSTALLATION

▶ **See Figures 80 and 81**

1. Raise and safely support the vehicle.
2. Remove the wheel and tire.
3. Remove the inner fender or splash shield as required.
4. Beginning at the sensor end, carefully disconnect or release each clip and retainer along the sensor wire. Take careful note of the exact position of each clip; they must be reinstalled in the identical position.
5. Disconnect the sensor connector at the end of the harness.
6. Remove the bolt holding the speed sensor bracket to the knuckle and remove the assembly from the vehicle.

➡ **The speed sensor has a pole piece projecting from it. This exposed tip must be protected from impact or scratches. Do not allow the pole piece to contact the toothed wheel during removal or installation.**

7. Remove the sensor from the bracket.
   To install:
8. Assemble the sensor onto the bracket and tighten the bolt to 9 ft. lbs. (12 Nm).
9. Route the cable correctly and loosely install the clips and retainers. All clips must be in their original position and the sensor cable must not be twisted. Improper installation may cause cable damage and system failure.

➡ **The wiring in the harness is easily damaged by twisting and flexing.**

10. Tighten the screws and bolts for the cable retaining clips.
11. Install the inner fender or splash shield, if removed.
12. Install the wheel and tire. Lower the vehicle to the ground.

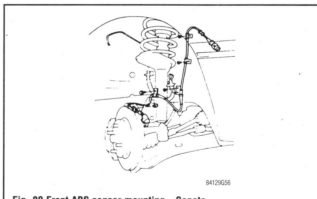

84129G56

Fig. 80 Front ABS sensor mounting—Sonata

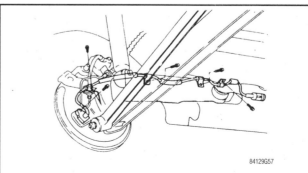

84129G57

Fig. 81 Rear ABS sensor mounting—Sonata

TORQUE SPECIFICATIONS

Component	U.S.	Metric
Anti-lock brake system components;		
Sonata:		
Bleed Screw	3–5 ft. lbs.	5–6 Nm
ECU connector bolt	2–4 ft. lbs.	3–5 Nm
Modulator mounting bolts	9–12 ft. lbs.	13–17 Nm
Modulator mounting bracket bolts	16–18 ft. lbs.	23–26 Nm
Proportioning valve-to-modulator	9–22 ft. lbs.	13–32 Nm
Sensor mounting bolts	6–8 ft. lbs.	9–11 Nm
Six brake tubes-to-modulator	13–17 ft. lbs.	18–23 Nm
Backing plate mounting bolt;		
Excel	36–43 ft. lbs.	50–60 Nm
Elantra	36–43 ft. lbs.	50–60 Nm
Scoupe	36–43 ft. lbs.	50–60 Nm
Sonata	36–43 ft. lbs.	50–60 Nm
Brake booster mounting nut;		
Excel	6–9 ft. lbs.	8–12 Nm
Elantra	6–9 ft. lbs.	8–12 Nm
Scoupe	6–9 ft. lbs.	8–12 Nm
Sonata	15–21 ft. lbs.	21–28 Nm
Brake booster hose fitting-to-manifold;		
Excel	6–9 ft. lbs.	8–12 Nm
Elantra	6–9 ft. lbs.	8–12 Nm
Scoupe	6–9 ft. lbs.	8–12 Nm
Sonata	11–13 ft. lbs.	15–18 Nm
Brake bleeder screw;		
Front:		
Excel	5–9 ft. lbs.	7–13 Nm
Elantra	5–9 ft. lbs.	7–13 Nm
Scoupe	5–9 ft. lbs.	7–13 Nm
Sonata	5–9 ft. lbs.	7–13 Nm
Rear:		
Excel	5–7 ft. lbs.	7–9 Nm
Elantra	5–7 ft. lbs.	7–9 Nm
Scoupe	5–7 ft. lbs.	7–9 Nm
Sonata	6–14 ft. lbs.	8–20 Nm
Brake hose-to-front caliper;		
Excel	18–22 ft. lbs.	25–30 Nm
Elantra	18–22 ft. lbs.	25–30 Nm
Scoupe	18–22 ft. lbs.	25–30 Nm
Sonata	18–22 ft. lbs.	25–30 Nm
Brake tube flare nut;		
Excel	9–12 ft. lbs.	13–17 Nm
Elantra	9–12 ft. lbs.	13–17 Nm
Scoupe	9–12 ft. lbs.	13–17 Nm
Sonata	9–12 ft. lbs.	13–17 Nm
Caliper assembly-to-knuckle;		
Excel	47–54 ft. lbs.	65–75 Nm
Elantra	44–63 ft. lbs.	69–85 Nm
Scoupe	47–54 ft. lbs.	65–75 Nm
Sonata	51–63 ft. lbs.	69–85 Nm

84129C01

TORQUE SPECIFICATIONS

Caliper guide rod bolt;		
Excel	16–23 ft. lbs.	22–32 Nm
Elantra	16–23 ft. lbs.	22–32 Nm
Scoupe	16–23 ft. lbs.	22–32 Nm
Sonata	16–23 ft. lbs.	22–32 Nm
Caliper pin bolt;		
Excel	25–32 ft. lbs.	35–45 Nm
Elantra	25–32 ft. lbs.	35–45 Nm
Scoupe	25–32 ft. lbs.	35–45 Nm
Master cylinder-to-booster mounting nut;		
Excel	6–9 ft. lbs.	8–12 Nm
Elantra	6–9 ft. lbs.	8–12 Nm
Scoupe	6–9 ft. lbs.	8–12 Nm
Sonata	10–16 ft. lbs.	14–21 Nm
Proportioning valve mounting nut;		
Excel	6–9 ft. lbs.	8–12 Nm
Elantra	6–9 ft. lbs.	8–12 Nm
Scoupe	6–9 ft. lbs.	8–12 Nm
Sonata	9–16 ft. lbs.	13–22 Nm
Wheel cylinder mounting bolt;		
Excel	4–8 ft. lbs.	6–11 Nm
Elantra	4–8 ft. lbs.	6–11 Nm
Scoupe	4–8 ft. lbs.	6–11 Nm
Sonata	9–13 ft. lbs.	13–18 Nm

84129C02

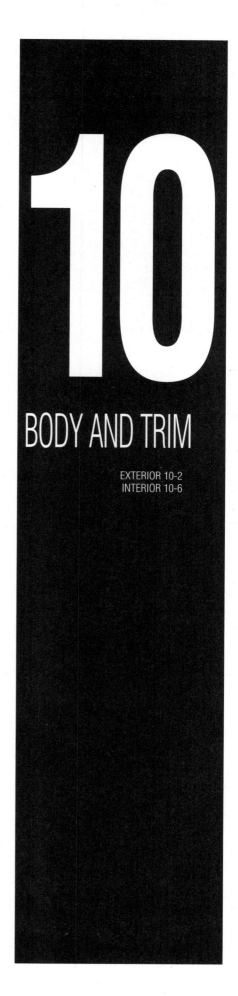

10

BODY AND TRIM

EXTERIOR

Doors

REMOVAL & INSTALLATION

1. Open the door.
2. Place some kind of support stand under the door or have someone hold it for you.
3. Remove the door trim panel and disconnect the door speaker wiring, power window wiring, power mirror and central locking system wiring. If equipped with manual window regulators, insert a screwdriver behind the regulator handle to release the clip and remove the handle.
4. Remove the hinge-to-pillar bolts.
5. Disconnect the door limiter strap.
6. Remove the door.

To install:

7. Support the door and connect the door limiter strap.
8. Continue supporting the door and install the hinge-to-pillar bolts. Torque the bolts to 26–30 ft. lbs. (36–42 Nm).
9. Connect the door accessory wiring and install the door trim panel.
10. Close and open the door several times to make sure it works properly and that it is properly positioned. As you do this, cheek for the following:
   a. A flush fit of the door with the body.
   b. Equal gaps on the front, rear, top and bottom edges between the door and body.
   c. Edges of the door and body are parallel.
   d. Door does not shake when closed.
   e. Door latches shut without slamming.
   f. Accessories work properly

ADJUSTMENTS

Door Position Adjustment

▶ **See Figure 1**

A properly adjusted front or rear door should exhibit the following characteristics:

- A flush fit of the door with the body
- Equal gaps on the front, rear, top and bottom edges between the door and body
- Edges of the door and body are parallel

If the door is not positioned as described above, then a door position adjustment must be performed.

Door position adjustment is made by means of Special Tool 09793-21000 at the hinges. When using this tool, make sure that the painted surfaces in the immediate area are covered with masking tape to protect the paint.

Striker Adjustment

▶ **See Figure 2**

If the door striker is adjusted properly, the door will not shake when closed and it will latch shut will minimal closing effort. If the door does not perform as

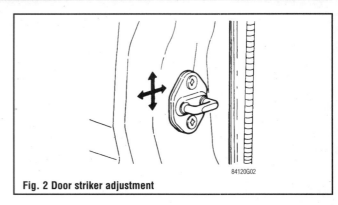
Fig. 2 Door striker adjustment

described, then the striker must be adjusted. To adjust the door striker perform the following:

1. Trace a thin pencil line around the striker plate for reference.
2. Loosen the striker screws.
3. Move the striker IN or OUT to make the latch tighter or looser.
4. Move the striker UP or DOWN to align the striker with the latch opening.
5. Tighten the latch screws and recheck. Hold the outside handle out and push the door against the body to make sure the striker fits flush.

Hood

REMOVAL & INSTALLATION

▶ **See Figures 3, 4 and 5**

➡ **Cover the front body area with a blanket for protection when removing and installing the hood.**

1. Open the hood and have an assistant support it.
2. Matchmark the hood-to-hinge position.
3. Remove the hinge-to-hood bolts and lift off the hood.
4. Install the hood in position and align the marks made during removal.
5. Install the hinge bolts and tighten to 16–19 ft. lbs. (22–27 Nm).
6. Check the alignment of the hood, and adjust as needed.

ADJUSTMENTS

▶ **See Figures 6 and 7**

1. Adjust the hood side-to-side and fore-aft fit by loosening the hood-to-hinge bolts and repositioning the hood as necessary.

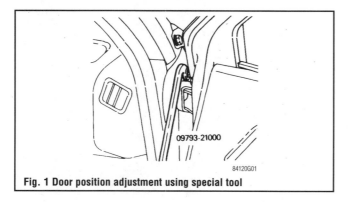
Fig. 1 Door position adjustment using special tool

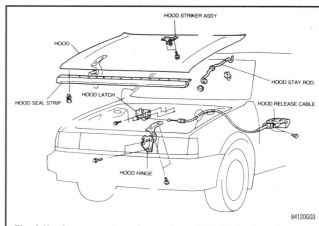
Fig. 3 Hood components and mounting—1986–89 Excel

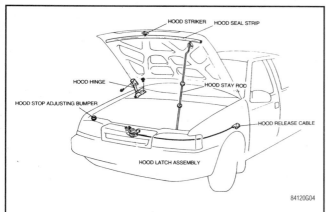

Fig. 4 Hood components and mounting—1990–93 Excel, Elantra and Scoupe

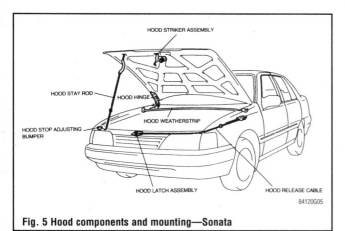

Fig. 5 Hood components and mounting—Sonata

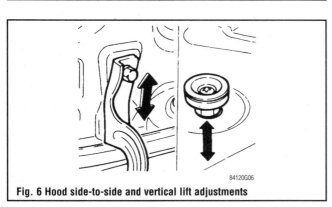

Fig. 6 Hood side-to-side and vertical lift adjustments

Fig. 7 Hood latch adjustment

2. Hood lock centering adjustment is made by loosening the lock plate bolts and moving the plate as necessary.

3. Hood vertical fit is adjusted by raising or lowering the hood stops.

Hatch

REMOVAL & INSTALLATION

Excel Hatchback

▶ **See Figures 8 and 9**

1. Disconnect the defroster grid wires and rear wiper wiring. The connectors for the wiper are found behind the quarter panel trim.

2. Disconnect the rear washer hose.

3. Have an assistant support the hatch. With the hatch fully open, unbolt the hydraulic supports from the hatch and C-pillar.

✳✳ CAUTION

Never attempt to unbolt the supports with the hatch closed or even partially closed.

4. Remove the hinge-to-hatch bolts and lift off the hatch.

5. Installation is the reverse of the removal procedure. Tighten the hinge-to-hatch bolts to 20–25 ft. lbs. (28–35 Nm). Lubricate the hatch latch with white lithium or suitable chassis grease.

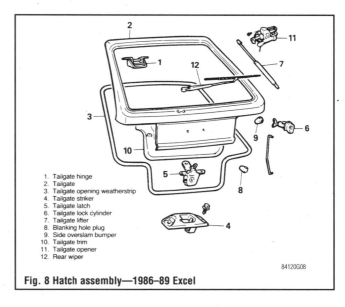

1. Tailgate hinge
2. Tailgate
3. Tailgate opening weatherstrip
4. Tailgate striker
5. Tailgate latch
6. Tailgate lock cylinder
7. Tailgate lifter
8. Blanking hole plug
9. Side overslam bumper
10. Tailgate trim
11. Tailgate opener
12. Rear wiper

Fig. 8 Hatch assembly—1986–89 Excel

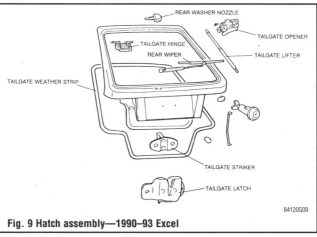

Fig. 9 Hatch assembly—1990–93 Excel

ALIGNMENT

Excel Hatchback

1. Side-to-side and fore-aft positioning can be adjusted by loosening the hinge bolts and moving the hatch as necessary.
2. Striker adjustment is made by loosening the striker bolts and moving the striker as necessary.

Trunk Lid

REMOVAL & INSTALLATION

▶ See Figures 10, 11, 12 and 13

1. Raise the trunk lid fully.
2. Matchmark the lid-to-hinge position.
3. Disconnect the main trunk wiring connectors.
4. Have someone hold the lid while you remove the nuts securing the lid to the hinges.
5. Install the trunk lid in position, aligning the matchmarks made during removal. Install the retaining bolts and tighten to 5–6 ft. lbs. (7–9 Nm). Lubricate the trunk lid latch with white lithium or suitable chassis grease.
6. Adjust the trunk lid as needed.

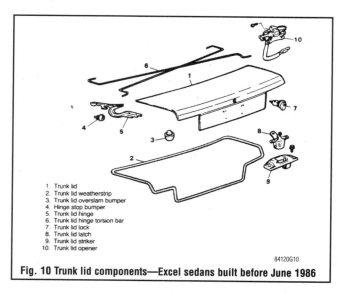

1. Trunk lid
2. Trunk lid weatherstrip
3. Trunk lid overslam bumper
4. Hinge stop bumper
5. Trunk lid hinge
6. Trunk lid hinge torsion bar
7. Trunk lid lock
8. Trunk lid latch
9. Trunk lid striker
10. Trunk lid opener

84120G10

Fig. 10 Trunk lid components—Excel sedans built before June 1986

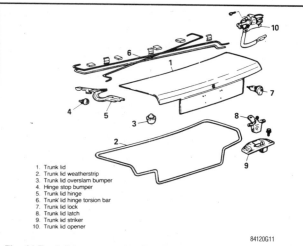

1. Trunk lid
2. Trunk lid weatherstrip
3. Trunk lid overslam bumper
4. Hinge stop bumper
5. Trunk lid hinge
6. Trunk lid hinge torsion bar
7. Trunk lid lock
8. Trunk lid latch
9. Trunk lid striker
10. Trunk lid opener

84120G11

Fig. 11 Trunk lid components—Excel sedans built from June 1986 through 1989

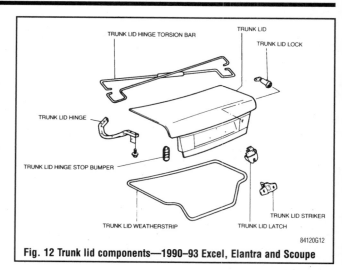

84120G12

Fig. 12 Trunk lid components—1990–93 Excel, Elantra and Scoupe

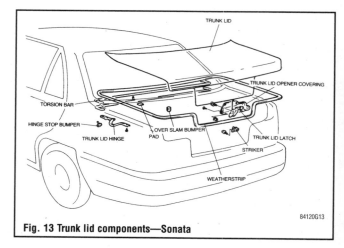

84120G13

Fig. 13 Trunk lid components—Sonata

ALIGNMENT

1. Loosen the trunk lid hinge attaching bolts until they are just loose enough to move the trunk lid.
2. Move the trunk lid for and aft to obtain a flush fit between the trunk lid and the rear fender.
3. To obtain a snug fit between the trunk lid and weatherstrip, loosen the trunk lid lock striker attaching bolts enough to move the lid, working the striker up and down and from side to side as required.
4. After the adjustment is made tighten the striker bolts securely.

Grille

REMOVAL & INSTALLATION

1. Open the hood.
2. On 1986–87 Excel, remove the six retaining screws and pull the grille straight out to remove it.
3. On 1988–89 Excel, release the grille mounting fasteners, using a small prybar, and pull the grille straight out to remove it.
4. On 1990–93 Excel, the grille is held in place by four self-tapping screws. Remove the screws and pull the grille forward.
5. On Elantra, the grille is retained by four screws and 2 clips. Remove the screws and gently pry on the clips, then pull the grille forward.
6. On Sonata, the grille is retained by three mounting screws. Remove these three screws to remove the grille.
7. Installation is the reverse of the removal procedure.

Fig. 14 Rearview mirror mounting—1986–87 Excel

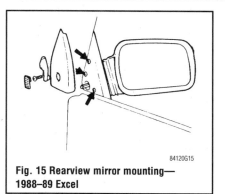

Fig. 15 Rearview mirror mounting—1988–89 Excel

Fig. 16 Manual rearview mirror mounting—Sonata

Manual Outside Mirror

REMOVAL & INSTALLATION

▶ **See Figures 14, 15 and 16**

1. Remove control knob handle.
2. Remove door corner finisher panel.
3. Remove mirror body attaching screws, and then remove mirror body.
4. Installation is in the reverse order of removal.

➥**Apply sealer to the rear surface of door corner finisher panel during installation to prevent water leak.**

Power Outside Mirror

The mirrors are controlled by a single switch assembly, located on the center console. The motors that operate the mirror are part of the mirror assembly and cannot be replaced separately.

The mirror switch consists of a left-right change over select knob and control knobs. The switch is ready to function only when the ignition switch is in the **ACC** or **ON** position. Movement of the mirror is accomplished by the motors, located in the mirror housing.

REMOVAL & INSTALLATION

▶ **See Figures 17 and 18**

1. Remove door corner finisher panel.
2. Remove mirror body attaching screws, and then remove mirror body.
3. Disconnect the electrical lead.
4. Installation is in the reverse order of removal.

➥**Apply sealer to the rear surface of door corner finisher panel during installation to prevent water leak.**

Antenna

REMOVAL & INSTALLATION

▶ **See Figure 19**

1. Open the trunk.
2. Remove the left side luggage trim by re. moving the five retaining screws.
3. Remove the two nuts that attach the antenna assembly to the support pillar.
4. Disconnect the antenna wiring harness.
5. Remove the antenna support cable.
6. Remove the antenna assembly from the support pillar and lift it out of the trunk.

To install:

7. Position the antenna assembly on the support pillar and secure it with the support cable.
8. Connect the wiring harness.
9. Install and tighten the two support pillar attaching nuts.

Fig. 17 Power rearview mirror mounting—1990–93 Excel, Elantra and Scoupe

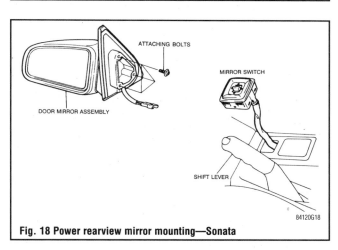

Fig. 18 Power rearview mirror mounting—Sonata

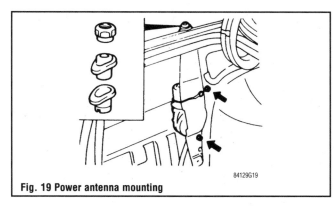

Fig. 19 Power antenna mounting

10. Place the key in the ignition and check that the antenna operates properly.
11. Install the left side luggage trim and close the trunk.

INTERIOR

Instrument Panel

REMOVAL & INSTALLATION

1986–89 Excel

♦ **See Figure 20**

1. Remove the steering wheel.
2. Remove the steering column shroud.
3. Remove the glove box.
4. Remove the steering column undercover.
5. Remove the lower instrument panel cover.
6. Unbolt the hood release handle mounting screws.
7. Unbolt the lower side dash pad and disconnect the wiring connector. Remove the main and supplemental consoles.
8. Remove the ashtray and lighter.
9. Unbolt and remove the main lower dash pad and unplug the wiring connector.
10. Remove the cluster housing, disconnecting the wiring and removing the cluster lamp.
11. Remove the cluster assembly.
12. Remove the radio.
13. Remove the heater control head.
14. Remove the bolts securing the main dash pad to the heater bracket.
15. Remove the upper dash pad cover and remove the main dash pad screws from underneath.
16. Remove the main crash pad.
To install:
17. Install the main dash pad and from underneath, install the main dash pad screws.
18. Install the upper dash pad cover.
19. Install the main dash pad-to-heater bracket bolts.
20. Install the heater control head.
21. Install the radio.
22. Install the cluster assembly.
23. Install the cluster housing with wiring and lamp.
24. Plug the wiring connector into the main dash pad and install the main dash pad.
25. Install the ashtray and lighter.
26. Plug the wiring connector into the lower dash pad and install the lower dash pad.
27. Install the hood release handle.
28. Install the lower instrument cover. On 1988-89 models, install the main and supplemental consoles.
29. Remove the steering column undercover.
30. Install the glove box.
31. Install the steering wheel column shroud.
32. Install the steering wheel.
33. Check all instrument panel functions to make sure they work properly.

1990–93 Excel, Scoupe and Elantra

♦ **See Figures 21, 22 and 23**

1. Remove the steering wheel.
2. Remove the upper and lower steering column shrouds.
3. Remove the hood release handle mounting screws.
4. Remove the lower fascia panel.
5. Remove the side lower crash pad.
6. Remove the glove box.
7. Remove the main lower crash pad.
8. Pull the instrument cluster forward disconnect all the electrical wiring and the speedometer cable.

9. Remove the heater control assembly.
10. Remove the front speaker grille from the main crash pad.
11. Remove the front speaker.
12. Remove the six retaining screws and remove the main crash pad from it's mounting brackets.
To install:
13. Position the main crash pad onto the mounting brackets and install and tighten the six retaining screws.
14. Install the front speaker.
15. Install the front speaker grille into the main crash pad.
16. Install the heater control assembly.
17. Connect the speedometer cable and the electrical wiring to the rear of the instrument cluster and install the cluster not the main crash pad.
18. Install the lower main crash pad.
19. Install the glove box.
20. Install the side lower crash pad.
21. Install the lower fascia panel.
22. Install the hood release handle screws.
23. Install the steering wheel column shrouds.
24. Install the steering wheel.
25. Check all instrument panel functions to make sure they work properly.

Sonata

♦ **See Figure 24**

1. Remove the steering wheel.
2. Remove the steering column upper and lower shrouds.
3. Remove the hood release handle.
4. Remove the side lower crash pad.
5. Remove the fuse box mounting screws and allow the fuse box and wiring to dangle.
6. Empty and remove the glove box.
7. Remove the lower crash pad center fascia panel.
8. Remove the radio and disconnect the electrical connector.
9. Remove the lower crash pad center skin.
10. Remove the main lower crash pad.
11. Remove the four steering column mounting bracket bolts and lower the steering column from its normal operating position.
12. Remove the cluster assembly and disconnect the electrical connectors.
13. Remove the air conditioner control assembly.
14. Remove the front speaker grille from the main crash pad.
15. Remove the front speaker.
16. Disconnect the defroster nozzle upper center cover from the main crash pad.
17. Remove the main crash pad.
To install:
18. Install the main crash pad.
19. Connect the defroster nozzle upper center cover to the main crash pad.
20. Install the front speaker and speaker grille into the main crash pad.
21. Install the air conditioner control assembly.
22. Connect the electrical connectors to the rear of the cluster assembly and install it.
23. Raise the steering wheel from the lowered position and install the four steering column mounting bracket bolts.
24. Install the main lower crash pad.
25. Connect the wiring to the radio and install.
26. Install the lower crash pad fascia panel.
27. Install the glove box.
28. Raise the fuse box and wiring into place and install the fuse box mounting screws.
29. Install the lower side crash pad.
30. Install the hood release handle.
31. Install the upper and lower steering column shrouds.
32. Install the steering wheel.

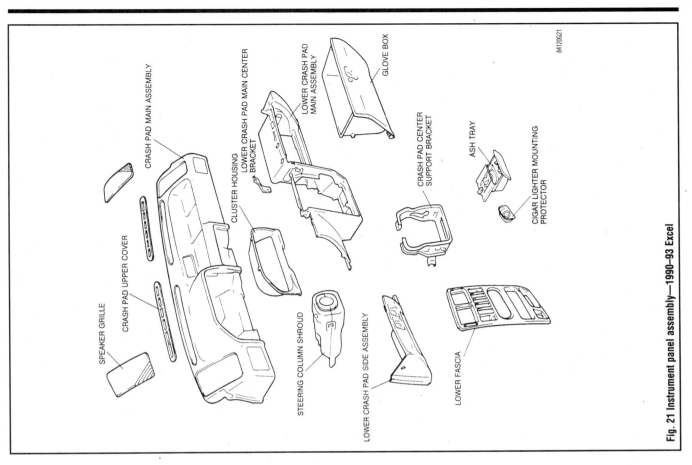

Fig. 21 Instrument panel assembly—1990–93 Excel

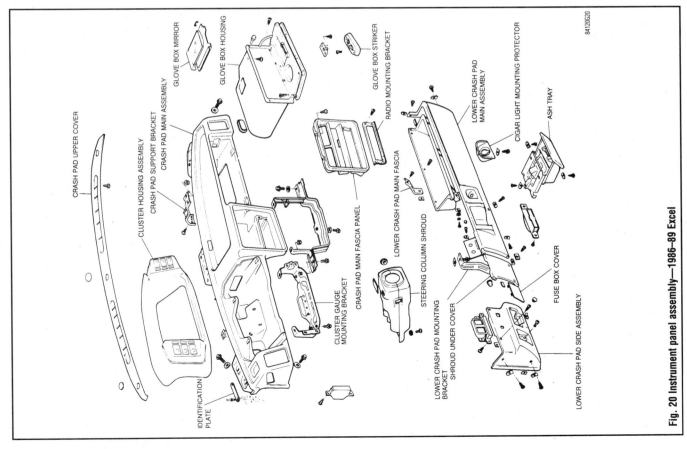

Fig. 20 Instrument panel assembly—1986–89 Excel

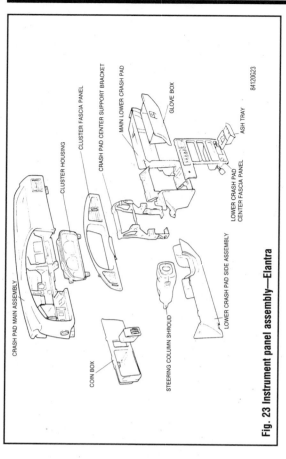

CRASH PAD MAIN ASSEMBLY
CLUSTER HOUSING
CLUSTER FASCIA PANEL
CRASH PAD CENTER SUPPORT BRACKET
MAIN LOWER CRASH PAD
GLOVE BOX
ASH TRAY
LOWER CRASH PAD CENTER FASCIA PANEL
LOWER CRASH PAD SIDE ASSEMBLY
STEERING COLUMN SHROUD
COIN BOX

8412OG23

Fig. 23 Instrument panel assembly—Elantra

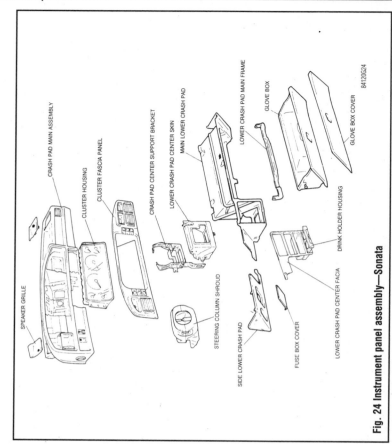

CRASH PAD MAIN ASSEMBLY
CLUSTER HOUSING
CLUSTER FASCIA PANEL
CRASH PAD CENTER SUPPORT BRACKET
LOWER CRASH PAD CENTER SKIN
MAIN LOWER CRASH PAD
LOWER CRASH PAD MAIN FRAME
GLOVE BOX
GLOVE BOX COVER
DRINK HOLDER HOUSING
LOWER CRASH PAD CENTER FACIA
FUSE BOX COVER
SIDE LOWER CRASH PAD
STEERING COLUMN SHROUD
SPEAKER GRILLE

8412OG24

Fig. 24 Instrument panel assembly—Sonata

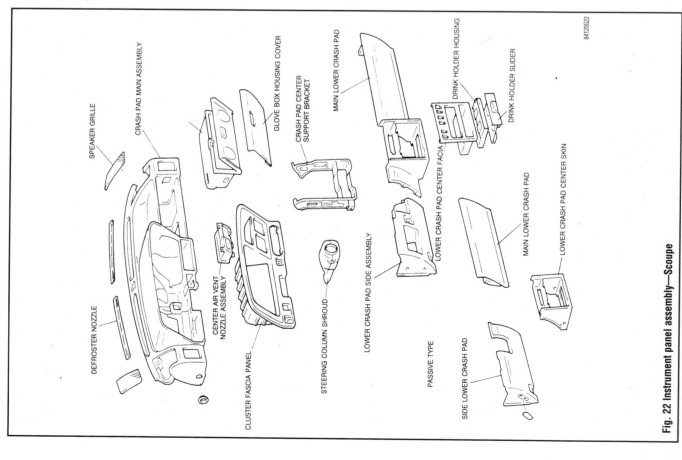

SPEAKER GRILLE
CRASH PAD MAIN ASSEMBLY
GLOVE BOX HOUSING COVER
CRASH PAD CENTER SUPPORT BRACKET
MAIN LOWER CRASH PAD
DRINK HOLDER HOUSING
DRINK HOLDER SLIDER
LOWER CRASH PAD CENTER FACIA
MAIN LOWER CRASH PAD
LOWER CRASH PAD CENTER SKIN
LOWER CRASH PAD SIDE ASSEMBLY
PASSIVE TYPE
SIDE LOWER CRASH PAD
STEERING COLUMN SHROUD
CLUSTER FASCIA PANEL
CENTER AIR VENT NOZZLE ASSEMBLY
DEFROSTER NOZZLE

8412OG22

Fig. 22 Instrument panel assembly—Scoupe

Console

REMOVAL & INSTALLATION

1986–89 Excel

▶ **See Figure 25**

1. Remove the four floor console section screws.
2. Lift out the console, disconnect the power window switch wires, if need be, and removing the shifter handle if necessary.
3. Remove the four upper console section screws, disconnect the clock wiring and remove the console section.
4. Installation is the reverse of removal.

1990–93 Excel, Elantra And Scoupe

▶ **See Figures 26 and 27**

1. Remove the rear console mounting screws and remove the rear console.
2. Unscrew the shifter knob from the shifter lever. Remove the shifter lever boot (manual transaxles) or the shift lever indicator plate (automatic transaxles).
3. Remove the front console retaining screws, disconnect the wiring and remove the console.
4. Installation is the reverse of the removal procedure.

Sonata

▶ **See Figure 28**

1. Gently pry the front console trim plate up on one side and loosen one of the retaining screws to gain access to the outside mirror control switch electrical connector. Disconnect the connector.
2. Remove the rear console by removing the two retaining screws.
3. Unscrew the shifter knob from the shifter lever.
4. Remove the four screws that attach the front console to the front and center mounting brackets.
5. Pull the front console out and disconnect the disconnect the ashtray lamp and cigarette lighter electrical connectors from their respective sockets.
6. Remove the front console protectors from the front bracket by removing the two retaining screws on each side.

To install:

7. Install the front console protectors.
8. Connect the cigarette lighter and ashtray lamp connectors to the front console and position the console onto the mounting brackets.
9. Install the front console mounting screws.
10. Screw the shifter knob onto the shifter lever.
11. Install the rear console.
12. Connect the outside mirror control switch and install the front console trim plate.

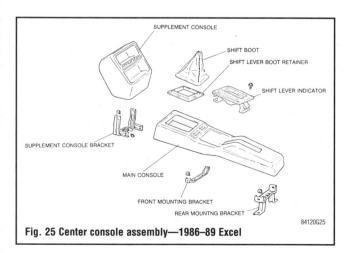

Fig. 25 Center console assembly—1986–89 Excel

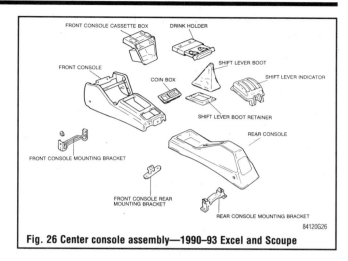

Fig. 26 Center console assembly—1990–93 Excel and Scoupe

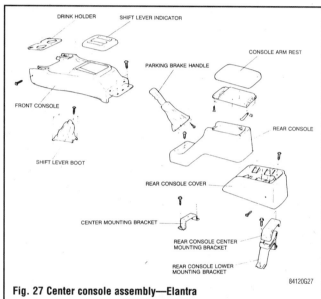

Fig. 27 Center console assembly—Elantra

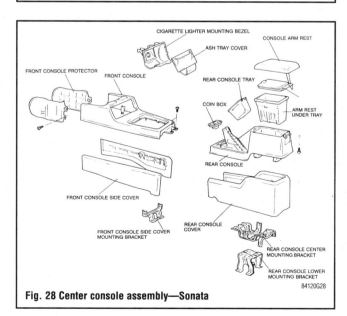

Fig. 28 Center console assembly—Sonata

Door Panels

REMOVAL & INSTALLATION

➡**Use care when removing the door panel, do not pull it too far back or use sharp objects to pry it off. There are tools designed to ease the removal of the trim panels, these can be found at any auto parts supplier.**

All Models

➡**Refer to the exploded views of the door assemblies found earlier in this section, for a complete view of the door panel components.**

1. Remove the door lock button.
2. Remove the arm rest (two screws). Pulling it downward aids removal.
3. Press in on the door trim panel and, using a needle nosed pliers or a soft cloth, pull out the window handle retaining pin. Slide the handle off the regulator stud.
4. Remove the door handle and handle trim.
5. Remove the outside rear view mirror mounting cover, remove the mounting screws and mirror. On cars with remotely controlled mirrors, remove the control knob.
6. Remove the door weatherstripping.
7. The trim panel is held to the door by means of snap clips. Slide a wood spatula or equivalent behind the trim panel edge and move it along until you come to one of the clips. Pry the clip out of its hole in the door. Pry only at the clip, never somewhere in between clips. The clips are easily torn from the door panel. Repeat this procedure for each snap clip.
8. Disconnect the speaker wiring and electric window wiring, if so equipped.
   To install:
9. Connect the electric window and speaker wiring to the door panel, if so equipped.
10. Position the panel onto the door frame. Carefully whack the snap clips into position with the heel of your hand. Take care that they are lined up right over the hole before inserting them.
11. Install the door weatherstripping.
12. Install the rear view mirror and remote control knob if so equipped.
13. Install the door handle trim and door handle.
14. Slide the regulator handle onto the stud and install the retaining clip. The window handle should be installed at a 45° angle up to the right, with the glass fully closed.
15. Install the arm rest.
16. Install the door lock button.

Manual Door Locks

REMOVAL & INSTALLATION

1. Remove the door panel and sealing screen.
2. Remove the lock cylinder from the rod by turning the resin clip.
3. Loosen the nuts attaching the outside door handle and remove the outside door handle.
4. Remove the screws retaining the inside door handle and door lock, and remove the door lock assembly from the hole in the inside of the door.
5. Remove the lock cylinder by removing the retaining clip.
6. Install the lock cylinder and clip to the door.
7. Install the door lock assembly and handles.
8. Install door panel and all attaching parts.

Power Door Lock Actuators

The power door locking system consists of switches, actuators and relays. Control switches are used to operate the system. Actuators are used to raise and lower the door lock buttons. These actuators are mounted inside the door assembly and are electrically operated once the switch is depressed. A control unit or functional relay is used to allow the system to regulate current, to function and to align all the actuators and switches with one another.

REMOVAL & INSTALLATION

1. Disconnect the negative battery cable.
2. Remove the door panel.
3. Disconnect the actuator electrical connector. Disconnect the required linkage rods.
4. Remove the actuator assembly retaining screws. Remove the actuator assembly from the vehicle.
5. Installation is the reverse of the removal procedure.

Door Glass

REMOVAL & INSTALLATION

1. Lower the glass fully.
2. Remove the door trim panel and door trim seal.
3. Remove the bolts securing the glass channel to the regulator.
4. Remove the felt strip from the window frame.
5. Push the glass up and lift it from the door.
6. Installation is the reverse of removal.

Manual Window Regulator

REMOVAL & INSTALLATION

Excel, Elantra and Scoupe

▶ **See Figures 29 and 30**

1. Remove the door trim panel.
2. Remove the door glass panel.
3. Remove the door regulator channel mounting bolts and remove the regulator, along with the retainer clip and spacers, through an access hole in the door panel. Note the positions of any anti-rattle pads. Make sure they go back in their original positions.
4. Installation is the reverse of the removal procedure.

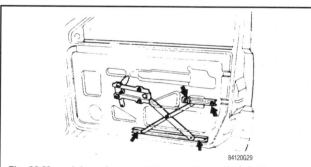

Fig. 29 Manual door glass regulator mounting—1986–89 Excel

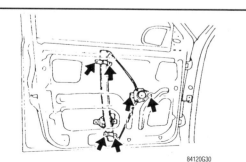

Fig. 30 Manual door glass regulator mounting—1990–93 Excel, Elantra and Scoupe

Electric Window Motor and Regulator

REMOVAL & INSTALLATION

♦ See Figure 31

1. Remove the mirror trim plate.
2. Remove the screws attaching the arm rest.
3. Remove the door trim panel by removing the attaching screws and the clips then pull it upward.
4. Lower the door glass until the mounting bolts can be seen.
5. Disconnect the power window harnesses, remove the screws then the arm rest.
6. Support the glass and remove the glass to regulator attaching bolts.
7. Remove the regulator mounting bolts, then remove the regulator assembly through the lower hole in the door.
8. With the regulator removed from the door, before removing the motor from the regulator, mark the sector gear and regulator position.
9. Move the window regulator to the original position by connecting a 12 volt source to the motor.

✴✴ CAUTION

The regulator gear will move suddenly when the motor is removed, because the regulator spring is tensioned against the gear.

10. Installation is the reverse of the removal procedure. Lubricate the sector and gear and rollers prior to installation.

Windshield and Fixed Glass

REMOVAL & INSTALLATION

If your windshield, or other fixed window, is cracked or chipped, you may decide to replace it with a new one yourself. However, there are two main reasons why replacement windshields and other window glass should be installed only by a professional automotive glass technician: safety and cost.

The most important reason a professional should install automotive glass is for safety. The glass in the vehicle, especially the windshield, is designed with safety in mind in case of a collision. The windshield is specially manufactured from two panes of specially-tempered glass with a thin layer of transparent plastic between them. This construction allows the glass to "give" in the event that a part of your body hits the windshield during the collision, and prevents the glass from shattering, which could cause lacerations, blinding and other harm to passengers of the vehicle. The other fixed windows are designed to be tempered so that if they break during a collision, they shatter in such a way that there are no large pointed glass pieces. The professional automotive glass tech-

nician knows how to install the glass in a vehicle so that it will function optimally during a collision. Without the proper experience, knowledge and tools, installing a piece of automotive glass yourself could lead to additional harm if an accident should ever occur.

Cost is also a factor when deciding to install automotive glass yourself. Performing this could cost you much more than a professional may charge for the same job. Since the windshield is designed to break under stress, an often life saving characteristic, windshields tend to break VERY easily when an inexperienced person attempts to install one. Do-it-yourselfers buying two, three or even four windshields from a salvage yard because they have broken them during installation are common stories. Also, since the automotive glass is designed to prevent the outside elements from entering your vehicle, improper installation can lead to water and air leaks. Annoying whining noises at highway speeds from air leaks or inside body panel rusting from water leaks can add to your stress level and subtract from your wallet. After buying two or three windshields, installing them and ending up with a leak that produces a noise while driving and water damage during rainstorms, the cost of having a professional do it correctly the first time may be much more alluring. We here at Chilton, therefore, advise that you have a professional automotive glass technician service any broken glass on your vehicle.

WINDSHIELD CHIP REPAIR

♦ See Figures 32 and 33

➡**Check with your state and local authorities on the laws for state safety inspection. Some states or municipalities may not allow chip repair as a viable option for correcting stone damage to your windshield.**

Although severely cracked or damaged windshields must be replaced, there is something that you can do to prolong or even prevent the need for replacement of a chipped windshield. There are many companies which offer windshield chip repair products, such as Loctite's® Bullseye™ windshield repair kit. These kits usually consist of a syringe, pedestal and a sealing adhesive. The syringe is mounted on the pedestal and is used to create a vacuum which pulls the plastic layer against the glass. This helps make the chip transparent. The adhesive is then injected which seals the chip and helps to prevent further stress cracks from developing

➡**Always follow the specific manufacturer's instructions.**

Inside Rear View Mirror

REMOVAL & INSTALLATION

Remove the screw cover from the mirror and remove the mounting screws. Slide the mirror from the bracket. When installing the new mirror, make sure that it is positioned properly on the mounting plate.

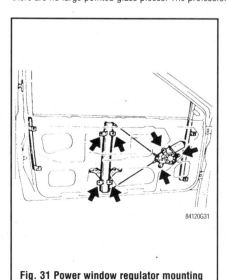

Fig. 31 Power window regulator mounting

Fig. 32 Small chips on your windshield can be fixed with an aftermarket repair kit, such as the one from Loctite®

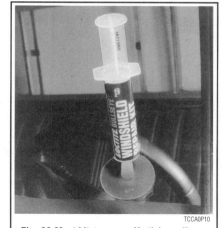

Fig. 33 Most kits use a self-stick applicator and syringe to inject the adhesive into the chip or crack

Seats

REMOVAL & INSTALLATION

Front

▶ **See Figures 34, 35, 36, 37 and 38**

1. Remove the seat adjuster cover screws and remove the cover.
2. Remove the seat track mounting bolts.
3. Fold the seat back forward and tilt the seat assembly back.
4. Disconnect the electrical leads and remove the seat from the vehicle. Remove components from the seat as needed.
5. Install the seat assembly into the vehicle. Connect the electrical leads and install the seat track mounting bolts. Tighten the bolts to 25–40 ft. lbs. (35–55 Nm) and the nuts to 17–26 ft. lbs. (24–36 Nm).
6. Install the adjuster cover. Test the operation of the seat on the track.

Rear

▶ **See Figures 39, 40, 41 and 42**

1. Remove the seat back mounting bolt from between the seat cushions.
2. Lift the lower part of the seat at the front to release it from the clips and pull it from the vehicle.

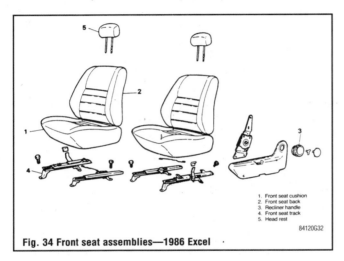

1. Front seat cushion
2. Front seat back
3. Recliner handle
4. Front seat track
5. Head rest

84120G32

Fig. 34 Front seat assemblies—1986 Excel

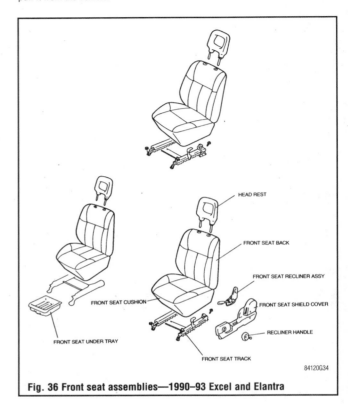

HEAD REST
FRONT SEAT BACK
FRONT SEAT RECLINER ASSY
FRONT SEAT SHIELD COVER
RECLINER HANDLE
FRONT SEAT CUSHION
FRONT SEAT UNDER TRAY
FRONT SEAT TRACK

84120G34

Fig. 36 Front seat assemblies—1990–93 Excel and Elantra

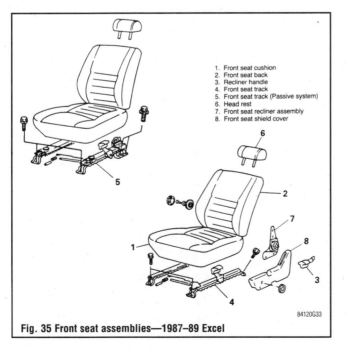

1. Front seat cushion
2. Front seat back
3. Recliner handle
4. Front seat track
5. Front seat track (Passive system)
6. Head rest
7. Front seat recliner assembly
8. Front seat shield cover

84120G33

Fig. 35 Front seat assemblies—1987–89 Excel

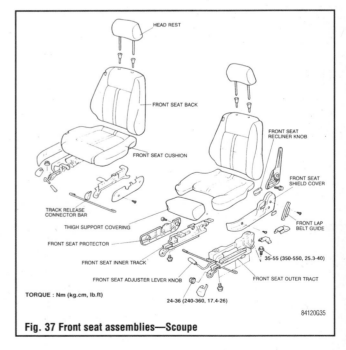

HEAD REST
FRONT SEAT BACK
FRONT SEAT RECLINER KNOB
FRONT SEAT CUSHION
FRONT SEAT SHIELD COVER
TRACK RELEASE CONNECTOR BAR
THIGH SUPPORT COVERING
FRONT LAP BELT GUIDE
FRONT SEAT PROTECTOR
FRONT SEAT INNER TRACK
35-55 (350-550, 25.3-40)
FRONT SEAT ADJUSTER LEVER KNOB
FRONT SEAT OUTER TRACT
TORQUE : Nm (kg.cm, lb.ft)
24-36 (240-360, 17.4-26)

84120G35

Fig. 37 Front seat assemblies—Scoupe

3. On late model Excel and Elantra, remove the 2 side seat back mounting bolts and pull the side seat backs up then out of the vehicle.

4. Tilt the seat back forward and remove the clips that retain the carpet to the rear of the seat back.

5. On early model Excels, remove the 4 retaining bolts at the seat back hinges and remove the seat back.

6. On models with fold down rear seats, remove the rear seat pivot hinge clips and remove the seat backs 1 at a time.

7. Install the seat back components in reverse order. Tighten the seat back hinge bolts to 12–19 ft. lbs. (17–26 Nm). Install all of the plastic clips and make sure that they are completely seated.

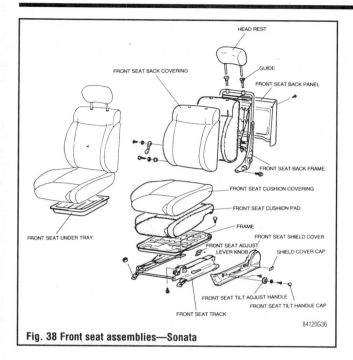

Fig. 38 Front seat assemblies—Sonata

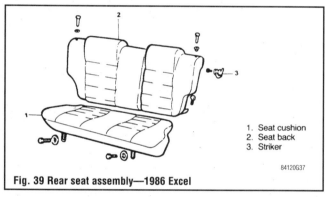

1. Seat cushion
2. Seat back
3. Striker

Fig. 39 Rear seat assembly—1986 Excel

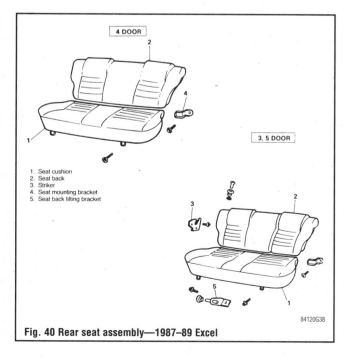

1. Seat cushion
2. Seat back
3. Striker
4. Seat mounting bracket
5. Seat back tilting bracket

Fig. 40 Rear seat assembly—1987–89 Excel

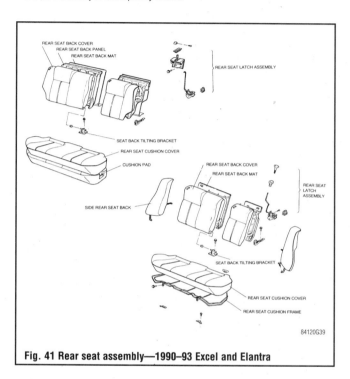

Fig. 41 Rear seat assembly—1990–93 Excel and Elantra

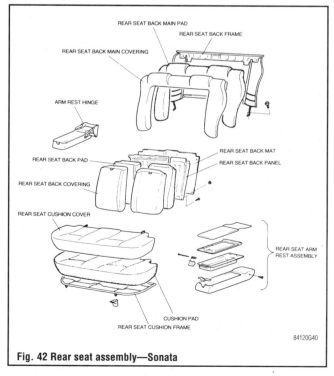

Fig. 42 Rear seat assembly—Sonata

GLOSSARY

AIR/FUEL RATIO: The ratio of air-to-gasoline by weight in the fuel mixture drawn into the engine.

AIR INJECTION: One method of reducing harmful exhaust emissions by injecting air into each of the exhaust ports of an engine. The fresh air entering the hot exhaust manifold causes any remaining fuel to be burned before it can exit the tailpipe.

ALTERNATOR: A device used for converting mechanical energy into electrical energy.

AMMETER: An instrument, calibrated in amperes, used to measure the flow of an electrical current in a circuit. Ammeters are always connected in series with the circuit being tested.

AMPERE: The rate of flow of electrical current present when one volt of electrical pressure is applied against one ohm of electrical resistance.

ANALOG COMPUTER: Any microprocessor that uses similar (analogous) electrical signals to make its calculations.

ARMATURE: A laminated, soft iron core wrapped by a wire that converts electrical energy to mechanical energy as in a motor or relay. When rotated in a magnetic field, it changes mechanical energy into electrical energy as in a generator.

ATMOSPHERIC PRESSURE: The pressure on the Earth's surface caused by the weight of the air in the atmosphere. At sea level, this pressure is 14.7 psi at 32°F (101 kPa at 0°C).

ATOMIZATION: The breaking down of a liquid into a fine mist that can be suspended in air.

AXIAL PLAY: Movement parallel to a shaft or bearing bore.

BACKFIRE: The sudden combustion of gases in the intake or exhaust system that results in a loud explosion.

BACKLASH: The clearance or play between two parts, such as meshed gears.

BACKPRESSURE: Restrictions in the exhaust system that slow the exit of exhaust gases from the combustion chamber.

BAKELITE: A heat resistant, plastic insulator material commonly used in printed circuit boards and transistorized components.

BALL BEARING: A bearing made up of hardened inner and outer races between which hardened steel balls roll.

BALLAST RESISTOR: A resistor in the primary ignition circuit that lowers voltage after the engine is started to reduce wear on ignition components.

BEARING: A friction reducing, supportive device usually located between a stationary part and a moving part.

BIMETAL TEMPERATURE SENSOR: Any sensor or switch made of two dissimilar types of metal that bend when heated or cooled due to the different expansion rates of the alloys. These types of sensors usually function as an on/off switch.

BLOWBY: Combustion gases, composed of water vapor and unburned fuel, that leak past the piston rings into the crankcase during normal engine operation. These gases are removed by the PCV system to prevent the buildup of harmful acids in the crankcase.

BRAKE PAD: A brake shoe and lining assembly used with disc brakes.

BRAKE SHOE: The backing for the brake lining. The term is, however, usually applied to the assembly of the brake backing and lining.

BUSHING: A liner, usually removable, for a bearing; an anti-friction liner used in place of a bearing.

CALIPER: A hydraulically activated device in a disc brake system, which is mounted straddling the brake rotor (disc). The caliper contains at least one piston and two brake pads. Hydraulic pressure on the piston(s) forces the pads against the rotor.

CAMSHAFT: A shaft in the engine on which are the lobes (cams) which operate the valves. The camshaft is driven by the crankshaft, via a belt, chain or gears, at one half the crankshaft speed.

CAPACITOR: A device which stores an electrical charge.

CARBON MONOXIDE (CO): A colorless, odorless gas given off as a normal byproduct of combustion. It is poisonous and extremely dangerous in confined areas, building up slowly to toxic levels without warning if adequate ventilation is not available.

CARBURETOR: A device, usually mounted on the intake manifold of an engine, which mixes the air and fuel in the proper proportion to allow even combustion.

CATALYTIC CONVERTER: A device installed in the exhaust system, like a muffler, that converts harmful byproducts of combustion into carbon dioxide and water vapor by means of a heat-producing chemical reaction.

CENTRIFUGAL ADVANCE: A mechanical method of advancing the spark timing by using flyweights in the distributor that react to centrifugal force generated by the distributor shaft rotation.

CHECK VALVE: Any one-way valve installed to permit the flow of air, fuel or vacuum in one direction only.

CHOKE: A device, usually a moveable valve, placed in the intake path of a carburetor to restrict the flow of air.

CIRCUIT: Any unbroken path through which an electrical current can flow. Also used to describe fuel flow in some instances.

CIRCUIT BREAKER: A switch which protects an electrical circuit from overload by opening the circuit when the current flow exceeds a predetermined level. Some circuit breakers must be reset manually, while most reset automatically.

COIL (IGNITION): A transformer in the ignition circuit which steps up the voltage provided to the spark plugs.

COMBINATION MANIFOLD: An assembly which includes both the intake and exhaust manifolds in one casting.

COMBINATION VALVE: A device used in some fuel systems that routes fuel vapors to a charcoal storage canister instead of venting them into the atmosphere. The valve relieves fuel tank pressure and allows fresh air into the tank as the fuel level drops to prevent a vapor lock situation.

COMPRESSION RATIO: The comparison of the total volume of the cylinder and combustion chamber with the piston at BDC and the piston at TDC.

CONDENSER: 1. An electrical device which acts to store an electrical charge, preventing voltage surges. 2. A radiator-like device in the air conditioning system in which refrigerant gas condenses into a liquid, giving off heat.

CONDUCTOR: Any material through which an electrical current can be transmitted easily.

CONTINUITY: Continuous or complete circuit. Can be checked with an ohmmeter.

COUNTERSHAFT: An intermediate shaft which is rotated by a mainshaft and transmits, in turn, that rotation to a working part.

CRANKCASE: The lower part of an engine in which the crankshaft and related parts operate.

CRANKSHAFT: The main driving shaft of an engine which receives reciprocating motion from the pistons and converts it to rotary motion.

CYLINDER: In an engine, the round hole in the engine block in which the piston(s) ride.

CYLINDER BLOCK: The main structural member of an engine in which is found the cylinders, crankshaft and other principal parts.

CYLINDER HEAD: The detachable portion of the engine, usually fastened to the top of the cylinder block and containing all or most of the combustion chambers. On overhead valve engines, it contains the valves and their operating parts. On overhead cam engines, it contains the camshaft as well.

DEAD CENTER: The extreme top or bottom of the piston stroke.

DETONATION: An unwanted explosion of the air/fuel mixture in the combustion chamber caused by excess heat and compression, advanced timing, or an overly lean mixture. Also referred to as "ping".

DIAPHRAGM: A thin, flexible wall separating two cavities, such as in a vacuum advance unit.

DIESELING: A condition in which hot spots in the combustion chamber cause the engine to run on after the key is turned off.

DIFFERENTIAL: A geared assembly which allows the transmission of motion between drive axles, giving one axle the ability to turn faster than the other.

DIODE: An electrical device that will allow current to flow in one direction only.

DISC BRAKE: A hydraulic braking assembly consisting of a brake disc, or rotor, mounted on an axle, and a caliper assembly containing, usually two brake pads which are activated by hydraulic pressure. The pads are forced against the sides of the disc, creating friction which slows the vehicle.

DISTRIBUTOR: A mechanically driven device on an engine which is responsible for electrically firing the spark plug at a predetermined point of the piston stroke.

DOWEL PIN: A pin, inserted in mating holes in two different parts allowing those parts to maintain a fixed relationship.

DRUM BRAKE: A braking system which consists of two brake shoes and one or two wheel cylinders, mounted on a fixed backing plate, and a brake drum, mounted on an axle, which revolves around the assembly.

DWELL: The rate, measured in degrees of shaft rotation, at which an electrical circuit cycles on and off.

ELECTRONIC CONTROL UNIT (ECU): Ignition module, module, amplifier or igniter. See Module for definition.

ELECTRONIC IGNITION: A system in which the timing and firing of the spark plugs is controlled by an electronic control unit, usually called a module. These systems have no points or condenser.

END-PLAY: The measured amount of axial movement in a shaft.

ENGINE: A device that converts heat into mechanical energy.

EXHAUST MANIFOLD: A set of cast passages or pipes which conduct exhaust gases from the engine.

FEELER GAUGE: A blade, usually metal, or precisely predetermined thickness, used to measure the clearance between two parts.

FIRING ORDER: The order in which combustion occurs in the cylinders of an engine. Also the order in which spark is distributed to the plugs by the distributor.

FLOODING: The presence of too much fuel in the intake manifold and combustion chamber which prevents the air/fuel mixture from firing, thereby causing a no-start situation.

FLYWHEEL: A disc shaped part bolted to the rear end of the crankshaft. Around the outer perimeter is affixed the ring gear. The starter drive engages the ring gear, turning the flywheel, which rotates the crankshaft, imparting the initial starting motion to the engine.

FOOT POUND (ft. lbs. or sometimes, ft.lb.): The amount of energy or work needed to raise an item weighing one pound, a distance of one foot.

FUSE: A protective device in a circuit which prevents circuit overload by breaking the circuit when a specific amperage is present. The device is constructed around a strip or wire of a lower amperage rating than the circuit it is designed to protect. When an amperage higher than that stamped on the fuse is present in the circuit, the strip or wire melts, opening the circuit.

GEAR RATIO: The ratio between the number of teeth on meshing gears.

GENERATOR: A device which converts mechanical energy into electrical energy.

HEAT RANGE: The measure of a spark plug's ability to dissipate heat from its firing end. The higher the heat range, the hotter the plug fires.

HUB: The center part of a wheel or gear.

HYDROCARBON (HC): Any chemical compound made up of hydrogen and carbon. A major pollutant formed by the engine as a byproduct of combustion.

HYDROMETER: An instrument used to measure the specific gravity of a solution.

INCH POUND (inch lbs.; sometimes in.lb. or in. lbs.): One twelfth of a foot pound.

INDUCTION: A means of transferring electrical energy in the form of a magnetic field. Principle used in the ignition coil to increase voltage.

INJECTOR: A device which receives metered fuel under relatively low pressure and is activated to inject the fuel into the engine under relatively high pressure at a predetermined time.

INPUT SHAFT: The shaft to which torque is applied, usually carrying the driving gear or gears.

INTAKE MANIFOLD: A casting of passages or pipes used to conduct air or a fuel/air mixture to the cylinders.

JOURNAL: The bearing surface within which a shaft operates.

KEY: A small block usually fitted in a notch between a shaft and a hub to prevent slippage of the two parts.

MANIFOLD: A casting of passages or set of pipes which connect the cylinders to an inlet or outlet source.

MANIFOLD VACUUM: Low pressure in an engine intake manifold formed just below the throttle plates. Manifold vacuum is highest at idle and drops under acceleration.

MASTER CYLINDER: The primary fluid pressurizing device in a hydraulic system. In automotive use, it is found in brake and hydraulic clutch systems and is pedal activated, either directly or, in a power brake system, through the power booster.

MODULE: Electronic control unit, amplifier or igniter of solid state or integrated design which controls the current flow in the ignition primary circuit based on input from the pick-up coil. When the module opens the primary circuit, high secondary voltage is induced in the coil.

NEEDLE BEARING: A bearing which consists of a number (usually a large number) of long, thin rollers.

OHM: (Ω) The unit used to measure the resistance of conducter-to-electrical flow. One ohm is the amount of resistance that limits current flow to one ampere in a circuit with one volt of pressure.

OHMMETER: An instrument used for measuring the resistance, in ohms, in an electrical circuit.

OUTPUT SHAFT: The shaft which transmits torque from a device, such as a transmission.

OVERDRIVE: A gear assembly which produces more shaft revolutions than that transmitted to it.

OVERHEAD CAMSHAFT (OHC): An engine configuration in which the camshaft is mounted on top of the cylinder head and operates the valve either directly or by means of rocker arms.

OVERHEAD VALVE (OHV): An engine configuration in which all of the valves are located in the cylinder head and the camshaft is located in the cylinder block. The camshaft operates the valves via lifters and pushrods.

OXIDES OF NITROGEN (NOx): Chemical compounds of nitrogen produced as a byproduct of combustion. They combine with hydrocarbons to produce smog.

OXYGEN SENSOR: Use with the feedback system to sense the presence of oxygen in the exhaust gas and signal the computer which can reference the voltage signal to an air/fuel ratio.

PINION: The smaller of two meshing gears.

PISTON RING: An open-ended ring with fits into a groove on the outer diameter of the piston. Its chief function is to form a seal between the piston and cylinder wall. Most automotive pistons have three rings: two for compression sealing; one for oil sealing.

PRELOAD: A predetermined load placed on a bearing during assembly or by adjustment.

PRIMARY CIRCUIT: the low voltage side of the ignition system which consists of the ignition switch, ballast resistor or resistance wire, bypass, coil, electronic control unit and pick-up coil as well as the connecting wires and harnesses.

PRESS FIT: The mating of two parts under pressure, due to the inner diameter of one being smaller than the outer diameter of the other, or vice versa; an interference fit.

RACE: The surface on the inner or outer ring of a bearing on which the balls, needles or rollers move.

REGULATOR: A device which maintains the amperage and/or voltage levels of a circuit at predetermined values.

RELAY: A switch which automatically opens and/or closes a circuit.

RESISTANCE: The opposition to the flow of current through a circuit or electrical device, and is measured in ohms. Resistance is equal to the voltage divided by the amperage.

RESISTOR: A device, usually made of wire, which offers a preset amount of resistance in an electrical circuit.

RING GEAR: The name given to a ring-shaped gear attached to a differential case, or affixed to a flywheel or as part of a planetary gear set.

ROLLER BEARING: A bearing made up of hardened inner and outer races between which hardened steel rollers move.

ROTOR: 1. The disc-shaped part of a disc brake assembly, upon which the brake pads bear; also called, brake disc. 2. The device mounted atop the distributor shaft, which passes current to the distributor cap tower contacts.

SECONDARY CIRCUIT: The high voltage side of the ignition system, usually above 20,000 volts. The secondary includes the ignition coil, coil wire, distributor cap and rotor, spark plug wires and spark plugs.

SENDING UNIT: A mechanical, electrical, hydraulic or electro-magnetic device which transmits information to a gauge.

SENSOR: Any device designed to measure engine operating conditions or ambient pressures and temperatures. Usually electronic in nature and designed to send a voltage signal to an on-board computer, some sensors may operate as a simple on/off switch or they may provide a variable voltage signal (like a potentiometer) as conditions or measured parameters change.

SHIM: Spacers of precise, predetermined thickness used between parts to establish a proper working relationship.

SLAVE CYLINDER: In automotive use, a device in the hydraulic clutch system which is activated by hydraulic force, disengaging the clutch.

SOLENOID: A coil used to produce a magnetic field, the effect of which is to produce work.

SPARK PLUG: A device screwed into the combustion chamber of a spark ignition engine. The basic construction is a conductive core inside of a ceramic insulator, mounted in an outer conductive base. An electrical charge from the spark plug wire travels along the conductive core and jumps a preset air gap to a grounding point or points at the end of the conductive base. The resultant spark ignites the fuel/air mixture in the combustion chamber.

SPLINES: Ridges machined or cast onto the outer diameter of a shaft or inner diameter of a bore to enable parts to mate without rotation.

TACHOMETER: A device used to measure the rotary speed of an engine, shaft, gear, etc., usually in rotations per minute.

THERMOSTAT: A valve, located in the cooling system of an engine, which is closed when cold and opens gradually in response to engine heating, controlling the temperature of the coolant and rate of coolant flow.

TOP DEAD CENTER (TDC): The point at which the piston reaches the top of its travel on the compression stroke.

TORQUE: The twisting force applied to an object.

TORQUE CONVERTER: A turbine used to transmit power from a driving member to a driven member via hydraulic action, providing changes in drive ratio and torque. In automotive use, it links the driveplate at the rear of the engine to the automatic transmission.

TRANSDUCER: A device used to change a force into an electrical signal.

TRANSISTOR: A semi-conductor component which can be actuated by a small voltage to perform an electrical switching function.

TUNE-UP: A regular maintenance function, usually associated with the replacement and adjustment of parts and components in the electrical and fuel systems of a vehicle for the purpose of attaining optimum performance.

TURBOCHARGER: An exhaust driven pump which compresses intake air and forces it into the combustion chambers at higher than atmospheric pressures. The increased air pressure allows more fuel to be burned and results in increased horsepower being produced.

VACUUM ADVANCE: A device which advances the ignition timing in response to increased engine vacuum.

VACUUM GAUGE: An instrument used to measure the presence of vacuum in a chamber.

VALVE: A device which control the pressure, direction of flow or rate of flow of a liquid or gas.

VALVE CLEARANCE: The measured gap between the end of the valve stem and the rocker arm, cam lobe or follower that activates the valve.

VISCOSITY: The rating of a liquid's internal resistance to flow.

VOLTMETER: An instrument used for measuring electrical force in units called volts. Voltmeters are always connected parallel with the circuit being tested.

WHEEL CYLINDER: Found in the automotive drum brake assembly, it is a device, actuated by hydraulic pressure, which, through internal pistons, pushes the brake shoes outward against the drums.

MASTER
INDEX

Chilton's Hyundai--Elantra, Excel, Scoupe, Sonata

Total Car Care, continued

Pick-Ups and Montero 1983-95
PART NO. 8666/50500
NISSAN
Datsun 210/1200 1973-81
PART NO. 52300
Datsun 200SX/510/610/710/
810/Maxima 1973-84
PART NO. 52302
Nissan Maxima 1985-92
PART NO. 8261/52450
Maxima 1993-98
PART NO. 52452
Pick-Ups and Pathfinder 1970-88
PART NO. 8585/52500
Pick-Ups and Pathfinder 1989-95
PART NO. 8145/52502
Sentra/Pulsar/NX 1982-96
PART NO. 8263/52700
Stanza/200SX/240SX 1982-92
PART NO. 8262/52750
240SX/Altima 1993-98
PART NO. 52752
Datsun/Nissan Z and ZX 1970-88

PART NO. 8846/52800
RENAULT
Coupes/Sedans/Wagons 1975-85
PART NO. 58300
SATURN
Coupes/Sedans/Wagons 1991-98
PART NO. 8419/62300
SUBARU
Coupes/Sedan/Wagons 1970-84
PART NO. 8790/64300
Coupes/Sedans/Wagons 1985-96
PART NO. 8259/64302
SUZUKI
Samurai/Sidekick/Tracker 1986-98
PART NO. 66500
TOYOTA
Camry 1983-96
PART NO. 8265/68200
Celica/Supra 1971-85
PART NO. 68250
Celica 1986-93
PART NO. 8413/68252

Celica 1994-98
PART NO. 68254
Corolla 1970-87
PART NO. 8586/68300
Corolla 1988-97
PART NO. 8414/68302
Cressida/Corona/Crown/MkII 1970-82
PART NO. 68350
Cressida/Van 1983-90
PART NO. 68352
Pick-ups/Land Cruiser/4Runner 1970-88
PART NO. 8578/68600
Pick-ups/Land Cruiser/4Runner 1989-98
PART NO. 8163/68602
Previa 1991-97
PART NO. 68640
Tercel 1984-94
PART NO. 8595/68700
VOLKSWAGEN
Air-Cooled 1949-69
PART NO. 70200

Air-Cooled 1970-81
PART NO. 70202
Front Wheel Drive 1974-89
PART NO. 8663/70400
Golf/Jetta/Cabriolet 1990-93
PART NO. 8429/70402
VOLVO
Coupes/Sedans/Wagons 1970-89
PART NO. 8786/72300
Coupes/Sedans/Wagons 1990-98
PART NO. 8428/72302

Total Service Series

ATV Handbook
PART NO. 9123
Auto Detailing
PART NO. 8394
Auto Body Repair
PART NO. 7898
Automatic Transmissions/Transaxles
Diagnosis and Repair
PART NO. 8944
Brake System Diagnosis and Repair
PART NO. 8945
Chevrolet Engine Overhaul Manual
PART NO. 8794
Easy Car Care
PART NO. 8042
Engine Code Manual
PART NO. 8851
Ford Engine Overhaul Manual
PART NO. 8793
Fuel Injection Diagnosis and Repair
PART NO. 8946
Motorcycle Handbook
PART NO. 9099
Small Engine Repair
(Up to 20 Hp)
PART NO. 8325
Snowmobile Handbook
PART NO. 9124

Collector's Hard-Cover Manuals

Auto Repair Manual 1993-97
PART NO. 7919
Auto Repair Manual 1988-92
PART NO. 7906
Auto Repair Manual 1980-87
PART NO. 7670
Auto Repair Manual 1972-79
PART NO. 6914
Auto Repair Manual 1964-71
PART NO. 5974
Auto Repair Manual 1954-63
PART NO. 5652

Auto Repair Manual 1940-53
PART NO. 5631
Import Car Repair Manual 1993-97
PART NO. 7920
Import Car Repair Manual 1988-92
PART NO.7907
Import Car Repair Manual 1980-87
PART NO. 7672
Truck and Van Repair Manual 1993-97
PART NO. 7921
Truck and Van Repair Manual 1991-95
PART NO. 7911

Truck and Van Repair Manual 1986-90
PART NO. 7902
Truck and Van Repair Manual 1979-86
PART NO. 7655
Truck and Van Repair Manual 1971-78
PART NO. 7012
Truck Repair Manual 1961-71
PART NO. 6198

Multi-Vehicle Spanish Repair Manuals

Auto Repair Manual 1992-96
PART NO. 8947
Import Repair Manual 1992-96
PART NO. 8948
Truck and Van Repair Manual
1992-96
PART NO. 8949
Auto Repair Manual 1987-91
PART NO. 8138
Auto Repair Manual
1980-87
PART NO. 7795
Auto Repair Manual
1976-83
PART NO. 7476

System-Specific Manuals

Guide to Air Conditioning Repair and
Service 1982-85
PART NO. 7580
Guide to Automatic Transmission
Repair 1984-89
PART NO. 8054
Guide to Automatic Transmission
Repair 1984-89
Domestic cars and trucks
PART NO. 8053

Guide to Automatic Transmission
Repair 1980-84
Domestic cars and trucks
PART NO. 7891
Guide to Automatic Transmission
Repair 1974-80
Import cars and trucks
PART NO. 7645
Guide to Brakes, Steering, and
Suspension 1980-87
PART NO. 7819

Guide to Fuel Injection and Electronic
Engine Controls 1984-88
Domestic cars and trucks
PART NO.7766
Guide to Electronic Engine Controls
1978-85
PART NO. 7535
Guide to Engine Repair and Rebuilding
PART NO. 7643
Guide to Vacuum Diagrams 1980-86
Domestic cars and trucks
PART NO. 7821